Chris van Houts

Julie Phillips has written about books, film, feminism, and cultural politics for *Newsday, Interview, Mademoiselle,* and also *Ms.* and *The Village Voice,* where her original articles on James Tiptree, Jr., appeared. Born in Seattle, she worked as a journalist in New York and now lives in Amsterdam.

Additional Praise for *James Tiptree, Jr.*

An American Library Association Notable Book
An *Austin Chronicle* Best Book of the Year
One of *Kansas City Star*'s 100 Noteworthy Books of the Year
One of *Publishers Weekly*'s 100 Best Books of the Year
One of *Salon.com*'s 10 Best Books of the Year
A *Seattle Times* Best Book of the Year
A London *Times* Christmas Book of the Year
A London *Times Literary Supplement* Best Book of the Year
One of *The Village Voice*'s 25 Favorite Books of the Year

"This thoughtful and meticulous biography provides both the expert and the novice with a Rosetta stone to the Tiptree catalog—an opportunity to extract from these stories the many layers of personal resonance they once held only for Sheldon herself."

—DAVE ITZKOFF, *The New York Times Book Review*
(front cover review)

"A crystalline reckoning of an enthralling life."

—JOHN MARK EBERHART, *The Kansas City Star*

"I'll be thinking about what biographer Julie Phillips has to say about women and writing for a long time to come."

—SUSAN LARSON, *New Orleans Times-Picayune*

"The sexual, artistic, and intellectual contradictions Sheldon mostly failed to accommodate in her own stormy life, Phillips captures and contains—in all their complexity—in this deeply intelligent and generous biography."

—JENNIFER REESE, from the National Book
Critics Circle Award nomination

"From the opening montage of contradictory scenes in her subject's amazing life, to its copious citations of sources, Julie Phillips's biography of science fiction's trickster genius is a wonder."

—NISI SHAWL, *The Seattle Times*

"Excellent . . . Julie Phillips combines diligent archival work with more than forty interviews to successfully portray one of science fiction's most brilliant—and tortured—authors."

—MARTIN MORSE WOOSTER, *The Washington Post Book World*

"Alice Sheldon's complex gender identity and sexual orientation is utterly fascinating, as is her remarkable life, which is made all the more vivid in this rich biography." —*BookSense.com*

"Phillips draws on extensive interviews with surviving relatives and literary colleagues as well as Alli's revealing letters to write a compelling, sympathetic portrait of one of speculative fiction's most gifted and fascinating figures." —CARL HAYS, *Booklist* (starred review)

"Journalist Phillips has achieved a wonder: an evenhanded, scrupulously documented, objective yet sympathetic portrait of a deliberately elusive personality. . . . Phillips steadfastly and elegantly allows [Sheldon's] star to gleam." —*Publishers Weekly* (starred review)

"A fantastically incisive study . . . Julie Phillips does great justice to the meta-sexual visionary in her page-turner biography."

—JOANNE MCNEIL, *Bookslut.com*

"A fascinating subject, an engrossing read. Phillips provides sharp, insightful portraits of the real Alice Sheldon, the fictional James Tiptree, Jr., and the complicated partnership of their work and lives. This is a biography written with equal parts sympathy, respect, research, and honesty. And a real page-turner, too."

—KAREN JOY FOWLER, *New York Times* bestselling author of *The Jane Austen Book Club*

"In this deeply thoughtful, rivetingly readable biography of James Tiptree, Jr., Julie Phillips traces the life and work of a woman whose self-presentation in her writing made her seem so much 'like a man' that she confounded our culture's myths of gender and genre, convincing even the most sophisticated readers that 'Tiptree' was and had to be 'really' a man. This is a fascinating investigation of a fantastic literary career."

—SANDRA M. GILBERT, distinguished scholar and editor of *The Norton Anthology of Literature by Women*

"*James Tiptree, Jr.*, documents not only an extraordinary life but all the fault lines of what it meant to be female in the twentieth century. I think this may be the rare case when a biography actually exceeds what I expect from a novel. I hope everyone reads this book."
—DOROTHY ALLISON, author of *Bastard Out of Carolina*

"It is a first-rate biography, important and rewarding to everyone interested in science fiction or Tiptree's work or women's writing or Alli herself. It's a solid, scholarly job, and shows great sensitivity to Tiptree's life and work."
—JOANNA RUSS, author of *The Female Man*

"Most compelling is Phillips's probing of why this intelligent, accomplished woman required a male persona to give voice to things she herself could not say."
—CARTER SCHOLZ, *Bookforum*

"Phillips clearly understands that the dramas of [Sheldon's] life are far more than neurotic scrawls on the tapestry of years. . . . May be the finest literary biography I've ever encountered."
—JOHN CLUTE, *SciFi.com*

"The complexity and brilliance of Phillips's treatment of Sheldon's gender and sexuality is this biography's most stunning achievement. . . . In elegant prose and with consummate understanding, Phillips shows us a life that was full, rich, and deeply contradictory."
—BETHANY SCHNEIDER, *Chicago Tribune*

"By revealing one of the most fascinating and complex personalities of the twentieth century, Phillips [has] quite possibly created a new standard for literary biographies."
—RICK KLAW, *The Austin Chronicle*

"This is an utterly absorbing and provocative book."
—CHARLES MATTHEWS, *The Baltimore Sun*

"The achievement of this biography is that it takes an extraordinary person and makes her emblematic of twentieth-century women and their struggles. Phillips is at Claire Tomalin's level, and this book is only her debut."
—LUCY SUSSEX, *The Age* (Australia)

JAMES TIPTREE, JR.

THE DOUBLE LIFE *of* ALICE B. SHELDON

JULIE PHILLIPS

PICADOR

ST. MARTIN'S PRESS

NEW YORK

www.picadorusa.com

Picador® is a U.S. registered trademark and is used by St. Martin's Press under license from Pan Books Limited.

For information on Picador Reading Group Guides, please contact Picador.
Phone: 646-307-5259
Fax: 212-253-9627
E-mail: readinggroupguides@picadorusa.com

Cover photo: Alice on her honeymoon at Antibes, France, September 1945, courtesy of Barbara Francisco.

Excerpts from the *Letters of Harlan Ellison* reprinted with permission of, and arrangement with, the author, and The Kilimanjaro Corporation. Copyright © 2006 by The Kilimanjaro Corporation. All rights reserved.

Book design by Jonathan Bennett

Library of Congress Cataloging-in-Publication Data

Phillips, Julie.
    James Tiptree, Jr.: the double life of Alice B. Sheldon / Julie Phillips.
       p.   cm.
    Includes bibliographical references and index.
    ISBN-13: 978-0-312-42694-1
    ISBN-10: 0-312-42694-1
    1. Tiptree, James.   2. Authors, American—20th century—Biography.   I. Title.

   PS3570.I66Z85 2006
   81'.54—dc22
   [B]   2006040095

First published in the United States by St. Martin's Press

First Picador Edition: June 2007

10 9 8 7 6 5 4 3 2 1

CONTENTS

To learn to write at all, I had to begin by thinking of myself as a sort of fake man.

—JOANNA RUSS TO JAMES TIPTREE, JR.

"For Christ's sake, Ruth, they're aliens!"
"I'm used to it" . . .

—JAMES TIPTREE, JR., "THE WOMEN MEN DON'T SEE"

JAMES TIPTREE, JR.

INTRODUCTION: WHO IS TIPTREE, WHAT IS HE?

No one [. . .] has, to my knowledge, ever met Tiptree, ever seen him, ever talked with him on the phone. No one knows where he lives, what he looks like, what he does for a living. [. . .] He volunteers no information about his personal life, and politely refuses to answer questions about it. [. . .] Most SF people [. . .] are wild to know who Tiptree "really" is.

—GARDNER DOZOIS, 1976

In 1921 in the Belgian Congo, a six-year-old girl from Chicago with a pith helmet on her blond curls walks at the head of a line of native porters. Her mother walks next to her, holding a rifle and her daughter's hand.

In 1929, the girl huddles under quilts in a cabin in the Great North Woods, reading *Weird Tales*. The candle by her bed flickers as an alien gently removes a young human's brassiere.

On Christmas Eve 1934, a nineteen-year-old in a white beaded evening gown makes her debut. At the party she meets a handsome, dark-haired boy in a tie and tails. She makes a joke; he laughs, and makes another. Five days later they elope and marry.

In 1942, a divorcée wearing three-inch heels and a fox fur jacket goes down to a Chicago recruiting station and enlists in the army.

Sometime in the near future, a woman and a man meet an extraterrestrial exploring party. The man tries to protect the woman. The woman says she doesn't believe in women's chances on Earth, and asks the aliens to take her away.

In 1970, a man who does not exist sits down at a typewriter. He writes, "At last I have what every child wants, a real secret life. Not an official secret, not a Q-clearance polygraph-enforced bite-the-capsule-when-they-get-you secret, nobody else's damn secret but MINE."

1

James Tiptree, Jr., appeared on the science fiction scene in the late 1960s, writing fast-paced, action-filled stories about rocket ships, alien sex, and intergalactic bureaucratic anxiety. He was a brilliant and original talent, with a voice like no one else's: knowing, intense, utterly convinced of its authority and the urgency of its message. No one had ever seen or spoken to the owner of this voice. He wrote letters, warm, frank, funny letters, to other writers, editors, and science fiction fans. His correspondence was intimate and revealing, yet even his closest friends knew little more about "Tip" than his address: a post office box in McLean, Virginia.

He was rumored to be a government official or secret agent. He did seem to know a lot about spooks around the water cooler: his characters worked in "an unimportant bit of C.I.A." or remarked, "Paranoia hasn't been useful in my business for years, but the habit is hard to break." He had opinions about fishing, duck hunting, and politics. He was courtly and flirtatious with women. When one of his friends, the writer Robert Silverberg, sent him a letter on his wife's stationery, Tip answered that he had "shaved and applied lotion" before reading on. Silverberg pictured Tip as "a man of 50 or 55, I guess, possibly unmarried, fond of outdoor life, restless in his everyday existence, a man who has seen much of the world and understands it well." Men looked up to him. His women friends fell in love.

The stories that came out of PO Box 315 became more and more brilliant and disturbing. It wasn't the sex, and it wasn't the death, but it was the combination of the two. His stories read like urgent messages from some haunted house on the corner of Eros and Mortality. Humans meet aliens—and abandon their very souls for a chance to sleep with them. A man in love with the Earth kills off the human race, including himself, to save her. A mission to the stars finds an alien egg for which the colonists themselves turn out to be the sperm.

Like Philip K. Dick, Tiptree used science fiction to talk about the importance of empathy and explore what it means to be human—though he was less likely than Dick to question reality. Reality is there; the human project is to learn to see it, or die. Or learn to see ourselves: the reality of human flesh and emotions was what terrified, and fascinated, Tiptree. Can the body be trusted? Will it betray us? What does it want? Can we get rid of it?

This masculine writer, who let his readers in on the technology of space flight and the inner workings of government, also showed a surprising sympathy toward his female characters. He wrote about women's alienation in a world of men, and was held up as an example of a male feminist, a man who understood. Still, his stories were so full of action, abstract thought, and desire for women that everyone knew they were dealing with a man. In 1975, in an introduction to a book of Tiptree's short stories, Robert Silverberg wrote of his friend, "It has been suggested that Tiptree is female, a theory that I find absurd, for there is to me something ineluctably masculine about Tiptree's writing."

He likened Tiptree's "lean, muscular, supple" stories to Hemingway's:

> Hemingway was a deeper and trickier writer than he pretended to be; so too with Tiptree, who conceals behind an aw-shucks artlessness an astonishing skill for shaping scenes and misdirecting readers into unexpected abysses of experience. And there is, too, that prevailing masculinity about both of them—that preoccupation with questions of courage, with absolute values, with the mysteries and passions of life and death as revealed by extreme physical tests, by pain and suffering and loss.

In the same year, another of Tiptree's letter-friends, the feminist science fiction writer Joanna Russ, wrote him that a professor at a party had "asked me if you were a woman (!) by which I gather he can't recognize a female point of view if it bites him." When Tiptree participated in a written symposium on "Women in Science Fiction" as a token "sensitive man," Russ told him he had ideas "no woman could even think, or understand, let alone assent to."

By then Tiptree had introduced a protégée, Raccoona Sheldon, who seemed strongly influenced by Tiptree's style. No one, not even herself, had opinions about Raccoona's sex: she was a former schoolteacher who published little and wrote, "As for me, really the less said the better."

Tiptree did reveal a few facts about himself. He had been born in Chicago. His parents had been African explorers and his mother a writer. He had spent part of his childhood in colonial Africa, and the Second World War "in a Pentagon sub-basement." He was reluctant to reveal his true identity because he couldn't have the people around him know he was writing science fiction, and because he liked his secret life.

Then in late 1976, Tiptree told a few friends that his elderly mother had died. More than one of Tip's correspondents checked the Chicago papers and found an obituary for Mary Hastings Bradley, novelist, travel writer, and African explorer. Under "survivors" was listed her only child: Alice Bradley (Mrs. Huntington) Sheldon.

Ten years later, shortly before her death by suicide, Alli Sheldon wrote, "My secret world had been invaded and the attractive figure of Tiptree—he *did* strike several people as attractive—was revealed as nothing but an old lady in Virginia."

ALICE HASTINGS BRADLEY DAVEY SHELDON, 1915–1987

As it turned out, Alice Sheldon, known as Alli, was just as attractive a figure as Tiptree had ever been, opinionated and theatrical, with a past that she revealed, bit by bit, in tantalizing anecdotes. The few friends she allowed into the home in McLean that she shared with her husband, Huntington "Ting" Sheldon, were fascinated by this eloquent storyteller. The writer Gardner Dozois called her "one of the most fascinating conversationalists I've ever met, brilliant, theatrical, far-ranging, strikingly perceptive." David Hartwell, her editor, said "Alli was electrifying, [. . .] enchanting both in person and in her fiction."

By the time she started writing science fiction she had already been a painter and an air force intelligence officer. She had eloped with the "beautiful alcoholic poet" who had been seated on her left at her debut. She had worked for the CIA. She had earned a Ph.D. in experimental psychology. She had published a story in the *New Yorker*. She had begun and thrown out essays, scientific works, and novels.

She was born in 1915 as Alice Hastings Bradley, the cute, blue-eyed only child of two extraordinary parents. Her father, Herbert Bradley, was a lawyer who led three expeditions into unmapped Central Africa. Her mother, Mary Hastings Bradley, was a highly successful author of travel books and popular fiction. Both adult Bradleys were charismatic, energetic, public people whose adventures gave the family an exotic air.

Mary Bradley was an enormous presence in Alli's life: magnetic, generous, theatrical, extremely long-lived. Tiptree described his mother as

> a kind of explorer-heroine, highly literate (Oxford & Heidelberg), yet very feminine whatever that is. You help her through doors—and then find out she can hike 45 miles up a mountain carrying her rifle and yours. And repeat next day. And joke. And dazzling looks. [. . .] I am still approached by doddering wrecks, extinguished Scandinavian savants or what have you who want to tell me about Mother as a young woman.

Alli called her

> a dazzling and formidable little person, a "queen bee" with two adoring males in addition to her husband. (In our Victorian culture they were Father's best friends.) She was gifted, beautiful, emotional, accomplished; a linguist, writer, spell-binding conversationalist—and a superb shot and brave endurer of considerable real hardships. [. . .] She didn't provide a model for me, she provided an impossibility.

Mary encouraged her daughter, first as an artist and then as a writer. But what Alli needed to say was not within the scope even of Mary's wide world, and what she did *not* learn from Mary's example was that women could say anything. She learned that women had to be very careful in order to speak at all.

Besides, Mary took up a great deal of emotional and creative space, writing her daughter's story, literally, in two children's books about the Bradleys' African travels. It took a radical subterfuge—taking on a new name, pretending to be a man, turning into a new person—for Alli to get that story back, to become someone else than her mother's daughter.

Tiptree wasn't only a trick for saying things Alli couldn't. Like all interesting people, Alli had many sides or selves, and Tiptree gave her more room to be those selves: worldly, analytical, independent, bloodthirsty, and funny. He let her play, make jokes, or, on a bad day, annihilate the human race. He gave her space to love women (though not always to like them). Sometimes he said things she didn't have words for, in the days when no one wrote honestly about women's experience. Many artists feel they have another persona who does their work for them, a secret self very much unlike the "me" of their daily interactions. Tiptree was that person for Alli: a writer who (he once said) longed to stop sweating over words and drafts and instead "storm naked with hard-on waving thru the world spouting whatever comes."

Tiptree helped Alli to write partly because he wrote science fiction. "Literature," with its famous injunction to "write what you know," cannot always help us discover what we don't know. Science fiction gave Alli a language for writing around the boundaries, for imagining what cannot yet be said. It has been seen as a masculine genre. And yet, with its metaphors for alienation and otherness, its unruly imagination, and its power to predict change, it is highly suited to talking about women's experience.

Alli chose her male pseudonym on a whim, in a supermarket, where a jar of Tiptree jam caught Alli's eye. She was sending out some science fiction stories as a joke, and she wanted a name "editors wouldn't remember rejecting." But the male name turned out to have many uses. It made her feel taken seriously when she wrote about what she knew: guns, hunting, politics, war. It let her write the way she wanted to write, with an urgency that was hers. It gave her enough distance and control to speak honestly about herself.

In 1931, when Alice Bradley was fifteen, Virginia Woolf wrote "Professions for Women," with its famous image of the imagination diving deep into the stream and the woman writer warily pulling it back. In one of Woolf's drafts, the writer explains to her imagination, "I cannot make use of what you tell me—about womens bodies for instance—their passions—and so on, because the conventions are still very strong. If I were to overcome the conventions I should need the courage of a hero. [. . .] I doubt that a writer can be a hero. I doubt that a hero can be a writer." Alli longed to be a genius, an artist who spoke the truth about her experience. But she didn't have the words for that experience, or the rare courage to become a literary heroine. Instead, late in life, she became one of our greatest literary tricksters.

Tiptree never pretended to be a man in person. Yet Alli's appropriation of the male mind is even more exciting. It's a much deeper challenge to the established narrative order, and promises a greater freedom. It questions all our assumptions about writing and gender. It changes how we look at our male writer heroes. As science historian Donna Haraway has suggested, Tiptree takes the figure of the Great White Hunter and reconfigures it for a postcolonial, postgender world. And Alli's performance speaks, in a way no other writer's life has, to the ongoing problem of writing as a woman. Which is not to say that Alli wrote only about or for women. She wanted to lose her gender partly because, like Woolf, she didn't want to write for half the world.

She couldn't always imagine her way out of the problems she raised. Tiptree's stories most often end in death—for the protagonist, the crew, the colony, or the planet. In the same way, Alli put an end to her own story. She and her husband Ting agreed to commit suicide together when they became too old to go on. On May 19, 1987, when she was seventy-one and Ting eighty-four, she shot him and then herself.

Since her death, her work has gone on finding new audiences and influencing new writers, from cyberpunk authors like William Gibson to those who imagine the future of gender and sexuality. Tiptree now stands alongside Philip K. Dick and Ursula K. Le Guin as one of the twentieth century's most important and exciting writers of fantastic literature in America. While new generations of readers are drawn to her prescient work, her passionate life and tragic death have much to tell us about what it means to write—and to be human. And her performance as Tiptree, with its reversal of everything we expect about men and women writers, may be her greatest achievement, her greatest influence of all.

NAMES

Certainly let us be on first names; mine is Alli. ("Alice" carries joyless connotations of "Alice, eat your spinach." "Alice, go to bed." [. . .])

—ALLI SHELDON

Alice Sheldon disliked her first name, which she felt did not belong to her. " 'Alice,' it was made clear to me early, *belonged* to my mother, who chose it *because it had no nickname.* How cruel can you get, unintentionally—I hope? But one's nicknames—they are one's own," she wrote Joanna Russ. She herself was an "inveterate nicknamer" who loved playing with names and was thrilled when her mother-in-law shortened her name to "Alli." She gave her own pseudonyms nicknames: "Tip" for Tiptree, and "Raccoona" for a woman writer with a mask. In writing this book I have called James Tiptree, Jr., "Tiptree" or "Tip"—he never used "James"—but Raccoona Sheldon by her first name to avoid confusion.

Like many women, Alice changed her name over the course of her life, from Alice Hastings Bradley to Alice Davey to Alice Sheldon. Alice Bradley Davey was her first byline. She also wrote as Alice Bradley, used the name "Ann Terry" on an early, unpublished science fiction story, and signed a rude letter "Mrs. H. D. Smith." In letters of feminist protest, on cream-colored stationery, she was Mrs. Huntington D. Sheldon, adding, "PS. I am not a 'radical' but a stuffy suburban matron who buys your advertisers' products." As a research psychologist she was Dr. Alice B. Sheldon. Franz Kafka's biographer can and does call his subject "Kafka" from infancy, but what can I call mine? I have tried to call Major Alice Hastings Bradley Davey Sheldon, Ph.D., by the names she used at different times, and have mostly taken the liberty of using the name she liked best: Alli.

CHAPTER 1: THE INNOCENT ADVENTURESS

And when you see even the outline of my dear, damnable mother you'll feel you were interviewing not only the wrong writer but the wrong woman.

—ALLI SHELDON

Mary Hastings Bradley is forgotten now, but in her daughter's lifetime she was a famous writer. She had stories in magazines that everybody read; she gave parties everybody attended. She was a socialite, an explorer, and a big game hunter. Her earnings kept her daughter in mink coats and finishing schools. She could be a blue-eyed beauty in a lace dress one day, an expert markswoman in khaki trousers the next. For a publicity portrait she posed in an evening dress, seated on the skin of a tiger that she had shot herself.

From her earliest childhood she wanted to write and have adventures. When she lectured on her career, she told her audience that her first memory of writing was of

> sitting before my dolls' house laboriously printing out the story of what I thought was happening there. It was an Indian attack, I remember, and I remember my dear Mother saying: "Don't you want to clean your dolls' house, Mary? Don't you want to change your dolls' dresses?" No, Mary didn't. She wanted to write about an Indian attack.

But for a long time she didn't get the chance to risk her life, and most of the exploits in her writing were romantic ones. Reviewing her 1921 novel *The Innocent Adventuress*, the *New York Times* called her "a well-qualified composer of literary confectionery" who had written a "little sugar-plum of a book":

> How Maria is lost on a mountain all night, who rescues her and bears her in his manly arms to his shack and whom she eventually decides upon as a husband ought to be fairly clear to the astute reader. The book

is written with verve, and [. . .] is not without sufficient interest to pass
an idle hour or two.

One of her early books, *The Wine of Astonishment,* was about "the seamy
side of life," and was banned in Boston, but it was about a boy's coming of
age. Her very first was a historical novel about Anne Boleyn called *The Favor
of Kings,* published in 1912. She later said of it: "I had the real stuff of history
in my grasp but I was much too well brought up then to make full use of my
robust material." Mary, too, was an "innocent adventuress": if she wanted to
have adventures, or write about them, she would have to keep up the appearance of propriety. The woman and the one who had adventures had to be two
different people.

Mary Wilhelmina Hastings was born in Chicago on April 19, 1882, into a
family that, on her mother's side, had come to Chicago when the city was new.
Mary's grandparents were proud of their pioneer spirit and their English and
New England blood. They taught Mary (who would later teach Alice) to admire courage, believe in progress, and climb socially. They passed on firm Victorian ethics and an American faith in self-transformation.

Mary adored her young mother, Lina Rickcords Hastings, but her father,
William Hastings, was a more unsavory type, a hot-headed Southerner who
may have been alcoholic and abusive. He died when Mary was about nine
years old, though Mary sometimes claimed he had died before she was born.
Afterward Mary's mother married a doctor named Arthur Corwin and had
another daughter, Sylvia, twelve years younger than Mary. A death in the family, a usurpation: this is the kind of early experience that makes a writer. It left
Mary with an enormous need to be seen, to be loved, to be a heroine.

By the time she graduated from Smith College in 1905, Mary was being
seen: she had already sold short stories to the popular magazines *Munsey's* and
the *Woman's Home Companion.* She told her parents she was moving to
Greenwich Village to live in a garret and become a serious writer. For a
woman, though, to be loved and to be a heroine are not always the same
thing. When her parents said no, Mary chose love over seriousness and returned to Chicago.

As a consolation, the Corwins offered a trip to Europe, chaperoned by an older cousin. Mary spent a whole year traveling. She visited Germany, France, Italy, and Egypt, where she took a boat trip up the Nile. This first glimpse of Africa made a deep impression. She then spent three months in Oxford, writing, sending her stories home for her mother to type, and researching her novel rehabilitating Anne Boleyn.

After she returned she used Europe as a background in stories such as "The Girl from Home." In this light romance, published in *Good Housekeeping* in 1911, an American girl studying in Paris discovers that romantic Frenchmen are not to be trusted. Her friend Achille declares:

> "I also have no such wish to marry—that is of an impossibility. [. . .] But the present we may have, and we are both young and poor together. Shall we not make life sweeter for one another?"
>
> She felt his hands stealing about her, felt him bending closer—she sprang from him, her heart hammering in sick dismay. [. . .] That he should think such a thing of her—should suggest—

After this, she finds that dull, dependable young men from home can have their charms.

Mary was all in favor of dependable men. In 1909, when she was twenty-seven and living with her parents, she met a thirty-four-year-old lawyer named Herbert Bradley. He had just come back from Montana and was setting up a respectable law practice in Chicago. He too liked travel and adventure. They married a year later, with a honeymoon on horseback in the Rockies.

Herbert Edwin Bradley was born December 20, 1874, in Canada, the third of six sons of an Ontario farmer. As a young man he worked his way through teachers' college, then law school at Ann Arbor and Chicago. At first he was a mining lawyer; by the time he met Mary he had started investing in real estate, putting up apartment buildings on Chicago's South Side. These investments would make him rich. He was good-looking in a dour way, sensible, practical, careful with money. He had a sensual mouth, Alli thought, that belied his Canadian reserve. He had a side that was spontaneous and funny and made off-color jokes, and a melancholy streak that he did not let people see. He approved of Mary's writing career and was prepared to support her, financially, practically, and emotionally. They were a good match.

In 1912, Herbert and Mary moved into the apartment they would live in
for the rest of their long lives. The building at 5344 Hyde Park Boulevard was
one of Herbert's investments, a plain, three-story brick apartment house between the University of Chicago and the lake. The Bradleys had the entire top
floor, plus a penthouse and roof garden. The apartment had plenty of room
for their servants—cook, chauffeur, a series of governesses—and later for the
Bradleys' collection of trophies, skins, and African souvenirs.

It had room for their parties and their many friends. Mary and Herbert
were social, gregarious people whose soirees and travels were covered on the
society pages of the Chicago papers. Where Alice would invent alter egos to
do her writing, Mary turned herself into a writer character, a figure in the
Chicago society columns:

> Mrs. Herbert Bradley, always one of the busiest women in town, finds
> her life complicated by the opera season. Her publishers make no al-
> lowance for opera-going when they set deadlines. [. . .] As a result she
> finished her last novelette by dint of staying up all night after an opera
> performance, and startled the household when she appeared for break-
> fast in her evening clothes.

Mary's energy, intensity, and generosity attracted people. She had a manner that was both grand and utterly sincere. She inspired loyalty: servants
stayed with her for decades. She inspired trust: people told her their life stories. Alice wrote wryly years later,

> There's always room for another person or project in Mary's life. If we
> went to the Antarctic desert, some lone Eskimo would appear and Mary
> would say, "Why, you remember George here, he's the man who—" and
> we would hear all about George's ancestors and descendants [. . .] and
> George would tell me what a terrific person my mother was.

Like many creative and exciting people, she created a magical world
around herself, drew her friends into it, and reigned inside it. The price for being swept up in Mary's charm was to leave something of yourself behind.

She was not an introspective person—keeping a diary made her feel "silly and self-conscious"—and didn't let people see inside. Mary's niece Barbara Francisco, the daughter of her half sister Sylvia, recalled that despite her warmth, "you couldn't get close to her at all. She was always on stage."

One of the few people allowed behind the scenes was Alice. Under Mary's gay and worldly air, Alice later wrote, "it was understood that she was enduring terrible grief."

The house on Hyde Park Boulevard had been meant for a big family. Instead, Mary had a series of miscarriages in the five years before Alice was born. (The probable cause, Rh factor incompatibility, was not recognized until years later. Alice survived because her blood type was Rh negative, like her mother's.) Mary was thirty-three when Alice was born, on August 24, 1915. Her birth must have given the Bradleys hope. But the worst was yet to come. When Alice was four, in 1919, Mary carried another pregnancy to term. Alice's sister Rosemary lived only a day.

In public, Mary was brave; in private, she never stopped grieving for her lost child. A death in the family raises the stakes: it makes the survivors more protective, more loyal, more frightened, more dependent. Alice became the sole and dutiful recipient of all Mary's hope, possessiveness, and love, and did her best to be the daughter Mary wanted. Sometimes she was afraid she was not that daughter: surely her dead sister would have been better than this flawed and disobedient living child. Death in the family may have made Alice a writer too, but first it nearly frightened her into silence.

Mary kept her surviving child close. Until she was six, Alice later claimed, she spent most of her time at home on the Bradleys' roof garden, with only nurses and a white rabbit for company. Mary distrusted the modern city, "where motors"—automobiles—"menace every curb and crossing, and where [Alice] could never for an instant be safely left alone on the streets."

Then the Bradleys went to Africa.

In 1921, to most Americans, Africa was still the Dark Continent, a wild, dangerous, and enticing last frontier. Theodore Roosevelt's 1910 book *African Game Trails* introduced America to the "great white hunter" and popularized the word "safari." In 1912, Edgar Rice Burroughs published his first Tarzan story. Stories also came out of Africa about colonial cruelty and exploitation.

In America in the early twentieth century, "Belgian atrocities in the Congo" was a familiar phrase. But Mary preferred the tales she had read as a child in Henry Morton Stanley's *In Darkest Africa,* "of a vast continent peopled with savages, of feverish jungles and mighty rivers, of treacherous beauty and swift death, of a primitive barbarism that had been going on from the beginning of time [. . .] unknown and untouched by trade or civilization."

Mary had also listened to the adventures of two family friends, Carl and Delia "Mickie" Akeley. Before the First World War, the Akeleys had traveled widely in British East Africa, hunting animals for Chicago's Field Museum and New York's American Museum of Natural History. (The elephants they collected still stand in both museums.) Carl Akeley had begun his career as a taxidermist, but became a legendary naturalist and hunter. The tooth marks of a leopard on one arm recalled an attack which he had survived by killing the big cat bare-handed. Mickie, too, was a courageous traveler and an excellent shot. A close friend of Herbert's, *Chicago Tribune* cartoonist John T. McCutcheon, had hunted with the Akeleys in East Africa in 1909.

Now the Akeleys were in the middle of a divorce and Carl Akeley was looking for companions and backers for a new and difficult expedition. He had plans for an African hall at the AMNH, and wanted to display the rare mountain gorilla, first seen by Europeans only nineteen years before. To get gorillas he would have to go to Central Africa—new territory for him—and travel on foot to their habitat in the eastern Congo. He also had another ambitious plan. No longer satisfied with collecting and mounting specimens, he wanted to film gorillas in the wild, using a new motion picture camera of his own invention. He suspected that gorillas were peaceful animals, and hoped to show they should not be hunted for sport.

The Bradleys were wealthy enough to help finance an expedition, and Akeley judged his younger friends hardy enough to make the trip. (Akeley was fifty-seven, Herbert and Mary forty-six and thirty-nine.) This would not be a tourist safari in British East, arranged by a professional outfitter in Nairobi. The area they were going to had first been explored by Europeans only thirty-five years before, and was accessible in about the same sense that the top of Mount Everest is now. Still, the Bradleys decided to take Alice with them, with a young woman named Priscilla Hall to look after her. Akeley's secretary, Martha Miller, would also join the party.

The idea of taking a six-year-old girl along appealed to Akeley. While Mary dreamed of a jungle frontier, he had become impatient with the Dark Continent myth. (Firmly contradicting Stanley, he called his memoir *In Brightest Africa*.) To take a child on safari, he felt, would be to undermine the image of Africa as a savage wilderness. He wanted Alice to be the witness to an Africa of peace and beauty, the lamb sent to lie down with a gentle lion, and hoped that Africa "seen through the eyes of a sweet little girl" would "all be much more beautiful than when seen through the eyes of rather blood-thirsty sportsmen and adventurers."

While Akeley was remaking hunting, Mary was preparing to remake motherhood. She wanted to be a mother and an adventure heroine both, to shoot lions and raise a daughter. There was pressure on her not to do this. When the Bradleys told the papers of their plan to go to Africa, Alice later said, editorials cast doubt on Mary's fitness as a mother or suggested that Akeley was taking the women along as decoys to attract male gorillas. To prove she was a good mother, Mary would have to do her best, not only to protect her daughter, but to raise an exemplary girl. She could have adventures, but only if Alice would compensate for them with white dresses, blond curls, a pretty face, and her best behavior.

When we first meet young Alice, not only is she a character in one of Mary's books—a children's book about Africa called *Alice in Jungleland*—she is wearing a disguise of Mary's making. It is August 1921, and she has just turned six, on board an ocean liner steaming from Southampton to Cape Town. The ship has announced a costume party for children, for which her mother has not come prepared. Improvising, Mary makes Alice a dress out of white crepe paper and pink ribbon, puts her in a child-sized wooden box, ties the box with a bow, and has two sailors carry it in to the party. The box is opened to reveal little Alice standing in it "like a French doll at a toy shop. [. . .] Every one had been afraid that she would never stand still, but she surprised them all by keeping perfectly quiet, just like a real doll in a box— in fact she felt so strange and shy that she didn't want to come out of the box at all."

According to Mary, Alice was thrilled when she won a prize, and perhaps even more excited by the company: she'd never been with so many children before.

For Mary, going to Africa was a way to prove herself. For Alice it was the site of a freedom she could not quite touch and a terror she could never escape. In Africa, she later wrote, she contracted "a case of *horror vitae* that lasted all my life."

CHAPTER 2: **AFRICA (1921-22)**

In Africa, Alice was an object of fascination to everyone who met her. When she was allowed to walk, Mary wrote, she

> danced along at the head of the line [of porters], holding her Daddy's or her Mummy's hand and waving a greeting to the native women in the fields. [. . .] [The Congolese] had never seen a white little girl before and Alice was very strange to them, with her blue eyes and long yellow curls. They used to crowd round her on the way, and in camp would wait hours before her tent, to see her having her curls brushed. [. . .] They felt sure that [her hair] must be some ornament she fastened on, and they used sometimes to touch it slyly, with a little pull, to make sure that it really grew on her head!

Her parents went to Africa to explore and observe. Alice got to be the baggage (she was carried most of the way by porters) and the view.

Later, when she got the chance to tell her own stories about Africa, she recalled being fascinated, indulged ("if I dropped something I was quite accustomed to clap my hands and have six large, naked cannibals spring to attention and pick it up for me"), occasionally miserable (looking at a photo of herself in a white dress riding a baby elephant, she remembered that she had had thin silk underpants on), and often extremely frightened. She had to be watched or she might be killed, by leopards or worse. If she even went for a pee in the high grass, her mother had to come along with a rifle.

As Mary liked to remind her readers, there were plenty of bad fates in Africa. In the adult travel book she wrote about the trip, *On the Gorilla Trail,* she lists gruesome endings for travelers, who are killed by leopards, crocodiles ("Some hunters say that he crunches down his prey at once; others, that he holds it under until it is drowned"), bugs, fevers, the sun. She visits the graves of Belgian soldiers who fought World War I in the colonies. She takes up the big game hunters' debate on which animal was deadliest, lion, elephant, buffalo, or rhino, and jokes, "Between the lion's chances for lunch and ours for a rug the odds were sportingly even." But Mary's story is about conquering death. Alice's is about feeling powerless in its sight.

As the party moved north by train from Cape Town, at twenty miles an hour, stopping at Kimberley to see the diamond mines and at Bulawayo to see the statue of Cecil Rhodes, Mary measured what they saw by its state of civilization—the wilder the better. Victoria Falls felt like the edge of the known world, with their "mad leap of water over savage rocks" and "barbaric blaze of red aloes on the banks against the white foam." Here they put on their pith helmets, which they had been told to wear at all times against the equatorial sun. But they still felt like tourists, staying at a hotel and being taken to the falls in little trolley cars pushed by local laborers along the tracks.

Mary had mixed feelings at Elisabethville, now Lubumbashi, 2,500 miles by rail from Cape Town, their first stop in the Belgian Congo and the last "European" town before Kampala. They arrived there on September 11, after more than a week in the train, and slept at their first "tropical hotel," with a veranda and a bar full of American mining engineers. Ten years before, Elisabethville had been a collection of tin shacks, but now it was a city built "for the future, well laid out, with wide streets and attractive administrative buildings. There are clubs and tennis and golf and motors—in spite of the dollar and a quarter for gasoline—good shops and Belgian and English libraries." Chicago had grown up in less than a hundred years from its own collection of shacks, and Mary must have pictured Elisabethville making the same progress, culminating in some Congolese skyscraper to rival the Wrigley Building, then rising on the banks of the Chicago River.

At Lake Tanganyika, too, Mary thought of Lake Michigan before the pioneers came, and foresaw factories, movie theaters, a whole dirty Chicago springing up along its idyllic shores. The scene she saw "was beauty itself, the perfect loveliness of beauty undespoiled. But it was beauty with a doom on its bright head, for already the white man had come. [. . .] In ten years, twenty or fifty, civilization and its gauds would be enthroned. The old Africa would go." Their very arrival on the frontier was the beginning of its end. Alice grew up, she once wrote, in a world "suffused with sadness; everywhere it was said, or seen, that great change was coming fast and much would be forever gone."

But if Elisabethville was a little too modern in some ways, it was not modern enough in others: they waited for an anxious week for lost luggage and searched in vain for trained local staff for their safari. In East Africa, a standard safari package included a crew of "tent boys" (personal servants) and "gun boys" (who carried equipment and provided backup on a hunt), plus an interpreter, a cook, and porters. But this was not the usual safari route. At last they managed to hire three men who had been house servants for the Belgians. One of them, Mablanga, became Alice's "boy" and watched over her protectively, while she impressed him with stories about how people lived in America.

At last they left Elisabethville on a train northbound to Bukama, where they embarked on a smoky little flat-bottomed wood-burning steamer, hardly more than a raft with an awning, with a Belgian captain and a Congolese crew. Pushing out onto the Lualaba River as a tropical rainstorm pounded the water, they felt they were "on the trail, really in Africa, headed up to the heart of it." They had their traveling clothes on now, the men and women in khaki shirts and trousers, Alice in a miniature safari jacket and pants tucked into leather boots. Mary had worried Alice would be careless about wearing her pith helmet, but Alice was as anxious as her mother was to prove herself in Africa. Not only did she never forget her own helmet, she reminded the others with irritating vigilance.

When Herbert held Alice up to the rail to see their first elephants feeding on the bank, she disappointed him by not being surprised. She had been told she would see elephants, and here they were. What was the surprise in that? Still, she followed the elephants eagerly through her father's field glasses, and stared at the hippos that came swimming around the boat and the crocodiles sunning themselves on the banks. When Akeley and Herbert Bradley fired guns into the air, the birds flew up in thousands from the trees that lined the river while Akeley filmed the scene. The adults also took potshots at the crocodiles, to make the river safer, they said. A Belgian steamer captain had been pulled under while swimming near his boat the week before.

After five days on the Lualaba they disembarked at Kabalo and took another train to the shores of Lake Tanganyika. There they camped on a windy hillside overlooking the vast blue lake, 450 miles long, with rough waters lapping a wide beach of golden sand. After a week of waiting they were picked up by the lake steamer *Baron Dhanis*. Crowded among missionaries and Belgian administrators, all of whom made much of Alice, they steamed north for five days to Usumbura (now Bujumbura in Burundi) at the northern tip of the lake, with a layover at Kigoma on the eastern side. There the Bradleys made an excursion to the place where Stanley had met Livingstone—not "in some dark and damp African forest" as Mary had always pictured it, but in the busy lakeside trading town of Ujiji, a "place of sunshine and dancing waves."

At Usumbura, a center of Belgian administration, they hired more "boys," and the Belgian officials sent out a request to the nearby chiefs for porters. Beyond this point they would have to go on foot.

By this time the delays were getting on Akeley's nerves. Alice later recalled Akeley as a genius, but also a difficult, cantankerous man whose crabbiness moved her parents to great feats of tact and polite denial. (She learned from this, she said, that survival depended on not speaking one's mind.) Alice helped by being a "sweet little girl": with her childish playfulness, she could cheer "Uncle Akeley" when the adults could not.

Fortunately, Herbert was calm and persistent, supervising the camp, negotiating with Belgian officials, keeping their luggage moving and their papers in order, while Mary's charm had a good effect on the local officials. On October 14, a month after they'd left Elisabethville, the porters finally arrived. At last their real travels could begin.

"In the Congo, the Eastern Congo," Mary wrote, "you sit upon a mountain peak and gaze out to other mountain peaks, like pastels with distance, and you do not wonder how you are going to those other peaks—you know. You walk."

And their baggage walked with them. It took two hundred men, each with forty to sixty pounds on his head, to carry everything they had brought: tents, cots, guns, folding bathtubs, formaldehyde, medical supplies, Mary's typewriter, sixty-five boxes of food, four porter loads of glass-plate negatives, and the evening clothes they would need again in British East. (To future safarigoers, Mary dryly recommended "lace [. . .] and heavily beaded georgette—the beads weight down the wrinkles.") On a traditional safari the whites themselves were carried in chairs on poles, but Akeley and the Bradleys mostly preferred to walk. Alice sometimes rode on a bicycle with a jerry-built child seat, pedaled by her "boy" Mablanga, but more often she was carried in a hammock, lying down, barely able to see out over the sides. As they changed porters along the way, Alice kept learning the local words for "Put me down!" and using them loudly.

At a rate of fifteen miles a day, this long string of porters and explorers followed the Ruzizi River north toward Lake Kivu, through a fertile, green country of villages and fields on the border between Rwanda and the Belgian Congo. Again, Alice had a calming effect, this time on the people they met, who were less suspicious of a traveling party with women and a child. Mary said the natives generally assumed that she and Alice were Herbert's favorite wife and child, traveling with him for safety's sake. Herbert's other wives might have poisoned them out of jealousy if they had stayed home.

This country, now a war zone, seemed to Mary then as peaceful as a park. Yet it was here, near Lake Kivu, that Alice had her first experience of death. On their march they came across elephants, and Martha Miller shot one. That night their porters and the local villagers feasted on the meat. The next day the porters refused to march and went off instead to hunt antelope. When they returned they had with them a prisoner, who they claimed had attacked and wounded one of their party. Akeley ordered the man held until they could turn him over to the Belgians. But that night the Bradleys heard screams, and in the morning the man was gone. The porters and villagers said he had escaped, but one of the "boys" told them he had been killed and eaten. In the tent she shared with her governess, Alice lay awake and heard the whole thing.

It was presented to Alice as a cultural difference rather than a crime, which confused and upset her: in Chicago her parents had absolute ideas about morality. There were more frightening stories. At Ujiji, Mary had explained to Alice for the first time about slavery in America. "It was too big a problem for a six-year-old to worry over, so Alice's mother soon started her talking of something else," Mary wrote in *Alice in Jungleland*. But Mary underestimated Alice's capacity for worry. If death was Mary's African theme, human cruelty would be Alice's.

Lake Kivu is 5,000 feet above sea level and 1,500 feet deep. It divides Rwanda on its eastern shore from the Congo on the west and is surrounded by green, fertile hills. "An African Switzerland," Mary called the setting, with wide-horned African cattle grazing on grassy slopes and the Virunga range towering above the lake's northern end. The three tallest mountains of the Virungas, Mikeno, Karisimbi, and Visoke, are the home of the mountain gorilla. Two others of the range are active volcanoes, and at night they could see the crater of Nyamlagira, or Nyamuragira, lighting the sky above the lake's northern edge. Every night Alice begged to be allowed to stay up until she could see the volcano glow.

The lake had first been seen by whites less than thirty years before; the Akeley party were the first Americans to reach its shores. In this pristine landscape, the little Belgian outposts, run by one or two white officers and their wives, seemed to Mary like "a stage setting waiting to be filled with the actors." She wasn't picturing refugee camps and armies, but perhaps an artists' colony settled along the lake's cool and pleasant shores.

Gisenye, near Goma, at the lake's northern end, was their destination, and they arrived there at the end of October, nearly two months out of Cape Town. There Mary and Akeley both came down with malaria, so they waited, and then waited again for porters. After she recovered, Mary continued her work of buying native baskets, bags, and ivory carvings—her own form of the men's museum collecting. Sometimes she used Alice as a trade object. When she asked to buy an ivory bracelet directly off a chief's arm, he said he would not sell even "for the price of two wives." But Mary produced Alice, and for the sake of the white child he accepted Mary's francs. At other times Alice played "gorilla hunter" on the beach, attacking the bushes with a native spear.

As soon as he could, Akeley took thirty porters and left on his hunting expedition. Shortly afterward the Bradleys left Alice and Priscilla Hall at a nearby Catholic mission (where a joke of Herbert's about sex between African women and gorillas got them a cool reception), and with Martha Miller followed Akeley into the steep, wet, densely forested, magically beautiful, and nearly impassable mountains.

Afterward, Alice loved to hear the stories from the hunt: how Akeley had fired at a gorilla above him on the hillside and was nearly crushed by the body as it fell; how they stalked Herbert's great silverback male through the bushes, crawling on hands and knees. When the silverback's body came to rest against a tree, with Mount Nyamlagira glowing behind it in the distance, Akeley said he would like to be given such a funeral pyre. Yet as the hunt went on, the adults began to be troubled by the gorillas' human faces. After Akeley shot a female, a guide speared her four-year-old son, and Akeley saw in the young animal's eyes "a heartbreaking expression of piteous pleading. [. . .] He would have come into my arms for comfort." They had a license to kill ten gorillas but were grateful to stop after they had taken five. Instead they used Akeley's new camera to shoot the first films ever made of gorillas.

There on Mount Karisimbi, the beauty of the landscape and the gentle strength of the gorillas touched something in Carl Akeley. Over the next few years, the former hunter worked hard, and successfully, to persuade King Albert of Belgium to set aside the area as a national park and wildlife preserve. In 1926, he returned to the Virungas to survey the park and study gorilla habitats, while an artist made sketches for the diorama in the African hall. There Akeley died of fever and exhaustion, five years to the day after he had watched Herbert's silverback fall and had envied the gorilla his funeral pyre.

Akeley became an important transitional figure in a changing relationship between humans and animals. The Akeley camera was used by his friends Martin and Osa Johnson to make their pioneering East African wildlife documentaries. Film replaced taxidermy as the way ordinary people learned about wild animals. And Akeley's push for preservation made him a forerunner of the great twentieth-century naturalists—Dian Fossey, Jane Goodall, George Schaller, Shirley Strum—who went to Africa not to hunt but to sit quietly and observe.

Alice received all of this mixed together: hope for progress, sadness about the passing of the old, the need for conservation, the longing for the bravery of the hunt. Asked to embody peace, Alice absorbed both the lamb and the lion. Among the conflicting currents in her writing are fantasies of peaceful societies (which she associates with the feminine, motherhood, and weakness) and a counter-yearning for a powerful, forbidden violence.

The party arrived back at the mission just in time for Thanksgiving, which they celebrated with the local pygmies. Offering payment in salt, they persuaded a group of Batwa to come to the mission to dance, telling Alice they were "little people."

"Am I a Batwa?" philosophical Alice asked Mablanga. "I'm little." No, Mablanga answered.

"Did you ever see Batwa, Mablanga?"
"No, Baby. No Batwa in my country."
"Then how do you know I'm not a Batwa?"

She watched the Batwa dance for hours until she was tired of them and glad they left.

The travelers moved on, with the porters now carrying the skins and bones of the gorillas they had shot. (The remains of the four-year-old were stored under Alice's cot every night, filling her tent with the stink of formaldehyde.) On the way north, the adults briefly explored Mount Nyamlagira and camped in its glowing crater. Then they went on to the savanna to hunt lions.

Next to their camp on the Ruindi Plains near Rutshuru stood a pile of rocks with a cross: the grave of an unlucky young English lion hunter. Because of baboons and leopards, Alice wasn't allowed out of the camp. When the adults left on a hunt she shouted after them, "Good luck—get a lion!" But she later wrote, "It was early impressed on me that I was viable only within the sheltering adult group, that the outside was dangerous and beyond my strength. [. . .] I never was allowed to learn to combat it; I lived helplessly inside, watching, learning the adult lore, wondering how I could meet each horrible challenge, and *never getting a chance to practice.*"

Mary got her lion on the Ruindi Plains. They stalked the young male through the grass: a risky way to hunt, but they got a bead on it from perhaps twenty feet, and the men let Mary take the first shot. She aimed at the head, fired, and the lion fell. Then she posed for pictures with its head in her lap—until the lion, only stunned by Mary's bullet, came to and started to roar. Mary jumped up, grabbed her gun, and this time shot it through the heart.

A few days later they received a message by runner that Mary's mother was ill, and on New Year's Day, 1922, they began the trek out. They crossed the unmarked border into British East Africa at what is now the southwestern corner of Uganda, then crossed Lake Bunyonyi in log canoes. Within a few days they reached Kampala, and their safari was over. Counting the ground they had covered hunting elephants and lions, Mary estimated she had walked a thousand miles.

Kampala was movies and formal dinners, "shops and hotels and clubs and telephones and ice tinkling in tall glasses." They unpacked their dress whites, and were invited to play golf and tennis when the sun was low. Herbert saw to the crating of the trophies and souvenirs: the buffalo heads and elephants' ears, the tusks, horns, and lion skins, the baskets, spears, and canoe paddles, the otter skins Mary had bought to make a coat for Alice.

In Kampala they visited another tourist site, the tomb of King Mutesa. Sixty years before, Mary wrote, Mutesa had held court here, having his enemies tortured or his friends killed on a whim. Now his house stood empty, and elderly beggars "gazed out with a flash of wonder at the little white girl with the fair curls who came to look at the tomb of their dead king, and then danced so fearlessly out into the spaces where once it had been death to approach."

In Mary's story, Alice is full of life and joy. The little girl had "peaked and pined [her] last year at home on all the sensible routine of her nursery fare," but in Africa she was "as hearty and healthy as a child could be. [. . .] Life was a continual excursion, an everlasting picnic."

Alice was happy and excited, but she was also frightened, and because the trip depended on her happiness, she couldn't tell anyone how scared she was. Toward the end of her life she wrote, "I think you could say that one of my hobbies is recovery from the status of Marginal Man—with no place to recover to except being my parents' dear little yellow-haired darling with its head full of Death . . ."

CHAPTER 3: **CHILDHOOD**

The mother-child interaction is the logical place to postulate the origins of human speech [and] empathy. [. . .] You can see mothers and children murmuring to each other, learning to understand each other's noises in a way and with a necessity that obtains in no other human relationship—if mother and child don't understand each other the child doesn't survive.

—ALLI SHELDON

You can understand why a system would seek information—but why in hell does it offer information? Why do we strive to be understood? Why is a refusal to accept communication so painful?

—JAMES TIPTREE, JR.

The Bradleys came back to Chicago in March 1922. Their return made national news. The *New York Times* ran a picture of Alice captioned "Youngest Explorer of Darkest Africa [. . .] the First White Child Ever Seen by the Pigmy Tribes." (Ordinarily the white explorers do the seeing, but again Alice was not the viewer but part of the view.) For the Chicago papers, they staged a photo session in the roof garden: beside a low table spread with a leopard skin, Herbert and Mary watched admiringly as Alice, with a look of sullen intensity, poured tea.

In New York, Carl Akeley mounted the five gorillas for a diorama at the American Museum of Natural History. He mounted Herbert's gorilla standing upright, its two fists at its breast; its image was reproduced everywhere from encyclopedias to comic book covers until it became Americans' idea of how gorillas look. Herbert had hoped their film footage, showing gorillas feeding peacefully, could be released commercially. But audiences for early wildlife films wanted charging elephants and cannibal chiefs. They weren't ready for an unstaged, nonviolent wildlife documentary.

Mary Bradley put her notes together and started to write. *On the Gorilla*

Trail ran serially for ten weeks in the *Chicago Tribune* and was published in book form that same year, 1922. When Mary spoke at the women's society of her mother's church, her tales of safari life found an eager audience: a reviewer said the listeners were "thrilled to the finger tips" by this "fascinating little lady looking every inch the society gentlewoman." At home the Bradleys uncrated their tusks, skins, spears, and baskets and put them on display in their penthouse, which they now called the African Room. Almost immediately they started planning a second trip.

Mary was able to be both women, the lion hunter and the "society gentlewoman"; to Mary, Africa existed alongside Chicago and enriched it. But for Alice, Africa opened a deep rift in her life, between her ordinary self and herself on safari. Africa made Chicago seem unreal, while in Chicago, the girl she had been in Africa, in khakis, boots, and a pith helmet, wielding a spear, was not permitted to exist. A photograph of Alice at about seven, roller-skating in a dress on a city sidewalk, shows her more uncertain than the girl of the year before—despite, or because of, the parental presence, the shadow of the photographer that falls across her path.

A few weeks after they got home, Alice went to school for the first time. It didn't go well. "I was already so spoiled, precocious and peculiar as to be unassimilable by other children, and was by most cordially loathed," she later wrote. This isn't quite true: she got along, and her schoolmates loved to visit the Bradley house with its fascinating African treasures. But she didn't understand them, or they her. One year her class learned about volcanoes and the teacher asked them what a crater was. Alice's hand shot up. "My Mummy spent the night in the crater of an active volcano," she volunteered. After that, she later claimed, most of the class stopped speaking to her.

From an early age, Alice felt like a displaced person. As a young bohemian she liked to quote Jean Cocteau: "There are some people whose passports are *not in order.*" Later, commenting on the story of the volcano, she added, "It is true that a great many episodes of my life have a fantasy-feeling to me when I recall them, a curious unconnectedness with me, like houses one looked at and didn't rent; sometimes it distresses me that experiences seem to have left no visible marks on me to confirm their reality."

In *Alice in Jungleland,* Mary admitted that the volcano was a hard story to believe.

For, of course, no one's Mummy ever spent a night in a crater. A volcano was something in a book, to study about. It didn't happen, not in real life. Of course not. At least not in *your* real life.

But all the time, over there in the heart of Africa, Mt. Nyamlagira was blazing away, pouring up into the air its dangerous, beautiful fire.

In Chicago, the death the Bradleys had defied in Africa caught up with them again. Mary's grandmother died not long after they came home. A few months later, her beloved mother died of cancer, painfully and horribly, in her daughter's arms.

In the spring of 1924, Herbert went into the hospital with a hemorrhaged ulcer. Mary kept up a courageous front: newspaper stories told how she saved his life by giving blood. In private she developed a chronic fear of Herbert's death. Three years later, a "tropical fever" nearly killed him. Alice grew up to the refrain, "Your father is dying." (It "was made worse when my behaviour 'broke his heart.'") In Mary's address book she kept a list with both birthdays and death dates. She was enormously vital and lively, but she never let Alice forget how narrow the strip of life is on which we walk.

In the face of all these deaths, Alice later wrote, Mary maintained "unremitting cheer and denial except when [she] broke down and unloaded on me." Alice was the audience for what she called her mother's "horror-recitals": over and over at low moments, Mary spoke about the deaths they had seen on their travels, relived her mother's suffering, or recalled the grip of her dying baby's tiny hand. Later Alice told Mary, "You 'taught' me, without meaning to, that love is the prelude to appalling pain."

Mary was deeply attached to her surviving child, and Alice to her: Mary seemed to be the only one who understood. Alice, too, mourned, and longed all her life for the sister who had died. But she was more anxious to console her mother, and their relationship was shadowed by Mary's need. She wrote, "Very early on it was branded in me that sin was not loving Mother. (And Father too, but less.) [. . .] Turning aside from one who loves you to get something else done is 'wicked.' Being interested in anything but the loving one is 'wicked.' Not loving back enough is wicked . . ."

When Alice was unhappy, Mary felt rejected, so she did her best not to be unhappy. But she couldn't really feel happy around her mother, either. Years later, it still seemed to her that "herself" was "in abeyance near [Mary]; instead I am some kind of response-machine. [. . .] I can't think of, much less talk of, what I am 'really' thinking."

She wrote that her relationship with her mother

> was marred by dishonesty—or rather, fear and lack of honesty—and also by my own terror of a frighteningly dynamic, unadmitted possessiveness from which I, her only surviving child, barely escaped alive when young. She was incredible—an epic, driven energy, much stronger than poor old long-drink-of-water here [. . .]. She had emotion enough for 10, but I got it all, and was always—perhaps wrongly—aware that had the others existed she wouldn't have cared much for me. Or perhaps we could *really* have been friends, if I hadn't been also her sole possession and projection into the future.

It may not be a coincidence that some of James Tiptree, Jr.'s, best stories are narrated by an observer who has no idea what is really going on.

In Alli Sheldon's stories about her childhood, Herbert is a lesser presence than Mary: less overwhelming, less available, less there. Alice aspired to his competent ease with guns and tools, and tried to prove herself to him, but he disappointed her by never teaching her what he knew. She thought her father would have preferred a boy, and that in his eyes she had been "an inferior variety known as 'only a girl.'" When Alice tried for the first time to build something out of wood and broke her father's saw on a nail, she recalled, her father "just gave up, because I was a girl."

Yet Alice valued Herbert's coolness, his appeal to abstract principles, unlike Mary's demands for attention and love. He was passionately on her side in any conflict. And he was funny and enjoyed her jokes, while Mary, with her lighthearted public persona, was serious at heart. James Tiptree, Jr., once wrote, "I was nine before anybody but Sr. laughed at anything I said." It was a recurring Tiptree joke to call Herbert "Tiptree Sr." One use of the Tiptree persona was to let Alice feel closer to her father.

Alice's parents believed in, and taught their daughter, old-fashioned Victorian virtues: achieve, be brave, be kind to others, champion the unfortunate.

(Later on, when she went in for socialist politics, she discovered that was not quite what her Republican parents had had in mind.) Alice liked these principles and found them reassuring. But they were also, when applied to the temperament of a noisy, exuberant kid, repressive. An emotion the Bradleys especially disliked was rage. "In my family anger and harsh words were an ABSOLUTE taboo. Ladies and gentlemen didn't raise their voices, yell at each other, say cruel things." In Alice's memory, her parents never fought—and when she got angry they reacted with hurt. "This must have given me the idea that anger was exceedingly dangerous and potent, a dreadful weapon one must never use."

If they had produced a houseful of children, Herbert and Mary might have had to relax their standards. As it was, Alice couldn't know that other kids squabbled, sulked, and did not act like miniature adults. She must have thought anger was her own particular sin. And so, while she was "lavishly rewarded for being passively dependent, obedient, verbally precocious, and 'sweet,'" she locked all her anger up behind a closed door. In the dark, her anger grew. When she acknowledged this closed door, she also wrote that behind it boiled "a fount of hot lava: fury, red revenge, indiscriminate murderousness. [. . .] I have trained myself to be 'nice,' humorous, hard to offend or irritate. [. . .] [But] I suppose, thinking it over, that I assume that everybody wants to wipe the world out a couple of times a day."

The closed door meant that Alice had no access to that anger, or protection against it, or knowledge of its power. Unable to use it, she felt weak. (Later in life, at depressed moments, she equated goodness with weakness: a decent person is a sitting duck.) Unable to confess it, she had no insulation against its secret burn. Unable to explore it, she never learned its limits or its strengths.

Aggression, too, was a Bradley taboo. In any dispute, Alice once wrote, Mary "is always for the underdog, but only as long as he is the underdog. The moment he gets on top, he had better watch himself." To Mary it was all right to kill lions, who were themselves violent creatures, but she went to great lengths to protect mice, chipmunks, anything that was small and weak. This might say something about the conditions on her love for Alice.

Alice tried to live with things and be a good daughter, until she surprised herself with sudden escape attempts. She recalled a childhood phenomenon that the servants called "Alice's little uproars": "Every so often I experienced a queer cold build-up of tension over several days, which suddenly took expression as an outbreak: 'I can't STAND this.' (Whatever 'this' was.) At such times, in later life, I would abruptly change jobs or do other sudden, drastic things, all with no emotion and a strange sense of unreality."

At a little older she began having "spells of intense melancholy," when the color and texture of ordinary life seemed to fade. They were replaced by images of every horror and tragedy she could name and every future loss she could imagine, all playing themselves out before her eyes. "When I was a kid I almost killed myself when I heard what happened to Carthage. And the burning of the Alexandria library," Tiptree wrote. Young Alice became anxious about age and morbidly fascinated with the passage of time. Her parents seemed old to her; frightened of their deaths, she hallucinated death and its reverse. "I looked in baby-carriages and saw old, old skeletons; I looked at the old men of the U.S. Senate and saw 96 babies. I was deeply puzzled by the existence of the past and future in the frail forms of the present."

Depression, too, was something she could not speak of to her parents, who wanted so desperately for her to be happy. And what reason did she have to be unhappy in her good, kind, loving home? So while she spent much of her life trying to find where her inner pain was coming from and make it stop, it was all in secret: "I didn't tell anybody any of this except that I found life painful. (Didn't everybody?)"

To admit her pain seemed to her "cowardly," though she felt a duty to comfort others. Years later she observed,

> I realize that my definition of being O.K. or normal was being able to conceal the pain I felt so as not to radiate it at other people, so as not to lay it on them because I assumed they already had all the pain they could take and were doing the same thing. And that there was sort of an unwritten convention that you didn't load onto somebody else or didn't break down or allow the pain to get out of control. [. . .] I really assumed this was general in life. Everybody was like me and could just barely stand what they had inside, and it was just noblesse oblige not to load more on there.

If comfort was offered, Alice pushed it aside. "When I feel bad I want to be ALONE," she once told Mary. "The encouraging pat on the back, the

shared glance of sympathy, make me run. They are the gasoline on the fire."
Yet she was determined to survive her depressions, and fought them with an
inner strength that might have had to do with her parents' love.

Later on, Alice generally said she had been a lonesome, unhappy kid. But
around the corner of this story peeks a different child, an affectionate, joyous
Alice, curious, adventurous, and never still. This child lived at the third important place in Alice's childhood, a summer house in northern Wisconsin
that the Bradleys called "the Lodge."

The Lodge was an old fishing camp with several tumbledown log cabins,
on a remote, wooded lake near the town of Florence. The Bradleys bought it
when Alice was a baby and spent two or three months there every summer. It
had no electricity and no phone. It had a dock with a little sailboat, a stable for
the horses they rented, and a raft for swimming in the lake, with a diving platform where Alice taught herself to do a back flip. In the first years, they still
heard wolves howling in the woods at night.

Like all good summer places, the Lodge was ramshackle, beautiful, and
full of the detritus of July and August freedom. During the week it belonged
to Alice and Mary. Mary had a cabin by the lake where she could work, while
Alice was looked after by more governesses (none of whom seems to figure in
her memories). When Mary wasn't writing, she taught Alice the names of
plants, how to hunt mushrooms, and how to ride. Herbert spent the week in
Chicago and came up on weekends on the train that ran to nearby Iron
Mountain, Michigan.

Alice's cousin Barbara Francisco was a frequent summer guest. "For both
my sister [Marilyn] and me, it was the ideal, most unreal place. And of course
Mary and Herbert created this; they were very good about creating these fantastic places. For a child, the African room was a *wonder,* and the place in Wisconsin was also.

"Each of the little cabins had its own wood stove, and the man came in
in the morning when it was freezing cold and lit the fire and you could stay
under your blanket and enjoy all the heat before you had to get up. They
had one of those big old wood stoves, that's all they cooked by, and in the
middle of the kitchen floor you could open up a trapdoor and go down into

a real cellar where they kept apples, a real McCoy. Oh, for a child, that was heaven."

In the city Alice wore white dresses and Mary feared for her safety, but in Wisconsin she wore trousers and could run and play, enjoy her strength and be alone. In the woods there were no people, no interactions that she didn't understand. Nearly every summer until Mary died, Alice went to the Lodge. At nearly sixty, as Tiptree, she wrote, "I love it helplessly, these woods; they presided over my first everything."

For the local residents, few of whom had ever even been as far as Chicago, the Bradleys were like royalty, arriving around the fourth of July in a big chauffeur-driven car to signify that summer had really started. They saw Mary as a glamorous eccentric, though Herbert was known around Florence as a "pinchpenny." Walter Sternhagen, who lived up the road and was a year younger than Alice, recalled that Herbert bought apples from the Stern- hagens' farm, but when Walter ate one he got yelled at: "These are our apples. You can eat your own apples at home."

In the mornings, Walter and his older sister Hannah would walk down to the Bradley place to deliver milk and butter from his family's farm. Then they were allowed to stay and play until noon. They and Alice would go swimming or clamming, or play in her playhouse in the yard or on the hammocks Mary and Herbert strung between the trees. As Alice got older, she developed a competitive streak. Once when Alice set out to swim across the lake Walter tried to go with her. "She turned around; she said I wouldn't make it."

But the Wisconsin woods were a pale substitute for Africa, and in 1924, when Alice was nine, the Bradleys went back to the Congo. By then, Carl Akeley was planning an expedition with a different backer—the one that would be his last. Martha Miller was exploring French Equatorial Africa with her new husband. The Bradleys decided to put together their own group.

They asked two friends to go with them: Arthur Scott, who taught history at the University of Chicago, and Harry Bigelow, who taught law. To give the trip some of the scientific air they'd had with Akeley, they planned for Bigelow and Scott to take notes on African law and history, while Mary would do some amateur anthropology. They decided to begin in British East Africa this time, cross over into the Belgian Congo, and explore an unmapped area west of the Ruwenzori Range, at the eastern edge of the vast Ituri Forest.

When Herbert's ulcer put him in the hospital that spring, they thought they would have to postpone the trip, but he recovered and insisted on going. The Bradleys found a governess for Alice, arranged to pick up supplies in London, and wrote ahead to outfitters in Nairobi. On June 28, 1924, the party of six sailed from New York on the *Minnewaska*. They planned to go on from Africa to India and the Far East, and make it a year-long trip around the world.

Their second trip to Africa was the high point of all three Bradleys' lives. For months they walked through unmapped wilderness, with "space and beauty flowing round [them] like a sea." It was, Alice said years later, as if they had seen "primeval America, while it still belonged to the Indians, and the great herds of buffalo were there, and the passenger pigeons darkening the sky."

Again Mary made a point of showing how easily things could go wrong. In the Red Sea, on the voyage out from England, they were hit by a heat wave and one of their fellow passengers died suddenly of heat stroke. While the man's baby son "played listlessly on deck, unknowing," his wife watched the crew lower his body into the sea. Mary talked to the hunters on board about lions and wrote down stories of hunts that had been fatal to the wrong party. She was getting ready for her return engagement with mortality.

The safari started this time in Nairobi, where they had lunch at the governor's house, admiring his tame cheetah and his English gardens. It was all part of the package supplied by the famous hunter and outfitter Leslie Tarlton, who also provided equipment and a staff of six "tent boys," four "gun boys," and a cook. The head gun bearer, Omali, had worked for Theodore Roosevelt's son Kermit on Roosevelt's 1909 safari.

They didn't hire a translator: Mary's Swahili was good enough now, and she had worked on her French for the Belgian posts. She had also done more reading on African cultures, and she spent more time on this trip talking to the Africans they met. Mary's book for adults about this trip, *Caravans and Cannibals,* is more serious and insightful than *On the Gorilla Trail.*

What they hadn't brought was the one thing nine-year-old Alice longed for, a gun of her own. In *Alice in Elephantland,* Mary's book for children about the trip, she wrote that the moment Alice heard an elephant trumpeting, she asked her parents excitedly if they were going to kill it.

It wasn't time yet, her father explained:

> "I haven't taken out a license to shoot on British territory. When we get over into the Congo, we'll all have licenses to shoot elephants."
>
> "Will I?" said Alice.
>
> "Don't be silly," said Mummy.
>
> "Why couldn't I have a little gun, with little cartridges? Daddy, why couldn't I?"

Herbert changed the subject. But to call Alice's wish for a gun "silly" is an insult to her capabilities. Any kind of gun, even the kind of air rifle that is commonly given to small boys, would have made her feel more powerful against the dangers of Africa. Alice was well equipped by her parents' lights. She had a governess and a "boy," books, paper, crayons, and the doll that she had won on board ship. (This time Mary had come prepared, and Alice's "old-fashioned crinoline costume" won first prize.) But Alice didn't have the one thing that would have made her feel like a real member of the party. When Alice drew the illustrations for *Alice in Elephantland,* she drew herself with a smoking rifle on her shoulder.

Instead, as they set out on foot from Fort Portal, on the western edge of Uganda, Alice was back in a hammock slung on poles, until a Belgian official finally made her a carrying chair. The adults occasionally let themselves be carried, but for the most part they walked, bringing up the head and rear of the safari with guns to guard against elephants and buffalo.

From Fort Portal the safari crossed over the Semliki River in log canoes and, step by step, passed westward into the great Ituri rain forest of the Belgian Congo. At night they camped at native villages, or at the little Belgian outposts with their one or two white officials and small garrison of Congolese troops. But gradually they passed into territory where the people had not formally submitted to Belgian rule. According to Mary they were cannibals who made war in order to eat the enemy dead; Mary stressed their cannibal nature partly to show that the Bradleys were entering the real, "undomesticated" Africa.

For three and a half months the party walked, circling west of Lake Edward and back down toward Rutshuru and the Ruindi Plains. Afterward they estimated that, counting hunting expeditions, they had walked 1,400 miles. They traveled until they began to have the feeling that comes on long trips, that home was a dream; they had always fallen asleep in canvas tents, then woken in the predawn chill and come out into a dusty campground, washed and put on boots and puttees and drunk campfire coffee in a forest full of orchids and chattering monkeys, or sat looking out from a grassy hill at the snowy Mountains of the Moon.

Into each new village the six whites, eleven "boys," and two hundred porters came, demanding eggs, chickens, corn, fuel, water, more porters, permission to go on. Sometimes they paid with francs, but deeper into the Congo, the only thing of value they could offer was meat, and the most valuable game was elephant. One large bull could feed a thousand people, and besides, the locals hated elephants for destroying their crops. So the party spent long, hard, dangerous days tracking elephants through deep forests, more often failing than succeeding. The few times they did manage to shoot a bull (their local guides were disgusted with their refusal to shoot cows), the meat went quickly. In one remote village, an eager mob stripped some fourteen tons of flesh from two elephants in a little over two hours.

On these hunts, Mary showed that she could walk as far, work as hard, shoot as true as any of them. And Herbert again kept the party together with his prudence, firm hand—he was in charge of keeping the porters from deserting—and hard work. Alice watched and took mental notes. In her memory her father was

> the official non-intellectual of the party, [. . .] a sweet, silent, sensitive, compulsive man of action. His action took the form of [. . .] holding everything together all the time, and required truly heroic exertions. Father got us through by dint of ceaseless vigilance, activity, versatility (he even learned to fill teeth!), checking and double-checking; ridden with malaria, burning with fever, he was the one who went back for a final

check and found the medicine box, or the ammo cans, discarded and about to be lost.

The family tacitly agreed that character, as exemplified by Herbert, was the only thing that kept the expedition from failing. The one relaxed and cheerful member of the party, Arthur Scott, apparently ran away with his gun during a buffalo charge and was "revealed as a weakling and a coward." To Alice, this was "a cautionary tale of major proportions."

In the Ituri Forest, the Bradleys were sometimes the first white people the villagers had ever seen, and they experienced what for most science fiction writers is only a story or a metaphor: "first contact" with the alien. In these contacts, Mary's sex did and didn't matter. Her skin color gave her a power that canceled out her femininity; but being a mother made her more approachable. She was called "Mama" by all Africans who saw her with Alice.

Mary's books about Africa fall into a female travel-writing tradition, one that emphasized ethnography and gently criticized male myths of exploration. Nineteenth-century white male travelers were lyrical on Africa's landscape and indifferent to its culture. In Livingstone's view, "There is nothing interesting in a heathen town." And early-twentieth-century "sportsmen" saw little else but the game. "Finally, I got a clear view of him and fired a finishing shot," reads an American account of hunting the giant sable antelope. "Imagine my joy when we came up to view a horn that measured sixty-one and a quarter inches in length and twelve inches in circumference at the base. It was well worth traveling half around the world and crossing a continent to have found such a trophy."

Western women writers in Africa seldom go on glorious quests or impose their will on a fertile, mysterious landscape. They tend to tell picaresque adventures full of comic mishaps, and to emphasize how foolish the whites appear to the natives. Mary in particular was careful to portray Africans in ways that a middle-class American would find sympathetic. Here she describes dinnertime in a village never before visited by whites:

> No word came about buffalo, and while we waited and watched the village grew much less concerned with us and reverted to its usual occupations. When we gave up hope of a hunt we went in to warm baths and

emerged in dinner costume of pyjamas overlaid with Jaeger bathrobes, and while waiting for dinner we sauntered slowly up and down the street.

In the gathering darkness fires were twinkling before the huts; savory messes of greens were bubbling, plantains roasting, and cakes of banana flour were baking. [. . .] Voices sounded continuously and though they hushed, at first, on our approach, they soon rose again and jests and laughter volleyed back and forth across the clearing, inspired, I fear, by our appearance in our muffling wraps. [. . .]

The women did not eat with the men but when the meal was over husband and wife sat about together before their hut, smoking in tranquil accord. I saw fathers holding their very little babies on their knees, dandling them with greatest pride. There was a tiny baby, not a month old, in the hut next to our tent, a fat, cunning little thing, with bright, shoe-button eyes. Sometimes the father cuddled it, sometimes the mother, sometimes the other young wife, who appeared as delighted as if it were her own. It was a much loved baby, and its little neck was so incased in wire charms [for luck and health] that it could not turn its head.

The appeal of charms for a baby's health must not have been lost on Mary. She devoted a whole chapter of *Caravans and Cannibals* to witchcraft and tried to portray it in a sympathetic light. She defended cannibalism as rooted in custom and a dietary lack of protein, and related the horror of the Congolese on being told that whites killed in war without even eating the enemy.

Between Herbert's and Mary's examples, Alice occupied a frightening middle ground. She could not aspire to Herbert's model: while the grownups hunted, she was left behind in camp with her doll and schoolbooks. And what to Mary was an ethnographic observation was to Alice a threat: she could all too easily picture people getting eaten. Besides, if even getting mad at somebody was a sin in Chicago, why was it all right to murder him in Africa? Alice "was finding out that these African cannibals are much like other folk," Mary wrote brightly in *Alice in Elephantland*. But Alice was drawing a different conclusion than Mary about human nature.

Sometimes she had the fun job of showing the natives Western technology. Villagers who had never seen a door before would ask Alice to open and shut the door on a lantern a hundred times in an evening; they could understand a candle, but not how it had gotten into its glass holder. They demanded endless displays of the prize dolly, which could open and close its eyes. "*Lala hapa*," Alice would say, "she sleeps," rocking the doll in her arms; then she would hold it up, its blue eyes wide open, and say "*Hapana lala*," "Not sleeping." Each time a murmur of awe and pleasure would go through the crowd. Alice was also allowed to trade the party's empty tin cans, highly valued as containers, for spears and arrows for her collection. But she was warned never to shine their flashlight on anyone by accident, lest she be accused of witchcraft.

Some of her encounters were strange in other ways. Most of the people they saw had no clothes on; later, when James Tiptree, Jr., professed a sexual attraction to "aliens," he wondered if it was "because of spending formative years surrounded by the socially-wrong-colored buttocks and pubes of Aliens you mustn't touch." And some were horrifying. Missionary nuns told the Bradleys about female genital mutilation; their stories, Alice wrote, "scared my immature soul sick." She saw grotesque diseases, too, including a girl her own age dying of leprosy.

At the same time, Alice's governess was dealing with Africa by telling her small charge graphic bedtime stories about how the "Red Indians" tortured their captives. It was these other tales about an alien culture (the ones that had figured so prominently in Mary's early fantasies) that absorbed all Alice's anxieties. "I would go to bed imagining each one, try to figure out how I could endure it, or die, and then after about a month of that ask her, Was that all they did? And she had a new one," Alice later recalled. "It wasn't that I wanted to be hurt more; [. . .] I was being told of a danger in the environment and I was in my own way trying to cope." In these stories she could be the hero, but not through great deeds, only through suffering and endurance.

Then one day when Alice was walking at the head of the party, they went around a bend and came upon two dead bodies hanging by the side of the trail. The men had been stripped naked, tortured, tied to posts, and left to perish in the sun.

Alice's parents hurried her away, explaining that the men had probably been accused of witchcraft. Alice got the message: these men were "just like other folk," too—and so were the people who had killed them. Mary didn't write about the dead men in her book, but the Bradleys took photos and put them in their album of the trip. Years later Alice could still recall the scene in detail: the flies that swarmed up as she approached; the rough, crooked little posts crawling with ants. "You think of a crucifixion as taking place on well-edged beams, straight from the wood polisher. No such thing."

Tiptree kept coming back to this story, as if it were an important part of his persona—or as if becoming Tiptree gave Alice enough insulation to speak of it. It was a "horror-recital" like Mary's, a way of talking about her own pain in the world's. She said of the incident that it made her distrust human nature: "Auschwitz—My Lai—etc. etc. etc. did not *surprise* me one bit, later on." She may have connected the men's fate as social outcasts to her own. In one version of the story, to the writer Joanna Russ, Tiptree added, "I was early impressed with the idea that 'orderly' societies can wreak considerable ravage on the deviant individual." Alice may have hoped that her correspondents would recognize both her fear and her brave endurance.

Mary again wrote of a healthy, happy Alice, "thriving as she never did in the sheltered, regular life at home; she was ruddy cheeked, ate like a young cormorant, and slept like a hibernating bear." Caught up in the excitement of the expedition, Alice probably did thrive; but she saved up the frightening parts of Africa to brood on at home.

Her stories of Africa are always more sinister than Mary's. In *Alice in Elephantland*, Mary wrote that one evening, after a long march, Alice "set to work making a labyrinth out of a knoll of tall grass which she called Rosamund's Bower." She urged the others to come explore it, but they were all too tired. Alice herself said she had been running away. "I got into a good patch of elephant grass and made a secret house by crushing the grass down. Mother led a search after me and hauled me back out." Where Mary described picaresque adventures, Alice seems to have gotten into a different book, something by Conrad or Haggard, a voyage into unknown and hostile regions of the human heart.

After the Ituri Forest the party traveled south to the Ruindi and Rutshuru plains, then south again, skirting the Virungas, to Kivu and Tanganyika. There they entered the Belgian territory of Ruanda and Urundi and met Belgians and Africans they knew from the trip three years before. But Bujumbura, the Belgian capital, at the northern tip of Tanganyika, was already much more developed, with new roads, new docks, even a hotel. Progress— including their own travels—was destroying the very wilderness they had come to see.

The travelers left Africa at Dar es Salaam and spent January to June 1925 touring India, the Dutch East Indies, Indochina, China, and Japan. After Africa, the rest was disappointing. Instead of walking they took cabs and rode on dusty trains. Instead of khakis they wore tropical white suits and dresses. Instead of drinking coffee in camp, they ate their breakfast in hotel dining rooms. Having been an explorer-heroine, Mary disliked being a tourist. The hunting was all staged for Westerners, she complained. Even the elephants were tame.

Mary especially hated India, with its crowds, filth, poverty, and purdah. In Africa they had seen neither wealth nor hunger, but here they saw the rich walk past beggars starving on the street. In Africa she had been curious about the local customs, but India brought out pragmatic disapproval. She was angry too about the child brides, veils, and restrictions on women's movements. They were warned not to let nine-year-old Alice go anywhere alone, not even from her room to the hotel dining room.

Almost everything Alice saw in India went into the category of "horror-recitals." In Calcutta, she said later, "As we went for some morning sweet cake, we'd step over dying people with dying babies in their arms." She saw "starving dwarf-children roving around racks of bones that were mothers trying to nurse more babies, toothless mouths and unbearable eyes turning on me from rag heaps that were people." Again she saw frightening scenes she was told were normal, such as "a man on the steps of the Ganges reverently—and quite inadequately—burning his mother's body, and then leaping into the water to fish up the still recognisable skull and pry out the gold teeth." She thought of her own grandmother, lying in a silk-lined casket in Chicago. She wondered if that was normal. She wondered if this was what it meant to be human.

From Calcutta the Bradleys went on to the Dutch East Indies, where they toured Java and Sumatra and unsuccessfully hunted tigers. In Sumatra, Mary went out of her way to visit villages of a much-studied matrilineal people, the Minangkabau. In a traditional Minangkabau family, married couples don't live together. Instead, adult men and women remain in their mother's house.

Men visit their wives, but care for their sisters' children as their own. Women can own and inherit property—to an early-twentieth-century Western woman, an enviable power. Later, on the lecture circuit, Mary often spoke to women's groups on the Minangkabau, under the almost science-fictional title "Where Women Rule."

The Bradleys left Sumatra tigerless and went on to Saigon, "the Paris of the Orient," with its patisseries, French fashions, and "sidewalks full of gayly dressed people, with electric lights springing out overhead and the long rays of motor headlights sweeping up and down the hill." In the interior, Mary finally got her tiger. Via Shanghai, Nagasaki, and San Francisco, they returned to Chicago in June 1925. War in East Asia was only a few years away—in Shanghai, the Bradleys witnessed a riot that was the start of the Chinese Revolution. But in 1974 Tiptree recalled a time fifty years earlier when he "rode a pony in peaceful woodlands in a place now called Vietnam."

By then all the colonies the Bradleys had visited had vanished or been transformed. But it was partly from colonial adventure stories like Mary's that science fiction was born. From the beginning, science fiction drew on Westerns and exploration stories. Sometimes the writers were the same: Kipling wrote science fiction, and while Edgar Rice Burroughs wrote of Tarzan's adventures in a fantastic Africa, he was also dreaming up the Martian kingdom of Barsoom. Even now, much of science fiction is about travel and hardship, technology and "magic," contact with the alien, outposts on the frontier. The first time Alice saw *Star Trek,* she recognized it at once as a story about her childhood.

But science fiction also has the power to rewrite the colonial narrative. It can acknowledge and even celebrate cultural confusion, bring human and alien together, change the intentions and the endings. For Alli, it became a way to take over the story and make it hers, to tear down the walls between herself and the grownups and the aliens. In science fiction, Alice was finally able to write her way out of her mother's box—with Tiptree as the narrator and the hero.

To grow up as a "girl" is to be nearly fatally spoiled, deformed, confused, and terrified; to be responded to by falsities, to be reacted to as nothing or as a thing—and nearly to become that thing.

To have no steady routine of growth and training, but only a series of explosions into unwanted adulation—and then into limbo.

The world was not my oyster.

—ALICE SHELDON

Back in Chicago, in the summer of 1925, the Bradleys again unpacked the trophies and souvenirs, the spears and arrows and thumb pianos from the Ituri Forest, the elephant's foot to make into an umbrella stand, the batik and cloth of gold from Sumatra. The papers photographed the three Bradleys posing with the tiger skin; the *Chicago Evening American* captioned their photo "Jungle Huntress and Nine Feet of Captured Ferocity."

Caravans and Cannibals ran as a serial in the *Chicago Tribune* in the fall of 1925 and came out in book form the next year. Then Mary wrote her two children's books, *Alice in Jungleland* and *Alice in Elephantland,* and a book about their travels through Asia, *Trailing the Tiger.* Twelve-year-old Alice illustrated the two children's books with lively silhouette drawings of animals and the safari on the march.

Mary turned out to have a talent for public speaking. Travel lectures with slides were a popular entertainment, and Mary began giving talks at universities, churches, and social clubs throughout the Midwest. The *Chicago Tribune* called Mary "one of the most gifted and natural speakers of the day, with a ringing voice and a vibrant personality, gallant and courageous, yet very feminine. [. . .] Mrs. Bradley takes one across Africa tense, yet safe: thrilled, mystified, enchanted." The *Cleveland Press* wrote, "Mrs. Bradley is good to look upon as well as to listen to. Her clear eyes sparkle, her smile is an illumination not soon forgotten [. . .]. She is aglow with enthusiasm, kindled by high adventure, which is peculiarly infectious."

The Bradleys now saw themselves as explorers. They got to know Martin and Osa Johnson. Roy Chapman Andrews looked them up when he passed through Chicago. Prince William of Sweden, an avid big game hunter, did the same. Herbert joined clubs for adventurers, such as the Cliff-Dwellers in Chicago and the Explorers Club in New York. Mary maintained her friendships with Mickie Akeley and Martha Miller.

And Mary became a member of the Society of Woman Geographers. An alternative to men-only networks such as the Explorers Club, the society was founded in 1925 in Washington, D.C., by a small group of adventurous women, including Marguerite Harrison (who collaborated on the classic documentary *Grass*) and Blair Niles (who exposed French Guiana's notorious prison camp in her 1928 book *Condemned to Devil's Island*). Its founding was reported under headlines such as "Women Brave Jungle Perils" and "Penetration of Wilds Necessary for Membership in Society." Early members included Mickie Akeley and Elsie Bell Grosvenor, who with her husband, Gilbert, ran the National Geographic Society. Eventually the society came to include anthropologists (Margaret Mead, Theodora Kroeber), photojournalists (Margaret Bourke-White), environmentalists (Rachel Carson), mountain climbers (Annie Smith Peck), and such all-around famous women as Amelia Earhart and Eleanor Roosevelt. Mary went to meetings in Washington and was active in the society until she was in her seventies.

By now the Bradleys knew most of Chicago society, literary and otherwise. Edgar Lee Masters and Carl Sandburg came to the house. They got to know the prominent Field and McCormick families: their close friend Chauncey McCormick was one of the richest men in Chicago and the cousin of Colonel Robert McCormick, the influential publisher of the *Chicago Tribune*. One afternoon a month they were "at home" to friends, and the friends sometimes brought visiting celebrities: Sinclair Lewis, Somerset Maugham, Ethel Barrymore.

Mary went to New York once or twice a year to see editors and friends, and hosted parties in Chicago for such New York visitors as Lila Luce, the first wife of the founder of *Time*. (The two women remained close long after Henry

Luce left Lila for Clare Boothe, and Mary would call on her friend's connections at least once to spy on Alice's love life.) Mary had many women friends, and was helpful to younger women in their careers. Yet Alice recalled her mother as a "queen bee" who liked male attention and surrounded herself with adoring men. Alice, too, learned that what men thought about you mattered more.

After Herbert, Mary's number-one adoring man was Herbert's best friend, Harry Bigelow. A widower, "Uncle Harry" lived just a few blocks from the Bradleys and came to dinner several times a week. When Herbert was out of town, Harry took Mary to the theater. When Mary was away he came over to see Herbert. Mary worried about Harry's stomach trouble; Harry worried about Mary's headaches. Comforting the sick was one of the great expressions of Bradley love; but when Mary had a sinus infection on one of their trips, it was Harry, not Herbert, who massaged her face. In Mary's date book, where she briefly noted each day's events, she called them "HEB" (Herbert Edwin Bradley) and "HAB" (Harry Augustus Bigelow), as if to emphasize that they were nearly interchangeable. With no children of his own, Harry devoted a lot of attention to Alice, and she returned the favor. When she was fourteen, he was still teasing her about her habit of climbing up him, choking him, or sitting "draped around my lap like an affectionate giraffe."

There was apparently a lot of physical affection between Mary and Alice as well. Mary often worked in bed, and had long talks with Alice there. When Alice was sixteen Mary could still close a letter to her with, "Much love, my dear girl—I shall be glad when I can get my squirmy child in bed with me and have a chatter with her."

The nicknames they all used for each other seem to blur the distinctions between Herbert and Harry, mother and daughter. To Herbert, Harry, and Alice, Mary was "Bunny" or "Rabbit." Alice was also "Bunny," or "Alice Bunny," or "Bunnette," or Mary called her "Child." In letters, Mary addressed both Herbert and Harry as "Darlint." Alice sometimes wrote to "Mummy and Daddy" or to "Darlings," but also to "Herbert and Mary." Mary often treated Alice as her best friend and companion. But at other times Alice was abruptly relegated to the position of child, or called upon to mother her mother, or left out of the adult triangle.

Mother and daughter were extremely close, and daughter got a lot of attention, but Mary was the one who had center stage. Alice's cousin Barbara Francisco thought there was a competitive streak in the family, one that had begun with the two sisters, Mary and Sylvia. She recalled that at family get-togethers and at Christmas, "Mary would gather all the men—because I think the women turned off—into another room. Then they'd shut the door and she would spout forth. She was a great—not raconteur, more than that, she really dished it out. [. . .] And people just listened, I mean, that's what you did with Mary, listened. It must have been the same with Mary and Alice."

Growing up in the midst of all this public achievement and unspoken emotion, Alice felt both doted on ("I got the feeling of being on a microscope plate, with all these enormous eyepieces goggling down at me") and disincluded. Her parents told her she was intelligent and beautiful, but compared to them and their friends she felt small and stupid. (Tiptree recalled one "awful moment [. . .] when I burst, age ten, into my parents' genteel gathering of most of the English departments of two universities, and [. . .] inquired loudly and loftily whether anyone there had ever heard of 'a man called Charles Algernon Swinburne?'") There were no other kids; Alice's cousins, Marilyn and Barbara Francisco, were ten and twelve years younger.

Adults compared Alice to her mother constantly, to Alice's despair: "I couldn't count the times I was patted on the head by some Eminence and told, 'Little girl, if you're ever half as talented, half as charming, half as good—capable—warm-hearted—plucky—beautiful—witty—(name ten)—as your mother, you'll be lucky.'" Alice grew up terrified of turning out "just an ordinary, medium-bright human. [. . .] If I wasn't somehow Somebody, it would represent such a failure I'd have to kill myself to keep my parents from knowing how I'd betrayed their hopes."

Years later Alice said,

A mother so able, no matter how dear and loving—and Mary gave real love—is still bad for a daughter because you identify with her. And without meaning to, you compete. And to be in competition with Mary was devastation, because anything I could do she could do ten times as well. It never occurred to me that I was a child and she was a grown woman and that was to be expected.

Alice blamed herself, but it's hard to believe all the competing came from one side. Mary even stole Alice's original claim to fame, her precocity. Approaching fifty, she took five years off her age, and now claimed she had sold her first story not at twenty but at fifteen.

Because of her talent for drawing, it had already been decided that Alice was going to be an artist, a creative person like her mother. "Mary foresaw happy years of her writings being illuminated by her little yellow-haired daughter," Alice later assessed. She was also good at science and mechanics. One Christmas Mary gave her an electric train set, and Alice's room "soon looked like a tool shop." She recalled staring for hours in science class at a set of prisms—the start of a long fascination with the science of seeing. But no one ever suggested that she could be a scientist, or study animals like her Uncle Akeley, or even be a lawyer like her father. She loved the cool precision of mathematics, and was good at it, but when her high school course load got too heavy, that was the class her teachers advised her to drop.

At twelve, she became a celebrity in her own right, as the protagonist and illustrator of *Alice in Jungleland.* The book was used in primary schools, and in Alice's memory whole classes of schoolchildren were brought to meet the girl who had been to Africa. But that only made it worse. Alice felt she suffered from what Ellen Moers calls "the warpage of gifted girls by an excess of domestic admiration." She was constantly fussed over and praised. She was so charming, everyone said, and her drawings were so lively and original. But she felt "valued only because I was my parents' child, not for myself." No one took her seriously enough to give her a real challenge. No one gave her room to make art for herself.

Mary, who knew how hard it was for a woman to have a career, did her best to open doors for her daughter. This frustrated Alice, who wanted to make it on her own. It also meant that when Alice broke with her mother, she didn't know where else to go. There were so few models, so few successful women. Mary's example couldn't make up for the rest of the world. Besides, a competition with a parent is doomed from the start: you're a loser if you fail, a traitor if you win.

Virginia Woolf once wondered what might have happened to her career if her writer father had not died when she was twenty-two. If that dynamic, demanding person had lived on, she thought, "his life would have entirely ended mine. [. . .] No writing, no books;—inconceivable." Mary and Herbert lived a long time—he died at eighty-six, she at ninety-four—and their long, long presence in Alice's life did very nearly kill off her creative career. It took Alice most of a lifetime to find a way out from under the shadow of their good intentions.

In the fall of 1925, ten-year-old Alice was sent to the University of Chicago Laboratory Schools. The Lab Schools was the private school for Hyde Park intellectuals, an experimental teaching workshop set up by the educator John Dewey. Classes were small and loosely structured, and children learned by doing. They studied geography by making maps, learned Latin in conversation, and did science by building thermometers or estimating the latitude of Chicago.

But even in a creative, child-centered environment, Alice's abilities to trade tin cans for spears or entertain a whole village with a doll didn't help her much. At first she made an effort in class. "I naively thought that I would win approval by excelling, and I was very competitive," she recalled. "My little hand would always shoot up if I knew the answer, and the more desperate I got the cleverer I acted." But by age twelve she was drawing and dreaming her way through school hours while the school sent concerned letters to the Bradleys. "Alice is a very gifted little girl with a great deal of linguistic ability which she is exercising just enough to meet the barest requirements and no more," her French teacher wrote dryly. "She withdraws from class activities at every opportunity into her own world of fancies and sketches." And her math teacher saw a pattern Alice would have throughout her school career: "erratic" study habits and "frequent periods of poor application" mixed with "intervals of intense work."

The rest of the time she worked at fitting in. Having spent a lot of time with adults, she was both precocious and babyish, "mature" and awkward with kids her age. Her intelligence made her clumsy. She saw through things that other kids didn't, and said things they couldn't understand. Barbara Francisco recalled, "You see people sometimes who have such a high IQ they're

stumbling over themselves. They never can get righted; it's like they're running on ice. Alice was like that."

Mary saw Alice's loneliness and tried to help. She and Herbert showed
their Africa films to Alice's class and encouraged her to invite schoolmates over
to the apartment. The girls were mainly impressed by Mary and the African
Room. One girl, who must have been visiting at the time Prince William of
Sweden came to town, remembered being told to play quietly because the
Prince of Wales was in the next room.

Another classmate, Cynthia Grabo, recalled that Alice "was a very talented artist, extremely smart and very pretty. [. . .] In Latin class, the rest
of us were struggling with Caesar, and the teacher would go around the
class, and we would all struggle, and then she would look at Alice, who had
probably been sitting there drawing, and Alice would rattle off the answer."
But there was something pro forma about her friendships. "I don't remember her having close friends in high school," Grabo said. "I was invited over
to her fabulous apartment from time to time, but we weren't intimate
friends." Alice did not have intimate friends, then or later. Almost everyone
who ever knew her found her wonderful, warm, charming, and funny, and
almost everyone begins their recollections with "I didn't really know her
very well."

By early adolescence Alice was keeping late hours, sometimes hardly sleeping,
sometimes sleeping around the clock. Mary jokingly called her "little Never-
Go-to-Bed and Never-Get-Up." She also had severe headaches. Between
classes she would go into the school bathroom and hit her head against the
tiled wall "to try to 'break' whatever was hurting so inside."

Summers at the Lodge were better, especially when Alice learned how to
ride. Riding was a real, physical challenge; she later wrote, "I dreamed horse
and lived horse and expected, if necessary, to marry a horse; for all practical
purposes I *was* a horse." The neighbors would catch sight of her streaking
down the road, her long hair streaming behind her like a banner. With a local
friend, a girl nicknamed "Johnny," she rode bareback, jumped, and practiced
circus tricks, riding standing up on two horses tied together. Later, in boarding schools, Alice jumped, fell, was dragged, got back on, and was thrilled

when riding masters complimented her on her courage. Mary approved, while Herbert warned, "Just remember that you are the only daughter we have." Yet it was partly Herbert she was seeking to please with her bravery. "Alice had a real danger streak in her," Barbara Francisco recalled. "That made her so different from me. She was like someone from Mars."

In the winter, like all too-bright, lonely children, Alice read. Curled up in a little cupboard under the stairs, eating soda crackers, she puzzled over the unexpurgated *Arabian Nights* and read and reread the complete works of Kipling. *Arabian Nights* was baffling with its graphic and archaic sexual language (Alice wondered what a "slit" was), but Kipling was her great love. Years later she wrote, "All of what I know about short-story writing and plotting came from Kipling, and will probably end there."

Kipling is a great writer about cultural confusion. Stories like *Kim* and *The Jungle Book* are about finding one's way in a foreign culture: a child who fit nowhere could imagine herself as Mowgli, at home among the animals, or Kim, "little friend of all the world." They are fantasies about "passing," with its promise of escape, transformation, and belonging. "Passing" allows Kim and Mowgli to be included, and yet they are always a little more important than the rest (Kim being white, Mowgli being human). For Kim, being in disguise is the opposite of being the doll in the box, in which all eyes are on you and you can't move. It lets him go anywhere, do anything, learn all the grownups' secrets while never revealing his own.

Unlike Mary, Alice didn't have a myth about herself as a writer. Where Mary had had her Indian stories, Alice was wary of her own fantasy life. "I never permitted myself an imaginary playmate (against the rules even then)," she once wrote. But she did have an ongoing secret story, about escaping into a world "where special sexual and empathic activities reigned—a world without unassuaged tears, without death and real pain."

And there were times when she longed for the sister who had died. Barbara Francisco felt she "had a romantic fantasy" about her sister. "For a while she tried to fit me into that, to make this cousin into her lost sister. That was Alice being dramatic, overdramatic." In Tiptree's letters, Alli changed her dead sister into a brother, suggesting that the identification was strong.

———

Alice's other great love, science fiction, belonged to summer and the Lodge. One year, she said, Uncle Harry went to get an order of literary journals from the local bookstore. When he returned with his package, out fell a large, cheaply printed magazine called *Weird Tales*. Its cover showed "a large green octopus removing a young lady's golden brassiere." Everyone stared.

> "Ah," said Uncle Harry. "Oh. Oh yes. I, ah, picked this up for the child."
> "Uncle Harry," I said, my eyes bulging, "*I* am the child. May I have it, please?"

From then on Alice and Uncle Harry carried on a conspiracy, trading issues, reading Lovecraft, discovering *Amazing* and *Wonder Stories* and the other pulp classics. They never talked about it; "It was just Our Secret." Alone in her cabin, huddled under the quilts in the flickering candlelight, Alice flew rocket ships to strange planets, battled monsters, or traveled in time, in stories that recalled her own visions of skeletons in baby carriages, her hallucinations of the future in the present. Science fiction, like the woods around the Lodge, was a secret space that Alice could explore alone.

In its early days, the genre had a strong positivist strain: rational man, represented by the white-coated scientist, could always defeat the monstrous alien threat. Alice, raised to believe in courage and reason (and frightened by humans' equal love of superstition and witchcraft), must have found this reassuring. Yet science fiction also embraces alienation. Its writers regard Earth from a faraway viewpoint, which they name Venus or Osnome or Barsoom. From such a distance in space or time, the ordinary world loses its hold. Like all fans, Alice longed to go to such a place, where she might feel at home.

The magazines themselves were a distant world, a paper universe inhabited by enthusiastic, argumentative fans. Not content just to read, the fans wrote long letters back to the magazines. They invented the fanzine (and coined the word), mimeographing page after page of their own opinions for anyone who would read them. And by the late 1930s, tribes of awkward, self-conscious youths—Alice's contemporaries, later Tiptree's editors and friends—were meeting in national science fiction conventions.

But Alice didn't go to the conventions. Why should she? She was not, in any visible way, an outsider. She was beautiful, well-bred, talented. If she was going to be unconventional at all, she intended to be charismatic, discerning, and bohemian, not scruffy, opinionated, and weird. And if she was unhappy in her parents' glamorous world, she only thought it was because she wasn't glamorous *enough*. She wanted to be more sought-after, more popular, more beautiful. She wanted to be like Mary, so impeccably feminine that she could get away with being herself.

In 1929, when she was fourteen, Alice left home. To get away from her family, and to ride horses all year round, she got herself sent to a chic Swiss finishing school and spent a disastrous year trying to learn how to be a girl.

CHAPTER 6: GIRLS' SCHOOL (1929-30)

There is the vanity training, the obedience training, the self-effacement training, the deference training, the dependency training, the passivity training, the rivalry training, the stupidity training, the placation training. How am I to put this together with my human life, my solitude, my transcendence, my brains, and my fearful, fearful ambition?

—JOANNA RUSS, *THE FEMALE MAN*

Les Fougères, in Lausanne, Switzerland, had thirty-five English and American students. Most of them were older than Alice. Some, the seventeen- and eighteen-year-olds, were already engaged to be married. They had come to Les Fougères to learn riding, good manners, and French. A year of French, Mary pointed out, would be useful for Alice's next trip to Africa.

Despite all Alice's travels, her Chicago society snobbery, and the shopping she and Mary did in Paris on the way, she arrived at her new school in September 1929 in braces, with socks instead of stockings, and felt desperately young and out of place. In a rare complaint to her parents, she wrote that the other girls' social sophistication made her feel like "a little calf among gazelles." "I'm such a square peg!" she lamented. "I'm so rude and rough and queer." Years later, in an interview with science fiction writer Charles Platt, she said that in her school days "I was known as That Girl and no one would room with me. [. . .] They didn't really loathe me; they just didn't count me as a girl."

So Alice did her best to be more like the other girls; that is, more girlish. She neglected her schoolwork and filled whole letters home with news of her new clothes: a pair of beige pumps, a hat and purse to match her fur coat, a jacket, a ski outfit, a peach crepe de chine dress. She was overjoyed when her parents sent her pearls for Christmas, and told them, "I'm going to be one of those people who are always in 'Unimpeachable good taste.' I am violently cultivating it." She affected what she hoped was a sophisticated accent, imitating her English roommates. (Later, when she repented of her class snobbery, she made an effort to lose it again, but she went on using British spelling: even Tiptree wrote "colour" and "realise.") She came to the school's New Year's Eve costume party dressed as an "old-fashioned girl" and once again won first prize.

She was good at leading mischief: late-night pranks during school trips, nighttime raids on the kitchen. (They were all hungry, and Alice saw it as her duty as an explorer to provide food.) Later on, she organized her schoolmates in a distance-peeing contest. But the girls who admired and followed her she thought of as "stooges," whom she "secretly despised." At the same time she had schoolgirl crushes on more glamorous girls and felt rejected when they were not returned. She didn't know how to talk to the other students. Either she tried too hard to be entertaining, or she blurted out her thoughts on horses or (later) Hegel, and they turned off. Trying to be honest, she came on too strong, was too serious or funny, too boisterous or withdrawn.

Alice had the bad luck to be extremely pretty. If she hadn't been, she might have given up the popularity contest. She might have studied harder, prepared for a career, and not cared what people thought. She and the other awkward, bright girls might have been friends. Instead she cared about appearances, practiced femininity and flirtation, and got addicted to the rewards for being a pretty girl.

She didn't do much schoolwork at Les Fougères. The school secretary wrote the Bradleys that Alice was attractive and bright, but had poor study habits and was "wayward and careless." Except for pictures of horses, she wasn't even drawing. One day, she later said, she climbed a tree and "stayed there all day crying, with the whole place upside down looking for me." She sneaked out at night and prowled around, sometimes "rejoicing to see the lighted windows, *they inside*, in the light—*me* outside, in the free and silent dark." Sometimes she went down to the railroad tracks to see how close she could stand when the train to Geneva came through.

Alice later saw her danger-seeking as covert suicide attempts, and she was desperate enough to make one deliberate try at suicide. She got hold of some razor blades, put them in the spine of a heavy history book, and brought them down hard on her wrist. Luckily she didn't know what she was doing and cut the wrong side. "I woke up tied to the rug with ropes of dry blood and got up & cleaned up and went to gym class," Tiptree casually told his friend Jeff

Smith; but Alice carried, for the rest of her life, thin scars on the back of one wrist.

In her sixties, Alice was diagnosed with cyclothymia, a form of bipolar disorder in which depression alternates with periods of high energy, or "hypomania." Cyclothymia is essentially manic-depression without the mania, but (at least in Alice's case) with all the grim emotional depths. Whatever the source of Alice's depressions, they came to her with a frightening persistence. No matter what she did to eliminate the causes of unhappiness, she would suddenly, without warning, without apparent cause, be overwhelmed by despair.

Alice desperately wanted to be her parents' happy daughter. Sometimes she was, especially at the times when she was "up," in a good mood, with its heightened energy and intensity. But she had no control over the other, unhappy Alice. And she literally couldn't tell her parents how unhappy she was. When she tried, she felt Mary didn't hear, or took her daughter's unhappiness as rejection. In a long letter Alice wrote Mary in 1961, she tried to explain:

> I was told I was happy, I was informed as to how a happy and affectionate person behaves, and I did my best, quite unconsciously and naturally, to behave so [. . .]. Whenever the internal commotion let up, I was indeed what I seemed. [. . .] But the continual evidence that something inside me was causing acute misery and alienating me wholly from life was so strong that I was faced with the choice—figure things out or die.

One of the central stories of Alice's life is of a solitary struggle with depression. Suicide is part of that story: when she couldn't stand it anymore, she promised herself suicide as a way out. She felt this made life a choice, not an obligation.

Like all girls of her generation, Alice wrote cheerful letters home, letters that concealed her real life behind a smokescreen of chatter and affection. In the first one, to Mary, she wrote, "I've got pictures of you and Daddy under my mattress [. . .] and posted all around. I'm getting a little reaction from the excitement and feeling punk, but that'll pass. [. . .] My roommates and the rest are awfully nice and all, and I'm so glad I came here." She talked a lot about clothes, a comfortable subject between Alice and Mary. News about dresses and shopping would fill Alice's letters home for years, while Herbert urged his daughter to be more careful with money. She worried about her dog Congo and her gold-fish, asked for packages of food, sent her love to the young Irish housemaids, Annie and Agnes, and patronized her parents, calling Mary "my silly darling."

Herbert, Mary, and Uncle Harry all wrote to Alice. Uncle Harry was af-fectionate, and Herbert funny, kind, and stern. In January, when Alice be-came homesick and lonely and asked if she could come home early, Herbert answered,

> If I followed the dictates of my heart I would send for you to come home
> at once and meet you with open arms. [. . .] I felt it was a long ways
> from home but having undertaken to do a thing you know your father
> well enough to know that he never wants to stop in the middle and I am
> very much afraid that it would not be fair to your school, nor to us, nor
> to you to come home in the middle of the year.

He reminded her, jokingly, "The traditions of the Bradley family have to be upheld and there is no one but you to do it."

This was frightening, but Alice also found the appeal to fairness and brav-ery reassuring. When she worried that she was "too temperamental," Herbert responded calmly, "I don't think you are at all too temperamental; all you need is a balance wheel. Temperament is a perfectly good thing if you just di-rect it a little bit."

Mary's advice seems less helpful to a moody, "square peg" daughter. When Alice complained of loneliness, Mary advised her to be more attentive to the other pupils. "Maybe, my dear girl, you aren't interested enough in *their* affairs—really interested—and they'd be more friendly if they felt you were. Don't put it on—just try to see their lives as interesting. You'll learn." She as-sured her, "You are taking life the right way, darling, if you keep jolly and keep going—that's all any of us can do. Some of my school friends who have the loveliest lives had to work the hardest to adjust themselves."

When Alice said she had argued with a teacher, Mary responded sensibly, "Don't scrap with little teachers who are set in their ways—great waste of time and energy and lack of understanding." But then she added, "Remember you are at the cocky age, little thing, and be retiring even if you think your little bean is right! It is more clever to be courteous than right! Also lovelier."

And when Alice asked if she could cut off her hair, Mary said absolutely not. Alice thought its weight might be causing her frequent headaches, and besides, long hair was old-fashioned—almost all girls her age wore a bob. "It marks me as a 'kid,' and so I get condescended to, and patronized, and oh how miserable I do get!"

Mary sent a telegram, then wrote a long letter urging Alice to keep her hair.

> My child, my child, you don't know what you'd be sacrificing. That hair is your beauty, Alice. I tell you truly, it is your style—you have something that others haven't. It means more than you know. [. . .] You don't know how people admire it. And the ones who suggest you cut it are often prompted by an unconscious desire—if they were psychoanalyzed—to do away with something more distinguished than they have or their children. Sylvia, for instance, would say cut it. She has tried vainly for her girls to have curls. I am speaking very frankly to you, just explaining, with no feeling at all. [. . .] It's the thing that gives you your charm and character and singles you out from the rest. Everybody has something. You have hair in particular.

Mary was possessive of Alice's looks (and clearly competitive about them with her sister), despite her claim of "no feeling."

Mary knew she was possessive, tried not to be, and usually failed. In one rather overwhelming letter, when Alice was starting her next boarding school at sixteen, Mary wrote,

> You needn't try to spare my feelings [about money], like Daddy's, for you and I are one and I want to know about things and change them if necessary. [. . .] But child of mine, I never want my love to be possessive or oppressive and you must never feel that it is—you are my dear girl and I want you to have your own life and as full as may be. I don't need to tell you how I love you. And I am deeply proud of you, Alice; your will to do right is a very precious thing to me.

Alice is "my dear girl" and "child of mine," while even her will itself belongs to Mary. And if Mary couldn't help loving too much, then Alice would have to make sure never to feel it.

While Alice was in Lausanne, Mary was working on one of her best and most acclaimed short stories, about a girl whose future depends on her ability to wear a mask of charm. "The Five-Minute Girl" takes place during debut season, when for days and nights of dinner parties and dances, young women compete for the prize of male approval.

The story's heroine is Judy, an only child who "seemed always to have been away at school, at camp or traveling. She was really an outsider to these sons and daughters of her parents' friends. All right for her fond parents to think that all they had to do was to introduce her." At their gentle insistence she goes to a debut ball, where the goal for girls is not to meet friends or find love, but to be disposable on the dance floor.

> If the men didn't give you a rush, grabbing you from one partner to another, you were sunk. If a man got caught with you, you had to dance on and on in an inferno of togetherness. [. . .] Getting cut in on, being a two-minute girl—that was the stuff. She didn't dare to hope that for herself—only a few pulled that off—but she longed, with all her frantic, passionate young heart, to be a five-minute girl—a girl that a man could be sure of getting rid of in a decently short time.

To achieve five-minute status the girls play a nervous masquerade: "All about her Judy saw girls' faces set in little masks of delight but with shafts of anxiety darting out the eyeholes of the masks—shafts of entreaty, of appeal, of fierce affronted pride." It doesn't work: Judy gets stuck with a boy, and no one will cut in. This nightmare calls for a Cinderella ending: even if all the other girls are lost, let Judy be saved. Instead, the author lets her character fall. So desperate is Judy to be liked that she lets a drunken older playboy lead her into a corner. He kisses her, someone sees, and her ruin is complete. The story has been told from her point of view all along, but at the end, while Judy lies in "the blessed oblivion of sleep," her parents talk sadly of the collapse of their dreams for their daughter.

The ending is a symbolic death—the death of Judy as an active, speaking subject. She fails and forfeits her voice—yet her subjectivity is a sham, since the popular girls are also trapped in the masquerade. There's only one way to survive: the exhausting balancing act of the five-minute girl, one who is liked enough to have the illusion of freedom.

This was Mary's way of surviving, and perhaps Mary was projecting onto Judy her own fear of losing her balance. Yet Mary's insight into the alienating aspects of a debutante ball didn't stop her from pushing Alice to make her debut.

"The Five-Minute Girl" won third prize in the O. Henry Awards for 1931. More importantly, it was published in the most widely read, best-paying magazine in America, the *Saturday Evening Post*. Mary had never before written for the *Post*, but Alice's year in Lausanne coincided with the start of the Depression. The income from Herbert's apartment buildings was starting to dry up. Mary's light fiction was about to become serious business.

By the end of the school year, Alice was pleading with Mary to come over and get her in Lausanne. The Bradleys asked her to come home with a schoolmate instead. Herbert wrote, "I'll trust you to be a good sport and see it through like a little lady. You know you are my only child and I'm very proud of you and for you." But Alice wanted her mother. "Maybe it's the traipsing about together and the comradeship. We could ride and swim together for a week here, and Paris and the boat. [. . .] I've made silly little plans and promises to myself all year about the day or two when you should come and I could tell you all about everything." At the same time she mothered Mary, writing, "I hope you're taking proper care of yourself? I'm dying to see you, but I don't want a tired-out bunny!"

Despite the expense—the trip cost five or six hundred dollars, the equivalent of about ten thousand now—Mary answered her daughter's pleas and came. They spent some time together in Paris and sailed for New York in July.

But intimacy with Mary had its price, in more ways than one. Years later, Alice told Joanna Russ that when she was fourteen, "in a steamy little stateroom on a boat," her mother "more or less openly invited me to bed with her. [. . .] I almost did but the gleam of her gold fillings put me off. (I have this horror of *age,* see.) Also, I didn't know how."

Alice mentioned this episode only one other time, in a diary, shortly before her mother's death. Recalling the real closeness and happiness she'd once had with her parents, she wrote,

> With Mary I must have had a real love affair going for many years; she had so much, she was great to be with, she so loved and understood. (Witness my lesbian impulse toward her later, in that ship's cabin— saved only by the gleam of her gold fillings.) It was Mother I wept for at Les Fougères. Even as I came to hate it, I loved and was vulnerable. Shall I blame her for being a seductress? She thought this was the way to bring up a child—her known intentions were only for my good. I cannot blame her. She created great, if lethal, happiness and tried to create more.

This time Alice shared credit for the almost-pass, but there would always be a "lethal" element in Alice's story about Mary.

The return home is one of the great recurring Tiptree themes: to be away from home is to yearn for it, to return is to be destroyed, or to destroy. Tiptree's short story "Painwise" describes an interstellar explorer whose pain circuits have been neurologically bypassed to make him a better research instrument. He tries repeatedly to kill himself because he can't bear to feel no pain: "I can't seem to feel, well, real this way." At last he is rescued by a group of furry telepaths who like his inability to suffer: he can't pass painful signals on to them. In their womblike ship they give him nice food, sex, and cuddling, but still he longs for Earth and the one forbidden emotion, pain. At last he leaves them and makes his way home, only to discover that his pain circuits have been wired to Earth itself: its once beloved smells and sounds now throw him into mortal agony.

Alli Sheldon assumed that the return home in her stories represented a return to childhood. But in "Painwise" home might also be the true self, neglected, terribly painful to inhabit, achieved at cost of separation from maternal love. "Jagged, ugly. Unendurable," the explorer says just before he passes out. "But real—"

In another story, "The Man Who Walked Home," an astronaut sent forward in time finds a horrifying nothingness and struggles frantically to get back.

> Whatever it was, that place into which he transgressed, it could not support his life there, his violent and violating aberrance, and he, fierce, brave, crazy—clenched into total protest, one body-fist of utter repudiation of himself there in that place, forsaken there—what did he do? Rejected, exiled, hungering homeward more desperate than any lost beast driving for its unreachable home, his home, his HOME [. . .]
>
> He walked.
> Home.

But the man's return will set off—or, in the logic of time travel, has already set off—an explosion that will annihilate the home he longs for.

Alice returned to Chicago looking more than ever like a young lady. At the Lodge, her childhood friend Walter Sternhagen saw the change and thought Alice was becoming more like her mother.

Mary Hastings Bradley on a promotional postcard for her novel *The Palace of Darkened Windows*, 1914. *(Courtesy of Barbara Francisco)*

Alice Bradley, circa 1916. James Tiptree, Jr., once sent a copy of this photo to an editor as a portrait of himself. *(Courtesy of Barbara Francisco)*

Mary and Herbert Bradley on their roof garden at 5344 Hyde Park Boulevard. *(Mary Hastings Bradley Papers, University of Illinois at Chicago)*

Herbert Bradley and Alice on the roof. Alice later claimed that she hardly left the roof garden until age six, when she went to Africa.
(Courtesy of Barbara Francisco)

Carl Akeley's exploring party about to sail for Africa, July 1921. From left to right: Akeley, Martha Miller, Mary Bradley, Priscilla Hall, Alice's governess for the trip, and Herbert Bradley holding Alice.
(Courtesy of Barbara Francisco)

Top: Belgian Congo, November 1921: Mary and Herbert with the gorilla Herbert shot on Mt. Karisimbi.
(Mary Hastings Bradley Papers, University of Illinois at Chicago)

Above: The gorilla, stuffed and mounted by Akeley, is still on display at New York's American Museum of Natural History.
(American Museum of Natural History Library)

Left: Mary and Alice crossing Lake Bunyonyi, Uganda, 1922.
(American Museum of Natural History Library)

Alice at a ceremonial dance of the Kikuyu, Kenya, 1922: Carl Akeley's version of the peaceable kingdom. *(American Museum of Natural History Library)*

Chicago meant dresses and tamer adventures.
(Mary Hastings Bradley Papers, University of Illinois at Chicago

One of Alice's drawings for *Elephantland*.
(Courtesy of Barbara Francisco)

Alice drew herself with a gun on her shoulder for Mary's book *Alice in Elephantland*. *(From* Alice in Elephantland*)*

Family portrait with elephant gun, Chicago, 1924.
(Chicago Tribune)

Belgian Congo, 1924: Nine-year-old Alice and one of the elephants the Bradleys shot on their second trip to Africa. The tusks were for the explorers, the meat for their Congolese hosts.
(Mary Hastings Bradley Papers, University of Illinois at Chicago)

Alice shows off her doll, 1924.
(*From* Caravans and Cannibals)

Alice and Mary in the African Room. (*Mary Hastings Bradley Papers, University of Illinois at Chicago*)

Les Fougères, the finishing school in Lausanne,
Switzerland, where Alice spent an unhappy year.
(Archives de la Ville de Lausanne)

Alice's first science fiction magazine: the February 1929 issue of *Weird Tales*.
(Copyright © 1929 by Popular Fiction Publishing Company.
Reprinted by permission of Weird Tales Ltd.)

At fifteen, on her third trip to Africa, Alice
was now taller than these pygmy mothers.
(Mary Hastings Bradley Papers,
University of Illinois at Chicago)

Chicago, August 1931: This photo of sixteen-year-old Alice "selling programs at the Stadium" was headlined "Like a Du Maurier heroine."
(*Chicago Daily News, Inc., Chicago Historical Society*)

The drawing Alice sold to *The New Yorker* in 1931.
(*Courtesy of* The New Yorker / *The Condé Nast Publications Inc.*)

A watercolor by Alice Bradley. (*Private collection*)

CHAPTER 7: LIKE A DU MAURIER HEROINE (1931)

The traveling/adventuring itself is not such a problem; I think the point of the Quest is that nobody has any idea of what a woman would find at the end of it.

—JOANNA RUSS

In December 1930, the Bradleys and Harry Bigelow left Chicago for yet another trip to Africa. They had arranged this time to cross the continent by truck, starting in West Africa and traveling east. Encouraged by their previous success among the cannibals, they told the papers they hoped to return with an entire pygmy village and its inhabitants, to be exhibited at Chicago's Century of Progress Exposition in 1933.

From New York the party went first to London, where Alice visited her roommate from Les Fougères, and then to Paris, where they saw Josephine Baker dance. Then they sailed from Bordeaux, and in early February 1931 reached the port of Douala in Cameroon. This time at the on-board costume party, Alice went in dress whites as the ship's captain.

In Douala they had arranged to rent trucks, and with letters from the French colonial administration at Brazzaville and Bangui, they set off for French Equatorial Africa (now the Central African Republic). Traveling by road this time, they passed through more developed areas and could not miss the effects of colonization. In many areas, Africans had been drafted into a labor pool for European corporations. At the beginning of the century, Belgian administrators had cut the hands off African villagers who failed to meet quotas of palm oil production for European export. Things had improved slightly, but Alice recalled seeing Belgian prison camps with horrific conditions. The Bradleys could no longer fail to acknowledge Africa's politics.

Then there were the usual horrors. Fifteen-year-old Alice was put in charge of distributing medicine, such as it was. Later, as Tiptree, she wrote,

I am probably one of the few people you've met who has applied Band-aids to fulminating syphilis and leprosy. (Yeah, leprosy, the kind where the person has five toes and his nose gone . . . A lot of the "persons" were like 5-year-old babies, too.) And there weren't Band-aids then; I made up nasty little things out of heat-sodden sticky tape and hard gauze.

To his friend Ursula Le Guin, Tiptree said that he had treated leprosy and tertiary syphilis with iodine, and elephantiasis with aspirin.

Even the trucks made them unhappy. As Alice later recalled, they all missed the stately slowness of entering the country on foot, "making those tiny thirty-inch human leg-steps, one in front of the other, very humble, setting off across the immense plain, knowing that it would be a month before even the faint blue scallop of the mountain ranges came over the horizon." The rough roads did make travel arduous and exhausting, but the old romance was gone.

It was still fun to arrive at the French outposts. Driving up in a cloud of dust, they would rattle to a dramatic halt at the French flag in the center of the post. The party of four Chicagoans and five "boys" would emerge, Mary and Alice rather shockingly wearing trousers. Porters would be summoned to unload the trucks, the governor's house would be opened for the guests, they would be invited to a formal dinner, and they would "hustle out of khaki into white silk and white ducks and sally forth." At Bambari on April 19, her forty-ninth birthday, Mary recorded a Sunday meal that began with lobster and wine and ended with mango pie and champagne. Alice was "a grand help socially," Mary noted: when Mary wanted to rest after lunch, she sent her to play tennis in her stead.

Alice was growing up, and getting a taste of what she was likely to gain and lose. Two events on this trip she remembered as essential parts of her coming of age. One she referred to as "the polite chase by the French administrator": while acting as her mother's stand-in, she found herself, perhaps for the first time, regarded as a sexual being. But in an encounter with a horse, Alice learned she was losing other kinds of independence. She was offered the chance to ride an Arabian stallion, and her parents publicly, in front of everyone, said no, it was too dangerous. Alice was outraged. All her experience with horses, her fearless jumping, all the hard work she had done to prove herself was swept aside. It was a profound humiliation, and she knew it had happened because she was a girl.

At least this time the ban on guns seemed about to lift: she'd been promised use of a rifle and a shot at the first lion they saw. But they never got a chance to hunt game. At the edge of the French territory the party left the trucks behind, crossed into the Belgian Congo, and entered the Ituri Forest, exploring on foot and making contact with the pygmies. (The pygmies were apparently willing to come to Chicago for the Century of Progress fair, but Herbert was never able to arrange the money.)

Then the expedition ran into danger. Because the Bradleys knew too much about the labor camps, Alice later claimed, the Belgians set a trap. They had the party given false information that led them on foot into drought-stricken country. When Herbert finally decided to turn back, it was almost too late. They walked out the last days on just a cup of water each.

After this they just wanted out, and fast, before the summer rains made the roads impassable. They headed into the Sudan, and at Juba on the White Nile they discovered an airstrip, a stop on a brand-new Cape-to-Cairo air service. Gratefully they flew out across the desert, putting this new, ugly Africa behind them.

But the aerial view of Africa helped destroy their last dreams of exploration. Later Alice wrote about her disappointment at the way it had ended:

> You keep remembering the wildness, the freshness, the unknown . . . now for the first time, never before this seen . . . it's different from the land with the gasoline smells in the rain-forest [. . .].
>
> [On the plane] our fellow passenger was Major Grogan, who thirty years before had been the first white man to go from the Cape to Cairo. It took him 3 years, one whole year in the marshes of the Sudd; his two companions died. It is said he ate them; I think so. He looked like a sensible man. But the whole 3 days up in the old De Havilland he sat silent with his face pressed to the [. . .] porthole, staring down as we roared over the way it had taken him so long to go. Little lions scattered like grasshoppers under us. He turned a couple of times and gave us and the interior of the plane a look that was just cold death laid over us. If we had had any taste we'd have died. Instead, we and the Japanese marquis and his aide and his wild cat all vomited for three days [. . .].

This trip not only taught her what a girl stood to lose in growing up; it showed her that all the joys of childhood were fragile, vulnerable to time and history, about to be lost.

Sometimes in later years she depicted herself as a child longing to escape from overwhelming parents. But sometimes she portrayed growing up as an eviction from paradise. Not long before Mary died, in 1976, Tiptree wrote his friend Craig Strete,

> My own childhood was a strange isolated little idyll of the 19th century, in which I was totally en rapport with a wonderful high-morale group of adults, who thought the great green world—as it was then—was their wonder-box. [. . .] And then the whole bloody thing was smashed—all the people we knew dead, my family sick and dying, the whole morning-of-the-world dream revealed as nonsense. Leaving me with no one who ever shared what had been so real, the last custodian of a dream of kindness and love and magic—like a survivor of Atlantis.

The Bradleys and Harry Bigelow were gone for half a year and returned to Chicago in July 1931. Again the papers came and took pictures in the African Room ("Heads, masks, ivory figures, pottery, basketry are everywhere. Just to step into the room gives the stay-at-home the thrill of a lifetime"), while Mary smoked cigarettes and charmed reporters with her stories. (She "doesn't have to be interviewed by questions," one journalist wrote. "She has so much to say that the words tumble out faster than water down a fall.") Then Mary settled down to writing and lecturing. That summer in Chicago she spoke on "Matriarchs of Sumatra" and "Black Queens" of the Congo to an audience that included Mrs. Adlai Stevenson, while Alice's illustrations decorated the walls.

Meanwhile Herbert joined the board of trustees of the Chicago Zoological Society, which was planning a new and modern zoo in Brookfield, just outside Chicago. The society's president was Herbert's old friend and golfing buddy John T. McCutcheon, the *Tribune* cartoonist who had hunted in Kenya with Akeley, and the board included Fields, Piries, and other prominent Chicagoans. For the next twenty years Herbert chaired the zoo's Animal Collection Committee. He did some of the collecting personally. When the

Depression made a return to Africa impossible, he and Mary took winter trips to Central America and the Caribbean, where Mary gathered material for lectures and Herbert collected birds for the Brookfield Zoo.

In the fall of 1931, Alice went away again to boarding school, a tiny place (just sixteen girls, she later said) called Andrebrook in Tarrytown, New York. In her first letters home, Alice told Mary she was happy. The teachers were "sweet," and a new friend, Janet, was "a dear. We have the most fun of anybody here." The headmistress, Miss Weaver, wrote that the art teacher was "delighted with her originality," and that she was "so ambitious and so responsive that [. . .] it takes some watching to keep her from overworking." But Alice was still getting headaches and was having trouble socially. Miss Weaver wrote: "The task of adjusting herself to her contemporaries is not an easy one."

Alice was coming of age, and it was nothing like the adventure she imagined. Growing up for a girl was frightening, confusing, with splits in the soul between who she really was and what she was supposed to do. At sixteen, Alice appeared to be a successful girl. She was very pretty and very vain. She was tall, five feet eight—she towered over Mary—and was developing a curvy, large-breasted figure that she disliked. (The boyish flapper look was still the fashion.) She wore high heels and cultivated straight posture and a strong, almost masculine walk.

She began to be featured in the society pages in her own right—usually as "Miss Bradley, who has penetrated the interiors of Africa and India," or "Alice Bradley, who knows the African jungles better than she does West Madison Street." The *Chicago Daily News* ran a picture of Alice selling programs for a charity event, wearing a white dress, white mesh gloves, and a lace cap over hair done up in an old-fashioned knot. Her head is lowered, but her eyes meet the camera in a knowing glance. The photo was headlined "Like a du Maurier Heroine."

Part of being a successful girl was getting male attention, and this part Alice enjoyed. Dates, letters, invitations, and dances were the biggest excitement in boarding school life, and the more of them you had, the more status you had among the other students. Boys were girls' future, and marriage what they were being trained to do. Romance, sex, and perhaps clothes were the proving grounds for girls' boldness and high spirits.

And Alice liked boys, with their experience of the world and their easy companionship. They were more interesting to her than girls, had access to a wider world, didn't talk about their emotions. (Alice always hated the way women complained about their troubles.) Unlike girls, they got her jokes. She would have liked to be friends with boys, but that was rare in those days. Instead she dated them, and learned to flirt.

Pursuit of boys was also an important part of Mary's plans for Alice. Mary wanted her daughter to study and have a career, but also hoped Alice would make a lucky marriage to some solid young Harvard or Yale boy who would support her financially and give her room to work. Mary would use her connections to get Alice's career started, Alice would live in Chicago, and her husband, a junior Herbert, would become another of Mary's admirers.

Part of Alice was happy to be an attractive, sophisticated, slightly arty subdeb. But like a du Maurier heroine, Alice had other sides, other selves, and secrets. While one side of herself was proud of her good looks, another side of her wrote, many years later, "I do not 'fit' my body. Never really have. When I was an 'attractive girl,' a 'beauty,' I didn't want to be a pretty girl. I didn't fit the interactions forced on me." And while one side of herself found other girls dull and silly, another kept falling in love with them.

All her young life and up until her second marriage, when she was thirty, Alice kept getting passionate crushes on women. She didn't act on them. She said later, "I hadn't a clue what to *do* about it." For many years afterward (when she was married, and knew fewer women to fall in love with), she told herself that her feelings had been adolescent infatuation, no more. But toward the end of her life, thinking it over, she told an acquaintance, "The 2 or 3 great loves of my life were girls." To Joanna Russ she wrote, "I *like* some men a lot, but from the start, before I knew anything, it was always girls and women who lit me up."

Only she didn't know how to speak about this desire that could ruin everybody's plans. She could hardly even recognize it: she had no mirror in which to see it, no language in which to make sense of it. Only as James Tiptree, Jr., did she try to write about her first loves. Even then she never finished the memoir she drafted, a handwritten document that she called "Tiptree's Dead Birds."

It didn't help that her first great love ended in disaster. In "Dead Birds," as

Tiptree, she wrote that "Adele," the daughter of family friends, had been "a thin, magically gawky girl with a Hepburn-Garbo face of extraordinary sensuality and a quiet, secret voice." Adele was a year older than Alice and had a "reputation," though Alice refused to believe it.

> I saw her in groups, slouching on a hassock with her tan arms around her long legs, her hair falling down on one side, listening quietly. [. . .] When I talked to her I said the wrong thing; my clothes were different from the boys she laughed with. I spent hours thinking of what I would say to her. I wanted to marry her. [. . .] I wanted to spend all my life looking at her, listening to her chuckle.

Finally Alice got to be alone with Adele, on the couch in a ladies' restroom at a party. They sat close together; Alice felt Adele's hair brush her cheek and was "paralysed with love." But when Adele spoke, it was to ask her if she'd ever been with two men at once. Adele had, and it was wonderful. She would never make love to just one again.

Alice had profoundly wanted to believe that the girl she admired was also a virgin, that within her beauty she, too, sheltered a shy, solitary intensity. Now Alice's own crush felt tainted and perverse. Then, as Alice was still trying to take in her friend's words, Adele became violently sick to her stomach. The vomiting went on and on, while Alice held her friend's head, until "there were phone calls to people I didn't know, and she went away, or was taken. A very short while later she was dead of septic abortion."

After the incestuous episode with Mary, this was if possible an even worse introduction to sexuality. And Alice had been helpless: she had had no power to rescue Adele and no right to mourn her. One of the very few borrowings from Alice's life in Tiptree's fiction is her crush on Adele, and her shock and grief at her death. In "Her Smoke Rose Up Forever," Tiptree gave them to his boy protagonist as the best and worst experiences of his life.

At Andrebrook Alice at last found a friend who shared her intellectual and artistic passions. She and Janet sometimes stayed up all night together, talking and painting. One night they got illicitly drunk and Janet let Alice put an arm around her. But when Alice tried to kiss her, she pushed her away and wrote on a scrap of paper, "No, no, go not to Lethe, neither drink . . ."

It was years before Alice read Keats and recognized the quote, but the words haunted her. She made a watercolor depicting a desk with a small bottle, perhaps ink or perfume. Hung on the wall above it are two Cubist-style paintings, one of flowers, the other of a cup. Tacked across these two paintings, and dominating the watercolor, is a strip of paper reading "NO NO NO no." It seems to be a prohibition of painting itself, as if those words had made painting impossible.

Sex and sexual attractiveness would mean a great deal to Alice as ideas. Tiptree's stories are full of sex, which is sometimes cheery and casual: when the characters are having fun it's often sexual fun. But years later Alli wrote Russ, "I never sexually 'let down' much with people—male or female. Perhaps because to me, as an only and over-loved child, I associated caresses with the threat of *possession*. And my yearning for love with vulnerability."

When sex in Tiptree's stories is serious, then it is drenched in alienation, pain, and loss. Tiptree's stories often concern an intense, erotic longing for a frightening union with another. This other is expressed as unattainably (and literally) alien; whether it is consummated or not, the yearning invariably ends in disaster.

Alice never had an affair with a woman; she was always drawn to girls and women who didn't return her love. She loved men, slept with them, married them, depended on them, sought their interest and attention. But loving women is one of her stories, a submerged plot within the public plot of her two marriages, another secret identity.

CHAPTER 8: AMBITION (1931–33)

I like the icy indifferent wind that blows across the flat fields of geological time. I like to think of geological time . . . it lifts the mind, it takes the weight off, it takes the weight off the nerves and the heart.

—STEVIE SMITH

At fifty, Mary only seemed to live more and faster. With Alice away at school, she lectured throughout the Midwest, had "lunch in Philadelphia with Mr Lorimer the nice old gentleman who owns the Sat Eve Post" (George Horace Lorimer was then the most important magazine editor in America), and went to dinners in Chicago for such visiting writers as Gertrude Stein and Vita Sackville-West. She became active in PEN, the Illinois Children's Home and Aid Society, and the Republican Party—parsimonious Herbert hated the New Deal. Theme parties were popular, and the Bradleys sometimes gave African dinners, setting the long table in the African Room with tin dishes and candles and serving native foods under the eyes of the stuffed buffalo.

"We had great fun at the Depression dance," Mary wrote Alice in November 1931:

> The Baroness von Hindenburg was there—she wants us to come and see her in New York. Not that we are going to be in New York but she seems to think so. [. . .] Tomorrow night I dine chez Uncle Harry while your father is out, and next night I lunch with a pair of Countesses and speak at the Quadrangle in the eve—father also and how he hates it!—and Friday night I speak all myself [*sic*] at the Fortnightly, father merely eating his dinner. [. . .]
>
> Now I must try and get a gleam for a serial—I write Edwin [Balmer, editor of *Redbook*] gaily that all is well but my brain is like a soup kettle—sometimes just a piece of fat floats up and sometimes a bone [. . .].

She only hinted at the hard work that went on underneath the bright surface. Alice later remembered that Mary's writing "was all 'effortless.' A charming and lucky accomplishment. The grim resolve went on deep out of sight."

The Depression changed the Bradleys' finances: now it was Mary, not Herbert, who earned all the money. Mary never wrote a book about the third Africa trip, probably because she couldn't afford to. Fiction made more money. While Alice was in Lausanne, Mary had written a predictable but entertaining mystery novel, *Murder in Room 700*. It ran in installments in *Redbook* and came out in book form to good reviews. More detective novels would follow, often skillfully mixing mystery and romance.

Mary was already well established with the women's magazines, but now she acquired an influential New York agent, Harold Ober, who helped her break into general-interest magazines such as *Collier's* and the *Saturday Evening Post*. These magazines were the country's most important mass media, published vast amounts of fiction, and paid extremely well. For a writer like Mary, the *Post* was the height of success and prestige.

Mary was never one of the *Post*'s top writers, commercially or critically, but she had her niche in romantic adventure stories—often with African settings—and tales of high society. (She would have liked to write about politics, too, but never had much luck selling reported stories.) She was perceived as daring and dynamic at a time when there was some encouragement for women to be these things, when women travelers such as Amelia Earhart and Margaret Mead were setting the tone. And she made enough money in the thirties to support the Bradleys without any sacrifices of style. In 1936, she recorded, she earned $32,000, her record up to that point and an impressive income at a time when 98 percent of American families earned less than $5,000 a year.

Still, she was careful not to let anyone know about the Bradleys' finances. To Alice at boarding school in 1931, she wrote that the two stories she'd just sold would pay a whole year's tuition, then added, "don't keep this letter or leave it about."

Mary may also have had more literary ambitions. At the peak of her writing success in the 1930s, she put a lot of energy into a more reflective novel, an earnest study of a troubled marriage called *Pattern of Three*. But the self-conscious attempt to be serious weighs down the book: its central characters—

husband, wife, and mistress—are too well intentioned to rise from the page. After that Mary went back to light fiction and her pose of giddy glamour. Now that her work mattered so much, she may have needed more than ever to think of it as play.

Mary encouraged Alice to think about her own career: "Not that you have to earn, child; but when one has a gift, drawing, painting, etc., one likes to do it professionally and have real standing." Mary and Herbert arranged for her to show her new African drawings at a Chicago gallery. And in her first year at Andrebrook, with help from Harold Ober, she sold an illustration. On December 5, 1931, the *New Yorker* ran Alice's spot drawing of a horse rearing up, spilling its rider in a spidery sprawl of arms and legs. It paid ten dollars, which Alice used toward a sleek white satin dress and a pair of evening sandals from Saks.

Aside from her illustrations for Mary's books, this was the only drawing Alice ever sold. She liked telling stories; she liked comic strips and cartoons. A job as an illustrator would have set her free from her parents. But Alice may not have been ready to break her reliance on them; and she certainly wasn't ready to forgo their level of material and social drama for a Greenwich Village garret and a day job. She was going to be nothing less than a genius.

Yet she was in a terrible double bind. She was extremely ambitious, desperately wanted to prove herself to her accomplished parents, even felt she had to achieve to earn their love. Yet she also wanted to speak for herself. After all, a genius had to speak the truth. But to speak her own truth, she would have to hurt the people she most needed to impress and please.

Besides, she was naive about opportunities for women, and knew little about the few hard-earned places a woman might occupy between dazzling success and married obscurity. She wanted to make it on her own, not as her parents' daughter; she had pure ideas about succeeding on talent, not self-promotion. Spoiled as she was, though, she had never learned to work at her talent or accept setbacks or mistakes. It was even harder for a woman to succeed as a painter than as a writer. Though Mary gave Alice career advice and tried to smooth her path, she apparently never warned her in so many words about the extra problems a woman might face.

Impatient and restless, Alice found it extremely difficult to choose, to take authority over her "world of fancies and sketches." She didn't want to have to give the truth a shape; she wanted to pour it straight from her mind onto the canvas or the page. The fragmentary truths that can be told in words or images seemed to her so inadequate next to the whole truths that fill the mind. Years later Tiptree warned a young friend about the headstrong "genius horse."

> He *knows* it is his destiny to make one great burning leap and carry you to shine forever among the stars. To your rightful place. He will chafe all his life at his inability to do this, at the idiotic small steps necessary even to shoulder among the earthly throng, [. . .] the endless miserable mechanics of attaining even a modest writer's career. Between that and the one great soaring leap he needs the difference is always almost too much.

Between Alice and that "great soaring leap" also came a sense that she wasn't ready, that she was still learning and preparing for the great work yet to come. All her life Alice would love new beginnings. She threw herself with enthusiasm into each new job, study, marriage. But when the future arrived with its limited potential, she tended to get restless and move on.

It was hard even for Alice to see her own truth, let alone express it. She had never encountered a language for her sexuality. No one talked about girls' frustrated ambitions and second-class status—except to claim that they would become better "adjusted" when they married and had children. All the painters girls studied at school, all the writers they read, all the intellectual heroes were men. A genius to Alice meant Rembrandt or Giotto; it was their subjects that seemed universal.

Alice did find a hero who seemed to come close to her own truth. In her senior year at Andrebrook she started dating a Dartmouth boy, the son of family friends in Chicago. Visiting him, she discovered the work of Mexican muralist José Clemente Orozco. Orozco was then painting a series of frescoes in the Dartmouth College library depicting a bloody history of North American civilization: ancient human sacrifice, modern warfare, revolution, conquest, Cortés, Zapata, rubble, bodies, gold, gods, guns. While Alice was drawing comic illustrations and painting emotional dead ends ("No no no"), the work she admired was violent, confrontational, angry at injustice in the world. She aspired to what she later also admired in the work of Max Beckmann: "the art of pure, complicated nausea."

If she didn't become a painter, Alice hoped to write. To Andrebrook's literary magazine she contributed light verse. In her college application, she said she "would like to be able to write acceptable fiction, or to develop writing as a side line for my art work."

Here, too, Mary encouraged Alice. But she and her daughter didn't agree on Alice's further education. Mary wanted Alice to follow her at Smith. Alice wanted a college with more art and fewer academic subjects. Besides, Smith required three years of Latin, and Alice had only two years left of school. She tried to catch up, but the four hours of Latin a day didn't last long. Alice's headmistress, Miss Weaver, suggested Vassar. (Imagine a meeting between Alice, Elizabeth Bishop, Vassar '34, and Mary McCarthy, Vassar '33.) Alice countered that she'd rather study painting abroad. The compromise was Sarah Lawrence, in Bronxville, New York, just outside New York City. Sarah Lawrence was then a two-year women's college with about three hundred students and an arty, experimental program. Alice later called it "the place for supposedly peculiar geniuses, and some of them actually were."

In her last year of boarding school, when she was seventeen, Alice went into a deep depression. Her friend Janet had left school early; Miss Weaver was lecturing her that "reading by flashlight at night and sleeping in study hours is not the way to do." "Alice's order is a sore point with us. We work on it all the time," Miss Weaver wrote Mary, but reassured her that "very often the most disorderly girls become the most punctilious housewives."

She wasn't painting much, Alice told Mary in a sudden outburst. "I'm stale, flat, dead, dry, fatuous, futile. [. . .] I may be an actress, I may be a writer, I may be—most probably—some man's grief. [. . .] Anyway, the art is a bother. It is such a human contact, and I'm not human here. I can't respond. Enough of ego. Oh, my dears, don't mind me."

She tried to work out in a poem her right to unhappiness, and concluded she had none.

Remember the ignoble one who sees the veniality of his sorrows, who can comprehend the superficiality of his plight, and who yet is utterly sick in his heart like to die of it. [. . .]

I do not deserve to die, and I cannot take refuge in life. [. . .]

And why should we have pity who are the wretched of the earth, for the really wretched are only to be hated,

And we can do nothing but cry out,

And that is wrong.

Instead Alice tried to shut emotion down. When she was very unhappy she would walk away from school, find a quiet place, preferably the cemetery, lie on her back in the cold grass, and look at the stars. She knew the name of one star, Sirius. She contemplated the vast separation between herself and that great sun. The thought of being "one dot of life among billions of brief lives on an insignificant planet" gave her a feeling of release. "My life, my death— Sirius was utterly indifferent," she later said. "And that was so comforting, the cold indifference of those stars."

It was a dangerous pleasure, Alice admitted. "While it makes pain bearable, it can make effort, love, life itself meaningless too." It was a fantasy of escape, not to a new frontier, but into powerlessness and death. Yet for a long time, for Alice, Sirius took the place of suicide.

CHAPTER 9: "WE HAVE FOUND IT QUITE IMPOSSIBLE TO PERSUADE HER TO LEAD A NORMAL LIFE" (1933–34)

[She said] she cared for the womanly ideal, sympathised with women and liked for them to come to her in their troubles, but while feeling near to them in one way, she felt far off in another—the friendship and intimacy of men was more to her. [She added that] when she was young, girls and women seemed to look on her as somehow "uncanny" while men were always kind.

—EDITH SIMCOX ON GEORGE ELIOT

I have terrible times with women—I don't know what to do with them. When I rush toward them, thinking, my sisters, my own people, they turn into a horde of stuffy little citizens, rebuking me with suburban eyes for my uncouthness. When I jump back, damning myself and them, they become sensible, great-hearted, the guardians of the heart of the race.

—ALLI SHELDON

At Sarah Lawrence, Alice was a school star, charismatic, mercurial, "different." Now it was she who wore high heels and made the other girls feel young. Her classmate Marjorie Kelly Webster recalled first seeing her when they both got on the train from Chicago in the fall of 1933. "She was tall, with a great walk. She had beautiful auburn hair piled high on the top of her head—long hair was unusual in those days—and she was very stylishly dressed. Finally one of us screwed up enough courage to go talk to her. She didn't come introduce herself—Alice was shy, for all her striking appearance."

Even on this artistic campus Alice stood out for her talent as a painter. Another classmate, Tayloe Hannaford Churchill, recalled her as "several years ahead of us" in maturity and sophistication. "I'm sure her family were very artistic and cultural; they must have been to produce a girl like that. She painted very, very interesting things; she had an unusual imagination. She was not an everyday child. Compared to the rest of us she seemed very aware of what she could do and who she was and what she wanted to be."

It struck Churchill that Alice didn't conform the way other young people of her social class did, or accept the limitations put on women. "In those days women were very subtly aware that we were second-class citizens. The best you could do, if you knew your way around, was be a first-class second-class citizen. And this is where Alice stood out. I never heard her talk about being a feminist but she just acted like one. She just was one. She was a very independent person."

Marjorie Webster recalled that Alice would invite other girls to her dorm room in the evenings, light candles, turn off the lights, and begin to tell "wonderful, scary African ghost stories. She scared us so we all had to go to bed holding on to each other. They were always about departed spirits returning and haunting people. You had to be very, very careful what you did. [. . .] She had a very dramatic way of talking, and flickering candles with the door closed and the curtains pulled—it scared the daylights out of us." In one of her most thrilling stories, Alice described the death of Carl Akeley, with her alone with him in camp, doing what she could, writing down his last messages, coping bravely in the shadow of death.

If Alice rewrote her stories to make herself the heroine, she may have had good reason. At least one college friend thought Alice's "bravado, this air she put on," was a way of catching up to Mary, who came to Sarah Lawrence more than once during Alice's freshman year, taking groups of girls out to dinner and giving a talk on Africa. Her friend suspected that her mother being an author was "a real cross."

Alice herself felt that all this drama was an effect that came and went with her moods. When her "vitality" was high, she once wrote, she felt herself "emanating some sort of radiant energy, and people occasionally can be seen to 'warm their hands' at it. [. . .] The remainder of the time something seems wrong." She recalled, "People came up to me years later and said how I seemed to be the one the sun shone on. They never saw the midnight."

Alice was still being "wayward" and moody. In her school reports, her painting teacher said she was the most talented artist in the school, her paintings "original, outstanding, pulsating with life"—only she hardly ever did her work. Along with charges for dry cleaning and lunches at sandwich shops in town, the Bradleys received bills for the removal of paint in a bathroom, a broken window, library books lost and defaced. In the spring of Alice's freshman year the college president, Constance Warren, wrote the Bradleys a worried letter. "Her habits of eating and sleeping are exceedingly erratic. Her headaches have been persistent and the oculist's tests showed that she needed glasses very badly but she has put off having his prescription filled." (Alice never got the glasses. She was too vain.) She had fallen and gotten a bad scrape, then neglected it so that it got infected. She had stayed up all night working on a play, "and would have done it a second night had not Miss Heinlein stopped her. [. . .] We have found it quite impossible to persuade her to lead a normal life."

Alice was especially impatient with sleep, and when she was caught up in work that excited her got as little of it as possible. Lack of sleep in turn exacerbated her moods, making her even more vulnerable to ups and downs. Yet, like Mary, she loved working at night. It suited her natural rhythm. Writing as Tiptree she explained, "I fling myself down and let sleep iron it all out, and then get up at some private hour, sometimes like 2:30 or 3, when the world is magical, and work then." She used to do all her work at night "and leave it on the professor's desk in the morning, like the elves." The night was for her another safe, secret space.

But what was all this studying for? The longer her education went on, the more it felt to Alice like a dead end. At Dartmouth, Princeton, and Yale, the boys were planning to go into law or medicine, business or politics. At Sarah Lawrence, the girls were working toward—what? The unspoken answer, Alice recalled, was marriage.

The post-suffragist thirties were a difficult time for young women. They were told that they could do anything they wanted, that the future lay before them like an open highway. Then they were handed, not the keys to a fast car, but the handle of a shovel, and saw that they would first have to build the roads themselves. It was hard for a woman alone even to support herself; to do so at anything above a subsistence level required a professional education and extreme dedication to a career. Besides, careers for women seemed to rule out Life, as defined by passion, boys, sex, and later marriage and a family. The threat of ending up an old maid was dire, the pressure to have children very strong. The women who succeeded were the ones who from the start knew exactly what they wanted. A woman seldom got the freedom to change her mind or go on a *Wanderjahr.*

Alice was so determined not to be found out as different that she too gave in to the pressures. She didn't work hard at her career. She later observed that a classmate, one of her "followers," had become a successful editor at a women's magazine. But that girl had been neither pretty nor popular, so the school stars could learn nothing from her example. And yet Alice hated what her shallowness made her. Being stuck in traditional roles for women was one of the great sources of Alice's anger.

Often that anger was directed at other women. About girls and women, Alice was always ambivalent. She wanted to like them, but was regularly disappointed by their failure to take their future seriously, by their artificiality, later by their reluctance to think politically and their willingness to put up with the status quo. She wanted women to join forces, but there seemed to be "so very many who cling to, [take] pride in their deformity of soul."

She had extremely high standards for life in general, and was impatient with people who did not live up to them. But her frustration with women in particular is a theme that recurs throughout her published and unpublished writing, from the very first stories she wrote (set at unnamed women's colleges, about girls who can't seem to "adjust themselves"). And it always also stands for the problem of herself, of whether or not she was like other women. If she wasn't, she might be in trouble, since "a certain degree of masculinity or boyishness" was said to be the outward sign of the female "sexual invert." Yet the only way to survive as an intelligent woman was to think of oneself as a secret exception—not really a woman at all.

Searching for something that did make sense, Alice tried politics. She didn't join the communist student group (thus unknowingly saving her CIA career), but she did become close to the school's resident socialist, the young and charismatic social science professor Max Lerner. He married one of her classmates, and they remained in touch, especially in the 1950s, when Lerner had become a prominent progressive thinker and a columnist for the *New York Post*, and Alice was again looking for political answers to the problem of how to live. Politics and philosophy appealed strongly to a rational, Victorian side of Alice that wanted to rid the world of injustice.

She tried passion: a crush on a sophisticated fellow student. In her unfinished memoir about her (or Tiptree's) first loves, "Tiptree's Dead Birds," she wrote,

> I had by this time managed to shed my virginity with the help of the usual friendly older heart who so often comes to the aid of the young; but that was screwing. This was *love*. [. . .] I couldn't sleep. I had no hallucinations about Cherie's virginity; the epic she was writing was said to be about the female orgasm. (The first time I had ever heard the word.)

Cherie finally called her, and Alice came running, but it turned out all she needed was someone to sneak her empty whiskey bottles out to the trash.

> As I was carrying them out, she casually let her robe fall open. I can still see that great black bush on that dead white (Y). I turned around, and a girl came in, a tall girl in a cashmere sports coat, slacks, and tie, and so help me, smoking a pipe. [. . .] Ah well. I got one more call from [Cherie], of a blurry nature, and then she was carted off, at nineteen, to someplace with a name like Happy Larches, which I discovered was for rich alcoholics.

In "Dead Birds," the young Tiptree ("I remember buying a Brooks Brothers silk ascot to impress her"; "I was in a *girls' dormitory,* you understand") can't have Cherie because Cherie likes women. Alice can't have her only because she's already taken. But Alice may also have been frightened, and didn't want these lesbians to be like her. By now she must have read *The Well of Loneliness,* with its portraits of mannish women doomed to live as outcasts.

Once again, Alice had failed to connect. But in one of Alice's stories set at women's colleges, two friends do try to break through the surface. Kent is shy and observant, but harbors a passionate nature. Her life to that point "had been chequered by occasional private agonies of disillusionment and reprimands from teachers for inattention and moods. Her intimacies were few, and cemented by a common inarticulateness."

The other girl, Shirly, is blond, high-heeled, and "socially precocious," while "her naturally inquiring mind had subdued itself to a fashionable vapidity." The energy she doesn't dare put into study, for fear of being thought dull, "she threw into the approved game of man-catching, where she did handsomely."

The two get drunk together and go back to Shirly's room, where Kent is touched by Shirly's sadness beneath her bright, daring manner. Shirly begins to cry. Kent comforts her, then, "moved by some nameless impulse," kisses her on the mouth.

> Instantly Shirly's body stiffened, and she strained back to give Kent one startled look—a look in which surprise and instant ugly appraisal were blended into the flash of a light going out and a blackness of resignation—the hideously meek and expert resignation of a depraved child who knows no other way to play.
>
> That look was to torture Kent whenever she thought of it.
>
> For then Shirly relaxed, and slid her arms up around Kent's neck as she lifted her face to be kissed again.

Here the story ends. Kent's desire for Shirly is motivated by kindness and dazzled love. But when she acts on it, her innocent love can only become "ugly" and "depraved."

One night, at two in the morning, Alice was in the art department trying to master photography under artificial light. She had on black velvet overalls and spike-heeled lizard pumps, and she was taking pictures of the department's anatomy skeleton, which she had arranged so that it was reclining on the floor, reading the Sunday comics, and drinking a can of tomato juice through a straw. As she adjusted the lights she was interrupted by "a plump little girl in a pink wool skirt, Braemar sweater and pearls" who looked at the photo session, looked at Alice, and said, "You don't live right." Before Alice could argue, she walked out.

The one sentence stuck with Alice; for years she argued with it in her head. What would the right life look like? How should she live?

Even more than other girls, Alice experienced growing up not as a straight path into the future but as a series of sidesteps and reversals (like the children's game "Mother May I?"); not a process of becoming whole but a series of doublings back and splittings off. It was not only her history that was divided, between Africa and Chicago. It's hard to know who you are when you have a beautiful outside and an "ugly," intelligent, angry interior; when your moods change in a rhythm all their own, when the familiar stories—the genius artist plot, the heterosexual romance plot—aren't yours.

Later Alice felt that her life lacked a pattern, that she was "diffuse" or "something that did not jell." She felt herself to be a mass of conflicting ideas and feelings. When she wrote down her ideas about painting, or about men and women, she often argued all sides of the same question at once. She could be self-assured or dependent, come across as girlish, masculine, or neuter, depending on who she was talking to. She had Herbert's pragmatism, Mary's theatricality, and an unruly sense of humor that was her own particular defense against despair.

Yet her life does have a pattern, the pattern of a woman writer. It's not Mary's pattern, of a creative spirit who knows from the beginning that she is meant to tell stories. It is another motif, characterized by long pauses, false starts, and late beginnings. It is the pattern of an unhappy person who took extreme measures in order to survive, and of a writer who—like so many women writers—concealed herself in order to tell the truth.

The summer after Alice's first year at Sarah Lawrence, she and her mother traveled together for the last time. Mary Bradley was part of the American delegation to the 1934 International PEN Congress in Edinburgh, and asked Alice to come with her. It was a politically charged event whose theme was "literary freedom." The previous year in Dubrovnik, the entire Nazi-led German delegation had walked out. This year, a group of German writers who had been banned by the Nazis attended; in his opening speech, PEN International president H. G. Wells called for writers to get involved politically, or to recognize that politics inevitably involved them. Like many Americans, Mary opposed U.S. intervention in Europe. But the whole talk of the congress was of the situation in Germany.

All this was lost on nineteen-year-old Alice, who spent most of the conference staying out late with a young Scottish journalist. In her date book for June 19, Mary Bradley recorded, "At meeting at 10 at the [illegible]. Alice at noon with Gilbert McAllister [. . .] PEN banquet in eve. Alice at Caledonia with McA." Two days later she wrote, "Could not rouse Alice for 9:10. Took 11:10 to Glasgow. Lunch Gran Hotel with McA. [. . .] Provost ball—very gay. Back 3:00."

Alice went on seeing McAllister until June 24: "A & McA. up till 4. Lunch here at hotel. A to tea with Harry & Mrs. Douglas—McA with me. A to Caledonia with McA. Much emotion."

Then on June 27 Mary noted: "Alice ill. I phoned McA that Glasgow off. [Illegible] to lunch. [Illegible] to tea. McA L[ater]—Caledonia. Alice distraught. I packed in eve."

This early try at independence didn't last long. Mary seems to have spoken or written sternly to McAllister. (McAllister wrote back saying his intentions were honorable and discussing his future earning prospects. Yes, he said, he was aware Alice cost a lot to maintain.) Back in Chicago, Alice became involved with another young man from Dartmouth, a practical, reliable, attentive boy from a good family—a junior Herbert. And Mary began talking to the gossip columnists about Alice's debut.

Mary thought coming out would be good for Alice. She would be invited to a whole season of parties, teas, and dances; it might help her make friends and a good marriage. (It would also, of course, reflect on herself: in the social class to which Mary aspired, a daughter was an accessory, like a hat or a handbag.) But if Mary had forgotten the cynical view of the coming-out ritual she had taken in "The Five-Minute Girl," Alice had not. Alice already knew what Mary had only hinted at in her story: that a debut was really an ending, the end of a girl's freedom, which "stops at the point where she would become the chooser instead of the chosen."

Yet Alice put up only token resistance. Most of her friends thought a coming-out party was something to be endured for their mothers' sake, but there was a part of Alice that thrived on parties, dresses, flirtation, and dramatic occasions. As it turned out, it was that part of her that managed after all to sabotage her debut.

On December 20, 1934, the Chicago papers announced that Alice Bradley would make her debut that afternoon at tea at the Casino. The society writers described Mary's African and literary achievements in detail, but also had room for "Miss Bradley," whose "poise is refreshing . . . for it is quite barren of snobbishness. [. . .] She speaks beautiful French . . . is an accomplished equestrienne . . . writes as a side-line and paints a great deal. And with all these attributes she is still as natural as can be, and very feminine."

But under every façade of an Alice who showed "poise" and fit in, there was another Alice who suspected it was all a fake and longed to escape. She once said that in emotional trouble, she had "a great weakness for the *simple* solution—the drastic one-shot magic cure. [. . .] I feel trapped, willing to do anything to break out. I despair of all reasonable, graduated effort. I give up—for Christ's sake, get me out!"

The day of the tea, Alice posed for the society photographers, seated before a screen of white-frosted Christmas trees. She wore a great deal of makeup beneath arched, plucked eyebrows, gripped a bouquet, and offered the readers of the society pages a stiff, effortful smile.

Mary was in her element. She was at the peak of her literary and social success, surrounded by friends, and enormously proud of her daughter. In her date book she recorded, "Alice's debut 3:30 Casino—photographers—4–7 tea—405 there—100 gifts flowers. Alice in blue taffeta. I in gray velvet. Lovely party."

The next step was a formal dance on Christmas Eve, again at the Casino, with Alice in a white beaded evening gown. Candlelight gleamed on silver and crystal. When the orchestra paused, the Bradleys' friend Chauncey McCormick raised his champagne glass and gave a toast. "Here's to Alice. May she always remain in Wonderland."

At that moment help arrived, in the form of the boy seated on Alice's left. His name was William Davey, he went to Princeton, and he was spending Christmas with his mother and stepfather in Chicago. He didn't want to be at the party, thought it was silly, and said so. Alice made a joke; he got it, laughed, and made another. He rode, played polo, wrote poetry, and wasn't a junior Herbert at all.

In 1941, William Davey published a novel called *Dawn Breaks the Heart,* a story of coming of age in the 1930s. In it, young would-be writer Philip Bentham gives in to his wealthy stepfather, puts on a tie and tails, and goes to the debut of a girl named Vivian Ashley. Phil stalls and arrives late. Amid a rain of disapproving glances he is ushered to a seat next to Miss Ashley. He expects to meet a shallow society girl, but immediately sees that Miss Ashley is different.

> She looked at him from wide gray eyes, expressive not so much of starry innocence as a lively intelligence in social abeyance.
> "I'm sorry I'm late, I—"
> She looked at him with a nervous smile. "Yes."

Philip asks her to dance. He says something that makes her laugh; she says something disparaging about the party, and he laughs, too. A moment of recognition passes between them.

The next day, with unfeminine boldness, she phones him at his parents' house and asks if he'll be at that night's party. " 'Because if you are, I'm going to be there too.' She laughed, a sudden frankness coming into her voice. 'This was difficult calling you up. I don't care. I want to see you. I'm going to be there. Come over. I want to see somebody I can get on with.' "

Phil does go to the party, a "huge cacophonous grinding nightmare of inflated gaiety" in a hotel ballroom. Searching among the five-minute girls with their false smiles, he finally finds Vivian. She's with a date but excuses herself, and she and Phil slip downstairs to the bar. They order whiskey. She tells him her parents are Arctic explorers. Phil is drawn to the frank expression in her eyes, and feels the same recognition he felt the evening before. He starts to say "I love you," but instead the words that come out are "Let's get married."

She stands up and says they should go get a taxi, immediately.

He panics and wants to think it over. "He had meant what he said, but he was not sure, now that she forced him to the point of instant action." But she looks at him scornfully and says, "I don't like people that are frightened of life."

> "Now wait a minute," he said, beginning to talk quickly, "listen. I meant everything I said, really. It's a funny thing. I love you. I mean it. I loved you the minute I saw you. I meant it about getting married, only . . . only there's a lot of things, a lot of other things . . . Good God, can't we . . . ?"
>
> "Sleep together? Oh, I'm through. Don't you want a different life?"

She walks away, but Phil follows and tells her he'll go. She puts on her ermine coat, and feeling a solemn thrill they step outside and ask a cabdriver where they can get married. He says Waukegan, forty miles north of the city. On the long drive they stop to buy a quart of scotch at a drugstore and Phil tries to find an excuse for them to go back, but Vivian insists they go on.

In Waukegan they wake a justice of the peace, marry, kiss, pay five dollars, are impressed by the words "Holy Matrimony" on the license, and get back in the taxi to go home. On the way, they decide to keep the marriage secret, and Phil hopes nothing has really changed. But when he gets home his mother is sitting up waiting for him. The justice of the peace has called the papers.

According to Mary Bradley's date book, Alice and Bill Davey saw each other several times before they married. On Christmas Day, the day after they met, Alice went to the next dinner dance on the calendar, and Bill escorted her home. Over the next three days, while the Bradleys entertained until the early morning hours, Alice went to more parties and saw more of Bill. On December 28 she went to a party with her Dartmouth boyfriend, but (like Vivian in the novel) abandoned him when she saw Bill. On December 29 Mary Bradley recorded in her date book, "Alice & Wm Davey married at 3 this a.m. at Waukegan."

Years later, Bill Davey himself told yet another story, in which the meeting and the marriage happened in the same night. He and Alice spoke briefly, he said, then got up to dance. "I'm a hell of a dancer. And the fanciest orchestras in the world, two of them alternating, were hired for the evening. But I always thought that I could do anything I wanted in conversation. And so we had a conversation. And I thought she was pretty damn attractive, and I suppose she thought I wasn't that bad. So after two hours I said, 'Will you marry me?' She said 'yes.'"

Bill said they drove out of Chicago "in the wee hours, almost frozen to death in the unheated cab, very silent, very unamorous, both secretly doubting the wisdom of what we were doing, found a justice of the peace, and, knowing we had made a mistake but both being too stubborn to admit it, got married, still shivering (and not from carnal desire), and then drove back to Chicago obsessed with doubts of the future."

Alice later told the story as a dutiful daughter's revenge. "When I was made into a debutante I thought that I was on the slave block to be married, so I married the first boy who asked me, three days later. He'd been seated on my left at the party, he was certified as a poet and gentleman by the president of Princeton, and so I ran off with him to Waukegan."

By the time Alice and Bill got back to Hyde Park Boulevard, Herbert and Mary had already been woken by reporters. Alice was met at the door by Mary, a gray-faced figure she hardly recognized, saying, "You have broken your father's heart." That morning, December 29, Alice and Bill's "secret" wedding was reported on the front page of the *Chicago Tribune*.

Later on the day of the wedding, four parents and two children met in emergency session in the African Room. Bill was not impressed by what he called "the Museum of Death" and took an instant dislike to his new parents-in-law, while Alice was grilled by Bill's mother and stepfather. They assumed she was after their money: Bill's stepfather was Cyrus McCormick, Jr., second cousin to the Bradleys' friend Chauncey and an heir to the International Harvester fortune. Eventually the parents decided that their children should finish school before setting up housekeeping. The problem was—as the *New York Times* helpfully pointed out when it, too, reported the marriage—Sarah Lawrence did not allow married students. Neither did Princeton.

Pending a solution, the McCormicks gave the young couple a fancy car, an open-top Packard, and sent them out of town. The Daveys spent their honeymoon in New York, at Mary's favorite hotel, the Seymour, and packed up their things. The society pages said they were considering the Sorbonne. (The marriage finally earned Alice a new society sobriquet: "Alice who has been to Africa" became "Alice whose romantic marriage was the surprise of the 1934 season.") But they decided on the University of California at Berkeley, where they could start the spring semester immediately. They returned to Chicago— Alice to Hyde Park Boulevard, Bill to the McCormicks'—and left January 12, 1935, for the drive to California.

Not only was marriage a time-honored way for a girl to get out of the house, marriage to Bill seemed to promise adventure. Her life with him would never be suburban, matronly, or dull. As they crossed the empty West, Bill driving (Alice didn't know how), they began to talk and to feel they knew each other. Alice saw in Bill a fellow soul, and thought that was enough reason to fall in love.

CHAPTER 10: LOVE TROUBLE (1935–36)

*To love her husband and to be happy is a duty [a young wife] owes to herself
and to society; it is what her family expects of her; or, if her parents have opposed her marriage, it is a way of showing how wrong they were. She commonly begins by living her married life in bad faith [. . .].*

—SIMONE DE BEAUVOIR

*You see me as Mr. Kindheart, but I've done my share and willed worse. [. . .]
Stomping on love, Christ, when love and sex get into it we do awful things
because. Because whatever is offered isn't IT—that terrible IT we can't define and the half-vision of which is killing us.*

—JAMES TIPTREE, JR.

Alice and Bill were married for six and a half restless, violent years. They tried
and failed to finish college; they tried to live together, separated, and tried
again. They were very young, nineteen and twenty-one; free of their parents at
last, they behaved very badly. They drank, they fought, they hurt each other,
they spent too much of their parents' money.

Except for the elopement (which made too good a story), Alli Sheldon seldom talked or wrote about her first marriage. But she occasionally admitted
that Alice Davey had not been a model citizen. She claimed to have been ar-
rested for kicking a Berkeley policeman in the crotch: "I did enjoy it (jail) a
little, in the sense that I could make a stupendous fuss." To Philip K. Dick,
Tiptree said he had experimented with "early opiates, wine, and—ugh—
thyroid extract. Took about a month to get stoned and another month to be
able to spell c-a-t." To a therapist, Alli wrote about trips to brothels, "perhaps
three I recall. One I went to play whore, another to play man, I mean I
dressed as a boy and went with some men and had to pay for having bitten a
woman's breast. Most confusing."

Bill, she said, had been "a brilliant alcoholic," "charming," "an angel possessed by demons." He was "very beautiful, as tempestuous and well-read and taste-ridden as myself. And we got on like Kilkenny cats, with magnificent reconciliations, until I came to. Anyone who shoots a real gun at you when drunk and angry is simply not husband material, regardless of his taste in literature."

Many years and marriages later, Bill Davey had equally mixed feelings about his first wife. He said she was beautiful, had "a great gift" as a painter, had cheated on him with both men and women. He called her a chameleon: in one of his old shirts, "a creative, paint-stained person"; dressed up in the Paris suits her mother sent her, vain and artificial. "Alice had a considerable amount of diamond in her and a hell of a lot of rhinestone."

From Alice's own point of view, she later wrote, she spent these years in "a process of rescuing myself from overwhelming chaos. Objectively, I resembled a bullet ricocheting blindly around the Grand Canyon."

Bill Davey was Alice's height, five feet eight, with dark hair and an athlete's strength. Like Alice, he was the ambitious and talented only child of talented parents. His father, Randall Davey, was a painter who had studied with Robert Henri, had been in the Armory Show, and was close to Ashcan School painters George Bellows and John Sloan. He was a charismatic figure, a charmer and bon vivant as well known for his parties as for his work. Bill's mother, Florence Sittenham Davey, was beautiful, generous, and strong-willed. Like Mary, she had lost a baby at birth and had an intense, difficult relationship with her only living child.

Bill was born in New York City in 1913, and spent his early childhood there and in an artists' colony in Gloucester, Massachusetts. When he was six, his parents and John and Dolly Sloan, leaving him behind, made an epic cross-country road trip to the sleepy Western town of Santa Fe, New Mexico. They liked it so much the Sloans bought a summer house there and the Daveys moved there permanently, buying a ranch at the end of Canyon Road and joining other artists drawn by the desert light. There Bill learned to ride and play polo; he also, like Alice, learned to associate freedom with solitude and wilderness. Like Alice, he was proud, private, "different," happier with horses than with people. Like Alice, he liked to look at the stars. "I wouldn't live in the house because there was all this partying all the time. I was a kid, about eight years old, and I insisted on living in a tent on a kind of little mountain-top above the house," he recalled. He wanted to be "out of earshot of all this exuberant success. I still recall how pleased I was by my own quiet failure."

When Bill was eighteen his parents divorced and his mother married Cyrus McCormick, Jr. Together the McCormicks became patrons of the arts, helping Sloan among others, and sending Bill up to Taos with parcels of food for the recently widowed Frieda Lawrence—Bill called himself "Ham-mymede, ham-bearer to the gods of literature." Money increased the shadow Florence McCormick cast over her son's life. It was McCormick who insisted that Bill go to Princeton, his alma mater, and threatened to sell Bill's polo ponies if he didn't comply.

Alice Bradley, the novelist's daughter, was going to be a great artist; Bill Davey, the painter's son, was determined to prove himself as a writer. He published a book of poetry not long after they met, and spent much of their marriage working on his novel. He and Alice shared a potent mix of isolation, loneliness, hunger for recognition, envy, creativity, and a sense of artistic purity that was dependent on money from home.

Brilliant, brooding, sexy, defiant, Bill was naturally extremely attractive to a young woman with a danger streak. But living with a Byronic antihero is famously not the same as being one, and Bill was not easy to live with. Helen Farr Sloan, John Sloan's second wife (and very much on the side of Bill's mother), recalled Bill as "very selfish, very self-centered." Another woman who knew Bill around that time described him as a "Jekyll and Hyde" who when he didn't get his way could change abruptly from warm and concerned to manipulative, demanding, and emotionally abusive.

Alice was in her own way a "Jekyll and Hyde." Marriage to Bill was a declaration of independence from her parents. It was, she believed, a choice for true connection. And it was her introduction to the exciting world of men. But it was also a choice for heterosexuality, financial dependence, "passing" as a traditional woman. From the beginning there was an element of bad faith in Alice's marriage to Bill, though fighting, drama, and parental defiance might have seemed to them both like emotional honesty.

In Berkeley the Daveys signed up for classes and moved into an apartment whose double bed made Alice feel vastly superior to the virginal Berkeley co-eds. Together they drove to the beach, explored the Berkeley Hills, gave parties, and laughed at each other's jokes. They deeply appreciated each other's sense of humor; that the other could also see the strangeness of what passed as normal life was a joy to them both. "Out of the beauty of youth, out of the intoxication of intellect and the abandonment of it to pure nonsense, out of love," they marched around the house making up silly rhymes in which each new pun threw them into ecstasies of delight and triumph, "a kind of tender delirium." They added to their ménage a red macaw named Major, "four feet long and colored like a fire engine." Major was an appropriate mascot, beautiful, noisy, affectionate, with a mean bite when offended.

Alice was amazed to discover that Bill thought his education meant something. He was as erratic a student as Alice, but unlike the women she knew, he took literature and philosophy seriously as a source of inspiration, pleasure, and understanding. He read poetry out loud in a beautiful, dramatic voice. He applied Epictetus to his personal troubles, quoted Sidney ("Leave me, O Love, that reachest but to dust") when he had a hangover, and borrowed from poetry to name his emotions. It had never occurred to Alice that this language could be used in real life.

"Contact with him has speeded up a lot of my slow gropings," Alice wrote in a journal toward the end of their marriage. "It was like running across a sailor when you are trying to fasten ropes together." He taught Alice to give up class for taste snobbery. She began cultivating what she thought of as a "universal" accent, read Important Books (Dostoyevsky, Ortega y Gasset), and affected a worldly tone in her writing. She shifted her admiration from "hereditary nobility" to intellectual passion and "a sort of brotherhood of man affair, with an aristocracy of energy, of positive life, to which I could conceivably belong."

Bill encouraged Alice to paint, told her she had talent, and urged her to focus her energy. When she hesitated to make choices, Bill reminded her to stick to the matter at hand. In her art, Alice put her faith in intensity. Genius was "the ability to soup-up indefinitely"; a truly great work was one that had "been done with 'all-out' powers." At the same time, in philosophy class, she scribbled wild notes in her copy of Spinoza's *Ethics*. If humans can recognize their emotions and understand their causes, Spinoza argued, they can embrace them rather than be controlled by them. People are free when they can think clearly, and lost when they do not know why they act. To a woman who felt like a ricocheting bullet, these were attractive ideas.

In Bill, Alice thought she had found someone she could really talk to. Many years later, she wrote that the greatest foolishness of young women was thinking that the man they love can ever understand them.

One trouble was that they had to share a house. Alice was nineteen, and had always had servants. It didn't occur to her to keep house; it probably didn't occur to her that Bill would expect it. Bill vaguely assumed that Alice would act like a wife, and was surprised and annoyed when she failed to shop, clean, or type his manuscripts. Money was another source of fights. They both spent too much of it, despite repeated lectures from both sets of parents. Alice criticized Bill's financial dependence on his mother, although she had escaped her own parents' money only by marrying his.

They also competed with each other constantly. They were in two of the same classes, and fought to outdo each other in grades. They bought a horse; Bill criticized Alice's riding but was hurt and angry when she didn't come watch his polo games. Alice wanted an equal marriage with Bill, but felt that when they were in competition, his male ego demanded victory.

Finally their parents came through with an allowance large enough to employ a housecleaner; and Bill said he eventually took over most of the cooking—when it happened at all. "I like to eat, so I thought, why not eat something decent, instead of opening a can of sardines on a piece of toast? I don't remember Alice ever cooking a damn thing. But we didn't do that much eating anyway. I think we mostly did drinking."

Bill denied that he had been an alcoholic but acknowledged that they both drank a great deal. This must have exacerbated Alice's mood swings and Bill's unpredictable temper. When Bill was in a bad mood, a woman who knew him recalled, he "put everybody down, didn't want anybody around, made life very unpleasant, and made you feel like you were nobody and nothing." One day Bill saw in the paper that Scott Fitzgerald had a new novel out and "went into hysterics: 'He's got another novel and I haven't finished anything.' Bill was always bitter." His temper was accompanied by an irritable sensitivity to loud radios and barking dogs and a susceptibility to sinus trouble and hay fever. When he got upset he would have violent asthma attacks. He was also prone to bloody fistfights.

In some ways Bill's anger may have been part of the attraction, a liberation from the Bradley taboo. And if both anger and independence were "wicked" in Mary and Herbert's eyes, it may have been hard for Alice to distinguish between the two. She was young enough to see volatility as an attraction and not a liability in love; and she must have appreciated Bill's capacity for scorn, particularly toward her parents. Friends describe Alice, in later years at any rate, as unfailingly kind and warm, but Alice's two husbands had in common both charm and rudeness. They would say what Alice would not.

Sometimes Bill's violence was directed against her as well. She said more than once that Bill had shot at her in a drunken rage. Bill denied this ("I never shot at her—and believe me, if I had, I'd say so") but admitted other acts of violence. And near the beginning of their marriage, in April 1935, Mary wrote that she'd heard rumors from out West "of the children's quarreling, of Alice being in the hospital, of guns."

All that spring Mary mourned her separation from her daughter. In a rare attempt at a diary she wrote, "I can't get used to it—never any of the good years when she was grown that we had so looked forward to. But if this only proves the right thing!"

She doubted it.

> Bill dislikes me and is hardening her to me, I know in my heart. He seems to lack the natural good feeling that any boy I know would have. And she is so pliable that for a time she will see through his eyes—she will have to, if she is to keep her feeling for him undisturbed. He must see me as opposed to him, as emotional, as having tried to separate them. It is a bit of irony, to have worked so hard for a child and loved her so dearly, and borne with so much, hoping always for her happiness, and then to have her find it with a man who will turn her against me.

Mary tried to convince herself that marriage was good for Alice's maturity, or, as her teachers kept saying, her "adjustment." But if Mary tried to reconcile herself to her daughter's choice, Bill didn't return the favor. Herbert, he decided, "wouldn't stand out in a crowd of two," while Mary was vain, self-promoting, and a bad influence on her daughter. With Bill's encouragement, Alice too indulged in disliking her parents.

The Daveys left academic incompletes behind and spent the summer of 1935 at the McCormicks' ranch near Santa Fe. The Bradleys visited; Herbert gave an interview on Africa to the *Santa Fe New Mexican,* while Mary used the setting for a romantic story she sold to *Ladies' Home Journal.* When Alice and Bill returned to California that fall, they rented an apartment in the Berkeley Hills, where they could watch the Golden Gate Bridge being built on the other side of San Francisco Bay. Alice took art and introductory psychology and actually finished the semester. They went to a costume party in the city for which Alice, looking gorgeous, dressed as a peacock's rear end. When the McCormicks came to Berkeley for Thanksgiving, Bill and Alice cooked dinner together and seemed happy.

But despite their parents' hopes, domestic happiness was not this marriage's strong point. And sharing a bed with a man didn't help Alice with her sexual confusion.

In resentful hindsight, Bill and Alice both said they'd had a lousy time in bed. Alice called sex with Bill "a mechanical farce." Bill called Alice "the greatest flop in terms of love-making with whom I was ever associated." Neither was a virgin when they married (though Alice's claim that Bill had been "maintaining half the whores in Trenton" may be unfair). For an artist, promiscuity was a sign of sophistication and radical intent; for a young woman, it was a time-honored way to be a bad daughter. Sometimes Alice really did think of sex, and herself, as evil, which could be a good or a bad thing, depending on how much she wanted to offend Herbert and Mary.

But in Alice's generation, sexual daring didn't include real frankness about bodies, or knowing what to do in bed. Early on in her marriage, Alice recalled, she got a case of cystitis "about which I was too embarrassed to speak for one agonising year." She also "went through the miseries of the damned" with another problem: despite everything Freud and D. H. Lawrence had to say about women's sexuality, she couldn't have an orgasm through intercourse. Eventually she discovered from other books that this was normal and not uncommon. But "frigidity" carried such a stigma that she could never bring herself to discuss it openly, and resorted to fake orgasms and surreptitious masturbation afterward.

She didn't relax easily with another person's body. Back rubs, she once wrote, she gave grudgingly but refused to receive: "I long to be touched in this way; hence my grudgingness. But I refuse to ask it, and if offered I tense up and do not submit." Sometimes she enjoyed the merger of self and other in sex, and she missed it if she went without, but she never achieved it (or perhaps trusted it) for long. Tiptree wrote that sex for him had been "a disaster area. [. . .] Mixed up with hopeless adorations for people who not only didn't but couldn't conceivably love back, who had no such needs. Also discovering I had not the easy capacity to take, to enjoy myself—that [. . .] there was in fact Something Wrong With Me Inside." Still later, Alli said simply, "I am (was) notoriously fucked up about sex."

As a sexual object—a beautiful woman—Alice was of course a success. But being a sexual object is not in itself an erotic experience, and models for women's sexual subjectivity—for wanting, and not just being wanted—were few and far between. She wanted to be equal to a man, purposeful and exploring, but didn't know how. The relative passivity of the clitoral orgasm made her impatient, and she hated it when she had masochistic fantasies or wanted to be "done to." She wondered later if she lacked "the machinery for active sexual pleasure (my fantasies from age 10 were of enjoyable things done *to* me—some painful and humiliating)."

Aware of the modernist equation of creativity with (male) potency, she saw a woman's (her own?) "masochist outlook" as a threat to her art.

To paint an object you want to seize, touch, fondle, penetrate, brutalize, and drown yourself in, is good and possible—one can handle such an object, it is specific—but to paint that which one wishes to be seized by, etc, is a sort of contradiction—one does not *know* it, and love it by that very knowledge, as a man does a woman—one wishes to be known by it.

In painting and in love, she feared that her sexuality was passive when she wanted it to penetrate, and masochistic where she most needed armored protection. Years later, in a note to herself, she wrote, "The curious indignity of female stimuli. Can I change this?"

Soon after she and Bill married, Alice began sleeping with other men. The decision to have an open marriage—Bill says it was Alice's—hurt Bill, but maybe they both thought this was how modern, creative people behaved. Within about a year of their marriage he, too, was having an affair.

For all her willingness to take sexual risks, Alice probably never had a serious affair with a woman. Most likely she didn't dare. Like women from Virginia Woolf to Daphne du Maurier (who called sex with a woman "going to Venice"), she knew about lesbians but needed to see them as something other than herself. She portrayed them as a dull lot: writing about women painters she remarked in superior tones, "I have yet to meet a lusty lesbian, mostly they are interested in a sort of pallid, attenuated Cranachy feeling, or else they go fishing in Yosemite." But she may also have read some of the sensational novels that portrayed "real" lesbians as a terrifying, depraved race of vampires and poisonous flowers. To dabble in bisexuality was accepted in artistic milieus, but a serious romantic and sexual relationship with another woman was not. Historian Lillian Faderman writes that while "a touch of lesbianism" could be "bohemian chic," living openly as a lesbian in the early twentieth century was a choice for only "the most brave, unconventional, committed, or desperate."

Then again, Alice's warmest feelings of love seem to have been contained in her unrequited crushes; maybe what she didn't know how to do was achieve the frightening combination of sex and tenderness. For whatever reason, the more intensely she loved, the more she kept her distance. She could be very frank about her desires intellectually while turning aside from the emotional consequences. She prided herself on her self-awareness, but didn't act on what she knew. Years later she again pled ignorance: "Since I looked and talked knowing, real gays were always throwing themselves at my once-handsome feet, and I hadn't a clue how to pick them up." Instead, if she met somebody she liked, she talked and talked and then fled.

But sometimes she did long to make love to a woman. In the middle of an otherwise blank sketchbook, in pencil, she scribbled a secret, probably drunken note:

> My god in so far as I am an artist I can wish for women beautiful women women women with soft asses (arses to you) and breasts goddamn I want to ram myself into a crazy soft woman and come, come, spend, come, make her pregnant Jesus to be a man to come in coming flesh I love women I will never be happy. [. . .]

Two other notes follow. One reads, "Oh god pity me I am born damned they say it is ego in me I know it is man all I want is man's life. [. . .] my damned oh my damned body how can I escape it I play woman woman I cannot live or breathe I cannot even make things I am going crazy, thank god for liquor." The other reads, "I am no damned woman wasteful god not to have made me a man."

At these moments Alice longed to have a man's body, a man's sexual agency. Years later, when she was thinking in a journal about a male side of herself she called Alex, she recalled kissing a woman "and knowing nothing else to do. [. . .] The weird shock and uselessness of two pairs of women's breasts. That was Alex, Tiptree's forerunner—who only knew he had the wrong body." To want to be a man, to want women—these longings are connected. But her longing for a man's body is clearly scary, unmentionable, and very much beyond the pale.

Whatever Bill saw of Alice's ambivalence, he did make Vivian's lack of femininity a problem in *Dawn Breaks the Heart*. Vivian can be extremely girlish, especially when she dresses in the expensive clothes her mother sends her. "No one wore such high-heeled shoes as Vivian." But when Phil refers to her as a "woman painter" she gets annoyed ("Oh, to be a woman! Jesus!"), and this makes him feel "uneasy. He thought women should like being women. Something was wrong otherwise."

In the beginning Phil enjoys Vivian's "[un]ladylike" enthusiasm, her "vividness, an occasionally masculine gesture." But these gestures also reveal Vivian's desire for equality with him, and Phil is quick to interpret them as a threat. Vivian lets her feet sprawl under the table and refuses to move them for his. Her muscular arms and habit of punching a fist into her other hand for emphasis give "a suggestion of masculinity unpleasantly at war with his conception of her as a woman." When he lifts her into the air, enjoying "upon her beauty the feeling of his own power," she is quick to show that she can lift him, and "that action, spontaneously exact with his, infuriated him. [. . .] A cold fury seized him, mingled with disgust. She couldn't once act like a woman, could she?"

Years later, Bill Davey commented only that in some ways Alice had a strong male side, both physically and in her approach to the world. "She had a very masculine nature, put it that way. [. . .] She was a beautiful man."

Wanting a man's body was forbidden; having a woman's body was dangerous. In the first year of her marriage, Alice got pregnant. Neither Bill nor Alice wanted a child, and Mary arranged for Alice to have a legal abortion, performed by a gynecologist at a San Francisco hospital.

Later Alice said that the doctor had discharged her from the hospital despite a high fever and she had started out with Bill on a trip to New Mexico.

> Bill had brought cases of whiskey and one canteen of water, and halfway through the desert to Santa Fe, with me getting hotter and sicker, the day about 120, the car broke down. He said, "This is the end!," emptied the water, drank a quart of the whiskey, and passed out in the back seat. Well, I drove that car the rest of the way to Santa Fe, found a sign that said "Doctor," and passed out on his steps. The next thing I knew, this doctor [. . .] was sitting on the side of the bed holding a tube in which was a fetus about the size of a lima bean. [. . .]

The D&C in San Francisco had been incomplete and she had developed an infection. Like her first love, Adele, Alice could easily have died.

When Alice got angry, it was not at the doctor, not at Bill, not at the culture, but at the female body. Probably around this time, she wrote an undated, unfinished essay that she titled "Femininity and Society: A Discussion from the Standpoint of the Atypical Woman." Her tone is typical of her writing under stress: the more emotional the content, the more desperately rational the style.

"For the purposes of this discussion," the essay begins,

> it is necessary to clarify the terms masculine and feminine. At this stage in the development of human civilisation, the male must be regarded as the basic human type. Actually of course, at least half of the population is female, but there is only one institution which is specially suited to them, the home. As soon as an impulse carries the individual beyond the home, physically or mentally, it must be regarded as a masculine impulse, although it operate in a feminine body. The feminine sexual impulse towards passivity, if it go roaming abroad in an effort to be satisfied, is operating in a masculine manner.

Though her language promises cool reason, Alice's ideas are troubled and contradictory. She argues that male and female are cultural categories, then that they are biologically determined. She suggests that women can choose the roles they play, then that they can't, then that her own temperament is freakishly divided. She also makes an argument she would return to throughout her life: that the sexes are divided, not into male and female, but into men and mothers.

To become a mother is to be consumed by a "vampire": the female reproductive system.

> A woman contains within her a mechanism hostile to herself, which without cause may wreck her health, which when operating specially will endanger her life, and which when diseased is a monster of malignancy; which is so bound up with her life force that its extirpation leaves her a sterile shell. [. . .] At the time when the machine comes to life, at puberty, the development of everything else is tremendously slowed up, and never recovers from the new tyranny. The muscles are neglected, the brain is checked, the stamina of every organ is sapped. It is as though a great muffling hand were clamped down over the young being, from whose stifling pressure many never emerge.

This didn't have to be a problem, Alice added. As long as the machine "governs the whole personality, there is no trouble. The creature acquiesces, develops her special virtues, is vivacious or placid but well adjusted, obtains a man to be the father of her children, and generally allows the mechanism to speak through her personality, adopting a maternal tone." But the real subject of her essay, she went on, was "a very frequent and much obscured conflict, the condition of those individuals who find themselves in approximately normal feminine bodies, which are yet imperfectly under the control of the feminine reproductive-nurturing organism." Where do the "atypical women" belong, who are physically not men and temperamentally not mothers? In other words, where did Alice belong? Could she refuse the "natural" roles? Could she escape this female equation of sex and death?

The trouble was, there was no alternative, no language for who she was and what she wanted to be: a woman with the agency and subjectivity of a human being. At the point where Alice begins to ask where the women belong who are neither men nor mothers, the essay falls apart into scrawled notes. It ends with a scribble in a corner of the page: "It is to be determined whether an individual can become 'normal' without more strain than under the abnormal condition. If a delicate tension has been achieved, through sublimation or periodic discharge . . . above all avoid further conflicts. Endless makeshift is the destiny."

Alice's whole life—the many changes of career, the unrequited loves, the strategy of Tiptree—has this feeling of "endless makeshift." One of her uses for her pseudonym was to slip out from under the patterns of gender, to escape the limitations of one sex and one desire. And one of her uses for science fiction was to find a language for an unspeakable trouble.

In her second year in Berkeley, in the spring of 1936, Alice ran into an old friend, now also at Cal. Her friend thought Alice "appeared to be sort of frightened of her husband, or not exactly frightened, but I got the idea he didn't want her to see any of her old friends." They met anyway, secretly, "about three times over the next three weeks in the ladies' room of Wheeler Hall. And then Alice said they were thinking about leaving, and maybe going to college back East."

Not long afterward, in the middle of the semester, the Daveys did leave. Alice may have been using Bill as an excuse not to see her friend, as she would later use her second husband, Ting, to get out of visiting Mary. But if she didn't have reason to be afraid of Bill then, it seems likely that she did by the time they left Berkeley.

The Daveys told different stories about how and why they left town. In one of Bill's versions he said he was defending Alice's honor. He had heard that an acquaintance of theirs, another student, had been going around town calling Alice a whore. He went over to the man's apartment and, "knowing that an assault on him in his own room would be legally more serious," dragged him downstairs and beat him up in the building's entrance hall. The police were called; Bill and Alice drove to Santa Fe.

In another version, Alice was the target of the assault. Bill said, "We gave a party—we used to love parties, like my father. There were about eighteen people there, it was a tiny little house, and there was a little bedroom that had a door. I had hay fever, and I began to sneeze, and I opened the door to the bedroom to get a handkerchief. And closed the door very quickly, and waited until everybody was gone, which took quite a lot of patience. Well then I— Alice's girlfriend had departed by that time, and then I picked her up and threw her through a glass window." What Bill had seen, he claimed, was Alice going down on another woman.

Alice was taken to the hospital, the police arrived, and Bill fled to New Mexico. This may not be the definitive exit from Berkeley (it may have happened earlier). Alice never spoke of it. But when Alice, as Tiptree, wrote of women's physical vulnerability to men, she was speaking partly from her own experience.

For some reason Alice got back together with Bill. In July 1936 they went to Chicago and spent a month at the Lodge. That fall they went to New York and tried again. But it was already clear that marriage to Bill wasn't the answer; it was part of the problem.

CHAPTER 11: SEX AND ARGUING (1936–40)

Every woman [. . .] I know has had in some way to give up being female (this means various things) in order to be a scholar, or intellectual, or even artist.

—JOANNA RUSS TO JAMES TIPTREE, JR.

In the radical 1930s, Mary McCarthy wrote, "the only pleasures that were considered 'serious' were sex and arguing." In Greenwich Village in the fall of 1936, the Daveys practiced both. They moved into a duplex apartment at 154 West Eleventh Street, stabled their horse in the Bronx, and stayed out late debating socialism, listening to jazz, and carrying on affairs. They went to burlesque shows, the Cotton Club, or Tony Soma's, a former speakeasy on West Fifty-second Street. One night at Tony Soma's, Bill remembered, "Alice was holding forth in a really brilliant way," but the woman seated next to them kept glaring at her and finally said to her companion "in an enormous stage whisper that filled the entire room: 'Who's *that?* Some damn amachoor?' " It was Gypsy Rose Lee, the intellectual stripper, who stormed out "flashing her eyes in indignation because most of the men were surreptitiously trying to listen to Alice."

They also hung around at the Marshall Chess Club in Greenwich Village. They took up chess together, but it turned out to be more Alice's talent than Bill's. "She could always beat the hell out of me. We had these two chess books only, and I never could quite figure it out. And then one day I found out that if I was reading Frank Marshall's book *Chess Step by Step,* Alice had secretly gotten two other books and was boning up on the openings there. I didn't know we were in competition, you see. But she was good at it." Alice was pleased to find she was good at chess. She liked seeing herself as a logical thinker, and she enjoyed the element of beating men at their own game. Not all men, she discovered, appreciated this: after she won one important game, her opponent tipped over the board and table on top of her.

Alice and Bill started 1937 and their third year of marriage with a fight.

Mary, who was visiting, wrote in her diary that on New Year's Eve "Bill was jealous of Christie who had sent Alice lilies and just walked out. Gone to a hotel, writing, for three nights. Alice dined with me each eve." Who Christie was, Mary didn't say, but concluded, "No use breaking my heart over it—the child has to learn to be pleasant and detached."

In the spring, the Daveys signed up for two courses each at New York University. But Alice only got halfway through Outlines of Art History and History of Philosophy before the next blowup came. On March 30, Mary wrote in her date book that Alice was in the hospital. On March 31 she wrote, "Alice left hospital. Left 154 [West Eleventh Street]. H & I took midnight plane." Whatever had happened (Bill recalled no hospital episode in New York), it was dramatic enough for Mary and Herbert to *fly* to New York and bring Alice back with them to Chicago. Bill stayed in New York and finished the semester, while Alice lived at 5344 Hyde Park Boulevard, painting and sitting in on classes at the Art Institute. In late April Mary wrote in her date book, "Alice & I shopped from dawn to dark for clothes [. . .]. Home in great cheer." But a few days later, after dinner at Uncle Harry's, she recorded, "Frightful discussion with Alice."

In June Bill summoned Alice, saying he'd rented a house in Taos for the summer. On June 26 she left Chicago on the train with Florence and Cyrus McCormick, headed for Santa Fe.

In August 1937, Chicago gossip columnist Martha Blair described in her column "These Charming People" the visit to the McCormicks' ranch of Henry Luce and his "flawlessly lovely" wife Clare Boothe. She went on,

No sooner had they gone than another raving beauty appeared, . . . young Mrs. William Davey, [. . .] daughter of Herbert and Mary Hastings Bradley. She too is a blonde but of a very different type of personality. Her mass of hair is worn in a coil at the back of her small head and curly bangs rest on a candid forehead touching her delicately arched dark brows. Her eyes are wide and violet and restless. Her gestures quick and nervous. She is slender and has a frail kind of intensity and gayety. She and Bill Davey are living at Taos this summer and come here for week-

ends. Bill, who is tremendously charming, is turning out some excellent
poetry these days and writing a book, and Alice Davey is a painter of real
talent, though both of them are barely over the twenty-year mark.

Alice was not quite twenty-two, and if her "gayety" seemed fragile, it probably was. To Mary, years later, she wrote that this had been a desperate time,
when she had taken desperate measures in order to survive.

I cast aside by turns everything of the systems I was given, I became a
nihilist on alternate Wednesdays, and a believer on Thursdays, [. . .] I
adopted every kind of temporary posture, and in general behaved like a
person trying desperately to lighten a sinking boat. When casting this
out hurt worse than leaving it in, I recanted. When it didn't, I went on
without it. As you know, I cast love overboard a thousand times only to
fish it back.

Sometimes she was outrageous, sometimes she cared too much what
people thought. She was torn between defying her parents and feeling guilty
because she had hurt them. She craved passion and connection, but when
things went wrong she was quick to retreat, physically (her arguments with
Bill often ended with one or another of them walking out) or emotionally. Bill
had a painful feeling that he was always excluded from her inner life.

She decided to try what her teachers had always recommended: "order,"
stability, structure. In the fall of 1936, while she was in New York, she'd had
a painting in a show of new American work at the Art Institute of Chicago: an
important break. Maybe painting would give her a hold on reality. In Taos
and Santa Fe, Bill was working hard on his novel: by that winter he was up to
1,500 pages. Alice lied to her parents that the character of the adulterous
young wife was based on Bill's ex-girlfriend and not on her, and began disci-
plining herself to paint.

For a while she took private lessons from Randall Davey's old friend John
Sloan. Sloan, then in his sixties, was an independent-minded painter of great
artistic integrity, who taught his students to avoid cleverness, facility, and fashion. Like Orozco, he had started out as a political cartoonist and liked figura-
tive, narrative painting. For most of his life he struggled to stay afloat critically

and financially. He was to Alice an important example of the starving artist, proof that reviews and sales weren't necessarily a measure of talent.

Alice's surviving paintings, all in private collections, suggest that she was still feeling her way through second-hand material, borrowing from other artists, working to develop her own visual language. She painted an Indian woman in profile, a powerful figure in a Thomas Hart Benton style, gazing out a window at a roiling gray sky. She painted a man with a long face and hands, also in gray. Like many women she painted herself. One of her works, Bill recalled, was a nude self-portrait mounted at the back of a velvet-lined box, with a window in the front, a self-portrait as peep show—or an adult version of the doll in the box. Describing her fear of age and death, she painted herself, with a frisson of horror, as she would look at forty.

She was impatient with prudery in painting. One of her texts for art class was an anatomy book with nude photographs, all of which had been delicately blurred around the crotch. In her copy, Alice took a pencil and carefully, in detail, restored to the male and female models their rightful genitalia and squiggles of pubic hair. Her surviving sketches are often of women, and she may have been searching for a way to look at and paint women's bodies. (She once complained of women painters "who appear to take such a wholesome male delight in bouncing breasts and rosy buttocks. [. . .] Describing someone else's infantile fixation for his benefit alone enrolls one right then and there in the world's oldest profession.") She also liked turning the tables of perspective, being a woman looking at men. Among her sketches is a tender colored-pencil drawing of an erection resting on a naked belly, framed by an unbuttoned pair of pants.

Her drawings reveal what her painting rarely does, an impulse to tell stories. (She named as her inspiration not only Orozco's murals but Will Eisner's comic strip *The Spirit*.) Often they are bitter, angry, and upsetting. One sketch shows a Madonna and child painted on a canvas stretched on a crucifix. Above the waist the painted Mary wears a nun's veil and a demure expression; below she wears a garter belt, high heels, and burlesque-show feathers. Another woman, presumably the artist, is at work nailing the painting onto the cross. Her face is hidden behind the canvas; her naked body is a wreck of ancient, drooping breasts, hairy armpits, and knobby knees, and she is dripping both menstrual blood and blood from a wound in her side.

In her painting Alice generally avoided this rich and frightening imaginary territory. She was starting to see rage as part of the condition of being female, but wrote in a note to herself that she hoped to keep it out of her art. If a woman "chooses to look upon herself as a member of the race of Women," Alice wrote, with an interesting "if,"

> she is automatically drafted into a fight which will absorb her whole life and embitter every day. [. . .] No home, no social life is possible to her. To merely attempt not to be slighted will engage all her time. [. . .] Wrongs have been done her as an infant, as a girl; slights have been endured. When their meaning finally breaks through the underlying, mute nausea, there is no more joy in life.

This anger could not be a source of energy in art, but could only make it petulant and particular. A painter, Alice went on,

> wants to lose himself in the colors of refracted light, his mind lives in his mute eyes—what is a meaning, an ethos, a history to him? (Him—her) Well . . . if the wound is deep enough it will probably cut the flow of blood into his work, only transparent ichor will fill his pictures' veins; these diamond visions of starvation will never be . . . universal.

By the 1930s, Taos was known for its women artists. Its residents and visitors included Georgia O'Keeffe, painters Rebecca (Strand) James and Dorothy Brett, Frieda Lawrence, and Willa Cather. O'Keeffe and Cather found in the Southwestern desert symbols of a female potency, like Cather's Panther Canyon in *The Song of the Lark,* with its fissures, hidden springs, and "V-shaped inner gorge." Exploring it alone, the singer Thea finds solitude and shelter but also feels filled with vitality and "a driving power in the blood."

There's little sign that either the women or the landscape influenced Alice. Though she sometimes longed for female solidarity, like many women artists of her generation she feared that working with other women, or making art about women's experience, meant resigning herself to second-class status. Years later she stated, "I am very strongly a feminist, but of the older school where we fought a lot of our battles alone."

Men were poor allies for a woman artist. In *Dawn Breaks the Heart,*

Philip refuses to pose for Vivian, and understands the request as a threat to his masculinity:

> As was usual with Vivian it seemed to reverse the procedure of the world. Lucienne Bourdeilles, a model, had posed for his father, a man, a professional artist. But here, he realized with extreme annoyance, his wife, a woman, looking not unlike Lucienne, would have it that he, the husband, should pose for her. He felt this always as a kind of psychic castration, serving the ambition of his wife. The world that he had known, his father and his models, seemed suddenly never to have existed at all.

Philip is not Bill, but he voices ideas that were not surprising or unusual in Alice's milieu. A modern man, Alice charged in an essay draft, "will acknowledge some women his equals, but rarely his wife—his father did not marry an 'equal'—is he to be less a 'man' than his father?" Even if Alice had been sure what she wanted to say, and had set out to say it, it would have been hard to break the male monopoly on painterly perspective.

Bill did believe it was the right if not the duty of an artist to offend the world. He believed that writers and painters were by nature "shits," indifferent to others, devoted at all cost to their craft. Years later, speaking of Alice, he said, "If you've got a great gift you should go on with it whether it makes you popular or whether you get turpentine in your hair." But Alice had moral qualms, and wondered for the rest of her life what to do with "the personal shit who can make great art."

Sometimes she longed to tell all. In a note to herself, Alice wrote, "I want to be like the drunk who wanders through the world, staggers into rooms, and utters truth. Transparent, embarrassing, unfaceable, irrepressible. I will never be like that; I will always be the prissy too-many-things-to-consider." She promised herself a compromise: "I will carry the drunk inside me, and draw my speech from him, a secret motor of truth." But how then to get the truth out?

Alice made very little effort to promote herself or show her work. She already felt more at home in anonymity—and the two big breaks in her career were

arranged for her, which made her feel they didn't count. The first was the
1936 group show of new American work at the Art Institute of Chicago—
where the McCormicks, the Bradleys, and Randall Davey all had connections.
And in 1939 she had another painting, a nude self-portrait, accepted for the
biennial "All-American" show at the Corcoran Gallery in Washington, D.C.

The Corcoran show was a large, well-regarded juried exhibition of contemporary painting, with a mix of unknown and established artists. Alice's
painting, discreetly titled *Portrait in the Country,* hung for six weeks next to an
Edward Hopper. But as far as Alice was concerned she'd only gotten there because her father-in-law was on that year's jury. That his regard for her painting might be sincere—he'd recommended her to the Corcoran as a painter of
"exceptional ability"—apparently didn't weigh strongly enough. According to
Bill, Alice never thanked his father for his help or complimented his work in
return. But Alice dreamed of a pure, impartial recognition, without expectations, back-scratching, or gratitude.

Instead she took shelter in high-minded artistic purity. Only second-rate
painters sold, she said, and Bill agreed. Not that they never competed with the
world: Tiptree later said that in his youth he had been "Scornful. Eat up with
envy. On fire to fault any work so it wouldn't make *me* (and I had done nothing) smaller."

The nude self-portrait from the Corcoran show sold, and Alice spent the
money on a shotgun, a "Fox CE double-barrel 12-gauge full choke." Alice had
taken up duck hunting, getting up before dawn on winter mornings to hunt
with Bill in the icy marshes around Santa Fe, and finally learning to use the
guns that had been denied her in Africa. Even Bill had to concede she was an
excellent shot. Later, in Tiptree's apocalyptic story "Her Smoke Rose Up Forever," the scene she used to depict intense happiness is of herself as a teenage
boy, "leaping down the rocks holding his ax and his own first gun, down to
the dark lake under the cold stars, forever."

She also acquired a .38 revolver, which she either bought or was given by
Bill at a time when a sensational carjacking and murder had made the New
Mexico roads seem unsafe. It was this gun, acquired for self-defense, that
Alice claimed Bill had used against her. (She also once suggested that she had
used it for a game of Russian roulette.) Nonetheless, she kept it. Later in life,

whenever she was depressed enough to think of killing herself, she always pictured doing it with the .38. The gun must have given her a sense of power over death.

In the spring of 1938 the Daveys moved again, this time from Taos to Carmel, California. Carmel was not yet the artists' colony it later became, but it was home to a few writers, among them the poet Robinson Jeffers. Bill had a letter of introduction to Jeffers, whom he and Alice both admired; they liked the town and stayed for three years, with winters in Santa Fe and summer trips to the Lodge.

Not long after they got there, Bill ended up in the hospital. They had gotten to know local character Ed Ricketts—soon to be immortalized as the marine biologist "Doc" in *Cannery Row*—and were invited to a party at his house in Monterey. Everybody had been drinking, Bill recalled, and the nearby canneries were making the whole house shake. "The machines were going woo-woo-woo, and Ed Ricketts' little rickety house was going back and forth. [. . .] And it was 3 in the morning, and I wanted to get back and go to bed so I could do some work the next day. But Alice wouldn't leave. She started taking her clothes off in public to take a shower—Ed had nothing there, just a shower head. And I became furious. Now what are you supposed to do? Are you supposed to sock somebody in the jaw and lug them off in the middle of a—what in the hell are you supposed to do? She wouldn't leave the bloody party. And so finally I left and [. . .] went around the corner and [tried to start] this little French car we had, with a hand crank." When the car backfired, the crank spun the wrong way, hit Bill in the face, and broke his jaw. "I ended up in the hospital in San Francisco for three months, a hundred miles away. Alice never visited me once."

Alice, who also liked a wild story, said Bill "laid off booze for one year, went around like there was a heavy beam over his head, wrote a book violently attacking me and my family, and then had a drink and within three hours was 400 miles away, had wrecked the car, assaulted me and two other people and a policeman, and was in jail with his jaw broken in six places."

The Bradleys, who came out in July, did visit Bill in the hospital, then went on to Carmel, where Mary made such notes in her date book as "A. induced conversation anent conduct—A vehement—M. Victorian" and "Explosion during br & forenoon. Much telephoning to Bill."

Hoping his novel would make him rich in his own right, Bill borrowed money from his mother, bought land on the ridge between Carmel and Monterey, and hired the modernist architect Richard Neutra to build a house. Neutra designed for the Daveys an angular, airy redwood house with a study for Bill, a studio for Alice, and huge windows overlooking wildflowers, fogs, and the ocean. It was finished in the spring or summer of 1940, but the Daveys didn't enjoy it much. On April 26, 1940, Mary wrote in her date book, "Letter from Alice. Finis to her marriage."

Alice got a place in Carmel and for the first time in her life lived alone. She rode in the mornings, painted, listened to music (Bach, Stravinsky, Duke Ellington, Count Basie). Herbert wrote, explaining what he felt were the emotional impracticalities of an open marriage and offering to put Alice back on an allowance so she wouldn't have to seek support from Bill. Alice began to think about abandoning her desire for communication. If human contact and intense emotions hadn't made her happy, she would try cold reason and isolation.

Living alone excited her at first, but as spring turned to summer she grew depressed. In July she wrote in a diary, "I have desires, and they seem absolutely doomed never to be attained. They have been denied so long I scarcely know what they are any more. I see bright sunshine, and a stirring in my soul, and then, crack, despair seems to knock me off my feet." Her painting was all she had, and it didn't seem to be keeping her sane. About to turn twenty-five, she pictured herself ugly, lethargic, "a stringy skeleton" who once was young. She wasn't working hard enough; painters were a dime a dozen, and she the same as all the rest. She was afraid of turning out a "freak," a "ghastly monument to ungifted ambition." She had dreams of lost luggage and missed trains. She decided to hang on to painting—"It is the skill which draws upon my whole nature; I can give it everything I have"—but renounce all else.

She again went into what she once called her "'excessive detachment' phase." Writing in the impersonal tone she resorted to in moments of panic, she drew up an outline titled "Plan."

> The first 25 yrs of life should contain every sort of violent experience, and strong sensations of the type which do not demand sustained effort in time. This will quiet the soul by substituting memory for desire.
>
> During this time work gathers force and all energies gradually center around it as they drain out of other vortices.
>
> All forms of sex should be explored, and many games should be learned. Relations with other people should be violent and experimental, with the idea of developing a mask to prevent erosion of the personality by other personalities.
>
> At the age of 25 a child should be conceived in order to bring the first period to a significant close. This is the last major physical experiment, at least for some time.

Before the child was a year old, "all the old life, including the child, its father and the old environments should be renounced, and a journey made to a new quiet place." The next twenty-five years "should be devoted to work, with life reduced to a minimum, which is now possible because of previous experimentation. Routine is glorified. Contacts are forbidden, the soul must stay alone." Age fifty, she foresaw, would mark the beginning of a new, as yet unknown phase.

She apparently did try to get pregnant—it's not clear with whom—but a year later was grateful it hadn't worked. Sometimes she went out, got drunk in San Francisco, slept with men. She went out of her way to sleep with black men, partly out of political solidarity, possibly as a way of replaying her parents' African adventures: "My contact with negroes [. . .] has refreshed all my early African memories."

But socializing made her edgy: "I never feel such a violent impulse towards self-destruction as when I have been seeing people. It is as if a hand was guiding my wrist to the gun. People upset me. [. . .] Restrain the desire for union with others, it is impossible; friends are not worth a —— in Hell, one's best friends are one's parents and they are apt to die first. Remember, when companionship appears possible, that it is an illusion." She even rejected truth, and wrote, "I am convinced that we are born with desires which it is impossible to satisfy, and only by a violent effort in the direction of artificiality and paradox can life be enjoyed at all."

One of the paintings Alice made in the spring of 1940 is livelier and more narrative than her other work, and might have something to do with her own truths about bodies and connection. It shows the interior of a lesbian bar, seen from behind the bar itself. In the background, customers talk and drink together in the booths; some are drunk, and the place seems run-down. In the middle ground, two women are dancing together. One has her head thrown back; she wears a look of great and simple happiness. In the foreground two drinks and a purse stand together on the bar.

Alice had reached the point where she had mastered all the technique she needed and was ready to choose her subject matter—to *say* something. At this point, she began for the first time to doubt whether she should paint.

She worked even harder at technique. She fiddled with chiaroscuro effects, studied the way a horse's coat reflected light, made notes about the golden California hills and the fog that ran south "like grey boxcars on topaz rails." She kept feeling something was missing, but she didn't know what. Instead of looking for it in content, she suddenly became fascinated with the question of form. She began reading books on aesthetics to find out what exactly, scientifically, made a painting "good."

Alice had discovered aesthetics in a philosophy class at Berkeley. The professor had drawn a figure 6 on the blackboard and asked if anyone perceived motion in it. Alice put up her hand. Of course, she said. If you saw it as a spool of thread, it seemed to wind up. If you thought of it as a tape measure, you could see it being pulled out. If you saw it as a fish with a fin, it swam left. If it was an Indian with a feather headdress, then it leaned over, and if it was a golf club . . . she stopped, because the professor was looking at her strangely. He said he wasn't looking for associations, but for a perceptual effect. Did the figure have an *intrinsic* dynamic quality? Thirty other hands went up, and the rest of the class asserted that the figure did seem to move in a particular direction—an effect Alice, with her quick mind sparking on full, couldn't see at all.

Then and there, Alice decided that aesthetics was the stupidest thing she had ever heard of. She scrawled the beginnings of outraged essays, snarling against critics, decrying academics' recipes for planes and colors, denouncing anyone who would tell artists what to paint. With the boundless indignation of a twenty-year-old she proclaimed art criticism a "great sacred system of mumbo-jumbo which has been fostered up among the harem-guards of art," and which "must be tackled if the simple artists are not to be frightened completely out of their natural powers."

Five years later, she was worried about her natural powers. Part of her wanted to paint as naturally and confidently as a racehorse, without calculation or thought. But she couldn't paint her own material with confidence. She didn't seem to see the same things other people did; she found so little to confirm her own point of view. She was drawn to the idea that one's own way of looking could be scientifically defended. She began thinking about studying aesthetics, maybe writing a book on forms or visual effects.

Aesthetics was one way out. History was another. In the spring of 1940, Europe was already at war. In May, the Germans occupied the Netherlands and Belgium. In June, Italy entered the war and the Germans entered Paris. In the fall, the Blitz began. The Bradleys were committed isolationists, and as late as May 1939 Alice had also opposed intervention. "As an artist I am very interested indeed in peace and isolation for America. No work gets done after succumbing to mob feelings." But now she felt she had to act. If she couldn't achieve one of her parents' ideals, a brilliant painting career, she would pursue another, serving a worthy cause.

I am not at all the sort of person you and I took me for.

—JANE WELSH CARLYLE

At the start of 1941, Alice and Bill, trying one last time, went together to Key West. But by May their marriage was falling apart for good. "My personal life is in a cold, scrofulous, moribund state," Alice confided to a journal. "Bill and I are passionless, friendly, irritated by too much intimacy, disaster, material objects. No friends, the war, the Neutra house, packing, travelling." Neither of them wanted to keep the house, or could afford it. Bill called it "a beautiful limb on a dead tree." Alice just wanted to "get somewhere and work."

In March 1941, Bill's novel *Dawn Breaks the Heart* was published—he took the title from a line by Rimbaud. It was "not a perfect novel measured by a conventional measure," said the *New York Herald Tribune*, "but through its very formlessness it succeeds in portraying a human being caught in chaos and bewilderment. [. . .] Davey writes with an intensity that burns deeply into the fiber of his main character." Not all critics felt the same: the *Hartford Times* review was headlined "Author Gives Up; Reader Does, Too, as Dawn Breaks." But all the reviews, even this one, praised him as a writer of power and promise.

Bill never fulfilled that promise. *Dawn Breaks the Heart* didn't make his name as he had hoped. He was enormously gifted, but though he went on writing until his death at age eighty-six and published poetry and short stories, he never had another novel published in America.

Alice was probably braced for the portrait of herself, but she did get angry over a hurtful scene involving Mary, while an unpleasant portrayal of Florence McCormick made Bill's stepfather furious. "All I ever got was criticism out of the thing," Bill recalled. He seems not to have been prepared for this.

The war in Europe hung over everything. Bill was thinking of enlisting. Alice wrote,

Reaction to the shocks of contemporary history rules our days. Liquor, ideas lost forever, time lost, quarrels, hell, reunion, heaven, vain violence—it is like a tornado. Too much mass movement, the individual's action is lost. Bill is my friend and comrade and lover, body and soul. I will never betray him or turn against him. His life is approaching some terrifying change, and I am caught up in the rush. [. . .] I am a woman and so exempt from active participation in the wars—often I wish it were different. [. . .]

Happy is the person who has never loved another. They can go on with their work, pure and free. But I cannot repudiate a man who has given me so much and who is in danger.

In leaving Bill, Alice felt she was giving up on artistic and emotional integrity. She felt like Peer Gynt, who had wanted to marry the troll king's daughter but refused at the last moment to wear a tail and so doomed himself to an in-between existence as a fraud, neither entirely good nor effectively evil. At the same time she became fascinated by the nineteenth-century abolitionist senator Thaddeus Stevens, whose angry refusal to compromise did more harm than good to his cause. She did a painting, called *The Negro at Billiards,* in which a black man took aim at a cue ball painted with Stevens's face.

Turning from a broken marriage to a shattered world, she filled her journal with notes on Oswald Spengler's *Decline of the West.* She was appalled by Spengler's thirst for war and power, his glorification of man's "animal" over his intellectual life. After six years of stormy marriage, Alice didn't think people had to get any closer to their animal nature. When she wrote, "Spengler's mania is the confusion of military offensives with all that is good strong and noble," she could be talking about Bill's and her mania, the confusion of emotional turbulence with love.

Alice had longed above all to communicate, to connect with another person. When she finally failed to connect with Bill, she felt it meant there was something missing in her. "I am not adapted for love or intimacy—at a certain point as I strain towards him, whom I really do love, I seem to vanish, or he does, it all goes up in smoke."

Bill too thought it was Alice's fault. Years later he said, "I have a theory that in some people the cells—and you can't control your cells—are sufficient unto themselves. They don't need anything else. Whereas somebody that falls in love with somebody, maybe the cells want to complete their inner voyage with some other thing, some other cells. [. . .] I think Alice's cells were just perfectly—I don't know, like an unmarked billiard ball. They were just fine the way they were, and I supposed it was a weakness in me, where I felt that I had to love somebody."

In the summer of 1941 Alice left Carmel for Mexico City, in the open-top Packard that had been their wedding present. She didn't say she was going away forever, but they both must have known it was so. Bill wrote from Santa Fe, trying to persuade her to come back, but she said no. He filed for divorce; by October he had remarried. At some point he destroyed most of the few possessions Alice left behind.

Alice arrived in Mexico City an attractive almost-divorcée of not quite twenty-six. She had claimed she was going there to paint, possibly to study with Diego Rivera. But in her heart she'd already given up on painting. She later said only that she had stayed in San Angel, the Mexico City district where Rivera and Frida Kahlo lived, and had been "mucking around on the fringes of the Diego Rivera/Orozco/Siqueiros crowd." She wasn't the only one: with Europe at war, a colony of young American writers and painters had descended on Mexico City. She did meet Orozco, her hero, and was disappointed to find not a god but an old, frail human being painting a portrait for a rich patroness. He was working for *money,* she saw, horrified. "He was not *pure,* like me—unmarried and supported on dividends from Chicago."

Alice stayed with friends for a while, but that was another disappointment; apparently she made an effort to shed her false liveliness and act natural and discovered they liked her less for it. There was some kind of falling out. "One expects painters to be better people," Alice wrote sourly in her journal, and set out on her own. At one point she ran out of money and lived for a week "on 1 bottle of tequila, 2 tuberculous eggs [. . .], quite a lot of tea leaves and some plain rice." She later recalled a "spectacular incidence of soliciting funds—consummated—from a perfectly villainous seven-foot-tall Nazi type," a German businessman "whose idea of sex included knife-work." She escaped by climbing out the hotel window and down the façade, searching for footholds among the potted geraniums.

This was dangerous territory, and she had enough self-preservation instinct not to go any farther along this line. In the end her adventures in marriage, sex, art, and rebellion hadn't given her any of the things they had seemed to promise: love, creative power, freedom from unhappiness. Her divorce from Bill went through on September 12, 1941; and Alice packed up the Packard and went back to Chicago. By the time she got there she had decided to quit painting.

Later she said her decision was a logical consequence of self-knowledge. All her hard work had only helped her to see that she wasn't Rembrandt or Giotto, and if she wasn't a genius, she had no reason to go on. She'd become "perceptive enough to realize I was a good grade B, no more, only with a quickness at new tricks which made ignorant souls call me an A. [. . .] I'd clambered up the foothills to where I could really see the mountains beyond, which I could never reach."

This doesn't sound like the whole answer. It's too cool a reason for giving up one's art. By all accounts Alice had talent. But she did lack other resources a woman painter needed.

She lacked patience. Her "genius horse" demanded quick satisfaction—or didn't want to take a chance on failure.

She lacked peers. Her "Dead Birds," the girls she had loved and lost, were not only beautiful; they were artists who never fulfilled their promise. In the fall of 1941, Alice's Andrebrook friend Janet came through town and asked her to lunch. "Immediately I thought God had sent her to me, the first woman I was ever friends with, loved, really, come to keep me company," Alice wrote in her journal. But instead of the talented painter she remembered, she found "a tall pale thin no-lipstick creature" who was "lovely enough looking, but absolutely cuckoo, quietly, restrainedly, weirdly, miserably nuts. Going back to her husband after a year's separation, mother of a child of three, no work done, talking of 'trying to control herself' and 'absolutely no self-expression.'" Alice was appalled. "O, my beautiful nineteen-year-old comrade, creative intelligence I was so jealous of, were you too another of my blind hallucinations . . . a lost dream?"

Alice was too strong to drift off into half-mad obscurity, suffocating marriage, bohemian poverty, or alcoholic oblivion. But she knew the extra price women artists paid just to work and stay sane. Painting, with its demands for emotional abandon, may not have been very practical as a hold on reality.

She lacked independence. Painting probably belonged too much to her parents. If she had seen it not as a collection of "new tricks" but as a way of telling her own truth, it might not have let her go so easily. Besides, it didn't seem to satisfy her analytic, opinionated side, the part of her that wanted to tell stories and explain the world.

Instead, Alice decided to try writing as a career.

Back at 5344 Hyde Park Boulevard, Alice felt contrite. She had been "selfish," a "louse"; she regretted her long estrangement from her parents and wanted to make it up to them. She once summed up this time, "I came back from what started out to be a rather good art career in Mexico to stand by and help [Herbert] and Mary get over that six-year debacle with early husband"—as if they, more than she, had been injured by her marriage.

Lonely, broke, and stuck in her parents' house, she thought she ought to do what most women did for money: marry again. She wrote in her diary,

> My work doesn't support me, I am a drain on my parents. They don't
> mind, but it's wrong. I should look for marriage. They don't want me to
> marry, but I can't live this way much longer. I'm no prize, either, I'm
> young, and pretty, and smart, but there are younger and prettier women,
> and what brains I have are a handicap. [. . .] All that must mean I can't
> hope for one of the more desirable husbands. Shall I settle for age, ugli-
> ness or stupidity? . . . Of love I say nothing . . . I should try more salable
> work; "commercial" art. The times being what they are, art is a failure fi-
> nancially, in case I fail to marry. . . . As to the mind, my lazy nature de-
> mands endless solitude and leisure to try to think, and between being
> nice to my parents, and these other affairs I have none. . . . I could just

try to make money and the devil with marriage, but my mind will crack
in this unnatural life.

Paradoxically, she hoped she could win her independence with motherhood. "Maybe if I marry I could give them a baby, a replica of me without the
black heart, maybe I could ransom my whole life. Anyone could stand anything for freedom."

Instead she found another outlet for self-sacrifice. On December 8, 1941,
she announced to her journal, "Have given up painting for the war. There are
two kinds of artists, those who paint during a war, and those who don't. The
second kind is me. There will be something to do soon."

While she waited to find out what her role was, she let her parents get her
a job. Marshall Field III, the department store heir and publisher of the liberal
New York newspaper *PM,* was starting a new Chicago daily to challenge the
right-wing, isolationist *Chicago Tribune.* Despite their *Tribune* loyalties, the
Bradleys pulled strings. Shortly after the *Chicago Sun* was launched in December 1941, Alice was hired as its art critic. The job paid a respectable salary,
$60 a week, and though Alice couldn't quite live within her means she made
an effort. She got her own apartment and became Alice Bradley Davey, journalist. "Amazing! I have an office, and a desk and two chairs. I go there at
nine, and stay. It is fine . . ." She finally cut off all her hair.

At first the tone of her reviews was stiff as she struggled to write deathless
prose. But as she went on she developed an enthusiastic, playful style. She but-
tonholed her readers: "Do not, please, pass by without an effort to like this
forceful work." She started a *New Yorker*–style listings section, promoted
Chicago artists, and praised a controversial show by her mentor John Sloan.
She discovered one of the great addictive properties of writing, the chance to
air one's opinions in print. She rarely gave poor reviews but couldn't resist criticizing one artist whose "works, now on view at the Arts Club, convey all the
aesthetic vitality of a dead mouse in the wainscoting."

Anyway, her editor wouldn't let her take reviewing seriously. She later described him as a classic drunken newspaperman who kept a pair of shears next
to his scotch bottle and, when she handed him a new column, "eyed it in silence with the reds of his eyes shining over the bags and then took up the

shears and cut off the last third, which was where the point was." She started to have fun.

She liked the atmosphere of the paper: "the raucous presses, the hectic blackened printers, [. . .] the wistful features editor," and the stern solidity of the building itself. She made friends at work, and found she enjoyed these easy, undemanding relationships that thrived on shop talk. She didn't feel her job was permanent. She saw the *Sun* as only a stop on the way to serving her country in the war. And she later dismissed her brief career as a critic: "That didn't count; that was just me talking about pictures." But after her time at the *Sun* she never stopped wanting to be a writer.

She had high ideals for America's role in the war. In April 1942, as the Japanese advanced across the Pacific and Allied forces surrendered at Bataan and Corregidor, she wrote a column criticizing recruiting posters that promoted the war as if it were a car or a new brand of chewing gum. "America deserves expression, not advertisement. [. . .] A lush babe in a cheesecloth flag, or a big strong Yank with a gun can't do it. We are not fighting for bathing beauties, or for power. We are fighting, if we mean what we say, for a soul, the free soul of a country of good will." In her enthusiasm, she sounds like the little girl who stood at the edge of an African camp and shouted, "Get a lion."

More and more men Alice's age joined up or were drafted. Bill enlisted in the army and was sent to the cavalry to teach equitation. He soon volunteered for the First Special Service Force, an elite Canadian-American commando unit that later fought with distinction at Anzio and Monte Cassino. But what could a woman do? Alice didn't want factory work, and as she reminded Mary, she was "not a nurse type." She didn't want a civilian desk job. She wanted to go overseas, where the action was.

By then even Mary was telling her editors she wanted to cover the war in North Africa, citing her African experience. A magazine assignment to Egypt almost came through in June 1942, but was dropped when the British garrison at Tobruk surrendered and Rommel's troops approached Cairo. Instead Mary stayed home and campaigned for war bonds, while Herbert grouched that the war was wasting his tax dollars.

For a while Alice hoped to become a pilot. A few American women were already ferrying planes in Britain, while others were calling for an American women's corps. In the spring of 1942 she began taking flying lessons, despite the high cost, $10 an hour. But her eyesight wasn't good enough. She got through the eye exams by memorizing the answers of the person ahead of her, but after "landing the plane 20 feet above or below the ground several times" she washed out of flight school.

Then in May 1942, after a year of debate, Congress established the Women's Army Auxiliary Corps. The prospect of women in the army was wildly controversial. The army opposed it. Women on the pacifist left opposed it. Ministers warned that it would be bad for women's morals. Newspaper editors made cracks about "Fort Lipstick" and printed insulting cartoons. A congressman from New York protested, "Think of the humiliation. What has become of the manhood of America, that we have to call on our women to do what has ever been the duty of men?"

Congress's compromise was to make the WAAC an auxiliary. That way the military wouldn't have to grant women the same rank, authority, or benefits as men. (When this was changed a year later the WAAC became the WAC, the Women's Army Corps.) Despite the lower status, when the army recruited its first group of WAAC officers, more than 13,000 women applied for a few hundred positions. Many of them were greeted at recruiting stations by crowds of jeering men and shouts of "Are you one of them Wackies?"

None of this was likely to dissuade Alice; on the contrary. But first she wanted to see if women would really be given skilled positions, if the WAAC was going to be "just another chambermaid and pantywaist organization" or "the real thing." (The army had hoped that Waacs would cook and clean for the men, a division of labor that the WAAC's director, Colonel Oveta Culp Hobby, successfully resisted.) She wrote much later that she'd also wanted to wait until the women's army truly belonged to women: "It was important to me to go in as an ordinary G.I. with *women officers.*"

In the spring of 1942 Alice was dating men and nursing another crush on a woman, a "red-haired gazelle" from a wealthy family who became one more in Tiptree's gallery of "Dead Birds." "[Her] only use for me was to phone me at 4 AM to come at the real risk of my life and extract her from the Chicago underworld and drug scene," Alice later wrote. So Alice went out in the middle of the night, got Maggie, and brought her back to her apartment. There she gave her a bath, washed her all over, and, when she passed out, hoisted her out of the bathtub, staggered over to the bed, laid her down naked and gorgeous, and, in a fit of adoration, covered her body with peacock feathers. She lost Maggie, too, to a private sanatorium.

That summer she began seeing a newly commissioned lieutenant named John Michel. The Bradleys must have been wary—they didn't trust Alice's taste, and he was Jewish and not one of their crowd—so she made a point of telling her parents what a good influence he was, lively yet steadfast, with a "slow, heavy quality [that] operates as a calming agent to my furors."

She began removing her love for women to imaginary planets; over time, she came to think of herself as attracted only to aliens, ghosts, beings that appeared in dreams. Years later, James Tiptree, Jr., described himself as

> a hopeless xenophile, victim of something in my head . . . all my life. In fact, what draws me is so damn xeno it's not really here, the whole thing has gone on in my head, no way to act it out: like a wind or a word blows from someplace, echoes and shudders in my nerves and I faint for some presence, to touch something or somebody Out There. [. . .]
>
> *And* it's all mixed up with basic sex . . . Maybe some of us try to find it through sex . . . And then there's the twin theme [. . .] that actual sex kills the chance, closes some door. Contact with reality. Ossian gets down off the horse, Psyche's candle drips wax on Eros' cheek; the knight possesses the faery—and zap, the gate clangs to forever. [. . .]
>
> I bet it's partly the same thing that once gave me terrible dreams of reaching out and . . . touching . . . *Emily Brontë* . . . and drawing her closer and closer . . . Really dreams; in one of them I was in an elevated train station in January and the snow started to melt and they started to play music and everybody waiting there frozen began to dance, gently— and there she was in a funny scruffy brown muskrat coat, but *her*—and with *eyes* . . . and we danced, too happy to talk, and—the dream broke slowly apart, both of us knowing it, goodbye, goodbye . . .

The story of Tiptree's that Alice considered her most romantic was "With Delicate Mad Hands." It tells of a woman who all her life has heard voices from the stars. She steals a ship, crash-lands on a strange planet, is greeted by the telepathic female alien who has called to her—and both die within a week, one from radiation poisoning, the other from grief and shared pain. Alli thought of this as a lesbian story, yet she also told an editor that "the lesbianity (!! word??) isn't really important between beings so alien—so very alien."

In August 1942, Alice wrote Mary at the Lodge that she was serious about the WAAC. It was so new, she wrote, that it had to offer some chance for talented women to prove themselves.

> I believe it will be a fine experience, a worthwhile experience, an experience offering some possibility of accomplishment, and which is in line with my principles. I have always asked for work for women, for responsibility, for a part in things. This is far from ideal, it is only a beginning, but it is the beginning from which any future we have will come; as a woman who has always spoken for these things, I believe that it is my place to be in it and do what I can to make good come of it.

"I want work," she told her parents. "I don't want to be on the outside, foisting my little brainwaves at a world gone mad." She also hoped to write about the WAAC, maybe as a series of letters home.

Mary worried that Alice would not accept the army's authority, that she was a "racehorse" not suited to the long haul. Alice retorted, "If I were a man, with the same temperament, the Army could use me [. . .]. If I were a man, would you dissuade me from enlisting? [. . .] I know I am depressible but I rise to occasions. This is one of the greatest occasions in life, a total war. I was good in Africa, wasn't I?" Besides, she added snidely, "I should think you'd be in favor of some discipline for me."

Part of the appeal of the army for Alice was the same discipline that Mary worried about. She went into the WAAC intending to throw off the passionate self she had been, and hoping to find the combination of independence and stability that her first marriage had so disastrously failed to provide. Besides, joining the army—like eloping with a stranger—would put distance again between Alice and her parents. And almost certainly it was her version of Africa, her chance to be a hero.

In August 1942 U.S. Marines were fighting on Guadalcanal and German troops were driving the Red Army back toward Stalingrad. Rumors were leaking out of Poland of Jews deported to "labor camps." And Alice Davey put on her best girl suit, "three-inch heels and my little chartreuse crepe-de-chine designer thing by Claire somebody, and my pale fox fur jacket," and went down to a recruiting station. There an unshaven second lieutenant with his feet on his desk laughed at her for the benefit of his noncoms and, when she asked to enlist in the WAAC, told her, "Ah, hell, you don't want to go in *that* goddamn thing."

On her enlistment form, Alice Davey wrote that she was twenty-seven years old, five feet eight and a half inches tall, a divorcée, fluent in French with some spoken Swahili. Her occupations were "artist" and "critic reviewer." Her "active hobbies" were hunting, horseback riding, chess, and writing. She asked to be assigned to motor transport or cryptography.

She stored her paintings at her parents' house. She gave Major, the red macaw, to the Brookfield Zoo, where he was inspired to lay an egg, and so turned out to have gender troubles of his own. She packed a suitcase with improving books: aesthetics, mathematics, Schopenhauer. At the Lodge she gave an unappreciative county librarian all her stacks of science fiction magazines. And at the end of September, she reported to Des Moines, Iowa, for four weeks of basic training.

CHAPTER 13: **FORT DES MOINES (1942–43)**

It is morning, Senlin says, and in the morning
When the light drips through the shutters like the dew,
I arise, I face the sunrise,
And do the things my fathers learned to do.

—CONRAD AIKEN

Fort Des Moines was one of the WAAC's main training camps, an old cavalry post, with red-brick barracks and a muddy, tree-lined parade ground, which had been hastily remodeled for the women's army. On the dark, rainy night that Alice arrived by taxi from the station (it hadn't occurred to her to look for the army's truck), she was thrilled to find exactly what she'd hoped for: a place where women were in charge.

"What an awakening," she wrote in her journal,

> seeing for the first time in my life a world of women—women glimpsed through doors of canteens offices barracks kitchens guard-posts— women plowing through the black mud into the pools of light—women in uniform, looking as though they owned the place—and owning it! Women seen for the first time at ease, unselfconscious, swaggering or thoughtful, sizing everything up openly, businesslike, all personalities all unbending and unafraid.

Alice was assigned to a barracks and issued a uniform: olive-drab jacket, tie, skirt, and underpants; a handbag, since the uniform had no pockets; and a "foundation garment," which the army felt was necessary to keep its women looking military. Wearing a girdle and carrying a purse didn't make Alice feel more combat-ready, nor did the regulation pumps or the skirt that crept up during drills. On the other hand, she wrote in her journal, the ensemble had "a certain lunatic chic, which I intend to exploit." Like most women in the service, Alice came to like the authority of olive drab.

Alice had been in all-female worlds before, but the WAAC included more kinds of women: schoolteachers, farmers, a sixteen-year-old from New Jersey who had delivered singing telegrams, a newspaper publisher, "a lady executive who probably made more than Eisenhower, and an opera singer and a girl from the Ozarks who was never on a train before coming here." Alice had never heard women joke so much, or be so raucous and lively. For fun, she started a rumor there was saltpeter in the food. She felt she was among free women for the first time.

Her letters home were always rosy, but she probably meant it this time when she told her parents, "The girls are *swell,*" and even wrote warmly about a morning on KP:

> I was South Dishwasher, I tended Bertha the Bathtub, a machine, and yanked scalding trays of crockery out of her maw and sent them flying down the ways. There was so much noise we laughed and sang and became hysterical and collapsed every 3 hours for cigarets and sun. [. . .] Of course, I expect it will be dull after a bit, but there is such enthusiasm here, such spirit, it is buoying. And I love being a private. The very orders somehow amuse me, I scurry to obey.

She was frankly stirred by the order of the camp: the drills, the ceremony, the military music played by an all-female band. She wrote in her journal of how affected she was by

> the long grey-green lines of *women,* for the first time in America, in the rain, under the flag, the sound of the band, far-off, close, then away again; the immortal fanny of our guide, leading on the right, moved and moving to the music—the flag again—first time I ever felt free enough to be proud of it; the band, our band, playing reveille that morning, with me on KP since 0430 hours, coming to the mess-hall porch to see it pass in the cold streets, under that flaming middle-western dawn; KP itself, and the conviction that one is going to die; the wild ducks flying

over that day going to PT after a fifteen-mile drill, and me so moved I
saluted them. [. . .]

Overworked and overexcited, she hardly slept. One day she was so tired
she fell asleep while marching to class and keeled over in the formation.

She soon got a crush on "two rather mannish girls in the Company,"
though she wondered if she wasn't drawn mainly to the idea of them, "a half-
there image of danger and daring, a mirage." She hoped she could learn to act
natural, to have the ordinary, uncomplicated friendships other women seemed
to have. "I hope I will brace up and quiet down. I want to be nice to people,
but not too personal, not too fey."

But even here, Alice discovered, her brains, ideals, and desires set her apart.
All of the women in the WAAC had something to prove, and made a point of
working harder than the GIs. But no one was as idealistic as Alice. The
women she met seemed too caught up in individual goals, too resigned to in-
equality. In disgust she wrote, "The great betrayal of women by women.
Rigour, responsibility, ruthlessness, all sold for gewgaws and pottage."

One weekend she went with a few other women to Des Moines, where
they got hotel rooms, bought and drank most of two quarts of bourbon, and
went to a bar where they could dance. But the jukebox, the spittoons, the effort to have a good time only made Alice depressed and withdrawn. She ended
up in a long, drunken talk with a fellow Waac "in which I remember trying
and groping to find out what really was going on, whether this was supposed
to be fun, whether there was any language we spoke in common. The net effect was like banging your head on a stone wall." The trip ended in a jealous
blowup between two of the women, who were lovers. On the way back to
camp Alice "tried to lecture the one on putting her energy into something
other than these romances, but of course to no avail."

The only one of her improving books that helped was Louis Untermeyer's *Modern American and British Poetry*. Climbing into her uniform at
dawn, with the last stars passing from the midwestern sky, she thought of
Conrad Aiken's "Senlin": "And I myself on a swiftly tilting planet / Stand
before a glass and tie my tie." When she felt sorry for herself she quoted from
the nineteenth-century romantic Ernest Dowson's "To One in Bedlam":

"Know they what dreams divine / Lift his long, laughing reveries like enchanted wine / And make his melancholy germane to the stars'?" The lines
stuck: as Tiptree, she would quote the same verses, or use them as titles for
stories.

Because of poetry she fell in love. A twenty-two-year-old former theater director from Georgia spotted the book and asked her about it. Alice and Becky
talked for hours about literature. At night they roamed the parade ground under the trees, telling ghost stories or declaiming e. e. cummings's battle hymns
of the consumer republic: "from every B.V.D. / let freedom ring."

Nothing happened. "I always spoil things with my over-emotionalism,"
Alice wrote.

> But I can't help feeling strongly about everything. I have been alienating
> my Georgia friend. Too much seriousness. But the light touch is only
> good with something deep behind it. [. . .] Somehow any human feel-
> ing except simple protectiveness, any feeling between equals, is a symbol
> which is still written: ?

Instead, she wished she could give herself up to a life of virtue. Thinking
about her crushes on women, she wrote, "Somehow I must weed out this
wilderness. Somehow something true must carry me on, there must be in me
something that will make the world a better place." John Michel, her lieutenant friend, came to visit, and she went with him to Chicago for a few days'
leave. There they stayed up late talking, and the next morning she wrote,

> Feel very happy and a little incredulous—last night something I never
> thought could happen came off. I never thought I would ever have such
> physical closeness with a man, or a woman either for that matter, though
> I always hoped for it more from the latter. The real point is that it was a
> lot more than physical, and I guess that's the only way such things hap-
> pen to people like me.

She added that she could suddenly "see a perfectly normal happiness possible for me—and I feel normal!" Still, she cried when Becky graduated and
left the post.

Alice finished her four weeks of basic training in early November 1942, as fresh Allied troops landed in North Africa—the first American move in the European war. But Auxiliary Davey, Company 81, was "assigned, to my deep misery, not overseas but as a Publications Artist, drawing Waac Christmas Cards! Christ! Today I designed the Membership Card for the Waac Officers' Club!" Casting off her egalitarian ideals, she applied to Officer Candidate School. In the meantime she was made an acting sergeant, and her company commander told her she had "leadership qualities." She began to see herself as officer material.

At the end of November Alice began studying for her gold bars at Fort Des Moines. She learned about the issuing of orders and memoranda (with proper numbering and correct margin width), defense against chemical warfare, accounting, "mess management," history. She took it very seriously, and was especially pleased when Herbert said she'd been right after all to enlist.

"Bunny was right about the strain," she wrote home. "They try to make you over, you know, you are plunged, or rather, jerked by the ears up into a rarified air, and you see cosmic eyes of Weighings in the Balance staring at you—Now or Never, Real Life—and also you get sick." Everyone had the flu, and it snowed, and Alice worked. She wrote letters to John. In the barracks in the five A.M. darkness, she listened to radio reports on the siege of Stalingrad. She tried to act like officer material, and sometimes failed. Asked to give a brief lecture on "Paragraph Ten of the Infantry Drill Regulations," she "climbed onto the two-foot-high speaker's stand, announced my topic, glanced at the hall of faces, threw up decisively, and fainted crash to the floor, blacking both my eyes. (I was later told it was voted Most Interesting Format.)"

Alice also learned what men could do when faced with an independent group of women. That winter Eleanor Roosevelt came to Des Moines to inspect the WAAC troops. As the women marched in formation through the city streets to receive the first lady, they drew a crowd of men who kicked slush at them and bombarded them with garbage. This run-in with open hatred left a mark on Alice. Man, she concluded, "has never forgiven woman for existing."

Alice learned that she too was capable of violence. One day, one of the phys ed teachers, whom Alice had come to hate, made one snide remark too many and Alice flew into a blind rage. Before she knew what she was doing she had the larger, stronger woman down over a footlocker and was trying to strangle her. It took several other women to pull her off her victim. As strongly as her fury at the rain of garbage stayed with her, so did the joy of acting on her anger. She remembered it years later as a moment when she had "felt fully alive."

In January 1943 Alice graduated from OCS and became a third officer, the WAAC equivalent of a lieutenant. Mary came down for the ceremony, charming everyone as usual. Shortly afterward Alice got a few days' leave, and a Chicago society columnist reported sighting

> Third Officer Alice Bradley Davey, Waac, looking better dressed in her
> G.I. uniform than any of a group of well-dressed women with whom
> she was lunching at the Arts Club. Blond-gold hair curling under her of-
> ficer's cap, a new erectness to her shoulders under her olive-drab jacket,
> gray shirt matching the gray skirt, olive-drab tie.

Alice had a new name, too. By now she was universally known as "Davey."

When Third Officer Davey finally left Fort Des Moines in March, though, it wasn't for North Africa or the Pacific but a dusty army post in the Virginia hills. Camp Pickett was getting ready to receive the 55th WAAC Post Headquarters Company: 150 typists, filing clerks, accountants, radio experts, and motor pool drivers. Davey, the company's new mess and supply officer, was sent ahead to make housing arrangements. From being surrounded by women at Fort Des Moines, she went to being the first and only one at Camp Pickett, "a fact which the troops marching past did not let me forget. 'Hey, look, fellas, there's a WAAC! There's a WAAC! Yahoo, the WAACs are here!' "

She was putting this politely. Now it wasn't civilians but the male soldiers who harassed the Waacs at work and made catcalls on the post. Thousands of men streamed through the camp on their way to Britain and the Mediterranean, and as they passed they felt free to jeer at the 150 Waacs who had joined the army to support them (or, looked at another way, to free them up for combat). After the war Alice recalled,

The Regular Army, which turned purple in the face and nearly blew up when we first appeared, soon accepted us as soldiers and gave us a very square break. It was a certain type of he-man draftees who really loathed us to the bitter end. They had a fund of bottled-up resentment against fate and they took it out on the women.

To prove herself, she worked even harder. Through the snowy end of winter she stood shivering in unheated barracks, supervising crews of men as they installed beds, shelves, sinks, toilets, window shades, and lightbulbs. She signed for blankets and pillowcases, ordered filing cabinets, typewriters, and trash cans, and made sure the company mess hall had enough dishes, aprons, buckets, and brooms. The work did appeal to a Herbert side of Alice that loved building and maintaining. She later said proudly, "My first act as a commissioned officer in the Army of the United States was to repair a toilet." She told her father she finally understood all his worries as a landlord.

When her company arrived, she supervised their first march to mess (gawked at by every man on the post), implemented a procedure for enlisted women to sign out on dates, requisitioned 1,350 pairs of stockings, and tried to sort out the new problems of rank and protocol women brought to the army. "It is a question," she wrote her parents, "this business of is she a lady, or is she a looie?" She herself hung around the officers' club with the men, drinking beer and learning to play poker. The male officers were politer, on the surface at any rate, than the enlisted men.

John Michel still wrote nearly every day, called once a week, and was, she told her parents, "awfully sweet and devoted. [. . .] Always interested in everything I do, and very solid." But it was easy to drink too much, flirt, and play the sophisticated divorcée. When a junior officer from post public relations, Lieutenant Johnny Crosby, "extracted from me the story of my life and invited me to a dance," they began a friendship that turned into an affair.

Crosby was a newspaper writer in civilian life, and he helped Davey write her first article about her WAAC experience, a short, bright, uncomplicated piece that Mary's agent, Harold Ober, helped her sell to *Mademoiselle*. She couldn't talk for a women's magazine about her hopes for women's future, so she summarized her work, described the Waacs' reception on the post, and spoke of "gaining an experience that no other job today can give: the experience of working together in the cause of our country's victory."

But then it all blew up—and it was a woman who betrayed her. The trouble started when the 55th WAAC Company's commanding officer finally arrived. Third Officer Miller was younger than her twenty-seven-year-old supply officer and equally inexperienced. The company were accustomed to Davey as their CO and looked to her for orders; Davey was used to doing all the work and getting all the attention. By the time she saw the fight coming and tried to smooth things over, it was too late. Davey went to Washington to deliver the *Mademoiselle* article for army review on April 19, 1943. When she got back the next day, Miller called her into her office. Alice summarized the results in her date book: "Miller blew top, I blew top, me confined to qrs for a week."

Miller accused Davey of resenting her, refusing to carry out her policy, and going to Washington to agitate against her. It also happened that Davey had borrowed money for the trip from an enlisted woman, a real breach of army regulations. When Davey lost her temper, Miller ordered her confined to her quarters in the evening. She spent the next three days doing her work, writing a falsely cheerful letter home, and waiting for judgment to come from Washington. Thirty years later she said it was "the lonesomest and roof-fallen-in-most time I ever had."

No charges were filed. Instead, Third Officer Davey was transferred to Newport News, where the WAAC company at Camp Patrick Henry needed a supply officer. Within three days she was doing the same job in a new place: sitting in a shack in the sticky Tidewater heat, typing out forms, filing memos gone limp with humidity and sweat. She had a fling with a fellow officer, and wrote in a journal, "Jesus it was good to get my legs around a young man again!" But a week later she had a serious case of depression, "like vomiting in a wash-room on a train going through the Holland Tunnel. Meaningless, lightless misery."

As she often did when she was angry and despairing, she indicted politics and the world. In a fragment called "The Women's Army Auxiliary Corpse," she wrote that the WAAC had brought out in all its officers and enlisted women "a surge of released inner hope. It was as if desires so deep and frustrated that the individual had ceased to admit them were suddenly to be granted. In each one's eyes a personal vision flamed, a vision of honour, of a high destiny in a new world." Now she saw that the army didn't care about women's hopes. It didn't even share the democratic principles it was setting out to defend. Observing the soldiers at Camp Pat, Davey concluded that most of them were on their way, first to fight the Germans, "and secondly and most heartily to kill or trample over Jews, Negroes, women, Indians, and anything else that they fancied as a menace to their Aryan male prestige."

Worse, solidarity between women had given way to backstabbing and spite. Davey wasn't a hero or a leader, she was That Girl again. And the real feelings she had about women, of love and anger, were almost impossible to write or even think about in 1943.

Even Mary had trouble writing about women in the army. After Alice enlisted, Mary became a passionate supporter of the WAAC and its successor, the WAC. Like Alice, she hoped that if women proved themselves in the army they might win more rights in the civilian world. She joined the WAC Mothers' Association of Chicago. And after a visit to Camp Patrick Henry, she wrote a short story that was published in the July *Cosmopolitan*. "The Lieutenant Meets the WAAC" is narrated by a male officer who is assigned a Waac assistant. Outraged at having to work with a woman, he refuses at first to speak to her: "As far as Lieutenant Nicholas Barclay was concerned, the Women's Army Auxiliary Corps was composed of nonexistent females." Through his cool, critical eyes, we watch insults being heaped on the Waacs: the scorn and catcalls from men, the hostility from civilian women. In the end, Barclay's assistant is unfairly transferred from her post for knocking down a soldier who made a pass at one of her fellow Waacs. But by then her hard work and forbearance have converted Barclay to her cause.

Mary knew more literary tricks than Alice did for conveying men's prejudice and women's anger. But this was the only piece on the WAC that even Mary was able to sell. In January 1944, *Collier's* asked her to report on the WAC's progress. She went to Washington to tour army installations and wrote several articles, including one called "Daughter in the Army." None ever made it into print—though the magazine did buy a spy yarn with a male protagonist called "Incident in Berlin." Most Wacs drove jeeps or sorted mail; the

WAC had none of the excitement of bomber bases or battlefields. The WAC's real war was against its own country; this was difficult to express delicately in the pages of *Collier's*.

In July 1943, the WAAC was disbanded. Its auxiliary status had caused too much bureaucratic confusion, in everything from the chain of command (could Waacs take orders from male army officers, or vice versa?) to veterans' benefits (Waacs had none) and medical care. It was re-formed, with full military status, as the Women's Army Corps.

At that point Waacs could choose to leave with an honorable discharge, and almost fifteen thousand of them, nearly a quarter of the force at that point, quit the army. As dissatisfied as she was, Alice couldn't think of an alternative and decided to reenlist. Herbert and Mary both encouraged her to stay in the army. Alice believed Herbert came to respect her joining up as something his son would have done.

But Lieutenant Davey, as she was now known, gave up on the idea of being a leader of women. It brought out a competitive side of herself she didn't like; and for all her ambitions to be like Herbert she suspected she wasn't steady enough. She set out looking for another kind of work.

In April, after the blowup at Camp Pickett, she'd written to Washington asking for a transfer. At the end of July 1943 it came through, and Davey left Newport News for WAC headquarters at the Pentagon.

CHAPTER 14: IN A PENTAGON BASEMENT (1944)

Washington in 1943 was a boomtown. Its population had nearly doubled since 1940, and its streetcars and rooming houses were overflowing with officers in uniform and single women looking for jobs in the vast bureaucracy of the war. Housing was expensive and Alice's salary, $171 a month plus housing allowance, relatively small. She found space first in a house with five other Wacs, two Navy Waves, and some civilians, and later in a series of women's residence halls.

She had been assigned to do clerical work for WAC public relations, but was soon bored by the undemanding work and feeling "full of frustrated self-importance." John Michel came to visit in August for her twenty-eighth birthday, but they broke up not long afterward. She worked too hard and ended up in Walter Reed Hospital twice. The first time it was a kidney infection; August 11 she wrote her parents: "Got out of hospital today, and celebrated by working late." The second was appendicitis. After that the army gave her sick leave and she went back to Chicago. When she returned to Washington, she had a plan for the assignment she wanted.

She'd read a newspaper article about the new military specialty of photointerpretation. Britain's Royal Air Force had worked out how to take photographs from high-altitude reconnaissance planes, then realized that it took training and experience to read them—to tell a road from a railway when both looked no bigger than a scratch, or distinguish a Messerschmitt from a Junker at pinhead scale. The work required patience, intelligence, and an ability to make sense of seemingly abstract shapes. In Britain it had attracted academics—archaeologists, geologists, geographers—and a high concentration of women, who were said to have the necessary attention to detail.

Some interpreters were based at front-line airfields, where they gave on-the-spot analysis. Others, back at headquarters, used months' worth of "covers" to select bombing targets and monitor enemy activity. In September 1940, RAF photointerpreters watched barges for the invasion of Britain being readied in Dunkirk, Boulogne, Ostend, and Antwerp. By June 1943, they were puzzling over a small airfield that seemed to be a test site for some kind of rocket, near a village on Germany's Baltic coast called Peenemünde.

The U.S. Army Air Forces, Alice concluded, must have a similar department. By November 1943 she had found it—"one major (a forester) and one lieutenant (a geologist) in a coat closet in Gravelly Point"—and was putting in extra hours there as a volunteer. She studied photos from the Far East, learning to use a stereoscope to make a pair of pictures look three-dimensional. The first time she stared at a blurry photo of shadows on a riverbank and suddenly saw the squadron of fighter planes camouflaged beneath the trees, she was hooked. By early December 1943 she'd gotten herself formally transferred to air force photointelligence.

The USAAF took photointelligence less seriously than the RAF, and a transfer to this obscure, undervalued specialty was not exactly an upward career move. But by now Lieutenant Davey was looking forward to doing something technical and quiet, far away from competition and command. She wrote her parents, "It looks like a grand job for me, peaceful and yet fascinating." It also put her farther away than ever from her all-women world. Unlike the British, the Americans were not yet using women in intelligence work. Alice told her parents she would be "the first Wac in this field, and one of the first 3 or 4" in air intelligence.

Most men who actually worked with Wacs accepted them, and in her office, Alice was liked for her enthusiasm and respected for her dedication. "Once I discovered my type, my battles with authority figures were over," she later wrote. "I never again reproached myself for not being a leader in the shark-pack." She had happy memories of "the jokes and the sexy fun and that whole loopy little ingroup that everybody peed on."

Nor was she sorry to leave an army camp for a city where officers commuted to the war in pressed uniforms and shined shoes. Family friends invited her to parties, colonels took her riding on Virginia estates, and though single women far outnumbered men in wartime Washington she never seemed to have trouble getting dates. Her office gave her the comfortable work friendships she liked, and from now on she worked with men, dated men, and never mentioned another crush on a woman.

For Alice the next two years were a time of calm at work and restless experimenting in love. She was torn between unconventional, difficult men and stable, dull ones. She feared that any love capable of sustaining her through her darker moments must come at the cost of the wild energy of the upswing. She pictured herself as the Little Mermaid, and love as "the mad craving of the dislocated soul for a normalcy that revolts him as he plucks out his bright tortured wings to obtain it." Being herself—all sides of herself—with anyone seemed impossible.

In the fall of 1943 she started dating a lieutenant in navy public relations, formerly the assistant director of the Corcoran, where Alice's self-portrait had hung four years before. Bob Parsons took her to a party at a private club, "very social," then on a picnic in the country, where she got poison ivy. By that time he wanted to marry her, but she didn't think he was equal to her intensity. "Bob is very charming and pleasant, in a grave, slightly stuffy, very well-meaning way," she wrote home. "I like him thoroughly—and he appeals to me. But he keeps making me feel like a lady tigress, and that is not promising." They settled on a friendship in which he was still smitten and she was holding him in reserve.

Conventional types weren't always so predictable, she discovered. Another of her friends, a staid lieutenant colonel with a car and an apartment in Arlington, promised "an easy conquest, a kitchenette, a drive to work—altogether, the ideal improvisation." Then he turned out to be a tiger in bed; then he dumped her for someone else. Alice was shocked and miserable: she'd never been left before. It was mostly just offended pride, she knew, but her unhappiness still felt like a punishment. Not the first woman to feel damned if she didn't enjoy sex and damned if she did, she thought her hurt feelings were "the evil fruit of evil life, of low cheap lust, and gifts wasted." Her answer was self-sacrifice: "I must find something greater than myself, and give my allegiance and all my actions to that light, or perish."

But within a few weeks, passion won out over resolve. Her tempestuous affair with a young lieutenant lasted only a month or so (just long enough to help her avoid Mary when she came to Washington to do research on the WAC). He was another Bill Davey, brilliant, seductive, and temperamental, and at first Alice was attracted enough to consider marriage. But afterward it seemed to her that their relationship had been built on competition, defensiveness, and mutual distrust, and that she hadn't learned anything in love.

She took refuge in her work, and work repaid her by getting her out of town. Her department had decided she needed formal training, and in February 1944 she was told to report to the air force intelligence school at Harrisburg, Pennsylvania, to study photointerpretation.

Alice was one of only two women in her class, but again, in this intensely focused group, her sex wasn't much of an issue. No one noticed: they were all floundering in the flood of information their instructors poured out over them. Alice wrote home,

> They taught us to have at least a tentative opinion about almost anything which man can photograph, from Rome to Nome and from the Susquehanna to the Yengtze. [. . .] They taught us the organization of our enemies' military and naval forces; they taught us what to do if by any chance we should find ourselves in the Pyrenees or points north; they stuffed us full of average dimensions of everything from soccer-fields to hopper-cars; they taught us what sort of locomotives the Japanese liked to buy; they taught us the location of the main steel, oil and coal deposits throughout the world; they even attempted to teach us the towns which the Russians were trying to take, which was nothing but futile, as we always woke up to find that the Russians had not only taken them, but twenty-five more besides all equally unpronounceable, and were advancing on a wholly new set of hyphens.

The students routinely went home at three or five in the morning, Alice claimed, to come back again at eight-thirty.

Alice would always keep long and late working hours, but seldom more so than during the war. She pushed herself hard, then on days off collapsed and slept twelve or fifteen hours straight. Sometime that year, an army doctor diagnosed "fatigue" and prescribed a new wonder drug, Benzedrine. Eager to hang on to her productive highs, Alice took to speed as naturally as a bird to a current of air. She quickly realized she was in trouble and stopped using the pills. But from then on she was vulnerable to amphetamine temptation.

Alice graduated in April and went back to Washington and her old group. It was now formally called the Evaluation and Library Branch, Photographic Division, AC/AS Intelligence, and had moved from Gravelly Point to the basement of the Pentagon, but the work was the same, long-term assessment of enemy activity and recommending bombing targets. For a while she agitated to get sent overseas, and later claimed she'd nearly been assigned to parachute into occupied France. Her boss wouldn't let her go—just as well, since in fact she was terrified. Instead she studied the war in pictures, getting to know the streets, parks, and factories of cities in Japan and occupied China. It was only when the airplane factory she had put on a list of targets was bombed—along with the school next to it—that she remembered that the scenes she saw from the air were real.

She liked the "strange town of 30,000 inhabitants" that was the Pentagon, with its long, anonymous corridors and gray cafeterias under the fluorescent lights. And she liked keeping secrets. The concept of "intelligence" was being born—before World War II, spying on a large scale had been considered not done—and along with it came the idea of "security": if foreign secrets were vulnerable, then so were our own. The War Department was constructing an elaborate classification system for documents, with separate procedures for Restricted, Confidential, Secret, and Top Secret. As Alice explained to her parents,

> There are things like weighting a classified parcel if you travel or send it over the ocean, so it will sink; a whole routine of locking, checking and double checking safes at night, numbering and registering and coding the titles of certain material [. . .]. And everything, carbons, envelopes, etc., that come in contact with confidential material are treated just as it is, that is, they are filed and burned under an authorized officer's supervision and the destruction certified. Impressive, no?

Top Secret was applied mainly to plans for D-Day. "Of course such a thing as an invasion involves such terrifically wide preparations, down to the guy who pastes the labels on the boxes of Spam, that it is a very interesting matter to afford military security to all the moves." But even the procedures for her own Restricted and Confidential work excited Alice with their private ceremony. She was a natural spy, drawn to an atmosphere and an ethic that permitted her to reveal no more than she chose.

In the time Alice had left over from work and parties, she continued writing. After a few tries at journalism—a piece on chess and military strategy that Harold Ober couldn't sell, an article on photointerpretation that she didn't finish—she began work on a novel.

It was to be a tale of turbulent love, one that would connect the chaotic experience of coming of age in the thirties to the chaos of the war. In an early version, she gave the central role to "the boy wonder of literature, of polo, of Princeton [. . .] Lt. Donald Kelsey, of the Cavalry, assigned on special duty in Washington." Kelsey has an intelligent and literate girlfriend who is about to arrive in Washington and whom he is planning to kill.

In a second version, Alice made the girl the protagonist. "There is this girl, coming from nobody knows where, a sort of wanderer. Typifies young, strong qualities of this generation. [. . .] She appears, roams around, causes a lot of trouble, finally gets killed in a race riot. Plenty of talking."

She got furthest with the novel's third version, giving it a full outline and cast of characters and drafting several pages. This time she planned it as a gothic fantasy, "a sort of mystery tale à la *Rebecca*." It was called *The Victories of Light* (after a line from one of the gloomier offerings in Untermeyer, by Lionel Johnson), and was set, she wrote her parents,

> in Wash. DC, time: the present. The gal has a Horrid Secret. Wish I knew what it was. As I see it, the guy, a stuffy bachelor, falls for her in a condescending way; the gal turns out to have a no good spouse, and was about to commit suicide when run into. (They find a loaded revolver in her pocket. [. . .]) So the husband turns up, and is repulsive, and the good guy is stuffy, and the gal shillies a bit and then repudiates both of them and goes out to Do Good By Herself—all in the middle of World War No 2.

Alice experimented with different versions of the Horrid Secret. One was a front-page scandal in the girl's marriage. Another was a celebrity past as "the

Angel Child," her father's darling and the survivor of the plane wreck that had killed her stunt-flier mother. (There may have been some wish-fulfillment in this.) To the good guy, George, and the violent husband, now called Donald McDermott, Alice added a fourth character, a shady mutual acquaintance named Dupuy who provides snide psychological commentary and speculates that if the girl doesn't kill herself, she'll "probably [turn] Lesbian in an effort to imitate her father."

But the girl refuses to fulfill any of their expectations: "to pity herself with George, abdicate herself with McDermott, or explain herself with Dupuy." Instead she proclaims her sanity, tells all the men to go to hell, and goes off with yet another man, a "small, gnarled, rather shabby-respectable" person whose "long nose and strong jaw" make him look faintly like her father. This gnomish deus ex machina has offered her a job doing Good Works in a slum school.

If the Horrid Secret can be read as all of Alice's own—depression, brains, anger, desire—the men might express her choices. With "repulsive" Donald she can be the bad daughter, with "stuffy" George the obedient one. Dupuy is the oppressive voice of self-criticism. To repudiate the men would be to reject all the daughter roles. But then what? What would she look like as no one but herself? A du Maurier story might have ended in murder, but Alice doesn't choose death; nor, having rejected men, does she choose women. Instead she fantasizes being swept up by a sexless father figure and escaping into a limbo of working for others. The ending suggests Alice's own paradoxical hope that she could win her freedom with self-sacrifice.

The Victories of Light shares with Tiptree's science fiction at least one stylistic trick. It's narrated by the "good guy" George, the character who knows least about what's really going on. From his point of view, we read a story of a mad, troubled girl who excites him and serves as his inspiration—until she abruptly refuses to play her part. Tiptree's stories often contain a similar rebellion: a woman rejects her secondary role and takes over, while the sympathetic male narrator turns out to be just another part of her problem.

And in a way the story anticipates Tiptree himself, the mysterious gentleman who would remove the heroine to a better life.

That summer Alice moved at last into an apartment of her own: two rooms in Georgetown, down at the end of M Street, with a café on the corner where she could buy cigarettes. She set up a desk and let her thoughts stray to pink chenille bedspreads from Sears. At the same time she was promoted to captain, generating "a combination stream of house-warmings and congratulators who managed to destroy all my time and fill my icebox with beer."

She had meant to hole up and write, but she got very busy at work, helping compile a series of illustrated manuals on different industries—oil, munitions, aircraft—to be used by interpreters in the field. Typical of Alice in a determined phase, the manuals are extremely thorough. July 1944's *Photo Industrial Study No. 2: The Petroleum Industry* explains refining at the molecular level, shows different kinds of oil field camouflage, and includes a brief guide to sabotaging an oil well from the ground. And by the fall she was going out almost every night. In November she wrote home, "More of the horrors of war, or how did you fight the Great War, Mamma? My dear, the popping of champagne corks was terrible, but your parent struggled through, armed only with a pair of nylon stockings and an electric hot-plate."

Alice also became involved in the American Veterans Committee, a new organization for active-duty and returning servicepeople. Leftist and activist (but explicitly not communist), the AVC was conceived as a postwar alternative to conservative "beer and pretzels" groups such as the Veterans of Foreign Wars and the American Legion. Its objective, as stated in one of its first newsletters, was to make returning soldiers more politically aware and to "achieve a more democratic and prosperous America and a more stable world." Its broad progressive agenda included veterans' housing, economic justice, and a United Nations. Unlike the VFW, which denied Wacs full membership, the AVC was open to women and minorities. The group briefly enjoyed a large and active membership, including Ronald Reagan of the Hollywood chapter, who wrote a piece for the newsletter supporting labor and the moderate left. Captain Davey served on the advisory board and tried to find ways to get more Wacs involved.

She wrote her parents she was already planning her postwar career. "Fundamentally I am a sort of literate Girl Friday with an organizational flair. I feel sure that I could get one of several jobs, but which do you think I should try

for? I want to write mostly, but I was also thinking of the bread and butter."
Yet she still considered getting married as a means of support. In September
1944 she asked Mary, "What would you think of Bob [Parsons, from the
Corcoran] as spouse? He will earn around 11,000 after war which isn't much,
is 37, I don't love him but like him—or didn't you get a good look? I'm not
sold, merely considering before passing over."

Around this time, Alice had a revelation: maybe the key to stability was to
treat life as a "technical problem." If she hurt, then she should figure out why.
Not getting an answer to a letter, not being as successful as her mother—these
were concrete problems, not reasons for panic or despair. She felt proud of the
"scar-tissue" she'd grown, in love and at work, and of having cast off her
"selfish weak loneliness." One afternoon at the Lodge, on her two weeks' leave
from the army, "all of a sudden something *clicked* in my head . . . and after
that I, well, I trusted myself just a little more. The bottom just never quite fell
out altogether the same way again."

In the spring of 1945, Alice made a last attempt at writing about the WAC,
in two fictional sketches for the popular Sunday supplement *This Week*.
Dropping her narrative tricks, she tried to write as simply as she could about
the women she had seen. But in trying to write honestly, she didn't write
about her own, real longings and disappointment in the women's army. Instead, she produced sentimental stories, set in the Virginia army camps of two
years before.

One, based on real events, describes WAC Private Priebe, a meek, consci-
entious "housewife in an ill-fitting Army suit." She is walking across her post
thinking about her son, who has just been killed in Africa, when she runs
into two male officers who call her an "old bag" and laugh at her anxious
salute. The anger at the injustice runs deep, but the story takes its tone from
Private Priebe's "watery" niceness. It achieves not protest but defenseless
sadness.

The other was about a friendship between two Wacs, a six-foot-three-inch
Minnesotan who cooks in the company mess and a mouthy little New York
redhead who works in the motor pool. But what do two women do together?

How does their friendship make a story? Alice didn't know, and the story dissolves into light comedy. Both sketches were turned down.

The flip side of emotional control is sentimentality, and it was Alice's Achilles' heel as a writer. All her life, whenever she felt that she was being "watched" in print, she would retreat into excessive concern for other people's unhappiness. Only as someone else did she feel free to take control of her anger at the world and shape it into fiction. As Tiptree, she once wrote, " 'Ouch' simply is not a story."

In March 1945, Mary got her overseas assignment at last. *Collier's* sent her to Italy to write on the WAC's contribution to a theater of war. On the way, she came to Washington to visit Alice.

Afraid Alice might be jealous of her overseas posting, Mary made a point of being nice to her, and understanding about her latest lover, an RAF officer with a wife at home in England. Afterward she wrote Alice, "I wish you weren't always getting companionable in ways with a No Thoroughfare sign. [. . .] All right, I won't say any more—you two know it all and are acting on it—I just don't want you hurt, even the least little bit. Not any more." It seemed to pay off. Mary wrote Harry Bigelow: "I am so glad to know Alice's life and she is touchingly glad to have me know it." She went on,

> That child has got stuff in her. She is too good for this world, and I
> mean that—she has such wealth of love and trust and admiration to
> give, and her acumen prevents her giving it, now, without the conviction
> of her mind. [. . .] You and I and Herbert are her only loves. That is a
> little poignant. But I haven't seen any one here that is what we'd choose
> for her—no young Harry Augustus [Bigelow]. I spect there is only one
> of those.

It sounds as if Mary would have preferred to keep Alice in her family of four.

To Herbert, Mary contracted her family again from four to two: "We have Alice and if anything should happen to either of us, the other would have to live for her but that isn't like having each other." But a few days later, to Harry Bigelow, she wrote, "You know, I'd like to adopt a child, a little lame boy some day. I have a feeling about that." At this unsettled moment, she wished for a child very much unlike Alice: a small boy who would always need her.

Mary left New York on March 8, flying to Italy via Bermuda and Casablanca. She spent nearly a month in Italy, visiting Rome, Florence, Leghorn, Siena, Caserta, and the Apennines. She stayed "in a tent with the Forward Wacs" for a few days, toured the battlefield at Monte Cassino, and at one point came within a thousand yards of the German lines. She was in her element, traveling rough and listening sympathetically to the enlisted Wacs. When she took up residence in a commandeered seaside hotel—"my marble foxhole"—she quickly had the male officers charmed and the Wacs running errands for her. There, on April 19, she celebrated her sixty-third birthday.

The trouble was, the Italian front was last year's news, and by now every journalist in America was scouring Europe for stories. Mary's assignment was very specific: to write about the WAC at war. But even at the front, most Wacs' jobs were repetitive, clerical, and dull. ("You don't know how lucky you are," she told Alice.) And a critical story on the misuse of women's talents, or on the difficult readjustment the Wacs were facing at home, was not in Mary's brief. She told Alice, "I am having a horrible time trying to make the overall account of the Wacs come alive and sound interesting to the unappreciative world." In the end, *Collier's* never printed Mary's WAC stories. President Roosevelt's death on April 12 pushed all other news aside, and V-E Day made them obsolete.

After Italy, Mary moved on to Paris, and then to Germany and a horrific tour of some of the newly liberated concentration camps. Her powers as a writer were not equal to the appalling experience, and her stories about the camps never ran. But she later used the material for lectures, urging Americans not to discount the death camps as exaggeration or propaganda. And she never let her family forget. At low moments, the camps became another of her "horror-recitals."

Then Alice got sent overseas after all. On V-E Day, May 8, she received orders to report to air force intelligence in London for a special assignment.

It made no sense: she'd spent the entire war working on the Far East. But she gave up her M Street apartment, put her things into storage, packed a suitcase, and flew to Greensboro, North Carolina, to be processed for the trip out.

CHAPTER 15: **TING (1945)**

The war in Europe was over, but army regulations hadn't yet caught up: at the end of May 1945, Captain Davey shipped out from Brooklyn fully outfitted with a helmet, first aid kit, and canteen. (The beach outfit she'd bought in Greensboro would turn out to be more useful.) "The Red Cross gave us coffee and doughnuts" on the pier, she wrote home, "just like the movies." And so she went to war at last.

In Alice's childhood the transatlantic voyages had been luxurious and exciting, but like so much in the army this trip was only damp and dull. "Where the old cabins were are now bare cells [. . .] lined and filled with double or triple-tiered steel bunks. [. . .] The lights are dim, and it is deathly cold. One can go on deck during the daylight hours, but there are no chairs, rugs, etc. Merely a broad and windy expanse." After a crossing of eight or nine days and another few days in England getting her orders straight, Alice arrived in London on June 9. There she reported to air force headquarters, called United States Strategic Air Forces in Europe, or USSTAF (Rear), to be briefed on her new assignment.

During the war, the German military, especially the Luftwaffe, had developed technologies the Allies badly wanted, including jet aircraft and the V-2 rocket. It also held maps and other valuable intelligence on Russia, in case Stalin should become the new enemy. In the fall of 1944 the U.S. Army Air Forces had set up an "exploitation division," headed by Colonel Huntington Sheldon, to evaluate captured German science. By the spring of 1945 all branches of the military plus the Office of Strategic Services were competing to get information and informants out of the ruins of the Third Reich.

To understand the information, the air force needed specialists in the relevant fields, so the Pentagon sent over a group of fifty assorted technical experts, among them one photointerpreter. (Alice was also the only woman; she always wondered if a clerk hadn't accidentally overlooked her WAC serial number.) By the time she arrived, the project had been moved to USSTAF

(Main), in the Paris suburb of Saint Germain-en-Laye, and Colonel Sheldon sent an assistant, Captain Walter Pforzheimer, to London to brief the specialists and fly them over to France. When Captain Pforzheimer got back, he mentioned to Colonel Sheldon that the Pentagon had sent them a good-looking WAC. Sheldon suggested he invite her over for dinner at the senior officers' château.

Huntington Denton "Ting" Sheldon was a tall, graying, gracious senior officer, formerly of Yale and Wall Street, but neither his social class nor his charm kept Alice from confronting him to protest her assignment. She had been sent overseas in the wrong direction, she told him. For the past two years she'd been studying Asia. It was in the Pacific, not in Paris, that the army needed her. When she finished yelling, she challenged Colonel Sheldon to a game of chess, played blindfolded, and won. He fell in love.

Two weeks later, back in London, Alice wrote home that she was being heavily romanced by her new commanding officer, with expensive dinners and evening walks on Wimbledon Common. "I am getting a terrific rush from Huntingdon [sic] Sheldon, Col. AC," she wrote, meaning that she was being pursued. "I don't know what to do about it. He has been married twice, has 3 children, is 42 and distinguished and more or less broke and charming and was educated at Eton etc. He is SERIOUS."

Ting Sheldon was nearly as complex a character as Alice, but they were not, at first glance, a logical match. In his youth he'd distinguished himself as an athlete and socialite whose Eton, etc., education had largely been a waste of books and paper. Where Alice once compared herself in her twenties to "a bullet ricocheting blindly around the Grand Canyon," Ting at the same age had been conservative, unoriginal, unquestioning.

Still, he and Alice had more common ground than it seemed. They were both brilliant outsiders beneath their social façades. They'd both done a lot of experimenting in how to live. And they'd both joined the army on the rebound, to live a more honest life.

Ting was born February 14, 1903, in Greenwich, Connecticut, and grew up in London, where his father ran the foreign office of a New York investment bank. The Sheldons were an old New England family, good-looking, aristocratic people with, Ting said, a weakness for drink. (His father's sister Betty also lived in London, where she led a glamorous, rather alcoholic life as the wife of Sir Anthony Hope Hawkins, who wrote *The Prisoner of Zenda*.) He had a younger sister, Helen, to whom he was close. From age six he went to English boarding schools, where he was beaten up for being an American. In response he underachieved in the classroom but became the first American to play on Eton's senior cricket team. In the 1921 Eton-Harrow match at Lord's, his crucial catch helped Eton win the game.

Like Alice, Ting felt foreign, and learned to hide it. By the time he started at Yale in the fall of 1921, he seemed to be just another rich jock with a skin-deep personality. He joined the varsity squash team and planned to go into banking like his father. To his freshman roommate, the future pediatrician Benjamin Spock, he was an example of the kind of superficial Yale student who "care[d] more about social life and secret-society fraternities than academic achievement. These scions of wealthy families dressed in ties and jackets and didn't seem all that concerned with worldly matters outside their small circle." Spock remembered Ting as "a haughty lad fond of playing bridge."

Ting's "haughtiness" didn't hide only his foreignness. Alice thought it also hid physical pain. As a child Ting had suffered a series of illnesses, including appendicitis—in the days when abdominal surgery was life-threatening and recovery took weeks—and chronic, painful sinus trouble, which was treated with even more painful operations. As a junior at Yale, he contracted typhoid fever and lost months to hospitals and convalescence. Emotionally he had little to fall back on. He was not introspective. His parents were kind but distant. And though he claimed not to have minded the boarding schools, they hadn't encouraged openness or warmth. People who didn't know him well found him cold and unapproachable. He could be protective, but also distant and hurtful to those who loved him.

He graduated from Yale in 1925 and went into banking as planned, working for his father's firm, Blair & Co., on Wall Street. In New York, the same qualities that had annoyed Ben Spock made him an eligible bachelor, and at twenty-five he married Magda Merck, known as "Markie," an heiress of the Merck drug company fortune. They had a son, Huntington, called "Skip," a daughter, Audrey, and another son, Peter. Ting became president of an industry interest group called the Petroleum Corporation of America. They moved into a large Park Avenue apartment that belonged to Ting's parents. Ting continued his athletic career as a top-ranked squash player.

The trouble may have started with the Crash of 1929. The Depression didn't affect the Merck millions or Ting's own relatively modest salary. But Ting's parents' paper fortune collapsed with the Dow Jones. After Ting's father took early retirement in 1931 the Sheldons lived comfortably in Biarritz and Vermont, but the Park Avenue apartment was sold, Ting and Markie moved in with Markie's parents, and Ting lost his sense of himself as a member of the privileged class.

A few years later he severely injured his back. He came out of the hospital in a steel brace; his career as an athlete was over. He started to do something he'd never done before: question his life. For the first time he thought he wanted to do something serious. Maybe he didn't belong on Wall Street and Park Avenue after all.

Markie had seemed unstable before; now, after their son Peter's birth in 1935, she was hospitalized for postpartum depression. When Ting went to visit she didn't recognize him. She was diagnosed manic-depressive and given shock treatments. Ting withdrew, letting doctors take over his wife's care. When they said she might not get better, and that he should leave "for the sake of the family," he followed their advice. Markie Sheldon went into a private institution and Ting went to Reno to sue for divorce. Peter Sheldon said, "He ran out on us really."

A year and a half later in Palm Beach he married another heiress, Frederica Frelinghuysen, granddaughter of sugar baron and art collector Henry O. Havemeyer. One rumor had it that they'd met on a boat going to England and Frelinghuysen had offered Ting more than his job was paying him to marry her. He kept his job, but talked of becoming a doctor. The new Mrs. Sheldon didn't care to be married to a med student and left Ting in 1941.

The war rescued Ting the way it had Alice: it gave him a chance to do something serious. In April 1942, at age thirty-nine, he enlisted in the army. With his standing he could have been automatically commissioned and given a desk job. Instead he concealed his back injury and reported to officers' training school. During a workout he hurt his back again; with typical stoicism he got a civilian doctor to prescribe morphine, secretly wore his brace, and carried on.

Commissioned a captain, he was sent to the intelligence school in Harrisburg, then stationed in Belfast, Northern Ireland. There he trained new U.S. pilots in procedures for the European theater: formations to fly in, what to do after bailing out over enemy territory, how to avoid friendly fire. In early 1944 the operation moved to England, where they were involved in dropping leaflets over occupied France and supplying the French Resistance.

Walter Pforzheimer, who came to work for Ting in August 1944, called him an efficient decision maker with a "tremendous mind." He was strict—"he would bang my head on the sink if I had screwed up somewhere"—but also stuck up for his staff, recommending them for medals and getting them in on plum assignments. Cameron La Clair, who also became a lifelong friend, joined Ting's group as a lieutenant near the close of the war. La Clair found him at first capable but "forbidding" and "frosty." Over time he discovered behind the coolness a likable and unconventional man, with a quirky sense of humor and "some rather eccentric ideas."

Sheldon moved rapidly up the ranks to full colonel and in 1944 was transferred to the intelligence staff of USSTAF. There he was put in charge of what was first called the "the post-hostilities project" and later, in a pessimistic moment after the German Ardennes offensive, renamed the "exploitation division." At first he had five people under his command. By the summer of 1945, his section had grown to six hundred.

As the Allied armies advanced that winter and spring, Sheldon's group came behind them, gathering documents, maps, and experts. They didn't get the V-2 scientists, who surrendered to the rival OSS, or a valuable wind tunnel that they lost to the navy. But one of their coups was seizing ten Messerschmitt 262 jet fighters, crating them up, and shipping them back to Wright Field in Ohio. Another was a lightning trip to the Zeiss photographic works in Jena to pull out key documents and personnel just ahead of the advancing Red Army.

Asked to join this treasure hunt, Alice quickly got over her initial protest. At Saint Germain, coworkers saw a "wildly enthusiastic" researcher who began "dancing with excitement" when they heard that the German photo library had been found in a barn near Berchtesgaden. When she was sent to Ninth Air Force headquarters in Bad Kissingen, Germany, Davey flirted with the American officers and went riding in the country, but she also worked hard, turning out reports and charts on the organization and history of German photointelligence.

Davey had no lack of male attention, but as she was sent back and forth that summer—London, Paris again, Germany, Paris, London—she and Ting kept crossing paths, and at Saint Germain she started spending a lot of time in the senior officers' château. She was impressed by Ting's integrity and dedication to his work, and as she got to know him she began to see, beneath the strict boss and the social charmer, a loneliness she recognized and a sense of humor that matched hers.

From Bad Kissingen, a spa town set in green farm country that reminded Davey incongruously of Wisconsin, she drove south across Bavaria in a jeep with a male U.S. air force captain, a British WAAF officer, and a driver. They spent a night in the "utter rubble-heap" that had been Munich, met up with Patton's Third Army at nearby Bad Tölz, slept in what was left of four-star hotels, found some documents in a coal mine, interrogated a German colonel, and ended up at Berchtesgaden—seeing everything, she wrote her parents, through

> a constant downpour of rain—magnificent mountains, chalets, and waterfalls [. . .]. A sorrier pair of women officers you never saw—or a happier one! Absolutely marvellous! [. . .] A constant series of excitements, emergencies, scenic wonders, hilarities, rain, champagne, people of every description, food—everything. Then we arrived [in Berchtesgaden] to see another P/W, and found 2 hotels—one for small fry, one for big fry. I had just succeeded in convincing the hotel officer (the 101st Airborne Div—Arnhem—is occupying at the moment) that we were big fry in spite of looking like bums—when Col. Sheldon and party walk in from St. Germain. Tableau!

A day or two later she went with Ting to the ski resort of Garmisch-Partenkirchen, where an American had put up a sign that said "If there is Heaven on Earth, it is here" (and another had marked the elevator to the scenic overlook "Senior Officers Only"). In London a week or so before, they'd made love for the first time. Now, on July 4, less than four weeks after their first meeting in Saint Germain, Ting and Alice decided to get married.

For Alice the decision wasn't completely spontaneous. While part of her was letting herself be romanced, another part was fitting Ting into a plan. Marriage meant children, which she wanted, financial security, respectability, an excuse not to go back to Chicago. Her approaching discharge from the army scared her. So did her age: on August 24, her thirtieth birthday, she "really expected to wake up as a pile of dust." When Ting presented himself as a suitable candidate, she took a deep breath and dived into a new life.

But she didn't leap as blindly as she might have in the past. Ting really was in many ways a suitable candidate. He respected her brains, wit, and ambition. He wasn't competitive: he didn't mind that she played better chess. He wasn't afraid of her moods but didn't have many of his own; he was dependable without being dull. He understood her foreign travels and social background—they later worked out that they were something like tenth cousins. He valued the same qualities she was brought up to admire: loyalty, good judgment, articulation, integrity, insight.

When Alice was sick in London, Ting brought food and showed concern—to a Bradley, a sign of true love. When she was depressed in Paris, mourning the visible evidence of war, he gave her balance and perspective. He reassured her with his confident assumption that life was worth living. Yet he wasn't demanding or invasive: with him she could be cared for without losing her independence. Nor did she feel shut out by his stoicism; it was a familiar Bradley quality, and she respected it. When his back went out again that summer and hurt so much he could barely move, he impressed her by telling the doctor firmly, "Captain, I have a head cold. Report me on two-day sick leave." He had the reliability and reserve Alice loved in Herbert. In some ways he was the deus ex machina from her story the year before, the father figure who takes the heroine away to a life of virtue.

He was also the kind of husband Mary had always wanted for Alice, a stable provider who would make space for her to work. (Alice once told a marriage counselor that when she married Ting, "In a sense I couldn't lose: either I got the 5-star protector [. . .] *or* I proved to my folks that their direction of me ended up in a bunch of Roquefort.") When Alice's cousin Barbara Francisco first met Ting she found him "self-sufficient, closed off." But she also saw him as a secure, stable presence who "didn't interfere with what Alice was doing and ambivalently kind of enjoyed it." Being married was important to Alice, she felt: "Alice's need to have a man front for her to the world, and to be an old-style woman, was very, very strong." Yet Alice also wanted an equal marriage, and Ting agreed to try.

Ting's son Peter felt that Alice and Ting were both veterans of heartbreak, washed up on the same exhausted shore. "I think both of them were emotionally bankrupt when they met, and what they found in each other was what they couldn't find in anybody else. Emotionally, they found some solid ground."

But while one Alice wrote ecstatic letters home—"Ting continues to be the ideal man of me heart, and all is happier and happier"—another Alice already saw trouble coming. Ting drank heavily, a disturbing echo of life with Bill Davey. And the sex was a disaster.

After their first nights together, Alice wrote out in a journal a series of meetings between two characters named H and S (he and she?). For "S," she wrote, sex with "H" had been an "entirely unshared experience. Woman's presence apparently a nominal excuse." H's sexuality was "masturbatory"; he was clumsy; he pecked like a seagull when he kissed. "It is apparent that his desire for her is of a very fragile order, unresilient and barely reaching to the physical."

(In notes to herself thirty years later she put Ting's problem more succinctly: "Him and women: Had to get drunk—then of course impotent.")

When Alice tried to talk to him about it she didn't get far. She found it hard under the best of circumstances to talk about bodies, and Ting was even more defensive than she. She decided to resign herself, renounce her desires, "live internally and accommodate in all externals. H is worried by possible consequences of such a course. S is too, but makes a flat case for it as a good thing." Alice began to see marriage to Ting as the self-sacrifice that would make her "good." Over time, their relationship grew and deepened. But ten years later Alice wrote, "Surely [our marriage] began as a masochistic 'painful discipline leading to a new life.'"

Ironically, Ting's friends assumed that the relationship was based on physical attraction. Ting and Alice were going around holding hands and smooching in public; what else could it be? Ting's friends knew him as a hard-working, unemotional type with no time for love or any other nonsense. They felt this cute girl had come out of nowhere and bamboozled him; they worried he was fussing over her at the expense of his career. Eventually they resigned themselves to the attractive and temperamental Wac who was hanging around their boss, and saw that Ting was attracted to her brains most of all. "She was difficult as hell," Walter Pforzheimer observed, "but he liked difficult people. She fascinated him, I think."

The Bradleys were worried, too. As soon as Mary heard the news she wrote her friend Lila, the former Mrs. Henry Luce, and asked her for the New York low-down on her prospective son-in-law. Sources at *Time* could find nothing terrible on Ting in their files, however. In her letters home Alice reassured her parents that she still intended to work.

Ting handled the situation diplomatically. On a brief trip to Washington in August, he arranged to meet Mary on the East Coast. Mary approved, then formally announced the engagement: all the Chicago gossip columns ran an item on the romantic wartime couple. Back in Paris, Ting's second in command, a high-powered lawyer in civilian life, helped get the couple's divorce papers in order for the French officials. Ting bought rings and rounded up a bouquet and an elderly relative; and on September 22, 1945, in the mayor's office in Saint Germain, Alice Davey shed the name of her wild youth and became Mrs. Alice Bradley Sheldon.

The army gave them a week's leave at an estate at Antibes that had been requisitioned as a vacation home for generals. Alice unpacked her Greensboro beach clothes and gave Ting chess lessons, and they took and developed pictures with equipment confiscated from the Germans. (Another thing the Sheldons shared was a fanatical approach to hobbyism, from photography to gardening to tropical fish.) Immediately afterward they were sent to Germany, where USSTAF was setting up a headquarters at Wiesbaden in the American Zone.

Wiesbaden in the fall of 1945 was a gloomy city in a gloomy, defeated nation. It had been only lightly bombed, but made up for it, in Alice's opinion, with rain and haut-bourgeois bad taste. The houses in the officers' billet area were covered in "plaster eagles, lion gate posts, fake caryatids, and iron cupids relieving themselves in fountains." The ruined houses were grotesque, while the undamaged ones "exhaled an air of sullen sculleries and apoplectic parlors."

Their inhabitants seemed no better. In November Alice wrote home, "This German atmosphere is worse than 3 skunks. Everywhere the broken-backed snake, not too broken, and snapping viciously in sidelong looks, leering and unrepentant, changing from jeer to servility to jeer fast as lightning." She wouldn't even get her hair cut: "I won't have a damn German touch me." In other letters she asked for things she couldn't get in Germany: shoes, underwear, cigarettes, makeup. "If you can find some Princess Pat Liptone (Liquid Lipstick) in orchid, 'gay plum' or cyclamen, I would appreciate it for Xmas." At the same time she told them Ting was "nicer every day and I am happier every day. Life is wonderful."

Army regulations did not allow them to live together, but by now Ting was deputy director of air force intelligence in Europe, under General George McDonald. His boss liked him, rules were bent, and they moved together into a house assigned to senior officers. (Two future bosses of Ting's were also sharing quarters in Wiesbaden, a couple of young OSS agents named Allen Dulles and Richard Helms.) All fall and winter, while Ting wound up the exploitation project, Alice worked on her own project, an exhaustive report on the state of German photointelligence. She later claimed that it had run to "three volumes, thirteen appendices and 600 pounds of exhibits" and when she saw it again ten years later had been read by two people. When she tried to reread it "it was like eating a hairbrush"—despite the dirty jokes she put into the footnotes to see if anyone would notice.

Unlike Captain Davey's work, Colonel Sheldon's required him to meet and socialize with various senior officers. "Ting could play the social game when he had to," Walter Pforzheimer recalled. "But he didn't play it very much after he met Alli, and I think he was glad to be rid of it." Alice told her parents her new husband was "charming the whole evening, and then comes upstairs looking like a Regency gent muttering 'I *hate* that sort of thing!!!' Which suits me fine." Afterward he did unflattering imitations of the people he'd been with and gave them funny names to make her laugh. Alice gave Ting room to question and rebel; they shared a keen sense of the absurd and a slight sense of superiority to the rest of the world.

Alice rarely left the house, with its red velvet wallpaper and morose servants, but occasionally ventured outside with Ting, who insisted she keep regular hours and get exercise and fresh air. Sometimes they went out with the cameras, taking pictures of ruined gardens or people searching for firewood in the rubble. For now at least, the camera gave Alice some distance from the ruins. While she wrote happy letters to her parents, part of her was taking in the shattered cities, the death and displacement that she had helped to make, and storing them away in her private horror museum. Later, at depressed moments, she would recall that she had been "right in the thick of things, seeing it raw"—the human race at its worst. "The lesson of my time is, If it is inhuman, cruel, and unthinkable, it'll happen," Tiptree wrote. Alice spoke of it so vividly to her friend and editor Jim Turner that he believed she had "never really recovered from the horrors of the Second World War."

She started to wonder what, if anything, separated the good guys from the bad guys. For her report she had spoken to a German photointelligence officer, a Colonel Ruef. Instead of one of the devils she'd joined the army to fight, she saw a "calm, sensible, dedicated man whose problems in winning his country's atrocious war were exactly those I had been struggling with in my country's heartfelt crusade." Even worse, with his long jaw and deep-set blue eyes, he looked exactly like Herbert Bradley. "To hear the hard military-Nazi words coming out of that mouth was as close as I care to come to experiencing alien possession," Tiptree later wrote, commenting on another statement he'd made: "If one of the important things to know about a person is the face in his nightmares, I give you the blue eyes above the death's-head insignia, that look so much like mine."

Alice kept working for the American Veterans Committee. "We of the Military Affairs Advisory Committee—which I am on by virtue of being the senior WAC member!—keep writing each other rather interesting letters," she told her parents. About her own future she wasn't sure. She didn't want to be a critic again, although Marshall Field himself had written to offer her her old job back. She thought she might like to write for *PM*, Field's left-wing New York daily, where her former professor Max Lerner was now editorial director. If she'd dared, she probably would have said she wanted to be a real, literary-type writer.

Alice's only published fiction before Tiptree is set in the wreckage of postwar Germany. "The Lucky Ones" is another story about women in war, this time three displaced persons, or D.P.'s, who lived and worked in the Wiesbaden house. They were Polish girls who had been forced laborers on German farms and were now assigned as maids for the Americans. The oldest was twenty-two; the youngest, now nineteen, had been just fourteen when the Germans shot her parents and took her away. While Alice learned what their lives had been like under the Germans, she also discovered how little her own "liberating" army cared about their future.

Harold Ober submitted "The Lucky Ones" to the *New Yorker*, where it appeared November 16, 1946, under the name Alice Bradley. It is a thinly fictionalized account of her interactions with the three D.P.'s, especially the youngest, Sophie, who became pregnant by an American soldier. She had probably tried to induce abortion, and was deathly ill by the time she came to Alice for help. It was yet another childbirth horror story, but Alice and another, male officer ("He gave me that I-hope-you're-not-going-to-cause-trouble look which women in the Army get to know well") got Sophie into a German hospital and she survived. The ostensible point of the story was that these were the lucky D.P.'s, the ones the Allies had not yet put into camps, the ones who hadn't starved or frozen while waiting for their fate to be decided.

But it's also about the narrator's contradictory responses as a woman and an army officer. Like Alice's earlier WAC fiction, "The Lucky Ones" is a dramatic account of injustice. But this time it is told in a cool, reserved voice. The narrator feels compassion, but she is also a captain with a report to finish, a place in the military hierarchy, and a strong habit of saluting colonels: "I never did get used to my husband in full regalia." Being a woman, she is the one the D.P.'s come to for help; being an army officer, she can only do so much. She is describing what it means to be in the WAC. But because she is not speaking directly about the WAC, the emotions are safe to handle: there's less pressure for an honesty that would spiral into rage or be deflected into sentimentality. The experience of a woman in the army is there, and it powers the story—but only when it has been hidden and changed.

In the summer of 1945, in a journal she called "Letters to My Sister," Alice wrote,

> I find, in all the writings of women, a strange muffled quality, as if the living word, as it left the lips, had been hastily suppressed and another

substituted, one which would conform to some pattern imposed from without. [. . .] I am trying, from the living urge of my own life, to force open channels of communication so far mostly closed. [. . .] To press out naked into the dark spaces of life is perhaps to build a small part of the path along which others like myself wish to travel.

She didn't want to be careful in print; she wanted to be the drunk uttering truth. Or as Tiptree once wrote, she wanted her writing to be "serious, tortured, tragic, self-convinced, outraged and outrageous."

But honesty in writing has to do with admitting complexity, too, and there is more to fiction than a raw emotional response. Even the "drunk uttering truth" that Alice once wanted to be is a persona, a voice that the writer assumes, not the writer herself. Honesty isn't always deadly earnest; it can be comic or contradictory. Then again, there were truths Alice wasn't prepared to tell at the expense of respectability, or emotional stability, or love.

In the end, the WAC didn't give Alice much of what she had hoped to gain. If she had wanted to become a lover of women, she hadn't had the courage, or the encouragement, to act on her desire. If she'd planned to become a writer, she still hadn't found (or claimed) a voice that she could use. And if she'd hoped to become a heroine of the good war, she'd discovered that doing good was harder and more complicated than she thought. It did give her more confidence in her own capabilities, but as an experiment in what it meant to be a woman, or what it could mean, it was highly inconclusive.

Ironically, Alice's time in the WAC would end up making it easier for her to pass as a man. In the 1970s, Tiptree's casual references to his Second World War service seemed to confirm his masculinity. Like many things Alice had done, the army made more sense in a male biography than a female one. By then the role that a couple hundred thousand Wacs had played in an army of 15 million had nearly been forgotten.

CHAPTER 16: **GOING UNDERGROUND (1946–47)**

Solely in the public interest, the disordered fantasies of the masculine-complex woman should be combated.

—FERDINAND LUNDBERG AND MARYNIA F. FARNHAM, M.D.,

MODERN WOMAN: THE LOST SEX

The Sheldons stayed on in Wiesbaden until early January, when Ting's boss, General McDonald, was relieved and they got to go home with him by plane. They flew via Paris, Casablanca, Dakar, and British Guiana to Miami, where they arrived on January 13, 1946. Alice celebrated by downing a quart of cold milk. Like most U.S. soldiers she'd been told not to drink the milk in Europe, which was said to be tubercular, and she was craving that bit of wholesome American normalcy. It gave her indigestion. On that inauspicious note Alice came home from the war.

The Sheldons went to Washington first. Ting got them a room at the elegant Shoreham Hotel—her first taste of his higher standard of living—and for a couple of months Alice tinkered with her German photointelligence evaluation while Ting did some work for Central Intelligence Group, the new coordination agency for military intelligence. A couple of Ting's army friends went to CIG as well, including Walter Pforzheimer, who became its legislative counsel. In 1947, he helped draw up the National Security Act to transform CIG into CIA.

As soon as the Sheldons could get leave they took the train to Chicago. From Wiesbaden Alice had requested a quiet homecoming: "PLEASE NO PARTIES! At least, the very minimum possible. We are a leetle weary!" The minimum possible was a cocktail party for fifty at the Casino, covered by the society press. For a photographer for the *Chicago Herald-American,* Ting and Alice posed in uniform and smiled with resigned charm, a new couple on show. "Alice received without her overseas cap," the paper reported. "Her mother's hat was a sheer black frou-frou, worn with a black afternoon dress and sables." The contrast between young Alice who had looked so cute in her WAAC jacket and the thirty-year-old air force captain just back from Germany was sharp. This was Alice's last major appearance in the Chicago society pages, and was not so much her welcome home as Alice Bradley's final farewell.

As the excitement and momentum of wartime drained away, even her army self, Captain Davey, began to fade. She had to find and furnish an unfamiliar new self; it was more difficult than she had expected. What she did finally acquire, after all the years of being Alice, was a nickname. When her new mother-in-law, Mimi Sheldon, started calling her "Alli," she was delighted, and adopted it as her own.

But that fall, when the army retroactively promoted her to major and awarded her a Legion of Merit, the official recognition made her feel like a fraud. She had gone into the army to do something all on her own, and now she felt she had gotten the medal not for her work but because of Ting. (Ting's jealous friends were inclined to agree.) Starting out to prove herself, she'd ended up back in someone else's shadow.

In April Alice and Ting left the army and spent a month in New York City, staying at Mary's old hotel, the Seymour. While Ting went around to his Wall Street connections to ask about jobs, Alice looked up friends and had fun spending her discharge pay. Having told Mary "I am resolute about shopping; NONE," she wrote two days later that she had ordered an expensive set of matching accessories—hat, purse, belt, umbrella, cigarette case, platform pumps—in mustard-yellow lizard skin. But there wasn't much work to be had, or much to buy. Rationing was still in effect, and everything from shirts and shoes to sugar and toilet paper was in short supply. Unemployment was high. Many, including Ting, feared the coming of another crash.

Ting thought Alice should invest her mustering-out pay and war bond savings in art. "Under extreme conditions, jewels and paintings represent the soundest assets," Alice assured her parents. Shyly, she went to see her old teacher, John Sloan, at his Greenwich Village studio and chose about twenty etchings and two paintings from his most recent work, sending most of them to Chicago for safekeeping. She herself never painted again. She gradually lost contact with most of the people she'd known before and during the war. Ting shared with his wife, and perhaps reinforced, an easy willingness to cut ties with former selves.

Bill Davey did make one last appearance in Alice's life. For a while after the divorce they'd kept in touch. "I wrote her a few mournful letters," he recalled. "And she said that my writing had always had an effect upon her or something, but I suppose that's politeness.

"Then just after the war I was in the Hotel Lowell in New York. I was with my wife at the time. We'd been arguing, she'd been crying, and I had a pimple on my nose. The elevator stops and who gets on but Alice, looking stunning, with this tall, handsome social type. We all rode down to the lobby together in stony silence, and that's the last I ever saw of her."

Ting and Alli spent the spring and summer of 1946 first at Ting's parents' farm near Rutland, Vermont, and then in Wisconsin. In Vermont Ting fished—one of the few sports he could still do with his bad back—while Alli read, chatted with her new mother-in-law about gardening, and, in answer to Mary's questions, said they hadn't yet begun making babies but were "planning for hows and whens." At the Lodge, Ting fished some more with Herbert, listened to Mary's stories, and took on the very useful role of buffer between Alli and her parents.

They started getting to know Ting's children. In New York in April they'd had a polite lunch with the two youngest, thirteen-year-old Audrey and ten-year-old Peter. Ting tended to favor his confident oldest son, Skip, who was away at prep school, but Alli took to Peter, whom she found charming, bright, and appealing in an underdog way. Audrey was the odd one out, an unhappy and rebellious child still mourning her father's desertion. "It is apparent she adores Ting," Alli wrote Mary, and said they were planning "an Audrey reclamation and regeneration program"—on which they never quite followed through.

They started getting to know each other, and found that they were not a perfect fit. Ting didn't read and wasn't self-sufficient. When they were both in a mood to talk they could have a lot of fun together, but when he wanted company and she wanted to work he got on her nerves. She had enjoyed her own family most at quiet moments, when they all sat in the same room and read. She associated silence with company, talk with being bored and overwhelmed.

And though he'd agreed to strive for an equal marriage, he didn't realize what it involved. He had always had servants, and was as vague about housework as she once had been. They compromised partly by employing housekeepers. But Ting's more expensive taste in houses and neighborhoods made it impossible for them to have an equal marriage financially.

Sex was still the worst problem. To friends they seemed physically passionate: Ting's friend Cameron La Clair recalled seeing them "in the air club in New York; they were holding hands, and at a moment they thought nobody was looking they were hugging and kissing each other quite madly." But even before they left Washington, and just six months after they married, Alli wrote Ting a letter saying she had made up her mind to leave him.

> When we decided to get married I liked you and admired you. Now I really love you as a person. But it has become increasingly clear to me that I married you for what were essentially selfish reasons. I wanted to escape from a situation which was too difficult for me, and it seemed that by marrying you I could make everyone happy, and put myself in a sort of Nirvana world with no pain and no joy where all I had to do was to work and carry out my duties toward you and control myself until I became a good person. That was an impossible delusion.
>
> When I told your parents I could and would make you happy if staying by you and loving you would do it, I meant it. I thought all I had to do was to go on and it would be done, twenty or thirty years of just going straight ahead. [. . .] I do love you; but I don't think I can make you happy. The staying by is tougher than I thought.

She loved Ting as a friend, but not "as a wife," she wrote; their being together physically "has from the first been a mistake for me." And sex mattered to her more than she'd thought. "I know, sadly enough, what should be and isn't. Nothing at all would be better to take than the shadow without the substance."

"All I know for sure is that I am in pain and am afraid I am going to cause pain," she wrote in a journal. "I want, I want, I want, I want. I want to be alone, to be in a crowd, to work, to have children and love them fully, to be fulfilled in body and mind and to carry each of those fulfillments to a point entirely contradictory to all the others." This is a familiar puzzle for women: how to combine work and children, body and mind, love and independence. But it was not much spoken of in 1946—or if it was, it was called neurosis— and Alli felt she must sacrifice herself not to hurt others. In a dramatic and self-dramatizing outburst she continued,

> What shall I do? Lie and deceive, put on a bold face and knock the bottom out of everything? Drift in this void and try to work? I cannot hold the beast that is me in check much longer . . . This is all nonsense. It is not honest. This writing is a farce. Can one not be honest? [. . .] If I could dissolve myself into a single desire to work, all would be solved and life would proceed in a noble orchestration of work by me and decisions and desires by other people. Oh, but I can't do this. [. . .]
>
> The crime is worse than you imagine it. [. . .] I sin, not in delight, but with the most vivid, relentless and heartbreaking images of the pain I cause ever in my mind. [. . .] My own pain is I feel an integral part of me. [And yet] inextricably mingled in me is a strong vein of life, and though I do wrong and nothing but wrong, I know that I do in some sense what is strong and independently good. [. . .] So continues the blind ambivalent charge into life, headed for no goal but the center of a—perhaps dead—fire. I can try not to hit out sidewise with my elbows as I go, but I can't help the ones in front. [. . .] I commit us all to life, surely a superfluous gesture. We are committed . . . Maybe those who follow us will be better. Or perhaps much worse, and me partly to blame.

Alli wants to erase her desires, knows she can't, half wants to claim them as "sin" and "crime" and knows that they are not. A line like "I cannot hold the beast that is me in check much longer" appears self-revealing but even to her sounds silly if she thinks about it, as if the drunk who had set out to tell the truth instead burst into maudlin self-accusation. She can't imagine being herself around anyone else. She can't picture release in the here-and-now, only hope for the future.

Her letter to Ting ends unfinished and unsigned. It may be she never gave it to him, or that she did and they were able to talk honestly. Apparently they compromised: Alli did her best for a while to be a housewife, and they eventually agreed to an open marriage. But for a long time she looked on Ting as a temporary arrangement.

Later that year Alli drafted a ghost story: a woman falls in love with a man she has seen in a dream. The woman is unhappy in her marriage, Alli explained to Mary. "Suddenly her various longings boil over into this intensely real fiction—the idea made real. But not there." Will the woman forget her dream lover? Will she go mad? Alli chose to leave the ending unclear. But this is another version of the story she kept retelling: the romance of the Belle Dame (or Homme, or Alien) Sans Merci, the doomed love affair with a ghostly, unreachable other.

In 1946, along with writing fiction, taking photographs as a hobby, and working on "The Lucky Ones," Alli revived the essay on aesthetics she'd begun in 1940. During the war she'd done informal research on visual associations: after Hiroshima, she'd surveyed thirty of her fellow officers on what color they thought uranium was. ("The majority said they saw it as silvery-grey, although one major really felt it was yellow and black. This I believe was a verbal association through *pitch-blende*.") Now she read all five volumes of Ruskin's *Modern Painters*, made forty typed pages of notes, and started dreaming of herself as a great theorist of art.

Her original essay had been an indignant, passionate defense of the creative imagination (meaning her own imagination). Now she found herself turning for reinforcement to science: physiology, physics, and especially psychology. To all the aestheticians who were cataloguing forms in art, she answered that the place to begin was not the painting but the mind of the observer. "To understand what he sees in art we must understand how he sees the real world in which art is one ingredient." What psychological forces were at play in our perception of a painting? Could these be tested? Why not search for beauty in the eye of the beholder? She decided she wanted to write a book on visual perception and its role in aesthetic judgments, to be called *The Psychology of Value in the Graphic Arts*.

For the next fourteen years, Alli saw this book as her life's work. Where painting and fiction seemed so frighteningly large and vague—where to begin?—the vision project appeared to be concrete, limited, and existing outside herself (although in fact it was none of those things). It felt like a "technical problem," the way she wanted life to be. Like life, it was a technical problem of vast and nebulous proportions, but the notion of a technique gave her the illusion of control. She suspected she was "attempting to gain security by systematizing the universe of perception."

Over the years she wrote many introductions explaining what her book was going to be. In one, she said she wanted to write about

> why red was chosen for "Stop," and what colors and designs are used in neckties, and how we feel about Night, and which way is Up, and what shape Sex is, and the mysterious attractions of certain numbers. All these things are seen; and in describing the seeing of them we will find, I believe, that we have laid a basis for discussing how we see Art.

Her initial research should have discouraged her: she kept coming across more or less scientific versions of the old saying "To each his own." Physical perceptions turned out to have little in common:

> Anthropologists can point to cultures in which almost any severe pain is regarded as part of some larger "good"; psychoanalysis shows us that we as individuals often seek sensory pain. [. . .] Only where we find extremely severe pain can we unhesitatingly qualify it as affectively unpleasant on the perceptual level. In no case can we go on to describe it as "bad."

Perceptions of the world around us are equally subjective:

> A forest situation has certain affective qualities, among which are remoteness, organic nature, and so on. But is it "peaceful" or "delightful"? To some, yes; but anyone who has ever been lost in one, or seen a city-dweller floundering about in one for the first time, knows that forests can be exasperating, frightening, hostile and boring. Hence we are not justified in any evaluative labels.

The vastness of the subject, plus the unacknowledged presence of herself, made the essay impossible to write. She had too many ideas, went in too many directions at once. She lacked the confidence to generalize, or the training. (She thought of studying psychology under the GI Bill, but was afraid academia would rob her of her voice.) The harder she tried to organize her material, the more she got seduced by interesting details. The book on vision never got written. Even so, it was an important part of Alli's long apprenticeship in communicating with the world.

From October 1946 to May 1947 the Sheldons lived in New York City, in a small furnished apartment that belonged to Ting's sister at Sixty-fifth and Madison on the Upper East Side. It was a long way from West Eleventh Street, physically and culturally, but it was what Ting liked, and given the housing shortage they were lucky to find anything at all. They adopted the first of several cats, and Alli got her books out of storage. Markie Sheldon lived nearby, and Ting's son Peter began stopping by after school. His visits were furtive and uncomfortable: his mother was jealous, his father never much at ease with his kids, his stepmother well intentioned but awkward. Alli still wanted kids of her own, and in January wrote her parents, "I thought last month I was pregnant but I wasn't. Ah well! Better luck next time."

Alli spent time in the Columbia University library, reading up on the physiology of vision. She got back in touch with Max Lerner. And she started volunteering at American Veterans Committee headquarters. She made one lasting friend in the AVC: Gus Tyler, a thirty-six-year-old writer and political strategist. He was political director of the powerful International Ladies' Garment Workers Union and was helping the AVC block a communist takeover attempt. They became friends in the way Alli liked to be friends with men: they debated politics, flirted, and didn't talk about her personal life at all.

Alli didn't end up writing for *PM*. But she did make one more serious try at journalism. Once again, what she really wanted to write about was women.

The first year after the war was a time of economic anxiety but political optimism. In 1946, Americans felt that they had fought for a just cause and justice would come of it. Congress was debating legislation on equal pay for men and women. The gap between the nation's rich and poor was much narrower than in 1940. In India, Gandhi's nonviolent resistance seemed to be succeeding. Utopian ideas were in the air. For a few short months, Alli later wrote, she and her friends "believed that the way to the Millennium was at last under our feet."

It was as if history had stopped, waited, balanced—and then slowly, heavily, come down on the wrong side. Black and Asian veterans returned to discrimination at home; the AVC began having its consciousness raised about race. And Alli was surprised by a violent backlash against women.

By 1947 almost all the economic and social gains women had made during the war had been swept away. These gains had not been based on an ideology of women's rights; all along, women had been encouraged to see their well-paid jobs as temporary. One War Department brochure had explained that a "woman is a substitute" in a factory job, "like plastic instead of metal." After the war, women factory workers were laid off en masse. And returning Wacs, including Alli, found their new skills worth little. Trained technicians and experienced managers were offered the same poorly paid jobs as typists and dime-store clerks they'd had before the war. Issues such as day care were being publicly debated, but there was no real political force behind them. The Senate voted down the Equal Rights Amendment, 38–35. And while militant (and mostly male) labor unions held bitter strikes during the period of postwar retooling, women never united to demand their rights. As a group, they confirmed Alli's old judgment that women didn't think politically enough for real solidarity.

Psychology books now pronounced working women "neurotic," unmarried women "unnatural," and educated women "sexually unfulfilled." When Alli read the popular 1947 book *Modern Woman: The Lost Sex,* she learned that women who worked outside the home were "masculinized," a condition which endangered their marriage, children, and sex life. If women were unhappy in the home, she read, it was the fault of feminism, which ranked with Communism, anti-Semitism, nihilism, and anarcho-syndicalism as one of the "organized movements of the modern world gathered around the principle of hatred, hostility and violence."

These books were accompanied by a stream of hostile articles in the mainstream press. The country may have been trying to go back to what it thought of as normal life. Or the returning soldiers, having been bullied by their officers and shot at by their enemies, may have wanted wives and children whom they could bully in turn, and from whom they could demand love. In any case, in 1947 the press spoke with the voice of the slush-kickers of Des Moines.

Collier's published an article, "The Trouble with Women," comparing woman's nature to "that of preadolescent children and of men inclined to criminal propensities." The author, a psychiatrist formerly employed at Sing Sing prison, warned, "Women have gone too far too fast. They cannot maintain the burden of what we might call an uneven ascent without disaster." In the *American Mercury,* Alli read that GIs preferred German women to their "domineering-demanding" counterparts back home. In the *New York Times Magazine,* a former GI compared Wacs unfavorably to European women. The American women wanted to run things and have careers, and they insisted "on a loud and full share of the conversation with their escorts while the French girls would let the men do most of the talking, adding only a word or two now and then to show their interest."

Alli was appalled—and one day while she was arguing about the "woman problem" with her friend Gus Tyler, it came to her that you didn't need Freud or hormones to explain women. You just had to look at power relations. If you saw women as an oppressed group it all fell into place. These articles described women exactly the way she'd heard Belgians talk about Congolese, anti-Semites about Jews, or American whites about blacks. Years later, as Tiptree, she wrote,

> Incredible how the top dog always announces with such an air of discovery that the underdog is childish, stupid, emotional, irresponsible, uninterested in serious matters, incapable of learning—but for god's sake don't teach him anything!—and both cowardly *and* ferocious. [. . .] The oppressed is also treacherous, incapable of fighting fair, full of dark magics, prone to do nasty things like fighting back when attacked, and contented with his place in life unless stirred up by outside agitators. [. . .] Once I learned the tune I stopped believing the words—about *anybody.*

Armed with this insight, Alli sat down to write an angry essay about the magazines' "barrage of rock-filled iceballs" at women. As she pointed out, it was no use trying to refute the absurd allegations, or even object to them. "What the average woman does, of course, is to laugh it all off. [. . .] A certain percentage of woman readers, whose cheeks have become stiff from laughing it off, write letters to the editor. The editor interprets this as 'reader interest' and promptly prints an even ruder article, which draws more letters, and so on and on."

Instead, Alli tried to turn the psychological argument back on men. It was men who were infantile, she stated—and not, in Philip Wylie's popular theory, because of their overprotective mothers, either. "It is directly due to man's concept of society, and 'Mom,' where she exists, is the end product of this regression, not the cause. Men get the kind of women they ask for." Even women who truly wanted a traditional home and family felt "cheated in their inmost souls by this paranoid athlete, this scorner and competer with the sealed unhappy face and bathroom jokes who is palmed off on them as a man's man and a real guy." It was these hostile, insecure men who had created the "woman problem," who saw women as at best a convenient scapegoat, at worst an active threat. A year or two later in France, Simone de Beauvoir would come to the same conclusion—women are the Other—but Alli ended simply on a plea to the papers not to stir up more hatred: "The customers are already oversold."

Harold Ober was enthusiastic about Alli's essay, "The Women-Haters," which was succinct, insightful, and dryly funny. But the *Saturday Evening Post* returned it, Alli reported to her parents, "saying how much they liked it or rather, my spirit, but that it generated more heat than light. This made even Harold mad, since the other stuff hating women which they have published was exclusively infra red not to say infra dig." Ober tried, but no one would print it, and "The Women-Haters" vanished into Alli's files.

Having a political analysis made Alli less vulnerable to the pressure on women to return to the home (what Tiptree later described as the "kuchen-kids-and-kimono media onslaught"). And her scientific curiosity made her a little less vulnerable to the imputation that she was "not fulfilled as a woman," that is, not having vaginal orgasms. She had read enough to know that her orgasms were a physiological, not a psychological phenomenon.

But her political analysis didn't tell her how it felt to be one of the oppressed. It didn't tell her how it felt to have her voice go unheard, her work discounted, and everything she had striven for in the WAC be erased. It didn't tell her how to live with anger, self-doubt, and loneliness. Later, in the 1970s, Alli was never as hopeful for the future as her younger women friends. She didn't see women's history as a constant, rising line.

After "The Women-Haters" failed to sell, Alli seems to have given up on journalism. At any rate she didn't look very hard for a job, and there's no evidence she submitted more freelance work. She'd made a good beginning with "The Lucky Ones," but the *New Yorker*'s heavy editing apparently put her off, and she didn't try to sell to them again.

She missed working—but as what? "Why have a child? Why work? Why live?" she wrote in her journal in February 1947. "I find no work to my hand. I don't seem to give a damn for others any more, for the great events of my times. I am shrinking up. I don't want money, or fame. I need a place in the scheme of things. Yet all my places were temporary . . ."

Even for Ting, finding a job was harder than he had expected. Prepared to go back to Wall Street at least for a little while, he called on his old social network, but nothing turned up. General McDonald tried to get him back into air force intelligence, but he didn't want to return to the military. Then in May 1947, a *New York Times* want ad caught the Sheldons' eye. It offered a chicken hatchery for sale in rural Toms River, New Jersey.

The hatchery, Alli wrote her parents a few days later, "nets over $25,000 per year, AND YOU ONLY WORK FIVE MONTHS A YEAR, Dec to May! [. . .] They hatch a million eggs in five months, and it runs like clockwork. [The owner] has made enough to buy a Cadillac and live in Hawaii, and they want to sell." In her next letter she wrote, "The thing that interests us about this is that literally, in no other field of work we can find are there any such possibilities for savings, living pleasantly, and doing interesting and not nerve-racking work."

The work involved taking in eggs from poultry farmers, hatching them in incubators, and returning the chicks, with potential sidelines in selling chicks or immunizing hens. The more the Sheldons investigated the business, the more it appealed to them. It would in theory make more money than a New York City desk job. They could work together in an equal partnership. Alli would have time to write. After war and Manhattan, the idea of making a living from the land, and raising kids there, sounded soothing and earthy. And the move must have appealed to their shared sense of the drastic: they could turn their backs on their earlier life.

Ting checked out the place financially, consulted with the agricultural department at Rutgers University, and concluded that the deal was sound. Then he and Alli asked their parents for loans. The Bradleys were surprisingly supportive; by now they must have been resigned to Alli's strange changes of career. Ting's father would have preferred the State Department or international finance, but he too came through. Within three weeks of seeing the ad, Ting and Alli agreed to buy Kiefer's Hatchery. They would work for the next four and a half years in what Alli later euphemistically referred to as "a small country business." But in her emotional and creative life, Alice would spend nearly a decade underground.

CHAPTER 17: **RUNNING A CHICKEN HATCHERY IN NEW JERSEY (1948–52)**

You're afraid of writing what you think about life, because you might find yourself in an exposed position, you might expose yourself, you might be alone.
—DORIS LESSING

Rhetoric is the attempt of the will to do the work of the imagination.
—W. B. YEATS, PINNED UP OVER ALLI'S DESK

The Sheldons agreed to take over the hatchery at the start of the new hatching season, in February 1948. They spent the summer at the Lodge. Then, in October 1947, they found rooms in New Brunswick, New Jersey, and reported to Rutgers University for a course in poultry farming.

Alli was thirty-two, Ting forty-four. Excited again by the prospect of a new life, Alli wrote Mary and Herbert about her lessons:

> One gent after another gets up and reels off yards of literature pertaining variously to breeding, recognizing, judging, feeding, managing, diagnosing, marketing, housing, and generally raising havoc with The Chicken, or Gallus Domesticus, as we have come to know her. [. . .] "What are the symptoms of Newcastle disease, Mr. Sheldon? The host? Any others? Are pigeons affected? What post-mortem lesions?" [. . .] And so on and on, we've only had virus diseases so far, with bacteria, protozoa, parasites, deficiencies and molds and fungi and poisons still to go. And this is just one course. Highlights of the others are double-entry bookkeeping, Mendelian theory, judging hens for laying condition, the economics of the egg, theory of crop rotation, chemical nutrition, and legislation affecting the poultry industry. In the afternoon we rush out to the [Rutgers] farm, where we do all sorts of things with chickens, including as I mentioned killing and dressing them. [. . .] Of course

(thank god) we won't have to know all this to run our hatchery, but it is what we need in order to make a place in a poultry raising community. And it includes our stuff—oh Lord, I used to think an egg just hatched or didn't. Now I know that it breathes, leans about, turns into this and that, emits gases and God knows what all. [. . .]

Isn't this wonderful?

Most of their fellow students were veterans like them, though several were on their way to Palestine to lend their farming skills to the proposed new state of Israel. Alli liked the conspiratorial frisson these men gave the class. As in basic training, she was enjoying being among the People—though probably not many poultry farmers would begin their career equipped with a box of Chanel No. 5 talcum powder, Mary's Christmas gift to Alli that year.

The Sheldons spent the first week of the new year helping out at the hatchery. They calculated feed prices and the prospects for a fall broiler season, and Alli grew even more excited about having her own business. "When you candle 22,000 eggs and those eggs are worth $2\frac{1}{2}$ cents each to you there is an extra element of satisfaction!" she wrote her parents. The place consisted of a plain, two-story white house and a few sheds, separated from the road by an expanse of half-dead crabgrass. But to Alli the feeling of ownership was "colossal—I walked out in the snow and scuffled up a piece of our own earth (sandy) and nibbled a leaf of our own wintergreen and felt very good. [. . .] We have signed a 50-50 partnership agreement, and Ting calls me his Pard. I like parding!"

Alli graduated from Rutgers with the highest grade point average in the class and won the overall citation for "best poultryman." Ting came in second, and the *Newark News* reported the awards under the headline "Poultry Honors to Wife." Not that the people they would be doing business with paid much attention to grades—or women. When Alli got an all-time high grade on a qualifying test, the county agricultural agent who wrote to congratulate her pointed out, "Your husband didn't do bad either. I expect Mr. Sheldon could have really beat you but wanted to be real gallant and diplomatic and let his wife win." Alli filed the letter with her draft of "The Women-Haters," her unpublished article from the year before.

After graduation they took over the farm, and from February to May they worked so hard they scarcely had time to think. Ting drove around the county picking up eggs, Alli scheduled orders, and they both did everything else: hiring help, hustling for business, ordering supplies, keeping the books, turning the eggs, running to check on the incubators when the temperature alarms went off. Alli thought she had finally found a balanced life. In February she wrote her parents, "The work is fun—simple, restful and interesting. It is a good way to make a living—no tearing oneself inside out, no emotion."

For Alli the next few years were a time of hard work and isolation. She and Ting played chess together in the evenings, adopted more cats, and if they weren't happy together there's no record of it. Ting's two younger children came out on visits from New York; the awkwardness between them and their father and stepmother never completely wore off, but Alli made an effort, taking Audrey to buy records or taking both kids for a swim. Mary visited when she came east on business. Alli and Ting kept in touch with New York friends, but the very social, party-going Alice began to disappear.

Alli began experimenting with the domestic: building shelves, fixing things around the house—she was proud of her ability to repair toasters—and reading *The Joy of Cooking*. She recommended to Mary a new invention, aluminum foil, very handy for lining roasting pans. And she discovered a new and lasting passion, gardening. When she was a painter she had sneered at gardening, calling it a "materialistic," "pseudocreative" activity. Now she studied nursery catalogs and sketched elaborate plans. She planted daffodil beds, lilacs, and a hedge in front, raspberries and vegetables out back. She put in peach trees, dogwoods, larches, magnolias. When six new pine trees arrived, she became so excited she couldn't sleep and got up to mulch them at 5:30 in the morning.

The prose that she once lavished for her mother's benefit on clothes, she now spent on meals—steaks, scallops, asparagus, broiled chicken in cream, a luncheon party with lobster and avocado salad—or, more often, on her crabapples, her lilies, her four hundred tulips. "The fading tapestry of mums is really beautiful in its smoky decline, all the lovely glowing colors of the orient dying out in the afternoon sun, resting their heads on the luminous lawn." Alli's letters keep Mary in her life, but they also pile up all the paraphernalia of the domestic—cats, recipes, plants, husband—as a barrier between them.

The Sheldons still went to the Lodge every summer. Ting liked the place as much as Alli did, and Peter sometimes came too—though when Ting tried to bond with his son by taking him fishing, he ended up casting a fishhook deep into Peter's hand. Herbert had always maintained the Lodge: Alli recalled him as "constantly busy fixing this and that, [. . .] caretaking, planning ahead. 'Think I'll put some more wire on that dock, a bad storm could carry it off.'" Now Alli began taking over some of Herbert's work. She typed up garden plans, drew maps, wrote away to nurseries, sent away for government pamphlets on a new pesticide called DDT. For several years she kept an elaborate, color-coded temperature and weather chart, with special symbols for storms, frost, and fish. Her efforts were out of proportion to any possible result, since few nursery plants could thrive on the shady floor of a pine forest or withstand the long winters. Alli's relationship to the natural world seems a little like her relationship to her own nature: she loved the wild loneliness of the woods but at the same time put herself through exaggerated efforts to tame and control them. Like Herbert, she was always wary of the storms that could carry the place away.

One of Alli's domestic plans was never fulfilled. In February 1949 she wrote her parents that she and Ting were "engaged in planning me out of the business next season, as this thing is a going concern now and it's time for me to get back to creating preferably children and books." But month after month, Alli didn't get pregnant. When she went for tests, they showed blocked Fallopian tubes, probably from the infection that had followed her abortion. An operation didn't help. Surrounded by eggs and incubators, in an era when every magazine ran glowing articles on the joy and fulfillment of giving birth, Alli was unable to conceive.

She mourned, went through "severe convulsions of angered pride and guilt," and in the end allowed herself no more than a lasting, ambivalent regret. At forty-one she wrote, "I recognise that my pleasant conscious life would be mortally interfered with by procreation, and my own childish nature would be severely threatened by the demand to nurture a real child. So I am resigned, in a complicated way which seems solid." The word "mortally" seems to recall her old association of childbearing with death—now never to be countered by any happy experience.

Mary, in her sixties, carried on as she always had, writing, lecturing, and entertaining. She had gotten to know Carl Sandburg, and helped him with drafts of his vast historical novel *Remembrance Rock,* published in 1948. In October 1950 she escorted T. S. Eliot to a PEN dinner. Every winter the Bradleys still went to Central America, where Herbert collected for the zoo while Mary gathered material for lectures. But Herbert was sick more often now. Lest the Sheldons ever consider passing up August at the Lodge, Mary reminded them each summer that it might be Herbert's last. In 1950 Harry Bigelow died; he was the same age as Herbert, seventy-five.

In 1951 the two elderly explorers went on safari one last time. They sailed to South Africa, then went to British East Africa, Rwanda, and their old lion-hunting grounds, the Ruindi Plains. While Mary made notes for a travel book with a political slant, to be called *Africa Old and New,* she also looked at nationalist movements and made a formal report to the State Department on her return. But investigating the "inroads of communistic thought" (as Mary told the Society of Woman Geographers) couldn't bring back the African wilderness they'd walked across thirty years before. When they tried to go back to the village they'd visited in 1924, where they had walked between the huts in their bathrobes, they found it was no longer there. Mary never wrote the new travel book (nor another book she contracted for around that time titled *They Work for Stalin*), and in Uganda their jeep crashed in a ditch, injuring Herbert's back. "Progress more terrifying than the primitive," Mary assessed. After his injury, Herbert was often in pain.

The Sheldons never did get the six months off per year they had been promised. But during the four and a half years they lived in Toms River, Alli wrote whenever she could. She tinkered with the book on vision. She drafted bits of a spy novel. She worked on a historical novel about her old antihero, Thaddeus Stevens. She wrote poems about unrequited love.

And she kept circling around the question of women: who they were, who they could be, whether they were the problem, the enemy, her sisters, or all of those. As in the vision project, when she wrote objectively about "women" she was always also writing about herself. And as in the vision project, she easily got lost in the details, evaded emotional truths, and adopted a falsely rational tone. The result was a series of essay fragments that are provocative, inconsistent, idiosyncratic, and humming with a steady, low-level anger. The "I" of

the essays is prepared to acknowledge the anger, but keeps denying that it is
the point.

In one of these essays, Alli concluded that most of her troubles had come
from being a woman. Had she been a boy, she probably would have become
"a rather prosy young engineer or research scientist," a "sober, solid junior citizen" with a wife, kids, and "a promising future."

> Instead of which, I was born a girl, and my life has been quite different.
> I find myself today a young citizen with a promising future, and there
> the similarity ends. I have had about four different and disparate careers.
> I have been married twice. I have seriously upset a great many of the
> people who came close to me. I rejected the one child I almost had, and
> a subsequent illness has made it unlikely I shall ever have any. I have
> been called brilliant, beautiful, neurotic, suicidal, restless, amoral, anar-
> chic, dangerous, diffuse, weak, strong, perverse, and just plain nuts. I
> have never had a "nervous breakdown" nor needed actual mental help,
> but I have been through quite sufficient periods of despairing confusion.
> [. . .] And it is my belief that at least ninety percent of all this has been
> traceable to my being of the female sex in this place and time.
>
>   [. . .] I can trace out so clearly the manner in which I was derailed,
> time after time, from what seemed to be my basic life pattern. [. . .] My
> "brilliance," my passionate intellectualism, my anarchy, are to me artifi-
> cial traits, like the neck of the giraffe; I would never have normally de-
> veloped them had I not had to feed on tree tops in order to survive.

She seems about to confront her own experience as a woman—which is "a
card-hand full of jokers, a life work, a source of endless amusement, an un-
charted, undespoiled kingdom of the mind." Then she turns away and starts
attacking other women for their complacency. She likes women but is "bored"
with them, she writes, and impatient with their "lack of an intelligent approach to a male-dominated society." She complains that Woman puts up
with her slavery, resists change, and "shows, en masse, the ignominious personality of the Quisling."

She condemns a kind of woman she calls the perpetual little girl. This
woman suffers from a neurotic desire for the approval of a father figure, which

makes her vain, frivolous, and afraid of success. The "little girls" include chess players she's known who "would go ahead full steam until they began to get that giddy feeling that they were actually going to win some section. Then, bang, all of a sudden they start to play erratically and end up safely in second place. [. . .] What would they do, all alone at the top?" It includes talented women who end up as men's assistants and women who pursue men with the "deep, all-pervasive feeling of ivy-looking-for-an-oak."

Is she one of these women? She seems to be rejecting these fates, yet she too believed she was not aggressive enough to play top-level chess. She knew she cared too much about men's opinion. And she played little girl to her father-figure husband. Years later she told interviewer Charles Platt that she was the vine and Ting the oak tree. A few years later, looking back at her "little girls" essay, she wrote, "Made me feel very insightful [. . .] right proof against such shenanigans myself. So why didn't I use my insight?"

Women's bodies are especially unknowable, she writes. Women

are more apart from their bodies than men are; having a woman's body is quite something; it is like being the owner of a large and only partly tamed animal, day and night the damn thing is being itself, with its own semi-inscrutable operations. Even to the owner, a woman's body partakes of something of the perverseness and animism of the primitive Earth. It is like being attached to a sleepless, amoebic, oozing, urgent, swelling, welling, vegetable animal, forever slipping out of control and leaking its pseudopod round the corner. [. . .] An unpredictable, volcanic, treacherous, merry, rather overpowering thing to live with.

She argues for "a great deal more homosexual activity on the part of women," to be punctuated by wild, masochistic episodes with men—"the 'grand piano smash' which is the only thing capable of putting the thing [the female body] in order for awhile," and which will punish the body for its "unpredictable" desires.

Returning to her ideas about "men and mothers," she tries dividing the human race into five sexes: "Men, Women, Children, Mothers and Human Beings." Again, she isn't sure which one she is, or wants to be. "I would like to be something in my own right. I would like to be a 'woman.' And yet, I look in vain for women—that is, persons who are something characteristic which is neither childish, male nor maternal." Instead she suggests that it would be easiest "in most of the waking hours of a non-pregnant woman to consider her a kind of man."

She swings back and forth between two traditional feminist positions: that gender divisions are artificial and should be rejected, and that women have innate qualities, such as a talent for nurturance, that should be more highly valued. In 1950 this debate was at least a century old, yet Alli never acknowledges these as formal positions, suggesting she was poorly read in women's history. A list of intellectual heroes she made around this time is all male: Spinoza, William James, Yeats, Proust, Freud, Ibsen, Rembrandt, Dostoyevsky.

And she knew so few other women, especially in Toms River. De Beauvoir interviewed women for *The Second Sex.* Betty Friedan based *The Feminine Mystique* on interviews and surveys. Alli drew on no experience but her own.

All Alli's, and Tiptree's, writing about women seems to circle around a hole at the center: everything she doesn't say. One is what she wants—her own desire. Another is how she feels about her parents: Mary and Herbert are conspicuously absent from Alli's discussions of parenting as a "natural," biological force. Another is where she stands. She never explicitly identifies with men, but she doesn't feel like a woman either. She often seems to be trying to get free of gender entirely, as if her "scientific" inquiry is a way of climbing out of her own skin.

During her time in Toms River, Alli wrote two letters to editors on the question of women. In one, to the editor of *Chess Review,* she speculated that women did not become chess champions because of their hormonal makeup, which denied them the winner's "tenacity of purpose."

> Women have the mental agility, the interest in puzzles, the scientific spirit, the pleasure in intellectual beauty, and they have the energy to sustainedly move mountains [. . .] but they do not, I believe, have that sustained combativeness. Only at times [. . .] did I ever feel the compelling, hunting spirit that drives one to work doggedly in preparation for a tournament. [. . .] I think that top women chess players will always be drawn from a small minority of women with a constant metabolic level characterized by—in a layman's concept—a high adrenaline output.

Here she seems prepared to generalize on women's biology. On the other hand, confronted with arguments even more hormonal than her own, she took the opposing view. In 1952 Ashley Montagu published an article in the *Saturday Review* called "The Natural Superiority of Women." In it he suggested that women were genetically better made than men (the X chromosome being larger and more complete than the Y) and therefore morally better as well. In response, a Mr. J. M. Martinez maintained that men were naturally more creative than women. He argued that "the secretion of the testicles acts like a catalyzer or spark on the brain of man, fires his imagination, and drives him to create or to conquer. [. . .] The mind of woman, like the egg, is more passive, usually centered around the home and children as it should be."

Alli couldn't help herself, and wrote: "I salute Mr. Martinez. His testicular juices certainly must be all over his brain." Then she called for an end to biological distinctions, arguments for group superiority, and comparisons of which sex had produced which artists.

> How would it be if the gentlemen would come out from behind Michelangelo and check their zip guns, while we for our parts descend from the heights of Balaclava and the noble aegis of Miss Nightingale and Universal Motherhood, and drop the sarcasm? Rather than belaboring each other over the head to prove that we are the real lovers of humanity, let us just look at each other, plain and simply, as individuals, and realize once and for all that even if the rest of our respective sexes were composed of burning geniuses, it would not mean a thing to us, as individuals. [. . .] Every other woman on earth could be a shining light of intellect and love, and I might still be a mean-souled moron. Even Mr. Martinez's testicular ethers cannot save him from being Mr. Martinez, no more, no less.

The diffident letter in *Chess Review* was signed "Mrs. H. D. Sheldon." The irreverent and graphic second letter was written by somebody else, someone ruder, funnier, and more daring. It was signed "Mrs. H. D. Smith."

This playful side of Alli appeared in another kind of writing she did in Toms River, genre fiction. She wrote the first five pages of a mystery novel set in a chicken hatchery. It was narrated by a male protagonist in a parody of hard-boiled style and was called *The Incubator Murders*. Continuing the poultry theme, she wrote a fantasy story about a farmer breeding invisible chickens, "The Secret Egg." And she started writing science fiction.

She'd started reading SF again, reserving it for late nights as a "forbidden indulgence," and found it had changed since she was a kid. In the early 1940s, science fiction went through what is sometimes called its Golden Age, when it moved beyond pulp fantasy to deeper levels of scientific speculation. In fiction such as Isaac Asimov's *Foundation* sequence, it dealt for the first time with the social consequences of technological change. Sometimes the future even had a domestic setting, as in Judith Merril's 1948 tale of a post-holocaust family, "That Only a Mother."

By the early fifties, new magazines such as *The Magazine of Fantasy and Science Fiction* and *Galaxy* were introducing a higher literary tone. Ray Bradbury wrote as if SF were poetry. C. M. Kornbluth and others added black comedy. Writers reacted to the shocks and worries of the age: materialism, McCarthyism, the Kinsey report, and relationships between men and women, a.k.a. "the sex wars." Almost all the important writers of this period—Asimov, Bradbury, Merril, Kornbluth, Robert Heinlein, Arthur C. Clarke, Leigh Brackett, Cordwainer Smith, Frederik Pohl, Alfred Bester, Theodore Sturgeon—were Alli's age or even younger. As a writer, Alli belonged to a later generation, one that wrote more sophisticated fiction still. But if many of Tiptree's stories comment on science fiction in sly and subtle ways, it's partly because Alli knew the field like no other novice. By the time she finally started publishing, she had been a fan for forty years.

Some of Alli's own early drafts are pure space opera. ("Something had gone wrong; the ship was not making the speed which they had expected," began a story that she later filed away marked "material for parody.") Others are earnest, wooden little cautionary tales. One is about a hard-hearted young man who wishes for power and instead receives the terrible gift of empathy. Another deals with a recurring concern of Alli's: could humans evolve a nonviolent society? If so, how would they defend themselves? In this cold war parable, a future race of humans has achieved nonviolence—until their fear of being attacked causes them to reinvent armed conflict.

But her best draft is a playful fragment called "The Mind Mice." Two schoolboys and a teacher from Duck Bluff, Ohio, fall through a hole into a parallel dimension, where they are found by parallel (but larger) schoolchildren and placed in a fishbowl as pets. Their captors then try to breed them by adding two adult males: an Oxford-educated African diplomat and the murderous local gangster of Duck Bluff. The story is not deeply original, but it is funny, energetic, and full of entertaining inventions, from the half-subjective quality of the other dimension, in which even their thoughts appear as blue blocks or bits of pink hay, to the characters' puzzled encounters with each other.

Alli couldn't find a way to end the story, and she hadn't yet mastered the stripped-down narrative style that would be one of Tiptree's trademarks. But she was exploring SF's possibilities and developing her material, particularly the humorous culture clash. Even the structure of the other dimension reads as a metaphor for her work on perception. In science fiction, she could visualize, play with, and enjoy what she couldn't pin down in an essay, the puzzles of sex, identity, and perspective.

Of all the fiction Alli wrote during this time, only two drafts seem to have seen the light of day. In the fall of 1952 Alli sent parts of the Thaddeus Stevens novel to Mary's friend Carl Sandburg. Sandburg wrote Mary, "She can write, she CAN. I dont go along with her terrific interpretation of the face of Thad Stevens. [. . .] Yet some who knew him in life [. . .] would say she has done him to perfection. [. . .] You can have a quiet pride in her style and imagination." Then he added: "What a mother or father must do in such a case is to pray and pray that the daughter KEEPS her flame. I will pray with you." Mary must have told him she doubted Alli's seriousness. Maybe she was right, as far as Alli the writer of great literature was concerned. The Stevens novel disappeared.

That same fall, Alli asked Harold Ober's office to send around a somewhat lower-brow manuscript. "Phalarope," a ninety-three-page novelette, is described in the Ober agency's records as: "Science Fiction story. Space ship from planet in another constellation arrives on earth. All women 8 feet high. They like our men because their men are the inferior sex. Do the housework etc." The story was to be submitted to magazines under the pseudonym

"Ann Terry," and returned not to Alli but to her mother. Did Alli not want Ting to know?

Harold Ober Associates had no experience selling science fiction, but after "Phalarope" was rejected by *Redbook,* they gamely looked up the addresses of various SF magazines and sent the story around. Over the course of 1953 it gathered rejection slips from *Galaxy, Thrilling Wonder Stories,* John W. Campbell's celebrated *Astounding,* and Lester del Rey's short-lived *Space Science Fiction.*

If the story had a chance anywhere it was with the editor of *Galaxy,* Horace Gold. Gold was one of science fiction's most talented and strangest editors. His army service in the Pacific had left him with agoraphobia, and he never left his apartment in New York City's Stuyvesant Town. In those three rooms he presided over both the magazine and a series of parties and poker games that might include not only SF writers and editors—Sturgeon, del Rey, Pohl—but also Martin Gardner or John Cage. Gold helped bring the social sciences into the field; he liked humor and cared about character and style.

Gold was interested in "Ann Terry" and "Phalarope." Alongside all the rejections, someone at the Ober agency noted *Galaxy's* comment: "If lengthened and strengthened (more plot) possibly suited to Galaxy novel. (Feel DO before sending anywhere.)" Maybe if Alli had sent the story out a year or two earlier, she would have tried a rewrite. Instead "Phalarope" went into a drawer, to be reused fifteen years later for one of Tiptree's first stories.

As a writing apprenticeship, the years Alli spent in New Jersey seem to have been a mixed period. Ag school fed her growing scientific curiosity, and running a farm helped her grow out of her debutante-flirt-bohemian youth. The isolation allowed her not to care so much about appearances.

But she still couldn't find a kind of writing that fit. As with painting, she could do several styles well but couldn't choose between them, or find one that accounted for the whole range of her experience. A few years later, thinking about why she hadn't liked writing for the *New Yorker,* she concluded that its polished professionalism and "disciplined first-rateness" made it "self-consciously the voice of civilised urban man." Admirable, restrained—but not her voice.

> I am not like that, for better or worse. I am not a civilised man, maybe not a civilised human being. I am in this culture but not of it. I am a much more savage state of affairs, more simple, less able, more able— different. Somewhere in the back of my mind there is a female wolf who howls, and a gross-bodied workman who moves things and sweats, and a thin rat-jawed person who is afraid and snaps, and a practical woman, and one of those monkeys with big haunted eyes gazing at an equation with love, and a Miss Fix-It, and an Anglo-Saxon lady who joined the CP for an education, and—my own favorite—a disastrous comedian who every so often comes roaring out of the wings and collapses the show. Now it seems clear that while one might get one or two of these characters to write for a living, most of them won't go along, and the co-median's opinion is unprintable. At the present time I have a working truce in which the navvy is helping the monkey take the equation apart . . . The wolf nobody can fix, but the equation will keep her quiet for a time.
>
> [. . .] The only thing I can do in prose is wrenches and transposi-tions through several keys, I can sometimes serve up many spectra of connotations at once. Usually it's best when there's a kind of a joke or something a little coarse in it.

It helped to imagine herself writing to a reader, preferably a powerful, benevolent one who looked approvingly on her work. In a note to herself, she mused that she couldn't imagine being a genius.

> The lonely eminences are not easily occupied by women. Men accept the admiration of the inferior; the wife and family are all they need. But I can with difficulty imagine myself satisfied with being a king. I would want to impress a bigger king, or at least an equal, strong king with whom I could have small rivalries, and who was essentially friendly and admiring.

In Toms River, Alli got into a lifelong habit of writing letters to strangers. She wrote protest letters to politicians, opinionated letters to editors, and detailed, intelligent, critical fan letters to writers. Alli explained these last letters as a way of "venting admiration" and expressing gratitude to the people who had furnished her head. When Orozco died in 1949, she realized she had never thanked him for his work. Even a brilliant artist, it occurred to her, might live "in considerable solitude and anguish and the mailbox might contain, not a daily stream of Nobel prizes but complaints, soap samples and tax bills. And it wouldn't hurt to drop a card, to put my money where my head was."

It was true: writers did like it. Answering an admiring note from Tiptree in 1970, Italo Calvino wrote, "A letter like yours is actually the best present a postman can put down in my mail-box. It is for the unknown reader that any author writes, but it is a rare chance to meet him, even by letter, and to discover that he is such a nice and witty person." But these letters were also a way of taming envy and allowing Alli to dream up a readership of her own. Tiptree once explained his prolific letter writing as a warm-up exercise: "The only way I can possibly heat my so-called mind up to working temperature is to imagine I'm talking to someone I admire."

The hatchery was never the easy life the Sheldons had hoped for, and by the start of the 1951 season, when Alli described her routine to Mary and Herbert, country life had clearly begun to pall. There was the new night man who had to be sat up with, the incubator alarm bell next to their bed that rang all night, the days holding down the fort while Ting was out delivering chicks:

> Mrs. Sheldon, Jimmy's sick and has to go home—Mrs. Sheldon, there's a man trying to get in the office—Mrs. Sheldon, the infertile man is here—Mrs. Sheldon, we just broke the last gallon of Germodex and now we can't wash the trays and we have to transfer onto them—Mrs. Sheldon, the humidity is low on S-1—Mrs. Sheldon, the draft board wants to see me can I have the afternoon off my grandmother just died—Mrs. Sheldon the man is here to fix the ventilator—Mrs. Sheldon the hot water has given out and the oil-burner won't turn on—Mrs.

Sheldon the truck has a flat tire—Mrs. Sheldon, where do we pick up eggs today?

Even being in business (Alli later wrote a friend) had begun to feel "somewhat dubious. It didn't seem like the sort of thing a grown person should spend time at. Just counting a lot of things, competing with people one had no impulse to compete with . . . somehow false and peculiar." Besides, Ting's back hurt. It was time to move on.

Ting still had his Washington connections. The CIA was looking for analysts and adding a photointelligence section. In the summer of 1952 the Sheldons sold the hatchery at a loss, left behind the cats and the daffodils, and moved to Washington, D.C., to take jobs in the CIA.

CHAPTER 18: THE AGENCY (1952–55)

I have a cold mind and a warm heart, whereas most people have cold, troubled hearts and warm, muggy minds, which they mistake for sincere feelings.

—ALLI SHELDON

From the beginning of James Tiptree, Jr.'s, career, he was rumored to work for the CIA. And ever since, eager science fiction historians have speculated about that work, lengthening Alli's CIA career from three years to fifteen, adding overseas postings that never happened, or claiming she took part in "illegal, clandestine investigations inside the United States." Alli sometimes abetted these speculations. Tiptree populated his early stories with government agents and implied that he was busy with undisclosed assignments. Later, Alli liked to tell tales from the spy business. "You should have seen how much trouble we had to go to to get Khrushchev's urine sample," she would drop into a conversation. Ting would neither confirm nor deny.

In fact, Alli's CIA career was brief and modest. It was Ting who worked at the Agency for seventeen years and became an important force behind the scenes. Alli was hired at a much lower level, doing work that, for all its aura of mystery, felt hardly more creative than hatching chickens. As a woman, she would never get a chance to rise to Ting's level. It didn't take her long to figure out that the CIA wasn't what she wanted.

But the Sheldons' circle was their CIA colleagues, the Agency was their world, and it all kept a hold on Alli's imagination. The CIA fed her fantasies of exploration, mastery, masculinity. When he wasn't hinting at being a secret agent, Tiptree liked to portray himself as someone who had coped with the obscure demands of faceless institutions, "a midwesterner who batted around jungly parts of the globe when young and worse jungles with desks when old." The atmosphere of the Agency would reappear in her fiction: the mystery and macho on the outside, the reality of memos, carbon copies, and reports born to be filed unseen.

The CIA was also the perfect place for someone who would someday take on a false identity: it confirmed all Alli's habits of self-concealment. The Agency's founders believed passionately in the covert, and the Agency has tended in turn to attract secretive natures. Ting and Alli were both in their own ways hidden, private people. Ting's son Peter believes that the CIA became "one of the great masks they could wear. They didn't have to say anything about anything, because everybody knew you didn't ask Agency people questions."

But the Sheldons were not sinister "operations" spooks. They worked on the analytic side, in the part of the Agency that collected, interpreted, and evaluated intelligence data. At the end of the Truman administration, the CIA was a relatively small agency, housed in various Washington offices, and its atmosphere was liberal, passionate, and idealistic. Most of the analysts were, like the Sheldons, upper-class intellectuals prone to speaking foreign languages, playing chess, and voting Democratic. Tiptree compared the atmosphere to "a rather activist faculty tea," and claimed, "The CIA parking lot had the highest percentage of [Adlai] Stevenson stickers east of Illinois. One of their jobs used to be to keep the Joint Chiefs from bombing (a) Russia, (b) China and (c) San Francisco." The Sheldons' colleagues had helplessly watched the rise of fascism, remembered Pearl Harbor, and wanted America never again to be so ignorant of what was going on outside its borders. They believed the knowledge they were gathering could be used to promote peace.

Not long after the Sheldons came to Washington, however, Eisenhower became president, and the Agency began to grow and change. Truman had been wary of clandestine operations, but Eisenhower, his secretary of state, John Foster Dulles, and his new CIA director, Foster's younger brother Allen, had fewer qualms. Allen Dulles had a Yale degree and a good game of tennis; he seemed tweedy, handsome, and utterly unsinister. But by the summer of 1953, the Dulles brothers had already orchestrated their first coup. It brought down the Iranian nationalist government of Muhammad Mussadegh, restored full power to Shah Muhammad Reza Pahlavi, protected U.S. oil interests, and was much too easy to pull off.

Ting knew of these covert operations but was not directly involved in them. He had been hired as director of current intelligence, one of the top analytic positions. His job was to produce a daily report on world affairs, which was given to the CIA director to help him brief the president and Joint Chiefs of Staff. Its readers weren't always interested, especially if it contained information they didn't like. But Ting sat in on meetings with the National Security Council—where he watched Eisenhower draw insulting caricatures of his vice president, Richard Nixon—and in a crisis might well be called out of bed at two in the morning.

Ting kept a low profile, didn't take sides, and was respected by various warring factions in the CIA, the State Department, and Defense. Though his social credentials were in order, he didn't go to parties or push for power in the Dulles clique; in his circle were either old friends like Walter Pforzheimer or junior people on his own staff. Cameron La Clair, now in Operations, recalled, "Ting having gone to Andover and Eton would have been accepted by that ['social'] group, but he was so odd that he would have gotten on with another group as well, the intellectually interesting and challenging. Ting was really quite sui generis." When Ting began growing orchids for a hobby, because the warm damp was good for his sinuses, he could talk shop with fellow orchid grower James Angleton, the reserved counterintelligence chief. Because of his Eton connections, he was often used for liaisons with British intelligence. But La Clair recalled that he "also got along quite well with some of the rough tough operators."

Like all his colleagues on the analytic side, he did not express strong political opinions but saw his job as the neutral interpretation of events. He opposed the Vietnam War, not on ideological grounds, but because he believed it wasn't working. His son Peter said Ting "admired Johnson, Kennedy to some degree, had a low opinion of Eisenhower, and hated Nixon." He had a fair amount of common sense about world events, worked hard, valued good judgment, and wasn't easily swayed by emotion. He was close-mouthed even for a CIA man. Pforzheimer said that when Ting went to London on business he studiously avoided the Eton friend who had become foreign minister. "There were so many things neither of them could talk about, they didn't even want to meet. Ting was a terribly cautious guy, terribly security-minded. He was a very cool person and he played things very coolly, whatever he may have been feeling inside." Ting's one enemy was Allen Dulles, who cared about parties and social connections and disliked independent-mindedness in his subordinates. Dulles had a slapdash enthusiasm for the covert side that clashed with Ting's integrity and caution.

Alli had been brought in separately from Ting—they had come looking for her, she said, under her old name, Major Alice Davey—to help set up a photointelligence section. Like Ting's, her initial work was analytic, "clean," with "no more moral ambiguity than looking over the neighbor's fence and counting his laundry." Later, after the first photos from the U-2 spy planes arrived in 1956, and then the satellite images, photointelligence became an important department, growing to some 1,200 employees. But in 1953 it was a sleepy office, where about twenty interpreters were kept busy evaluating captured German air photos of the USSR. Once it was up and running, Alli asked to be transferred.

She must have suggested that she use her African experience, because in 1954 she was sent to the Johns Hopkins School of Advanced International Studies in Washington for their "Summer Session on Contemporary Africa." After that she worked on tracking African nationalist movements. She told Mark Siegel, who interviewed her in 1982,

> I was in the CECI—Counterespionage-counterintelligence—for a while. I was supposed to keep records on these Africans because countries were being taken over by these people, and we'd been relying on the British sources—the colonial occupying power—for everything we knew, and all of a sudden these guys we'd never even heard of would be in charge of the place.

While one part of her still remembered Africa as an untouched Eden, another now turned out papers with titles such as "The Pattern of Soviet/Communist Activities and Interest in Africa" and subheadings on "Contact Through International Organizations" and "Travel of Africans to the Bloc for Conferences or Tours."

Sometime in 1954 Alli also went through basic training in Operations. "They sent me down to a training area to put me over on the clandestine side, because of my African experience," Alli told Siegel. She told Charles Platt that her clandestine work had consisted of "working up files on people. [. . .] It was not James Bondish, really. It probably would have eventuated into a little

James Bondism, but . . ." In her own files are only copies of memos, stamped "secret," haranguing the director of training about the disorganized courses and offering to produce a better training manual.

Alli once again made friends among her coworkers, and enjoyed the easy company and the shop talk. With men she was flirtatious, but also loved arguing about politics and philosophy. She had given up on finding soul mates. Tiptree once told Joanna Russ there was no use expecting to be " 'among your peers,' part of a real 'sacred band.' You have to find your peers in this or that facet, [. . .] making a network of part-sharings serve the lonely need for a group of true fellows."

At heart she now felt like an outsider. She was not and had never been a communist, having just missed joining the John Reed Club at Sarah Lawrence. But in the repressive political and cultural climate of the early 1950s, she thought of herself as a "deliberate and convinced non-conformist." She later said she once went down to the McCarthy hearings with her old .38 in her pocket, "to make sure one could still get close enough if it came to that."

Even having a job made Alli suspect. In the fifties, working women were underpaid, underpromoted, and harassed, on the logic that they shouldn't be working at all. Alli's old grade school friend Cynthia Grabo, who was working in military intelligence (she sat on committees with the close-mouthed Ting Sheldon without ever learning that he was married to her old friend), recalled that most women in government were resigned to the middle and lower ranks. "We didn't expect to be equal to men. We were satisfied with the jobs we had. We hadn't been brought up to think we should run the office." Besides, most of them needed the income and couldn't afford to quit. But Alli couldn't stand not to be taken seriously, or to see Ting enjoy an authority that she could never have.

Like other women in male fields, she learned to act like a good sport and be one of the guys. She could still, on rare occasions, be stylish or girlish or get dressed up for parties. But at work she wore flat heels and neutral clothes. She felt the result was more attractive anyway for a woman of nearly forty. "Boyish clothes look younger, or healthier, because they contrast a woman's features with a man's, rather than with a girl's. In a clean white shirt I still look like a perverse young boy, and this is about my best effect, from the stand-point of attraction. The other effect I enjoy is to look like somebody's healthy aunt, sort of clean-cut and active." In Toms River, she had had surgery to lift and reduce her breasts. She had always felt they were too big, and she hated even more the way they sagged with age. The operation, she wrote, had cor-rected "the defect of my decadent breasts" and given her "a slendered, more boyish shape."

At SAIS in the summer of 1954 Alli met a married CIA man named Ed. They carried on a lively correspondence (Alli kept some of the letters) and may have had an affair. She also managed to build her own version of her par-ents' triangle. Each year in August and September the Sheldons spent a few weeks at the Lodge, and from the mid-fifties on they were joined each year by Ting's friend and colleague Bob Koke. Koke was in his late thirties, Alli's age. Like Alli, he was well traveled: before the war, he and his wife, Louise, had run the first beach hotel on Bali. Koke loved to fish, but Louise didn't care for the outdoors (or for Alli). So for years, Ting, Alli, and Bob Koke spent their sum-mer vacations together. If Ting was Alli's version of Herbert, Bob Koke was clearly Uncle Harry.

Alli's AVC friend Gus Tyler occasionally came to Washington on business, and he and Alli would go out for a drink. In Tyler's memory they mainly dis-cussed strategies for the AVC: she enjoyed keeping in touch with grassroots politics, while Tyler got a chance to bounce ideas off an informed and percep-tive listener. He knew little about Alli's work or private life, and never met Ting. She did tell him her husband worked for the CIA, and he assumed she did as well. Not knowing what the work involved, he half assumed she was re-porting on their conversations, but decided he didn't care.

Tyler recalled Alli as "a beautiful woman, very attractive and very stately. She had a bit of a regal manner about her. Not snobbish at all, but she looked like she was a member of the elite." In a slight upper-class drawl, her voice deepened from years of smoking, she talked the way she wrote letters, vividly, eloquently, and originally. "She spoke in full sentences and full paragraphs and had a marvelous choice of words all the time. And she had a lot of infor-mation and a lot of insights. You could talk about anything with her, litera-ture, politics, philosophy. Delightful."

Like all Alli's friends, Tyler felt he only knew a few aspects of Alli. "I always had a feeling there were big things going on in her life that she would share with nobody. She could have been living three or four lives all at once. There were always multiple ulterior motives that I didn't know about, didn't want to know about. She was always cheerful when I saw her. But every once in a while I had a feeling that there were things in her past that she just couldn't get out of her system." Tyler didn't ask, and Alli didn't explain.

They differed on the possible scope of human action. Tyler insisted that everyone must make choices, that each person can only act within a human-sized world. "If you want to save the whole universe, the only way you can do it is step by step." But Alli disagreed, and would not choose. Later, recalling their debate, she claimed that "despite Ting and everybody," her small world and the people in it didn't have a strong enough hold on her emotions. "My keenest, most vivid relationship, umbilical cord, or whatever you want to call it is to the race as a whole, to the planet as a whole, more than to any single individual or group."

More and more, Alli couldn't stand to be around people. By her third year in the CIA, in 1955, she felt worn out by so much human interaction. She had a charismatic energy that she used to attract people and get things done—except that it seemed to come and go on its own schedule. When it went, it left her utterly unprotected. Office mates, friends, family, she wrote,

> overload my circuits [. . .] It is as though I had an uncontrollable leakage of energy in response to any electromagnetic circuits in the vicinity [. . .]. Other people seem to have better insulation. Ting urges me to develop insulation; but I have spent ten years—more, counting the Army—and I have no insulation to speak of.

Writing about her parents she lamented, "I have no mechanism of resisting people's presences except by flight." She started having migraine attacks.

She was working too hard at the office. She was trying to do the vision project in her spare time. She was sleeping too little. And she got into trouble with an old friend, speed.

At some point, the CIA issued her and everyone else on her project Dexedrine. Years later, Tiptree told his friend Craig Strete that it had been the army and Benzedrine all over again. But he had assumed this was a different pill and

> pop-pop-pop. Shit, I thought I had found a new way to live without
> sleep. (I hate sleep. [. . .]) What I didn't do in that glorious six weeks.
> And then one day while I was taking notes at a lecture all of a sudden
> my hand with the pen in it just began to waver off the page like a dying
> encephalograph and . . . I was a walking zombie. [. . .] Also I was a
> prey to huge roiling paranoid fancies. There ensued two months I can't
> recall, but friends said the average bed-pan had me beat on personality
> and activity. I was DEPRESSED. Suicidal . . .

To Philip K. Dick, Tiptree wrote that he once "fell repeatedly into the clutches of Dex—and did the insane bit of trying to come down with barbs. All, all by myself, and keeping up work in the world. . . ." Amphetamines were widely prescribed in the 1950s and thought to be harmless. Alli knew they were addictive: Tiptree wrote Strete, "When I get tolerant to one pill a day, that's it. Dry out. Bunk in with the blinds shut and cringe when an ant breathes." But in 1975 she reported two decades of steady, low-level use, at about 260 to 300 mg. per year.

Alli loved speed. It helped her get through the lethargy that came with her depressions. It helped her recapture the periods when she was *up,* excited, productive. It helped her lose herself in work. Amphetamine burns the candle at both ends and in the middle; it's a drug for the genius horse, the one that wants to leave all else—including its own mortal body—behind.

But speed mimics both the manic and the subsequent fall. It depletes serotonin levels in the brain, leaving steady users in a state of permanent dysphoria or depression. It surely contributed to her later medical problems, especially heart trouble. (Her lifelong smoking habit can't have helped either.) In the end it may have removed even more of her protective covering against the world, until she was haunted by the evening news—and by her own fear of death.

Years later, Cynthia Grabo asked around about Alli among her CIA friends. No one claimed to have known her well, Grabo recalled, but "one of the things they all said was that she had these mood swings."

By the summer of 1955 Alli wanted out. She liked the work she was doing, the challenge, the structure, her independent income. But it exhausted her—and it wasn't her own work. She wanted to go on with the vision project. She borrowed books from the National Institutes of Health library and tried to study in her spare time. She joked that she was spending fifty hours a week "impersonating a dedicated government worker." On August 24 she would turn forty.

She was edgy with Ting and unhappy at home. They were living in the Greenbrier Apartments, at 4301 Massachusetts Avenue NW, an expensive, anonymous high-rise surrounded by a parking lot. Their living room was full of tropical fish tanks, Ting's latest hobby, and it was full of Ting. When Alli came home, she wanted to rest, read, and work. When Ting came home, he wanted to have a few drinks, be served dinner, and talk. Alli resented it. She felt it gave her a "second job of entertaining him every night," one that kept her from writing. It seemed to emphasize her lesser status at the office and the unimportance of her writing.

Dexedrine can't have made Alli much fun to live with, and Ting, who had his own office stress, was drinking heavily. It made him demanding and un-reachable. He often blew off steam by laughing at people behind their back, but if he'd been drinking he might do it to their face. He didn't criticize Alli, but she was hurt by his distance. Mary said Ting looked to her like "a man floating away on an iceberg."

Then again, Alli's heart was as ambivalent and wary as his. She was having affairs, including sleeping with a neighbor at the Lodge, which she described as "unsatisfying from the orgasm point of view but as exciting as mating with a stag or a bear—really, I suspect to me a concrete sexual expression of the woods." She had never really tried to be all of herself with Ting; part of her was only waiting until it couldn't bear it anymore.

She started renting a place of her own, "a little studio with a garden" where she could work. She told Ting she wanted to leave the CIA and write full time. Ting didn't want to give up their second income—and if she did quit her job, he thought she ought to "cater to him" more in the evenings. This was what most wives did, but Alli understandably found the phrase in-

sulting, especially when Ting said he would be supporting her while she was
"doing nothing." "O, for the chance to do my work I'm to be your paid en-
tertainer," she snarled. She was "hostile to the idea of being a service institution. [. . .] The *society* doesn't tell others to make a nice setting for my life,
while it tells me I must make a nice setting for his."

She drew up a "life plan," like the one she'd made at twenty-five. Only this
time she called it "Operational Analysis" and used the language she'd learned
on the job to talk about her fears.

> *First, statement of problem (symptoms):*
>
> Sense of unbearable conflict between
>   a) Self and husband in terms of interests, long range goals, daily life
>   habits
>   b) Work in Agency and personal work
> Feeling of doom ahead if present course continues
> Sense of urgency, continual pressure beyond productive degree; time
> shortage
> Sense of helplessness, dependence taking two forms:
>   a) Inability to earn income while doing personally chosen work
>   b) Oversusceptibility to environment; inability to retain concen-
>   tration and mood during "office" and "husband" impinge-
>   ments; consequent inertia without resolution of conflict

She listed her "present occupations in terms of time": "Office 43 hrs per
wk," "Own work app. 24 hrs per wk," "Husband talk 5 h p wk," "Sleep 45 h
p wk" (a "necessary evil"). Her five hours a week of social life she rated "1st in
terms of tense pleasurable emotion, [but] minor in attention; overall a tiring
& futile activity contributing little; goals too divergent."

Under the heading "Husband Situation" Alli listed Ting's drinking, plus
"incompatible mental outlooks," requiring her to suppress all interests Ting
didn't share. The list went on:

> Inability to concentrate, relax or find peace in husband's presence
> Inner resentments, fears of

(a) male

(b) possessive person who "loves" me

Fear of being eaten & locked up & used as psych. doormat [. . .]

Intense desire for never-experienced personal freedom; husband as jailer

Oversensitivity making husband's every normal act "overbearing"

Competition; jealousy of husband's poise, calm, dominance, financial self-sufficiency, prominent position in office

Resentment at husband's childishness especially when drinking; having no child resent having to mother grown man who dominates me

Boredom

Under "Positive" she wrote a much shorter list, including "Admiration of husband's qualities," "Sympathy for his attack on life," and "Enjoyment of husband's company when sober and seen occasionally—i.e., not obligatory." But she added, "Personal factors [. . .] show me as unsuited for 'team' situation regardless of husband's qualities."

In July 1955, Alli wrote her friend Max Lerner a long, feverish letter about, among other things, Eisenhower and the Geneva disarmament talks, Piaget, Walter Lippmann, mixed marriage (she was for it), and lying alone and forever in one's grave: "Damn, you're really of the upper bourgeoisie if you can guarantee that. [. . .] Nowadays few can afford to lie in their graves any length of time, and it's rather an exotic Western custom to be buried alone. [. . .] You'll find yourself with plenty of company in the stucco of somebody's rumpus room in less than fifty years is my bet."

Then she confessed,

You see, I haven't quit for two weeks yet, but my psyche has, and last night a strange and wonderful thing happened. I went to bed about 12, after working on a paper, and . . . I never slept all night. I have never had this experience before. I don't mean those "I never slept a wink" things where you actually woke up a couple of times to pee and slept 6 hours, I mean I lay there thinking pleasantly but unexcitedly, and the luminous dial clock went slowly, but visibly around and around from 12 to six. For an hour or two about 3 I was worried, because I have had to work all day, but finally I gave that up and just enjoyed it. I would like to do this a lot when I quit punching time clocks. . . . I didn't think about anything awfully significant; a few rather solid paragraphs on the future of the nationalist movement in various parts of [word deleted,] an hour or less experimenting with after-images and watching behind my eyelids to see if I could catch any hints on the field structure of vision . . . and a period of great interest in something I never thought of before—the question mark. What a wonderful thing! One of the most truly human phenomena. Think of it. How did it start? Were there question marks in Greek? In pictograms? And in Russian? The odd shape [. . .] kinetically expressive. O classicist—whence come question marks?

Something was about to snap.

CHAPTER 19: **A DISAPPEARANCE AND A RETURN (1955)**

O, how I want to be loved, me myself—and how I fear it—and what bliss it might be—brrr!—and how easy to shelve the whole thing.

—ALLI SHELDON TO "DR. K," 1955

One day in the summer of 1955, Alli left Ting and disappeared for a while. "I was all choked up with Ting because I was having to submerge myself to help him," she told Mark Siegel in 1982,

> And so I ran away. I used my clandestine training to disappear. In a day I had a new name, a new bank account, had rented a house and really destroyed all traces of my former personality, including sanitizing my books and everything else. I was really a different person in the bottom of this little house where I lived for about six months. And Ting never found me, though he really hunted for me. And then finally he did, and actually came and courted me for the first time.

Alli told Charles Platt a similar story, including the name and bank account.

> I left a safe open one night. Twenty minutes later, I checked it and caught it. But I'd never done that before in my life, and I said, "My innards are telling me something." I wrote a two-line letter of resignation and departed. Actually I ran away from everybody, I ran away from Ting. [. . .] I wanted to think. So I thought, and then I got back in touch with Ting, who seemed to be really suffering, and I was suffering, and then we thought together and decided we could work things out.

To Joanna Russ, Tiptree wrote, "I once had to live as someone else for a short and ENTIRELY unglamorous time, the strain is extraordinary. And this was in a friendly territory [. . .]."

Once again, Alice had run off, made a hiding place in the long grass, become someone else. But like the other story about hiding, this one seems to be embellished for dramatic effect. Alli left the CIA in the summer of 1955 with at least two weeks' notice—or so she told Max Lerner. By then she already had the little apartment at 2619 Green's Court NW that she planned to use as a studio. She lived there, separated from Ting, for almost a year, but she can't have disappeared for more than a few weeks. By mid-August she and Ting were speaking again, and were seeing a marriage counselor. At the end of August they went together to the Lodge.

Brief as it probably was, this disappearance was a turning point in Alli's life. She had always tried to be a good daughter, virtuous wife, servant of her country. She had never been herself around anyone else. Now, turning forty, she again shut her eyes and jumped into a new life. But this time when she became "someone else" it was not someone's daughter or wife or junior officer or business partner, but herself alone.

She leapt—and Ting, who really did love her, caught her and pulled her back. Whether he found her or she got in touch with him, they started talking to each other. She stopped trying to "submerge" herself for Ting, or her writing for her day job. After ten years, she came up from underground.

For a long time Alli wanted a divorce. At the Lodge, while Herbert and Mary hovered in the background, Ting urged her to stay and Alli insisted she couldn't live with anyone. "I've learned my lesson, it's not for me, and there are plenty of women who live alone and I'm one," she wrote their marriage counselor, a man she addressed as "Dr. K." She didn't have to be lonely, she said: "I figure that I have enough sub-personalities so I can build one up to where it is quite companionable, and displays divergent views, the ability to question, argue and hold opinions."

She loved Ting, she wrote Dr. K, and "his going will leave a hole. He is a familiar figure, walking up the sunlit bluff with his pail of minnows, coming in from the woods to smile and joke, looking out at the eagle and the osprey, knowing and living in the land I love." But she didn't know how to resolve their problems—which, coming down out of her analytical cloud, she summed up as work, sex, Ting's drinking, and money. Letting her parents support her was out of the question: she couldn't face "the guilt I would incur by repudiating being a 'sweet normal woman' after they had put money into it."

For over a month Alli hung around the Lodge, writing and brooding. She took photos to illustrate "radial forms among plants," kept irregular hours, refused to come to dinner, refused to tell Mary her troubles.

> I blurt out bits or go into kind of abstract rodomontades, and I demonstrate tension and hostility all around at times, but I keep "me" covered with a pretty heavy blanket of silence as a defence against being reduced to edible infancy. [. . .] (They all agree that dear Alice who is so talented is terribly tense and upset and Our little Girl and My dear Wife presents problems but everything is going to work out all right and We are all so mature.)

Mary wanted to help. But what Alli liked, she told Dr. K., was constructive advice, while Mary's way of offering comfort was rehashing emotional situations, recounting, repeating, dwelling on troubles—and at the same time, Alli thought, fulfilling her own need to have an audience. "I do slink about avoiding talk, but on the other hand if you show yourself too much she opens up a harangue," Alli complained.

> All you have to do is stand still and you get everything from her mother's death to a description of the tribe living where they shot the big elephant. Mary I think partly wishes to dominate by talk—it does no good to say you remember every word from the last nine times you heard it— and partly feels she must entertain to be loved. [. . .] And her feelings get so appallingly hurt if you don't want to listen.

This way of talking, Alli felt, "wipes out any different approach. [. . .] I can't buck the verbal surf." She knew she could count on her parents' loyalty: even taciturn Herbert came through with " 'blood is thicker than water,' or some such ancestral, murky, prideful and you-and-me remark." But understanding seemed as hopeless as ever, and Alli asked, somewhat rhetorically, "Why do I get so hostile to my sincerely sweet, sensible, hard-working and lovable friend who is my Mother?"

In her own way, Mary did know something about appearances, deception, and hiding behind a façade. That summer, while Alli was moping around the Lodge, Mary was correcting page proofs for what would turn out to be her last book. It was the as-told-to autobiography of a young woman who used the pseudonym Reba Lee, and was called *I Passed for White*.

Reba Lee was the fair-skinned daughter of a black woman who had worked for Mary as a seamstress. At seventeen she had run away to New York, changed her name, and begun passing. Mary portrays her as a girl Gatsby whose looks and magnetic personality—men fall for her instantly—hide a carefully spun web of lies about herself, her family, and her past. She marries a rich white man and goes to live his country-club life, but is not happy: Mary makes clear that for Reba, being a traditional wife is also a kind of passing. In the classic passing-story manner, she gives herself away in childbirth: while still half delirious, she asks, "What color is it?" The baby dies, and Reba quietly returns to her family in Chicago.

Passing stories were popular in the fifties. They were a safe social criticism, indicting the "color line" while ultimately reinforcing it: in the end, the white life is seen to be false and must be given up for any real chance of happiness. Yet when Reba exclaims, "I was sick to the bone of lying and pretending," she is surely speaking for the many people who were passing in that decade: gays pretending to be straight, geniuses working as housewives, token women acting and thinking like men. How much did Mary know?

When Alli returned to Washington in early October 1955 it was not to the Greenbrier Apartments but to her studio. She often spent weekends with Ting and wasn't talking quite as seriously about divorce, but she wanted to keep her independence.

Sudden freedom gave her a rush of creative energy. She had been hungry even for time to read, and now she sat down with coffee and cigarettes and consumed every book she could find on the psychology of perception. She got out all her years' worth of notes on vision, took more notes, organized her card files, made work schedules. She read Gestalt psychology, which deals with the problem of wholeness and looks at organisms and processes in their entirety. It answered some of her frustration about aesthetics, with its cutting up of paintings into planes and lines. She drafted and redrafted her introduction.

She loved the nights she could work as late as she wanted, the mornings when she could go straight from bed to her desk. She wrote Max Lerner, "Life moves so fast here; I feel I'm living 3 years each quarter. That comes of learning. I am perhaps growing like a starved something at last let out."

She still disapproved of science fiction as a guilty pleasure, and told Ting it was "pure escape, [. . .] my form of self-indulgence and self-nursing, being 'soft' with myself, like your having an extra drink or two, and just as damaging." But while she tried to be serious and study perception, wild stories kept sneaking into her head, or out of it. "A symptom of opening this ingrown moon-jungle of a mind is that everything in the world is coming out," she wrote in her journal; sometimes the plots came to her in dreams.

She wouldn't give in to them; she was determined to produce something real this time. She felt she had been too "undisciplined," too easily satisfied with

isolated reflections, not bothering for structure, production, communication. In fact, not brave enough to try for communication. [. . .] I live way within, in the unformed, unchallenging deeps, occasionally lashing out at someone with a tongue-whip of words, a severe glitter—"See, I contain marvels!"—then whisk, back into the hole.

But her serious work, the vision project, would not be tamed. The more she read, the more the subject grew. When she wasn't getting distracted by fascinating minor phenomena she was finding that the data she needed didn't exist. In January 1956, Lerner came to visit, looked at her work, and told her that the world at large saw autodidacts as crackpots. To be taken seriously she would need some credentials. She began thinking about graduate school.

She began to see that telling the truth was a question of making choices. Once, like Borges's cartographers whose map covers the entire area of the country it depicts, she had longed for impossible, everything-at-once, 100 percent brain-to-page reproduction. And still, in writing or in life, she hated to discard anything. She wrote, "I as a person have some sort of block against total commitment; like Peer Gynt, I cannot choose, cannot abandon potentials. So my effort in any line has a kind of foot-dragging quality, heels invisibly dug in just before the threshold."

But reluctance to choose is an indirect kind of self-censorship; it keeps the writer from the page. There were other kinds of self-censorship of which Alli was faintly aware, although she tended to think and write about them in the third person. For one thing, she hadn't forgotten her old problem of the "writer as shit" and truth-telling as betrayal. "His [the writer's] understanding is an act of aggression," she wrote in a particularly bad mood in a fragment called "Tales of a Paranoid." "A writer is fundamentally exploitative in personal relationships; to create the Brothers Karamazov how many human beings went into the grinder?"

The pattern of Alli Sheldon's life from thirty to fifty is one of making up her mind to speak. Her year alone was an essential one, partly because she began to make choices, to abandon the infinite possible for the limited real. She chose to commit herself to psychology. She chose to move back in with Ting.

Ting agreed to support her while she was getting her degree, and she gratefully let go of her financial independence, concluding, "I am a unique, specialized and virtually non-marketable object, and the attempt to incorporate Puritan economic virtues into this structure is grotesque." He stopped relying so much on her for company, and spent more time with friends and coworkers. He cut back on his drinking.

Alli learned to see Ting's requests for dinner and company not as intrusions but as expressions of his own need for love. And if he sometimes lacked empathy, she thought, it was because no one had ever shown him any until she came along. Their intimacy didn't look the way she had thought true love would, a passionate meeting of bodies and minds. Ting would never share her wild moods and flights of imagination. But when she came down to earth again he gave her stability, encouragement, laughter, and love. He was tender and kind to her in a way he was to no one else. They never got tired of talking to each other.

Maybe, having studied Gestalt theory, Alli was more able to see a dynamic, argumentative marriage as forming a satisfying whole. In a letter to Ting in March 1956 she wrote, "You never get the thing fixed up so it runs automatically. A big, complicated, fast marriage like ours is just like those big fast delicate motors—it's 25% of the time in the shop."

In trying for equality, she added, they were fighting not only social pressure but their own feelings about how men and women were supposed to behave.

> Part of us will always view what we are doing as abnormal, a little wrong, a little dangerous. [. . .] The joker is that these feelings are only a part of us. We cannot go back and give in and be happy by living according to the stereotypes. And we can't be entirely easy living against them. We are transitional types who have one foot in the past and one foot in the future and our fannies will always be a little uneasy about it. When we're tired and cross the thing gets on top of us, it seems too hard a fight. When we're strong we feel quite different—we lean happily into the future.

At that moment, being strong, she felt she could accept all the complications and arguments as signs of life being lived.

> Certainly my inner world will never be a peaceful place of bloom; it will have some peace, and occasional riots of bloom, but always a little fight going on too. There *is no way* I can be peacefully happy in this society and in this skin. I am committed to Uneasy Street. I like it; it is my idea that this street leads to the future, and that I am being true to a way of life which is not here yet, but is more real than what is here.

In the fall of 1956 the Sheldons bought five wooded acres in the little farm town of McLean, Virginia, near the rural spot where the CIA was planning its new campus. They began designing a house and garden. They put a lot of work into it and had a lot of fun together.

They knew now that they could count on each other: they had pulled as hard as they could and their love didn't break. Besides, Alli once said, "as we went through life tripping each other and wrangling about why, how it had happened, in the smallest things, it finally began to dawn on us that we were enjoying it immensely, and that everybody else seemed dull by comparison." She liked to tell people they had been married ten years before they fell in love.

Alli didn't regret her choices. But still she sometimes dreamed of being able to contain more. The first summer after they got back together, Ting went overseas for work and Alli went alone with her parents to the Lodge. From the Lodge, in a letter to Ting, she tried to explain another feeling she sometimes got from looking at the stars. When she was unhappy she saw Sirius as a cold and distant light, but when she felt alive and full of wonder she took part in the glory of the distant sun. In the middle of one night she went outside and saw through the branches of the hemlocks

Sirius, the magnificent, the great white-cold diamond blazing in cold space, the brightest star we see. I thought, *pinpoints,* we call them. And I thought of the reality of the stars, of Sirius, an inconceivable fountain of energy, greater than six of our poor sun, [. . .] pulsing, beating, boiling, flinging continuously on every side this expanding turmoil of force, unknowable billions of miles away, for unimaginable billions of years past and to come; and this fantastic rush of energy was descending on me, and out of that tremendous cascade, those particular minute electrons which my wretched little eyes could focus on passed through my lenses and made "pinpoints" on my retinas; but meanwhile the flood swept past my eyes, past my head and rained against the earth. [. . .] And I looked at the other stars, the whole sky dense with suns beyond suns, each one pulsing out these great shells of energy. [. . .] And I stood amongst this like a tiny stick of flotsam which for a second holds itself upright amid a torrent of ocean, myself minutely upright on a spinning ball of rock, caroming through this universe of suns. [. . .] Oh, Ting, I can understand the soul which would hold out its arms and its heart to the stars, and offer out its life just to leave this earth and make one wild and exultant rush out into that vortex of force. The Stars . . .

There must be other races out there, watching our tiny yellow sun glimmering in their unknown field of sky. Do they desire us as we desire them?

When Alli went to work full-time on her vision book, she started writing to other researchers about her project. She approached neurologists, psychologists, the art historian Erwin Panofsky, anyone whose work she liked, expressing admiration, offering feedback, and asking questions about her own work. Not all of them responded. But one who did became Alli's friend and mentor, and gave a sensible answer to her questions about choice and communication: "I think the thing for you, to use your drive and talent, is to pick a limited phenomenon and work on it intensively. If you are good you will catch the whole in any part you deal with, whereas you may simply dissolve your powers if you undertake to juggle with the globe." Her correspondent was the psychologist Rudolf Arnheim, who became the benevolent audience she needed for her work, and who encouraged her to choose psychology as a career.

Alli first wrote Arnheim in May 1955, just before she left the CIA. She had read his *Art and Visual Perception,* an important new work on psychology and aesthetics. She saw that he taught at Sarah Lawrence. She wrote him a three-page letter mentioning her Sarah Lawrence connection, commenting on his book, and raising some of her own questions about visual perception. Arnheim answered encouragingly.

In November 1955 she wrote again, politely asking if he would look at her work. He said he would be glad to. "I am, of course, interested in your subject and, to judge from your letters, reading your writing is likely to be pleasurable. Perhaps that some time after I have read your piece you happen to be in New York so that we could meet and discuss my reactions *con viva voce.* You shouldn't neglect your Alma Mater anyway."

A more conventional academic might have steered clear of the potential crackpot who signed her letters Mrs. H. D. Sheldon, but Rudolf Arnheim hadn't followed a standard career path either. Born in Berlin in 1904, he studied psychology, philosophy, and art history at the University of Berlin and received his doctorate in 1928 under the founder of the Gestalt school, Max

Wertheimer. By then he was caught up in the cultural energies of the Weimar Republic: seeing premieres of plays by Brecht and exhibitions by Expressionist painters. He became a film critic for the leftist, anti-Nazi weekly *Die Weltbühne*, writing on silent film as an art form. In 1933 he left Germany and got a job in Rome, compiling a film encyclopedia for the League of Nations. In 1939 he went to London, where he worked as a translator for the BBC.

It was only after he arrived in New York in 1940 that he returned to psychology. He got a teaching job at Sarah Lawrence and received a Guggenheim grant to write a book on the application of Gestalt psychology of perception to the visual arts. Like Alli, he discovered that no one had ever tried to link art and psychology. It took him twelve years to research and write *Art and Visual Perception;* by the time Alli wrote to him he knew something about long-running projects as well as changes of career.

Art and Visual Perception and the subsequent *Toward a Psychology of Art* were influential works in a long and brilliant career. Arnheim was a clear, direct writer and astute synthesizer of ideas; he was also a warm, generous person who replied with serenity and humor to Alli's excited letters. (Alli admired the "natural lucidity" of his prose; her own, she said fondly, was "like a dogfight in a tunnel.") At a time when American psychology was full of behaviorists taking apart responses into their component parts, Arnheim believed in whole beings and the power of art to move people and convey experience.

At first Alli didn't take him up on his invitation to visit. All winter and spring she sat in her little house, taking notes and writing, until in May 1956 she wrote Arnheim that she had something for him to read. By that time she had decided Max Lerner was right: she should study psychology, starting with the undergraduate degree she had never received.

Arnheim agreed, and again suggested they meet. This time Alli accepted. In June she took the train to New York and spent an afternoon with him at his home in Bronxville. The meeting was exciting for them both. He found in her a brilliant, imaginative, and critical thinker who had good ideas and could help him in working out his own. She found a catalyst. "I must have learned how to use somewhere between two and three hundred words," she wrote him after she got home. "Here at last is the language I would like to live in and build on."

Arnheim understood her language, too: for him she filled her letters with her best and most exuberant prose. That summer, she joyously described driv-

ing her parents to Wisconsin—a trip that had "most of the features of the removal of Soviet industry beyond the Urals, played in a Corot setting." It began with

> the mass exodus, the bent figures bearing loads of electronic communi-
> cations equipment, uprooted zinnias, melons, hatboxes, schipperkes,
> egg-beaters, back issues of the *National Geographic* [. . .]. Then the
> Dash for the Pole, in which I played forward scout position; culminating
> in the unlocking of the forest refuge, the dispersal of the deer, the light-
> ing of the icebox (talk about conflicting sensory associations, here one
> cools with flame) and then all the blurred first week, which really groups
> into select short subjects: [. . .] a devastating tragedy known as Garage
> Delenda Est—the porcupines have conquered; the moral decision about
> exterminating mice; is Warfarin really painless? The beauty of the
> Skunk; the Skunk is eating out of the little dog's dish; the hired girl is
> being seduced at the Fourth of July fireworks; the eagle has not returned
> to the lake—the eagle *has* returned to the lake; the thunderstorms, the
> sunsets, the intoxicating air, the stillness, and the almost maudlin sen-
> sual loveliness of everything.

She went to work on her book, argued by mail with Arnheim over the
physics of color perception, and felt, she claimed, almost boringly happy, "like
the joke about the bird who said it was such a nice day he wanted to walk."

Alli was still fascinated by the most subjective class of visual effects, associations, such as judging one color to be warmer than another, or seeing the
figure 6 as a tape measure or a fish. She began to regard "The Psychology of
Value in the Graphic Arts" as a three-volume work, with the first volume devoted to cataloguing associations. Arnheim had warned her that associations
were so personal she might end up with an "encyclopedia of curiosities." So all
summer she did her best to confine herself to an essay on the perceptual effects of certain dots. She drew turbines, hung them up around her desk, and
tried to catch glimpses out of the corner of her eye, hoping to see for a moment as a "naive subject" and catch some innate motion.

But her drafts are full of lists—the zinnias and schipperke dogs of

perception—and she couldn't keep her mind on dots and lines. She noted that
the world of the Average Observer

> contains in addition to "real" objects several sub-classes of dreams, fic-
> tions, verbal reports, and so on, which are perfectly "real" in their re-
> spective class. Examples would be the bottom of the ocean, germs, the
> forests of the Amazon, the Land of Oz, the closets in the White House,
> the gloves left in the car, and the sound of an unseen bird.

Her science was drifting dangerously close to poetry.

At the end of the summer she and Arnheim saw each other again in
Chicago, at the annual meeting of the American Psychological Association.
Arnheim had encouraged Alli to go see what the academics did, and though
she felt intimidated by so much scholarship, she saw that there were people
who did not conduct their intellectual life as if it were a private vice, and that
she could perhaps be one.

Afterward, she finally sent Arnheim part of her manuscript. He responded
that it showed "lots of visual imagination. It is appetizing. That is a rare quality, and it augurs well for your work in this field." But he wasn't sure exactly
what her thesis was, and he saw that she'd been drawing mainly on her own
perceptions for phenomenal data.

> Now, of course all of us have done that, but while the method is always
> risky it becomes most precarious when you are tackling the problem of
> what is seen "between the lines." It's a beautiful problem, but the phe-
> nomena are so delicate and labile that expectations, sets, and all sorts of
> context are likely to have a tremendous influence. [. . .]
>
> If you were a student of mine, I would say: You have laid out a fine
> hypothetical survey; now let's try with some of your patterns to find out
> whether people see what you assume they see.

Just for a moment, Alli fell in love. She had chosen for Ting, but she still
longed for a meeting of true minds, and was drawn to this "magical creature,"
this "Ariel," with his elfin, expressive face and intellectual passion. In a note to

herself, she wrote that her new friend made her feel "slow" and "dull," like "a freight train which becomes derailed at every corner and has to be reassembled on another track." She ached with clumsiness, she wrote. "I prefer to admire from afar where I can do no harm to what I admire."

The feeling quickly passed. Alli chose instead to think of Arnheim as an ethereal and benevolent protector of her intellectual life, and he became her close and enduring friend. Long after she had lost touch with other friends and colleagues, she and Arnheim went on corresponding. Sometimes they met, or the Arnheims visited the Sheldons, when Alli didn't find it too terrifying. "I suffer so actually seeing people I like," she confessed after spending a morning with Arnheim in Washington. "It's wonderful looking forward and remembering but at the time I suffer agonies."

Mostly they carried on a lively exchange of letters. Alli's are written in a persona that could be a forerunner of James Tiptree, Jr. She debates politics and aesthetics and has fun dramatizing her life. In talking about her work, she plays the eager, argumentative, yet respectful student, with Arnheim as the approving senior scholar. Arnheim did not object to this. As a teacher at a women's college he was perhaps used to continuous low-grade female adoration. He wrote to "Alice," she to "Dr. A." It would take another eleven years, until Alli got her own Ph.D., before she could bring herself to call him by his first name.

Back in Washington in the fall of 1956, Alli found that her local universities were not lining up to give homes to stray researchers. She wrote Arnheim, "I cannot describe the lack of enthusiasm with which persons interested in research are greeted here as undergraduates. The lady professor to whom I spoke said there were so many 'fringe personalities.' The word 'art' seems also an unfavorable stimulus." Besides, it turned out she would need more undergraduate education than she thought. Between the semesters left unfinished and the incompletes never made up, her three and a half years of higher education added up to maybe a year's worth of usable credits.

But she confronted the sins of her youth, got her transcript from Berkeley by paying a twenty-year-old tuition bill, and was accepted at American University, not far from the Sheldons' apartment. There, in January 1957, a forty-one-year-old Alli signed up for undergraduate courses. This time around, she was more enthusiastic about her education. She read and wrote in vast quantities, occasionally with the help of Dexedrine. Unlike her earlier self, she got straight A's.

She began to lose her fear that academic training would make her just like everyone else. "Idiosyncratic energy can go only so far—after that you have to have the common speech," she now concluded. "I was not an 'undisciplined genius' seeing true—I mostly didn't *see*." Though a year later she still worried: "I wonder, has this escapade in legitimacy ruined my mind?"

Sometimes she complained of pedantic professors and dull classes. But when she was happy she beamed tolerantly down on her education. A few months into it, in April 1957, she wrote Arnheim, "You know, this is the funniest, most touching endeavor. All sizes and ages and conditions of people, all propelling themselves with outcries in the general direction of learning." In November, she imagined the academic year as a voyage of exploration:

> The first semester is like an arctic trip; in the warm weather you sign up for the long plunge into the dark tunnel of winter, and you sail North with the weeks; the trek across the campus growing colder, the inside of the night bus hotter; darkness coming earlier, and finally closing in to the tough struggle of the exams, an inhuman time—and suddenly the lights and confusion, the camp of Christmas . . . And then the voyage home out of the darkness, back up the tunnel to the great blaze of Spring ahead. . . .

Alli liked the other students, the kids young enough to be her own children, though she told Arnheim she did seem to attract a weirder element.

> I try to mix with my young classmates, and have made friends. [. . .] But everytime I think, Ah, now here it comes, I will learn the pure essence of the young of 1957—it turns out I have latched on to another social deviate like myself. Really! It's uncanny; they come to me—the one just out of shock therapy, the one in love with an older woman, the one who drove a taxi for five years and only goes out at night, with big dark eyes. Girls . . . It's plain, now no more than ever, will I meet the

normal sunshine people of this world. [. . .] How will I ever understand my Average Observer?

But she enjoyed feeling older and wiser, and was generous with sympathy
and advice. She was determined not to coast into complacent middle age; instead she felt a new confidence and vitality. She realized she was no longer as
frightened of death as she once had been.

At first, all this reinforced her conviction that life and even self-knowledge
were "technical problems." In May 1957, while Ting was in Thailand for
work and she was studying for exams, she wrote in her journal, "All through
my life happiness has followed more *tech.* understanding [. . .] Not focus on
people (There're always enough people.) . . . Truth sets free. Augustine on
highest felicity of man. [. . .] When people are unhappy there is something
wrong with their philosophies—they *use mind wrong.*"

But by September she had found something new to worry about. What
good was her private contentment? Of what use was her work to anyone else?
She became so anxious that she took the unusual step of asking Arnheim for
advice, first for a "friend," and then for herself. All her other work, she explained to him—the army, the CIA, even hatching chickens—had contributed to the general good. Whenever she put in long hours and got some bit
of "drudgery" done, she thought "Well, maybe this will be useful to someone." But now that had changed.

It started to come to me this summer. I was walking home, after having
worked to tiredness, and got another of these absurd "As" in the math
exams, and I started to sigh, in the old way, and well, maybe this will be
useful—and it came to me, Useful? Useful to what? To whom?

Only to yourself.

You are working *only for yourself,* said the voice.

For the first time.

So then I quickly said, Well, remember what Augustine said about
the greatest felicity of man . . . And I pushed it aside.

But this is what has now jumped out of the bottom of the trouble
and I can't push it aside.

How can I go on, putting light into my own head, enjoying the greatest felicity of man? What is the aim of making my own perishing brain-jelly into a self-pleasing machine? When I feel it die, what will I be able to say? That I was happy?

Dear Dr. Arnheim—what is the answer? How does one get this happiness back into the general pool?

I think that you are not one just to be resigned to personal pleasure as the goal . . .

This is poisoning me. Please say something if you can.

Arnheim answered with a tender, professorial, philosophical talking-to.

What is so "only" about "yourself"? Is not the first thing one has to learn in this respect that to do something for yourself—I mean, the right kind of thing—is just as valuable and ethical than [*sic*] to do it for somebody else? Wouldn't you say that the good feeling we get simply because we did "it" (whatever) for somebody else is cheating, in that it postpones the question: what is it good for?

We are all in one and only one business: the realization of man. To eat and to drink is a beginning: to think because you are able to think, to be "fully alive" or "fully open" [. . .] these things are so true that the words that express them tend to become embarrassing. But they are true, nevertheless.

And to do things for others, Alice, is little else but a spilling over. You can do things for others because you have become what you are (little as it is, with most of us). But do you think I teach out of a mission that impels me to help the young? Or rather because some things I have known and thought about are exciting enough to want to be said: and because the young are beautiful and energizing and my way of loving them is to tell and show them things. Teaching is to be (moderately) in love with man [. . .].

Certainly, the greatest favor you can do to others is being yourself as much as you can. [. . .] Don't let your friend think that Utopia is better than the small furnished room within his own heart.

Arnheim's answer was a first sign from a new time, anti-Victorian and very un-Bradley. To Alli's surprise, it made sense. She wrote back, "This sounds terrible—but you know; one thinks maybe someone can help, but one doesn't really believe it, one is so used to people not being any use. Then when one receives solid and straight words this is startling."

Alli almost accepted the idea that she could do something for the sake of her own pleasure. But she couldn't quite let go of her ideal of self-sacrifice— partly because she saw it as a weapon against her old enemy, time.

She began to explore a theory that could reconcile her pleasure in learning and making things with doing good for others. If her enemy was time, she argued, then it was also the second law of thermodynamics. That law, sometimes called "time's arrow," states that the universe is entropic: it tends to lose energy, become disorganized, move toward death and decay.

But Earth supports a local condition of negative entropy: its life has evolved from lower to higher states of organization. Mathematician and cyberneticist Norbert Wiener, among others, had suggested that negentropy, and perhaps life itself, could be defined as everything that adds to information or organization.

In this view, to learn is to abet the forces of life—to turn time's arrow back. To teach and research are even better. Altruism is a more organized behavior than self-interest, understanding more complex than ignorance. Alli adopted negentropy as her goal in life. A fervent atheist, she used it where another might use faith in God. When she was depressed, she told herself that to keep building and contributing to knowledge was reason enough to live, regardless of her own joy or pleasure or capacity for happiness. Even if she were trapped in her life, she could still work to make "some future Door through which some future people could go, if one here and now helped build."

But negentropy is an unforgiving faith for a writer. A belief in working and building doesn't allow for wasted efforts, setbacks, fallow periods—the paradoxical entropy of creation. And which is more negentropic, honesty or politeness? Negentropy was also for Alli another form of self-sacrifice—a faith for a good daughter.

In Tiptree's fiction, the moral imperative of working for others is often contrasted with a deadly dream of release. Both Tiptree and Raccoona Sheldon wrote about people who must choose: either work, suffer, and struggle toward the future, or leap out into a freedom that is also a kind of nonbeing, a kind of death. In Tiptree's story "On the Last Afternoon," a man prepares to sacrifice his life to save the colony he has founded. Then he is offered another choice: to abandon the others for disembodied immortality among the stars. "To go out, forever out, to meet . . . strangeness . . . to go *alone,* his essence, his true self free forever from the blood and the begetting and the care. [. . .] To be free of the tyranny of species. To be free of love. To live forever . . ." In the end the man cannot choose, and fails to save either the colony or himself. But his is a temptation that runs through Tiptree's work: to stop struggling and hoping, and instead find freedom in suicide.

When she was happy, though, Alli loved the future and the present, "our life and efforts, our strange, tangled, exciting, deplorable, ever-changing condition of profit and loss, trial and dream and struggle." Reading an art historian who seemed to disapprove of the modern age, she wrote Arnheim in 1958,

> What we have here is the sickly hankering after Daddy-god, who made the world safe and interesting for little boys—a point of view which every humanist, materialist, cynical and female fibre of me rejects. [. . .] The relativist view, the empirical view makes us disjointed, unhappy, uncomfortable, and undoubtedly vulgar and inartistic, but I have a great faith that the solution is ahead and not behind, and that the chains once broken can't be got back into, no matter how musical their clanking. [. . .]
>
> Being, I imagine, must be very simple. It is Becoming which is so messy and which I am all for.

CHAPTER 21: **CHEZ WOMEN (1950s)**

> *All I can say is that laughter is my music; I would deeply suspect an argument which hadn't laughter. The very effort to be fully serious, really dealing with love and awe in the great things, is itself lovable and funny, in the true sense. Leave out the fun and you become a spectacle like the King's clothes; a little figure sternly parading in the light of the giggling stars.*
>
> —ALLI SHELDON

In Washington, Alli studied and was happy. But in Chicago, Mary and Herbert were growing older, more frail, and more and more dependent on their only child. Even Mary's writing, which had seemed so unquenchable for so long, was finally starting to dry up.

In the first years after the war, Mary had published short stories and a series of high-society mystery novels. In a 1952 *New York Times* review, Anthony Boucher wrote,

> Mary Hastings Bradley is an astonishing woman—among other things, probably the only mystery writer who has personally stalked gorillas. And among her astonishing qualities is an ability to blend the woman's-magazine type of mystery-romance with shrewd legalistic plots. [. . .] *Nice People Murder* is one of her best—fine romantic goings-on on the Maine coast, with believable motives and people [. . .] and a neatly constructed plot turning on testamentary technicalities.

The books were serialized in the *Saturday Evening Post,* so they kept money coming in and Mary in the public eye. At seventy, admitting to sixty-five, she wasn't planning to retire from writing. In 1953, a reporter for the *Milwaukee Journal* came to the Lodge for an interview and admired this "slim, small woman with the youthful step and the very young enthusiasm for life."

I Passed for White came out in 1955 and was a huge success. It was serialized in six parts in the *Chicago Tribune* and generated hundreds of letters, mostly from people who wanted Mary to hear their story. It even sold to the movies, which no story of Mary's had done since the silents, though the film version suffered by comparison with Douglas Sirk's *Imitation of Life* and did not do well.

Then in the late 1950s, Mary's market disappeared. Television replaced light fiction as mass entertainment. *Collier's* folded; the *Saturday Evening Post* went into decline. And though women's magazines such as *Redbook* and *Ladies' Home Journal* still published fiction, it was no longer about independent women. "You just can't write about ideas or broad issues of the day for women," one women's magazine editor stated; they wouldn't be interested. Another said, "If we get an article about a woman who does anything adventurous, out of the way, something by herself, you know, we figure she must be terribly aggressive, neurotic."

Besides, the time of African exploration was over. To Americans, Africa no longer represented safaris and pith helmets but poverty and political unrest. The Russian satellite Sputnik entered orbit in 1957; America's Explorer I followed in 1958. As Africa faded from the public imagination, people began to look to the stars as the last and greatest frontier.

And as the civil rights movement began in the mid-1950s, Americans discovered that alienation began at home. In this sense, Mary was right on target; but she didn't have the resources or energy to follow up on *I Passed for White*. She thought of writing a new Anne Boleyn biography—the book she had been "too well brought up" to write properly in 1912—or a book about Chicago. But by then Herbert really was chronically ill, with a bad back that left him nearly bedridden. She felt she couldn't leave him to make research trips.

She did go on lecturing. In May 1955 she spoke on the Mau-Mau revolutionary movement in Kenya to her old literary club, the Society of Midland Authors. In 1957 a society columnist reported that Mary would be the first woman ever to speak at the fifty-year-old Sunday Evening Club at Orchestra Hall, and added that "her acceptance of an invitation always is a delight to a hostess and is a guarantee of a party's success." As Herbert's health failed, Mary tried for his sake to pretend they were still the young, glamorous couple they had been. She began getting beauty treatments: not her style, she told Alli, but "Herbert hated to see lines."

At the same time Mary was so frightened for Herbert that she neglected herself, barely ate, couldn't sleep. For energy she took Dexedrine; at night she took barbiturates. She began having accidents. In the spring of 1956, she tripped over the lion-skin rug in the African Room and broke her arm. The newspapers got word and ran the story as a novelty item, with headlines such as "A Lion's Revenge" and "Big Game Hunter Felled by Trophy."

In the summer of 1957, Alli went to the Lodge as always, watching as Herbert drove "firmly on the left side of the road at 30 mph. [. . .] Fifty years ago the road had been two ruts with grass between, as far as Pa was concerned the 4-lane concrete didn't exist. Perils of time-travel . . ." But she had to go back early to start classes, so Herbert and Mary had to close the place alone. Hoping to spare Herbert, Mary went on packing late one night, slipped on a step with her arms full, and smashed her hand on the door catch. Determined not to hold up the return, she tied a scarf around her arm and wouldn't let it be looked at until four days later in Chicago, when she was admitted to the hospital with a badly fractured wrist. A few weeks later, Herbert developed pneumonia. He was in the hospital until February and nearly died.

Alli came to Chicago when she could, and when she couldn't she wrote long letters full of advice and affection. "I love you so damn much it hurts," she wrote, and her parents' friends were impressed by her loyalty. She did love them, but it did hurt. She resented the work of caring for them: making arrangements from a distance, flying back and forth to Chicago when she needed to study. She missed their strength and protection. Conversations at home had once been witty and wide-ranging, but now Mary insisted on "telling the old African stories over and over in a loud voice all during every meal." Older people do repeat themselves, but Alli had no patience for it.

She hated how hard it was to say no to Mary. Her annual trip to Wisconsin now coincided with the American Psychological Association convention. In August 1958, having given up the APA for the Lodge, she complained to Arnheim, "It is a question of Father and Mother's plans and his sickness and Ting's only possible leave dates and there is no way out . . . so long as I retain a façade of civilisation. Why do we play the roles we play? Why is a perfectly good oral dependent cast in the role of Occasional Comforting Presence?"

Alli disliked her mother's emotional stories and called them "harangues," but Mary used the same word for Alli's response, which was to send letters full of practical advice, urging her parents to hire more help or Mary to set aside more time for her writing. In 1957 Mary wrote Alli, "Sometimes you harangue me a bit like a professional exhorter—I don't mean that unkindly in the least—what I mean is your zest for penetration and criticism finds me a vulnerable target and you warm to it." Mary added that she didn't need more help: "If you think your mother is a fragile flower you should have your head examined!"

Herbert and Mary accepted Alli's new academic career, though they never understood Alli's new love of isolation and study. Answering one of Alli's letters, Mary wrote,

> Your description of your teachers makes me feel again that your real work is writing and that you will come to it some day, in some form— historic, scientific, biographical—who knows. But you have the power. A very real gift of words. A feeling for the unusual, the penetrating. You will use that gift, I think, Alice, if you do not seize on too many worlds to penetrate.

One of Mary's dreams was that she and Alli might write together. She hoped they might collaborate on a play. But it was only after Mary stopped writing that Alli started to feel freer to tell her own stories—and to see that there were other ways of being a woman writer.

Aside from her mother, Alli still didn't have much contact with other women. In her journals during this time she mentions only one woman friend: Ava Dilworth, known as Dilly, a nurse she had met in the army camp in Greensboro while waiting to ship out overseas. Dilly also lived in Washington, where she became director of nursing training at the federal Public Health Service (later part of the National Institutes of Health). She lived with another woman and talked frankly to Alli about her sex life and her own troubles with Dexedrine.

What Alli finally discovered in the 1950s was women's work. She read Hannah Arendt, who led her to Simone de Beauvoir. She studied Rebecca West and Mary Wollstonecraft. In 1955 she told Dr. K that she was reading Lady Murasaki and that a man friend had just given her Virginia Woolf's *Orlando*. The playful fictional biography of a man who becomes a woman—part lesbian love story, part celebration of the diversity of the self—thrilled and delighted Alli, who had never read Woolf before.

Being happy, she began to have more hope for women. At the start of 1957 she bought and read a *Life* magazine special issue on "the American woman." Serious and respectful in tone, with a working mother on the cover and an article by Margaret Mead, it said women could do anything they wanted—but reminded them that marriage and children were still the ultimate fulfillment. Articles such as "Changing Roles in Modern Marriage" acknowledged that many housewives were unhappy, but conjured a "primitive biological urge toward reproduction, toward homemaking and nurturing," plus a high incidence of divorce for working women, to show that women were still best off not "rejecting the role of wife and mother." Fortunately, the rising birth rate showed that women were starting "to comprehend the penalties of 'feminism' and to react against them."

"Jesus Christ. I puke," Alli wrote Max Lerner.

> Those Psychiatrists or whatever they are—mouthing the same old stuff. Of course there are casualties. This is transition. Nobody knows how to do it yet. But tell you what—this whole imputation of trouble with or chez women is just 90% one thing—*projection*. You hear the same thing every time a class frees itself [. . .].

In 1945 Alli had seen the writing of women as "muffled" and self-censored. Ten years and much reading later she thought of it as having its meanings in a different place. In a 1954 letter, she took Ed, her married CIA colleague, to task for complaining of women's disorderly prose.

> Our style *is* anarchic, to you, because we either reject or have never accepted many of your traditions. [. . .] When a woman begins to think, she perceives at once that a great deal of male thinking—verbalised—is symbolic of the male processes; she does not share the roots. So she can go on to acquire the knack of writing imitation male prose—which is pretty dead; I can write good, solid, dead male prose. Or she can start trying to strike to the shape of fact as she sees it. [. . .] A proper woman accepts nothing from the male world without putting it to the test of the

Emperor's clothes. Do I see it? Where is it? That way much error is avoided, but the resulting thought always strikes the conventional man as peculiarly uneasy-making. The thing is at a bias; he has a sneaking suspicion the pillars of society are being regarded with levity. So they are—except that they are only funny if you have a strong stomach. Most women have. [. . .] We are strangers; we write as individual captive Martians.

It's ironic that the same woman who wrote this should end up being acclaimed for her "male prose." But Alli might argue that a woman's way of looking at the world persists under any name: as she once put it, "everything but the signature is me." Besides, what's important in her stories is this very questioning of perspective. Who's looking? How does who they are influence what they see? The "pillars of society" in Tiptree's stories are always being sawn (seen) through.

Levity started to slip into Alli's writing. Sometime in the 1950s, possibly for the benefit of this same colleague and pen friend Ed, Alli wrote a parody of Tom Godwin's 1954 short story "The Cold Equations." In that famous story, the pilot of a small spaceship, carrying serum to stop an epidemic, must jettison a pretty girl stowaway. Her extra mass would overload his fuel reserves and doom his vital mission. From one point of view, Alli admired Godwin's story. She saw the girl as illustrating "one side of humanity—the touching disregard for the environmental facts, the magical hopes. Silly, darling and doomed."

From another, she poked fun at it. In her story "Please Don't Play with the Time Machine," Captain Red Herring discovers a monstrous alien hiding below the control panel of the *Ocarina III*. But this unwanted passenger laughs at the pilot's efforts to eject it: " 'Ah, stow it, Buttons,' said the Thing composedly, picking at its toenails. [. . .] 'The way you flow this pig you need some ballast.' " Instead it snuffles his neck, appalls him with its monstrous fleshiness, then reveals its terrifying true nature: " 'Don't you really know what I am, Reddy dear? [. . .] You poor deprived engineer! I'm a w____n!' "

It wasn't hard to notice that the icky-sticky aliens who attacked the handsome heroes of the pulps were often suspiciously female (though perhaps only Alli was well versed enough in both *Astounding Science Fiction* and *The Second Sex* to make the joke back then). Her parody is cheap, but its playfulness gave her a way to speak. The first stories Tiptree sold weren't lengthy constructions like "The Mind Mice"; they were fast-paced bits of silliness like "Time Machine." The story also anticipates by twenty years Alli's own coming out as a science fiction stowaway.

In the spring of 1959 the Sheldons settled into their new house in the woods, at 6037 Ramshorn Place, McLean, Virginia. An unpaved driveway led down to a comfortable and idiosyncratic house with a study for Alli, a greenhouse in the middle of the living room for Ting's orchids, big windows looking out into the trees, a fireplace, and a porch where they could sleep outside in the summer. Later they enclosed the porch to make room for Alli's books. The house had Danish modern furniture, including a chaise longue in the study that Alli liked to lie on to write, a John Sloan nude over the fireplace, and such practical features as polished concrete floors that could be washed with a hose. It was remote and ramshackle, and Alli's cousin Barbara Francisco recognized it at once. When she came to visit she told Alli, "You found the Lodge."

To Rudolf Arnheim, Alli described her new home as "a large transparent shell full of space and healthy plants and food and water and fire. Walls around a way of life. [. . .] People exclaim it is beautiful, but you will know it is just superlatively convenient. Like me." But it was never quite as practical as it was meant to be. "Only living room I know that had to be weeded," she once said, and its close-to-nature design caused other maintenance problems. The drainpipes from the living room greenhouse were a two-way street, letting out water and letting in bugs, lizards, and snakes. (In 1981 the Sheldons had the greenhouse replaced with an indoor koi pond and fountain.) The concrete floors and picture windows made the house miserably cold in winter. The roof leaked, and condensation from the greenhouse accumulated in the ceilings until, on at least one occasion, it came down again in an interior cloudburst over Alli's desk.

Like the Lodge, the house on Ramshorn Place was in a constant state of becoming, or possibly decay. Alli saw it as her job to supervise all maintenance, and wrote Mary, "I guess I do around here a lot of what Herbert did in the Lodge and 5344." Maybe the lover of maintenance deliberately built a house that would always need maintaining.

In June 1959, at age forty-three, Alli graduated summa cum laude from American University. That fall she moved downtown to George Washington University, which was expanding its psychology program and was a slightly better school. She received a fellowship from the Public Health Service to work on the vision project. She muttered about her adviser pulling strings, but she was deeply proud of predoctoral research grant number 10,907. She'd gone through a door at last, and it was one she had opened for herself.

Not that her work was likely to fit the government's ideas on closing the science gap with the Russians. She wrote Arnheim, "My idea of research was time to think and an educated brain to think with, and maybe access to some students or subjects to do a few simple experiments. I really don't need $50,000 worth of rats to think with. [. . .] Can you tell me, is there still room for one brain, sans rats?" She was already anticipating the trouble she would have with academia. Even so, she was about to become the happiest of all her selves: Alice Sheldon, research scientist.

CHAPTER 22: PREDOCTORAL RESEARCH GRANT NO. 10,907 (1960–62)

A grant, official status: at one time Alli might have gotten cold feet and run. But this was different. In July 1961 she wrote Arnheim:

> The last years have been passage rites for me, I think there is little of me left unmodified by unremmitting effort. (Except my spelling.) It is remarkable; if one spends every day from sleep to sleep earnestly endeavoring to change oneself in structure and function, to form new habits and patterns, and new patterns of the new patterns, and to absorb a sufficiently large number of unfamiliar concepts, and to reorganise, and rechannel, and discard what is useless—and if one is assisted in all this by a variety of instructors who have many different notions of what is missing, but are united in the aim of changing one somehow—and if one is heart and soul interested in all this with the deadly intent of a boy scout learning to patch canoes which he is actually going to paddle in—
>
> Then suddenly one month you realise that there has been a displacement at the center.
>
> I have been feeling that very keenly. What I needed I no longer need, what I need now I do not quite know. I am what I hoped to be, or almost, and yet I am not used to it!
>
> Of course just time itself does these displacements—you know. It is strange to realise the continuity of self—you know undoubtedly a thousand times, having changed countries and languages. The puzzle of seeing those same hands grasping a pencil here, that grasped a horse's mane—was it a week ago or a century ago that one was fourteen? And yet that same crooked thumbnail endures, my same round shadow of a nose goes before me in the scene.

To Mary, she wrote that she had found a stability in her scientific work that she had found nowhere else—a detachment that allowed her to survive.

> My way of finding identity and social intercourse is simple and limited. I speak with those I can learn from or teach. [. . .] I am willing to represent to people that limited segment of their lives which is comparable to looking through a lens or into a book. [. . .] For the rest, my favorite social milieu is a nice quiet library stack-room, where the other inhabitants grunt if disturbed.
>
> This I have identified as the best way to make my peculiar personality socially useful, and my little brick to be laid in the general effort. When thus engaged I do not have emotional upsets or try to suicide, and this is the only way of life I have found of which it is true. The government work was almost, but fatally not quite. Science is my home, the eye is my channel to life.

No place was as pure as Alli wanted it to be. Even in graduate school, she discovered, she would be called on to compromise some of her ideals (or, looked at another way, her insistence that talent was more important than playing by the rules would get her into trouble). But for a long time Alli felt she'd found the place where she fit at last.

She also discovered a group of graduate students and young faculty she genuinely liked and respected. For once, she was working with women, intelligent women who took their careers seriously. She became friendly with several of her colleagues: Ann Milne, who was just out of college; and Lila Ghent (later Braine) and Jacqueline Goodnow, who were at GW with research grants. (Women who had moved to Washington because of their husbands' jobs formed an important talent pool for GW.) Alli made the kinds of casual, "shop-talk" connections she liked, but they mattered to her more; for the first time in years she felt she was really making friends. She had occasional dinner parties at her house and saw her colleagues socially long after she left GW.

Her adviser was Richard D. Walk, a young professor who had made his name with the famous "visual cliff" experiments in perceptual development. He recalled being impressed by Alli's enthusiasm and intensity. "She was the only student I had who could write faster than I could read. She would come in all full of something, and we would talk about it, and then a few days later she'd come in with a twenty- or forty-page paper which I had to read in the next day or two." She also had strong opinions and liked to give advice. "I remember Alice upbraiding me for eating a peanut butter and jelly sandwich. She said that I should not eat peanut butter because it had incomplete protein. Alice was fierce."

Milne, too, recalled Alli's "extraordinary boundless energy," and thought she got it from Mary. "She clearly admired her mother, although she made her sound like a kind of wild woman. But every time she gave that description I would think, Alice, that's yourself you're talking about."

Her new persona was not flirtatious but straightforward and practical. "Alice had style," Goodnow recalled, with her straight posture and strong walk. But in the psychology department her clothes and manner were as neutral as possible. She wore skirts, slacks, and sweaters of high but unostentatious quality. Walk recalled seeing her once when she dropped by her office "in her war paint" before an evening out with Ting. The contrast between her makeup and her businesslike manner startled him; it was the wrong persona for that set of clothes.

She was becoming almost monastic in her study, her determination—she once wrote that in her forties, the melodramatic depressions of youth had given way to the "dry-lipped depressions of resolve"—and her sexual life. Vain as ever about her looks, she hated the thought of losing them to age. Rather than go on having affairs, she later wrote,

> I resolved to stop wanting sex before I became undesirable. (I was always acutely aware of the power-relations between the sexes.) I formed a vague plan of meeting age by "migrating into my mind." As 50 came around I applied this to discontinue sex, partly by trivialising it into sensation (masturbation) and mainly by sublimating it into the successful drive of work.

Maybe in a way this abdication from her physical presence prepared her for becoming the genderless, unseen Tiptree.

When she first started graduate school, she threw all her energy into visual perception experiments. In one burst of enthusiasm, she drew forty-eight different spirals and turbines, made up booklets showing the figures covered in transparent plastic, rounded up student test subjects, and had them mark in red grease pencil the movement they saw in each shape. She wrote yet another outline for the vision project, a paper titled "Introduction to the Psychophysics of Form."

But other kinds of science began to tug at her attention. The woods around the Sheldons' new house were full of birds, deer, opossums, raccoons. Alli started putting out food for them and observing their feeding patterns and behavior. Once she caught a four-foot-long black rat snake and brought it to GW for Walk to try out in his depth-perception experiments. It didn't do much—snakes have poor eyesight—so Walk took it with him to a lecture to illustrate a common emotional phenomenon, the groundless fear of snakes. When he took it out of its cage in front of the class it bit him. Afterward Alli told him her sympathies were entirely with the snake.

For all Alli's ambitions to transform herself into a neutral scientist, and her pride in what she saw as a "strongly scientific 'hard-nosed' approach" to the world, observing animals quickly turned into half-taming. She couldn't resist slipping out at night to give the raccoons peanut butter crackers. She fed the raccoons for many years, and told Charles Platt she thought it was maternal instinct. To another friend she wrote, "I'm afflicted with [. . .] sentimental tendencies, [. . .] the womanly chute-de-toute when confronted with something small, curved, weak, big-eyed and furry."

Not everyone saw this side of Alli. Walk, for one, thought of her as utterly unmaternal. But Milne remembered a woman who was "very warm, very giving." Lila Braine said of Alli, "I always felt that she had a very tender side to her—because of the way she acted toward animals, and her very real pleasure and delight in them." Jacqueline Goodnow agreed: "She was very vulnerable underneath it all."

Goodnow recalled Alli as "a woman who cared passionately about the topics that took her interest and took no notice of the rest." She thought this was both Alli's talent and her weakness as an academic. Her monastic fantasy of research, study, writing, and perhaps a little teaching simply didn't fit with the tasks of university professors, at least not at GW.

Goodnow felt Alli was "impatient with what she saw as the needless conventions of the way theses were supposed to be designed and written. Alice, to my mind, would have been perfectly at home as a female Darwin: one of the great Victorian naturalists, with a capacity both for observation and for original interpretations of behavior. She was like them also in being able to draw on financial resources that few graduate students could count on. Her goal at the time was to be on a university faculty, but it was a goal that had little to do with the small details of university commitments: the right ambition for her but at the wrong time and in the wrong country. Her sense of academic posts was closer to what obtains in a few European universities, and even there is restricted to people at the very senior level.

"I liked her enormously as a person. As an academic colleague? The circumstances would have had to be very special for that to have worked well. She had a vision of what life should be like, and it was, I know, a disappointment for her—that is, I think she found us disappointing—when we turned out to be more 'rule-bound' than she thought we should be.

"All in all, you would not think from the surface that here was a James Tiptree, Jr. If you talked to her about the animal observations and the naturalistic experiments she was carrying out in her own woods, you would not have found it so surprising."

Those observations introduced Alli to ethology, the study of animals in their natural environment. It wasn't much done at GW, but Alli was always vulnerable to new ideas—especially if they were unpopular with the people around her. During her graduate coursework, her idea of what she wanted to study started to change.

Then Herbert died.

For years the Bradleys had spent each Christmas with Alli and Ting, then gone south to Central America. In the late 1950s, when Herbert was no longer up to their old kind of roughing it, they switched to wintering in Acapulco, in a cabin at a beachfront hotel. They liked the American community and the tourist comforts, and the warmth was good for Herbert's back.

In Acapulco, in April 1961, Herbert caught a cold that turned into pneumonia. Mary asked Alli to send medicines. Alli flew down with them herself. On Mary's birthday, April 19, the three of them sat out on the veranda drinking champagne. But on the morning of the twenty-second, as his wife and daughter sat by his bed listening to his shallow breathing and waiting for him to wake, Herbert's heart stopped. He was eighty-six.

Ting flew down for a few days to help, though it must have been a difficult time at the Agency: on April 17, as Alli headed down to Acapulco, a group of CIA recruits had begun their disastrous invasion of Cuba at the Bay of Pigs. Afterward Alli went home with Ting while Mary stayed on in Acapulco, wanting to be alone. From McLean, Alli helped Mary with everything from taxes to car insurance to a death notice ("postcard size, no black edges," Mary requested. "About one or two hundred"). Alli reminded her mother to eat and tried to write cheering letters. Mary replied, "How I love your sweet notes full of delightful garden items and little philosophies of life." Without Herbert, she wrote, "nothing seems very important. Nothing but you my Darling."

Herbert's death hit Alli much harder than she had expected. She wrote Mary, "There was no 'me' before Herbert; something I scarcely identified as separate from me went crashing." To herself, later, she wrote, "To admit his death is to close the door on all that was"—and maybe all that never was, the recognition he didn't give. But Mary put her grief ahead of her daughter's, Alli felt, and demanded comfort when she too was suffering. Alli sought refuge in studying and solitude. Mary took her daughter's withdrawal as a deliberate rejection.

That summer at the Lodge, it seemed to Alli that Mary couldn't get enough of her old subject, death. She talked about the concentration camps. Alli asked her to stop, but Mary went on. Alli told a cute story about a newborn rabbit. Mary replied—and Alli knew her response by heart, saw it coming on like a speeding car—"You know, when they are shot they cry like babies."

After she got home, Alli worked up all her courage and wrote Mary an eleven-page letter. As if to anchor the letter more firmly in her own reality, she dated it to the hour: "Thursday 8 AM, 7 Sep 61." Halfway through, she added, "It has taken me a month to get up the courage to write this letter, and although it is a cool day I am pouring sweat down my sides and onto the chair which is luckily plastic."

She tried to explain that what looked like distance or disloyalty was really unhappiness and desperation. She wrote that the trouble between them was not lack of love, as Mary seemed to think, but lack of understanding. "To put it jokingly, it is as if a porcupine loved one dearly—how do you draw his attention to the fact that your face is full of quills? [. . .] Again jokingly, it is as if A has the measles, and B says, you do not love me or you would not be all over those loathsome spots."

Mary had accused her of "bottling up" her feelings, but she explained that not feeling was the way she survived.

> What I do with emotion is not, strictly, to "bottle it up." I parcel it out. I make it drive me in work; I try to use it to understand the world; I occasionally try to form or express little bits in objective writing or drawing; I try to stay out of situations which encourage it; I take it out in physical exertion—and what still can't be handled I do "bottle up" and sit on. What else can one do? [. . .]
>
> Your way of finding your identity and your sense of being, among people, is to evoke an emotional response from them, to develop a wide empathic atmosphere of shared love and communication, and to converse by ranging over a broad spectrum of emotionally charged topics, expressing each one fully, and evoking response from the audience.
>
> When the audience does not respond, you repeat, often louder. You have dismay, you feel alone and rejected and deprived of identity.
>
> This style of sociability is to me the continuous plucking of utterly raw nerves, which cumulates into sick exhaustion and precipitous flight.

She tried to explain to Mary how frightened she was of her depressions and her visions of time and death. She described to Mary how she saw "the end in the beginning," the corpse in the baby carriage, all events and lives hurrying onward toward their end.

> I walk on our concrete floor, and the thought comes to me that one day I shall fall alone on this floor and perhaps die so, as many solitary old women do. I see its texture close up, as I will see it then, and I try to accept.
>
> Mostly I do accept. But sometimes the thing runs away with me, and the best way I can put it is to say that I live as a skeleton, among skeletons. [. . .] The time-sense of the Present, which fortifies most people I think, is weak in me. The collapse rushes on me, the solid ground falls

out. This is not easily understood unless you experience it. I live in fear
of these total collapses which leave me helpless and drive me to death.
[. . .]

Maybe if I put it very concretely you can get it: When I envisioned
driving you to the Lodge, I knew that most of the way I would be struggling with the howling urge to drive us straight into every tree or concrete wall along the route. I even wondered if this was what you wanted.

If you can "get" this, if you can believe it is real, you will get the ker-
nel of the thing.

I am riding an internal destructive force that I cannot completely
control but can only outfox.

Mary couldn't get it. As desperate as Alli's plea was, it wasn't written in any
language Mary understood. In so many ways Mary and Alli were alike. Even
their voices, on tapes they made for each other, have the same deep timbre, the
same smoker's rasp. They loved each other profoundly. But a few years later
Mary wrote Alli sadly, "We never seem to know what the other is truly feeling."

After Mary's death, Alli donated her own long letter to an archive along
with the rest of her mother's papers. Across the top of page one she added a
postscript: "Result of this letter: zero."

Shortly after she wrote this letter, for unknown reasons, Alli abandoned the vision project. She may have given it up for practical reasons: It was hard to narrow down to dissertation size. No one in the department knew enough about
visual perception to supervise her work. Walk was demanding quantifiable research results. Or it's possible that she got cold feet: she still had terribly high
standards for herself, hated to accept her limitations, and would rather turn to
something new. On the other hand, if writing about vision was a way of defending her own perceptions against her parents', Herbert's death may have
freed her from it at last.

Yet writing as James Tiptree, Jr., also let Alli feel closer to her father—who
had, after all, always wanted a boy. As Tiptree, she once wrote, "I keep the 'Jr.'
kinda as a magic, like it makes him still alive."

CHAPTER 23: RAT SCIENCE (1963–67)

You know, exams are like war—the birth rate of ideas goes up. Anything to keep from this dismal regimen, says poor mind, and hopefully tosses up another distraction.

—ALLI SHELDON TO RUDOLF ARNHEIM, 1957

Alli finished her course work in the spring of 1963 and spent the next four years working on her dissertation. She was in no hurry to finish. She wasn't quite sure what she would do with a Ph.D. She was happy where she was, doing research, and wanted to prolong her grant and her grad student status. She began to hope that she could somehow stay on at George Washington.

The trouble was, her research fit neither her adviser's work nor the university's needs. Lila Braine, like Jacqueline Goodnow, thought Alli was utterly oblivious to career politics: "She didn't see the realities of how departments are organized and how people get jobs. It would have been extremely unrealistic of her to think that she would be a fit at George Washington." She probably felt that pure talent ought to get her hired, not adjusting her research to fit what other people wanted. Maybe she could no longer give up being an outsider. Whatever the reason, when she abandoned visual perception, she took up an equally unpopular subject, the problem of novelty.

Novelty is an important concept in perceptual research: many developmental and perceptual tests are based on the assumption that animal and human subjects will spend longer looking at something new than at something familiar. Some of the prevailing ideas about novelty bothered Alli. Is novelty really, inherently appealing? Are animals (and people) always attracted to it? Alli refused to believe it. Animals in the wild are wary of the unfamiliar, she pointed out. "If you want to attract wild animals, you don't present them with novelty. You make yourself look like a swamp or a bush." Only if you want to attract lab rats, who sit around all day in cages, do you show them something new.

Humans too, she argued, are balanced between their drive to explore and their longing for security. Travelers in a foreign country are glad to run into neighbors they can't stand at home. Children in a strange environment clutch familiar blankets and toys. Even art lovers, Alli argued to Arnheim, prefer established genres to true innovation.

One theory proposed that animals would approach when the amount of novelty was small and retreat when it became overwhelming. But is the absence of overwhelming strangeness the only goal, or are we actively attracted to what we know? When a man prefers an old, battered hat to the new one his wife buys for him, Alli said, surely he isn't frightened of the new stimulus, but finds comfort in the old one.

And so contrarian Alli ended up doing a rat study after all: a study of reaction to novelty as a function of context. It wasn't what she had set out to do, but it did let her look at problems of perspective: the contradictions of cultural identity, the problem of fitting in or being different, the mystery of not seeing what everyone else saw. She spoke from experience when she wrote in her thesis, "Adult humans who appear different, behave in a novel manner, or propose new views have learned to expect aversive reactions from their fellow men."

Her "fellow men" may have included Dick Walk. Alli's thesis adviser thought she was a brilliant student. But he was a conventional academic who didn't know what to make of an advisee who went her own way. He was jealous of the Sheldons' money—he thought other, poorer students deserved a grant more—and suspected Alli of being a dilettante. "I don't think Alice had any long-term interest in psychology," he eventually concluded. "Maybe her aesthetics business might have been something. But I was doing research at the time on concept formation in art with children, and though Alice certainly knew about it she never got involved with it. I had other students who did, and who did their dissertation on it, but not Alice. She was off by herself, wherever it was; I was never sure."

Her thesis topic, Walk felt, was a one-shot idea: it did not open up a line of research on which to build a career. And besides, it brought Alli into conflict with the department's underlying philosophy. The department was traditionally minded, behaviorist, applying itself to stimuli and responses. Alli, the budding ethologist, was impatient with behaviorist theories that didn't treat animals as thinking, feeling creatures.

There is a side to behaviorism that's very liberating: if the human psyche begins as a blank slate, then we can change anything. But what if you can't change things in yourself? What if you feel emotions you can't explain, that arise in you unexpectedly and refuse to be told they aren't real? To say that animals have emotions is to suggest that our emotions are also in some sense animal, that they operate on a level beyond conscious control. A feeling that emotion must be controlled and cannot be controlled—that alien signals are coming from within—was very strong in Alli's way of looking at the world.

Ethology also demands empathy, which Alli began to see as an important part of negentropy—that force of life, growth, and organization that she felt was our purpose on Earth. Empathy meant watching a butterfly instead of squashing it. It meant sharing another's pain. It meant flinching when you watched the evening news. Alli saw empathy as rare, fragile, and necessary. She wondered if it could be bred or taught. She thought it might save the world.

Yet she saw it as a one-way process: one should not speak of one's own unhappiness, only share others'. Later on, to a therapist, she wrote that empathy was a painful duty: "It is wrong to be happy when others suffer." Yet she added, "Question, how much of this preoccupation with pain and horror is reaction-formation, denial of own sadistic and aggressive impulses? [. . .] Difficulty: No middle ground. Callousness seen as sin."

Studying lab rats in their natural habitat was a strange sort of ethology, but once Alli started watching her rats she fell in love. She drew pictures of the ways they reacted to the edges of their environment: "edge-peering," "gap-straddling," "shadow-crouching." She especially liked one rat she named Snedecor, after George Snedecor, author of the influential 1937 text *Statistical Methods*. After she finished her experiments she handed the rest of her rats on for other research but brought Snedecor home to McLean. He became "wildly affectionate, kept rushing up and clasping my ankles in the can." But she let him outside at night, and a wild rat gave him encephalitis. The vet had to put him to sleep, "mad as a hatter but still hiding his head in my hand on the huge steel table."

Liking rats, Alli became even more disgusted with the kind of experimental psychology that involved cruelty to animals. Later, in a story called "The Psychologist Who Wouldn't Do Awful Things to Rats," Tiptree filled a university lab with gruesome scenes of vivisection, electrodes, and researchers slicing off baby rats' heads. Walk denied that this was a portrait of the GW lab. He himself stopped by the lab on weekends to make sure the animals were fed and believed that cruelty to animals disqualified a student for the field. Like Alli, he handled lab rats gently without gloves and was rarely bitten. However, he did recognize himself as the academic bureaucrat "R. D. Welch," who demands from his hapless grad student "a major project outline that we can justify in terms of this department's program."

Alli had to conduct many experiments, with different kinds of stimuli and many, many groups of rats, before she finally got clear results. In her last and most conclusive trials, rats were allowed to get acquainted with two small objects, a ceramic figure of a professor and a brass turtle. Alli then built a Y-shaped runway leading to two different goal boxes, one containing the familiar stimulus, the other a novel one (a washcloth, a plastic cube, or, with Alli irony, a mousetrap). She put a rat on the runway and watched which box it chose.

She conducted one trial a day, washing the runway between each subject to eliminate scent traces, for thirteen days. In the beginning, most rats went to the box that held the familiar object. With each trial, as the rats got used to the initially unfamiliar environment, they began to show more interest in the thing they had never seen before. In trial fourteen, the last, she let one group of rats play in a novel environment, a monkey cage full of toys, for an hour. While the rats who had not played in the monkey cage still tended to be drawn to the novel object, the ones who had just explored a new environment reverted to a preference for the familiar.

At last Alli had clear, conclusive results, so clear that even Walk and the department head had to concede that her research had been a success. She was overjoyed. She had defended what she knew and been proved right by the world itself. She felt she had stood "bare-faced in front of Nature" and asked it a question. And Nature had grumbled, stalled, made her rephrase the question, then finally answered yes. It was, she recalled, "the most thrilling moment I have ever had in my whole life."

Early on in her graduate career, even before she had finished her course work, Alli was asked to teach psychology, and led courses at both American and

George Washington universities. She liked the idea of teaching. She liked young people, and saw teaching as a compensation for not raising children of her own. Unfortunately, the reality of teaching was, like so many realities, a disappointment to her. She was assigned the giant lecture classes no one else wanted, in subjects like statistics and educational psychology, full of education majors who "could barely count their toes." Incapable of doing things by half measures, she was determined to educate and inspire her students, but calculated that, with the time she was putting in, she was wearing herself out for something like seventy-five cents an hour.

> Stupid kids come up and say I've been here three years and you're the first faculty member that ever TALKED to me—and bang goes three hours. Or bright kids, and you find they went to some progressive so-called school and can't read or write an English sentence, and want to. And piss goes ten hours. And they aren't getting the material so you re-vamp your whole series. And you give real exams, essay exams, and READ them. Yeah, $.75 with your fucking Ph.D.

She simply couldn't keep up these interactions; they exhausted her. Years later, in a depressed mood, she wrote in her journal that teaching was "over-empathy with lame ducks."

And Alli had another exhausting new responsibility, her mother. Mary was still active, spending summers at the Lodge and winters in Acapulco. In 1968 she talked of going back to Rwanda to visit a friend there, Rosamond Carr. In 1975, when she was ninety-three, she was still planning to help Carr with a book about her life in Africa. But physically she was declining, and she needed more and more help from her only child.

Mary had many friends and, like Alli, loved being with young people. When Ting's son Peter and his new wife, Ann, moved to Chicago in the early sixties, Mary asked Ann to be her secretary and treated them both as her own grandchildren. Peter recalled, "She was a wonderfully loving, sweet person, really someone we adored, my wife and I. She had fallen and I think broken her hip and was in a wheelchair. But when we had our daughter in Pittsburgh she flew out and came to us. She was very capable, and just a very nice, generous, we didn't think very complicated person."

To Peter, Mary's big apartment was a "time capsule," not only because of the African Room with its forty-year-old trophies, but because of its other collection, Alli's paintings. "Alice was a presence in that apartment. Her art hung everywhere. It was like Mary had created a museum; she treasured these things from Alice." Yet Ting and Alli treated Mary badly, he felt, "just talking back to her and being generally unpleasant. There was a deep love there, between mother and daughter, but there was also a jealous rivalry."

Still, it was Alli and Ting that Mary called on most—to assist with her finances, hire nurses and household help, find doctors and repairmen. By the late sixties Mary was keeping herself going on a steady diet of amphetamines and sleeping pills, until Alli (who thought at first her mother was going senile) found out and persuaded her to cut back. Alli never stayed long in Chicago; she apparently told Mary Ting wouldn't allow it. But at a distance, she did her best to empathize, in her own sense of a one-way flow. She felt it was her duty to write cheerful notes, listen, respond, express concern, and watch her brave, strong mother slowly lose her hold on life.

Alli herself still went through occasional bouts of depression, and sometimes a general malaise that left her feeling weak, queasy, headachey, and "like a motor that won't start." She tried diets (she thought for a while it was low blood sugar), more sleep (a cure she hated), and the Dexedrine her doctor prescribed for "adrenal insufficiency." She suspected she was "a low-stress-tolerant type with high-stress ambitions. Too much motor for the chassis." She was impatient with low moods, and preferred her more energetic states, when she could burn the candle at both ends. Her body repaid her neglect by regularly breaking down.

When she was depressed, the world gave her plenty to worry about. In the sixties the Sheldons started spending their summer vacations deeper in the wilderness. They and Bob Koke would drive up to Quebec or New Brunswick and have bush pilots fly them to remote lakes, where the men could fish and Alli could write, explore, or sunbathe nude in sheltered coves. But it seemed they had to go farther every year to be alone: even the wilds of northern Canada weren't free of beer cans and fellow tourists. Wisconsin's North Woods were fished out and overrun, rural McLean rapidly being developed. Alli mourned her lost wild places and feared for the environment. If the human race didn't destroy itself in a nuclear holocaust, biologists now warned, it was likely to die slowly of starvation in a poisoned, exhausted wasteland. Alli had disturbing visions of the Calcutta she had seen at age nine and feared overpopulation would lead to war. "Man is not humane to man, let's be frank," she once stated. "Not naturally humane to man, and does not remain humane to his fellow man unless he has lots of room and nothing is frightening him."

In politics, too, these years were hard on Alli's hopes. The Cuban missile crisis brought the world to the brink of destruction. The resistance to the civil rights movement showed America at its worst. The Kennedy assassination made Alli fear the country was doomed. Even the CIA, who had seemed to be the good guys—Alli had seen her work there as a contribution to peace—lost their white hats at the Bay of Pigs. The bungled invasion wasn't all bad for Ting, since it cost his nemesis, Allen Dulles, his job. But Ting was deeply disillusioned with what Alli on his behalf called "the bloody clowns of the covert side."

As the Bay of Pigs tarnished the CIA, so Vietnam tarnished all America. In early 1965, as Alli was building goal boxes and breeding rats on H Street, the fighting in Southeast Asia began to escalate. The first student antiwar demonstrations were held. In Washington, GW students found themselves unable to sleep or study because they had twenty other demonstrators sleeping in their room. At times the shrubbery reeked of tear gas, the smell lingering in the bushes to be revived by the rain. Alli was of course on the side of the students; later, in 1971–72, she briefly helped the Quaker Vigil, a round-the-clock antiwar protest in front of the White House, keep going during the winter nights.

Ting abetted Alli's worries by always assuming the worst: economic crash, world war. During the Cuban missile crisis he stocked the basement with canned goods in case of a nuclear attack. Later he hid gold coins around the house. More and more, Alli alternated between left-wing idealism and its corollary, a fear that the human race was doomed. She once described her politics as "knee-jerk liberal verging on apocalyptic."

Inevitably, all this made its way into Tiptree's stories. James Tiptree, Jr., was born not only into the end of Alli's career as a psychologist and her mother's slow decline, but into the violence and drama of the 1960s. His sensibility has in it some of that time's passionate hope and realpolitik paranoia, its despair and its wild visions of a new world.

Throughout the sixties, for Alli and many others, those visions were embodied in humans' progress toward the stars. In April 1961, as Alli was flying down to Herbert's deathbed, Yuri Gagarin became the first human to orbit Earth, completing one full circuit in 1 hour and 29 minutes. The next month, Alan Shepard made a fifteen-minute suborbital flight in Mercury 3. In February 1962, John Glenn circled Earth three times in a flight that lasted nearly five hours.

Alli and the country watched, listened, hoped, and were moved by the messages from Mission Control. The great adventure of humans leaving Earth reminded Alli of her own longing for the stars, her belief in human evolution, and the Bradleys' long-ago vision of a civilizing journey into the unknown. In the 1960s, Americans looked at the moon with a surveying eye, the way Mary had once stood on the shore of Lake Tanganyika. The first landing, they felt sure, would be followed by exploration, then outposts, then movie theaters, libraries, industry, and settlement of the lunar frontier. Asked about the significance of the moon landing, Wernher von Braun compared it to the moment when life first emerged from the sea.

Alli's old love, science fiction, began to seem less like an escape and more like a discourse as necessary as the news. After the narrow, stifling fifties it offered new, longer perspectives. It was "different," and that was suddenly a good thing. Robert Heinlein spoke of sexual revolution, Kurt Vonnegut of absurdity. William S. Burroughs borrowed from science fiction, which in turn borrowed from his explorations of sexuality. A generation of young writers—Harlan Ellison, J. G. Ballard, Thomas M. Disch, Joanna Russ, Samuel R. Delany, Ursula K. Le Guin—began to insist that SF be taken seriously as literature, or wrote as though it already were. SF acquired real characters, atmosphere, social criticism, style. And it joined these qualities to what it already had, a vocabulary uniquely suited to imagining change.

In painting, journalism, and fiction, Alli had found few words or images for her sexual longings, her midnight despair, her dreams of escape. But all this time Alli and science fiction had been growing toward each other, until at last it could express something like Alli's angry, loving, scatological, moral, political vision of the world.

The stories started coming to her when she was writing up her dissertation, studying for her orals, skimping on sleep, and using as much Dexedrine as she dared. To relax, she wrote up a few plots, in a different style from the fiction she'd written before. Where her earlier drafts had rambled or been sentimental, the new stories were fast-paced, taut, energetic, and entertaining.

Why now? It may be that working on her thesis gave her a hold on the world that allowed her to let another part of herself go. With her thesis engaging all her rational mind, her imagination was free to play. And after all her years of messing around with drafts and ideas, writing unfinished stories and introductions to books that didn't exist, it taught her to look outside herself and focus her energies. Finishing such a large work must have given her confidence.

It probably helped that she was writing genre fiction, and not the literary novels she had struggled with in the forties and fifties. Genre gives the writer a narrative framework to shelter in, a structure, a place to start. For Alli, it removed the obligation to say the right thing or make a serious point.

And Alli could write fiction because she didn't need to. Since the last time she had submitted a story for publication, in 1952, Alli had had two successful careers and was about to earn a Ph.D. Her earlier writing had had her whole identity riding on it; these stories were just a goof. Alice B. Sheldon had become a scientist, a serious researcher who presented papers, attended conferences, studied rats, and contributed to knowledge in the world. It was another, less serious, less public person who sat up at night scribbling science fiction—a person closely related to the silly, spoofing author of "Please Don't Play with the Time Machine."

One of the stories, "Birth of a Salesman," was a farce about troubles at the office. A bureaucrat at the department of "Xenocultural Gestalt Clearance" is in charge of inspecting interstellar freight, judging it for cultural offensiveness at all transit points. His long day of miscommunication seems inspired by Alli's cross-cultural childhood and her years of writing memos, and is a cheerful variation on the SF chestnut that one creature's meat is another's poison, religious symbol, spaceship, or spouse. The story's good qualities are its manic energy and the way it wastes no time explaining the situation, but sets off in the middle and lets the reader catch up.

"Fault" was equally slight but more serious. It plays with the double meaning of its title by describing a man who, as punishment for a crime, is "slipped" in time. His "temporal friction" is reduced, so that he falls behind the rest of the world: if his wife embraces him, he feels it only hours after it happened. The story is told by the man's commanding officer, in a sort of I-was-there voice Mary had liked to use in her stories, and might be inspired by Alli's own sense that she was not firmly anchored in time.

Alli later said she never really believed the stories would get published. But she was starting to think about new lives, and she was willing to try something crazy. Sometime in the spring of 1967, Alice Sheldon, a fifty-one-year-old research psychologist, typed them up to send out to science fiction magazines. Because of the precarious scholarly career she'd built, she decided again to submit her work under a pseudonym.

She later claimed that all she had wanted was a name no one would remember rejecting. But the alias she chose was not forgettably anonymous, like "Ann Terry" or "Mrs. H. D. Smith." It was flamboyantly anonymous—an absurd name that marked this science fiction business as strictly a joke. She and Ting were shopping in Giant Foods, and she saw a jar of Tiptree jam. She said "James Tiptree." Ting said "Junior." After they stopped laughing, she decided she liked it—and after all, a male byline was more common in science fiction than a female one. She went home, put the stories in envelopes, wrote cover letters using the new name (and her own street address, 6037 Ramshorn Place), and sent them off.

CHAPTER 24: **THE BIRTH OF A WRITER (1967)**

The cosmos is the most radically open and non-enclosed space the female imagination could wish for, large enough to accommodate the ghosts of the past and the embryonic hopes of the future, and unknown enough to comprise both the familiar and the alien.

—INEZ VAN DER SPEK

Just as James Tiptree, Jr.'s, first stories only hinted at the haunting, subversive, many-layered fiction to come, the name on the cover sheet did not summon out of thin air the sexy and appealing Tiptree persona. Alli had not been trying to dream up a new identity that day in Giant Foods, and she didn't recognize it as such when it arrived. Later Alli sometimes wondered if Tiptree hadn't been in her all along, waiting to be given a name. But he doesn't seem to have been a deliberate plan—and certainly if he was the writing voice she had always sought, coming to her suddenly among the condiments, he arrived in the shape of trickster rather than prophet.

Tiptree liked to make his writing career sound even more accidental than it was. In his first and only interview, conducted by mail at the end of 1970, he wrote:

> Couple of years back under a long siege of work and people pressure, I set down four stories and sent 'em off literally at random. Then I forgot the whole thing. I mean, I wasn't rational; the pressure had been such that I was using speed (VERY mildly), and any sane person would have grabbed sleep instead. [. . .] So some time later I was living, as often happens, out of cartons and suitcases, and this letter from Condé Nast (who the hell was Condé Nast?) turns up in a carton. Being a compulsive, I opened it. Check. John W. Campbell.
>
> About three days later I came to in time to open one from Harry Harrison.

Now, you understand, this overturned my reality-scene. I mean, we know how writers start. Years, five-ten years, they paper a room with rejection slips. It never occurred to me anyone would buy my stuff. Never.

Alli probably didn't write the four stories all at once, and she certainly didn't forget about them—though it's true she wasn't expecting much from this odd new phase of her writing career.

On the other hand, some of Tiptree's readers have assumed he was a carefully thought out, undercover secret identity. "Using techniques that she had learnt whilst working in the CIA in the 1950s, Sheldon established Tiptree with a bank account and a postal address in Virginia (Sheldon herself lived in Washington, DC)," one critic explains. Another tells us Alli took a pseudonym partly because of "the habit of excessive secrecy" she had learned while conducting illegal investigations. Though Alli did have habits of secrecy, she neither "established" Tiptree in advance nor went out of her way to hide him. Two years later, after one of Tiptree's new letter-friends came to her house looking for him, she rented a post office box in McLean. And she did set up a (legal) bank account under her working name. But when Tiptree wrote, "I'm so spooky that I get a cut-out to open my mailbox," all that meant was asking Ting to pick up the mail.

Tiptree wasn't a deliberate plan; yet he wasn't a complete accident either. Alli did apparently see him as something separate from her old literary ambitions: he was not a Writer who struggled and bared his soul, but a guy who tossed off low-grade work without thinking about it too hard, the literary equivalent of a Sunday painter. Yet his writing was also something she had, in a sense, been working her way toward for many years: not just the authority to speak, but the courage to play games, to be bad at something, to stop trying to be polished and perfect but to be amateurish and silly and have fun. It was typical of Alli to take this step in a way that made sure she wasn't quite admitting it even to herself.

For months, Tiptree led a flimsy existence as a name on some cover letters, while Alli wrestled with her own life. In February 1967, she defended her thesis and became Dr. Alice B. Sheldon. She gave a party at her house for her colleagues and the members of the examining committee. Her thesis was published in the prestigious *Journal of Comparative and Physiological Psychology*. She was now a research scientist, with formal credentials, ready to begin a career. Rudolf Arnheim read her thesis, enjoyed it, but thought to himself, "Now that she will be on her own she will produce the real Alice!"

But what career, which real Alice? She could have gone on researching novelty and familiarity, but she couldn't face the grantsmanship and didn't feel her department would help. Some of her colleagues, including Ann Milne, became freelancers, taking government contracts to do research on whatever subject came along. This was not Alli's style. Lila Braine got tenure at Barnard College and had a distinguished career as a developmental psychologist; Jacqueline Goodnow returned to Australia, where she became a professor at Macquarie University and achieved considerable eminence. But even if Alli had wanted to move (Ting was due to retire in two years), she couldn't face the thought of teaching full-time. That spring she led a forty-student section of educational psychology for GW and concluded, "I cannot teach—if I teach as teaching should be I become so exhausted I nearly die, I seem to have no middle gear."

She got back in touch with Arnheim and began a detailed critical reading of his latest manuscript, *Visual Thinking*. He sent her the chapters as he finished them, and with her old mentor for an audience, Alli wrote long, passionate letters critiquing his structure and arguing with his style. He was grateful: "All that work you put in! What shall I do with you? Carry you around in procession as the people of Siena did with the Duccio madonna, if I remember correctly?" He told her she should get a job as an editor.

Alli didn't look for a job as an editor. She never quite got around to going on in psychology. Still, though she had never missed her other old careers—painting, journalism, the CIA—she was always a little bit angry that she didn't get more support from GW, and sorry that she didn't stay in science.

That summer, both Sheldons got sick. On their annual fishing trip, in the wilds of New Brunswick, Ting developed kidney stones and had to be flown out, while Alli packed the station wagon and drove all night to get to the hospital. Then Alli's own steady diet of coffee, cigarettes, amphetamines, and physical neglect culminated in a perforated ulcer. After surgery the doctor instructed her to drink milk, avoid stress, and reform her ways. Around this time, for unknown reasons, she also underwent a hysterectomy.

But that spring and summer, with unusual persistence, she went on writing, submitting, and resubmitting stories. One day in the spring while she was teaching, Ting, who thought she was working too hard, got her to knock off for an afternoon and go with him to the racetrack. Extrapolating the experience into interplanetary terms, she wrote a fast-paced farce about a group of Earth exiles running an off-world racing empire. She submitted the story to the magazine *Analog,* whose editor, John W. Campbell, turned it down with a friendly note saying sports didn't sell in science fiction.

A few weeks later, in July 1967, Campbell returned another story, "Your Haploid Heart," along with a two-page critique asking Mr. Tiptree to speed up the action and make his hero more resolute. "One of the troubles with a majority of modern stories," he remarked, "is that nowadays the idea of an heroic Hero is considered gauche or something." Campbell, who had been editing *Analog* and its predecessor, *Astounding Science Fiction,* for thirty years, passionately believed that scientific man would save the world. Neither he nor Alli yet knew how thoroughly Tiptree would undermine science fiction's heroes.

Alli put "Haploid" aside; but over Labor Day weekend, at the American Psychological Association convention, she found herself awake before dawn drafting yet another story. In it she used her old idea of the eight-foot-tall women, but added a CIA setting. She called it "Mama Come Home." Tiptree mailed it off to Campbell.

In September, the ceiling collapsed in Alli's study. She packed all her papers into boxes, where they stayed for weeks while workmen dealt with condensation in the attic. Describing the start of his writing career, Tiptree made this sound romantic: "I was living, as often happens, out of cartons and suitcases." For Alli it was a depressing nuisance.

Then in October, just as Alli was starting to set up her office again, go through the boxes full of papers and unanswered mail, and comment on another section of Arnheim's book, two envelopes arrived. In one, Harry Harrison, editor of *Amazing Stories* and *Fantastic,* offered Tiptree $25 for "Fault" and asked to see more. In the other was a check from Condé Nast. After some confusion (in some versions of the story, Alli said she thought the envelope was junk mail and Ting had to rescue it from the trash), Alli realized that Campbell had bought "Birth of a Salesman."

A month later, after Campbell rejected "Mama Come Home" as implausible in its science (an eight-foot-tall person would be too fragile), Frederik Pohl, the editor of *Galaxy,* picked it up for *Galaxy*'s second-string sister publication, *If.* At *If*'s and *Fantastic*'s rate of one cent per word, James Tiptree, Jr., wasn't rich, but with three stories accepted in six weeks he was a selling science fiction writer.

By now Alli had already received several letters addressed "Dear Mr. Tiptree." She didn't correct anyone. If the whole thing was a goof, she must have thought, then why not be Mr. Tiptree a little longer? But a check made out to James Tiptree, Jr., gave him a certain practical substance. He didn't need a social security number: under the rules then, the amounts of money were too small to be declared. But should he have a bank account?

Alli decided to take the deception a step further. She went down to her bank and said she wanted to open an account under another name. Patiently, she explained to the manager that there were no laws against assuming an alias or working under a business name. Eventually, the manager agreed. For the next few years, a set of checks and deposit slips imprinted "James Tiptree, Jr.," would be the most substantial sign of the writer's existence.

Alli must have practiced signing Tiptree's name, because she gave him a flowing signature that looked very different from Alice Sheldon's neat, careful one. And she did go out of her way at first to make his letters sound like a man's, adding casual details about Tiptree's fishing trips, his "professional responsibilities," even his long-ago flying lessons. When Pohl accepted a story because he "decided if you were content with it I probably ought to be," Tiptree answered that it made him feel "like the time I was in flying training and I thought the instructor was flying it and he thought I was." Alli asked Ting to read some of these first letters to see if they sounded masculine enough. On the other hand, Alli didn't like being addressed as "James" or "Jim." When Tiptree got on a first-name basis with Harrison and Pohl, he asked them (on the model of "Ting"?) to call him "Tip."

Later she wrote, "Tiptree kept taking on a stronger and stronger life of his own; if I were superstitious I'd say Something was waiting for incarnation there in the Giant Foods import section . . . maybe I do anyway. This voice would speak up from behind my pancreas somewhere. *He* insisted on the nickname, he would not be 'Jim.' " It seemed to Alli, at least in retrospect, that Tiptree was creating himself.

Tiptree's second logistical problem came when Pohl accepted "Mama Come Home." "Mama" is about a freighter crew of three giant humanoid women from somewhere near the star Capella who come across Earth and decide to drop in. On their home planet, women are the dominant sex. On Earth they concoct a nefarious plan to kidnap and enslave human men.

The story's narrator, a CIA photointerpreter named Max, is not crazy about this idea, but his coworker Tillie has a certain sympathy for the plan. She was brutally raped as a teenager, distrusts all men, and is drawn to the powerful Capellan women. Only later, when she discovers that the Capellans also plan to send Earth back to the Ice Age until they can return for more slaves, does she agree to work with Max to drive them away.

To a casual reader, the appeal of "Mama" lies mainly in its narrative style—quick, vivid, no space wasted on explanation—and the insider's portrayal of a CIA setting. "We really aren't a big secret thing," Max says of his "shop." "Not a Biretta [sic] or a cyanide ampoule in the place and you can get into our sub-basement any time you produce front and profile X-rays of both your grandmothers. What's there? Oh, a few linguists and old war leftovers like me." Asides about United Nations politics and rivalry with the Joint Chiefs made it all sound grown up and knowing, and so did the Chandleresque metaphors: "She gave me a long look as though she were trying to make out a distant rider on a lonesome plain."

But from the beginning, Alli's adventure stories had more to them than meets the eye. Though "Mama" is narrated by a man, the plot centers on the actions of the woman, Tillie. And underneath the yarn about spies falling in love and saving the world, the story asks questions about Tillie's identification with power. The large, murderous Capellans seem to represent Tillie's desire for power and control. But that desire is connected to her revenge fantasies, and it frightens her. In the end, Tillie chooses to ally herself with men, turning away from the strong, cruel, alien women.

The logistical problem was this: in December 1967, Fred Pohl, having accepted "Mama" and complimented its author ("You handle science-fiction backgrounds very well indeed"), asked for a brief biography he could print with the story. It was easy enough for Tiptree to set up a bank account. But who was he? Did he have a profession? A past?

Alli didn't reveal herself; nor did she give Tiptree an imaginary résumé. She didn't even give Tiptree her own life. Instead, she invoked silence. Tiptree wrote Pohl that he was thrilled to have the story accepted, but "re the biographical details: Sorry, but for reasons which are, I trust, insufficiently clear, I don't have any to offer right now." He added coyly that he would finish and send his next story "as soon as Big Brother glances elsewhere for a bit."

Pohl picked up on the "Big Brother" reference and on Tiptree's return address: by then McLean already had strong associations with government in general and CIA in particular. Pohl had edited other secretive writers, including a mathematician at the Institute for Advanced Study who was so closeted about his pen name that he didn't even cash the checks for his stories. He assumed that what his new writer was hiding was "the kind of work one is required by the work itself to conceal. I supposed that Tiptree most probably reported for work every day at an inconspicuous little office [where] the staff seemed not to hear the question when asked by outsiders what they did for a living—that Tiptree, in short, was an assumed name, and that the person behind that name was a CIA (or similar) spook."

Tiptree let him believe it, and went on dropping offhand hints about his real work. To Harry Harrison he wrote that his next story "may take a little time as my so-called legitimate employers have this foolish notion as to what I should be spending ergs on." To Pohl he grouched, "This damn plot business is driving me up the wall, Fred, they keep busting up in working hours. I am becoming a candidate for No. 1 Cesspool of Waste of the Taxpayer's Dollars." And to Campbell he worried, "What happens when I get my briefcases mixed?" Since Alli was trying to sound like a man, maybe she took her tone from the men she knew best, Ting and his friends. Or maybe she couldn't resist giving Tiptree the glamorous CIA career she hadn't had. While Alli was feeling like an outsider in science, Tip could be the insider she had never been. Whatever her reasons, the CIA hints turned out to be the perfect red herring. For a long time, it didn't occur to anyone that Tiptree might be hiding anything else.

This didn't quite solve the logistical problem. Pohl understood Tiptree's wish for secrecy, or thought he did, but he didn't see why he and his new writer shouldn't meet. He met with other pseudonymous authors, such as Cordwainer Smith; pseudonyms were routine enough in SF and not generally the sort of thing one kept from editors. He wrote back to say he'd be in Washington for a conference in a month. Why didn't he and Tip have a drink?

What would Alli have thought about this? Surprised? Anxious not to disappoint? Reluctant to let her game become real? Embarrassed to be caught writing science fiction? Unwilling, when it came down to it, to give up being a man? She was apprehensive enough seeing somebody like Arnheim—it had taken her a year to work up the courage for their first meeting. This time she decided to stay in hiding. Tiptree wrote Pohl back telling him he wasn't going to be in D.C. (not quite a lie, from a McLean point of view) and making some general remarks about business trips. The pseudonym had begun to pay off.

"Birth of a Salesman," Tiptree's first published story, appeared in the March 1968 issue of *Analog*. Having a science fiction story published, then and now, meant appearing in a cheap-looking, digest-size magazine, probably edited by another writer who was trying to make a living at this day job. *Analog* and *Galaxy* were the most respectable magazines—they could afford offices in New York—while the low-budget *Amazing* and *Fantastic,* and later also the *Magazine of Fantasy and Science Fiction (F&SF),* were "cottage industry" magazines, published out of their editors' homes. Pohl and Harrison in particular were excited about this promising new writer, not because his stories were so spectacular, but because they always needed new writers. On their rates, no professional could survive.

It was a small and scruffy club that was accepting Tiptree as a member, but he was thrilled. In early 1968 he had three more stories accepted, for a total of six. Fred Pohl took "Help," a sequel to "Mama Come Home" (with a raise to two cents a word), plus the racetrack story Campbell had rejected. And when Campbell wrote accepting a revised version of "Your Haploid Heart," despite doubts about its scientific basis, Tiptree wrote Pohl, "What kind of argument did he expect to get after administering about 100 ccs of pure euphoria? After that first sentence [accepting the story] I would have agreed with him that Planck's Constant was god's hat size."

Alli was delighted—and surprised to find herself taking it all so seriously. To Campbell, in March 1968, Tiptree wrote, "You must have seen many beginners who thought they could take it or leave it alone and then find themselves increasingly hooked on the craft of fiction." Not only was writing addictive, it seemed within reach. Alli began to feel that writing fiction wasn't magic but a craft she could work at and learn.

Tiptree was still writing relatively conventional stories. Almost all writers start out imitating what they've read; it takes self-confidence and experience not to copy what has already been done. Yet right from the beginning, Tiptree had original ideas—and scared people. John Campbell could feel it, and responded to it by questioning his new author's science, first in "Mama," then in "Your Haploid Heart." That story's action-packed plot of political intrigue, kidnapping, and a dramatic rescue by rocket sled can't conceal speculations straight out of Alli's anxiety closet—speculations well beyond Campbell's vision of rational man and the scientist hero.

"Your Haploid Heart" describes a planet inhabited by what seem to be two warring humanoid species, one cruelly oppressing the other. These turn out to be the two reproductive phases of a single species, one sexual, the other genderless. The lumpish, unappealing creatures of the genderless phase appear to be fully human and are petitioning the interplanetary authorities to be classified as such. In their anxiety to be seen as the norm, they have begun repressing and persecuting the small, fragile, wildly sexy creatures that are their own parents and offspring—in a sense, their own sexual selves.

Campbell told Tiptree his premise was implausible: two interdependent forms of the same species had to be symbiotic, not competitive. Reproduction is a matter of instinct, he explained, and "the inherent characteristic of an instinct is that it feels deeply right, satisfying, the only natural and proper way of doing things. [. . .] The emotional tension relationship you've suggested [. . .] simply wouldn't exist. On *their* world, that system of reproduction was the 'only natural way.'"

As Tiptree, Alli argued back that social tension might easily imbalance the system and produce "a drive by the asexual form to control the sexual form, destroy its human identity, and reduce it to a physical breeding-phase—a 'baby-factory' so to speak." Alli knew whereof she spoke, but science fiction was only just starting to question the assumption that familiar human sex roles were "right, satisfying, the only natural and proper way of doing things." So Tiptree added lusty, human, male heroes and squeaked the story in under Campbell's radar. Tiptree was turning out to have subtle advantages. His male name and manly voice made Alli's ideas seem a bit less subversive—maybe even to Alli herself.

The more stories Alli wrote and the more letters she sent, the more real James Tiptree, Jr., became. She had invented Tiptree as a disposable cover, like "Mrs. H. D. Smith." But pseudonyms are not always easy to kill off. Looking back on the start of her career ten years later Alli wrote, "And then it all sold and I was stuck with it. What started as a prank dreamed its way into reality."

But by the time Tiptree's "Birth of a Salesman" appeared in print in March 1968, Dr. Alice B. Sheldon was depressed. She was still working on Arnheim's book, but she wasn't teaching that spring. On March 7 she wrote her old friend that she felt like a "fishbone in the world's throat, going neither up nor down."

She had already confessed to him that she was writing science fiction under an assumed name—just a few stories, in between serious projects—and now she was unusually frank with him about her state of mind. She was having "fits of collapsed time" again, "seeing old people as infants and aged skeletons in every baby-buggy." And how could an unemployed academic contribute to negentropy, or hold back time? She used to believe she was building for the future, and used that hope to keep off the depressions.

But recently the strain on the illusion reached some critical mass, and it went. A friend of mine told me that a couple of Fridays ago she was in National Airport and suddenly it seemed to her everything was in a dark-yellow supersaturated solution which was going at any moment to crystallise and everything would come down as a pile of . . . junk. Mine isn't quite like that. I just have come to see the odds against any improvement as so very great, and the possibilities of disaster as so very large. [. . .] Of ending as a dulled mass, recycling forever on a used-up planet, locked in a state of endless exhausted strife. [. . .] The worst is relatively better, holocaust. Ting says—and he has kindly been questioning generals to relieve my mind—that as things stand, an all-out nuclear war would leave survivors in the Southern Hemisphere, and they would, as he points out, be really better off than Cro-Magnon, and look how well he got on. . . . I guess so. It is just that the reality of a great dark age ahead, of the futility of building before the tidal wave, got to me.

Then she said never mind, it was just the winter weather making her unhappy. Besides, she'd found her own form of "occupational therapy." "My 'illness' has taken the form of writing some more science-fiction stories. They are very mechanical and banal so far but cheerful, but not worth your seeing. [. . .] I am going to finish the series with one about a man who kills EVERYBODY, that will make me feel better."

It may not be a coincidence that this depression coincides with the moment when Alli began to speak and work not for others but for herself. Her story about the "man who kills everybody," "The Last Flight of Dr. Ain," could be read among other things as a story about Alli's complex feelings about what was coming out of her typewriter, and its ending as a fear of what writing might destroy—or maybe a longing for what it might begin.

CHAPTER 25: **DR. JEKYLL AND MR. SPOCK (1968)**

In publicly presenting acceptable façades for private and dangerous visions women writers have long used a wide range of tactics to obscure but not obliterate their most subversive impulses.

—SANDRA M. GILBERT AND SUSAN GUBAR

When I was dissatisfied with my single unfurnished room I took a luxurious flat for him in Piccadilly. When my cheap rug got a hole in it, I ordered him an Aubusson carpet. When I had no money to pay my bus fare I presented him with a Daimler double-six, upholstered in a style of sober magnificence, and when I felt dull I let him drive it.

—DOROTHY L. SAYERS ON LORD PETER WIMSEY

"The Last Flight of Dr. Ain" was Tiptree's real debut, the moment when he found his own voice and his own material. It is very short, just 2,500 words, and like all Tiptree's best stories, it combines exhilarating speed with unsettling shifts of perspective and resonant moral and psychological depths. His fellow writer Robert Silverberg later wrote that while Tiptree's previous work had been unremarkable, "Ain" was something new, a story that, "while of unpretentious scope, opened trapdoor after trapdoor for the reader and ultimately shoved him neatly into a bottomless abyss."

The story is reported in a cold, anonymous voice, with sudden flashes of a more human perspective. "Ain was not identified en route to New York, but a 2:40 jet carried an 'Ames' on the checklist, which was thought to be a misspelling of Ain. It was. The plane had circled for an hour while Ain watched the smoky seaboard monotonously tilt, straighten, and tilt again."

Gradually we discover that the story is a murder mystery, and the victim is us. Dr. Charles Ain ("C. Ain") is a biologist in love with a female Earth. She has long been his secret mistress; now she is dying of pollution and he is determined to save her. As he travels, via New York, Reykjavik, and Glasgow, to a Moscow conference, he deliberately spreads a potent new strain of influenza that within a few weeks will kill him and everyone else on the planet. The story hints that Ain is an instrument of Earth herself, helping her do away with a troublesome species.

As the anonymous voice reports on Ain's movements, we are given glimpses of the people who have seen him: a young mother pushing a pram, a scientist who was once jealous of his grants, colleagues making friendly jokes. Soon all these people will be dead. We also see Ain as a young biologist falling in love with a vision in the woods, contrasted with a cold world of international conferences, airports, investigations. The shifts of tone and perspective disorient the reader, and so does the story's moral ambiguity: we don't know whether the writer thinks killing everybody is a bad or a good thing. This moral disequilibrium is typical of Alli's stories, both as Tiptree and as her second alter ego, Raccoona Sheldon. From the beginning, Tiptree spoke for both an Alli who worried about human cruelty and an Alli who contained "a fount of hot lava: fury, red revenge, indiscriminate murderousness," and believed that "everybody wants to wipe the world out a couple of times a day."

Though "Ain" went through several drafts—as would almost all of Alli's stories—she later said its writing felt strangely natural. For the first time, she experienced the writer's sense of an inner voice, as if someone else were telling the story and all she had to do was write it down. It's tempting to think this has something to do with her change of name. Alli wrote "Ain" in the spring of 1968, after Tiptree had begun selling stories and corresponding with editors. It was the first story she wrote *as* Tiptree. A few years later, Tip wrote that a "big hunk of Tiptree is in 'The Last Flight of Dr. Ain,'" and called the story "screaming from the heart."

Science fiction writers have used pseudonyms for many different reasons. Prolific writers have used them to keep from flooding the market: the magazines used to have "house names," like a restaurant's spare necktie, for when a writer had two stories in the same issue. Collaborative writers have published under shared pseudonyms. Writers with day jobs have hidden behind pseudonyms, like Paul M. A. Linebarger, a State Department expert on China who wrote science fiction as Cordwainer Smith. Women have written under genderless or male names, including C. L. (Catherine) Moore (who also collaborated with her husband, Henry Kuttner, as "Lewis Padgett" and "Lawrence

O'Donnell") and Andre (born Alice) Norton. SF has known hoaxes, such as the black science fiction fan "Carl Brandon," a 1950s invention of white fan, writer, and editor Terry Carr. Like Tiptree, Carl Brandon lived only on paper, but the SF world very much wanted to believe he existed, and mostly did.

A new name can allow a work to be judged on its own merits, or, conversely, add cachet. Certainly Tiptree's mysterious name, not found in any phone book, contributed to his aura. Some people thought he must be Native American. His friend David Gerrold said the name "was elfin. You imagined something magical."

But whether it happens deliberately, casually, by marriage, or as a prank, a change of name can be powerful writing medicine. It can give access to that inner voice that dictates. It can allow a writer room to play, try out new ideas, or explore forbidden emotions. Multiple pseudonyms, like all the characters who spoke for the poet Fernando Pessoa, can give voices to many sides of the self. A writer may speak of being "possessed" by a pseudonym, as Terry Carr told Alli. When he wrote as Carl Brandon, he said, "ideas and phrases would come to me that didn't seem to be part of my own psyche at all."

For a woman, a pseudonym can be a way of getting published at all, or of avoiding public disapproval. "George Eliot," for example, put some distance between the respectable novels and the "fallen woman," Mary Ann Evans, who wrote them. "Currer Bell" put distance between Charlotte Brontë and the words of poet laureate Robert Southey, who told her that writing "cannot be the business of a woman's life." A male name can confer a power and authority, in the eyes of the reader, that a woman might not have as herself.

It can confer that authority even in her own eyes. It is a strategy for getting around self-censorship, for, in Virginia Woolf's phrase, "killing the Angel in the House," for claiming creative potency, for following the imagination into deep waters. The tightrope walk of play, control, power, openness, and confidence that is writing has everything to do with gender, and it's not only a nineteenth-century phenomenon. Throughout the twentieth century, women writers have adopted male or genderless pseudonyms, from H.D. (Hilda Doolittle) and Isak Dinesen (Karen Blixen), both of Mary's generation, to Carson McCullers (two years younger than Alli, born Lula Carson Smith) and Flannery O'Connor (a decade younger than Alli, dropped the first name Mary). Few have taken the deception as far as Alli, but many have used male protagonists: as Dorothy L. Sayers pointed out, Lord Peter Wimsey could have much more fun than she. For a long time Ursula Le Guin (fourteen years younger) wrote about men, and told Alli, "My Daemon just wouldn't produce a woman-hero."

Joanna Russ, who was a generation younger than Tiptree, once told him,

> You know, it's extremely difficult for a woman to become an intellectual, or to have intellectual authority as (some) men do. [. . .] To move into the intellectual community at large you practically have to repudiate your sex [. . .]. It really results in having to tear oneself in two. [. . .] To learn to write at all, I had to begin by thinking of myself as a sort of fake man, something that ended only with feminism.

Alli herself felt more authority as a man: she felt she could write about sex, science, and violence without being second-guessed. She felt the events of her own life—in Africa, as a hunter, in the army, even her crushes on women—taken more seriously. After all, the stuff of literature as it was then defined—exploration, war, fistfights, free love—really was Alli's experience. Yet, as Raccoona Sheldon once wrote, "There is a faint feeling that a roaring adventure story *by a woman* isn't quite as, well, *interesting* as if it was by a man. There's a felt absence of some wildness, some threat. (What does *she* know?)"

Alli didn't feel she was imitating male writing styles. The intensity in her stories was her own. But she did feel freer as a man to take her readers on a roller-coaster ride.

> As Tiptree, I had an unspoken classificatory bond to the world of male action; Tiptree's existence opened to unknown possibilities of power. And, let us pry deeper—to the potential of evil. Evil is the voltage of good; the urge to goodness, without the potential of evil, is trivial. A man impelled to good is significant; a woman pleading for the good is trivial. A great bore. Part of the appeal of Tiptree was that he ranged himself on the side of good *by choice*.

Tiptree didn't have to be a good daughter. And as Tiptree, Alli could get out of her impossible project, writing about what it meant to be a woman.

"Tiptree solved matters by leaving it all out," Alli once wrote, meaning all the experience of growing up a girl. "Tip," this slightly off-kilter representative of manhood, allowed Alli to be, as Charlotte Brontë wished, neither male nor female, but "an author only."

It almost certainly mattered that Tiptree was a man, but he also helped Alli write simply because he was secret. In anonymity, she felt safer to be herself; she could submit her manuscripts the way she used to leave her college papers on the professors' desks "like the elves." Tiptree was a cupboard under the stairs, a nest in the long grass, a secret life. To Alli, one of the most important things about being Tiptree was that his achievements were "pure": she was finally recognized, not for her family or her looks, but for her work alone.

Like the genre itself, the Tiptree name also allowed Alli to play, to take her writing less than seriously. It freed her from the need to be a genius. The stories that came out at first were often silly or scatological, as if Alli were testing her freedom: Can I really say anything? Make bathroom jokes? Tell dirty stories? A year after she wrote "Ain" she brought forth "The Night-Blooming Saurian," in which a group of time-traveling scientists, angling for grant money, connive to reproduce dinosaur tracks in the wrong geological era. For verisimilitude, they must also personally produce a large quantity of fresh "dinosaur" dung. Alli said she wrote it in response to stories that didn't take care of the details. The story acquired a small cult reputation. Some part of Alli must have enjoyed doing something in such poor taste.

Another use of Tiptree was to rein in all the incredible diversity of Alli's ideas, to mediate between the empty page and the overfull mind. Tiptree habitually referred to his writing in the third person: a "big hunk of Tiptree," not Alli, is in "Dr. Ain." Alli used this third-person figure to make choices: confronted with a problem, she could think, "What would Tiptree do here? What would he write?" In a way he gave her the courage to face the failure at the heart of the act of writing—the failure to put the whole truth on the page. As Tiptree she was no longer responsible for a universe of truth, or women's truth, or even her own truth. Responsible only for Tiptree's fiction, she no longer, as Arnheim once put it, had to "juggle with the globe."

Yet Alli's best stories as Tiptree (and Raccoona) are intense, layered, complex: all the different writer selves that Alli once listed for Arnheim are present in one way or another in Tiptree. Years ago, to Dr. K, she had described herself as "six characters in search of an Author." Maybe Tiptree was that author. He was clearly a lie who helped Alli to speak the truth, and a psychic division that helped her put all of herself into her work.

Writing as Tiptree must also have helped Alli get out of the competition with her mother. Alli didn't keep her writing secret from Mary, but did claim never to have told her mother her pseudonym. In a sense, Tiptree was another man, like her two husbands, that Alli could put between herself and Mary. At the same time, Tiptree changed Alli's relationship to her father. With the "Junior" in her name, she took a place in the hierarchy of fathers and sons. When she referred to Herbert as "Tiptree Sr.," she insisted on his responsibility to her. But Tiptree didn't take his father's name. Instead, Alli renamed her father after her writing self.

"The Last Flight of Dr. Ain" ran in *Galaxy* in March 1969. A year later it reached the final ballot for the Nebula science fiction awards, alongside stories by Theodore Sturgeon, Larry Niven, Harlan Ellison, and Robert Silverberg. It established Tiptree as a writer to watch, with depth, worldliness, and narrative style. His voice seemed new and exciting—maybe, as Harry Harrison speculated with hindsight, because it was a woman's voice. Yet Tiptree had other qualities that were then unusual in SF: a degree in psychology rather than the "hard sciences," age, sophistication.

After "Ain," Alli had a burst of writing energy: in 1968 and 1969, Tiptree submitted thirteen stories. For fun, he tried writing space opera. And he experimented with some comic fragments that were rejected as too trivial or too obscure. Tiptree's later pen-friend Barry N. Malzberg, who briefly edited *Amazing* and *Fantastic,* returned one with the comment, "I'm just not sure that I get this and not entirely convinced that it's my fault."

Tip's occasional serious "message" stories yielded mixed results. An early attempt at revenge on the GW psychology department is "I Have Come Upon This Place by Lost Ways," about a young, idealistic scientist who horrifies his elders by wanting to explore a new planet instead of taking readings from the ship. This talky, moralistic story ends on Tiptree's refusal to let his hero win. He does make a new discovery—a gateway, a door leading Out—but dies before he can pass through. Real scientists, Tip argued, never get to go through—just as real geniuses perish unknown. "They just [. . .] look and call and point unheeded, and die looking on what they've found."

In "The Snows Are Melted, the Snows Are Gone" the message is planted in a narrative compressed to almost pure action. Gradually we discover that the main characters, a girl with no arms and an intelligent wolf, are part of a small group of apocalypse survivors, who are peaceful and sensitive but suffer from physical mutations. Coming across another colony of survivors who are dim brutes but physically sound, they kidnap one of their men for breeding purposes. But will his healthy Y chromosome bring back with it the old human afflictions of aggression and war? "Snows" is an almost comic-book treatment of an old worry of Alli's: the problem of how to achieve, or breed, a peaceful human race. It also plays subtly with genre convention. The heroes are physically weak, while the strong, purposeful male (who is captured while taking his morning pee) is revealed to be a grunting barbarian as likely to destroy the colony as save it.

Harry Harrison returned "Lost Ways" for rewrites and gave useful advice: cut down the talk, delete unnecessary characters, make the symbolism clearer. "Use similes, like Graham Greene [. . .]. Spell out some of the abstraction in not-too-abstract terms." In other letters, he pushed him to take his prose style seriously. "Let's have stars do anything but 'wheel,' too cliché," he suggested, and "I think 'big shimmery' on page 26 too purple. Or girl-writer term or something. Substitute?"

Harrison left *Amazing* and *Fantastic* in the summer of 1968, but started buying stories for an original anthology series called *Nova*. (Original anthologies were an important outlet for SF. They gave writers more freedom than the magazines, which were aimed at a teenage readership, and were literally more durable.) He also edited a series of "year's best" anthologies that reprinted several Tiptree stories. His patience with this new writer earned him Alli's gratitude and loyalty, and in the beginning she sent almost all her stories first to him or Fred Pohl.

Pohl was also very sympathetic to Tiptree's voice, which impressed him as "urbane and cosmopolitan." Pohl assumed Tiptree was a younger writer. In fact Pohl was in his late forties, and Alli fifty-three, but Tiptree was new, and Pohl had been working in SF, as a writer, editor, and agent, for thirty years. He suggested rewrites, gave career advice, and tried to steer Tiptree toward better-paying markets. After he accepted "Ain" for *Galaxy,* he sent the story on to *Playboy,* which was buying science fiction; he wanted to see Tiptree get the money and exposure. *Playboy* didn't take it, but Alli found out about the gesture and was moved. In return, Tiptree acted like the promising young writer everyone thought he was. He wrote burbly letters explaining his stories, complimenting Pohl and Harrison on their work, and going on about how thrilled he was to be writing science fiction.

Though he was now a published author, Tiptree still led only a minimal existence, as a name on title pages and a return address on stories. The accompanying notes were getting slightly more personal—Alli could never help trying to charm—but it was all still business. And while Tiptree was typing up his stories late at night, Alli was still in limbo. She worked on Arnheim's book. She worried about Ting, who had gout, and about Mary, now facing double cataract surgery. She went to Chicago often. In July 1968, Tiptree muttered to Barry Malzberg that he was doing his writing "in spare time, airports, conference waiting-rooms, etc."

But by then Alli was hardly even going to conferences. She had just tried to attend a psychology seminar at GW, but found the department parking lot reserved for official attendees. When she couldn't find parking on the street, she drove back to McLean. Disappointed, she wrote Dick Walk, "Confirms my view there is no place for outsider in Organised Science." She signed her postcard, "Cordially, Outsider (A.)"

She worried about politics. Martin Luther King, Jr., was assassinated in April 1968. The riots that followed filled Washington with smoke, and sandbags were placed around the Capitol. Presidential candidate Robert Kennedy was shot in June, and Tiptree wrote Pohl, "Like everyone else who spent the weekend scrubbing off bumper stickers, can't think of much small talk." In August Rudolf Arnheim wrote from his summer house in Michigan, "A Japanese friend gave me a tiny radio, the size of a Liederkranz cheese, out of which sounds, raspily, the nomination of Nixon, the occupation of Prague, and the announcement of church bargain sales in Sturgeon Bay, Wisc." Alli responded with a gloomy summary of the Chicago Democratic convention: the tear gas, the police brutality, the sad inadequacy of Hubert Humphrey as a candidate.

On September 1, instead of going to the American Psychological Association convention or the Lodge, the Sheldons flew to Scotland for a three-week fishing vacation in the Outer Hebrides. The trip was organized by one of Ting's boyhood friends, who had arranged for a group to stay at Amhuinnsuidhe, a nineteenth-century castle on the island of Lewis and Harris. Leaving behind their tent and duffel bags, the Sheldons boarded a BOAC jet in style: Ting in an orange turtleneck, Alli in a brown leather sheath dress and brown silk stockings. While Ting fished, Alli walked in the hills, swam naked in deserted lochs, longed for American cigarettes (having bought and smoked the last carton of menthols on the island), and admired the otherworldly Pictish standing stones at Callanish.

In Chicago, Mary had her eye surgery, and Alli made two long tapes for her mother, describing the vacation in detail. In an answering tape, Mary said, "I'm grateful to have such good friends but I hate to bother them so very, very much. It's wonderful that you'll be home so soon."

To Fred Pohl, Tip said only that the Outer Hebrides had been "strong on mana, weak on fish." Pohl assumed this "fishing trip" was some kind of cover but still used it as a gossip item in *Galaxy:* "James Tiptree, Jr., one of our more peripatetic writers, is just back from a fishing sojourn amid the primeval rocky lochs of Northern Scotland. Saw no Loch Ness monsters, he reports: also no fish."

Around this time, Alli fell under the spell of a new story about exploration. She started watching *Star Trek,* and saw in the crew of the *Enterprise* her childhood traveling party, crossing the starry unknown. Kirk was the fatherly leader of the expedition, while Mr. Spock, with his pointy ears and rational reserve, fit Alli's dream of the unattainable alien. To her surprise, Alli developed a violent crush on Spock. As Tiptree, she wrote a long fan letter to Leonard Nimoy explaining Spock's appeal. Since humans were exogamous, tending to marry outside their own group, and xenophilic, or naturally attracted to foreignness, a crush on Spock was an instinctive and almost biological reaction to his alien appearance: "the touching shoulder-blades, the tremor, the shadowed and infinitely effective squint." To Harry Harrison, Tiptree sighed, "If Spock had a sister—"

One of Alli's responses to the show was to write a treatment for a *Star Trek* episode. If Tiptree could write stories, then why not TV scripts? But the show's producers returned "Meet Me at Infinity" with a form letter saying they didn't read unagented material. And when Tip appealed to Pohl for help, just before he left for the Outer Hebrides, Pohl asked,

> Are you sure you want to do this? Writing a script for any TV show almost certainly involves spending a month or two in LA, eating up your profits on motels and tacos. Almost impossible, especially for a first-timer, to do it from the east. [. . .]
>
> I almost put my name on it as collaborator and mailed it off to Roddenberry; I expect he would read it that way. But I could foresee complications and heartburn, even if you approved of so cavalier a gambit.

Tiptree thanked Pohl and backed off: Alli put the script aside. But she was still strongly under the influence, and immediately wrote two more stories on *Star Trek* themes.

One, "Happiness Is a Warm Spaceship," is an affectionate parody. A freshly commissioned space lieutenant, the son of an admiral, is assigned to a patrol ship as its only human. His adventures with the nutty but lovable aliens of his crew show parallels to Tiptree's writing career: the son escapes his famous parent, is accepted on his own merits, throws in his lot with the oddballs and misfits, and decides he doesn't want to go home.

Pohl picked up "Happiness" for the lower-end *If,* making up for his sense that it wasn't much of a story by offering Tiptree as little money as possible ($250 for 18,000 words). For a while Alli thought of turning it into a comic novel, but lost interest as she began taking her work more seriously. At least the story added to Tiptree's reputation as a writer who could handle hardware. A new acquaintance, Anne McCaffrey, asked Tip, "Where in hell did you extrapolate all that marvelous gunboat-type equipment? That's one of my main problems. I can't make that kind of technology *sound* plausible." Alli hadn't written all those reports on aircraft factories and oil refineries for nothing.

Tiptree's other, stronger, more personal response to *Star Trek* that fall was called "Beam Us Home." In a few compressed, skillful scenes, it describes a boy deeply alienated from the violence that he sees all around him, and that everyone else seems to consider normal. He comes to believe he is not native to Earth, but has been stationed here as a researcher. "All I had to do was sort of fit in and observe. Like a report. One day they would come back and haul me up in that beam thing [. . .]. And there I'd be back in real time where human beings were." In the end, just before it's too late, the future does beam him home. Like "Happiness," this story concludes with the most rare of Tiptree plot devices: a happy ending.

Tiptree didn't end with "Ain," as Alli had intended. But Alli still wondered what exactly it was that she was doing and how far she was willing to take it. At the newsstand in the Glasgow airport, she had been startled to find a stack of *Fantastic* with her story "Fault" in them and Tiptree's name on the cover. Tip wrote Pohl that he had had a "Jekyll/Hyde" reaction:

> As Dr. Hyde, I started to kick the thing under the counter—and found Jekyll nudging the stack into a better display position, grinning and panting. What goes on?? It sure ain't the minuscule fame, nor the micro-money; it's only partly the magic of print. It's something about the old, old story-teller's urge, isn't it? The Ancient Mariner syndrome. [. . .]
>
> But agents scare me, Hollywood terrifies me, my own urge to think up plots horrifies me—and what is laughingly known as my work here has a couple of fangs in my collar too . . . Reason yells stop, something else hisses cop-out . . . See the clandestine writer, colour him green.

Oddly, Tiptree mixed up the names of the respectable Dr. Jekyll and the hidden Mr. Hyde, as if even Alli weren't sure whether Tiptree was her bad or her good side.

But by the end of 1968 Tiptree had decided to stick with science fiction—at least enough to pay five dollars to join the Science Fiction Writers of America. This gossipy, contentious professional guild was founded in 1965 to represent writers' interests. Among other things, its members vote on the Nebula science fiction awards. Tip was proud of his membership, and later had postcards printed and an address stamp made that read "James Tiptree, Jr., SFWA."

Meanwhile, Alli spent the last days of 1968 glued to the TV and radio, as the three astronauts of Apollo 8 left Earth's orbit to circle the moon. Apollo 8 was in a way an even greater mission of discovery than the Apollo 11 moon landing: these were the first humans to leave the shelter of Earth, the first to see the planet whole. Alli watched "the perilous lumbering lift of that appalling rocket" and saw it as the *Niña, Pinta,* and *Santa Maria* of its time. She watched footage of the crew chasing a toothbrush in zero G. She saw their pictures of the Earth as a "big blue marble." She watched on Christmas Eve as Houston broadcast Apollo 8's pictures of the moon, while the crew members took turns reading from Genesis. She felt she would have given her life to be on that voyage out from Earth.

Everyone's greatest fear was that the capsule would fail to kick out of its lunar orbit and the men would be trapped there, in full radio contact, until their oxygen ran out. Alli imagined how devastating it would be "if we had to watch them die for two weeks, whirling forever around the moon. [. . .] But it's not intolerable, or even really *wrong*—when you think of the skulls lying along man's routes of discovery—the graves we camped beside in the Congo, the bones in the Donner Pass."

The engines didn't fail. By the end of 1968, the first lunar explorers had come home.

CHAPTER 26: FIRST CONTACT (1969)

There does seem to be a surprise when people just speak honestly. [. . .] It always startles me because I can't imagine what value non-communicating communication has. Of course you know that my tell-all is temporarily chopped at the one limit that leads directly to my mundane persona, but since I regard that persona as kind of an insignificant accident, it isn't much of a limit. Anything real, just ask me—and jump back before the flood. I suspect most of us are just like that, why else are we in the word game? To communicate . . .

— JAMES TIPTREE, JR., TO JEFFREY D. SMITH

By March 1969, when "The Last Flight of Dr. Ain" appeared in *Galaxy,* Tiptree had been selling stories for over a year, and the close-knit world of science fiction writers and readers was starting to take notice. When "Ain" came out, Tip's friend and later agent Virginia Kidd recalled, "*everybody* noticed that story and was impressed by it." Damon Knight wrote asking Tiptree to submit to *Orbit,* his influential series of original anthologies. In an interview in the May issue of *If,* Lester del Rey singled out Tiptree as a new writer to watch.

Tiptree's new colleagues were curious about him. Knight invited Tiptree to another of his projects, the Milford Science Fiction Writers' Conference. In January, Harry Harrison suggested Tip come up to New York for a few days and socialize. "You can meet the writers, talk things up, go to a couple of parties, meet some people (editors) for lunch, get the feel and the swing and the feedback of your peer group."

Alli let Tiptree decline on grounds of secret business.

N.Y. sounds great, if Ground Control will kindly press the right buttons. They may not. Did I mention that writing here is done in time filched from what are laughingly known as my legitimate responsibilities? (That's why you keep getting mss typed at 3 AM.) No one here

knows me as a writer, and for reasons I hope you won't make too close a
guess at for awhile, it's got to stay that way.

But despite himself, Tiptree was getting more and more involved, not
just with writing, but with the intense, gregarious, garrulous world of science fiction.

Science fiction is interactive. Writers (and their fans) meet at conventions,
argue all day, drink together all night, and influence each other in a way unlike any other literature. They talk about ideas, stories, politics, and recipes.
They work in and from a rich soup of letters, gossip, affairs, rivalries, and
friendships. They draw from a common pool of images and imaginary settings, using spaceships, androids, and aliens to build the genre that Tiptree
called a "towering, glittering mad lay cathedral."

Science fiction is inclusive. It is read by boys with faces full of acne and
brains full of cyberspace, girls with stringy hair and fierce imaginations, awkward people, brilliant people in search of like minds. Damon Knight, in his
history of the 1930s fan and writer group the Futurians—a shadow bohemia
living in the same New York cold-water walk-ups and burning to tell a different kind of story—concludes that fans are "more intelligent and articulate
than the general population, and somewhat less mature." As in many subcul-
tures, fans reinvent themselves. Cy Chauvin, who wrote for a fanzine called
Gorbett that Tiptree subscribed to in the early 1970s, recalled that its mimeographed pages were full of his friends' in-group fantasy and masquerade. "We
were all part of that secret life then, fandom, that Tiptree had stumbled on,
and really if she took on an invented persona, she was just behaving like everyone else."

Alli liked this world but wasn't quite sure what to do with it. Part of her kept
safely above the gossip and politics and contemplated science fiction from a superior height. Tiptree claimed no attachment to his work—"I came to my own
mediocre efforts so late that my ego isn't invested"—and often expressed a condescending affection for "the world of Camelot-people this attempt at writing
seems to have landed me in." Barry Malzberg recalled being put off by the way
Tiptree behaved "as if it were a pretend life and we were all pretend people."

It helped that writing was a game for Alli financially. She liked being paid,
but didn't mind being paid pennies a word or waiting months for a check.

(Tiptree was also famous for not cashing the checks he did get, to the despair of editors trying to balance their books.) At first she spent Tiptree's minuscule earnings on "his" expenses: magazine and fanzine subscriptions, SFWA dues, typewriter repairs, and post office box rent. Later, when Tip's funds started to add up, she sometimes used them to buy jewelry or other presents for herself, and joked about "money for jam."

Tiptree was friendly, of course, and flirtatious with women. When he was grateful to Judy-Lynn Benjamin, Pohl's assistant at *Galaxy*, he wrote, "It's probably lèse-majesté to tell a Managing Editor she's a superdoll. You are, though." When he paid his SFWA dues he enclosed complimentary letters to Anne McCaffrey, that year's secretary.

With young people he played one of Alli's favorite roles, the wise older friend. When Tip was still thinking of submitting his *Star Trek* script, Harrison put him in touch with David Gerrold, an enthusiastic twenty-four-year-old in Los Angeles who had broken into SF with the famous *Star Trek* script "The Trouble with Tribbles." Gerrold asked Tiptree to contribute to an anthology he was editing, and the two writers began a sociable correspondence. To this non-threatening youth Tiptree could make jokes, free-associate, use dirty words. On what could and couldn't be said in SF, with its teenage readership, he commented, "Yesterday the *Washington Post* had a main editorial about how it was more or less okay to print mother-fucker on the front page. (They used * * *, but so what?)" It's hard to imagine Alli writing that to Max Lerner or to Arnheim.

Another part of Alli took science fiction much more seriously. When she wasn't feeling embarrassed about her science fiction habit, Alli was thrilled to be writing it, deeply grateful to her first editors, and very much in awe of other writers.

One way Alli coped with this mix of admiration, envy, pride, and fear was by generously giving out compliments. Robert Silverberg complained about Tiptree's habit of "professing [. . .] high regard for colleagues not fit to change his typewriter ribbons." Sometimes the compliments came from a feeling of relief, after years of reading academese, bureaucratese, and bad fiction. Alli once wrote Joanna Russ, "You are like me—when something strikes you right you are so happy to be *able* to like it that you spill all over generosity." Sometimes they were a deliberate seduction of a writer Tiptree admired. Tip's fan letters were so charming they made Barry Malzberg think for a while that this new writer was a plant. "The best way to get to writers at a distance is to write them letters saying nice things about their work. I thought this might be the CIA setting up a persona to investigate a lot of scruffy people who didn't fit in."

The compliments always deflected judgment from Tiptree's own work. To Damon Knight, who also complained about Tiptree's intemperate praise, he wrote, "Damon, if I'm going to be clear-eyed enough really to judge the sheep from the goats, I can't write. *Because I am one of the goats.*" Despite her claim that her ego wasn't involved, Alli was almost certainly terrified of writing. She was afraid of having talent, not having talent, being seen, not being seen, being the writer and not her daughter, having her game turn out real.

At the same time, Alli tried to connect with writers whose work she respected. SF might be a game, but she hadn't lost her longing for an audience, or her desire to be liked by people she admired. Almost all Tiptree's closest correspondences, when they didn't begin with an editorial relationship, started with a fan letter to another writer.

At first, Alli also used Tiptree to write to mainstream figures. He wrote to Tom Wolfe praising *The Pump House Gang,* Anthony Burgess, Italo Calvino. Wolfe and Calvino wrote back, and Calvino asked to see Tiptree's stories. But Tip didn't answer their letters. Instead, he got himself into a short, intense, messy correspondence with Philip K. Dick.

In 1969, Dick was forty years old and at the height of his influential, controversial career. Using the conventions of science fiction, he was asking questions as basic as: What is real? What is human? His protagonists are ordinary men who struggle to stay sane as reality shifts underneath them. Like Alli, he believed that empathy was a defining quality of humanity.

Alli read a lot of Dick and tried to learn from him. She admired the way he bared his soul, explored emotion, yet never lost a gentle sympathy for his characters and creations. (He was less sympathetic toward women, but in those days most women readers were less attuned to misogynistic portrayals. Well, Alli would have thought, some women are like that.) Besides, the raw energy of his writing lit up her own imagination like a switchboard. After reading anything by Dick, Tiptree told Jeff Smith, "I start walking round and round it talking to myself and bashing my head and spitting on my typewriter while this incredible flood of invention and alternate-reality grinkles glittering and oozing like radioactive Ajax lava playing Bach and smelling of hash and gear-oil out all over the floor."

In January 1969, Alli stayed up half the night reading a 1966 Dick novel, *Now Wait for Last Year,* about a man whose wife becomes addicted to a time-traveling drug. The next day, Tip wrote Dick a fan letter. Like Alli with Arnheim, Tiptree came bearing the gift of detailed, intelligent praise. But Tiptree's tone with Dick was much more awkward, as if he admired him so much he didn't know how to talk to him—and as if Alli hoped that a manly tone would help.

Tiptree complimented Dick on the book's portrait of a charismatic dictator named Molinari, and interpreted Kathy, the bossy wife, as an echo of the same character:

> That jolt when hero meets Molinari was just right. [. . .] I've watched you trying (I think) to make believable human great men, and these really hit it. It's so damn *hard.* [. . .] I've met a few such, the worst luckily on opposite side of bars; you've *got* it. And coupled with the Kathy embroidery on the theme, it really does it. Brrr. [. . .]
>
> And the tremendous richness of plots, the stuff thrown away that would serve us lesser mortals for a week's menu. [. . .] The endless jerkiness of people worrying about their own stuff, each mind its own ant-castle. [. . .] Of course the bit that really sticks—that damaged cart hiding in the zinc bucket. *That*'ll be around in my head until I get a new brain!
>
> You know, thinking it over, it all raises the problem of how much human reality the sci-fi fabric will bear, doesn't it? (E.g. the what-do-I-do-with-a-mad-wife theme.) I think you've brought it off perhaps by keeping it low-pitch. But since I started writing the stuff meself I sometimes wonder. Especially since I don't have the Magic Electric Fireworks fountain you must have in your head!

Tiptree added a PS: "This doesn't call for answering—am just gratifying own desire to vent admiration."

Dick answered anyway, thanking his new fan for the feedback.

> I would judge from your comments that you read the novel in a very cre-
> ative way—I don't mean that you saw things that weren't there—I just
> mean that yours is not a passive kind of reading but an active one which,
> I strongly guess, implies creative writing ability on your part, in terms of
> writing your own novels and stories. You are quite perceptive . . . a little
> *too* perceptive and analytical than a mere reader.
>
> Thank you again, and I would enjoy hearing from you again, not
> necessarily on the topic of my writing (which would be okay, of course)
> but perhaps on general literary subjects.

But having a writer he admired invite him into a friendship must have
been terrifying, because Tiptree quickly pushed Dick back up onto his
pedestal. He wrote back babbling about how thrilled he was to get a letter
"from a real live writer whose works I've been admiring and chewing my lip
over for years." At the same time he made fun of himself for getting so excited.

> Funny about that thrill; finally realised what it comes from: Subcon-
> sciously, a conviction that the really good writers aren't human. That the
> works are messages in bottles from the writer's world. You know? So
> when Sturgeon or Bunch or somebody turns out to be an actual Terran
> primate using—of all things—the U.S. mails, with a zip number, for
> god's sake—I get about the same kick the Ozma people would if one of
> the pulsars began to rap out binary Yeats.

To be told that you are not human is disconcerting, however—especially
when you are suffering from such earthly troubles as writer's block, a dissolv-
ing fourth marriage, and a violent amphetamine addiction. It took several
months and several more fan letters from Tiptree before Dick finally responded again, in September, with thanks and a request for an explanation.
"As far as your remarks go on my general work, I am humble and a little net-
tled. How does an author reply to such compliments? Do you really mean
them?"

Tiptree answered again that he wasn't talking to a fellow writer, just responding to a work of fiction. "To me the work is objective, in a sense detached from its author—it's *out there*— and there it sits, oozing or glittering or exploding, or whatever. [. . .] Frankly, all I really expect you to say is yeah, I thought it was pretty good too!"

Eventually, after about a year of letters from Tiptree, Dick reached out and grabbed his fan by the lapels. Although Tiptree had mentioned his own writing, Dick apparently didn't take him seriously until he was sent copies of the stories that had been nominated for that year's Nebula Awards. One was "Dr. Ain." Dick wrote to say it was "damn good" and would Tiptree be interested in collaborating on a novel?

Dick had been looking for a collaborator to help him break his writer's block. But whatever Alli wanted from an exchange with Dick, it wasn't anything as intimate as this. Tiptree bolted. "You want to lose a fan from heart failure?" he responded. "The idea couldn't be greater but the glaring question is, what in hell could Tiptree contribute to Dick's processes?"

Later, in a letter to another friend, Tiptree said that Dick had once made "an offer of collaboration to a writer far inferior to himself" and that this writer, metaphorically speaking,

> got down, banged his head on the floor, and said, "Lord, you've scared the pants off me, and maybe in about a thousand years when I know how to write I'll come back and offer to erase a few commas with you or something. But meanwhile please be assured that I consider this to be some kind of an honor that descended on me in a dream and is not to be taken seriously."

Alli couldn't have collaborated with Dick or anyone, and was also, humbly, excusing herself. But after this the correspondence dwindled, unable to bear the weight of so much admiration. Alli's deference, which worked so nicely on Arnheim and Lerner, didn't play as well when she was writing as a man.

To people who didn't scare him so much, Tiptree was able to talk more honestly about his life and troubles—more and more, his troubles with his mother. In early 1969 he began corresponding with Virginia Kidd, a longtime

SF fan who had just started an influential literary agency. After "Ain" appeared, she wrote complimenting him on the story and fishing for a new client. Tiptree didn't get the hint, but he did write back. In April he dashed off a postcard on the way to Chicago: "Absence indefinite, Big White Father's business now complicated by emergency with Aged Parent. (This is no country for old men—)"

In June he described to Kidd the "heart-wringing" scene of Mary's decline.

> My returns to McLean and desk are beginning to resemble the awakenings of Dr. Hyde after a bout as Jekyll. You know, the dawn light on shambles, the piles of reproachful corpses, agonised messages from friends in mortal offense, vague sounds of police without . . .
>
> So he tries to explain, I have this problem, see—
>
> I have a problem known as a catastrophe-prone ma, Virginia. And let me go on record, I never adequately realised what the girls in a family do. "Sis is taking care of ma." What a comfort. Well, I've no sis, nor living brothers neither, and the old lady—who is fiercely compos mentis much of the time—rejects any attempt to move her out of a mad midwestern eyrie—and how you get nurses, ambulances, doctors, drugs, more nurses, more ambulances, more everything from orthopedic beds to adequate protein at long distance is What I'm Learning. [. . .] Nothing my normally elliptical style can cope with.

This time when Tiptree mixes up Jekyll and Hyde, the writer is the better self. And Kidd fell in love with this kind older man who cared about his mother. Kidd's marriage to writer James Blish had ended a few years earlier. Tiptree appeared to be a bachelor. She hinted he would be welcome to visit her in Pennsylvania, and recalled, "I fantasized about meeting this man and being swept away by him." But here, too, alas, "hints did no good whatsoever."

Alli's own tangled feelings about writing and her exchanges with writers—not to mention her surprising crush on Mr. Spock—led her to think about fame and desire. In the spring of 1969 Alli began work on a story about "that fantastic misdirected adoration one is sometimes struck by for actors or public figures." She was also thinking about "The Little Mermaid," with its moral about the price of dreams, and Damon Knight's SF classic "The Handler."

The result was a Jekyll-and-Hyde story about a female monster: "The Girl Who Was Plugged In."

The story's heroine, a monstrously ugly seventeen-year-old named Philadelphia Burke, is offered a Faustian bargain. If she will allow herself to be wired with electrodes and locked naked in a cabinet, hidden from the world, she will be taught to animate the artificially grown body of a perfect girl. She accepts, and becomes Delphi, a ravishing, yellow-haired, elfin teenage movie star. Among other things, the story seems to echo the uneasy relationship between Alli and Tiptree: the inadequate private self operates the attractive persona by remote, and division is the precondition of a complete self.

Another ambitious story Alli wrote in late 1968 she called "I'm Too Big but I Love to Play." It describes an alien, little more than a vast, disembodied energy force, that tries to understand human experience by taking human forms and participating in human encounters. Because the being is so large, primitive, and unstable, it can't sustain its imitations of people, but at moments of tension detonates violently into its original form. The monstrous, amorphous real self can communicate only if it takes on a presentable exterior—an inherently volatile situation that is always threatening to explode.

Tiptree implied to all his correspondents he was working hard in the spring of 1969. Yet there's no record of Alli teaching at either American or George Washington. Tiptree sent stories around: "I'm Too Big" was rejected by *Galaxy/If*, *F&SF*, and *Playboy* before it finally sold to *Amazing*, and "The Girl Who Was Plugged In" was rejected so many times that Tiptree temporarily shelved it. (Damon Knight said the ending didn't work; Ed Ferman at *F&SF* said it didn't "jell.") Meanwhile, Alli lived an everyday life that she kept out of Tiptree's letters: letting in the roofers, finding paste wax for the cleaning lady, fertilizing the lettuce, buying a dress at Lord & Taylor to go see Mary in.

Ting was getting ready to retire that year, and was looking forward to more travel and fishing. His life, too, was changing. His father had died in 1960, his mother in 1967. When his sister Helen, who had never married, went to their home in Biarritz to settle the estate, she suffered a heart attack and died too. Ting missed his mother, and his sister even more. But he came into some money, about two hundred thousand dollars, and he and Alli were better off than they had been. In 1969, along with the usual vacation in Canada, they made a short spring trip to Mexico, spending a couple of weeks in a beach house in a remote hamlet on the Yucatán Peninsula. The fishing was good, and they made plans to return the next year.

It wasn't until the fall that Tiptree again had Alli's attention. By then he had turned up one very enthusiastic audience: the editorial and writerly phenomenon that was Harlan Ellison.

Ellison was thirty-five, good-looking, cocky, combative, magnetic. He lived in Los Angeles, where he made a good living (rare among SF writers) writing for TV series such as *Route 66, The Outer Limits,* and *Star Trek.* He spoke out against the Vietnam War and in support of civil rights and (later) the Equal Rights Amendment. He was publishing some of his best fiction, stories such as "A Boy and His Dog" and "I Have No Mouth, and I Must Scream." He encouraged younger writers, male and female, tried to make science fiction look sexy, and was in the midst of editing *Again, Dangerous Visions,* his second anthology of "New Wave" science fiction.

"New Wave" is a controversial term in SF. It was coined, some argue, purely for promotional purposes, on a par with Ellison pronouncements such as "speculative fiction is hotter than sliced bread." Yet it did convey the sense that there was a new energy in the genre, that more could be said better, that much "contemporary" literature was already old-fashioned, whereas science fiction had its finger on the pulse of the times. Ellison was looking for stories with stylish writing, thematic sophistication, and daring subject matter.

He had put out a call for submissions, and Tiptree had sent in two of his fragments, including a revised version of the old parody "Please Don't Play with the Time Machine." Months later, in July 1969, he received a rejection letter on dove-gray, gold-embossed stationery:

> Dear Mr. Tiptree:
>
> Your credentials precede you. The respect and admiration in which you are held by other writers and at least two editors who have mentioned you as "brilliant," allows me to return these stories with-

out qualm. You are considered—even for a newly published author—quite a comer. And as such, I don't have any sadness about sending back what are obviously two quickies cobbled-up late at night. You can do better than this, and I expect you to do so.

Ellison promised to hold the book open until Tiptree sent work worthy of his true talent. When Tip wrote back to say he'd try, Ellison repeated his instructions to

> bust your ass [. . .]—brilliant new idea, incisive characterization, original attack of style, boggling ending. [. . .] A story on which to build a first-rank reputation. The best story you ever wrote. Don't worry about time. I'm patient. (You see what undeniable talent buys you, friend?) Don't disappoint either of us.

Sensing that Tip needed more confidence, Ellison gave him some. His verve and theatricality reassured Alli that this was still a game. And he didn't need any pushing to stay on his pedestal. On the Sheldons' vacation, at a lake in northern Ontario, Alli sat down, thought about what it might take to blow Ellison's mind, and wrote a story called "The Milk of Paradise."

"The Milk of Paradise" describes a young human who was raised by an alien race. He has been reprogrammed to fit into a human world, but they haven't been able to erase his longing for his first home, the planet Paradise, with its dim ruby sun, its towers, its sweet music.

The story opens with a blast of sexual revulsion:

> She was flowing hot and naked and she straddled his belly in the cuddle-cube and fed him her hard little tits. And he convulsed up under her and then was headlong on the waster, vomiting.
>
> "Timor! Timor!"
>
> It was not his name. [. . .]
>
> "I'm sorry. [. . .] It's no good. It's never any good."
>
> "But you're Human, Timor. Like me. Aren't you glad you were rescued?"

Timor is tricked into going back to Paradise, only to discover that the towers of his memory are mud huts, their inhabitants "gray rotten little things [. . .] humping towards [him] out of the walls." Yet he realizes, as his artificial conditioning falls away, that this hideous place *is* his paradise, his home, ugly, maybe deadly, but his, and he will stay.

From beginning to end, the story startles, disorients, and turns the tables on the reader. SF critic Steve Brown recalled that when it appeared in *Again, Dangerous Visions* in 1972, "I read the first two sentences and felt like I'd fallen off a high tower. [. . .] I had read many stories that were far more sexual and/or 'shocking' than anything Tiptree wrote. But it was the contrast. The intense burst of sexuality immediately coupled with violent physical rejection. These combined to instill a profound sense of alienation before the story was underway. Alienation, and a distrust—the story's ground had become shifting sand, and I picked my way through uncertainly and in doubt of everything, which is exactly how she wanted me to feel. That story was a deep and unsettling experience that still resonates to this day."

Alli often thought of herself as writing purely abstract fiction, a look at a social problem or an exercise in impressing an editor. But "The Milk of Paradise" doesn't feel like it is coolly under the writer's control. It is too upsetting not to be personal. It delivers the effect Alli had once aspired to in painting: the "pure, complicated nausea" of Max Beckmann, or Orozco's blood and guts and righteous anger.

In September 1969, just after Tiptree had tried to persuade Dick that praise had nothing to do with its recipient, that the work was "out there [. . .] oozing or glittering or exploding, or whatever," he received a gold-embossed letter of acceptance from Harlan Ellison.

Dear Jim:

> Dear mother of God!
> I just tried to call you from LA. You aren't listed. Now listen to me, man, because this is where the bullshit stops:
> You are the single most important new writer in science fiction today. Nobody *touches* you! Not me, not Delany, not Blish, not Budrys, not Disch, not Dick . . . none of us. [. . .]

["Milk"] is so good there are no superlatives. It goes beyond. It's absolutely new, absolutely fresh, unkind to everything that went before because it is its own *rara avis*. You are another new wave. If each new wave is one man—as I contend—then you are what's coming bursting breaking cresting now, and I am so fucking destructed by what you've allowed me to read, I don't know how to say thank you.

What he did offer was a place of honor in *Again, Dangerous Visions,* as the last story—and two and a half cents a word, or $75, plus royalties.

"I've learnt to take Maalox before I open those gold things but this time it should have been digitalis," Tip wrote back. "They found me six feet up in the curtains trembling, my large tarsier eyes vacant and crossed."

Then Ellison wrote again, demanding "complete autobiographical and bibliographical information on you" plus an afterword to "establish that rare writer-to-reader liaison." Tiptree tried to wriggle out: "You've got it wrong, it's the readers who convince the writer of his own reality." Ellison answered, "I will, of course, respect your feelings in the matter, but I ask that you seriously reconsider. In other words, Tiptree, don't be a goddamn trouble maker."

A few weeks later Harry Harrison, who had picked up "The Snows Are Melted" for a reprint anthology, also asked for a biography. "School, army if there was, jobs, training, hobbies [. . .]. Just blurt it out. Reveal all." For Harrison, Tip coughed up the first few bits of real data, soon to become part of the Tiptree myth:

World War II, yeah, mostly locked in a Pentagon sub-basement. [. . .] Birth, yeah, flat-r midwestern and north Wisconsin lakes, plus a bit of trekking around to odd spots, am still trying to figure out what war was going on in Shanghai when I was there age 10, and I can say bring me a small teaspoon in Swahili if anybody's interested.

To Ellison, he wrote a long explanation of why a story has nothing to do with the everyday business of its writer, which Ellison, pragmatically, used as the story's afterword.

Then David Gerrold came looking for Tiptree—and showed up on Alli's doorstep.

Tip had promised his young friend he'd buy him a drink sometime. So when Gerrold and a friend drove back East for a convention in Philadelphia, they decided to look him up. They couldn't find him in the phone book, but they had his address. So, Gerrold wrote afterward,

> we did the really gross maneuver of dropping in unannounced. That is, we tried to. Apparently you out-maneuvered us. We couldn't find 6037 Ramshorn Place. Are you sure you live there? (We did find a 6037 Ramshorn *Terrace,* but the lady there couldn't help.) Harlan said you were mysterious, but this is ridiculous!

The two long-haired kids had of course rung the right doorbell. But when Alli opened the door and they asked for Tiptree, she told them the first lie she could think of. The streets in the area were winding and confusing, so the story was more or less plausible.

That same week Alli went out and got Tiptree a box at the McLean post office. Then Tiptree sent Gerrold a bouquet of excuses: what a shame, it would have been lovely to see you, but I just moved, and the McLean street map is terrible, and I'm in Chicago half the time anyway. You weren't at the right house, and besides, I wasn't home.

By that time Gerrold was less sure he had been at the wrong address, and was wondering about the lady at "Ramshorn Terrace." Anyway, the story made good gossip, and he told it several times at Philcon. Most of his hearers concluded that Tiptree was a CIA agent, and wondered why he didn't show up so they could tell him they liked his stories.

Meanwhile Tiptree was sending out change-of-address cards and trying to make it look like he was mostly on the road. This wasn't too hard: in early December Alli went to supervise the rewiring of 5344 Hyde Park Boulevard, and she and Ting visited Mary again at Christmas. When Tip wrote Pohl in January 1970, Alli used stationery from a Chicago hotel and forwarded the letter to be mailed from Chicago.

Most of Tiptree's acquaintances decided not to pry. Anne McCaffrey wrote, "Did have a bit of a chuckle when your [. . .] address change arrived. Bit too much on the heels of David the Gerrold's abortive attempt to find you." But at Philcon she had "loyally insisted that you were not female gender . . . I could be wrong but then that never bothers me particularly. Someone else remarked that you prefer to be anonymous so I will leave it lay, as the saying goes."

Tiptree wrote back, tongue invisibly in cheek: "I'd be honoured if [Gerrold] wishes to class me in the sf female contingent, for whom I have hair-raising respect—but I trust he comes off the CIA kick. [. . .] I am not, retransmit NOT, employed by CIA."

A few years later, in a letter of confession to be opened by Tiptree's agent in case of his death, Alli included an apology to Gerrold. "You looked fine. It killed me to be too scared to speak."

Yet Alli wasn't ready to give up her new project. On November 3, just before Gerrold rang her doorbell, she wrote Arnheim sheepishly that she'd done no new work in psychology.

> I really totally dropped out. Like a hopeless drunkard whose last virtue is to manage a clean shirt-collar, all I have done is punctiliously to send out reprints of my articles when requested. [. . .]
>
> But Rudy, it's been such fun. How many times in one's life does a door open to total escape, utter newness? I was so profoundly dispirited, alienated [. . .]. And suddenly I was in the middle of a different light, a new me, first having a good joke of being someone else, and then as the stories went on and out, having started genuine friendships among delightful people whose native language—crude, childish, humourous—rational—was *mine* . . . And that wonderful experience, when one is *new*, of that trembling freshness of perception on all sides—each new friend *listening*, and oneself *listening*—you know, when one is starting a new correspondence, each word received or sent adds—doubles—the known area. . . . And *honest*. The funny little Camelot-world of these writers and enthusiasts is extraordinarily honest. One corresponds with strangers, old, young, male, female, without caution or disguise, and without false needs. About the stories, about other writers, trivia, politics, death, price-per-word—
>
> [. . .] What I have written are mostly somber, simple little tales of passionate revolt and doom. Also jolly ones . . . But as I went on from

telling a story like an anecdote to telling one in the present tense, with some life in the words, I became fascinated with the techniques. . . . (Rather late in the day for fresh loves, what?)—and young people seemed to like them. This is a TERRIBLE seduction—when 20-year-olds start writing you that you have spoken their dreams, the grey-head is landed like a trout . . . So you write about their dreams and reality, and the 20-year-old locked up inside one takes you by the hand, and you forget death.

And you may say a lot of things about science, and cruelty, and make jokes you were never allowed to make.

Well Rudy now I have told someone—you are the only one except Ting to whom I have told, what actually I am just trying to understand myself. I have just been going on somnambule, doing the stories and experiencing . . . It was not until I realised some sort of explanation might be due that I tried to sum it up. Should I just giggle and say, I've been *bad,* or fake-earnest and talk about a pleasant rest-period, so good for one, or jaunty and say I'm hooked. . . . What the hell *has* been going on nearly two years here? Probably just a shallow, over-stuffed, childish mind, a lazy slob-soul, bright enough to understand real excellence, too self-indulgent to take the hard and only route, and rushing through a miraculously-offered bypath to esteem.

Well, with 3.5 billion people riding with me on this rock-ball, I don't see that it matters much. [. . .]

(—I hope you realise, this whole letter is predicated on the idea that you and yours are well, are all right, that you would tell me if otherwise, so that one can babble on as if psychic adventures were the only realities [. . .])

Yrs wildly,

VOX POP

CHAPTER 27: **THE YUCATÁN (1970)**

I don't identify with "normality," not in this world. I don't hold, nor do you, illusions about the great dazzling sanity of sf, no, it's more a matter of looking for the direction in which the darkness gives way to something that may be, someday, sunrise.

—JAMES TIPTREE, JR., TO BARRY N. MALZBERG

We must do the undoable! Think the unthinkable! F— the ineffable!

—FAN MOTTO

In 1970, Alli set Tiptree aside in favor of her own life and travels. Ting had retired in the fall and wanted to go back to the place in the Yucatán they had been to the year before. It was a coconut plantation at an inlet called Boca Paila on the Caribbean coast of the Quintana Roo Territory, between the border with Belize and the fishing villages of Cancún and Cozumel. The owner had some cabins that he rented by the week to tourists and a separate little house on the beach that he agreed to lease to Ting and Alli.

At the end of January, the Sheldons packed their duffel bags, added Ting's fishing gear and a spare typewriter, flew via Miami to Mérida, then took a small plane to Tulum on the coast. At the Tulum airstrip they were met by a driver who took them to Boca Paila. "Chevy dived up a stream bed, teetered among boulders, and went on teetering and growling and jolting incredibly at a walking pace . . . occasional sand stretches over which Raúl drove like a demon, stopping just before various chasms," Alli noted in a journal. "Sheldons injudiciously seated on rear seat, slamming about and holding on with hands and feet."

While Ting pursued sport fish, Alli walked on the beach, snorkeled, and tried out her phrasebook Spanish on their landlord's employees. They toured the Maya ruins at Chichén Itzá. And Alli worked on Tiptree stories, one of them a brief fantasy called "The Man Doors Said Hello To" that is probably the most cheerful piece of fiction she ever wrote.

The Sheldons came home at the end of May, tanned, happy, and holding a ten-year lease on their new winter home. In July they left McLean again to drive up to Canada and the Lodge, where they stayed until November. Altogether they were gone more of the year than they were home.

Though they never again went away for quite so long, this would be their pattern for the next ten years: two or three months each winter at Boca Paila and several weeks in the summer up north. Tiptree liked to make his vacations sound like world travels, erasing the suburban retiree. "The ranch owner is a friend who lets me sit in his old house when I come by," he would write offhandedly. "He has a fishing camp tourists visit." And Alli really liked the raggedy shack on the beach and the feeling of lighting out for the wilderness.

But she also missed her house, her garden, and her office. Supplies such as typewriter ribbons and even paper were hard to come by there in the mangrove swamps, and she was cut off from Tiptree's medium, the mail. She couldn't get letters at Boca Paila, and when she got back in May she discovered that none of the letters Tip had sent via the Mexican postal service had arrived.

If travel was bad for Tiptree, it was good for Mr. and Mrs. Huntington Sheldon. Ting and Alli were sixty-seven and fifty-five, and they had developed the closeness of a couple who have fought and compromised and worn grooves into each other with use. "They watched over each other constantly," Alli's friend Jeff Smith recalled. "While you talked with one the other would lean forward and drink in the scene with pleasure and admiration." Another friend, David Hartwell, said, "They were always calling each other 'my sweet, my heart, my dear.' If he were in the room she had to touch him."

They had probably given up sex long before: they still shared a bed, but with Alli's late-night hours she was often just getting up as Ting was going to sleep. To Joanna Russ, Alli once wrote, " 'platonic marriage' with a really solid male friend has good points . . . I should know." But their bond of affection, loyalty, and trust mattered more. Alli had always relied on Ting for stability, and she leaned on him heavily in the years after she left the structured world of graduate school and was writing as Tiptree. More and more, as she put it, she became the ivy and he the oak tree. After he retired, she found it easier to withdraw from the world. Ting, too, depended more on Alli after his mother and sister died. Hartwell felt that the bond between them "was the single most important and determining factor in both their lives." Peter Sheldon called them "a one-to-one couple—anyone else was *de trop*."

Ting didn't take much interest in her writing, and didn't read it, though he was glad she was enjoying herself. (He certainly didn't believe in any kind of personal writing, Alli once noted. His reaction, she thought, "would be, (a) why write about one's personal life; (b) nobody could understand it; (c) if they did understand it they wouldn't need it.") But he helped her name her characters, and she filled her writing notebooks with "HDS-isms," including puns ("Actual Mouse coffee"), rude speculations on the domestic habits of Richard and Pat Nixon, and a line that must have been delivered in a little-old-lady falsetto: "My dachshund is terribly old and he voted for Hitler. That's why I won't buy him a new Christmas suit." This was part of that side of Ting that was reserved for Alli, his own half of their secret strangeness.

Alli had always said about herself and Ting that what mattered was how they would be with each other when they were seventy. Time seemed to bear her out. In 1980, when she was sixty-five and Ting seventy-seven, Alli looked back on her marriage after Ting's retirement and wrote, "Since the last 10 years we are so as one it's ridiculous. Without agreeing on how to do the simplest thing, like open a jar, we arrive at the same basic life-conclusions and perceptions." To another friend she wrote, "The thing about the right stranger, you love each other tenderly across a gulf of trivia, and it's always fresh because your different worlds bring in different news. But that love doesn't strike, it grows."

Yet she also wrote, "I've lived so deep under masks, my interior was built to satisfy me alone—I have lived 60 years almost totally alone, mentally, and quite content to have it so. I'm fond of a hundred people who no more know 'me' than they know the landscape of Antarctica. [. . .]

"Even Ting."

Another reason Alli wrote so little in 1970 is that she was rethinking her writing style, or perhaps thinking about it for the first time. Readers were taking Tiptree's stories seriously, so she started taking them more seriously, too. She moved away from the action-adventure plots that had endeared Tiptree to John Campbell and the readers of *Analog* and started writing more serious fiction. As a result, Tiptree's stories weren't being accepted as readily as they had been, especially after Fred Pohl left *Galaxy* in 1969. Several of the more avant-garde tales were now making the rounds of editors, collecting rejections. Yet after Ed Ferman at *F&SF* turned down one story, "Painwise," as too baffling, he found it still haunting him months later, asked to see it again, and bought it unrevised. "Like any original author," Ursula Le Guin later commented, "Alli did have to teach people how to read Tiptree."

In January 1970, just before Alli left for Boca Paila, she experimented with putting more personal content in a "hard SF" story. "Mother in the Sky with Diamonds" is a fast-paced adventure with an autobiographical twist: a frustrated bureaucrat patrols the asteroid belts while trying to keep his senile parent out of a rest home. She was a space explorer who long ago abandoned her son for the stars. Yet he loves her, remembers her youthful beauty and courage, and hides her aboard her old spaceship until she gets a chance to play the hero one last time.

Alli wrote it partly as a joke on her own new Serious subject matter, and the story is a noisy, entertaining mess. But Alli really was trying to see, as she told Phil Dick, "how much human reality the sci-fi fabric will bear." For her material, she drew more and more on her work in psychology, and sometimes rationalized her writing as a mission to broaden science fiction's horizons beyond rocketry and engineering. She stopped imitating other people's work. Her plots became more complex, her stories more subtle and compelling. Tiptree was entering his subversive and exuberant prime.

One quality Tiptree's fiction already had was narrative speed. For sheer flow of information at the reader, for inventiveness, for ideas thrown away that would serve lesser writers for whole novels, Tiptree was unequaled. Critic Steve Brown has observed that Tiptree could "write in eight words flat what anyone else would take three pages to convey." After Alli gave Rudolf Arnheim a copy of "Your Haploid Heart," he wrote her, "It is as cleverly written as I expected it to be, and the basic idea is a truly ingenious invention." But he teased her about the story's pace: "Remember that you think 99% faster than the rest of humanity, and therefore you better write with one nostril closed like that fairy tale giant who was always about to blow the whole landscape to pieces."

Tiptree's stories are not only fast but intense. Their narrators grab you by the lapels and blurt out wild tales; what stays with you afterward is the juice and energy, the sexy humor and defiance of the telling. The moral message of her fiction is often complicated by its roughshod tone. The new stories used unusual perspectives: a brainwashed traitor in "The Peacefulness of Vivyan," a giant bug struggling to reach a higher consciousness in "Love Is the Plan the Plan Is Death." The emotions in a Tiptree story almost always belie the "official" point of view.

Tiptree had done this from the beginning, in stories such as "Dr. Ain" and "Mama Come Home," but now it was much more a deliberate strategy—not because he wanted to write great literature, Tiptree claimed, but because putting in details that the reader might catch only on a second or third look

> strikes me as a way of being like life. Life plunks you amid strangers making strange gestures, inexplicable caresses, threats, unmarked buttons you press with unforeseen results, important-sounding gabble in code . . . and you keep sorting it out, sorting it out, understanding five years later *why* she said or did whatever, *why* they screamed when you—

His trick, Tiptree said, was to "start from the end and preferably 5,000 feet underground on a dark day and then *don't tell them.*" It worked. Tiptree's and Raccoona's best stories are urgent, explosive, and troubling. Like Alli herself, they refuse simple readings. Instead they sweep the reader up into a "gabble" of emotional discord, the voices of Alli's own tangled truth.

"A Tiptree story was like a crystal ball. I always felt Tiptree was taking us into a private space," David Gerrold said of his friend's work. Critic John Clute writes that when he discovered Tiptree,

> I felt as though I had stumbled [. . .] into some unbearable drama. The stories themselves engaged me at every level I was capable of responding to; but more than that, their profound obscurity seemed itself a kind of willed death that I (that any reader) had to violate. Despite their brave gaiety, the visible genius of their telling, it felt that simply to read a Tiptree story was to yank it bleeding from its dark home.

In her long-ago stories and essay drafts, Alli had veered between cool science ("this is just a theory, it has nothing to do with me") and an unmodulated wail. Now it was Tiptree who gave her distance and control, who could handle the darker emotions, who helped her shape pain into stories. "I had to take the sentiment out, because Tiptree was not sentimental," Alli once told Jeff Smith. Tip himself wrote, "I am aware that my own personal damnation is of not the slightest interest to the outer world until it has been forced up to form figures in the fire, dream-artifacts into which reader can for a moment live."

Often the pain is in the longing for connection, communication, union with another, and the fear of being destroyed by that union—a fear that, in Tiptree's stories, almost always comes true. Love (between men and women, humans and aliens) is an inexorable, biological drive; but it is frustrated, impossible, and almost always deadly.

In "And I Awoke and Found Me Here on the Cold Hill's Side" (the title is from Keats's "La Belle Dame Sans Merci"), humans have found life on other planets and all they want to do is screw it. A man addicted to alien sex recalls the first time he saw an extraterrestrial dancing:

> Her arms went up, and those blazing lemon-colored curves pulsed, waved, everted, contracted, throbbed, evolved unbelievably welcoming, inciting permutations. *Come do it to me, do it, do it here and here and here and now.* [. . .] Every human male in the room was aching to ram himself into that incredible body.

He warns us, "Man is exogamous—all our history is one long drive to find and impregnate the stranger. Or get impregnated by him; it works for women too. Anything different-colored, different nose, ass, anything, man *has* to fuck it or die trying." Humans can no more help lusting after aliens "than a sea worm can help rising to the moon." This desire is so strong that humans will give anything for it, even abandon their culture and society in a "cargo cult of the soul." Humanity is dying of yearning, the narrator says. "Our soul is leaking out. We're bleeding to death!"

Throughout Alli's fiction, sexual desire is portrayed in this way, as something instinctive, "natural," and therefore terrifying. Sex is "the vulnerable link in the behavioral chain," the place where humans are most at risk. It is where we are open to the enemy, which is not a monster from a distant star but an obscure signal from the human brain stem.

In 1970, all this graphic sex didn't make Tiptree unusual in SF. Writers such as J. G. Ballard (*The Atrocity Exhibition*), Samuel R. Delany, and even William S. Burroughs were already taking the genre out of the chaste world of men and their machines. What Tiptree had that other writers didn't was his frankness, not about the mechanics of sex, but about its anxieties.

Often it is reproduction that is the killer. In "The Snows Are Melted, the Snows Are Gone," the need to reproduce may allow a deadly strain of aggression to enter the population. In "Your Haploid Heart," the haploid generation dies on giving birth. Even in "On the Last Afternoon," when the colony is being wiped out by giant lobsters, it is because the humans have accidentally built their homes on the lobsters' mating grounds. Alli argued that this was just science.

> The arrival of death is synchronous with the arrival of sex in the biological world. As soon as you start multiplying by different gene systems the parents then die, whereas if you stick to budding, you simply have two people. 'Haploid Heart' grew out of my wondering about this. We come trailing not clouds of glory, but shreds of placenta on which are written pain, suffering, and death.

Yet Alli also had less abstract reasons to see death in giving birth. She wanted to see her reasons as science, but was able to imagine them fully only in metaphors of the monstrous.

Though her stories grew deeper, Alli went on using the paraphernalia of science fiction: spaceships and time machines, aliens and planetary settlements on the brink of destruction. In July 1970, Tiptree started discussing science fiction backgrounds with Damon Knight, who had invited him to contribute to *Orbit* but was now writing him detailed rejection letters. Turning down "The Peacefulness of Vivyan," Knight wrote, "All that alien-planet apparatus that we have clung to so long . . . not to mention the robots, laser guns, girls in tinfoil brassieres, etc. . . . honest to god, what is it for and who needs it?" Rejecting "Painwise" a few days later, he again urged Tiptree to throw the "goddam apparatus [. . .] out the window and start over."

Tiptree answered that he was trying to make a surface of SF paraphernalia and hide the real story beneath it. Defending "On the Last Afternoon" to Knight a year later, he argued, "the monsters were merely the human condition writ large, the 'cliché colony' was only human life."

Knight grouched back, "Putting symbols into a cliché is a little like trying to reform Mayor Daley's administration from the inside. [. . .] I did see, *of course,* that you were writing about the fershlugginer human condition, but so were the authors of all those other stories about frontier planets, and so what?" Knight wanted a new kind of science fiction. But Alli had finally broken into the candy shop, and she wasn't about to trade her gumdrops for foie gras.

Besides, she used the "apparatus," like her layers of narration, like Tiptree himself, as a way of negotiating the real story. Adrienne Rich has said that the formalism of her early poetry was such a protective covering: "Like asbestos gloves, it allowed me to handle materials I couldn't pick up bare-handed." ("A later strategy was to use the persona of a man," Rich adds.) Decked out in space suits and tinfoil brassieres, Alli's ideas didn't seem so dangerous even to herself. And Alli really did do new things with the clichés of science fiction: a space pilot rescued by—his mother; a hero who can't tell the difference between the girl and the monster. Alli's stories are almost all, among other things, loving and brilliant commentary on the SF genre. She sometimes bit the hand that fed her, as the writer Michael Swanwick has pointed out. In "And I Awoke," science fiction itself is shown to be a deadly addiction, and the "very xenophilia and sense of wonder that fuel the science fiction enterprise" a danger to the human race.

Yet the more Alli began to speak for herself in writing, even in the dis-
guised and limited voice of James Tiptree, Jr., the more she cut off the dream of escape in her work. Almost invariably Tiptree's and Raccoona's stories end badly. Escape is frustrated, hopes for the future come to nothing, death claims the protagonist, the colony, or the whole human race.

Writing science fiction, Alli told Arnheim, was a "revolt" against her life. But Tiptree's own stories warned that revolt didn't lead to freedom. Tiptree once sketched the basic plot of a Tiptree tale: "There's this backward little type, and he's doing some grey little task and believing like they tell him, and one day he starts to vomit and rushes straight up a mountain, usually to his doom."

All this time Alli had been writing short stories. SF had, and has, a strong market for short fiction, but the novel is still the more prestigious (and profitable) form, and by 1970 editors were telling Tiptree that he ought to be writing one. Harry Harrison wanted him to expand "The Snows Are Melted": "I got eager editors lined up for your novel." Terry Carr, at Ace Books, reprinted "Your Haploid Heart" in *The World's Best Science Fiction: 1970* and encouraged Tiptree to submit something longer. (Tip replied, "I'd like to get [a novel] good enough for you, but I am slow. Very slow. If you'll have patience, one will be along but we may both have white beards." Or not.) Tip did pitch a novel to Ace later that year, based on "Happiness Is a Warm Spaceship." But a year later, when Carr's fellow editor Donald Wollheim wrote offering him a contract, he had moved on.

Alli did seriously consider making a novel out of "The Snows Are Melted." The Vietnam War was going on and on. The son of friends had come back with a brain-damaging injury. Alli thought more and more about the Second World War and her belief that she had been fighting for an ideal. She remembered Colonel Ruef, the German officer she had questioned at Bad Kissingen who looked just like her father. How different were he and she? How had America become the bad guys in "this travesty of a war"? In October 1969, Tiptree described himself to Harrison as a "grizzled primate whose inside is still focussed around the great lesson [. . .] that erupted out of Germany": that a few small changes might "have landed sacred white-hatted ME in the proud deathshead uniform, or the dirty goat-skin, just as easily." A few weeks later, antiwar protesters held a huge demonstration at the White House, where they read the names of all the 40,000 American dead. That month, the story broke of some 300 old men, women, and children killed by American soldiers in the South Vietnamese village of My Lai.

To David Gerrold, Tiptree wrote that he longed for someone to fight, the way he and his generation had fought the Nazis. He was frightened by how pervasive and elusive evil in the world now seemed to be—and how close to home. The old ways of fighting it weren't enough; it wasn't

> a question of conserving grease, of obeying the anti-litter laws. It's today
> a question of massive conversion to new ways of life, new values, the
> dimly-glimpsed necessities of total change in our most primitive—
> Ah, SHIT.

Human evolution is an old science fiction subject: if you look at the distant future, inevitably you wonder how people will have changed. Alli never did write the novel based on "Snows," but the future of the species is a problem she would return to again and again. If there are no heroes in her stories, it is often because everyone is implicated in a cycle of violence that we must evolve beyond. Alli wanted people to become better than they were, and feared for the human race if they did not. She wanted to build the door leading out—though as always she had more hope for others than for herself.

By the fall of 1970, after a year of traveling, Alli was depressed. Her ulcer was still bothering her, and a new problem, painful arthritis in her right hand, was making it hard for her to type. In June she had tapped Tiptree's bank account to buy an electric typewriter, which helped for a while, and she took a lot of codeine for the pain. At the Lodge, where she had once gone to rest and work, she now had to cope with Mary and her needs. (On subsequent Lodge trips, Alli got sick or had accidents and ended up being nursed alongside her mother.) From Wisconsin in October, Tiptree called himself "a writer temporarily blocked by rigor mortis." But that was about to change.

CHAPTER 28: A DECADENT INTELLECTUAL FAKED UP IN A WOODMAN'S SHIRT (1971)

I meet somebody who says "youre this or that," and I dont want to be anything when I'm writing.

—VIRGINIA WOOLF

During her year on the road, Alli did stay in touch with the SF world, partly through Tiptree's subscriptions to the SFWA newsletter and one or two fanzines. She enjoyed getting to eavesdrop on such characters as Richard E. Geis, a fortyish fan who lived with his mother (or said he did) in Portland, Oregon, wrote pornography for a living, and published fanzines called *The Alien Critic* and *Science Fiction Review*. In late 1970, Tiptree wrote that he envied the kind of writer, like Norman Mailer or Harlan Ellison, who wrote about himself, "whose life forms into narrative as it is being lived, so that at every act of unveiling, at putting the naked squirm of the inmost flesh into words, another level of reality forms behind and beneath in which the living [writer] exists just one jump ahead of the audience." Alli wanted to hide, but more and more she wanted to reveal herself too.

Tiptree generally insisted that all anyone needed to know about him was in the stories. In an introduction to "Dr. Ain" in one of Harry Harrison's best-of anthologies, he again proclaimed the work's independence from its author.

Writing about your own story reminds me of those tremendous floats you see in small-town Labor Day parades. You have this moving island of flowers with people on it being Indian Braves or Green Bay Packers or Astronauts-Landing-on-the-Moon (Raising-the-Flag-at-Iwo-Jima has happily gone out of fashion) and great-looking girls being great-looking girls. That's the story. Under each float is an old truck chassis driven by a guy in sweaty jeans who is also working the tapedeck and passing cherry bombs to the Indians. That's the author. Now Harry wants me to crawl out and say hello. Well, I love saying hello. But my feeling is that the story is the game. Who really needs me and my carburetor troubles up there blowing kisses with Miss Harvest Home?

It's a lovely, odd image, with the supernumerary girls—or are they by definition part of the masquerade?—and the author who, if he were to climb out, would become like one of his characters, an incongruous—and powerless—beauty queen.

Tiptree gave Alli a safe space to write in, but sometimes she yearned for her life and stories to be part of a whole. She still wanted to be the drunk speaking truth, the woman "pressing out naked into the dark spaces of life," the writer who could "storm naked with hard-on waving thru the world spouting whatever comes." So when a young fan in Baltimore asked Tiptree to do an interview by mail, he cautiously said yes—and then wrote pages about himself.

Jeffrey D. Smith was a quiet twenty-year-old who worked in a bookstore and put out a fanzine called *Phantasmicom*. It was a typical small, mimeographed fanzine, with a print run at its peak of about three hundred copies. Smith and his coeditor, Donald Keller, wrote most of the first issues themselves, and were noticed in fandom for their "youthful enthusiasm." Harlan Ellison liked an interview they'd done, and suggested they do Tiptree.

Smith wasn't a great Tiptree fan, though he "had read several of his stories and had liked some of them." But at that point Tiptree was being claimed by both the old guard, the John Campbell types, and the New Wave, the Ellison types, and Smith could see there might be a story in that. He asked Donald Wollheim at Ace Books to forward a request for an interview. Tiptree didn't answer.

Smith assumed his letter hadn't arrived. (It had, but Alli had been away, or had ignored it.) He got hold of Tiptree's address and tried again. Although Tiptree lived only an hour's drive from Baltimore, Smith suggested they do the interview by mail—not because he knew Tiptree was reclusive, but because he himself was too shy to interview a writer in person or even by phone. He said he wasn't going to try to talk Tiptree into it. "I don't want you to enter this with any reluctance at all; if you have any doubts about this, tell me 'no.' Fanzines are fun things and non-obligatory."

All the defenses Tiptree had built up for corresponding with people like

Dick, the pushing onto pedestals and insistence he wasn't worthy—it all collapsed in the face of Smith's unassuming honesty. He wrote back, saying that he couldn't give much "census-type biographic data" but would be happy to talk about "real matters like sf, personal hang-ups and Spiro Agnew." Over Christmas 1970, in Chicago, Alli sat down at the typewriter to answer Smith's first question: "How about telling us what you *are* willing to let us know about you?"

For the first time, Alli gave Tiptree a biography: her own. "Well, I was born in the Chicago area a long time back, [and] trailed around places like colonial India and Africa as a kid," Tiptree began. He said that because of the war, his career had been "derailed" into the army, government, "business," academia. He had become a writer more or less by accident, after "hidden years of writing crap headed MEMO, SUBJECT, TO."

When Smith asked why he was keeping his private life secret, Tiptree said he thought his new game was "overdetermined." A few reasons were his professional reputation, his childish enjoyment of secrecy, his reluctance to tamper with a way of writing that seemed to work, his wish to keep his new friendships separate from the "real world."

So, how to reconcile that with honesty? Well, who is honest? You? Or You? [. . .] You know as well as I do we all go around in disguise. The halo stuffed in the pocket, the cloven hoof awkward in the shoe, the X-ray eye blinking behind thick lenses, the two midgets dressed as one tall man, the giant stooping in a pinstripe, the pirate in a housewife's smock [. . .] So who the fuck cares whether the mask is one or two millimetres thick?

Who he really was was easy enough to read in his stories, Tiptree added: "Anxious, somewhat niggling; aggressive instincts well repressed, converted to possibly spurious sympathy; inhibited but daring in a furtive way [. . .]—in short, a fairly typical Who, me? guilty face behind a typewriter . . . And, in case it isn't clear, a clown. Man, if you can't laugh at it, what good is it?"

But mostly Tiptree talked about science fiction, writers he liked, his current work. Over the course of several months, Smith edited Tiptree's letters and sent them back to be checked, and asked for a bibliography, and got a short story, one of the unsalable fragments. When Smith first asked about a story, Tiptree said no, he wrote too slowly. Smith replied disarmingly, "I sympathize with your 'stupid problem of writing slow and painful.' I share it; and I have an additional one. When I finish a story, it isn't as good as yours and no one will buy it."

As they went on exchanging letters, the correspondence grew more personal. Smith confided in Tiptree about his fear of being drafted, his troubles with his boss, his relationship with his girlfriend, Ann. (The next year, Tip politely declined an invitation to their wedding: "Would really like to loiter in shadows and peek . . . however fear not, will be loitering in Chicago.") They talked about music: Tip recommended Tom Lehrer, Smith sent tapes of the band Yes. After a while, Smith began to think of Tip as one of his best friends, and simply accepted that he was friends with someone he had never seen. "Tip was so warm, so open, that it made absolutely no difference that I never saw his face or heard his voice."

For Alli, the interview and correspondence seem to have broken through a distance she felt from her persona. In the previous year, she had written very few letters as Tiptree, presumably because of her travels, and maybe because of all Tiptree's frightening encounters—with Dick, Ellison, David Gerrold. Now she began to give Tiptree more detail. Over the course of 1971 and 1972, she started letting him make friends.

It was exciting to have an audience, one that asked real author-type questions such as "What writers have influenced you?" She'd been too shy to discuss writing with Phil Dick, but she wasn't afraid to ask Smith for feedback. To her young fan, Alli found herself thinking out loud about her work. Who did she want to be in her fiction?

Meaner and more daring than she'd been so far, she thought. When Smith passed on Virginia Kidd's remark that Tiptree was a nice guy, Tip yelled back, "SEE? THAT'S WHAT'S WRONG WITH ME!! What kind of a writer his every word is likable yet? A pink-shit writer, that's wot . . . I wanna be hateful, loathsome, impossible." Commenting on Robert A. Heinlein's attempt to write from a woman's point of view in *I Will Fear No Evil,* Tiptree noted, "Maybe having the macho to do such a horrible bad taste disaster is the mark of a real writer. [. . .] The good taste that holds your tongue from making the little *unlikable* lapses is also the castrating inhibition that keeps you from really saying anything."

Tiptree did take more risks. His stories began selling not to *Analog* but to the more avant-garde *F&SF,* or to original anthologies, with their greater editorial freedom. (He submitted several times to *Playboy,* but they always judged his stories too obscure.) If an editor suggested a rewrite he was now likely to ignore the advice and send the story elsewhere.

He began selling to Ted White, a young editor who had succeeded Harrison and Malzberg at *Amazing* and *Fantastic.* If no one else would buy a story, Tiptree sent it to White, usually with a cover letter saying that it had been sent around, no one else had understood it, and he hoped he could count on White's discerning taste.

At first White took this to mean " 'I tried this story on the higher-paying markets and they didn't buy it, so I'm trying you . . .' At that time my magazines paid the lowest rate—one penny a word, on publication—so this did not surprise me, but I was bemused by someone coming right out and *saying* that in a letter of submission. My impression then was of a young, talented, but arrogant writer—someone in his twenties or thirties probably, and so brimming with talent that he could get away with a certain amount of brashness.

"It was obvious to me that 'Tip' was a major find, and one I couldn't keep to myself (as an editor). She was in fact selling to the higher-paying markets. I had only one thing going for me: I had fewer editorial restrictions. I was willing to buy the more off-beat stories. And it was on that basis that I continued to receive stories from 'Tip,' often accompanied by letters complaining about how a given story was being misunderstood by other editors." Although White lived and worked just a few miles from Tiptree, in Falls Church, Virginia, they never met. Tiptree promised to buy White a drink someday, as he did several of his men friends. White never pressed the point.

Knowing she had one or two appreciative editors, as well as one critical-yet-respectful fan, gave Alli more confidence to experiment. In 1971, in a burst of writing energy, she produced a series of remarkable short stories.

She was still exploring human evolution, morality, and sex, and wrote a story in which all are intertwined. "Love Is the Plan the Plan Is Death" is a haunting, tragicomic tale told from the point of view of a giant bug. The bug speaks according to its primitive perceptions, in what Tiptree intended to be the overripe, heavily symbolic prose of pornography circa 1920: "Oh, beautiful you became, my jewel of redness! [. . .] my tiny one, my sun-spark." (Tip told Smith, "I wish it was more like Nabokov, but since the aliens are quite primitive and so am I, they can be grateful it's a cut above Me Tarzan, You Jane.") It's the ultimate read-twice Tiptree story: the spiderlike alien's tale of coming of age, courting and winning a mate, and being eaten by her is filled with cryptic hints of an underlying shift of climate or consciousness. The alien struggles to understand its instincts ("the Plan"); seeing through its eyes, we feel its murky, limited knowledge of its own purpose. We also see that if it cannot abandon the "Plan," it and its species will die. Not to know oneself is to remain the slave of one's animal nature.

Another 1971 story is the joyous "All the Kinds of Yes," the finest—and last—of Tiptree's purely comic stories. John Clute has said that the story "refines and darkens and speeds up and in the end utterly transforms the comic clatter of Tiptree's earliest work," taking confusion and remaking it into an exalted, joyous embrace of life. An alien—seemingly just a tourist—lands in the middle of Washington, assumes human, male form, and is adopted by four college kids for fun and sex. The story is told in snatches of dialogue and scraps of poetry (the title is from e.e. cummings), and is all goofy juxtapositions, happy xenophilia, and affection for the enthusiastic and accepting youth. "I guess it's indecent," Tiptree wrote Jeff Smith, "but what I was really interested in was to tell a story about us by what the kids *didn't* do—or mention."

But even this happy romp ends with a hint of reproductive disaster. The alien turns out to be (in its true form) pregnant, and has come to Earth looking for a place to deposit its 30,000 voracious offspring. "It's not like with you," the creature explains, its jazzy voice changing to a teary feminine wail. "I mean, the first phase is like almost crude energy. They just f-fight and eat, you can't even *see* them and they're dreadfully fast. They destroy everything. That's why we use special planets now. And we send in *soldiers* to collect the survivors. [. . .] There wouldn't be anything l-left." Fortunately, the alien has learned to like humans. At the last minute it—she—finds another planet and moves on.

At the end of the year Alli rewrote and resubmitted "The Girl Who Was Plugged In," her story about an ugly girl in a beautiful body. This story too has a lot of what Clute called "clatter"—an aggressive, rapid-fire rain of bits of information, asides, opinions, all meant to keep it from sounding too sentimental. It lurches and stumbles with the clumsy walk of its heroine, the hideous Philadelphia Burke, who, locked in a closet and wired into a network, animates the luscious body of Delphi the movie star.

Like the astronaut in "Painwise" who can't feel pain, the beautiful Delphi is physically not all there. Delphi's artificial body has no sexual feeling; to save bandwidth, her creators have left that out. If Delphi makes love, P. Burke can't feel it. It doesn't matter. All P. Burke wants is to leave her own body, "to close out the beast she is chained to. *To become Delphi.*" Then Delphi/Burke falls in love with a real man, who discovers that Delphi is being manipulated and undertakes to "set her free." When he finally reaches P. Burke, he accidentally kills her, believing she is a monster who has possessed his girl.

"The Girl Who Was Plugged In" has been called the first cyberpunk story; William Gibson has cited it as an inspiration for his novel *Neuromancer.* Certainly "The Girl Who" shares cyberpunk's, and Gibson's, sense of disastrous longing for a technologically mediated transcendence of the self. Like some of Tiptree's characters, Gibson's have been emptied out by unattainable desire, by a "cargo cult of the soul."

But "The Girl Who" is also a horror story about performing the feminine: the beautiful, numb outer self, the female impersonator, houses the unacceptable true self. (It has been said that the woman's body is the third party in any seduction; "The Girl Who" makes this literal.) In the classic fairy tale, the lover discovers the true beauty beneath the ugly surface: the prince in the frog, the princess in Cinderella's rags. In "The Girl Who," Tiptree says the reverse: the world loves the beauty on the surface and can't abide the monster in the mind.

"The Girl Who" may also reflect Alli's longtime use of Dexedrine. The drug is said to push the mind far ahead of the slow body with its needs for food and sleep. Gibson has implied that speed is behind his own characters' yearning to transcend the physical world: "It's probably no accident that Case, the protagonist of *Neuromancer,* eats Dexedrine until his criminal employers have his metabolism altered to bypass the stuff." Certainly Alli was careless and impatient with her body, especially as it got older. A few years later, as Tiptree, she wrote, "I am increasingly coming to resist *being* my body [. . .]

although I know perfectly well that I am it and it is me, as age comes on and I feel it start to fail under me like a tiring horse I have to disassociate myself from more and more of it."

Alli didn't write on large doses of speed. She tried, but said it "produced garrulous and minute diary-like effects, very dull," or else generated "paranoia [. . .]. Like I become convinced room is a huge set of jaws, furniture teeth, chimney a gullet, fireplace is *out to get me*." But she used small doses in order to work, and it may have reinforced her growing sense that embodiment is an iffy proposition—the body likely to betray the mind, the mind at best an uneasy passenger of the body and its desires.

One striking thing about Tiptree's stories is how full they are of men looking at women. Some of this might be imitation of "male" writing—except that Tiptree's sex scenes don't seem copied from standard action-hero models. Often we see an innocent boy gazing at a woman and becoming "paralyzed" with yearning. In "Dr. Ain," the picture of young Ain meeting Earth for the first time is straight out of a Swedish movie circa 1968, and at the same time goofily sincere:

> Squatting under a stump to watch a shrewmouse he had been, when he caught a falling ripple of green and recognized the shocking naked girl-flesh, creamy, pink-tipped—coming toward him among the golden bracken! Young Ain held his breath, his nose in the sweet moss and his heart going *crash—crash*. And then he was staring at the outrageous fall of that hair down her narrow back, watching it dance around her heart-shaped buttocks, while the shrewmouse ran over his paralyzed hand.

A more sophisticated 1971 story, "Forever to a Hudson Bay Blanket," centers on a teenage boy's gentle fantasy of rescuing a girl lost in the woods and making love to her in his lonely cabin, on his wool blanket. His fantasy is convincing enough that when some of Tiptree's friends began to wonder if he might be gay, others cited this story. How could he be gay when his male characters were so hot for women?

Alli may have been describing how men see women, or speaking about her own desire, or both. "And I Awoke," with its pictures of alien longing ("Every human male in the room was aching to ram himself into that incredible body"), portrays men's desire from a critical distance, yet it also echoes the Alice who in her twenties wrote, "I want to ram myself into a crazy soft woman," and who had lusted after "unscrewable" girls.

Was Tiptree's truth Alli's truth? Was it a female truth? To put concealed stories into ostensible ones, or to undermine narrative authority, is, one could argue, a female literary strategy, a way of challenging the dominant story. (Alli herself argued this in the 1950s, when she told her friend Ed, "Our style *is* anarchic, to you.") The way Tiptree told stories, as much as anything he said, seems to reflect Alli's experience. But even a confessional writer like Mailer or Ellison, Tiptree pointed out, is never revealing himself completely.

One trouble with Tiptree as a writing strategy is that it may have put too much distance between Alli and her work. It helped her to find her talent, but not to recognize it for what it was. She wrote that while she admired other people's stories, "I have zero feeling about my own, something out there or under my pancreas is dictating. I mean, that's nice, but it doesn't fill me with wonder." When she talked about stories coming naturally to her, she insisted it was "not at all psychoanalytic" but a question of pulling down ideas that were in the air, out there, not part of her. This disowning of Tiptree's writing voice was not such a problem when he was just a "revolt," but in the end it seems to have made Alli feel she couldn't share in his achievements or keep his writing voice when the Tiptree mask was lost.

Ironically, part of Tiptree's appeal lies in his uncovering of secrets. From his very first stories, Tiptree conveys an enormously attractive sense that we are being let in on the underside of the world's business. Alli claimed to have borrowed this quality from Rudyard Kipling. As a child, reading in the cupboard under the stairs, she had been entranced by his "glamorous adult world of secrets, of the Insider—Kipling is expert at making you feel he is writing from some mysterious inside knowledge of how things really work, by hunch, accident, malice, momentary love, as apart from the Official View." Tiptree's heroes tell the truth about human limitations, too. They don't always have a great time in bed. They don't always understand what is going on. They are prone to longings and sadness.

And on a basic level, Tiptree combined a mastery of the genre's materials, the rocket ships and laser guns, with a questioning intelligence that made his work into SF for grownups. He was good reading for those who loved traditional SF and credible when he challenged it. He worked from the true science fiction tradition of scientific extrapolation, of "What would happen if": What if people were haploid? What if we really could have sex with aliens? Where women readers often talk about Tiptree's startling feminism, men admire him for his moral vision and the sense that he's doing real, scientific thought-experiments. When William Gibson came back to SF in the late 1970s, he found in Tiptree one of the genre's few truly "passionate" and innovative writers, and at the same time "a 'classic' practitioner, whatever that means. I felt she did it the 'right' way, strict rules of golf, no cheating, but full-on. She was terribly exciting, in the way that great 'real' sf had been exciting for me as a kid."

Harlan Ellison said she was simply his idea of good. "I resist the demeaning of Alli's talent by saying, well, she was popular for this or that reason, or because she was a perceptive-sounding guy, or she was a guy who was able to examine his softer side. Bullshit. It was simply and purely that these stories were spectacular. This was one of the really imaginative writers of our time. And the quality of Alli's talent, and the insight, the brilliance of her writing, was what sold her. You can fool the readers, but you cannot fool the writers. The writers will know. And unless the person talking to you is a complete asshole, it has nothing to do with sex. So I firmly and adamantly go against trying to find other reasons for this woman to have been as popular as she was. She was just terrific, that's all. She was a hell of a writer."

Tiptree's persona as well as his fiction was manly and appealing, and it became more substantial when Jeff Smith asked Tiptree to write a column, on any subject, for his 'zines *Phantasmicom* and *Kyben*. In the fall of 1971, Tiptree sent in some short pieces about his recent trip to the Canadian Rockies and the Lodge. The travelogue was Mary's territory, but in his letters and columns, Tiptree made it his own. Like Mary, he sometimes used it to lament the disappearing wilderness, while making himself sound adventurous. In a letter to Lester del Rey, he noted that going fishing in the wilds of Canada

> used to be a fairly seclusive endeavor. Today you drive north 'til your springs break, transfer into a bush plane, flap a hundred miles or so into the unnamed and barely charted, set up camp—and within a day pink and purple Cessnas are landing all over you to borrow beer or Bandaids or just jaw. [. . .] Seeing 9 people on my lake in a week is NOT my idea of privacy.

But for Smith, Tiptree was able to laugh about Canada's tourists:

> Old, old tourists in their millions, bus-loads of geriatric specimens, singing "You Are My Sunshine." [. . .] Old old men hung with cameras, dressed in weirdo mod stuff their pantsuited old ladies have put on them. Man, if they were all stripped I bet you'd only see three navels visible west of Ontario. Not to mention other organs.

He described tourists interacting with the Athabasca Glacier: kicking it, breaking off bits, taking pictures, kicking harder. Race memory? he wondered. A last shot at humans' old enemy, the Ice Age?

And Tiptree made fun of the heroic warrior in a fragment he called "Spitting Teeth, Our Hero—." At the Lodge that summer, Alli had gotten hurt: she had been helping Ting take down shutters and had dropped her end. The heavy planking caught her square in the mouth, knocked her teeth loose, and badly cut her lip. Ting had to drive her to the hospital for stitches and pills. She was miserable. But what about all those space opera heroes? Didn't they get bashed in the face all the time without even slowing down? What was that fantasy all about?

Tiptree, a "decadent intellectual faked up in a woodman's shirt," starts comparing himself to fictional characters who

> get their faces stomped in or shot off and leap up gamely and—
>   Steal an alien rocket ship, and—

Figure out a vector-mathematical language and/or the secret of the universe, and—

Fuck at least the bad girl and the good girl during surgery, while—

Making a half a dozen brilliant psychosociophilosophical speeches.

Man, I couldn't. [. . .] I couldn't do anything but sit down and sluice my face and accept a ride to the hospital. [. . .] I wasn't interested in the nurses and the only speeches I made were something like " 'Anksh 'Oc" and "Fflthh."

The essay is a fair imitation of male anxiety, the thoughts of a mild-mannered writer comparing himself to his fictional heroes. At the same time, the "decadent intellectual" is faking it in more ways than one.

But despite the secret jokes, Tiptree said what his readers wanted to hear. Here was a guy with all the masculine credentials, who wrote about fishing, spaceship hardware, Q clearances, and the jungles of Africa—who was finally admitting that it was all hooey. As Tiptree, Alli was at last establishing a connection with men—her colleagues, her readers—that was not based on sex or competition but on a shared understanding of human vulnerability.

At the end of 1970, Tiptree had been stalled. A year later he had written seven more stories. He had a new admiring editor, Robert Silverberg, who had accepted "All the Kinds of Yes" for his influential *New Dimensions* series of anthologies. In an introduction Silverberg announced that "a major new short-story writer is in our midst: deft, original, vigorous." The next summer he bought the revised "Girl Who."

To help keep things going while Alli was in the Yucatán, Tiptree acquired a real New York agent, Robert P. Mills. There wasn't much money in a short story writer, but Mills took Tiptree on Harry Harrison's recommendation. (Tiptree had asked about Virginia Kidd, but Harrison had said she was not professional enough.) Fred Pohl, now an editor at Ace Books, suggested a paperback collection of Tiptree's stories.

Tiptree would never again equal the intense production of 1971. But over the course of 1971, 1972, and 1973, he started on a new project: writing letters. Through Tiptree, Alli began to make friendships that were distorted by her persona and at the same time very real. Many of these exchanges were with men. Yet if Alli had become Tiptree partly to be "one of the boys," the outcome was ironic. She never had so many woman friends as when she became James Tiptree, Jr.

CHAPTER 29: **FRIENDSHIPS (1971–73)**

I sympathize with your desire for the incognito, although I hope to break through it erelong as far as myself.

—PUBLISHER JOHN BLACKWOOD TO GEORGE ELIOT, 1857

After her exchange with Phil Dick, Alli had laid off the fan letters for a little while. But in the spring of 1971, while Tiptree was getting to know Jeff Smith, Alli read Ursula K. Le Guin's new novel, *The Lathe of Heaven*. She admired it enormously, from its opening image of a jellyfish adrift in the open sea—the sleeper, dreaming—to the story of George Orr, whose dreams can change reality. Orr is a true antihero, a man who patiently, almost passively, seeks balance rather than change. The book influenced Alli even more in her questioning of hero figures—though she saw herself in the idealistic villain, Dr. Haber, who puts too much trust in the intellect and fatally underestimates the unconscious mind.

As Tiptree, Alli drafted an effusive fan letter, then decided she didn't like its tone: "aggressive admiration, endless citations of beauties (showing I'd read every single word twice), fatal fluency." It sounded, she thought, like Haber. Instead, on April 17, Tiptree sent a short, admiring note. As he often did in his fan letters, he urged Le Guin not to write back: "Please, it would distress me to think I'd wasted your writing time answering this."

A few weeks later, Le Guin replied:

> Dear Mr. Tiptree,
>
> You categorically forbade me to answer your letter, so you must understand that *this is not an answer*. It is not to express appreciation of your letter, and it doesn't say how tickled I am that you liked the jellyfish. (Very few people seem to share my feeling for jellyfish.) It also doesn't say how much I like your stories.

Yours, insincerely,

niuG eL alusrU

Her letter set the tone of the correspondence: affectionate, comic, inventive, admiring, and, in the beginning, not very serious. Le Guin made drawings of jellyfish and squid (because they hide in clouds of ink). Tip sent squidlike postcards: as new ideas came to him, he would add lines around the edges or on bits of correcting tape stuck to the front of the card. Tip played games with "Ursula," translating it into "Starbear" or "Bear." Le Guin replied with "Tree," and drew cartoons of trees and bears.

Le Guin was in her early forties, married to a history professor, the mother of three children, living in Portland, Oregon. Like Alli, she was the daughter of talented parents, the anthropologist Alfred and the writer Theodora Kroeber. Like Alli, she had had a long writing apprenticeship: her first published story, in *Fantastic* in 1962, came after a decade of false starts and rejections. But Le Guin was by far the better-known writer—especially after her novel *The Left Hand of Darkness* was published in 1969. Part adventure story, part fictional anthropology, part work of political philosophy, it takes place on a planet called Gethen where people have no gender most of the time, and is one of the first works of science fiction to explore the difference gender makes in human society. Le Guin's books were read outside SF, for which she was envied within it, and she had a more literary sensibility than most SF writers, which was part of her bond with Tiptree.

Throughout 1971 and 1972, the two writers exchanged notes and postcards. Then Le Guin, like Dick, put Tiptree on the spot by reading his work. In November 1972 she sent him a postcard saying that "On the Last Afternoon" (which had just appeared in *Amazing*) was "the best sf short story I have read in years."

After Alli got done dancing around the post office, Tiptree answered with a five-page letter telling Le Guin please not to admire him, since her response to his obviously second-rate story had nothing to do with its merit. Artists and writers, Tip asserted, go around with these big invisible radar-rigs overhead, turning and tuning, seeking all the time (in the dentist's chair, picking their noses, fighting with their loved ones, cowering before their enemies, filing by their coffins). *All the time.* Which makes some people correctly conclude that really good writers are inhuman shits. And this rig is pulling in hints, visions, unsung songs, marvels, apparitions, garbage, angel's grocery lists, junk unending quite unperceived by others, but essential to the writer. His nest-building material, his making-a-charm-against-death supplies, I don't know. *You* know; whatever.

But it isn't only bringing in, this antenna. The bloody rig is energised. It's active, it digests, projects. What the owner gets, coming down the wave-guide, is not raw stuff, but a mix. Sea-gulls' jabber comes in as a conversation about Hegel, supermarket shelves come in as a bleacher full of aliens betting on how fast Atlantis will sink. [. . .]

So what happens when the writer reads other writers' work?

[. . .] The words hit the tuned field and flash! Transmogrification! All alarms ring! And down the spout comes pouring—not what the fellow wrote, but a combined product with auras dancing around it!

A product which might be loosely labelled, Oh Jesus, Oh Dammit-to-hell, how—what—this is, this is WHAT I ALMOST WAS GOING TO SORT OF WRITE!!!

Over-valuation is I believe the jargon.

The fellow writer then broods, paces, and is overcome by admiration or envy, all of which may or may not have anything to do with the qualities of the work. Finally, Tip explained, he asserts control over these feelings and this frightening "combined product" by writing an admiring letter. But there is no room in this image of "aggressive admiration" for two writers working together or exchanging criticism—let alone two women forming a creative partnership.

Le Guin replied, after a long pause, with a letter defending her taste and gently inviting Tiptree into a literary friendship. She said there were so few science fiction writers she truly admired—Dick, Stanislaw Lem, Cordwainer Smith—and when she included Tiptree in that group, she knew what she was doing. "I love sf and writing sf but sometimes I feel horribly lonely—morally lonely, psychically lonely—an outsider born. [. . .] You can't keep on reading Borges and pretending it's science fiction because you feel so lonesome, indefinitely."

Tiptree didn't accept the invitation. But he had a strategy he hadn't had with Dick. He answered:

Dear Starbear,

Your letter of 8 1 73 just arrived and only by the grace of fate and some minor automotive problems have you been spared from receiving an incoherent telegram proposing immediate elopement to Madagascar.

You are beautiful.

But after sobering up I came to the sad conclusion that there could be certain problems for example with your spouse and children, and it might be that they do not sell Geritol in Madagascar, or oil for my wheelchair, and so on. And that perhaps even if these obstacles could be overcome, I could probably expect at best to receive a ticket saying No. 142, kindly wait turn . . . But the vision of us strolling forever beneath the giant blossoming urp trees, while ring-tailed lemurs weave around us in orchestration of our discourse of agreement . . . will remain with me.

By which I mean, dear Lady, that every word of your letter fell into my ears with the silvery plonk of total understanding.

Tiptree evaded the question of art and competition not only by flirting but by describing himself as being too scarred by life for art to really matter. He wrote of the German officer who looked like his father. He described the crucified bodies he had seen in the Congo. He called himself "an old battered Airedale, one-eyed and droop-eared, whose scarred paws have travelled a lifetime of lava plains." He claimed he couldn't take the gossip, infighting, and jealousies of the science fiction world any more seriously than "the squabbles of a cloud of brightly colored butterflies." At the same time, in the same letter, he said it did matter: "it has been almost literally a life-saver, this writing."

After this, Le Guin and Tiptree went on alternating serious letters and silly postcards, in a relationship that was sustaining to both writers. They told each other stories and jokes. Tip asked what it was like to raise children. Le Guin wrote about her family and her "real life" as a Portland housewife—though the Portland housewife was also one of her letter-writing voices. Tiptree was always anxious not to get in the way of Le Guin's work. In May 1974 he worried his postcard would get him "elected No. 1 Person from Porlock." Yet Le Guin enjoyed the correspondence, and often wrote at times when she was stuck with her fiction.

Tiptree gossiped discreetly about his other correspondents, and sent Le Guin the old parody "Please Don't Play with the Time Machine," which made her weep with laughter. Le Guin discussed subjects from the religious conversion of Philip K. Dick (when he wouldn't talk about it: "Oh hell I don't blame him, I suppose anybody who gets within letter's length of me scents the Voltaire lying in wait") to the dropping of hyphens in compound words ("Dos shitholes con salsa verde por favor!"). They talked about Blake. Le Guin wrote about Shelley: "He is like oysters; you do, or you don't; if you don't, he makes you sick to look at; and if you do, he is simply in a class by himself." Tiptree wrote about his dissatisfaction with the *New Yorker:* "They have such a high floor beneath which they never sink. A high ceiling too—but I think the answer is that there *is* a ceiling, there is an escape-proof ceiling, commanding you to call it the common sky."

They did talk about work sometimes. Tiptree urged Le Guin to write angrier, darker fiction in the style of *The Lathe of Heaven.* They discussed a novelist's responsibility to her creations: Tiptree had no trouble killing off his characters as a lesson or a warning, while Le Guin felt a moral obligation to the people she had brought to life. "Listen—do you believe everything you write? In this horrible, irrational, occult, secret way? I do and that is why I pull my punches."

But when Le Guin asked difficult questions about writing, Tiptree tended not to answer. He preferred to cast her as a serene, distant literary mother. After he got to know Joanna Russ in 1973, he wrote her that Le Guin "radiates something [. . .] maybe it appeals to my Victorian background, in which crises were handled in the third person. Some kind of invincible non-immediacy." At one point Le Guin accused Tiptree of "pedestalizing" her. He replied, "But I put all kinds of people on pedestals, no sexist bias there. You just have to be comfy, all you pedestalees, I assure you Tiptree's pedestals are

the very best and most modern, TV and coffee-machines on every one, occu-
pant has no obligation to keep their socks up or anything."

When the correspondence first started to get serious, in late 1972, Le Guin
had just finished writing *The Dispossessed* and was feeling unsure of her new
material. In February 1973 she complained to Tip that her new stories were
collecting "batches of polite rejection slips, all remarking that I write well. If
anybody else ever says that I write well I am going to hit them with an 18-
pound 1950 Underwood Standard. For Chrissake at my age would I be writing if I didn't write well?" Determined to set her above him, Tiptree found it
difficult to respond to this. Yet when she was wrestling with writing, his
warmth and courage often gave her heart.

"He was an extremely charming persona, and I think aware of his charm,"
Le Guin recalled. "The flirting was certainly mutual. The charm consisted
partly in vivid intelligence, interestedness, epistolary wit and elegance and humor and good humor—really good letter-writers aren't common, after all—
and partly, like all charm, was mysterious, irrational, irresistible. It is flattering
to be written wonderfully clever, admiring letters to.

"Tiptree's letters combined lavish praise with personal reticence, also a rare
combination. He courted, flirted, joked, charmed, and evaded. Masterfully.

"The praise did get in the way of open friendship. He refused equality, in
that he was always writing as the admirer. This is perhaps why I always felt a
certain element of play-acting, of performance, in my side of the correspondence. I had to play up to Tiptree, and it was fun to do so; but a plain frank
friendship would have been even lovelier. But that, of course, is denied to a
persona."

And so Le Guin was reticent with Tiptree, and didn't pry. Like some of
Tip's other correspondents, she wondered if homosexuality might be his secret. But she didn't know how to ask, and later confessed she had felt this as a
"sort of vast lacuna or gap in our Meeting of Minds." Still, it was nice to have
"this man friend who understood more than most men."

Over the course of 1972, Tip opened up and wrote personal letters to
other friends. He renewed a friendly exchange with Barry Malzberg, the
gloomy author of pessimistic fiction questioning the nature of reality. Tip
gave the younger writer (Malzberg was thirty-three in 1972, and Alli fifty-
seven) advice on treating chronic sinus trouble, something Alli knew a lot

about from living with Ting. They talked about horse racing: would Secretariat win the Triple Crown? Malzberg urged his friend to concede his own talent: "I mean *stop* this bloody deference already. You know your value and so do I." Tip admired Malzberg's "capacity for uninhibited obscure outrage," his "exasperated scream" at the humiliation that was sentience.

Malzberg longed for more recognition for his work, and Alli tried to teach him all her tricks for dealing with competitiveness and envy. Over and over Tiptree told Malzberg that he was good and that recognition didn't matter. "Life is fair. Some people have talent and other people get prizes." The Nebula Awards were a running theme of their correspondence. When Malzberg withdrew his stories from consideration, because of his disappointment at not winning in the past and sense that the enterprise was unfair, Tiptree yelled at him for it. If a writer won an award he deserved it, and if he didn't, so what? Deep down, Alli wanted to win too. Years later she confessed to Charles Platt that "winning a Nebula was an actual salivating, don't-even-think-of-it-dear goal." But to Malzberg Tip insisted, "I absolutely refuse to hope I might win or care."

In a spirit of resistance, Malzberg refused to use Tiptree's requested nickname and began all his letters "Dear Jim or Tip." Yet he felt in retrospect that the persona had permitted Alli a certain kind of honesty: "There was an openness and accessibility in her letters that I'm sure wasn't in her ordinary dealings with people."

Tip's business correspondences were warm and rich—the epistolary equivalent of Alli's old work friendships. Tip wrote his agent, Bob Mills, worrying about his stories, talking about literature, and complaining about his ulcers. Mills replied with brevity, wit, and reassurance. And when Tip agreed to do the short story collection with Ace Books, he corresponded at length with his young editor, Albert Dytch. (Fred Pohl had left Ace just after he signed up Tiptree.) They went from discussing story revisions and titles to frankly exploring sex and literature. Dytch sent Tiptree Sylvia Plath's *Ariel,* which Alli hadn't read, and recommended Thomas Pynchon, whom Alli didn't like.

Tip sent admiring letters to Harry Harrison, telling him he was a great writer, a "suppressed wild crazy poet. Walking around making like a for god's sake businessman." Harrison thanked him, and went on giving him writing advice.

He resumed flirting with Judy-Lynn Benjamin (now del Rey). When she asked him for a photo, he eventually sent one of Alice age one: a curly-headed baby of indeterminate sex.

In the fall of 1972, he began corresponding with a young writer out in Seattle, Vonda N. McIntyre, who was volunteering for SFWA's Nebula committee. He talked to her about feminism, and McIntyre noticed that this older man seemed to "get it" in a way most men didn't. He got to know another young writer in Berkeley, Chelsea Quinn Yarbro.

For all these people, Tiptree was an extremely likable character, generous with compliments, with stories for young editors, with advice and sympathy. Tip gave people what they wanted, but Alli enjoyed doing that as a man, enjoyed what that made her, more than she did as a woman. It was fun to be urbane, competent, cheerfully knowing about sex and power; yet Tip was always kind. If for men he tried to be a "guy's guy," for women he was a man who understood. Other women, Alli told Jeff Smith, "had to brace up and respond to my courtly compliments—Tip was quite a flirt—and they knew somebody quite different valued them. Whereas just another woman coming in with sympathy and admiration tends to dissolve in a mutual embrace of woe."

All that sympathy and charm were less exhausting when Alli was Tiptree. As herself, she sometimes felt like "a 12-volt battery trying to power an entire city." But when Tiptree's batteries ran down, he could be switched off. Tip once wrote Le Guin, "I am VERY shy. I've had to pretend not to be shy, to develop a 'cool' persona, and I hate every minute of it. In our sf world it is wonderful to be able to be as recessive as I please." This contradiction—belonging to "our sf world" but still "recessive"—is essential to all Tiptree's correspondence.

Tiptree seems to have been fairly truthful: maybe her awareness of the big lie made Alli reluctant to add little ones. And Tip could tell the truth without getting anyone in trouble. He let Alli be a writer and a good guy, too. Alli once told Russ that her only solution to "the question of the personal shit who can make great art" was "to put man and work in totally different universes of discourse and state the facts."

Charles Platt, who interviewed Alli in 1982, said of her, "You have someone who was the classic example of the small child completely dominated in an adult world and wanting to get her life under her control. And I think she felt that so long as she was anonymous and could do everything by mail under this assumed identity, it was on her terms." But while Tiptree kept Alli's friendships under control, he also made them unreal. He may have contributed to what Alli once described as a "hopeless sense that people don't give a damn about you yourself, they only like your act, your outer shell, the cool charismatic myth you put about." He also contributed to an extreme case of writer's isolation: over time, with no one to talk to about her work, Alli got lonely.

Alli seldom mentioned her correspondence in her journals. In the autobiography she drafted for a psychologist in 1974, she wrote, "Probably I should put in a note about the score or so epistolary friendships I've formed with fellow sf writers. They're real—yet unreal insofar as they're carried on under an assumed name and gender. A lot of genuine relation comes through, but it's tainted to an unknown degree by falsity. Here I seem to have contrived another odd trap for myself." Yet shortly afterward Tiptree wrote Le Guin, "There is somehow a feeling of homecoming about our converse."

Alli must have wondered how different she and Tiptree were. At some point she and Ting came across a handwriting-analysis computer. Ting signed one punch card and Alli signed two, one as Alice B. Sheldon and one as Tiptree. When the machine spat out a list of characteristics, she tallied the differences. She and Tiptree (24 similar, 5 different characteristics) came out much more alike than she and Ting (10 similar, 21 different). Yet where Alli was "philosophical" and detail-oriented, Tip was "enthusiastic," "methodical," "sophisticated," and "diplomatic." Oddly, Alli was "creative" while Tip, her creation, was not—and it was Ting, not Tip or Alli, who had "original ideas" and a sense of humor.

Tiptree made things Alli did look better. In the winter of 1972, Tip sent Jeff Smith a new column from the Yucatán. It was the fourth winter the Sheldons had spent in the shack on the beach. They had electricity put in and bought a small boat. Alli snorkeled on the reef and visited Mary in Acapulco for a week. Bob Koke came down for two weeks. So did Ting's daughter, Audrey.

For Smith, Tiptree wrote about Mexico as the wilderness—and again, his writing from the frontier was nothing like Mary's. His scenery was wilder than hers:

> This is not [. . .] an "idyllic" beach like the Acapulco side, this is a raving brilliant blowing beach, storms of glittering coral dust, torn skies tumbling by, the surf creaming and blowing spume, the bay inside the reef has a million white lemmings running and plunging over it, everything glinting and gleaming and shrieking turquoise and jade shrieks, palms sweeping, grackles going ass over endwise, only the noble frigate birds demonstrating calm.

Tip saw the politics and power relations in his surroundings. He wrote about the locals who worked on the ranch, running the rented cabins, scavenging the beach, taking the tourists fishing, caring more for their irreplaceable outboard motors than their interchangeable gringo passengers. Most of them were Maya; Alli read up on Maya history, tried to learn the language, and admired their compact, powerful build and aristocratic profile.

And Tiptree put sex into the story, stopping to admire a sixteen-year-old Maya girl named Rosa, "running like a deer in a blizzard of blue moonlight, her long black hair flying from her small elegant head. [. . .] She wears a short white tubular thing from which her classic Maya legs emerge in a way that makes me happy I don't wear contacts, they'd fall out." But Tip was quick to deny any alien lechery. He said he was in love with freedom, "one three-thousand-year-free girl running forever in my brain in the wind and the moonlight . . ."

The trouble was, while Tip was mastering the wilderness, Alli had to do all the work. She and Ting had spent weeks before the trip planning and packing—and hiding all evidence of Tiptree from the house sitter. They had decided to ship down some of the many things they couldn't get in their remote outpost: a typewriter, paper, pens, books, pots and pans, bug spray, a battery charger, even a secondhand car. The entire shipment went missing for two months before it finally turned up in Belize.

No mail was bad enough for Tiptree's existence; no paper meant he was reduced to drafting stories on cardboard boxes. Alli missed her office. Her ulcer hurt. Their guests tired her out, and so did the other tourists. She complained to her journal about "impingements, over-intimacies, material chaos and entropy, 'invasions' by somewhat hostile strangers. [. . .] Nothing happens as planned. Maddening, we are *helpless*." Then she laughed at herself for wanting "the unblemished, private, virgin paradise—with service, yet!"

Later that year, returning from the falling-down Lodge to a messy, mice-ridden house in McLean, Alli wrote Mary: "I keep trying to keep this place up AND the Lodge AND travel AND go away to the sun in the winter—and it's insane."

Discontentment turned to panic in April, when the Sheldons came back to McLean. First they went to Chicago for another Mary crisis. Then their doctors told Alli her ulcer didn't need surgery, but sent Ting into the hospital for a double hernia operation. Hospitals scared Alli. On May 20, in an eight-page letter to Jeff Smith, Tiptree wrote, "I'm having troubles of my own now—too many people impinging, changing life-conditions, desire to flee, health a bit eroded, writing-time loused up—VERY sorry for myself—and our correspondence is sort of a hole in the sky, a nice blue honest sunshiny place where no barracuda has ever bitten me . . . and I love to linger there."

But if anyone scared her, she shut the door, the way she had with David Gerrold. In May 1972, the day before he wrote Smith, Tiptree rolled a sheet of paper and a carbon into his typewriter to answer a letter from Harry Harrison. Harrison had been urging Tiptree to show his face, saying that everyone in science fiction was in some way a misfit—Phil Dick "manic-depressive," Judy-Lynn del Rey a dwarf—and whatever was wrong with Tiptree, science fiction could accept that too. Now he said he would be in Washington in July and was prepared to stake out Tiptree's post office until he found him and could buy him a drink. "Someday you will have to emerge and I can think of no better emerger than me. [. . .] Really, it has to be done sooner or later and you be a better Tip for it."

Tip's reply begins with a sly allusion to the truth, then builds to a terrified wail.

> Now listen, Harry. If I promise cross my heart and also Bob Mills' and Gloria Steinem's that if and when I go public YOU WILL BE THE FIRST TO KNOW—
>
> —WILL YOU LAY OFF? In point of fact I'm going to be on a

small mountain in British Columbia in July, if plans work out. But let's
get on the same wavelength with this. I really really have to stay reclusive
for awhile more. When all this started, I had one set of reasons. Now my
life is changing, and I have a different set. Harry, listen. You've been a
great friend and I value it more than I can say. My life is a mixed-up
mess right now. I have personal problems like other people have ter-
mites. I'm barely viable. You and my other friends in the sf world, and
the writing, are all that's keeping me sane, under a surface normality. I
know from experience what I need: to get in a hole away from everything and everybody and stay there awhile. *Not* new vivid experiences
and meeting great people. Christ, I start shaking when I read the paper.
I've been through this before, see. The last time well-meaning pals tried
to cheer me up I ended sitting around with my .38 in my mouth. I was
brought up as a real loner, see. At a given point if I don't get off alone I
end up maniacal. This isn't an easy world for low stress types, and I've
only been able to go thru decades of organisational hassles and keeping
up a façade of calm and normalcy by keeping my escape routes open.
[. . .] As it is, I'm so spooky that I get a cut-out to open my mailbox; if
somebody really comes looking for me I'll just take off for good . . . Saying this kind of thing hurts. Harry, there isn't any interesting secret or
goodie here at all, just one real neurotic . . . Peace?

Harrison recalled recoiling from this letter, thinking "This guy's on a twist."
Later, after Alli's identity was revealed, he concluded that his friend had not
been "nuts" but "a woman who was just being very female about it." Whether
or not one sees this as "being female," there were moments when some of Tip's
correspondents sensed that the tone wasn't right—when, as Le Guin described
it, "the disparity between Alli's pretended gender and her real feelings was really
confusing and bewildering. It's kind of upsetting, that insecurity in a man."

Of course, Tiptree would never let anyone worry about him too much,
and ended his letter to Harrison, "Yours for the ultimate horselaugh." But her
writing game was starting to become more serious, more like real life. For the
first time, there was trouble in Tiptree's paradise. And one of the troubles was
women.

CHAPTER 30: THE WOMEN MEN DON'T SEE (1972)

One can speculate endlessly on the reasons for the pervasiveness of male pro-
tagonists in Tiptree's fiction. [. . .] It may make more sense to simply con-
clude that, for whatever reason, many of Tiptree's stories cannot bear to
articulate directly the pain and the desire of women, and therefore require
more reading between and behind the lines ascribed to male voices.

—INEZ VAN DER SPEK

In April 1972, frightened for Ting, Alli did what she always did when she was
depressed: despaired of man's future. Exposed as she was to government's
coldest levels of plotting and indifference, she worried about America's
"gerontocracy," old men who made policy based on "greed and fear." Tip
wrote Jeff Smith that he feared "the runaway growth of tribal militarism and
its take-over of our economic activity. A ten-year-old cub scout can define the
evils and dangers in our institutionalizing of our aggression."

She wondered if we could evolve beyond that aggression, "close out the
Stone Age," and make a new society. In a note to herself, she wondered if aggression was inevitably male.

> Certainly males are the main carriers of the defect; designed as aggres-
> sive intruders, and expansively territorial; and with inbuilt hierarchy.
> (The sin of women, by the same token, is over-nurturance. The drive to
> nourish and protect the runt, the defective, the deviant, whatever need-
> ful thing gets into their arms; to protect the killer even, to find satisfac-
> tion in filling his sick needs; and to find vicarious expression of their own
> aggression through him . . .) If the male could be eliminated, the prob-
> lem would be vastly reduced; the relatively gentler nature of women, the
> relative rarity of power-obsessed women, might slow down the crises.
> [. . .] But [. . .] the loss would be very great; many virtues also are car-
> ried by males . . . Can eugenics work, the breeding-out of the savage?

A month later, giving Smith marriage advice, Alli accused women of "over-nurturance" in a slightly different sense.

> Women I think—being very wary of saying sentences starting with "Women are"—but I really believe they are less nasty-aggressive, less apt to turn toward punishing others—but they suffer more sometimes. Parents really seem to build it in deep to daughters. And maybe there's some sort of natural care-taking feeling in women more than in men, which makes them suffer more when they make parents suffer.

In 1972, a new wave of feminism was gathering force. Young feminists were claiming that women didn't have to suffer, for their parents' or anyone's sake. Part of Alli was delighted, but part of her was frightened, as feminism challenged her ideal of self-sacrifice and confronted her with her oldest question: What are women and am I one?

For women of Alli's generation, feminism did feel threatening. They had gotten along by pretending not to notice their second-class status, "laughing it off," being proud of how much they could take. They had been careful never to expose themselves, never to complain. Now feminists were telling them to do all those things: talk about it, say it hurt, refuse to get along.

Alli had always liked women in theory, and she embraced feminism immediately as a political program. She joined the National Organization for Women. She subscribed to *Ms.* as soon as the first issue appeared in July 1972. After the American Psychological Association established its Division 35, for the Psychology of Women, in 1973, she switched her APA membership to that division. She started referring to all women as "sisters." But "consciousness-raising" made her uncomfortable. She believed in introspection, but personal confession felt (as it did for many women of her generation) both alarming and sloppy. She thought her young feminist friends complained too much. In an unfinished advice manual for young women that she drafted in 1983, she wrote:

> Train yourself to be tough-minded about the injustice of it all to you personally. This doesn't mean being tough or unsympathetic about wrongs done to other women—it means stop wasting time sympathizing with yourself, deploring your lack of self-confidence, weeping about

How *could* he—But I *trusted* him—etc. etc. [. . .] And beware of load-
ing down other women with your woes; chances are they have enough of
their own.

As Tiptree she remarked, "I don't have an urge toward personal liberation
from stereotypes, probably because I'm old and very peculiar and have done a
lot of my own liberating or at least living with my neuroses." As herself, she
put herself in the category of "women over 50 who have had their consciousness raised for 30 years, and are looking for someplace to put it." But you can't
raise your consciousness in a vacuum, without other women doing the same.
And Alli's official support for feminism contrasts, as always, with her unadmitted hostility toward women. As Tiptree, she now offered to write a column
for Smith on an old idea of hers from the fifties: the modest proposal that
women should be lobotomized at birth. Why not? It would end their troubles
with the brains they were not allowed to use.

Sometimes she was wary of women. To Ursula Le Guin, Tiptree wrote
that though he was "for the Lib," he didn't think it would help him much personally. "Entre nous & sub specie aeternitatis, I am one of those that always
get accidentally guillotined when the Great Day of Liberation comes, because . . . I guess . . . I am full of parentheses. Revolutions can't abide parentheses." Besides, he added, no revolution was going to help the real problem,
which was being "that obscene joke known as alive and conscious."

Sometimes she was anxious for women. After reading a pamphlet on the
lack of structure in the women's movement, she wrote its author, Jo Freeman,
wondering

> how far this wave of the movement will go. I'm old enough to have lived
> through the death of the first hopes—in the post-WW2 misery—and
> I'm frightened for this one. It is a wonderful thing to have seen women's
> liberation reborn, but we have so far to go and with so few tools. Also, as
> an organisation veteran I've seen something of how power works and
> I'm terrified of women's innocence.

Reading her NOW chapter newsletter, Alli found it "sadly childish. My
sex seems so trivialized . . . If one could somehow evolve a race of trained,

'hard' women?" Yet maybe women's liberation confronted her too much with her own anger. The more loudly women demanded their rights, the more Alli worried about empathy, thought about mothering, and tried to define femininity as nurturance.

Tiptree had his own response to feminism in the spring of 1972. He sat down and wrote his ironic, many-layered, pessimistic, comic masterpiece, "The Women Men Don't See."

The story opens with a man emerging from the men's room. "I see her first while the Mexicana 727 is barreling down to Cozumel Island. I come out of the can and lurch into her seat, saying 'Sorry,' at a double female blur. The near blur nods quietly. [. . .] I continue down the aisle, registering nothing. Zero."

The man, Don Fenton, is a federal agent of some unspecified sort, on his way to the Yucatán, ostensibly to fish. The women are Ruth Parsons, a government librarian, and her daughter. The three agree to share a chartered plane, setting in motion a classic drama: The plane crashes in the wilderness. The man struggles to protect the group. Then the UFOs arrive—but in a reversal of the classic SF plot, the man doesn't save the women from alien kidnap. Instead, the librarian tells him she'd rather go with the aliens than stay with him.

Throughout the story, Don misreads the women. Trapped in his adventure yarn, he can't see that they are playing out a very different plot. He assumes Ruth's daughter, Althea, will not want to be left alone with the Maya pilot; Althea is intent on seducing the Maya pilot with a view to offspring. He can't help sizing Ruth up sexually; her mind is on a different rendezvous. When Ruth goes to speak with the aliens, Don assumes they are under attack and yells for Ruth to get behind him. He pulls his gun and fires—and in his panic shoots Ruth, grazing her arm. This last scene is pure black comedy: Alli making fun of science fiction. ("I hoped somebody would snort," Tip wrote Le Guin.)

But in the crucial central scene Don asks Ruth about "women's lib," and she emerges from the shadow of Don's narration to say that feminism has no more chance than their campfire, which has gone out in the rain.

> Women have no rights, Don, except what men allow us. Men are more aggressive and powerful, and they run the world. When the next real crisis upsets them, our so-called rights will vanish like—like that smoke. We'll

be back where we always were: property. And whatever has gone wrong will be blamed on our freedom, like the fall of Rome was. You'll see.

Ruth concludes, "What women do is survive. We live by ones and twos in the chinks of your world-machine." Then the two women depart Earth with the alien exploring party. They leave Don behind to ask, "How could a woman choose to live among unknown monsters, to say good-bye to her home, her world?" They leave us to ask, "Whose world? Who are the monsters?"

On one level, this was a story about feminism that men could understand. By showing women longing to leave Earth for the stars, it describes women's alienation in terms any male science fiction reader can instantly recognize. Everyone was impressed by how well Tiptree had understood the women, though Alli later said she had worked hardest for the male tone. "Shit, I knew Mrs. Parsons, all I had to do was keep her from talking too much. But Don Fenton—!" In other words, the hard part was to achieve the cool, calm, uncomprehending voice that indirectly communicates Ruth's anger.

But this is not just a story explaining feminism to men, and as usual, it's not at all clear which side Tiptree is on. Are we meant to believe Ruth Parsons's view of the world? Ruth's outburst was one of Alli's many opinions on women: her remark about the fall of Rome comes from Alli's 1947 essay "The Woman Haters." But Ruth's position is insanely extreme, and her abandonment of Earth for the unknown an act of desperation.

Are we meant to hate Don? Surely not: he is too likable, and too much like Alli's own alter ego, Tiptree. Being Don is clearly more fun than being Ruth, who beneath her competent exterior is all rage and pain. Don is not just a straw man, like the narrator in Mary's story "The Lieutenant Meets the WAAC." He is not only there to have his prejudices overturned or keep the anger under control. He must also bear witness to Ruth's otherwise unspeakable despair.

It would be easy to read "The Women Men Don't See" as a polemic, like Mary's story, or as a game played on the reader, with the author emerging at the end laughing and saying, I was cheering for the women all along. But maybe it is really about what it says it's about: the writer's difficulty in speaking of, or even seeing, women's experience—including her own. (One part of the story that remains completely unspoken is the relationship between mother and daughter, who barely interact at all. And yet Alli, at the same time, was writing her mother almost daily.) Tiptree's story says much more about women than that men don't understand them. It says that to be a woman is so painful it's not safe to take their side.

Tiptree sent "The Women Men Don't See" to Bob Mills in June 1972, with instructions to submit it to *Playboy*. The story was rejected by *Playboy, Cosmopolitan,* and *Penthouse* before it sold to the first SF editor who saw it, Ed Ferman. It ran in the December 1973 issue of *F&SF*. Along with Tiptree's growing correspondence with women friends, it gave him the reputation of being that unique creature, a male feminist. "Tip listens (or reads, to be more accurate) and really tries to see the trouble from the woman's side," Quinn Yarbro wrote. It was a time when many women and some men badly wanted to discover that men could be feminists. Again, Tiptree worked because he gave people what they wanted.

But to really take women's part, Alli would have to stop giving people what they wanted. She could stay, like Tillie in "Mama Come Home," and side with the men against the alien women. Or she could give up the advantages she had gained from being Tiptree, ally herself with the women, and, like Ruth Parsons, go forth into the unknown with no hope of return.

After Alli finished "The Women Men Don't See," in early June, she started to feel better. When Robert Silverberg bought "The Girl Who Was Plugged In" for *New Dimensions,* Tip told Smith he was "euphoric." Even a three-day storm from Hurricane Agnes that got through the leaky roof and rained all over Alli's desk didn't seem so bad. By July, when Alli began revising her stories for the Ace Books short story collection and (with Smith's help) was trying to think of a title, she was in a cheerful, roll-up-your-shirt-sleeves mood. The one thing that was bothering her was her arthritic hand, which made it hurt to type. To his agent, Bob Mills, Tiptree grumbled, "If mankind's intellectual rise was based on the opposable thumb, I expect to be back with Pithecanthropus shortly."

The summer trip was to Canada again, this time a cabin, reachable only on horseback, in the Rocky Mountains near Banff. Tip told Smith it was bliss: "This is practically a new Tiptree speaking, the last 3 weeks have been mountain air, sleep, gorgeous geology, sleep, horses-bears-marmots-snow-flowers-blisters—and SLEEP. Also sound food and no worries greater than 1 blister, 2 saddle-sores and is-the-camera-focussed." Tiptree didn't write a travelogue, but did draft four (unpublished) pages on the history of equitation and the worthlessness of the Western saddle, concluding, "The natural, instinctive way to do anything is usually the worst way possible."

As Tiptree narrated Alli's day-to-day life, he gave it extra magic. Where she was tagging after her husband on fishing trips, Tiptree was having wilderness exploits; where she was doing some work around the house, Tiptree was showing off his mechanical competence. On the way back from Banff Alli and Ting went to the Lodge. In a letter to Smith, fixing a table at the old fishing camp became an epic undertaking:

> My typewriter table is part of an o-o-o-old Singer hand-sewing-machine base, wrought iron legs—and every time the carriage returns the whole thing waves a foot sideways for ten minutes. So I put in diagonal wire braces and turnbuckles, and now it only vibrates 6 inches; typing is like watching very small fast midgets playing pingpong. Also I repaired my typing chair, which is a swivel fishing seat clamped onto a crude bench of 2×4s. [. . .] I installed splendidly measured braces, which only required the insertion of several shingle ends to fit. Ho ho, now I can swivel, sway, lurch—let's try leaning back? . . . Gee, that didn't hurt much. Anyway, I'm a great carpenter. If some day posterity cares to collect my artifacts they'll have no trouble recognising them.

But if even household repairs belonged to her male alter ego, what was left for Alli? With her professional and, more and more, her personal life happening on paper and in secret, Alli Sheldon had less and less substance. She wasn't using her Ph.D. She had already banished her sexual self. By day, she was a Virginia housewife who went to parties with her husband's friends, made sandwiches when they came over to play bridge or watch Redskins games, worked in her garden, and shopped at Lord & Taylor (or, since she had started working at home, ordered corduroy shirts from L.L. Bean). Parts of her intellectual life, like feminism, couldn't properly belong to Tiptree and had no outlet at all. After five years of being Tiptree, she began to wish that she could write as herself, or at least as a woman. She decided to set up a female pseudonym.

The new persona, she wrote in her journal,

> has to be me.
> I can't afford another pseudo-personality.
> But what stories would *I* tell?
> It's hard. "I" am not a writer. "I" am what is left over from J.T. Jr., a mindless human female who "lives" from day to day, converses with H.D.S. (usually about my malaises)—"loves" H.D.S.—watches Walter Cronkite, has opinions about politics and the probable value of the Swiss franc, cleans up the garden, orders daffodil bulbs, repeatedly washes, clothes and reclothes my body, makes a visual presentation of self to world, worries about repairs to the roof. "I" haven't a story in my head—all that went to J.T. Jr. And became, or was born, somewhat deformed or deracinated, by being his.
> Can I get the parts back together? Does the described "I" have any interest for anybody, even any self?
> Dreadful thought: maybe "I" am a serious small mainstream writer [. . .] an item in surplus supply. Nothing unique, and peculiarly transparent. [. . .] JT at least has a satisfying large-frog-in-small-puddle identity. [. . .]
> (Oh, I could salvage "unique" anecdotes, ransack my interminable biography. But with what labor! And to what point?)

As "herself," Alli didn't want to write feminist stories necessarily—although that later became a job for her new persona. But she wanted to try out a new kind of narration, one she associated with the feminine. Having written in Tiptree's unsentimental style, she wanted to explore what her new persona called "bare-faced pain."

In November 1971, Tiptree had mentioned to Jeff Smith a female artist acquaintance who might like to do fanzine illustrations. In the spring and summer of 1972, the female friend began to write stories and was given a name: Raccoona Sheldon.

This time Alli set the pseudonym up deliberately. She decided that Raccoona would be an old friend of Tiptree's from Wisconsin. At the Lodge in late August, she went into town and rented a post office box in Raccoona's name. She bought Raccoona a typewriter, an Olivetti with sans-serif letters and a black ribbon instead of Tip's trademark blue. She invented a signature, a small, cramped one that was very different from Tiptree's flowing, confident hand. She practiced it, and put samples into a new file for Raccoona's correspondence. Then she typed out three stories and sent them off, one by one, to Ed Ferman at *F&SF*.

In her first cover letter, Alli gave Raccoona the bits of her history that were left over from Tiptree, along with some of his mix of shyness and arrogance. "I used to sell feature reporting and travel type pieces. I guess my status peak was the *New Yorker*. Then I got locked into teaching and research, which shows in this story. But sf is my true love. Please be warned, I'm going to learn to write it, *ruat coelum!*"

At the same time, Tiptree wrote Smith again about his old friend who could draw, this time enclosing "a sheet of doodles I extracted from her pad." This artist friend, he added, "may try writing again, she did once. Doesn't take herself seriously."

When Smith wrote to say the doodles looked promising, Tip added more detail:

> I think she once sold book illos, she is even more recessive than me and hard to talk to. Just as the conversation starts getting somewhere she begins madly rewiring her house or weeding her drive with a blowtorch. (Fire: very ecologically sound.) It is difficult to persist in a subject when your partner is armed with a four-foot blowtorch. [. . .] I don't guarantee anything will come of this but it'd be nice for her, I think.

His friend, Tiptree wrote, "goes by the name of Raccoona, her own name having been, she feels, used up by a high-voltage media star so it no longer belongs to her."

This is startling, the assertion that Raccoona—who was to have a voice closer to Alli's own—has already been wiped out or overshadowed by somebody else. (Alli was probably thinking of the actress Ali MacGraw.) It's also odd that Raccoona took more shape in Tiptree's descriptions of her—shades of Ruth Parsons—than in her own voice. But it's not an accident that the first characteristic Alli gave her female persona was a first name that did not belong to her. The combination of obvious whimsy in the first name and straightforward truth in the last—Raccoona also used the name "A. R. Sheldon"—was probably a deliberate game of revelation and masquerade. "Raccoona" was also, as Alli intended, the name of an animal with a mask.

But Raccoona did not help Alli decrease the distance between writer and work—especially since Alli had already given most of her history to Tiptree. Raccoona did have some of Alli's past. She had been an artist. She had had an abortion. She knew the "technology of chickens," and once told Vonda McIntyre she was sketching out a plot about "a chicken hatchery set in the asteroids, run by women in competition with a huge processed-foods corporation." Later she became an outspoken feminist. But she was a thinner character than Tiptree: shy, unsure of her talents, with an oddly childish voice. She told Jeff Smith she was a retired schoolteacher with a large family, "a Wisconsinite these years, clinging to a fading patina of sophistication from the days when I lived in your East." When she sold stories she said things like "My goodness, I can't believe it." She corresponded little—maybe it was just too difficult for Alli to be close to the same people in two different personae—and required more outright lying to maintain. She used her fictitious family as an excuse for her frequent absences, which were really caused by Alli's illnesses, her trips to Mexico, and delays in forwarding Raccoona's mail.

The three stories Raccoona submitted in the fall of 1972 were all set in Wisconsin. One was a light parody of small-town radio talk shows called "The Trouble Is Not in Your Set." Another, "Press Until the Bleeding Stops," was a tale of bulldozers wiping out the innocent creatures of the forest. It has a jokey tone, but portrays nature as utterly victimized by human greed, and is a much weaker story than the morally complex "Ain." If Alli took the name "Raccoona" out of love for the natural world, the name allied her with what Alli saw as nature's powerlessness.

Earth destroyed is also the subject of Raccoona's most substantial early story, "Angel Fix." An alien lands in a cow pasture and asks to meet the local "good guys"—anyone who cares about the fate of the world. He brings a gift: a portal to an empty planet, fertile and green, "a secret beautiful place free from evil and greed" where decent people can refresh themselves after struggling with the world's hurts. It turns out the aliens want Earth for themselves. If all the good people go away, the bad people will kill each other off in a few generations.

"Angel Fix" is funny and its characters well drawn, but it is talky and sentimental, without the fast action and moral depths of even Tiptree's most primitive stories. Raccoona's characters do not philosophize while climbing mountains or fighting giant lobsters. Instead they are confined by Alli's sense of obligation and speak of the duty to empathize with others' pain. Raccoona would go on to write two of Alli's best stories, including the coolly gruesome horror tale "The Screwfly Solution." But at first she seems compelled to sympathize with the world's victims, of whom she is one.

Raccoona's early work went the course of most of Tiptree's first stories. The two slighter stories were the kind of pastiche Tiptree had never been able to sell either; they were rejected by form letter from *F&SF* and *Amazing*. Eventually Tiptree sent "Press Until the Bleeding Stops" to Jeff Smith as a favor to Raccoona, and Smith published it in a new fanzine, *Khatru*. "The Trouble Is Not in Your Set" never saw print in Alli's lifetime.

For "Angel Fix," Raccoona got a brief, encouraging rejection from Ed Ferman ("I did like the writing [. . .] and I'd be glad to see others"), a four-page letter from David Gerrold offering to buy it if she made changes, and a scribble from Ted White ("Try us with something new . . . Your writing is quite good"). After a year of bouncing around acquiring coffee stains, the story was finally accepted by the new editor of *Galaxy,* Jim Baen—though only after Tiptree had added a cover letter recommending his friend.

David Gerrold recalled finding Raccoona's first stories "too light, too fluffy, too delicate" and having "no bite." Ted White remembered them arriving "with little hand-written notes on flowery notepaper," and said, "They read like the work of an entirely different author—one whose stuff left me cold. There were maybe two or three of them, and I can't help feeling I failed a test when I rejected them. Not that I'd have published them under anyone's name; but I feel Alice had decided in her own mind that if she presented herself as a man, I'd buy her stories, but not if she presented herself as a woman."

In the early days, Tiptree had gotten plenty of manuscripts back with coffee stains. But Alli had gotten used to Tiptree's new status as a writer in demand, and now it made her mad to see editors like White and Ferman, who were asking Tiptree for stories, rejecting Raccoona's. On the other hand, she once claimed deliberately to have given Raccoona minor stories that would seem to have come from a beginner. Maybe more important was that no editors had come forward offering to befriend Raccoona the way they had Tiptree.

Alli came to feel that Raccoona wasn't taken seriously because she was a woman, and it's possible this was true. Yet Raccoona was not the many-sided woman that Alli Sheldon was, either in her fiction or in her correspondence, nor was she as appealing as Tiptree. She did become close to one or two people, particularly Vonda McIntyre. And some people recognized Tiptree's style in Raccoona's stories and suspected them of being the same person.

But almost everyone was put off by the name. "Tiptree" sounded magical, but Le Guin found "Raccoona" "klutzy" and a "self-put-down"; McIntyre thought it was embarrassing. And men weren't the only readers who were put off by the work. After the revelation of Tiptree's identity, Le Guin wrote Alli that she had suspected Tip and Raccoona were the same person but had liked Raccoona's stories less. "Raccoona, I think, has less control, thus less wit and power."

Tiptree closed out the year 1972 with another attempt at the novel everyone seemed to want. "I'd love to see [a novel] for consideration as a serial," Ted White said (shortly before rejecting "Angel Fix"). "Aren't you ready for a novel now? You're one of the five or six writers around this genre for whom I have respect," Barry Malzberg asked. Harry Harrison gave advice: "Plot your characters. Classicly. A hero. Got room for a heroine? If not—get another male in second position. [. . .] Get it straight in your head just what the fuck is going to happen to your hero. [. . .] Accept the fact that the first page or pages will be shit and get on with it."

But her idea didn't pan out (she completed it the next year as the novella "A Momentary Taste of Being") and instead she began work on a story for an anthology called *Final Stage*. The editors, Ed Ferman and Barry Malzberg, had asked each contributor to attempt the "ultimate" story on a science fiction theme, and had assigned Tiptree the theme "Doomsday." The story Tip turned in, "Her Smoke Rose Up Forever," was inspired by the work of British psychic researcher Whately Carington, who had speculated that human souls might live on after death as patterns based on their strongest emotions. He had assumed that these emotions would be joyous ones. Alli wondered, what if they were not? What if souls survived as shreds of broken heart and grief, Gettysburg and Ravensbrück, "atrocity without end or comfort, forever"?

In "Her Smoke," Alli gave bits of her own life to the story's teenage boy protagonist. She gave him a morning of joy and disappointment hunting ducks in the tule reeds near Santa Fe (with her own gun, the Fox CE double-barrel twelve-gauge). She gave him her love for the beautiful Adele and her horror at her death. Then she smashed it all—the human race, and her alter ego within it. At the end of the world, in some catastrophe it's too late to comprehend, the young man's very self is reduced to mere scraps of consciousness in a windstorm.

CHAPTER 31: A GLASS GETTING READY TO CRACK (1973)

How can we live, being half beast?

—JAMES TIPTREE, JR., 1973

Several important Tiptree stories were published in 1972: "And I Awoke and Found Me Here on the Cold Hill's Side" and "Painwise" in *F&SF*, "The Man Who Walked Home" in *Amazing*, "All the Kinds of Yes" in *New Dimensions II*, "The Milk of Paradise" in *Again, Dangerous Visions*. By 1973, Tiptree was being talked about. Other writers started sending *him* fan mail; the prominent British SF writer John Brunner asked if he could come to McLean. Tip was writing to more and more people. His social star was rising, and so was his literary one. In *Again, Dangerous Visions*, Harlan Ellison announced that Tiptree was the man to beat for the year's short story awards. "[Kate] Wilhelm is the woman to beat, but Tiptree is the man."

By now Tip had stopped hinting that he worked for the government and had begun insisting that he didn't: "I do not, repeat it, work for the CIA, the FBI, NSA, the Treasury, the narcs, or the Metropolitan Park Police." Even so, rumor had it he was some kind of high-placed official. His travels seemed to confirm this: even Jeff Smith joked that summer, "Canada again? Don't they ever send you anywhere different?" So did what Silverberg called Tiptree's "obviously first-hand acquaintance with the world of airports and bureaucrats." When the Watergate scandal broke in the spring of 1973, the temptation to connect Tiptree with Watergate was not resisted.

"It made for wonderful speculation games," Quinn Yarbro recalled. "Basically, take almost anybody in the Senate or the White House who'd been in Europe after the war, or anything like that—because that's what we knew about Tip—and at one time or another somebody would have suggested they might be Tiptree. Sure there were rumors he was really a woman. There were also rumors he was Henry Kissinger. We took them about as seriously."

The tales about Tiptree's sex did have one bit of corroborating evidence. In September 1973 Harlan Ellison teased Tiptree, threatening to blow "his/ her" cover if "he/she" didn't come up with a novel. His proof was an exaggerated story about David Gerrold's 1969 trip to Virginia. Ellison wrote that his "operatives" (Gerrold and his friend)

> did a reconnoiter of your home in Alexandria, Virginia. Or, at least, what was *purported* to be your home. Huge, rambling, Beverly Hills-ish home in a deeply wooded area. Door answered by a woman described in my operative's report as "striking dark-haired woman in middle thirties, approximately 5'5" in height, average weight for the size, wearing blouse and slacks," a woman who seemed nonplused when Gerrold asked for you.

In his reply, Tip ignored Harlan's speculations and mentioned casually,

> Yeah, Gerrold told me about his trip around the Washington suburbs, I tried to explain him a little but I don't think he understood. At least he has given up the CIA kick. He's a fine lad, I wish I could turn out to be Dick Helms or even Elizabeth Drew for him. [. . .]
>
> Of course I can tell YOU the real shit Harlan, how I really am an escaped nun working in the FBI Gatorade concession . . . but on third thoughts . . .

On her guard now, Alli took steps to laugh off the question of her identity. To Albert Dytch, the young editor at Ace, Tiptree griped that Ellison's "latest is that he with the help of [Gerrold] now believes I am a woman, he writes me using he/she. Well it's a relief after the last which was believing I was a CIA creep." To Jeff Smith he joked that Gerrold must have "leapt out of the shrubbery onto some slinky suburban housewife who claimed she was me."

People made mental images of their friend Tiptree. Ted White pictured him as "tall, thin, with an easy-going grin on his face." Dytch imagined a man "like Ichabod Crane, tall and stoop-shouldered, or else like a very thin Joseph K." Fanzine publisher Richard E. Geis, asking for an interview, tried to lure Tiptree into conversation with a description: "I think of you as a tall, lean, intense young man who doesn't yet need glasses. You like wild shirts and ties.

You smoke a pipe. You type fast and grin a lot. What is the real Jim Tiptree, Jr. like?" Later on, Joanna Russ told Tip, "I bet you're (in a quiet way) immensely handsome."

In his own letters, Tiptree began to acquire a detailed physical presence. He paced back and forth. He stayed up late nights pecking at the typewriter. ("I type with one (1) finger, when I worked on the Chi. *Sun* people used to gather round and gape.") He taught Barry Malzberg how to do exercises for a bad back. To Dytch, he complained frankly about his own back pain: "I personally have spent the last week strapped to a plank, something went croink down in that region where we so unwisely abandoned tails. [. . .] This is the first day I've been able to type for a couple of hours and . . . and . . . and my ass hurts." Describing the same sore back to Harry Harrison, he wrote, "I have encountered that which comes to all men, a busted sacroiliac." Even Alli's illnesses—ulcers, back trouble—seemed to fit a male biography.

Tiptree had appetites as well as ailments: he liked to joke about the bodily pleasures Alli had written off. To Dytch he threatened to call his book "Future Fellatio" or "Understated Jizzums," and described a reading binge in sexual terms: "Like your dark questing after nooky, I too, with decorum suitable to age, nose after literary labia."

To Robert Silverberg, worrying that a story was overdue, Tip wrote, "My mother must have absorbed a jolt of guilty juice along with Tiptree Sr. rest his soul." To Ellison, just before an operation on his arthritic thumb, he signed a letter, "Love, one-ball reilly." And to Terry Carr, just after the annual trip to the Yucatán, in May 1973, he grouched, "I swear, vacations don't pay, a week after you stride back in bronze and horny—you're back worse than you were."

In lines like that one, Alli did use Tiptree's physicality, very deliberately, to mislead her correspondents. Afterward, she said about her performance, "I have never told a lie or modulated my natural voice [. . .]. It wasn't calculated. (I'm lousy at that.) All my letters have been just first draft typed as fast as I can go [. . .]. I can't help what people think sounds male or female." But she eventually admitted that certain phrases were "very carefully chosen [. . .] to suggest masculinity—but only to the hasty, stereotypic reader."

She loved to sneak in private jokes about her own identity. When Tip told Jeff Smith he loved gardening, he added that he was glad the natural world was back in fashion. "Ten, fifteen years ago if I revealed such feelings I was a kook . . . A *bird watcher*, a nature nut, probably wore space shoes and ladies' underwear."

To his friend Craig Strete, in June 1974, insisting that he should charge money for his fanzine, Tip wrote, "The only place this doesn't apply is if the subscriber is a beautiful nubile young human female, which I assure you is not the case here."

And to Ursula Le Guin, continuing on the theme of age, Tiptree commented archly,

> Virginia Kidd wrote me that I must be 46, when I wrote back that she was under by about 15 years I haven't heard boo from her since. If she doesn't watch out I'll lodge a discrimination complaint. [. . .] I can see refusing to go *out* with an aged gent, but I don't see what my *typewriter* can't do that it couldn't 15 years ago.

Tiptree clearly had something of Herbert Bradley in him: the tall, thin, respectable gentleman, liked by men, protective of women, with a sideline in raunchy jokes.

At the same time, Alli wasn't sure how much longer the strategy of Tiptree would last. In April 1973, submitting a revised version of "The Women Men Don't See" to *F&SF*, Tiptree worried to Ed Ferman about the story's "honky flatness." As with white writers speaking for blacks, he said, "the day when male writers can speak for women is speeding by. Fast."

In November 1972, in a fan letter to Joanna Russ on her short story "Nobody's Home," Tiptree wrote, "Find myself turning to women writers now. Specially in sf. Something inside me, behind my Islets of Langerhans, responding to cryptic signals of unguessed-at freedom. New paths out of hell, a new fight. Lead us." In a non-SF letter Alli wrote, "I'm getting fairly tired of being a man; so much one can't say."

Instead, in the spring and summer of 1973, Alli abandoned science fiction for another project: a book under her own name, on the nature of women, to be called "The Human Male."

Alli had come up with a new angle on women, another way to write about them without including herself. In answer to all the "scientific" studies men had produced over the years on Woman, Alli proposed to write a book on Man. It would review current research on gender differences while serving as a guide for young women to the male world and the male agenda. It would be, she hoped, "the book someone should have handed me thirty years ago. [. . .] Even today girls launch into life so ill-informed about the male." Learning from experience "can be traumatic; it almost always wastes years and energy." In other words, "Who *are* all these others, these boys and men? Why are they acting this way? Are they crazy, or am I?"

At the same time, by talking about men from a woman's point of view, it would illustrate women's way of looking at the world. In an introduction, Alli wrote that everything we know about the human male comes from his own mouth and is suspect.

> Consider how odd it would be if all we knew about elephants had been written by elephants. Would we recognise one? What elephant author would describe—or perhaps even perceive—the features which are common to all elephants? We would find ourselves detecting these from indirect clues; for instance, elephant-naturalists would surely tell us that all other animals suffer from noselessness, which obliges them to use their paws in an unnatural way. [. . .] So when the human male describes his world he maps its distances from his unspoken natural center of reference, himself. He calls a swamp "impenetrable," a dog "loyal" and a woman "short." [. . .]
>
> The only animal who can observe man from the outside is of course the human female: we women who live in his house, in his shadow, on his planet. And it is important that we do this. This incompletely known animal conditions every aspect of our individual lives and holds the destruction of Earth in his hands.

Women had been told that to be human was to be "man." Now they must look at how their experience and their nature set them apart from the dominant point of view.

Alli planned to open with a section on male reproductive biology across the animal kingdom; she felt a detached, scientific beginning "cools the mind" and takes women out of their daily struggles with boss or boyfriend. "We cannot exchange [our human male] for a gibbon or a lobster but we may see him with new interest, in new lights." She proposed chapters such as "Getting It There: The Central Drama of the Male" and "Beyond Sex: Dominance, Territory, Bonding and All That." The second half of the book would be about humans, and would cover the cultural consequences of men's biological makeup, with chapters titled "Men's View of Sex: Are Women Necessary?" and "Things That Go Wrong With Men."

In January 1973, Alli wrote a letter to Harold Ober Associates—Ober had died in 1959, but his agency was still in operation—introducing herself as Mary Bradley's daughter and sketching out her idea for the book. She said she was writing science fiction under an (unnamed) male pseudonym. In a later letter she added that she was really a slumming scientist "ready to get back to something a bit heavier on the brain after my sf vacation."

Mary's current agent, Dorothy Olding, wrote to say she was interested, and in July Alli submitted the introduction, a table of contents, and two chapters. In her first chapter, as promised, she looked at alternative sexualities in the animal kingdom: "Many worms and the common land-snails are hermaphroditic"; "Oysters are alternately male and female." She touched briefly on human male homosexuality, noting that it was a common behavior that seemed to be of psychological or cultural rather than biological origin. This was one of the few behaviors she did ascribe to culture—thus putting it safely outside the bounds of her study.

In the second chapter she began to look into reproductive behavior as the origin of male character. Before she got lost in questions of sexual dimorphism in penguins and hamsters, she made an important assumption. In direct contrast to most feminists at the time, Alli argued that "evolutionary concepts are still the best tool we have in thinking about sex differences."

Appeals to "women's nature" had so often been used to argue that women belonged at home that most feminists in the 1970s rejected any appeal to biology out of hand. Joanna Russ later told Tiptree that humans had no biological cues to maternal behavior at all, only "customs, traditions, learning, illusions, myths, power politics. [. . .] There *is* no human biology." Vonda

McIntyre wrote, "I tend to think that primate 'instinct' stops at about the level of pissing when they need to."

But Alli embraced evolutionary biology as a source of hope. Only when people understood their biological drives, she believed, could they transcend them, learn to control their emotions, and achieve real cultural change. She wasn't dreaming of breeding a race of supermen. Empathy and negentropy were the qualities she wanted to give the human race, and she began to look for them in the human behavior of mothering. Mothering as a state of mind (not necessarily as an activity) might be an antidote to male aggression.

By next summer, Tiptree was telling McIntyre,

> I am beginning to see this "manly" life as an enormous parasite on the true *life* of the group: the humanmaking life. Did you know that the average mother and child—child say 2 to 5 years—communicate with each other something like 500 to 600 times in a half hour? No man can do that. And every poor bloody mother since we came out of the trees has carried on years of this, literally making human people. Not pleasure. A different order of life.

Of course Alli also saw sex roles as the product of cultural conditioning. In October 1972, she wrote a long letter to the editor of *Ms.*, commenting on the November issue. In it she professed a "lifelong suspicion that roles produce much of what we know as minority personality." Assessing the psychic damage done by the role of housewife, she added, "Did you ever look into the personalities of male cooks, Army, logging camp, etc.? They're all supposed to be crazy, incomprehensible, contemptible. And angry. The *act of feeding adult males* seems to have strange personality effects."

But biology gave Alli a way of talking about men and women that let her off the hook. If gender roles were determined by biology, then she wouldn't have to look at her relationship with her mother, her own anger, her own desire, even her own writing (which belonged to the "parasitical," "male" world of cultural activity). Since she was neither a man nor a mother, she wouldn't have to talk about herself. And writing in a scientific, gender-neutral voice—or as Tiptree—she could say "women" without meaning "me."

Alli was romanticizing women again, but still didn't entirely like them. In her notes for the book she observed that women "never seem to be zesty connoisseurs—Life not there for my savoring." But if women don't sit around talking about wine, whiskey, cars, or horses, she scrawled angrily, "What do they deal in? Are they alive?" It was around this time, while Alli was working on "The Human Male," that Tip wrote about his longing not to be so careful in his writing, but "to storm naked with hard-on waving through the world spouting whatever comes."

Olding liked the chapters and encouraged Alli to write more. But the book soon met the fate of the vision project: Alli got lost in too many details, while discovering that the research she really needed had never been done. She tried writing letters to ethologists, including Jane Goodall, asking among other things about frequency of orgasm among apes in the wild. Goodall replied that no one had ever studied this. Alli realized sadly that she could have spent a lifetime just gathering the necessary information.

In the end, Alli abandoned "The Human Male"—though her evolutionary view of feminism would influence Tiptree's writing on the subject. One of the ironies of Alli's career as Tiptree is that she insisted most on the biological, essential nature of gender at the moment she seemed to be proving that it was all an act, that gender was what you said it was after all.

In April 1973, "And I Awoke" came in second in the Nebula balloting, losing by just a few votes to Joanna Russ's classic "When It Changed." Tip wrote Russ another fan letter and told Malzberg he was "delighted" he hadn't won. "Tiptree is going to emerge from the shadows on his own sweet timing, not be winkled out by some damn award however kindly meant."

Meanwhile, Alli, Ting, and their friends were all enjoying the first flower of the Watergate scandal. The Senate Judiciary Committee had begun investigating the White House's connection to the Watergate burglars. Nixon's closest advisers, John Erlichman and Bob Haldeman, resigned on April 30. A few days later Tiptree told Vonda McIntyre,

> Many here are reduced to happy-jelly. After 25 years of watching that
> dingy murderous clown weavil [*sic*] his way up—to see the spotlights
> suddenly go on—FLASH!—and the vermin scuttle. And the apparently

genuine gasps of revulsion from those who voted him in. Vonda, I thought they knew, I thought that was what they *wanted*.

To Ed Ferman, Tip said he'd been "hanging on the TV like a sucking puppy [. . .]. I never believed that so many senior Republicans would actually *object* to real illegality and corruption." Alli began writing to congresspeople to demand Nixon's impeachment, and in a fit of joy sent $50 to the night watchman who discovered the break-in by noticing a piece of tape on a door.

In July, while she was working on "The Human Male," Alli went through another burst of political letter writing. She wrote to state legislators, calling for Virginia to ratify the Equal Rights Amendment. She wrote her congressman, opposing antiabortion legislation that had been drafted in the wake of *Roe v. Wade.* Getting out her most conservative stationery, she wrote the head of CBS, William Paley, to protest the hiring of anti-ERA figurehead Phyllis Schlafly to present a radio program.

After reading an article in *Ms.* about a women's camp in Denmark, she wrote a letter, published anonymously in the December 1973 issue, offering to donate the Lodge after her mother's death to an organization that could make a "liberated space" for women. *Ms.* forwarded several proposals, none of them serious or professional enough for Alli.

While she was at it, she wrote a fan letter to William Masters and Virginia Johnson, who had just been profiled in the *Washington Post,* thanking them for their work on human sexuality.

As Tiptree, too, Alli was corresponding more than ever. Even as Alli told Dorothy Olding she wanted to get out of science fiction, Tiptree kept getting deeper in. He thanked Jeff Smith for a Rod Stewart tape, and promised Firesign Theatre in return. He wrote a column for *Phantasmicom.* And Tiptree's book from Ace came out, under the title *Ten Thousand Light-Years from Home.* Tip got a box of free copies and sent them to friends: Smith, McIntyre, Le Guin, Yarbro, Fred Pohl.

To Alli's dismay, Ace had done a shoddy job on the book. It was full of typos, it had no table of contents, the stories were crammed together with no page breaks, and the cover illustration of a spaceship docking resembled, Tiptree once wrote, "a road-mending vehicle having intercourse with a laundromat." Still, Alli was pleased that the book existed, and what reviews there were

were favorable. In a British review, John Brunner politely passed over early stories like "Birth of a Salesman" and praised Tiptree's "extraordinary and varied talent" and "the quite astonishing freshness of his best work."

By the end of July, between Alli's writing and his, Tiptree said he had been working for the previous thirty-two hours straight. All this frantic activity was also Alli clearing her desk for the annual summer trip. Mary was ill again, and instead of going to Canada Alli and Ting had decided to spend most of August and September at the Lodge. Then, as they got ready to leave McLean, they got word that Mary had had a heart attack and had been rushed to the hospital.

Though Mary was mostly confined to a wheelchair now, she was still reasonably active, and there hadn't been any recent crises. But for Alli the situation was becoming unbearable. For more than ten years, she had worried, phoned, written, come running to her mother's bedside. She felt old herself at fifty-eight, and later described herself and Mary in these years as "competitive Lears raving upon the heath." Their relationship was still full of dissimulation: Alli had only recently discovered Mary's true age, ninety-one. Even Mary's independent spirit had begun to tarnish in Alli's eyes. Like many older women, Mary resisted the new wave of feminism, and Alli now described her as "distinctly unliberated."

And she was as unreachable as ever. A few years later, looking back, Alli wrote Jeff Smith, "We were close, even through those godawful years at the end after Father went, when I could barely stand to look upon the wreckage. 'Close' in the sense of empathy; I respected and understood her generous heart and witty mind. And her vulnerability . . ." But this suggests that the closeness went one way, in the sense that Alli understood empathy, of her obligation to give but not her right—or obligation—to receive. She also wrote Smith, "I am not 'mother-fixated'—far from it, we were aliens to each other."

At first Mary's heart attack looked like the end, but she made a quick and courageous recovery. Before she left the hospital she was already dictating letters to her secretary. Even so, Ting and Alli ended up staying at the Lodge for nearly three months. Instead of resting and working, Alli found herself hosting well-wishers, getting a phone put in, and hiring local women for round-the-clock care. When Alli could still joke about it, Tiptree wrote Le Guin that he felt like a minor figure in a decadent Roman deathbed scene. "I struggle to retain a protective, quasi-authoritative image; one finds oneself being cast in the role of one of the fruit-bearing slaves."

But as the weeks went on, Alli grew more desperate. In early September Tip wrote Le Guin again:

> I always thought dying was vaguely dignified. Maybe it is for the dyee; for the bystander it is total immersion in large, talkative, kind-hearted, ignorant, violently idiosyncratic NURSES. Who each have their own dynamic lives, which they recount in loud voices at 4 AM when one is furtively snatching coffee in order to (laugh) work.

Then there were the local friends, Tip went on, "who pay their respects by long sieges of sitting at coffee and cake [. . .]. Every woman who comes Brings Something; I think we have fourteen applesauce and/or lemon coleslaw cakes. [. . .] Mother eats soup, I eat Maalox." It was exactly the kind of emotional theater Alli loathed, and that exhausted her.

By the end of September she was a wreck. The Lodge was as beautiful as it had always been, with its familiar, battered cabins at the water's edge. At dawn, Tip wrote Harlan Ellison, "The mist is rising on the lake now, it's 5 AM, a skunk waddles by; a bat is coming in to hang up in the corner . . . The earth I grew in before they yanked me into the Congo." But he also wrote that he was sitting around with his .38 in one ear and mixing the Maalox with gin. *"Jesus I hate nurses,"* he snarled. "I am going to send a donation to that guy who shot 8 of them, who—Richard Speck."

Underneath was Alli's grief at watching Mary, the lively, warm, impossible, charming, capable woman she had loved so long, slowly slipping away. With lonely horror, Tiptree described to Le Guin "the dreadful faltering physical functions, who was always so fastidious; the babbling; and then, heartbreakingly, the sudden snatch of normal voice saying, 'We'll go no more a-roving . . .'"

Alli coped by pilfering Mary's Dexedrine and barbiturates and sitting up all night at the typewriter, writing letters. Tiptree corresponded with Vonda McIntyre about a feminist anthology she was planning to edit. He made excuses to a French editor who wanted to meet him for lunch. He recommended stories for the Nebula Awards. But Alli couldn't hide her troubles behind the cool Tiptree façade. From now on Tiptree was not immune to Alli's suffering.

Friends worried about Tiptree. Ellison saw through the tough display and told Tip he sounded "like a glass getting ready to crack under an icewater tap." He advised Tiptree to use his pain to write a novel, and tried, on his gray-and-gold stationery, to help: what if Tiptree broke up the work into linked novellas? Would that make it manageable? "You do not need to waste all that frightening grey naugahyde and 24-carat heraldry on poor old Tiptree," Tip replied. "The only thing that would help my production is a signed statement from god saying I'll outlive my mother which does not now seem probable."

To Barry Malzberg, he wrote, "I can see no way of turning all this into anything of literary value. I mean, after you've said *I'm trapped and dying* you can only repeat." Malzberg responded, "Whole scene there sounds grim and produces a helpless feeling. I can't and won't intrude on that privacy of yours however by attempting advices that would certainly be beside the point. Hope it works out. What can I say? *Can* you get out of there?"

Le Guin helped by asking for writing advice: she sent Tip an early version of her novella "The New Atlantis." This haunting story, told by a Portland housewife in an impoverished world, promises the return of lost cities and the awakening of a people who have forgotten even themselves. Le Guin, too, was thinking about feminism. Tiptree read the draft and urged Le Guin to tell more about Atlantis, to dare bring it into the story.

And Alli wrote. On September 24, in the midst of the worst struggles to find help for Mary, Tiptree sent Bob Mills a final draft of the novella he'd started a year before, "A Momentary Taste of Being."

"Momentary" is long, nearly a hundred pages, and moves at a slower pace than Tiptree had used before. It seems at first to be a conventional space opera: the tale of the spaceship *Centaur,* which has left a dying Earth in search of a new home. Ten years out, the ship is approaching a planet that seems habitable. In sight of land, tensions rise among the crew. Will the fatherly captain be undone by his secret drinking? What's going on between the beautiful, cerebral Dr. Kaye and her brother? And why does the planet's plant life exert such a mysterious attraction?

Aaron Kaye, the story's narrator and the ship's doctor, distrusts the plant samples that have been brought on board, while his sister, biologist Lory Kaye, feels irresistibly drawn to them. The tensions between Aaron and Lory run deep: they were in love with each other as teenagers and are still traumatized by their overwhelming, unregainable, incestuous passion. Lory, like other women in Alli's fiction, has renounced sex and love and gone out to do good in the world. Uncompromisingly moral, she believes that humans must evolve beyond the body and its base drives. She quotes Tennyson: "Grow upward, working out the beast, and let the ape and tiger die. . . ." She's related to P. Burke, of "The Girl Who Was Plugged In," who longs to "close out the beast she is chained to" and become Delphi. But Lory wants no body at all. She asks her brother, " 'Why do they use the word *human* for the animal part of us, Arn? Aggression—that's human. Cruelty, hatred, greed—that's human. That's just what *isn't* human. It's so sad. To be truly human we have to leave all that behind.' "

In the end, all the other conflicts on the ship are just a setup. The story takes the metaphor of thrusting into the unknown and makes it sexual and literal: the alien plants turn out to be ova for which the aura of the human mind is the sperm. One by one the humans surrender to their zygotic destiny. All "the evolving, the achieving and fighting and hoping," all human consciousness, history, and desire culminates in interplanetary sex, fertilization—and silence. Because what use is a sperm's tail, after it's done its one and only job?

"A Momentary Taste of Being" surely has an element in it of black comedy: Earth not as a womb but as a "planet-testicle," humanity as a giant jizzball. But it is also a sad story of great psychological richness, filled with questions about what it means to be human. It seems fuller than almost any other Tiptree story of Alli's own worries, ambivalence, "xenophilia," sense of being "trapped and dying," and yearning for escape. Lory, like one side of Alli, longs only for the stars. But like "The Women Men Don't See," "Momentary Taste" casts doubt on this yearning for nonbeing. Because Lory cannot live being "half beast," she embraces the destruction of the human race as we know it. But Aaron refuses to give up on individual humans, each one with "a face, a name, a unique personality, and a meaningful fate." It is he, like Don Fenton, who stays behind to tell the story. But he stays behind alone.

A few months earlier, when Alli was working at the peak of her energies, she also wrote of abandoning the mortal body. But in his column for *Phantasmicom*, "Going Gently Down," Tiptree described it differently, as a joyous fantasy of becoming all voice, all truth, burning up the body to fire the soul.

Suppose in old age, he wrote, you could somehow escape into that place that is fuller and richer than it's ever been before, the inside of your own head?

> By the time you get sixty (I think) the brain is a place of incredible resonances. It's packed full of life, histories, processes, patterns, half-glimpsed analogies between a myriad levels—a Ballard crystal world place. One reason old people reply slowly is because every word and cue wakes a thousand references.
>
> What if you could *free* that, open it? *Let go of ego and status,* let everything go and smell the wind, feel with your dimming senses for what's out there, growing. Let your resonances merge and play and come back changed [. . .].
>
> But to do it you have to get ready, years ahead. Get ready to let go and migrate in and up into your strongest keep, your last window out. Pack for your magic terminal trip, pack your brain, ready it. Fear no truth. Load up like a river steamboat for the big last race when you go downriver burning it all up, not caring, throwing in the furniture, the cabin, the decks right down to the water line. Caring only for that fire carrying you where you've never been before.
>
> Maybe . . . somehow . . . one could.

CHAPTER 32: "HOUSTON, HOUSTON, DO YOU READ?" (1973–74)

Why don't you write about women? my mother asked me. I don't know how, I said.

—URSULA K. LE GUIN

Alli finally got back to McLean at the beginning of November 1973, exhausted and depressed. She was anticipating Mary's death, Ting's, the world's. She saw herself aging and dying slowly like Mary, but utterly alone. On Election Day, she drew up a list called "What I Worried About Today." It included a polluted Earth, the human habit of war, her mother's nursing bills, her own health. "My stomach hurts. Is my ulcer reopening? Will Mother outlive her funds? Will Mother outlive me? Will I live to die alone in a VA back ward? Are cigarets killing me? Why aren't cigarets killing me *faster?*" She worried about the elections, the energy crisis, Israel, and Ting's beloved Washington Redskins. She worried about her work: "Why haven't I opened 8 inches of mail in personal in-box? Why haven't I answered Bob Mills? [. . .] Why doesn't Harlan Ellison realise I am not writing a novel? Why am I not writing a novel?"

In July's burst of energy she had written about living in the mind, but in November, looking at a pile of half-finished projects including "The Human Male," she felt she would die with everything undone. She wrote her old friend Rudolf Arnheim,

> Rudi, I have behaved as if every day had 48 hours, as if I were not only immortal but tireless. And meanwhile my mortal body has been weakening and slowing, while the foolish head imagines yet more fascinating projects and leisurely prepares to start.
>
> [. . .] Even to live I must give something up. What shall it be? The garden? Writing stories under pseudonym A (the man)? Writing letters to the host of friends I have acquired under that name? Writing under

name B (the woman)? The house? Travel? *Something* must go—but which? *I can let none of them go,* Rudi [. . .]. When I try to stop *anything,* this terrible mourning comes over me, I cannot kill it. I cannot even let a tree die. So I am dying instead.

Arnheim told her gently, as he had long ago, that to write was to choose, to "seize upon one of those bits and nurse it and feed it and polish it and get it to that final shape. Having a Ph.D. in psychology, you know perfectly well that you are running after all of them because you are afraid to run after one of them." But Alli couldn't let go—or Tiptree, with his letters, his friends, his promises to editors, wouldn't let go of her.

"I'm used to bouts of despair that go off in hours or such," Tiptree wrote Ursula Le Guin in February 1974. But this time he had "found myself lying 36 hours in a darkened room, unable to eat or sleep, hating the possibility of sound or light, wishing only to cease." To Jeff Smith, Tip wrote, "This fall and winter have been rough. I've been under a cloud of sourceless, almost meaningless depression. [. . .] As you know I'm a gloomy character, but this one was something new. It didn't exactly paralyse me, I've functioned work-wise, but what came out when I tried to write people was such a thick clotted cloud of despair that I usually tore the letter up."

Alli's doctor prescribed her an antidepressant, the tricyclic Triavil, which made her feel so stupid and slow that she quit taking it after a few weeks. Tip wrote Le Guin, "They never regard brain damage as a side-effect worth mentioning."

One reason for Alli's depression was surely Mary's decline. Another was her growing sense of Tiptree as an obligation. Yet another was probably feminism. Alli felt she ought to be writing about women. She was trying to come up with a story for Vonda McIntyre's feminist anthology. She was trying to write about her crushes on girls for Jeff Smith. And Tiptree had started talking about women with a thorny and brilliant new friend, Joanna Russ.

At the end of August 1973, in the midst of the scene with Mary, Tiptree had received a fierce two-page letter from Russ, forwarded from McLean. He had already written Russ several fan letters, including the one in May congratulating her on her Nebula for "When It Changed": "Sometimes something goes right, like Haldeman getting canned. [. . .] The reason I'm pleased is not because I love you (I do) but because it was NEW." In July, he had sent Russ a copy of *Ten Thousand Light-Years from Home,* along with a note apologizing for its sloppy layout and its cover illustration, which he said looked like an "abortion."

In her letter Russ thanked Tiptree for the book, complimented him on his stories, but told him his choice of metaphor was sexist: "The cover isn't an abortion. It's obviously a premature ejaculation." She went on,

> You see, I'm not nearly as amiable as you may think, and before you send me any more admiring letters I'd better let you know. I once reduced an MLA [Modern Language Association] meeting to surprised silence by correcting a gentleman about that "abortion" metaphor—it annoys me very much to hear my sex's reproduction used over and over again in metaphors as if men didn't have organs and biologies. It's part of the sexism of our whole disgusting culture (and most of the world). And I get very angry at it very often.
>
> That's usually the point at which former friends and admirers draw back and say in surprise, "But you're *hostile!*" Which, of course, I am.

The letter was an invitation to write more, but it was also a caution: "If I blow up in your face later, don't say I didn't warn you. And don't cherish and revere too much; I may not be what you think. Nobody's ever all of her/his facets in a correspondence."

Russ was thirty-six and teaching English at the State University of New York at Binghamton. Along with Ursula Le Guin, she was emerging as one of the most important science fiction writers of her generation. A perceptive critic, she explored the genre in academic essays and in book reviews for *F&SF,* while in her series of "Alyx" stories she created science fiction's first and most influential feminist heroine: a time-traveling mercenary, autonomous and in charge of her own story.

"The Women Men Don't See" opens with a man seeing women as a blur. "When It Changed" opens with a woman watching an individual woman. "Katy drives like a maniac; we must have been doing over 120 km/hr on those turns. She's good, though, extremely good, and I've seen her take the whole car apart and put it together again in a day." Russ's story is a reply to SF narratives of all-female planets "saved" by a spaceship full of men from Earth. Here on Whileaway, the arrival of men is an alien invasion that will destroy a self-sufficient world.

In his four-page reply to Russ's letter, written from the Lodge in early September, Tip said he didn't understand why Russ was objecting to abortion as a metaphor. ("Should I regard involuntary abortion as something a woman does, for which she is in some way blameworthy so that the term reflects on her?" he replied, missing the point.) But Russ's anger was hard to miss, he wrote:

> Do you imagine that anyone with half a functional neurone can read your work and not have his fingers smoked by the bitter, multi-layered anger in it? It *smells* revolutionary—no, wait, not "revolutionary." Not the usual. It smells and smoulders like a volcano buried so long and deadly it is just beginning to wonder if it can explode. [. . .] What the hell do you think sends some readers like me so?

Alli wanted to talk about anger, at least as long as it was tamed and harnessed for a just cause. She wanted to talk about feminism. But to talk about feminism with Joanna Russ, Alli had to go through Tiptree; and in order to arrange this game of gender Telephone, she had to invent a reason why James Tiptree, Jr., was interested.

So Tiptree told Russ that although he was "an old type with no near woman to oppress or free," he was concerned about stereotypes in his stories and welcomed a feminist education. In any case, he'd learned from his "crazy upbringing [. . .] which side I was on. The bottom side. When the jackboots kick in the door, it's *me* they're coming for. My fantasies are of escape, not of wearing the jackboots."

What Russ saw most in this letter, and what moved her, was that Tiptree understood her anger. "You really seem to know. That feeling of mingled horror and deadliness—something at once strong and good to the ego and very, very frightening." Dismissing the overheated rhetoric, Russ acknowledged the rare and powerful gift of being seen.

I suppose my fantasies are of taking off the Nazis' jackboots and whapping them over the head with them. Or better still, growing tall as a house and picking them up in two fingers by the scruff of the neck and sneering very much at them with teeth about 10' long and a smile as wide as a city street. [. . .]

The terrible thing is, when I get a letter (or a reaction) like that—from a man—I tend not to grow 10' teeth but to start crying. Which makes me feel muddled, humiliated, grateful, humiliated that I feel grateful, and most of all—*recognized.*

She didn't quite believe Tiptree's explanation of his feminism, and wrote, "Can I ask you if you are gay? Anything like this I've ever met before has come out of that particular kind of oppression. I wouldn't be that blunt to anyone I didn't really know, usually, but your letter just laid me out flat."

Tiptree answered, "No, I'm not gay so far as I know. [. . .] I'm more or less non-sex, it was a disaster area."

And so they set out the themes of their correspondence: sex and sexuality, frankness and disguise, power, anger, recognition, feminism, and growing up a girl. They exchanged intense, wide-ranging letters, with Tiptree playing gallant older man and admiring audience for Russ's emotional and intellectual fireworks. Russ dealt with Tiptree's hazy identity not by being guarded or reticent, but by making him whatever she needed him to be: a confidant, a compatriot, a punching bag.

At the same time Russ talked about problems Alli recognized, and that scared her. One was Alli's old question of how to be a woman. Russ said she had found it hard as a kid to identify with women. "Women never did anything even remotely interesting, so I identified with the men in all the books and films and in life, too, almost—which leaves you with an awful split sort of life." She couldn't find any women like her, she wrote. "So I decided I would be an exception, but one can't use that as a model or guide to real living."

Another was anger. Alli believed in righteous anger, but Russ wanted women to acknowledge harsher emotions: aggression, competitiveness, hostility. (Whileaway, the all-woman world of "When It Changed" and Russ's novel *The Female Man,* is full of women getting angry, fighting duels, killing wolves. One of its utopian aspects is that it has socially acceptable ways for people to dislike each other.) Russ's verbal violence made Alli very uncomfortable. Tiptree frankly admitted that he had violent thoughts. At that moment, October 1973, he was guiltily cheering on the Israeli tanks in the Yom Kippur war. But he didn't like his thoughts, and told Russ they made him "not a fit citizen of utopia."

Tiptree and Russ were both working on stories for McIntyre's anthology, *Aurora: Beyond Equality*. McIntyre and her coeditor, Susan Janice Anderson, wanted fiction that explored what the world might look like after equality between the sexes had been achieved. Tiptree told Russ that he'd had a disturbing thought: what if equality didn't equal utopia?

> I'm not going to yield to the fallacy that Women Will Save Us. [. . .] Nobody is going to save us. Things would be different if we could run this world on some other basis than greed and power . . . but Beyond Equality boggles me. Equality is necessary, but it isn't sufficient, you still have people. When they come to get me—if we achieve equality first— I can see just as many ferocious mindless grins coming at me on female faces, right along with the males.

If Alli was hoping for a denial, she didn't get it. Russ answered that, though she believed in *cultural* evolution, she was prepared to accept human nature as it was. And what was so bad about greed and power? Russ confessed to a Sirius of her own: the feeling that

> if humanity isn't viable, then it isn't our responsibility. Every once in a while I think that to myself and the weight goes right off me; after all, it's not our business to keep the species going. All we can do is the best we can. And maybe learn to enjoy, if possible.
>
> The world will always be run on the basis of greed and power—but I don't think we should badmouth either, since they are obviously as much part of us as our arms and legs. [. . .] Power and desire are both necessary, unless we all start growing chlorophyll and live off sunlight. And then we'd discover what vices plants have.

Tiptree protested that there really were good and bad people in the world, lambs and lions. Russ responded that there were only people, who behaved differently under different circumstances. "Really none of us are lambs, are we? We're just smaller lions."

"Touché," Tiptree replied—and yet, and yet. There were still more and less empathetic people in the world: the child who watches a butterfly versus the one who kills it, Shirley Chisholm versus Phyllis Schlafly. The creator of Dr. Ain knew this was not an easy question; a few years later, Tiptree and Russ repeated the same argument but switched sides. But the idea of accepting human nature for what it was deeply frightened Alli.

Russ's zeal scared Alli, too: it reminded her of her own early disappointments. She wanted Russ to cultivate indifference, not risk rage. To Le Guin, Tiptree assessed Russ as "vulnerable and unaware of the everyday mechanics of power and survival, while studying their apocalyptic forms. [. . .] Not yet settled into her own strength, not assured, unhurtable; not wily." Alli also thought Russ talked too much about her troubles, and once told her disapprovingly, "You seem so *surprised* when everything hurts or disappoints."

Another problem was that while Tiptree believed in niceness, Russ very often refused to like the nice self Tiptree offered. Not only would Russ not stay on her pedestal, she wouldn't let Tiptree stay on bended knee. She wouldn't accept him as an admirer, only sometimes as a sympathetic figure, and as a feminist not at all. And she wouldn't buy his attempts to define men and women so as to leave himself out.

She had a startling ability to see through Tiptree to the problems of Alli beneath—maybe because she was traveling on a parallel course, as when she spoke of her growing fascination with transformation and dissimulation. In November she wrote, "I keep coming back to the theme of the person-in-disguise—the Christian among the pagans, the woman disguised as a man [. . .]. Of course it's the bright child among the dullards," she wrote. In her next letter she went on,

> The whole point of a disguise is that you are both the inside and the outside—Rosalind is both her role and her person. It allows one to be everything. [. . .] Growing up in the 1950s was growing up in disguise—I remember it as a period in which all sorts of strange and arbitrary standards were forced upon me. In order to remain alive I had to

disguise myself even from myself—the really awful thing about having a cover, I should think, is that you must *be* it (in order not to betray it) so it ends up being not an act but a schizoid split in your very soul.

At the same time she kept reminding Tiptree that he was a man and couldn't understand. When Tiptree said he'd been brooding on "the problem of trying to write from and about women," Russ answered, "WHY on earth should you write AS a woman or from the p.o.v. OF a woman? You're NOT a woman, kiddo. Not as far as I can tell. Your own viewpoint is the only one you have. [. . .] Write your own stories!"

On one hand, Tiptree was a man designed by a woman, and that made him as appealing as any Darcy or Heathcliff. "I was madly in love with him," Russ later told Alli, "and sensed uneasily that this was odd, since no real man, and no real-man-as-truly-revealed-in-literature has ever had that effect on me of intimacy and 'I know *you*!' Though I kept trying to persuade myself over and over that Such Men Existed." On the other hand, his maleness kept Alli and Russ from understanding each other, and made it easier for Alli to resist Russ's insights about being female.

With Le Guin, Tiptree came alive as a flirt, philosopher, and "man who understood." With Malzberg, he was a professional depressive and maker of black-humored jokes. With Jeff Smith, he was a wise friend and raconteur. But with Russ, Tiptree was often a third wheel. When Alli tried to express sympathy, Tiptree sounded patronizing. When she spoke of men's potential for violence, he sounded threatening. Alli would let herself, as Tiptree, get as exuberant or outraged as Russ, and Russ, reading that as masculine interference, would slam him down. Early on in their correspondence Russ asked Tiptree to participate in a NOW letter-writing action. Tiptree did, but complained about NOW's sloppy organizing: "Dammit, why don't you silly idiotic childish women put the goddam ZIP NUMBER" on the address? She thought Tiptree had demonstrated enough allegiance to the cause, but Russ snapped back: "You aren't one of the family, to joke like that—nor, if you were a woman, *would* you."

This tempted Tip to a sly apology: "I am very regretful to have angered you. It was just like a crass, presumptuous, raucous-mouthed old man." But the slaps hurt. Alli herself maintained, in certain moods, that women couldn't trust men, but she was still puzzled when women didn't trust Tiptree. A few months later Tiptree told Le Guin that Russ was brilliant but exasperating, with "even less manners than she realises. [. . .] Pees all over your leg, interspersed with the converse of angels."

To anyone else, though, Tiptree was quick to defend Russ. When Jeff Smith wrote of her "shrill" politics Tiptree told him firmly not to use that word, and said,

> I've been corresponding with Russ, it's like corresponding with a conflagration. An absolute delight. She rushes out and bites my ankles one sentence, the next paragraph goes into some towering and genuinely impressive metaphysics [. . .]. Next will be some slaughterhouse humour, suddenly a page of elegant analysis of some literary phenomenon—I tell you, Jeff, I had to jack up my epistolary style several notches every exchange. Uncle Tip has a conceited streak about epistolation, you know, I don't get out-epistolated too often. When I do I love it—and I sure do with Russ.

Over the next two years, Tip and Russ wrote as often as once a week, and Russ became one of his—and later Alli's—closest letter-friends.

Alli was thinking about her sexuality. For years she had filed her lesbian crushes under the heading "youthful folly." Now she began drafting the essay for Jeff Smith that she called "Tiptree's Dead Birds." Tip had first mentioned it to Smith as an idea for a column in July 1973, when Alli was working on "The Human Male." He wrote Smith about it again in November, when he and Russ were discussing growing up female: "Got to reminiscing about what went on in my late teens when I kept going crazy over beautiful, unscrewable, hideously rich and very ill-fated girls."

Tiptree might have been using the "dead birds" to pretend to be a man; more likely he was letting Alli write about a subject she could not touch as "herself." But the essay stops in the middle, letting the question it raises go unanswered: why was its writer drawn only to "ill-fated," "unscrewable" girls? Why were they "unscrewable"? All Tiptree says is that he didn't dare seduce them: "I couldn't! I couldn't! And I would have killed anyone who tried. [. . .]"

A month later, Albert Dytch, like Russ, asked Tip if he was gay. Tiptree replied, "I'm not gay so far as I know. [. . .] It's my bloody talkiness." If his stories showed a lot of "feeling or sensitivity," it was only because he was trying to find "some way of letting the long-suppressed real reactions hang out." A few months later, in March 1974, he wrote Dytch again: "Hey, I just thought. Now I know why I'm attracted to women. I always wondered. I mean, being a respectable xenophile. Well, if women aren't the last Martians, the really realest aliens, what are?" This may be one of Alli's strangest balancing acts as Tiptree: using Tiptree to speak of her feelings for women, using her attraction to women to make her male alter ego straight, and ensuring that her desire would never be fulfilled by banishing its objects to Mars.

At the same time, Alli was using Raccoona to talk about unrequited desire, in a December 1973 story called "The Earth Doth Like a Snake Renew." The story—which didn't sell and was published only after Alli's death—is about a woman who falls in love with the erotic potency of the Earth. The story insists on Earth's masculinity: Alli had no patience for romantic ideas about fertile, female Nature. But unlike "Dead Birds," or "Her Smoke Rose Up Forever"—in which the boy protagonist probably takes his early loves from Alli's real life—Raccoona's story feels contrived. Its tone is distant and ironic, its feeling for its main character fiercely uncompassionate. The young woman's unanswered and ultimately deadly love of a male Earth reads like an evasion rather than a true story about sex and sexuality. Writing as a woman, Alli seems to have fallen again into an emotional dishonesty she didn't have as Tiptree.

Meanwhile, Alli was struggling with her story for *Aurora*. All of the eventual contributors, including Le Guin and Russ, had a difficult time with McIntyre's assignment. How do you write about equality as the story and not the backdrop? If you don't know how to write about women, can you write about an equal world? Is equality utopia, or, as Tip said, necessary but not sufficient? Alli had written years before that she didn't know what women would look like in an equal society; now she was upset with herself because she couldn't imagine it. What had she been working toward, all these years? From Boca

Paila, in March 1974, Tip moped to Russ that SF writers were "limited, invisibly bounded at a ludicrously near line; we think our imaginations roam to the misty horizons, but do they? Ha. Here Vonda sets a simple story problem—describe this future some of us are actually working for, believe in. *And we (I) can't!*"

Sometimes Alli didn't believe humanity or Earth had much of a future at all. From the Lodge, in October 1973, Tiptree wrote McIntyre about his problem with the assignment:

> *I find in my heart I am so damn pessimistic I cannot imagine a better world.*
> I can't imagine people—men and women and children—just *living*. With everything ok. [. . .] This isn't age—I guess I've always been this way. Living in an essentially doomed world. [. . .] I care strongly that other, younger people should have a better life—but as for myself I can't imagine it. [. . .]
> Moreover I suspect that most of the organised world activities are male-structured (as well as male-dominated) so I can't believe that simply filling in the personnel-slots with women means anything real. And I don't think things would get much different unless women had a chance to build their own world . . . which ends up like Russ' "When It Changed" and not Beyond Equality at all. Everything else I try just ends up with Golda Meier running a space-station, the Heinlein jocks-in-skirts thing. [. . .] I REFUSE to fancy some stereotype like Women-Have-ESP or Only-Women-can-understand-aliens etc. etc.

Tiptree added with double meaning, "I would not feel threatened by an all-female power-structure any more than I do by an all-male one."

Russ had urged Tip to write what he knew. So had Harlan Ellison. But what did Tiptree, or Alli, really know about being a woman? In January 1974 Tip asked Le Guin, who was also having trouble writing for *Aurora*, "Is it possible that this stuckness is Telling Us Something???"

A few days later, the Sheldons left McLean for Boca Paila. But by now Alli saw female trouble even in Tiptree's jungle paradise. "In former years I beamed upon it as a fragment of Eden," Tiptree wrote Russ. "But now I have started to look at what it is for the women." He saw the pregnant thirteen-year-old whose husband beat her. He saw no education, no contraception, men who kept all the money, women afraid of the men.

At Boca Paila, Alli had a nightmare she felt was connected to her *Aurora* story. It began

> in some kind of fancy hospital [...] my mother arrived there (driving a car!) car key was stained (bloody?) [...] I took doctor (Larson? Parsons) aside to tell him she hurt all over (like me)—as we walked he scooped a small patient from a chair in the hall and thrust it into a wooden drawer. "It's time, in you go!" It was a very old woman, like a toucan bird, all head and beak—I said, but it's dark in there, no light, nothing! [...] "Can't you be kinder?" He shrugged [...] I tried to talk about Mother, about being kinder, I said I'd seen cruel untreated diseases—he seemed OK but then made the first peculiar or "ominous" remark—"Are you sure all that hasn't changed *you*?"—or "made you sentimental" [...] I protested, thought him convinced. [...]
>
> Then we came to an eating room, the doctor went to sit with several young nurses; I knew I was invited but I turned away [...] instead went to the dessert "line" to cozen some food—I was "irregular," lying, "I'm with—" Some men at one end like off-duty conspiratorial waiters or sailors offered me a dish [...] and drink, the drink was pinky-creamy, I felt awkward and left after drinking it—the men were joking evilly—
>
> And now the terrible chase-action part begins—
>
> First, drink in hand, I somehow yielded to some kind of temporary idle seduction or woman's room Saks sort of atmosphere—I went around and "down" with the women—till somehow I understood I was in a trap, running to some kind of slavery, and tried to resist—fought to turn around and go back [...]. Always the magic talisman was, "Let me pass, I must leave and go to my mother, she is dying up on the top floor, her doctor is Dr. Parsons? . . . They want me." [...] At first it was various "temptations" and threats, all by women—dressed as vampires, insects, whores, etc.—silks and weird spaces and hangings—always trying to get to the "up" ramp, get up it—"I can't be a woman, I must go to my mother!"

Finally she made a run for it, pursued by the pack of women, then turned: "One of the pack came at me, I grabbed her or she me, wrestling arms, everything in terrible slow-motion glue (I was lying on my face, on my arm I think) [. . .] couldn't talk or breathe—I bent only her finger, it withered—I awoke—"

It was, she noted, a dream that drew on "my fear of being a woman, [. . .] my fear of desserts (and men), Acapulco, the lost women I've seen, [. . .] age, cancer, Africa, the WAAC, all together. Whew." The day before she had "inspected my genitals (mosq. bite), noted the labia 'withered' like my assailant's finger. [. . .] *Also* worrying about my own story for Vonda, my sex-reversed role." She concluded maybe it wasn't a good idea to sleep face down.

She didn't note what the dream also suggests: she doesn't belong at the table with the women, but the girly pink drink the men offer her is worse. It seems to be the men's feminine drink—not the women themselves—that sends her down into the world of "vampires, insects, whores" (like Greenwich Village in a lesbian novel). As always, there is no alternative but asexual virtue, kindness, and remaining her mother's daughter.

Alli decided after all to write about an all-female world, as seen through the eyes of a male narrator. She wanted to know what women would be like as themselves, outside men's shadow. The world of "Houston, Houston, Do You Read?" is more peaceful than ours, and knows neither greed nor power. But it does not seem like a free or comfortable place—certainly not a utopia in which Alli could live.

Like "The Women Men Don't See," "Houston, Houston, Do You Read?" begins in a bathroom. But this time the man doesn't come strolling out of the "can." Instead, in a flashback, schoolmates push young Orren Lorimer into the girls' room. He stumbles back out, "his fly open, his dick in his hand, he can still see the gray zipper edge of his jeans around his pale exposed pecker." He hears the girls giggling, sees the boys' "grinning faces waiting for him [. . .]. You shitheads, I'll show you. *I am not a girl.*"

Years later, Lorimer becomes a physicist, goes into space, and, along with two other "Right Stuff" astronauts, is flung by a solar flare several centuries into the future. Rescued by an all-woman space mission, the astronauts discover that Houston is gone, and that an epidemic on Earth has wiped out all men. Earth is now governed by consensus, has no central authority, and knows no anger, war, or violent passion. Its two million people are cloned from a small number of surviving genotypes, so that each woman has many identical sisters, mothers, and daughters. Love and sex are casual, and family bonds are not strong, although each woman feels close to the other copies of herself. Men, not women, are the aliens in this world. They are not saviors, destroyers, patriarchs, or sex partners, but leftovers of history.

Alli later said she wanted to show a world with a "relaxed, cheery, practical" mood, in contrast to the "tense, macho-constricted, sex-and-dominance-obsessed atmosphere of the little all-male 'world'" of the men's mission. Lorimer hates it. Though he likes the individual women, their womblike spaceship gives him claustrophobia.

> The cabin curves around over his head, surrounding him with their alien things: the beading rack, the twins' loom, Andy's leatherwork, the damned kudzu vine wriggling everywhere, the chickens. So cozy . . . Trapped, he is. Irretrievably trapped for life in everything he does not enjoy. Structurelessness. Personal trivia, unmeaning intimacies. The claims he can somehow never meet. Ginny: *You never talk to me . . .*

He pictures the world's population as a "structureless, chattering, trivial, two-million-celled protoplasmic lump." In the end, when one of his fellow men commits rape and another tries to kill them all in the name of God, Lorimer sides with the women. But it's a choice that lacks conviction.

"Houston" is a story that raises many more questions than it answers, including "Are men/women really like that?" and "Is this society really happy?" Tiptree said at the time that he was enjoying imagining the world of "Houston." It's a world of cool, competent women who take care of practical matters while the men flounder in a useless search for hierarchy and authority. And it has qualities that must have been restful to Alli: no anger, aggression, passion, or pain, no one unknown or unrecognized, no one different, no visible breaks in the mother-daughter bond. (Although mothering is named as an important economic activity, all the actual mothering in "Houston" takes place far offstage.) This all-female place is vastly different from Russ's Whileaway, and seems among other things to counter a fear of an angry, unnurturing feminism.

The clone fantasy arose, Tip told Le Guin, from "my own loneliness and longing for siblings—sisters especially." It is also about not having to make choices. A world in which "each person has perhaps two thousand living versions and extensions of herself," Alli later wrote, might permit "great relaxation, almost a playful response to life—since what 'I' don't accomplish may be—or has been—accomplished by another Me." Besides, Alli had always liked women in general better than women in particular.

Yet the world of "Houston" is almost oppressively cozy—like the maternal world in "Painwise" that the hero must reject in order to feel real. ("The clone part seems almost to hide something," Le Guin commented.) In talking about the story, Alli made it clear that the world of "Houston" had evolved over time, and that she with her twentieth-century self could not have lived there. But that only means that, once again, she had managed to define men and women so as to leave herself out.

Alli later said she had based her all-woman world partly on her exciting first months in the WAAC, in the barracks of Fort Des Moines. She didn't mention that she had been disappointed by the women's politics, or that she'd felt stabbed in the back by her commanding officer. She did once say, according to the writer Gardner Dozois, that "Houston" was not a Utopia, but a "cautionary tale, an if-this-goes-on warning about what would happen if the sexes continued to war with each other," and that readers were meant to sympathize with Lorimer.

"Houston" ends with a suggestion that all three men, even Lorimer, are euthanized by the crew of the *Gloria*. Having taken a good look at men's sexual violence, god-the-father complex, and so on, the senior woman says, "We simply have no facilities for people with your emotional problems." Tiptree later denied the charge of killing off the men. He told Jeff Smith their fate was not death but "polite, kind isolation, like a zoo. The point is, they and all their drives and motives are now not bad or good but IRRELEVANT. The women don't relate to them in any way. [. . .] Much more chilly than hostility."

Either way, the story upset people. Tip's old friend David Gerrold read "Houston" as "a feminist ideology story gone sour. All men are bad, all women are wonderful, so the answer is to kill all the men. How is that morally superior? When she opened our eyes, when she forced both sexes to confront the relationships between the sexes, she was brilliant. But it felt like she had stopped writing for men as well as women."

Yet Orren Lorimer is so very much like James Tiptree, Jr. In a feminist world, what are the women going to do with him? And Lorimer, like Don Fenton or Aaron Kaye, might be the side of Alli that can cope and bear things. Now he too must go with the women, and suffer. Alli felt she ought to want to be a woman, and was often angry with men, but things being as they were she liked men better. The question is not only, What do we do about men? It is also, Will becoming a woman mean having to kill off half of myself?

The world of "Houston" pleased Alli so much she planned to revisit it in a story she called "The Warm World." It was going to be about a man who was in love with one of the original women who was cloned: when she died, he had himself frozen, and woke up "in a world with 200 of her. All quite different from the original." To McIntyre, Tiptree worried, "It'll deal a lot more with the women; I'm on risky ground, I may have to send it to someone for vetting."

But Alli never wrote "The Warm World." Instead she wrote a story that dismisses the hope of female freedom, and submitted it to *Aurora* as Raccoona Sheldon. In "Your Faces, O My Sisters! Your Faces Filled of Light!" a young woman *believes* she lives in an all-female world, where she is a courier walking through a deserted, ruined Chicago on her way to points West. "Left-right, left-right, her slim strong legs carry her Indian style, every bit of her feeling good now in the rain-fresh night. Not a scrap weary; she loves her tough enduring wiry body. [. . .] To be young and night-walking in the great free moonlit world."

To her observers she is a madwoman who has run away from her marriage, child, and charge cards, and who walks through the city in the middle of the night as if nothing could hurt her. The result of this double vision is death: the young woman is raped and murdered by what she perceives as a pack of wild dogs.

The story is much more skillfully and truthfully written than Raccoona's early fiction. Yet while the woman's delusion is a rare joyous vision of being female, "Your Faces" is extremely bitter about women. Over and over, it's women who refuse to help the nameless (!) girl. The message: any woman who throws her lot in with other women is delusional and a sitting duck.

But Alli felt more and more that she must throw her lot in with the women. She was losing Tiptree as a gender-neutral figure, a playful epistolary androgyne; her own feminism was forcing her to choose. The dream about her mother and the Pit of Women suggests that, like the sorcerer's apprentice, she'd called up real terrors when she wrote "Houston," and she didn't know how to make them go away.

CHAPTER 33: **A TIN ROCKET (1974)**

Creative people not infrequently experience periods of despair in which their ability to create anything new seems to have deserted them. This is often because a particular piece of work has become invested with such overwhelming importance that it is no longer possible to play with it.

—ANTHONY STORR

In the winter of 1974, as "Houston" started to take shape, Alli's mood improved. Sun, sand, and no American news helped ease the depression. A trip to Acapulco to visit Mary went well. And Tiptree caught up with old friends. He wrote Jeff Smith another travelogue. He promised Harlan Ellison he'd turn up one day with a bottle of tequila. He told Virginia Kidd the only news he'd had from the States, "except that That Man is still in the White House," was about the new fad of streaking. "I hope it will not turn out that this is something all right-minded pinko communist radical democrats have to do; Tiptree slogging down the GW Memorial Highway in the buff could be counter-productive."

Alli loved to show off her talent for roughing it, and Tiptree's letters from the Yucatán often warned the reader to watch out for tropical cockroaches. "PS, this paper has been stored on a roach-infested coconut ranch. Don't let it lie among your papers. If not sprayed or frozen, invisible eggs could hatch. They eat paper and book-bindings and cloth and electric insulation, they grow to 4 inches and breed like they were burning up."

Tiptree's friends reacted with gratifying alarm. Ellison replied to a smeary blue letter (sprayed with a "cucarachacida" that had made the ink run):

> That bruise purple horror from Mexico scared the bejeezus outta me, you loon! I read down to the place where you described in loathsome detail the hatching habits of the Palmetto Bug of Yucatan (something straight out of a fucking Island of Dr. Moreau nightmare), screamed, and ran and threw the entire letter and envelope into the freezer. [. . .] For two

weeks, every time I went in to pull out a steak, I saw it, trembled and left it there till it became a Tipsicle. People around the house would stand in the doorway to my office, stare at me as if I were certifiable, and finally ask, "Why is there a letter in the freezer?" Finally, got so *nuhdzed* by the questions, I started snapping back, "Hot Watergate evidence from Tiptree. Have to leave it there till it cools off." (By the way, you turn out to be that shithead Howard Hunt, I'll go open my veins with a can opener!)

Ursula Le Guin, in her Portland housewife voice, said she had read the cockroach warning out loud at the dinner table, to dramatic effect.

The sound of soup being inhaled ceased abruptly. My God, put it in the freezer at once! Charles said. [. . .] BURN IT, Caroline said, shrinking away from me. Hey, said Theo, Can I see the eggs? Can I? Can I hatch some in a jar? NO, everybody said very loudly.

I haven't any bug sprays, there aren't any in Oregon, bugs, I mean [. . .]. So I put your letter in a plastic sack with some cat-flea-powder, in the freezer, just behind the orange juice. Do you think that will do?

She was on her way to England, and added, "Shall I take your letter along, and release a Horde of Giant Cockroaches on London?" The letter is now archived among Le Guin's papers at the University of Oregon, still wrapped and tied in a plastic sandwich bag.

Barry Malzberg was less calm about the cockroaches. He returned "Her Smoke Rose Up Forever" without reading it, saying he was having a paranoid phase and couldn't use any bugs that might eat papers, livers, or sinus passages. Would Tiptree please have the MS retyped?

Tiptree answered that he didn't have time but had fumigated the MS instead.

HOWEVER—it takes one to know one, and you are probably now starting paranoid tremors about the insecticide, right? Okay. Please check last page of ms. and note corner missing.

I ATE THAT CORNER.

Okay?

Malzberg replied, "The piece looks fine to me—I read it from a moderate distance and then had a brisk shower; am planning to call my doctor for asepsis after the Easter Weekend."

Back in McLean, approaching a pile of roach-infested gear with a can of insecticide, Tiptree declaimed, "For each man sprays the thing he loves . . ."

At times like this, Alli still seemed immensely to enjoy being Tiptree. The trouble was, the best part, the glorious anonymity, was by now almost gone. In the past two years Tiptree had made so many new letter-friends that corresponding had almost replaced writing as Tiptree's work. The more letters Alli wrote as Tiptree, and the more editors who wrote asking for stories, the more people she had to please. Despite the jokes, writing was no longer a pleasant little hobby, and Tiptree was no longer a game.

Sometimes the performances in the letters are very strange. To Harry Harrison, Tiptree wrote that he'd been "mixing it with Women's Lib": working on a story for Vonda McIntyre's anthology. "I got into correspondence with her during the Nebula [recommendations] one year and she impressed me mucho. I dig the gals in sf. It's great to be of an age where I can say what I mean in a complimentary way without the lady taking it as an obscure move to the sack."

What was Alli doing here? Encouraging Harrison to look at feminism in a way she thought he would understand? Building up Tip's macho credentials, in case anyone wondered what he was doing mixed up with the feminists? Whatever it was, it seems like a very lonely-making strategy.

And the cheery letters notwithstanding, Alli was frightened. Mary's illness scared her. Her bout of depression that winter scared her. She concluded once again that she was not living right. On March 31, 1974, at Boca Paila, she drew up a six-page analytical document headed "The problem: Make a better life-plan for our last decades."

As the central problem for both Sheldons, Alli named her own "psychic pain and disarray."

> —A.'s symptoms: Continuous underlying dread of age and death making all small joys and efforts seem futile. Hence pain and desire to end or escape via sleep or alternatively to make effort easier by drugs.
>
> —Secondary symptoms not caused by basic problem: Poor scheduling

of daily life. This assists disorganization, makes achievement harder, lets in more fear.

—Cause of A.'s dread is only partly the real situation; it is amplified and deepened by past experiences with M. and H. It is also amplified by A.'s cast of mind and difficulty with time. It has been a chronic problem but is now overpowering because of *lack of central hope* of any kind, and the presence of too many acts which to A. symbolize death rather than growth, principally too many *total moves* and *deteriorating or uncontrollable environments*. And excessive social *isolation* from cheering influences. This last has come about partly through A.'s desire for solitude in which to write or think, and the physical problems of entertaining. (No servants, disruption of house.) It is now so great as to make T.'s life difficult too. (Another contributory cause is M., about which nothing can be done but avoidance; time will change that.)

How to bring back hope and growth?

One way, she wrote, might be to leave McLean. The former farm town was being overrun by development. Ting and Alli mourned the loss of fields and woods, now gone forever. They feared urban crime. Besides, the house they had lived in for fifteen years was as exhausting as ever to maintain. Only where would they go? Ting dreamed of moving to a place he could fish. But they needed medical services. Alli needed reliable mail.

Ting wanted friends and the chance to entertain them. Alli wanted books, her work, a garden she could manage, and "some controlled sociability" centered around her interests: writing, psychology, the women's movement, nature. She fantasized about a life in which she could "just take the day off and rest or think if desired without guilt." Strangely, though writing is listed among "A.'s" interests, nowhere is it mentioned as a source of hope—or trouble. The impression this document gives is that Tiptree's writing didn't count. But writing was starting to confront Alli with ideas and emotions she was scared of. Tiptree's work was no longer the refuge that it had been. And she had no one she could talk to about it.

It might have been time for Alli to make another dramatic change. But writing is addictive. It was the one thing she had wanted all her life to do. And at fifty-eight, with her closest ties to a husband of seventy-one and a dying mother of ninety-two, Alli felt that time was running out.

Several years later, on the far shore of a long depression, Alli wrote across the top of page 1, "Trying to be honest and factual produces this weird formalistic tone? I think not, I think there is a scream just below the surface. . . . It could all have been said shorter, ruder and truer." She labeled the document "SAVE as a sample of nutty prose and (maybe) nutty thinking." But for Alli, sitting down to list her troubles was still a sign of unbearable psychic pain.

The Sheldons returned to McLean in early April, then left immediately for Chicago, where Mary was having another medical crisis. Alli had just enough time before she left to answer a few letters from PO Box 315, including two from the new editor at *Galaxy* and *If*, Jim Baen. Before Alli went to Mexico that January she had sent him Raccoona's story "Angel Fix" with a cover letter from Tiptree, saying he was passing on a story from an old friend. Baen wrote Raccoona accepting "Angel Fix" for *If*, and later wrote Tiptree asking why Raccoona hadn't replied.

On April 8 Raccoona wrote back, "Your wondrous letter about 'Angel Fix' was waiting here when I got home last night—my mother had a heart attack down South." Four days later, Tiptree sent an offhand note:

> I can't imagine what has happened to Sheldon (Raccoona), unless she's been abducted by aliens, because I know she feels about being published by *Galaxy* or *If* like Bunyan felt about Heaven. (Didn't we all!) It's possible she dropped dead when your letter came, but she's a sturdy soul; more likely some of her multitudinous parasitic family has her tied up.

Not long afterward, Vonda McIntyre and Susan Anderson accepted both "Houston" and "Your Faces" for *Aurora*, and Alli began corresponding with McIntyre as both Tip and Raccoona. (McIntyre described Raccoona's story glowingly to Tip: "It has a vast number of levels to be read on, it's neat. You'll like it.") Raccoona was finally a published writer.

Alli began to fantasize about killing off Tiptree and living on as Raccoona. In July 1974, writing Dorothy Olding about the stalled "Human Male," she confessed that she was now working under two pseudonyms, male and female. "Eventually the man is going to get sand-bagged en route to New Zealand and fade out, see, leaving me at last one whole woman. Of course I could do it the cheap way and just confess all around, but that would be letting the game down."

But Tiptree's death would leave sorrowing friends behind. And how could Raccoona pick up his correspondence? Nor was Raccoona all of Alli, any more than Tiptree was. Had Alli ever been "one whole woman"?

Meanwhile, Tip was about to become more substantial than ever. Back from Chicago, on April 20, he reassured Vonda McIntyre, who had been nominated for a Nebula Award and (according to Le Guin) was very much hoping to get it, that awards were not correlated to talent, seldom went to deserving artists or lasting works, and didn't matter. Tip was up for two Nebulas, but wrote, "If I were to get one it would bother me . . . I'd feel that something was a little wrong with me."

But McIntyre did win the Nebula for best novelette (beating "The Girl Who Was Plugged In"), and already ticking unopened in Tiptree's mail was a small bomb: a letter from Kate Wilhelm of the Nebula committee saying that "Love Is the Plan the Plan Is Death" had been voted best short story.

Four days later Tiptree wrote Le Guin, wailing, "Oh, Bear, they got me."

I picked out a letter from Kate Wilhelm to open, it looked safe. Would you believe, half an hour later I was vomiting, before breakfast yet. (Does that really mean, Tiptree, that what you really are is beady-eyed sick with ambition, covetous creep, loaded with pious reaction-formation like a TV dessert with whipped sweetness, a whited sink of ego? What is the blood-guilt chum, what are you dreaming after? Sanctimonious invertebrate, your friends have to sympathise with you for *success,* yet? Why don't you pick up your socks, why can't you be NORMAL? . . . No good; you're just no good . . .) Oh, Bear, I don't want sympathy, I just want it to go away. It doesn't FEEL good. It feels like our real life is taking on the characteristics of that mess out there, that fake life. YOU should get Nebulas, YOU should bear up bravely. Not me.

A year earlier, Tip had told Barry Malzberg, "I absolutely refuse to hope I might win or care. [. . .] Remember the part in *Alice in Wonderland* where the heroine realises she is growing and that the others are just a pack of playing cards who can't possibly hurt her?" But you can't always call your friends and colleagues a pack of playing cards, or a Camelot world. The Nebula made Tiptree part of "that mess out there, that fake life" that Alli had fled in the first place.

To his letter to Le Guin, Tiptree added an extra page:

> Listen, I've been thinking about something for awhile and I want to make a peculiar-sounding statement which maybe you will keep to yourself and maybe also you will drop this page in the fireplace. The point is, if you should hear a rumour that Tiptree has emigrated to Tierra del Fuego or contracted galloping MS or been beheaded on the highways— please I beg you, *believe* it. In public. Believe it in private if and only if a note addressed to you personally and writ by me is delivered to you via my executor, one R.A. Koke. [. . .] All this is a bit of looking-far-ahead, not applicable for years if ever.

Le Guin wrote back immediately:

> Dear Tree,
>
> You frighten me. I know you didn't mean to. Only you do. Look: the trouble is this. There are facts about you I don't know. Don't *want* to know. Oh yes, of course, monkey curiosity, what is it? does it tick? etc. But not anywhere below the monkey level. I "know" a Tree and it keeps its privacy, like most trees, and that is more than its right, that is its *being* [. . .], that is the Tree Way. So that is lovely. Indeed it is one of the lovely things in my life the last couple of years. But: there comes the sudden fact, the fact to be burned in the fireplace—but it has no other facts to attach onto and fit into: and so it is very frightening. It just sits there (ashes or no) and stares at me. And says: Is my friend whom I know and do not know troubled beyond all touch or reassurance? Is he *in* trouble? Is there nothing his friends whom he knows and does not know can do, or say, or be? Nothing that would help?

She added that she had been getting through a depressed time partly on Tip's funny, affectionate letters; his note from Boca Paila, she said, "kept me going for the last 6 weeks." She was already worried about Phil Dick, another friend by mail. ("I have never met him either [. . .]. We are both scared to death of each other.") He'd just phoned from California after a stay in the hospital, "half seas over on sedatives, utterly enigmatic about what was actually wrong with him and whether he was out of danger, funnier than Charlie Chaplin, laying his soul bare in great swathes, absolutely overwhelming." Now Le Guin had opened Tiptree's letter and found more worry. "I ask you, what is one middle-aged Portland housewife to do with TWO mad geniuses?" Years later, Le Guin recalled that she had found Tiptree's response strange, a false note in the male register. "This was just too improbable, a man who didn't think he deserved a prize."

Tip answered with a telegram apologizing for the worry: "Nothing whatsoever amiss here nor mad genius neither merely your loopy friend taking catnip notions letter follows." In the letter he wrote, "I am torn between my usual retreat into whimsy when upset and coming right out with it—let no one say, 'Manfully,' this is what men don't do—and apologising weepily all over the mat." He talked a little about himself: his literate parents, his few years in intelligence, his "useless doctorate in the behavioral sciences." He confessed that he'd been feeling "not exactly hemmed in, but maybe over-organised? [. . .] Suddenly to be so 'in' disconcerts me. I'm a natural outsider." That was why he'd thought of killing off Tiptree and writing under a pseudonym—who would, in the course of things, start sending fan letters to Le Guin.

But Le Guin's concern only tangled Alli up even more in the Tiptree game. Alli may have felt safer with the less intimate responses from Barry Malzberg and Jeff Smith. When Tiptree told Malzberg he was thinking of disappearing, Malzberg simply accepted it, promising to protect his friend's privacy and again urging him to recognize his talent. Malzberg could understand how frightening winning a Nebula might be. Years later he said, "They give you an award and they make you a figure of substance. They strip from you the ability to take this on your own terms. [. . .] She wanted the Nebula to the exact degree she was terrified. She had to admit that she wanted it, that she had a real stake in it."

Smith wrote his friend, "Don't worry about it. I can assure you that a lot of people *still* don't like your writing. [. . .] There. That make you happier?" Alli laughed at herself, and for a moment felt better.

It didn't last. A few weeks later, Harlan Ellison wrote to congratulate Tiptree on the Nebula and ask him again for a novel, for a new series Ellison wanted to edit. "If you laid off writing letters to the ten thou correspondents who enjoy your postal favors, and started using that time to write [. . .], it would be done in a month," he helpfully pointed out.

> Everybody wants to see what you'll do in a sustained effort, and I'm frothing to be the guy who snags it for publication. The money is no object; I'll get you a *smashing* advance, and a fine package, and fame and glory and all the booze you can inhale, and the state of Vermont, and your own motorcycle, and . . . and . . .
>
> Please write and show me some light in this dearest desire of my life. Dammit man, I'm gonna be 40 on the 27th, you *can't* deny a man in the twilight years!
>
> All best, congratulations on the Nebula, good health, and write quick about the novel
>
> > the novel
> > the novel
> > the novel [repeated 30 times]

But the Nebula had raised the stakes: Alli was now struggling to write something worthy of an award-winning author. And Ellison, whose praise had helped Alli so much in the beginning, was without knowing it pushing too far. To Smith, Tiptree still insisted he didn't really care about writing: "I seem to be lucky in having most of my ego-involvement either somewhere else or so deep down it isn't easily got at." To Ellison, Tiptree wailed,

> Don't you realise man, Tiptree could write half a dozen novels, Tiptree has scads of sketches of lovely little piss-ass novels I planned to spend the next five of my unknown years daintily spewing out at the impervious public, [. . .] a dozen little exercises in self-masturbation, a quintet of gently amusing drawing-room-on-Planet-X wowsers, a faint-hearted streaking through the underbushes of youth transposed to Planet Y, in

fact all the farting asininities any goddam miserable beginning writer has a right to commit. Christ, I have a beautiful one with six subplots all neatly dovetailed and a most moving love story, all like wax clockwork. (I LOVE it.) But can I do it? Can I have the ordinary human freedom to crap around and figure my way? No! Why? Because Harlan, Harlan that iridescent maniac with the heart of fermented fermium, Harlan says that it has to be

Good.

Well, these ain't good. [. . .] Shit, I am trying. I sadly threw out the waxwork marvel. (Dammit, it was so nice.) I'll try . . .

But I feel like I'm walking off a plank in the dark.

Tiptree, the imaginary character whose stories Alli made up, kept becoming I, the I who was struggling and failing to write a novel. For ten more days, Alli held her subconscious hostage, demanding a plot. She tried Dexedrine, she tried no Dexedrine. She tried one of Le Guin's sources, the I Ching, but couldn't make sense of the result. She tried clearing the garden, but got poison ivy. Over Memorial Day weekend she locked herself in her study and said, "All right, Brain, do it. Here you sit and subsist on black coffee and crud until Tuesday and by that time YOU WILL HAVE A NOVEL PLANNED."

But at two in the morning on Memorial Day, Tip wrote Ellison that he couldn't do it. "I do not yet naturally incubate those longer rhythms and developments that make a decent novel; all I have is the high-intensity dash." To Jeff Smith two days later he wrote, "I realised—having worked each out—that *none* of [my] piss-ass plots were worthy [. . .]. So I started to grope for the real one, the right one. [. . .] And I found—

"Nothing."

Alli was not a natural novelist. She had always worked in short bursts of energy and lost interest in long projects; and her taut, epigrammatic style was impossible to sustain at length. But in a way Alli was also struggling with the notorious "second novel problem." Her first body of work had come out of nowhere, unbidden. Now, with all eyes on her, she was trying to write the second. And when she called, it wouldn't come.

For now, Alli turned to easier tasks, revising her more recent stories for a new collection, *Warm Worlds and Otherwise,* and finishing some drafts she'd sketched out at Boca Paila. But the stuff she wrote that summer had a shadow over it. "Beaver Tears," by Raccoona, was slight and gloomy. Even gloomier was "The Psychologist Who Wouldn't Do Awful Things to Rats," which Robert Silverberg bought for *New Dimensions.* An evocative depiction of the trials of a graduate student, it is also yet another story that offers nonbeing as a blissful escape from suffering. "She Waits for All Men Born" is a grim meditation on the power of death over life.

Alli threw herself enthusiastically into one new correspondence. In June 1974 Tip got a fan letter from a young Cherokee Indian writer named Craig Strete, along with a copy of his fanzine *Red Planet Earth.* Tiptree gave him publishing advice; he wrote back about his life and troubles; and the exchange grew into a warm friendship. "Uncle Tip" wrote Strete often, sending money (which Strete sent back) and concern. Alli liked Strete for his talent, inventiveness, and humor, was interested in his experience as a Native American, and felt protective toward a young man whose life seemed as out of control as hers had once been.

In August, Alli and Ting spent two weeks at a mountain lake in British Columbia. But the travelogue Tiptree wrote this time, for Jeff Smith's new solo fanzine *Khatru,* feels obligatory and tame. Oddly, it reads like Mary's writing, long on scenery, ethnography, and health hazards—mainly blackflies—and short on self. When Smith commented that the piece felt impersonal, Tiptree said that was because he'd left out the main note of the trip, his depression. "If I had put personal stuff in it it would have come out as a sort of supine wail. [. . .] Sometimes I get so that all the pain and misery in the world seems to be tied into my nervous system and hurting together." While reading up on Native American customs, he'd also read about the smallpox-infested blankets they'd been given by white settlers. Such stories "seemed to add up and build until I wanted to get out of the planet or out of the species, or out of my own malfunctioning nervous system. [. . .] Life just seems to be one long flinch."

Alli still expected to snap out of her depression, the way she had all the others. She just had to pile up the mental furniture against the door and wait out the assault. But not this time.

On Labor Day weekend of 1974, the World Science Fiction Convention, an annual gathering of several thousand fans, was held in Washington, D.C. It was just a few miles from Tiptree's PO box, and the rumor spread that Tiptree was in the audience. Tip's novella "The Girl Who Was Plugged In" was on the final ballot for the Hugo Award, which the fans would vote on at the convention. And Tiptree had joked before about turning up incognito. Earlier in the year he had written Bob Silverberg, "Some day I gotta sneak round to a convention and really see. Watch for the two-button suit wearing a beanie in the back row."

But that was before he won the Nebula. Afterward, Jeff Smith said he was getting more questions than ever about Tiptree's identity, and Tip reiterated that he didn't want to come out.

> I can't explain it, really. Partly stubbornness, I fear. I don't see who I'm hurting, why can't I squat in my cave in peace? I'm just a plain old mortal, I don't see why I have to present the knobby flesh to be scanned in vain for what makes the words come out. [. . .] And I guess I'm afraid, now. So many good friends on paper, spirits of the air. I somehow feel I would be, well, a disappointment, maybe. Sneezing and not hearing and saying things like Where does one park, yes, conventions are frightening.

To Virginia Kidd, Tip said that who he was in person was "totally meaningless beside the friendships that have so wonderfully come to me through the PO. What could the metabolising hunk that is me be but a disappointment?"

Friends went on teasing Tip about his identity. Malzberg wondered if he was really J. D. Salinger. McIntyre wrote, "I knew you weren't Charles Colson." Joanna Russ reported, "Rumors circulate that you are Henry Kissinger, are high/low in the Federal Gummint, are really the force behind Congress, &c.?" But the Nebula put an edge on the gossip. When Kate Wilhelm wrote Tiptree that he had won, she warned him, half jokingly, "You know, don't you, that after receiving a Nebula you'll be the target for all the thwarted detective instincts of the pack?"

By the time WorldCon came to D.C., Alli was either in British Columbia or at the Lodge. But the convention-goers began to fantasize that he was really in the audience. Ellison (who had himself been accused of being Tiptree) said he knew for a fact that Tiptree was there. Quinn Yarbro told Jeff Smith Tiptree must be a pseudonym, because Tip had told her he'd gone to Cal and she had found no Tiptrees in the records there. Fans talked about staking out the PO box in McLean. Members of the convention committee reported as truth that Tiptree was present. Speakers addressed remarks to him. At least one fan claimed he was Tiptree and began signing autographs. Then Tiptree won the Hugo for best novella for "The Girl Who Was Plugged In."

Jeff Smith, shy and unhappy in his role as Tiptree's contact, got up in front of three or four thousand people to accept the award and assured the crowd he knew no more than they did. This made some think Smith himself was Tiptree—though Ellison said, in Smith's hearing, that it couldn't possibly be "that little twerp." Even Smith half expected the award to disappear from his hotel room, replaced by a thank-you note from his mysterious friend. By the end of a long, noisy weekend, with still no sign of Tiptree, frustrated detectives began to claim that he could alter his molecular structure at will and had been assuming the form of Coke machines and ashtrays in order to mingle undetected with the crowd.

The Hugo, named after pulp publisher Hugo Gernsback, is science fiction's most important prize. It looks like a bowling trophy with an old-fashioned rocket on it, a long shaft propped upright on little fins. Smith couldn't think of a way to pack this strange object for mailing, so when the convention ended he and his wife Ann drove out to McLean, paid the postage, and handed it directly to the woman at the PO box window. "Mr. Tiptree's moved to Wisconsin," she said. Still, Smith felt guilty about treading on his friend's turf.

To McIntyre, Tiptree wrote that the "tin rocket" had sent him "up the drapes again."

> I wish I knew why "prizes" depress me so profoundly. If I had to analyse without regard for how awful and puling it makes me sound, I'd guess something about believing that *outsiders* are better, or freer, or more real and talented while *insiders* (awardees) are stuffed figures, phoneys, "them." I don't want to be a "them." Or maybe it's even worse—maybe it's guilt, like I've *stolen* this. [. . .] Or maybe . . . way down deep—oh, this is awful!—maybe it's that I want people to be kind and friendly to

me as one who deserves more than he gets, when if I *get* some of it I will become That Fat Shit and a *target* and no one will be kind and friendly and warm to me anymore.

Oh, mummy, don't leave me alone—!

Despite her complaints about awards, Alli put the trophy on display in her library, and when Ting's friends came over she sometimes showed it to them, with a mixture of irony—look at this game I'm playing—and real pride. At one point she added a nonverbal joke: she set the rocket ship on a shelf and stood a vibrator on either side.

Being Tiptree just kept getting weirder and weirder. That fall, Le Guin joked that they should share a pseudonym, so they could sound both male and female. "We can both use it and people will say, My, what a breadth of style this person has." Then Alli received a copy of Silverberg's introduction to *Warm Worlds and Otherwise,* with its generous praise for Tiptree's stories and its assertion that the writer must be a man. Alli enjoyed the praise. It felt as if a mountain range had suddenly addressed him by name, Tip wrote Judy-Lynn del Rey; however, to Silverberg he wrote, with double meaning, that he kept "looking over my shoulder to see who in hell he's *talking* about." But she felt guilty about her deception. And she was about to go in for surgery on her arthritic thumb: she would be unable to write or type for weeks. Tiptree's voice would go dead.

Just before the surgery, just in case, Tip sent a sealed envelope to his agent, Bob Mills, to be opened "if there doesn't seem to be any more Tiptree." In it was a letter confessing that Tiptree was a pseudonym for a woman (though Alli didn't give her name). It went on, "Tip has been conscious of no dishonesty. Not him. But I have. As I saw my brave sisters I went through terrible qualms. Everything sounded so much more *interesting* coming from a man. (Didn't it? Didn't it, *just a little?* Be honest.) I said to myself, it's the double-cross I am, the secret XX."

When she wrote this, Alli was about to begin the strangest episode of the whole Tiptree masquerade. Jeff Smith was organizing a symposium on women and science fiction for his fanzine *Khatru.* It was to be done in round-robin form, by mail: Smith would ask questions, collate the responses, and send them out again for more comment. The panel included Le Guin, Wilhelm, Yarbro, McIntyre, Virginia Kidd, Joanna Russ, and a new writer, Suzy McKee

Charnas. Tip had been encouraging Smith to do it, and now Smith invited him, along with Samuel R. Delany, to contribute the man's point of view.

To Joanna Russ Tiptree predicted, not inaccurately, that his contribution would be "a solo input from left field, I'll just scribble down some thoughts that'll probably offend everybody."

CHAPTER 34: A SENSITIVE MAN (1974–75)

Today I sense a fund of unresolved rage somewhere inside which is all too apt to turn against my condition and myself, and to blow out in suicide or who knows what. Is this the common condition or does it need some attention?

—ALLI SHELDON, FALL 1974

In the fall of 1974 the scene in McLean was not good. Nixon had resigned in August, the American troops had withdrawn from Vietnam, and a spiritual smog lay over Washington. One of the people drifting in it was William Gibson, not yet a science fiction writer but a kid who was "couch-surfing" the living rooms of Fairfax County. Among the children of the CIA analysts and technocrats, he recalled, "there was epidemic drinking, depression, drug-abuse, auto accidents, suicides . . . The psychic climate Tiptree wrote those stories in was charged in ways one would not necessarily imagine today."

Looking at an oil crisis, inflation, rising unemployment, and a falling stock market, Ting was once again predicting economic doom. The Sheldons worried whether Mary's investments would still cover her nursing costs. In September Tip advised Judy-Lynn del Rey, "Check your change. Dimes and quarters from 1964 and before have more silver in them than their face value—quite a bit more. [. . .] It looks like any little bit will help in what's coming."

Tip told Craig Strete that his entire circle of acquaintances believed the human race would destroy itself in the next hundred years, with a bomb or a biological weapon or some other new lethal item. "I don't know anybody who believes we will make it [through the next century] without a tremendous Dying. [. . .] I rather look forward to it," he wrote—then added, "Tiptree, you really are pompous and solemn . . . Looking forward to the great evolution of an arthropod culture. (Wash & wax job, Madam? Polish your feelers fifty cents extra?)"

In October, after another emergency trip to Chicago, Tiptree wrote Barry Malzberg, "Perhaps we are Entropy's instrumentation, set to register in the pain of our nerves the steady progress of the end."

Alli was about to go into surgery. Her arthritic right thumb had become almost too painful to use, and her doctors had suggested an operation to replace the joint. They added that it might be as much as six months before she could write or type again. (Tip warned most of his correspondents they wouldn't be hearing from him. Raccoona just said afterward that she'd been sick and busy with "family junk.") Alli was terrified of hospitals and of losing her epistolary voice.

That fall, Alli was overwhelmed with visions of death and thoughts of suicide. She began planning "accidents." Each time she drove—and Ting made sure she got fewer and fewer chances—she counted concrete bridge abutments, trucks, even school buses. She wondered if she could turn the wheel and drive into one. She wondered if she could stop herself. She pictured Ting and herself dead; she saw "images of corrupt politicians mingling with napalmed babies running non-stop" in her head. She couldn't stop feeling the world's pain.

She had always held suicide in reserve, in case the depression got too bad. But sometime in her thirty years of marriage she had fallen in love with Ting, and now she couldn't bring herself to hurt him with her death. She felt trapped. In her desperation she thought about taking him with her. "Two cold midnights I stood by our bed, looking down at his head, gun in hand, debating . . . Couldn't." Ting didn't share Alli's fear of age; she knew he didn't want to go.

Instead she began plundering the medicine cabinet, using amphetamines, painkillers, and tranquilizers to remove herself from the scene. Finally she asked Ting to lock up the pills and went to her doctor. He gave her antidepressants and urged her to go into therapy.

It may be at this time that she wrote two undated pages, titled "On Reading Other People's Thoughts." Contemplating seeing a psychologist, she seems to be wondering if he'll find anything in her personality at all (and maybe hoping he won't). She describes herself as a mechanical or biological collection of stimuli and responses.

I am a peculiarly transparent person—perhaps "flat," lacking some dimension. I contain no mysteries. I am not a vortex or node—not a dark knot in the flow of things, I do not add complications. My relations with the world, with people, are perfectly uncomplicated. The world is complicated—that is another matter. I don't seem to have this dark central node from which so many people speak so interestingly. I have, for example, very little GUILT [a year later she wrote in the margin, "O what shit"]; what guilt I have from time to time I understand perfectly—how it was put there, what has activated it. [in the margin: "But not how deep,—how much"] That is the trouble—I understand myself perfectly. I feel—oh, indeed, I lunge about now and then, red-faced, hoarse-voiced, I cry, I laugh—I droop, I wail—but nearly always—and certainly later—I understand perfectly whence these up-rushes. A chemical, a bad dinner, a stress, no sleep—a death, a remembrance of death, a rejection—perfectly simple, no mystery. I wanted A, I got B; etc. I am gloomy—perfectly natural. "Man is in love and loves what vanishes." I will die, I age. Unpleasant. Man is a member of a species whose triumph is built on the disappointment of the individual. The individual's doomed drives. We are not descended from the satisfied. Ergo, I hurt. No mystery.

She recalled the relief she'd felt seeing life "as a technical problem." But had it really helped? "It also seemed to me that when I achieved understanding— a necessary housekeeping act—life would somehow begin. I have achieved it. But what have I done since? What is to do?"

Like the "Better Life-Plan," this note quietly ignores the existence of Tiptree. "My relations with the world, with people, are perfectly uncomplicated," Alli writes, as if she weren't tied up in Tiptree's strange friendships. "I don't seem to have this dark central node from which so many people speak," she writes, denying the source of Tiptree's stories.

Around the same time, in October 1974, Tiptree wrote Joanna Russ about feeling "transparent":

It's odd, at my nearly-60 age—I feel everybody else, I mean everybody who counts, has Been Through Experience, has *lived*, while I have only, what, fumbled through unsuccessful apprenticeship, got ready to begin to start, and stand eagerly upon the brink of figuring out How to Live—

just as hook from shadows is snaking out to yank me off scene.

(I also have moments of believing I am transparent, something that did not jell. Everyone else seems to have so much density, self-organisation. Personality. If asked who they are, they *know*. I asked myself that the other day—could I write an autobiography just for my own amusement, OK, who you? And all that formed in my throat was, uh, uh, well, I guess just the something peering out from this totally random manifestation. Something *small* peering out. [. . .])

"How to Live"—"You don't live right"—the search for a "better life-plan"—as her world of false fronts was threatened, Alli tried to stand in front of the turning bookshelf and smile. One way to disown emotions is to name them animal instincts, another to say that they're not really part of yourself, that they're a "totally random manifestation." Russ, perceptively, suggested that knowing oneself was often a matter of "admitting."

And in the midst of trying to persuade herself that she was all biology and no history, Alli sat down to write what Tiptree thought about women.

By 1974, science fiction's "New Wave" had crested and broken, raising the genre's literary quality and popularity but leaving it uncertain about its subject matter. The moon landing had not altered history; there were no space stations, no colonies on Mars. Instead, to some people's surprise, the important changes were cultural, and were happening at home. In a letter to Vonda McIntyre, Tiptree said the "rocket jocks" of SF had better look around them. Feminism was "the very part of the FUTURE which is starting to move and crystallise right under their noses. [. . .] SF has moved on from asking How Do We Get There? and is and has been for some time asking What Do We Do When We Get There?"

One at a time, women writers and readers had been discovering science fiction. In the early 1970s, their number reached a critical mass—and at the same moment, feminism arrived. By 1974 and 1975, everyone in science fiction, for or against, was talking about women. The first anthology of science fiction by women, *Women of Wonder,* appeared in 1975. McIntyre and Anderson's *Aurora* appeared in 1976. Russ's remarkable feminist novel *The Female*

Man, written in 1969, was published in 1975. Feminist fanzines began to appear. WorldCon '74 featured a heated panel discussion on "Women in Science Fiction." It was followed by more discussions, more excitement. When the men talked too much, the women started women-only panels, provoking outcry and even more debate.

Suzy McKee Charnas's first novel, *Walk to the End of the World,* appeared in 1974; it depicts a post-holocaust dystopia in which women are men's slaves. Charnas recalled that the constant exchange in SF between writers and readers made the feminist conversation intense. "Instead of the lonely writer in her garret, there was this incredible 'bounceback' effect of ideas, right away. It was like a big consciousness-raising group of fans and writers. And we just talked ourselves blue."

The science fiction community as a whole was in an odd position regarding feminism. On one hand, most of the writers and fans were men. In 1974, women still made up less than 20 percent of SFWA's membership. And most of those men, even those who were using SF to address other social issues, were still not ready to question gender relationships. The "rocket jocks" (who had also hated the New Wave) insisted women couldn't write real, "hard" science fiction and probably shouldn't even be reading it. Other men were more open in theory, but had trouble understanding the problem.

Arthur C. Clarke, for example, had recently sent a letter to the editor of *Time* magazine agreeing with astronaut Mike Collins. Collins had told *Time* that women could never be in the space program, since in zero G a woman's breasts would bounce and keep the men from concentrating. Clarke proudly claimed he had already predicted this "problem." In his novel *Rendezvous with Rama* he had written, "Some women, Commander Norton had decided long ago, should not be allowed aboard ship: weightlessness did things to their breasts that were too damn distracting." When Joanna Russ tried privately to explain why this was insulting, Clarke, responding publicly in the SFWA newsletter, asked why Commander Norton shouldn't be attracted to women—didn't Russ want him to be? He added that though some of his best friends were women, the level of discourse of the "women's libbers" clearly wasn't helping their cause.

The whole exchange appeared in the *SFWA Forum* in February and March 1975. It drew a storm of comment from all directions, most of it expressive of how new feminism was to most men and how automatically many reacted by kicking slush. The newsletter's editor, Ted Cogswell, illustrated an issue with pictures of naked women—intended, he said, as a joke. Suzy Charnas informed him that this kind of "joke" was aggression disguised as humor. Some of the letters, from men and women, were open and intelligent, but even the more reasonable men often reduced the argument to the sexual or the physical, as if all sexism was about was, as one man put it, the shape of a person's plumbing.

On the other hand, the SF community had a great deal invested in the idea of tolerance. It was, and is, in principle sympathetic to all who feel themselves different. Science fiction itself is, at its best moments, a literature of difference, alienation, change. Russ said in *Khatru* that she wrote it because she could make it hers. "I felt that I knew nothing about 'real life' as defined in college writing courses (whaling voyages, fist fights, war, bar-room battles, bull-fighting, &c.) and if I wrote about Mars nobody could tell me it was (1) trivial, or (2) inaccurate."

Probably not by coincidence, two of the most important women writing SF in 1974 were two of Tiptree's closest correspondents, Ursula Le Guin and Joanna Russ. They were very different from each other; Tiptree described them to Russ as the Martin Luther King and Malcolm X of feminist science fiction. But they both provided uneasy-making examples for Alli: Le Guin talented and successful but avoiding writing about women; Russ embracing anger and demanding stories from life.

In 1974, Le Guin was wary of feminism. She was living happily in a traditional family, one that sustained her and made her work possible. She found mothering not a waste of her talent, as some feminists suggested, but "terrifying, empowering, and fiercely demanding on her intelligence." She also resented its debased status, and later said, "If I've called myself a housewife, it's in defiance." But liking motherhood made her feel unwelcome as a feminist. To Tiptree she wrote that when the discussion went beyond "plain social justice—equal pay, equal dignity of work, child care, etc.," she became "very shaky and unsure and am at once seen through as an Aunt Tom."

Like Alli, she admired and was frightened by feminist anger. When Russ's *Female Man* was published in early 1975, she complained to Tiptree: "Womanhood as power, sex as power, violence as power. And it's all power-over [rather than power-to]. It's a total role-reversal, but exactly the same game. [. . .] I reject it utterly—with so much vehemence, so much bitterness, that I know damn well that it strikes to something in me which I will not admit."

In her next letter she added, "The Old Eve leaps up and down deep within in the darkness chanting KILL em all KILL em all BANG BANG BANG. It's no good repressing her; but it's no good letting her out, as J. [Russ] wants to do, either. Somehow she has got to be *included*."

She often used male protagonists in her fiction. Like Tiptree, like Russ early in her career, she may have needed to imagine herself as a man in order to take possession of her creative power. Besides, she felt most at home among myths and archetypes, and we do not yet have a mythology of true female experience. But feminists, including Russ, had begun criticizing her for not writing about women. She later recalled, "I had lost confidence in the kind of writing I had been doing, because I was (mostly unconsciously) struggling to learn how to write as a woman, not as an 'honorary man' as before, and with a freedom that scared me." She came to think of this time in her life as "the dark hard place."

Russ, on the other hand, had embraced feminism from the beginning. Unlike Le Guin, she was a single professional woman who was daily faced with the inequalities of paid work and the sexism of academic institutions. Unlike Le Guin, she was confrontational. Alli admired her ambivalently, worrying among other things that she was indiscriminating in her choice of targets. In September 1974 Tiptree cautioned her, "My life-gained impression of revolutionaries—from early labor-unions to you—is that they have a tendency not to remember who their real enemies are."

Russ was angry with Le Guin for using male protagonists. It felt like a cheat, she told Tiptree. "It's easy to avoid sexism and the incredible ugliness of the whole business if you half-pretend you're really a man. I did it for years." She was even more angry with Le Guin because she admired and looked up to her. When Russ and Tip got onto the subject of mothering, Russ wrote, "You have obviously romanticized Ursula as a Mother. [. . .] I romanticize her the same way—which leads me to demanding an impossible standard of wisdom and protectiveness from her, and hence badmouthing her books."

Tiptree urged Russ to be patient with Le Guin. "Her style is the very quiet statement. [. . .] Quietly, persistently, she inserts the impression that there is something very wrong and absurd between the sexes." Russ replied that Le Guin "may include some troubled waters in her books, but I think one has to be as sensitive as you to see them; most reactions are simply that if U. K. Le Guin isn't complaining, why am I, Joanna Russ? [. . .] And I confess I do feel somewhat deserted by that."

At that moment, it seemed to Russ

> impossible to express oneself by characters as fundamentally different in situation as exchanging man/woman. None of the great female novelists have done it: not Colette, or Marian Evans, or the Brontës, or Jane Austen, or anybody else I know. [. . .] Not being oneself in any way at all exacts its price—look at all of Roger Zelazny's novels about big, flashy, achieving supermen. Some day (as somebody once said) he'll write about short, slight, frail little dark men who don't fit the heroic ideal—IF HE CAN. Because the minute one writes about that (or, if a woman, about women) you walk head-on into the cruxes of your own life, whatever they are. You, as far as I can tell, do write about you; and Chip [Delany] about Chip; and me about me; but Ursula's always indirect.

A literary point of view, Russ insisted in *Khatru*, "must be authentic and to be authentic it must be individual and to be individual it must be specific, and *therefore* male or female."

Autobiographical honesty was an important part of that wave of feminism: no more masks, no more pretense. But there's more to "authenticity" than Russ credits here. In Tiptree's and Raccoona's letters and stories, masquerade and truth do not exclude each other, but comment on each other and are interwoven. If it did Alli psychic damage to be Don Fenton as well as Ruth Parsons, "The Women Men Don't See" is also about that psychic damage.

Besides, what works, works; and both Tiptree and Le Guin were writing powerful and evocative fiction. Even Russ finally conceded, "The only thing one can put on the line in the arts is oneself. And you do that. And Ursula does that, too. [. . .] She's right there, risking everything."

But if Alli still thought she could enter the symposium without putting herself on the line, she was about to find out otherwise.

The symposium took a year to put together, from Jeff Smith's first questions in October 1974 to the 156-page mimeographed 'zine he published in November 1975. Smith's first questions were general: What has attracted so many women writers to SF in recent years? What problems are there in portraying characters of the opposite sex? But the symposium quickly went beyond science fiction to become a fierce feminist consciousness-raising session and debate.

Most of the symposium's most vocal contributors—Charnas, Yarbro, McIntyre, Delany, Russ—were in their twenties and thirties. Tiptree was the oldest of the group at fifty-nine, Smith the youngest at twenty-four. They were almost all, McIntyre later recalled, "just beginning to realize and under-stand the huge lies we had been told while growing up in the fifties and six-ties." As kids they'd read past science fiction's reduplication of fifties sex roles (and the thinly clad spacegirls on the magazine covers) to its implied offer of escape. They'd all come to science fiction, they agreed, not because of what it had achieved but because of its potential.

Then Yarbro began getting angry for all the times her mother had told her "to be less outspoken, not to let people know I was smart, not to 'scare' people so much." Russ submitted a reading list (Friedan, Firestone, Millett, Greer). Delany, who was gay, married to the poet Marilyn Hacker, and the father of an infant daughter, talked about writing and parenting. They won-dered if one should be a feminist or a "humanist" first. McIntyre, for one, felt that humanity in general was not her problem. "All of us must have been given the line about helping others before we devote ourselves to the 'trivial' cause of feminism." Delany talked about how hard it was to write beyond stereotypes: "The moment you slip your mind into their well-worn ruts, they take over you, your story, and a good deal of your world." Most participants believed that patriarchy would soon disappear, though Yarbro wrote pes-simistically that equality for women would take at least four generations to achieve.

Tiptree's "solo input from left field" was an essay on Alli's old idea that there were two patterns of human behavior, "men" and "mothers" (with somewhere in between them another, unknown pattern, that of women). At twenty, Alli had equated maternity with death. At twenty-six, she had imagined it as a bad daughter's penance. In her thirties she had wanted a baby she couldn't have. Now she hoped motherhood might save humanity.

Not long before the symposium started, Tiptree had been making rude remarks about mothering. Responding to Le Guin's feelings about her eldest daughter leaving home, he wrote,

> This is [your] mysterious Normal Mother incarnation and I respect it although being ill-equipped to share it. I am not one of those gents who go all misty seeing a radiant Mother swabbing off a Child, I mean, I appreciate the function profoundly and I realize it must be one of the great warm good-relations of all . . . but I am more apt to think Another damn good astronomer shot to hell.

A month later, in October 1974, he mentioned the male and mothering patterns to Russ, in a context of frustration with traditional sex roles and thinking about lesbian desire. Russ had observed that for women, brains and body canceled each other out: women could be either smart or sexual but never both. Tiptree responded with an odd chain of associations:

> About the either-or roles for women. Jesus, I read that with aching heart. Prescription for self-mutilation [. . .]. I hate to say this, but one of the most sexually sane woman friends I have had was—is—an almost complete homo. (Some disastrous early marriage attempt, soon over.) I begin to wonder if female sexuality isn't a biological accident, a nightmarish side-product of your inherent masculinity. (All women's, I mean.) Maybe there are only 2 sexes, men and mothers. (Oh, and two asexual sexes, children and the old.)

Apparently Tiptree belongs to the "asexual sexes"—while Alli's "men and mothers" theory, which had always been a way of getting out of thinking about women's sexuality, becomes a way of banishing it to the "nightmare" world.

Russ snapped back, "WHY do you say that 'female sexuality' is a biological accident? 'Inherent masculinity?' WASH YOUR MOUTH OUT WITH

SOAP, JAMES TIPTREE!" Yet she added, "I think you're just in a big yearn for mothering, which is only natural, as I am too. And who isn't?"

In his next letter, Tiptree struggled to explain what he had meant: in female primates, "genital gratification" and fertility are not connected. "Of course women—I suspect most women—have a drive for sexual-genital gratification, but in many of them it may not be linked to the mechanics of the procreative act, or even to men." About the "mother" pattern he wrote, "Would it surprise you if I said I am TERRIFIED of mothers (I had a cannibal one) and am made very uncomfy by mothering?"

A few days later, Tiptree turned in his essay on "men and mothers." It begins with a warning against dualistic thinking.

> Our view of men and women is infested with the vicious mental habit of seeing any pair of differing things as somehow symmetrical mirror-images of each other. I, man, am hot—therefore they, women, are cold. *I* am active—therefore *they* are passive. [. . .] My id grunts, "Me good"; therefore they are bad. Perhaps more perniciously, my superego whispers, *I* have selfish and destructive drives—therefore *they* are altruistic, compassionate and nurturant. (They better be.)

It goes on to describe two patterns in human nature, both of which could occupy one psyche: the destructive violence of males and the compassionate nurturance of mothers.

Tiptree portrays the male pattern as both aggressive—Vietnam, nuclear proliferation, John Foster Dulles—and "trivial" in the sense that males had just one evolutionary task to perform and too much time on their hands. He argues that male sexuality

> *shares the neural pathways of aggression.* The male primate pursues, grasps, penetrates with much of the same equipment which serves aggression and predation. This has the dire side effect that the more aggressive males tend by and large to reproduce themselves more effectively and thus intensify the problem. [. . .] We appear to be subject to an androgen-related overgrowth of the aggressive syndrome, with

its accompanying male-male dominance-submission conflicts, male territoriality, and all the dismal rest.

To this pattern, the essay opposes the (capital m) Mothering pattern:

> the female primate endlessly, tirelessly lugging her infant, monitoring its activities at every moment, teaching, training, leading it to the best of her animal abilities. Not for a day or a week, but throughout its whole infancy and into self-sufficiency. [. . .] Look at what Motherhood involves. Leadership without aggression. Empathy of a high order—can it be the true root of speech? Great environmental competence. Aggressive defense of the young. [. . .] Most important of all, it is a relation *between* animals which is totally outside the "male" repertory.

This is a picture of motherhood as both "animal" instinct and the ultimate negentropic behavior. That humans were capable of such behavior gave Alli hope for human evolution.

But to harness mothering for human improvement, the research psychologist said, we must know *why* people do it. "Maternal instinct" wasn't a good enough explanation. "What is mothering powered by? What 'goals' has it? What reward drives it? We don't know." Then, as usual when Alli talked about women—or mothers—she got scared and angry and started saying women were doomed. Because of women's "physical, political and economic weakness," Tiptree wrote, "the women's movement is *dependent on the civilized acceptance of men.* Are we sufficiently civilized? Will the hand that holds the club really lay it down? [. . .] Let us not kid, men have the power. [. . .] Is our civilization deep enough in the bone? I fear the answer . . ."

Was Alli warning women of men's aggression, or was she venting her own rage at women, or at women's fates? Who is "we"? Everyone in the symposium was baffled by this essay—even Alli. (Tiptree told Russ his ideas about biology were "in a sense foreign, tentative steps for me. This is a secondary level; I am going against my own deepest dogma.") It shows how isolated Alli was from other women that she came with this question to the symposium. Only Le Guin said she was interested and wanted to hear more. The others ignored

Tiptree's essay or dismissed it. McIntyre wrote, "Ah, Tip, you are the last person in the world I would expect to hand me the Baboon Theory of Human Behavior. I cannot tell you how much I despise that argument." About Tiptree's observation that "men have the power," Delany asked simply, "Who are you threatening?"

Russ did not argue with Tiptree in the symposium, but she beat up on him fiercely in private. In a long letter she accused him of believing "that there are two kinds of women (or, as you would say, two kinds of behavior patterns): mothers and men. That is, we are right back to the old split between feminine women and 'masculine' women only you have dressed it up in the worst kind of fake-biology frills."

Why did Tiptree (and Alli) respond to feminism by writing about mothers? Maybe Russ came close in her guess about a "yearn for mothering," in both senses: Alli was not childless by choice. Tiptree later wrote transgender SF writer Jessica Amanda Salmonson, "I have never held a baby. Have you? Isn't this pretty basic to taking a female role?"

To Le Guin, in March 1975, Tip wrote,

> Today there were two babes-in-arms in the dentist's elevator, one blue, one yellow-decked. (Liberated baby?) I gazed at them in turn. One hiccuped. Nothing happened. *Why* are we raised? No one will answer me. Yet it is gospel that behaviour must be motivated. But *what* rewards this endless lugging-about, this gabbling and care and interacting? Why don't I feel it?

Would Alli have felt it? What would it have been like? Maybe she was like Mary Cassatt, late in her career, painting and repainting maternal bliss, trying to see into it, needing to know if it was worth what it cost.

Meanwhile, feminism was still bringing Alli back to the unspeakable: her relationship with Mary. In some notes to herself about mothering, Alli said, "The sorts of things that can be talked about in the mother-child interaction are exceedingly deep, direct, biological, and un-sacred, and there are no taboos." This is surely wishful thinking. She also said simply: "If mother and child don't understand each other the child doesn't survive."

The unnurturing act of writing is conspicuously absent from the "men and mothers" pattern—as it was from Alli's descriptions of herself that fall. The pattern of men and mothers might also describe the split between Tiptree who wrote about violence and Alli who felt responsible for the world's pain. Was it Tip who whispered to Alli, "*I* have selfish and destructive drives—therefore *you* are altruistic, compassionate and nurturant. (You better be)"?

Legend has it that Tiptree got kicked out of the symposium for his sexist views. This is not quite true. After several rounds of letters, Russ wrote that Tiptree and Delany "have contributed a good deal, but it's true that they are time-hoggers and they—and Jeff—keep drawing our attention away from what (to me) is what is truly interesting: what *we* think." Tiptree, glad to have an excuse to stop, said he had only joined to be a straw man anyway. "Joanna, your piece inviting me out of the talk is exactly how I feel."

A few years later, Alli wrote cheerfully to Smith, "Things like being hooted at in the [. . .] Symposium really didn't bother me at all, because I doubtless would have done the same myself. [. . .] There are stages in all revolutions of consciousness where certain things are unsayable, because they sound too much like the enemy's line."

Yet Alli's thoughts on aggression and empathy, her feelings of powerlessness and her duty to suffer, are all also signs of oncoming despair. Like Le Guin, she was going into a "dark hard place." In a letter to Mary, in July 1975, she called it "the black pit with only one door."

CHAPTER 35: DEPRESSION (1975–76)

The greatest pain does not come zooming down from a distant planet, but up from the depths of the heart.

—PHILIP K. DICK

On November 5, 1974, Alli Sheldon had surgery to replace her right thumb joint. For a month she wrote nothing—except for a few mirror-image postcards to Ursula Le Guin, who had said that writing left-handed was easier if you did it backward. Then she began keeping a journal, because the doctor had told her it would help to exercise the hand. In it she formed the letters of the roman and Greek alphabets in a wobbly script, described her pain (which was all she could think about at first, holding the pen), and said she hoped to start writing down "ideas for a story or novel, or at least ideas about ideas. (Including whether to write a Tiptree or Raccoona next!)"

At the same time Alli started seeing a psychologist, Dr. Robert Harper. She had found him through her old army nurse friend Dilly, who had gone to him for her amphetamine addiction. He was Alli's age, which made her feel comfortable at first, and she liked his calm authority and eclectic approach. She asked him to help her with her periods of "apathy" and "lethargy," a problem she felt was physical, though compounded by "self-indulgence and the bad habit of waiting 'until I feel more like doing it.'"

Instead Harper suggested that her low moods might have a psychological cause, either (Alli wrote) "that some conflict or conflicts (unspecified—and better so) are blocking the natural access to energy, or that some psychic structure is in conflict with action—or perhaps that energy is being used in internal conflict." If her emotions were blocked, "it would be stupid to attempt to raise energy chemically. [. . .] Like pushing voltage through a leaky line." He suggested she try quitting Dexedrine for a while, and she agreed to explore a purely psychological approach to her depressions—though he also used hypnosis for short-term relief.

The cast on Alli's wrist came off in mid-December, amid the arduous packing for Boca Paila, and the Sheldons left the next day. Alli felt guilty—she and Ting had never before spent Christmas without Mary—and as always she hated being torn away from her work. But they'd been told the warmth would help her thumb heal faster; and it did help. By Christmas Day the joint hurt less than it had in years. Tiptree wrote Le Guin:

> I gaud, I am gaud-y, I am damn near impossible; no, I am not full of tequila [...] what I am full of is joy. THE DAMNED CAST IS OFF AND THE ONCE-DAMNED THUMB REALLY TRULY WORKS. Oh, I can write, I can unscrew peanut jars—have some peanuts, have some aceitunas, I have unscrewed everything! Ursula, it is joy unspeakable.

Yet by New Year's Eve 1974, having gone off Dexedrine, Alli was writing in her journal of flu, headaches, leg cramps (Ting massaged her legs), tension, and inability to work. She had already used all their supply of Numorphan, a synthetic morphine she was prescribed for migraine headaches, and was taking Demerol for the pain in her legs. On New Year's Eve she wrote,

> I tried intermittently to act "normal," walking, swimming, etc., got house all unpacked [...] tried to settle to thinking of work. VERY difficult—mind felt dead. [...] I want to note here the horrible day passed (yesterday) miserable abed, unable to rouse; when I read (poetry) I wept. Suffered thru incredible stupid hours, soaking head, half-crying. Main symptom—Total absence of motivation. No desire to *do* anything. Desire to stop, to die; very strong. (Had Ting lock up Seconal.) No desire to move, to go out, to eat, etc. Tried to "analyse," got nowhere. No trace of "Why?"—no thoughts of mother, guilt, anything. Sourceless woe.

One source was probably amphetamine withdrawal. Another may have been writing. Alli was again trying to plot a novel; in a letter to Bob Harper on January 8, she described a creative process in which she was not listening to her subconscious but trying to force it to generate something worthy.

About ten days ago I sent down the order to produce and started the usual routine of pacing and grunting and staring into space. And got the usual evasive results—amazing what the subconscious will come up with to get out of doing the job you ask of it. About four perfectly good un-needed short story lines, any amount of theoretical musings, but a story long enough and dense enough to carry a novel? Oh, no. The old hassle. Do it! I can't. *Do* it! Aw, take this instead, see how pretty. Screw you, *do it!* Silence . . .

That winter she did start work on a novel. But in her depression she began to associate the writing of it with her own death. She later told Charles Platt,

I would sit out in front of the house in Yucatán, under the diminishing shade of a little palm tree in the hot wind, and write three or four lines on the novel, and then look up at a grinning skeleton, and then think of my body wallowing in the formaldehyde tanks of GW, and then write three or four lines and look up again and see Ting floating beside me, white hair streaming as the corpse revolves. Then I'd write three or four more lines and spend an hour laughing gaily. It was that way, chapter af-ter chapter.

After a while the writing began to go better, and Alli's mood improved. "The moment I started working again on something objective," she wrote Harper on January 31,

EVERYTHING BECAME ALL RIGHT. The demons fled, the woes of life deflated and appeared as a non-threatening landscape.
    From which I deduce what I've always really known and what Ting has sometimes bitterly accused me of—I really only function when I'm working at something not myself. [. . .] Something *I* do which yet isn't me. In other words, if we can put me back to working industriously at something, everything else will be solved or solvable. [. . .]
    Of course writing fiction is a peculiar task. Maybe, in the long run, not the right one. I may be ending this phase and go back to something more factual. But not quite yet.

But for the next two years, the novel, her mother's illness, and Ting's and her own ill health all came together in a depression that this time would not lift. Sometimes she had a happy hour or day, "finding myself a lucky, healthy woman with an incredibly kind and beloved mate, in the best of circumstances." But then her world would go dark again, "as if some internal mood-switch was being flipped by an idiot." She felt, she thought, the way she had always felt before one of her sudden changes. Only now it wasn't a job or a project she wanted to abandon, but life itself.

She thought often of suicide, her old way out. Sometimes she saw it as a way of getting the dying over with. To Harper, she called this "the Second Shoe syndrome: Oncoming death has laid its hand on me, penetrated my defenses. All is about to be lost—for god's sake get on with it!" In her journal she wrote, "I have 'deadline-itis'—I've seen the end. Like IF YOU CAN READ THIS YOU'RE TOO DAMN CLOSE."

But to Le Guin, Tiptree wrote that fantasies of suicide came from guilt and "suppressed fury." "There is an indescribable quality to the mental act of finding Death *compatible*—suitable—to oneself which is the end-product of some intense psychic elision. Have you ever felt it? I have, strong enough to motivate action. It lies in wait for evil moments."

In one of those moments, she wrote in her journal, "The intent toward Death has a momentum of its own, it is like a vortex. It sucks all else around it and into it. (Do people realize the *life* of this idea of death? Its addictive, alluring qualities. [. . .])"

Part of her whispered that suicide was the only logical response to her condition. Another part shouted, "Something inside me is trying to kill me. Help!" She wondered if her depressions were not "merely the dramas of a childish woman seeking for attention with suicide threats." She thought maybe she ought to kill herself just to prove she was serious. She admonished herself, "Whatever the outcome, this is a great waste of time. (Funny; the idea of having 'invested' so much energy in suicide, it would be stupid to waste it.)" She always planned to use a gun, her old instrument of mastery and control.

More than ever, Ting cared for Alli, watched over her, and played the role of Leonard to her Virginia. He hid guns and pills, promoted reason and regular hours, bought groceries, made sure she ate. At one point, at the Lodge, he grabbed her old .38 out of her hand and threw it in the lake. There were times

Alice on the afternoon of her debut. She liked the attention her looks brought her but knew she didn't fit the part.
(Chicago Tribune)

Bill Davey.
(Courtesy of William Davey)

Bill and Alice at the Lodge, 1930s.
(Courtesy of William Davey)

Alice in uniform, early 1940s.
(Courtesy of Barbara Francisco)

Alice at a Georges Braque
exhibition in Chicago,
November 1939, when she
was separated from Bill.
(Courtesy of Barbara Francisco)

Diana at the Architects' Ball
. . . With a 'Beau' and Arrow

Alice at a costume ball in
Chicago, January 1940,
enjoying what Bill called
her "rhinestone" side.
(Chicago Herald-American)

Loveliest Diana at the Architects'
"Calling Out the Gods" ball last week,
Mrs. William Davey, the Herbert E. Bradleys' statuesque daughter, Alice, had a
host of admiring mortals in "gods' cloth-
ing'" waiting to dance with her at the

very gayest party of the Winter. Edwin
T. Meredith Jr., whose blond wig, halo
and maribou-trimmed ballet costume
stamped him an "angel from Des
Moines," was the Nat Owings' guest at
the ball . . . and one of Diana's fans.

Alice retouching a photo, probably in Antibes. She's wearing the beach outfit she bought while waiting to be shipped out to Europe.
(Courtesy of Franklin Berkowitz)

Alice and Ting in Wiesbaden, fall 1945.
(Mary Hastings Bradley Papers, University of Illinois at Chicago)

At a homecoming party in Chicago, January 1946,
Alice posed for the newspapers for the last time.
(Chicago Herald-American)

Alice, fall 1945. *(Mary Hastings Bradley Papers,*
University of Illinois at Chicago)

COL. HUNTINGTON D. SHELDON, U. S. A., and his bride,
Capt. Alice B. Davey, WAC, are party-going this week in Chi-
cago. They were married in Paris in September, and have just
arrived in America. Yesterday, Mrs. Sheldon's parents, the Herbert
Bradleys, entertained for them at the Casino, and today the
Chauncey McCormicks are their hosts.

The house and hatchery in Toms River.
(Courtesy of Peter and Ann Sheldon)

Rudolf Arnheim at Sarah
Lawrence, 1950s.
*(Sarah Lawrence College Archives;
photo by Mary Morris)*

A handsome family at the Lodge, early 1960s:
Ting's son Peter Sheldon, Peter's wife Ann,
Mary, Alli, and Ting.
(Courtesy of Peter and Ann Sheldon)

Mary, Herbert, and Alli at the Lodge, 1950s.
For this photo, Alli put on lipstick; other
photos from the Lodge show her working
on boats in a T-shirt and jeans.
(Courtesy of Barbara Francisco)

Top: Ursula K. Le Guin, 1971. She became one of Tiptree's closest correspondents.
(Photo Wes Guderian/The Oregonian)

Bottom Left: Harlan Ellison. Rejecting a submission of Tiptree's in 1969, Ellison ordered him to "Get off your ass and do me the best story you've ever done."
(Photo by William Rotsler)

Bottom Middle: Jeff Smith, Tiptree's young editor friend, in 1977, the year they first met in person.
(Courtesy of Jeffrey D. Smith)

Bottom Right: Barry N. Malzberg. As Tiptree, Alli wrote him about horse racing and back trouble. As herself, she preferred to flirt.
(Photo by Charles N. Brown/Locus)

Joanna Russ. More than twenty years younger than Tiptree, she did her best to give him a feminist education. *(Photo by Jay Kay Klein)*

Judy-Lynn and Lester del Rey, 1974. *(Photo by David Dyer-Bennet)*

Craig Kee Strete in Amsterdam, 1977. Alli felt especially protective toward a writer whose life seemed to be as wild as hers had been. *(Photo by Kuno Grommers)*

Alice B. Sheldon

AKA James Tiptree Jr.

AKA Raccoona Sheldon

On a 1984 contract with her new agent, Virginia Kidd, Alli signed as all three personae. Tiptree seems confident, Raccoona Sheldon reserved, while Alice B. Sheldon's signature combines the two. *(Courtesy of Virginia Kidd)*

In 1977, not long after Tiptree's identity was revealed, Alli posed for an author photo for *Up the Walls of the World*. For the book jacket, she chose a masculine-looking shot.
(Photo by James Reber)

When she signed a photo for Charles Platt, she chose a more feminine one.
(Photo by James Reber)

Ting and Alli at their home in McLean, Virginia, 1983.
(Photo by Patti Perret)

Alli in her office, 1983. On top of the pile of books is Joanna Russ's novel *On Strike Against God*.
(Photo by Patti Perret)

he worried so much about her that he cried. Alli's troubles and his concern seemed to bring them closer together than ever.

Harper's first diagnosis for Alli's depression was her worry and guilt about Mary. It was certainly true that the ordeal of caring for a dying parent, on top of all her feelings about this particular parent, was often more than Alli could bear. When she first started seeing Harper, Alli wrote a fifteen-page document for him that she called "The Relevant Biography." In it she said of Mary,

> I deeply feel that I should help her, companion her, love her, respond to her with empathy; that this is an adult DUTY. And at the same time I loathe doing so, I feel bled dry of empathy, I want to live the remaining bit of my own life. [. . .] My only solution—for years—has been to hope that she, or I, would die before it got worse. It is now getting worse.

In May 1975, Tip wrote Barry Malzberg that his mother was going blind, could no longer read, and was phoning constantly. "I'm bled of all emotion except empathic death."

As always, she expressed her pain by talking about universal tragedy. She told Harper, "*Reality* is the worst thing you can think of; everything else is agreeing to enjoy the dancing as the Titanic sails on." In her journal she wrote, "In my head, the 'bill of complaints' against life is all interconnected; when I weep for Mary, I'm weeping for Carthage and the baby shoes at Belsen. Thus trying to desensitize any particular instance ends having to desensitize all. Life *has* its saddening, tragic side, and any attempt to reduce this (past a point) flies in the face of reality." She felt, she wrote, a "duty to mourn."

Harper offered logic, suggesting that Alli learn to shut herself off from others' pain—an act she dismissed as "a deliberate atrophy of the empathic response." The person most deserving of Alli's empathy was perhaps herself, and her grief for the state of the world an expression of her own pain. But Harper didn't see it. He was a behaviorist by inclination, and urged Alli to do what she had always done: counter depression with reason. He tried to get her to "insert an intellectual 'joint' in the process, an evaluation change which would make tragedy merely unpleasantness." Like Ting, he emphasized her practical problems, erratic work schedule, and social isolation. He talked about "self-management" and encouraged her to develop an "interest in life."

Maybe because Harper was a man Alli's age, there were many aspects of her experience he doesn't seem to have understood. They didn't explore Alli's feminism or her life as a woman. They probably didn't talk about her sexuality. And he was very uncomfortable with what Alli herself felt was one of the roots of her depression, her anger. In April 1976 she wrote in her journal,

> I must tackle Bob on the anger bit. He is "blind" there because his problem is to get rid of or control anger. Is he confident that I'm a person abnormally low on anger? Or that my anger has all been converted to fear? (Or turned against self.) Get this cleared up. The conversion-to-fear explanation sounds likely to me. But it's a bit fishy. [. . .] The whole thing smells of something buried and unexamined.

As usual, it was Joanna Russ who went digging for the buried bone. Returning to their old discussion of anger, Tiptree asked her, "How can you get angry with the Second Law of Thermodynamics, which has stolen from me most of what I love, and is in [the] process of killing me?" Russ responded,

> It is my opinion that you [. . .] are not angry at the second law of thermodynamics but at something/somebody MUCH closer to home. [. . .] It is really *safer* not to get angry at people, to find reasons why not and reasons why you're really angry at God or at impersonal forces and so why be angry and it's hopeless, &c.
>
> Do you know, there's a good deal about you that seems to me more like women I know than like men I know in the way you handle your feelings?

To Harper and her other doctors, Alli dismissed her work as a cause of stress: it wasn't as though it were hard work to write a novel. At the same time, almost in the same sentence, she accepted that she suffered from "excessive achievement compulsion." Yet she generally insisted that she was a second-rate writer and didn't mind it. After all, she assured Harper, her own life was no more futile than anyone else's. "We and all our works are lemmings rushing to extinction. I am a lemming who has raised his head and cried, Jesus Christ, we're all marching to extinction. The other lemmings answer me, Shut up and march."

She no longer hoped her writing would change anything. "[Writing] seems pointless. Another cry of woe—so what? [. . .] I don't desire to dig deeper, burn hotter, express better—because I am reluctant to deliver again my message: Death; and I personally am dying."

Yet when she thought about her "duty to mourn," she wrote, "my writing work has been my main defense against this, because in writing you can handle grief, distance and pattern it." In July 1976 she noted, "Remember to tell Bob 'writing is my only connection to life.'"

She rarely discussed her performance as Tiptree with Harper or explored it in her journals. On the contrary, her journals mostly record the daily life she couldn't write about in Tiptree's letters: the garden, chats with neighbors, talks with Ting. When she thought in her journals about having a male side, she created a new persona, Alex, herself as a man in her daily life. She used Alex, rarely, in her journals when she was wondering how a man might handle various situations: "What would Alex do?" Alex seldom had an answer. Alli never asked Tip.

Throughout the spring of 1975, while Alli was struggling with her moods, Tiptree was contributing to the symposium and doing his best to be a feminist man. When "The Women Men Don't See" reached the Nebula Award finals, he withdrew it from the ballot with a vague excuse about giving other writers a chance. (In fact Alli feared its male byline would give the story an unfair edge.) He urged his male correspondents to take feminism seriously.

He also went on arguing with Joanna Russ, though he tended more and more to deny everything—even that feminism might demand changes in his life. He told her, "I have it easy, because at my age and solitude [feminism] doesn't mean rethinking actual on-going roles. I don't have to change or be threatened, and I do my own dishes anyway. I wish I had a daughter." He went on insisting on women's vulnerability. In February 1975 he wrote Russ that women (he said "you" for women, "we" for men) were "a little—a little— like a beautiful deer in a game park where they have temporarily suspended hunting season. There are few such parks and god knows how long this will last." In a subsequent letter he said he meant that women should consolidate their power base, watch their backs, and try to make their freedom last. But having made the deer park analogy, what agency can Tiptree imagine for the deer? He added, "If men did not exist, would you have invented them? I am making myself feel so unreal I shall shortly vanish."

Russ replied,

> There are times, Tip, when you're a very doubtful ally; you seem bent on
> proving that all is suffering, brutality, and horror, and that the goodies al-
> ways get it in the neck. I can imagine having you in the bunker when the
> shelling gets rough and all of us finally have to toss you out in the snow
> because you are subtly undermining our nerve by your constant weeping!

She later apologized, but went on alternately offering friendship and beating up on Tiptree for his sexism: "Oh, you Penis People are impossible! (All
right, you're an exception. Yes, you are.)"

Even worse, Russ kept writing about identity, sexuality, the difficulty of
being one's body. Russ was coming out as a lesbian, and in April, in a long,
thoughtful letter, she came out to Tiptree. She told him about the complexity
of her feelings, their refusal to fit into the definitions at hand. She'd had so
little lesbian experience; what did that make her? Her whole idea of herself,
she wrote, had been turned upside down. "It's not simply a 'sexual preference'
as so many gay people try to say, i.e. We're just like you except for this one
little thing. [. . .] It has everything to do with everything else."

Tiptree's reply was brief, sympathetic, and highly evasive. "And as for going officially Lesbian, more power to you," he wrote.

> Here of course I'm a bad advisor, because I long ago realised I would
> outlast my gonads and decided to move that part of my life up into my
> head before I became ridiculous. So it's a long time since I've passed wild
> nights of longing, or wilder ones of acquisition. I can only sympathise.
> But on the basis of memory and reports from friends, I must say I see
> nothing particularly two-headed about wanting both men and women. I
> myself don't [. . .].

"I myself" is apparently another person than the one of "memory." In his
next letter, Tip did say a little about his love life. Russ had written about men's
fear of women. He replied, "I personally don't really know what everyone is
so scared of. (I know what *I'm* scared of—everything, starting with the second law of thermodynamics. But I guess I don't count.)" Then he described

his unrequited romances with beautiful, "doomed" girls. Russ answered, "Do you know, those beautiful, doomed, delicate, appallingly rich and heartbreaking girls sound to me oddly like you? I mean the part of yourself that makes you scared of everything, starting with the second law of thermodynamics? Like an externalized soul."

Tiptree was frightened for Russ: he also responded to her coming out by urging her to withdraw, to protect herself more, to keep all her rage and genius to herself and show the world only "calmness and lucidity." It was the only way to succeed on the world's terms, he said. "It's expensive and it hurts, but it's the one that'll work."

And he went on insisting on women's vulnerability, until in February 1976, after a year of listening to Tip's worrying, Russ wrote angrily,

> I very much distrust your division of humankind into the Victims and the Torturers. I've never met a Victim yet who wasn't a Torturer in her own quiet way, and there's not a Torturer in the world who doesn't suffer and isn't driven. [. . .] It is, I would think, one way of handling anger, but it strikes me as an unfruitful way and certainly for your friends (of whom I am one) very frustrating.

Alli got this letter just after she was hospitalized for heart failure, and didn't answer it. Until then Russ and Tiptree had been exchanging letters as often as once a week. They didn't write again for six months.

While Tiptree was being a feminist, Alli didn't seem quite sure what to do with Raccoona. To Jeff Smith, in February 1975, Raccoona talked about their mutual friend:

> There seems to be some confusion about me and Tip Tiptree. Several people have written me as though I were an authority on him. I did know him when we were in the local 4th and 5th grades together, but I have not seen him in person for a couple of years. We correspond in fits and starts. I take care of his mail when he comes through here to see his mother. His letters have mostly to do with urging me to write or draw;

he is a dear person, rather protective—but I don't think anybody is an authority on him. I did not know of his [hand] operation until I got a card from somewhere in Mexico. [. . .]

As for me, really the less said the better. I'm a retired schoolteacher—how romantic can you get?—with a sort of messy peopled-up life. So I live in dreams.

Later that year Raccoona contributed letters, drawings, and a poem to a new feminist fanzine, *The Witch and the Chameleon*. There was talk of *WatCh* continuing the *Khatru* symposium, and Raccoona wrote its publisher, Amanda Bankier, to encourage this. But she added, "I don't think I could contribute anything of value. Everyone else seems to have thought of it all so much more. All I just know could be summed up, Ouch!" In passing, like Alli, she dismissed her own sexuality: "I'm so old nobody including me could care if I am gay or straight or queer for typewriters." Raccoona was in a way chillier than Tiptree, despite her nutty-old-auntie voice.

For most of 1975 and 1976, Tiptree wrote few letters. He *got* more mail all the time, from friends, fans, and editors asking him for stories. After Tiptree got back from the Yucatán in February 1975, he complained to Le Guin of "receiving a great body-bag like a dead horse" from the post office. To Craig Strete he added, "Half of it is ANSWER LAST WEEK OR WE WILL REPOSSESS YOUR PRICK."

But because he wasn't writing short stories, a lot of his friendly exchanges with editors—Silverberg, Harrison, Ellison—fell away. And other friends of Tiptree's had troubles of their own. Barry Malzberg was depressed; when Tiptree confessed his own depression, a misunderstanding made Malzberg take offense. It took him nearly a year to resume his letters and his expressions of circumspect concern: "You send grim and ominous signals [. . .]. I am in a difficult position of course because your identity and situation are still unknown to me and probably always will be (and I do not even speculate on them [. . .]) but if there is anything I can do to help you will nonetheless please advise."

Jeff Smith had a new job as a lab tech at a community college and needed less of Tip's advice. He was publishing less, too, so Tiptree was writing fewer columns for him. Their correspondence settled down to occasional postcards.

Craig Strete went on writing about his adventures, and "Uncle Tip" responded with long letters full of advice and encouragement, telling him his troubles came "from being a highly intelligent, highly *gifted* being, Indian or whatever, it's all the same. The far teeny end of the distribution curve is occupied at the price of continual shit and agony." For Strete alone among her correspondents, Alli didn't bother to disguise her concern and affection with a more "manly" style. Strete didn't ask, but he guessed early on that the letters were coming from a woman.

Le Guin was depressed and writing little. Tiptree advised her gently, "You are feeling your way toward something new [. . .]. I do not want you ever to be *really* upset because of the turning-round in place and slow ripening. You burn up a lot of living and thinking in each story. Takes time to accumulate the next bonfire." Avoiding questions about the symposium, Tip sent Le Guin warm, friendly rambles, and she responded with cartoons, jokes, and gossip about Nebula banquets. In the fall of 1975, Le Guin's husband Charles went on sabbatical, and they traveled, via World-Con in Australia, around the world to spend a year in England. All year, Le Guin sent Tiptree travelogues of Venice and Vienna, Stonehenge and London. But she also cited Yeats's poem on the inability to write, "The Circus Animals' Desertion," and said, "Well, here we are, anyhow, where all the ladders start."

Like Tip, Alli grew more and more isolated. She gardened, chatted with neighbors and Ting's friends, but had no more work friendships and little reason to leave the house. During the worst of her depressions, she told Mary, she could still "appear quite normal and jolly, a paragon of relaxation, brightness, health—for an hour or two together. People who see me then never suspect. God knows I've had practice. But then I start to tremble and have to break away fast." One evening, trying to be sociable, she went with a woman friend to see a play in the city. The next day Tiptree wrote Strete, "It was like squinting down [the] small end of binoculars. I couldn't take any of it seriously."

Alli certainly didn't want to talk to friends about her depressions. In her journal she wrote,

What is in me is death, is the grief-frozen acknowledgement of entropy triumphant—and some last gentlemanly scruple kills the urge to communicate it. I don't want to make others feel like me.

Not only a scruple. A sense of the total futility of it.

But in January 1976, at Boca Paila, Alli wrote in her journal, "Maybe I miss all the Tiptree letter-writing. They reinforced 'my' life."

CHAPTER 36: **MARY'S DEATH (1976)**

By July 1975, Alli was convinced—and had convinced her doctor, Charles Schehl—that her illness, depression, malaise, and struggles with writing were partly physical. Schehl again suggested antidepressants. Instead Alli went to a Chicago neurologist and family friend who confidently put her back on her old depression remedy: daily doses of Dexedrine.

All fall, Alli took Dexedrine, supplementing it with codeine and Seconal. The sadness and inertia abated; raving anxiety took their place. In October 1975 Tiptree wrote Ursula Le Guin that the way he felt was like having one's car horn get stuck, or like "going about one's business carrying a relentlessly screaming child. (Doubtless the child is me [. . .])." He quickly added, "I DO NOT want you to play the I'm so sorry game, this isn't an appeal for mothering. Not that I wouldn't love it, but don't *reward* me, if you know what I mean."

Later Alli concluded that Dexedrine "is only good when one has a definite desire to do something, a plan. It does not generate desires and plans. If one takes it in a state of anomie or despair it merely increases anxiety." But by now it was hard for her to tell the difference between Dexedrine anxiety and her normal state of mind. She told Bob Mills, "The stimulants that get me off my ass and moving also seem to render one more vulnerable to a sort of nightmare-panic-gloom effect, with which I've always been plagued. [. . .] There are practical ways to cope with this, but unfortunately writing highly emotional fiction is not one of them."

Still, over the course of 1975 and 1976, Alli became more and more dependent on prescription drugs. She kept records of her pill taking in her journal, partly to make her feel it was under control, partly to keep track of any combination that might yield a decent state of mind. In a two-week period in May 1976, she recorded using Seconal, phenobarbital, Dexedrine, Compazine, codeine, Percodan, Valium, Demerol, and Numorphan. More and more, the most tempting of these drugs was Numorphan, a synthetic form of morphine. It made her feel lousy: "flustered, vague, prone to elaborate sweaty

bad dreams; weakish, confused, unreal." Yet she craved the moments of exquisite "peace" and "normalcy" that Numorphan gave her, its "opiate euphoria"
and "glorious oblivion."

None of this did Alli's health any good. In January 1976, she started
having heart arrhythmia. In February, at Boca Paila, she got a salmonella infection, dysentery, and pneumonia, became dehydrated, and went into heart
failure. In the middle of the night, the ranch owner, Tony Gonzalez, found a
plane and a pilot to fly the Sheldons to Cozumel, and Ting rushed Alli to the
hospital. She lay there for three days hooked up to an IV. Then Ting took her
home to McLean.

Almost dying made Alli, for the first time in ages, write something funny:
a column for Jeff Smith called "How to Have an Absolutely Hilarious Heart
Attack." As Tiptree, she was able to describe her stay in the hospital as a comic
adventure: the kindness and inefficiency of the staff, the baby in the next
room that cried for twelve hours straight, the attempts to go to the bathroom
holding one's own IV bottle or remain decent in the absence of clean bedding
and clothes.

The more physical the story, the more tempted Alli was to play games with
gender. Tiptree describes a "lanky self" kept wrapped in a bedspread because
of a "strong feeling that beautiful young ladies, or young ladies, beautiful or
otherwise, should not be subjected to my grizzled, uh, nudity." Zapped by a
primitive X-ray machine, he "thanked my stars that my gonads had little future." Later, in a rare instance of admitting, Alli wrote that it was all deliberate, even the "uh," which "makes the [. . .] reader think I am ducking out on
the word or words uppermost in his mind, while in fact I was ducking out on
the different words describing the exterior appearance of the aged nude female crotch. [. . .] Is it my fault if people don't *read?*"

Alli could laugh about her own health, barely. But now they learned that
Ting had vascular damage in one eye and was slowly going blind. Alli thought
his anxiety over her might have worsened it, and was extremely upset. Bob
Harper wanted her to prepare for Ting's death, but she wrote in her journal,
"As to trying to build 'another' reality beyond Ting—I feel it wrong, I feel it
to be wrong. Reenactment of childhood guilt, the 'killing' of another dream."

As a writer, Alli was feeling more exposed than ever. The new blow to her artistic reticence came in March 1976 in the form of a critical essay on Tiptree's work. The critic was Gardner Dozois, another of Tiptree's young writer acquaintances; the essay was an introduction to a hardcover reprint of *Ten Thousand Light-Years from Home*. Dozois praised Tiptree's energetic style, talked about his mysterious identity, and pointed out certain themes in his work: communication, the longing to transcend the self, the search for home. In "Painwise," "The Milk of Paradise," "The Man Who Walked Home," and "Beam Us Home," Dozois noted, "the search for the Lost Home has become indistinguishably bound up with the quest for personal transcendence: transcendence can only be achieved by the finding of the Home, *is* the Homecoming."

Alli knew that Tiptree had been dealing with some themes that were close to her heart. But she thought she had written about them in the abstract. Now the search for a lost home, this very personal, private emotion, turned out to be something a perceptive reader could pick right up out of the pages of her stories.

She interpreted the lost home motif as an unadmitted longing for her childhood, and felt she had at last uncovered the source of her secret sorrow. Her parents had really loved and understood her, and had given her a deliriously happy childhood, "a Potemkin world of fairness and justice and joy." It was not her parents who had failed her, but time and adulthood. Because the Africa trips were no longer possible, a part of her reality, or even her soul, had "been snatched away into the garbage heap of history," leaving her the only survivor. On March 14, Tip wrote Le Guin that all his work was "just a wild attempt to build magical bridges somehow back, or out, or Do Something about the Unbearable."

In her journal on the same day Alli wrote,

> Certainly my early life "in the morning of the world" was at the time almost an idyll; so beloved and understood. En rapport, such high morale in our little group, and the world a great treasure pot to be opened. [. . .] Later I came to hate all that love and closeness, but it was in fact there, the dark side I now see was very hidden. Nobody should be so coddled in all good at the start [. . .]. And then, of course, it was lost; the world was stolen—destroyed, the people aged and fell away from the dream and died; I aged and looked for my own world, agonized with guilt at

betraying the idyll. [...] I became the official mourner and remem-
berer [...]. And when father died, the idyll, the dream, was finally ir-
revocably shattered and lost. To admit his death is to close the door on
all that was. And what was, was my first reality and compared to it, my
later identities are as puffs of smoke. [...]

Thus to let go, to cease to mourn is to kill—as the bereaved mother
cannot admit her child is really dead.

She really felt, she wrote, like one "of those bereaved mothers who 'never
get over it.'" But the "dead" child she is mourning might also be Alice, the
child who never dared to be herself, and whose last chance to be loved for herself was lost along with her childhood world. A week later she wrote, "The
story of my incapacity for the parental Eden is the problem of Utopia."

It could have been the start of a breakthrough for Alli—realization not of
childhood happiness but of childhood loss. But Harper couldn't see it, or
didn't understand it. A few months later Alli wrote in her journal, "No one
can 'help' me."

Even Tiptree (that child of Alli's) felt exposed, "dead." Dozois's "all-too-
perceptive gaze saw right into the springs of Tiptree, and barely left me one
faded figleaf to cover my artistic nudity," Tip joked to Virginia Kidd. But to
Le Guin he wrote, "I feel as if I'd just read my obituary."

Dozois had spoken of Tiptree's rapid rise to prominence. But several
months later (thinking partly of Phil Dick), Tip wrote Barry Malzberg,

Sometimes I think writers only last so long, if they are writing out some
kind of mine or vein of unconscious material. I may be one of these.
[...] There are people who erupt, grow brilliantly, sustain an unsus-
tainable level until you can't hold your breath any longer . . . and then
it's all over but the stick and shreds descending more or less gracefully to
earth.

Despite her depression and health troubles, Alli spent most of 1975 and
1976 working on her novel, now called *Up the Walls of the World*. In November 1975, Tiptree sent 25,000 words and a synopsis to the book's editor, Judy-
Lynn Benjamin del Rey. Del Rey had married writer and editor Lester del Rey

and had moved from *Galaxy* to Ballantine Books, where she was developing a very successful line of commercial science fiction and fantasy. She had edited *Warm Worlds and Otherwise,* and the contract gave her an option on Tiptree's first novel.

Months later, in May 1976, del Rey responded that she liked the book except for one problem: it was written in the present tense, a style she said was arty and didn't sell. Tiptree suggested she get a second opinion from Lester, who had praised Tip's work in the past. Lester told Tiptree that the present tense always "fails abysmally. Tell a first-rate story that way, and the readers vote it down to the bottom of the list—or don't read it or buy the book, mostly."

Tiptree pointed out that some of his most highly praised stories—"The Girl Who Was Plugged In," "The Women Men Don't See," "A Momentary Taste of Being"—were written in the present. He said he had put a lot of effort into making the present tense work. He said it felt right for the material. "You know, the world's best writer I'm not," he grumbled to Bob Mills, "but I do write things like they seem to ask, not like editors or beautiful women or god tells me." But Judy-Lynn wasn't having any "pseudo-literary tricks and gimmicks [. . .]. If you are writing for awards, for the critics, for the fans and for 'posterity' (whatever that is), I may be the wrong editor for you. If you are writing for readers, then you're in the right house." Tiptree decided to continue in the present; they could both judge when the book was finished.

In protesting the present tense, Judy-Lynn may have been responding to a sense that the novel didn't quite live. The overall tone of *Up the Walls of the World* is not angry, like Tiptree's earlier stories, or ruthless, like "A Momentary Taste of Being," but gloomy. The characters are divided into victims and villains, with a great deal of persuading us to be sorry for the victims. There are fewer emotional surprises in *Up the Walls*: no Dr. Ain murdering for the best of reasons, no saintly Lory Kaye engineering the rebirth of humanity. Above all, it lacks Tiptree's confident, electric narrative voice.

The two main human characters are again—as in "A Momentary Taste" and "The Women Men Don't See"—a man who can bear reality and a woman who longs only to escape it. But this time even the man can hardly stand to live. Dr. Daniel Dann is a physician whose wife and child have died in a fire (a cliché to which Tiptree at his best would not have stooped), and who medicates away his guilt and sorrow. He is painfully sensitive to others' suffering:

a sad confession "hurts him physically, in the way others' pain always does, as he assumes [it hurts] everybody." The woman is computer specialist Margaret Omali. The American daughter of a Kenyan father, she was subjected to genital mutilation as a child, and as an adult has fled into a cool world of mathematics and machines.

Dann and Omali are both working for an obscure Defense Department project, assisting at an elaborate ESP test. The test subjects are not very cheerful company. One young sailor is dying of leukemia. An elderly housewife calls herself a "surplus human being." A lesbian couple are described as vulnerable to the world's hostility, their lives "pervaded by some intrusive permanent menace, a lurking, confining cruelty like an occupying enemy."

The distant planet Tyree seems to promise freedom from such suffering. The Tyrenni do not even live on their world, but sail like giant manta rays in the winds high above it. They are physically insubstantial, almost all mind, and are wise and careful in balancing the mind and controlling their telepathic communications. In a synopsis Tiptree wrote, "Much of their culture is devoted to training, ordering and decorous control of their mental output"— making them sound like WASPs in space. The work of cultivating young minds has great status among the Tyrenni, so while the females are hardy and adventurous, the males, with their larger and more sensitive "life-energy fields," raise the children and have all the authority. Tyree's equivalent of feminists are the females who insist that they too are capable of caring for the young. "Can you imagine [a world] where the females are *Fathers?*" one says wistfully. Another answers, "But, but how could that be? [. . .] Males are bigger and stronger, they'd obviously keep the babies."

This was Tiptree's first experiment with world building, the science fictional practice of imagining an entire new planet, race, or culture. Sadly, Tiptree dreamed up this lovely, comical place only to destroy it. Tyree's sun is about to explode, and the Tyrenni are searching the heavens telepathically for a way out.

Alli hadn't lost her talent for writing action: the sequence of the Tyrenni making contact with the human ESP subjects and attempting to flee into their bodies is skillful and tense. It ends when the Tyrenni, plus some of the humans from the ESP group, find refuge within a sentient alien lifeboat. Omali fuses with the alien craft to become its pilot, and Dann ends, unrequitedly in love, standing eternal guard outside her virtual cockpit door.

Again, Tiptree fantasizes a disembodied escape. Together, the sad, lost humans and the doomed aliens set their course for the unknown. But the noisy, sexy, funny, painful real life of Tiptree's best stories, the rude noise in the face of injustice, is missing from the novel. Trying to write "from herself," Alli made a deeply personal catalog of her fears, defenses, and fantasies of escape—everything but her strengths.

In August 1976, Alli went to see her mother at the Lodge. Mary was very frail now, and Alli could hardly bear to be with her. She dreaded the visit and stayed only a week. Afterward Tiptree wrote Malzberg that his mother "spent the week begging me to kill her. She's not in pain but helpless. I couldn't."

At the Lodge, Alli had suffered for years from the encroachment of other vacationers. Each new house on the lake seemed to steal another piece of her childhood freedom. In 1955 she had written Dr. K, "I don't feel this place is 'mine.' I don't know what will happen to it. I have seen it largely spoiled by the influx of 'vacation-landers' since I have known it. I do not believe its solitude will last." Now she was convinced "thieves and vandals" would destroy the place before the coming winter. "It is ludicrous to have my self so entwined with a piece of terrain, trees, a light on the water," she wrote to herself. "It is not me that dies if the Lodge is sold or vandalized or burned." But she could not bear to keep the Lodge after Mary's death. Before Mary died, she and Ting found buyers for it, a family from Green Bay who promised not to subdivide the land.

At the end of September 1976, Alli finally completed *Up the Walls of the World*. Afterward, like many writers who have just completed a project, she felt depressed. She wrote in her journal that Tiptree seemed "finished" and her study "sad, purposeless." A month later, she felt on the verge of some new insight. "Yet my actual thoughts merely trot round the same dreary hurdles— Mary, Ting, Lodge, roof, undone work, messy self and home."

In his letters, though, Tiptree came back to life. He promised a story for an anthology Le Guin was editing with Virginia Kidd. He was talking to

Malzberg again. And in August, after a six-month lapse, he finally made up with Joanna Russ. Russ, who was now in Boulder teaching English at the University of Colorado, wrote that her chronic depression had cleared up, partly because she had come out as a lesbian. It had worked so well she wished she could recommend the same remedy to Tip. "Pieces of one's personality are attached to one's sexuality, I suppose, and things begin to fit together."

Alli even felt strong enough to send a letter to another writer. In October 1976 she wrote the poetry critic Helen Vendler, who had reviewed Adrienne Rich's *Of Woman Born: Motherhood as Experience and Institution* in the *New York Review of Books*. Rich's book was exactly what Tiptree had been calling for in the symposium, a critical look at mothering. Vendler read it as warily as if it were a biting animal, pointing out real flaws but also accusing Rich of complaint and sentimentality. As an example of Rich's "sentimental" prose, she cited a passage about mothers and daughters: "There was, is, in most of us, a girl-child still longing for a woman's nurture, tenderness, and approval, a woman's power exerted in our defense, a woman's smell and touch and voice, a woman's strong arms around us in moments of fear and pain."

Why was this sentimental? Alli asked Vendler.

> Her paragraph struck me as quite spare and sensible, the nouns are as plain as any I can think of, and there is only one adjective, "a woman's *strong* arms." What she is describing quite accurately is a *childish* emotion, and I think it is interesting that I can feel it in my own 60-year-old solar plexus. *I want my Mommy,* that's what she's talking about. [. . .] Are you saying that one must somehow expunge this childish need, blow it up, push it down some cosmic rat-hole?

Alli the scientist concluded, "The damn thing exists, we ought to look at it."

Vendler answered with a long, thoughtful letter, saying Rich was indulging an impossible yearning for childhood regained. Yet Rich was making a very different point, that girls don't get enough nurture or approval in the first place. Mothers don't have enough to give.

A few weeks later, on October 23, Mary fell into a coma. Alli flew to Chicago and her mother's bedside. She was there when Mary died two days later, at age ninety-four.

As she put Mary's ring back onto her cooling hand, Alli thought, "Rest, rest wild head on that cold bosom / that neither cares nor knows," and began to cry. The "wild head" was hers, and it was Mary who now would never know.

Shortly after Mary died, so did James Tiptree, Jr.

After Mary's death, Alli was plunged back into her parents' lives. For days she went through Mary's and Herbert's effects, talked to Mary's ancient lawyer, phoned Mary's friends. She had to dispose of all the old belongings, she told Jeff Smith: "letters from Carl Sandburg mixed in with grocery lists, [. . .] lace panties, .38-caliber automatics, irreplaceable diaries [. . .], correspondence with heads of state, unpublished poetry, old curtains, two thousand African moleskins each as big as a postage stamp," plus her own paintings and Mary's "letters to me which conjure up the laughing, brilliant, beautiful, incredibly active young woman I once briefly knew." She added, "I have to write documents to go with some of the historical stuff, which breaks me up again—all that youth and adventure and genuine gaiety gone to dust and a few aging—no, a mountain of aging trinkets and memorabilia." After the first days, Alli retreated to McLean and her medicine chest, and did as much as she could by phone. She sold Mary's ancient typewriter, auctioned the furniture, donated to museums most of the African souvenirs.

Then Alli escaped into one last blast of fictional fury. Three weeks after Mary's death, she sat down and wrote Raccoona Sheldon's breathtaking horror story "The Screwfly Solution."

She wrote it in about a week, from an old idea: aliens exploit a weak link in the human mating cycle as a form of pest control. The weak link is an aggression wired into men's sexual advance. Suddenly, in massive numbers, men begin to murder women.

The story is told in men's and women's voices, as a series of reports, interviews, diary entries, and letters. To most of these people, the killing of women seems eerily natural. A cult called the Sons of Adam begin to preach that

> man must purify himself and show God a clean world. [. . .] Some
> people raise the question of how can man reproduce without women,
> but such people miss the point. The point is that as long as man depends

on the old filthy animal way, God won't help him. When man gets rid of his animal part which is woman, this is the signal God is awaiting. Then God will reveal the new true clean way [. . .].

A Catholic cardinal states that women "are nowhere defined as human, but merely as a transitional expedient or state." Another researcher, not yet under the influence, comments, "Man's religion and metaphysics are the voices of his glands."

"The Screwfly Solution" is classic science fiction, a thought-experiment that reveals something about the human situation: that we do in some terrible sense find it normal for a man to kill a woman. Alli pasted the story's cover sheet with *Washington Post* headlines: "Woman's Battered Body Found"; "Body of Missing Girl, 13, Found in Fairfax Woods"; "Girl Found Slain." Notably, Raccoona neither condemns men (several individual men try to protect women) nor exempts women from the human burden of violence. The story ends with an epitaph for the female half of the human race: "Here lies the second meanest primate on Earth."

Killing everyone did make Alli feel better for a while. In her journal for November 18 she wrote, "There's no doubt, when I have some writing going tolerably, all else is OK."

On November 23, 1976, Alli submitted "Screwfly" to *Analog,* adding a cover letter from Raccoona's friend Tiptree. When she took it to the post office to mail it, she found a letter from Jeff Smith in PO Box 315.

Dear Tip,

Okay, I'm going to lay all my cards on the table. You are *not* required to do likewise.

You've probably heard from people already, but word is spreading very fast that your true name is Alice Sheldon.

Tiptree had asked Smith to print one of his letters about his mother's death in *Khatru,* so friends would know why they hadn't heard from him. Smith wrote back saying he thought it would be too risky. Everyone knew Tiptree's mother was an elderly explorer living in Chicago; an obituary might give clues to Tiptree's real name. Then Smith began to wonder how hard those clues would be to find. (Later he said, "I didn't expect it to be so important. I thought I was going to find out his name was really James Johnson, so what?") He went to the library at the community college where he worked. In the first *Chicago Tribune* he pulled out, he found Mary Bradley's obituary and saw "Mrs. Alice Hastings (Mrs. Huntington) Sheldon" listed as her only survivor. That night when he got home he found a postcard from a friend saying, "Is it true that James Tiptree is Alice Sheldon?"

Smith told Tip he felt deceived and confused. Tiptree had always seemed to him so male—and how did a woman get those mysterious positions with the government, and how had Tiptree pulled off the symposium? Yet even now he didn't want to pry, and added,

> This is not a demand for information. A postcard saying merely "Later" will not be the ending of a friendship. But one thing to definitely consider: I am going to be getting questions, and whatever you choose to disclose or to withhold from me, please pass along the Party Line that I'm supposed to tell others.

The day she got the letter, Alli wrote back. "How great. At last it's out, and you're the first to know, as I promised long ago you would. [. . .] Yeah. Alice Sheldon. Five ft 8, 61 yrs, remains of a good-looking girl vaguely visible, grins a lot in a depressed way, very active in spurts. Also, Raccoona." She said she had a husband. Other than that, she told Smith, everything she'd said about herself was from life. "You used the words 'deceiving me'—when I never *felt* deceptive. One knows when one is being devious and nasty and untrue, you know. I was always just being me." Then she asked him to hang on to the secret a little longer, at least until *Up the Walls of the World* came out. She was afraid readers (and her doubting editor) would like the novel less. She signed the letter "Tip/Alli."

Smith said it was already too late. "Rumors *are* spreading fast," he warned on November 26. "Harlan is one of the perpetrators." Alli didn't want Tip's closest correspondents to hear it from anyone else, and decided to come clean.

(Harlan Ellison later recalled that someone had sent him the obituary, that he wasn't the source of the news, and that he had thought it was already common knowledge: he had after all been saying for a long time that Tiptree was a she. He stressed that he would never knowingly have caused his friend pain—and in fact he probably wasn't spreading rumors. Robert Silverberg, for one, never heard them, though he and Ellison were close friends.)

Alli had already confessed to one other friend. On November 24, the day after she wrote Smith, she wrote a scared coming-out letter to Ursula Le Guin.

I want you, alone, to know first from me because of our special relation. I write this feeling a great and true friendship is wavering on the balance, about to slide away forever to the dark. [. . .]

Ursula, Ursula, I am petrified. All the friends, the sf world—will they take it as "deception"? Will I have any friends left? Will the women who mean so much to me see it all as an evil put-on? [. . .]

Well dear Starbear an old age is dead and time to begin a new. But I think I'm finished. [. . .]

Tip says goodbye to a very dear friend and all that is hers.

Let me know what you think if you're still speaking to
Tip/Alli

Le Guin answered,

Dearest TREE,

oh strange, most strange, most wonderful, beautiful, improbable—Wie geht's, Schwesterlein? sorella mia, sistersoul! [. . .] Do you know what? I don't think I have ever been *surprised* before. Things have happened but when they happen one thinks Oh, of course, this had to Be, etc., deep in my prophetic soul I Knew, etc.—but not this time, by God! And it is absolutely a delight, a joy, for some reason, to be truly absolutely flatfootedly surprised—it's like a Christmas present! [. . .] I want to laugh, also slightly to cry, because the whole thing now is on this huge and unexpected scale of real and total reversal—only what does reversal mean? Explain to me, my Gethenian Friend. [. . .] I don't know about people's reactions, I suppose there are some who resent being put on, but it would take an extraordinarily small soul to resent so immense, so funny, so effective and fantastic and ETHICAL a put-on.

She too promised to keep the secret, and did. Vonda McIntyre said afterward that she had been visiting Le Guin when Alli's letter came, "and aside from nearly falling off a chair when she was getting a book off a high shelf and I said 'What have you heard from Tip lately?' she never said a word."

A week later, Alli wrote Fred Pohl, though it had been a long time since they had corresponded. "Well, hell, of *course* we're still friends!" Pohl answered. "Friends come in all shapes, sizes, sexes and colors, and I am not so rich in friends, or in writers whose work I respect, that I can afford to worry about the packaging."

Alli wrote McIntyre and Quinn Yarbro, though she held the letters a day or two, awaiting Le Guin's answer. She wrote Craig Strete.

She screwed up the courage to call Joanna Russ. Russ recalled picking up the phone in her kitchen in Boulder. "I heard this gravelly voice, and the first thing she said was, 'Oh, you're going to hate me.' And I said, 'Who is this?' And she said, 'This is James Tiptree, Jr.'"

And so the word spread. By the end of December McIntyre reported she still hadn't heard any rumors about Tiptree's identity. But Alli kept writing more confessions. On December 20, she wrote Gardner Dozois and Robert Silverberg, "so they won't be left all over egg after writing all those nice introductions about how I had to be male."

Dozois replied that his whole mental picture of Tiptree was shot. "It's strange, like talking to somebody who keeps turning into somebody else before your eyes and then instantly flicking back again." He said he hoped that Tiptree was not, as Alli had told him, "written out." Tiptree had portrayed young, searching boys so convincingly, Dozois wrote. "Where in your fiction are the equally convincing portraits of what it's like to be a girl growing up? [. . .] It wouldn't surprise me at all to find that 'Tiptree's' best work is yet to come."

Silverberg said he didn't mind about defending Tiptree's masculinity. "I suppose I will eat some crow over that, but I'm not at all annoyed with you," he wrote. "*You* didn't fool me; *I* fooled *myself,* and so be it." He confessed that he felt intimidated by guns, fishing rods, politics, and tent poles, and had been taken in by Tiptree's competence in these matters. Tip had seemed the better man.

He then told Alli that he too was living a dishonest life: stuck in an unhappy marriage that gave him order and security, in love with another woman but afraid to commit. He invited her to write to him if she was in trouble. "For all I know you're really pretty content, [. . .] living a neat tidy life with one odd compartment in it called Tiptree, but somehow I don't think so." Or she could come out West, have a beer on him, "and we'll work on some more useful level of reality."

Alli answered by telling him a little about her two marriages, her past, her fears for Ting as he grew older. But she was wary of intimate confessions, especially about marriage and security. "Stay put in limbo," she urged Silverberg. "You are hemorrhaging from the conflict, from the not-right life. But Bob, there *is* no right life."

Alli wrote Barry Malzberg on December 28. He began his answer "Dear Jim or Tip or Alice or Allie," asked for Alli's phone number (she gave it to him, and they spoke), and concluded, "You are still the same person and I am still the same person and here we are."

Alli was still writing as Tiptree to other correspondents, including Judy-Lynn del Rey. But she had told the secret to too many people. Out in Berkeley, Silverberg told Terry Carr and Harry Harrison, assuming the news was about to become public anyway. Both men wrote Alli. Fantasy writer Elizabeth Lynn, who lived in San Francisco and knew Silverberg and Yarbro, wrote Alli a spontaneous letter of "welcome." So did novelist Marta Randall, who was involved with Silverberg at the time. Eventually the news got around to Charles Brown, editor of the science fiction trade monthly *Locus*. In the issue dated January 30, 1977 (and mailed to subscribers in early March), Brown ran a front-page item headlined "Tiptree Revealed."

Just as Alli was coming out to Tip's friends, the second shoe dropped: in December 1976, Judy-Lynn del Rey rejected *Up the Walls of the World*. She wouldn't accept it in the present tense; Alli refused to rewrite it. "Christ I worked over that thing like an engraver, it's a machine, I can't yank off a distributor cap here and run three wires there and turn the thing upside down for some reader's whim," she wrote Fred Pohl. She asked Pohl, now at Bantam, if he would look at it. Yet even he was not enthusiastic. "I'm not all that keen on present-tense stories, and I wouldn't be surprised to know that some of J-L's antipathy comes from what she learned at my knee, or Lester's. But of course there are present-tense stories and present-tense stories, and we will see."

Within weeks the book was picked up by David Hartwell, a young editor at Berkley Putnam. He suggested only a few minor revisions, which Alli agreed with and made. But Alli was hurt, by Pohl's lukewarm response perhaps most of all. She had been so grateful for Pohl's early support, back when she really felt like "one of the boys." Now it seemed to her she had lost it. Later she wrote that after the revelation "quite a few male writers who had been, I thought, my friends and called themselves my admirers, suddenly found it necessary to adopt a condescending, patronizing tone, or break off our correspondence altogether, as if I no longer interested them. (I can only conclude that I didn't.)" This is not true: almost all of Tip's friends wrote encouraging letters. But she was quick to feel slighted, and strongly felt the loss of Tiptree's masculine authority. One of the people she felt slighted by was probably Pohl.

By January 1977, the first excitement of the coming-out was over, McLean lay under snow and ice, a pipe at the Sheldons' had burst, and Alli was miserable. To Jeff Smith she wrote she couldn't feel Tiptree's voice anymore. "I feel as if some microphone had gone dead on me." To Joanna Russ she wrote, "I keep dreaming I'm dead and spending eternity in hell with a collection of failed financiers and Tupperware salespeople." To Terry Carr she wrote, "I have the feeling that when Tiptree dies for good, I will too."

As usual she didn't want comfort. To Craig Strete she grouched,

> Now you are adding me to your stable of lame horses to care for. [. . .] Funny; Uncle Tip thought for awhile he could be a strong point for weak others, help by holding hands. It worked when they saw Tip as strong, mysterious and male. Now . . . landscapes are shifting. My little band of helpees are struck with cold realisation of just how perishingly mortal

the reality behind Tip is, they are all trying to comfort me. Well, maybe it's good for them.

[. . .] I have to keep firm hold of the great joke Tip played, in certain lights I am made hilarious by all that went on.

But in April she told Gardner Dozois, "Alli Sheldon is maybe a mad woman, maybe an ex-good-researcher, but is not a science fiction or any other kind of writer. I am nothing. Must learn to be happy so." She was starting to realize just how bad losing Tip was going to be.

CHAPTER 38: "I LIVE IN MY BODY AS IN AN ALIEN ARTIFACT" (1977)

"I can't adjust to your being a female." Filomena gave him a hug.
"I—it's not—oh, it's all so complicated."

— JAMES TIPTREE, JR., "ALL THE KINDS OF YES"

One of Alli's first reactions to losing Tiptree was to make it part of the problem of what to write. On November 26, just after she got Jeff Smith's letter, she wrote in her diary, "I feel the sf writing is at, or coming to, an end. [. . .] But what do I DO inside? Try for 'mainstream' writing? A theory-research book? A diary? Some kind of weird autobiography? (Why, why?) I will NOT return to being a Bradley appendage. I feel I have one more go inside me, but what, what?"

The archivists who were organizing Mary's papers kept telling her she ought to write a memoir. Gardner Dozois told her she should write about growing up a girl. But as an "old lady in Virginia," she felt only self-loathing. ("By definition, an old woman is the lowest form of human life," she once wrote.) Suddenly she realized how much it had suited her to be a man.

All winter, at Boca Paila, she struggled to write but felt empty. Tiptree had had power, she wrote in a note on his "death." "And since I have none, I am nothing." As a woman, she had only the burden of empathy and "the dull interminable mission of [. . .] maintaining the very race"—while men and boys ruled the world.

Reading a report about child sexual abuse, she found herself aroused, and was upset. She wrote in her journal on February 2,

> The distasteful proof that my sexuality is bound up with masochistic fantasies of helplessness [. . .] depressed me profoundly. I am not a man, I am not the do-er, the penetrator. And Tiptree was "magical" manhood, his pen my prick. I had through him all the power and pres-

tige of masculinity, I was—though an aging intellectual—*of* those who own the world. How I loathe being a woman. Wanting to be *done to*. [. . .]

Tiptree's "death" has made me face—what I never really went into with Bob [Harper]—my self-hate as a woman. And my view of the world as structured by raw power. [. . .] I want power, I want to be listened to. [. . .] And I'll never have it. I'm stuck with this perverse, second-rate body; my life.

On writing from her own experience, she noted, "I don't *want* even to cry out, to explain how it is. Merely to end it."

She told Ting that her problem in writing was "somehow combining Tiptree back into ABS—who is 'nothing.'" She complained of loneliness. Ting suggested she stop "'putting on the act' socially and try to listen and make friends," but Alli rejected this as "imitating Mary." She dreamed she was

at a festival or convention, without the right evening dress to wear. [. . .] I saw it was a metaphor for exactly what I'm worrying over—trying to find a new persona, despair over what I have to show. [. . .] [There is] a fear that the reality isn't good enough. If I could only improve from within, that's what I must do. Get rid of self-hatred, fear, worry, indiscipline and sloth.

A little later she wrote, "No doubt about it, I do not 'match' my exterior. I live in my body and my social presence as in an alien artifact. It commits me to a way of life that is not mine; could I somehow bring the inside out, fuse it? Not so much sweetness and cordiality; not so much desire to be admired and loved."

She noted, "I thought the departure of Mary and the sale of the Lodge would free me. Instead it seems to have started by draining meaning from the world. [. . .] I identify with her: I am dead."

Again she thought of quitting writing, or at least giving up fiction with its "emotional plow-ups." "Maybe I've spent some years learning how to do an art that is fundamentally bad for me, for which I am unsuited. And all this inaction, introverted thought and despair; my 'farmer's' body is starting to malfunction under it."

One night, she dreamed of a "beautiful tall girl who came up to me naked (on beach) and said, 'Cut that out, it's nonsense.' Calming!" The next night, March 3, she dreamed of falling in love with a woman, then making love to ("initiating") a girl who was in love with her. It was not an erotic dream, she wrote, but an extraordinarily happy one.

> I lay in bed savoring the dream, hating to get up. My deprived sexuality, confused gender, and longing for penis—sex and prestige—to turn into a man—I guess those are the themes . . . Also came to me in half-waking a kind of inner voice saying cheerfully something like, "Well, now you understand all these inner things (mechanics), it's time to lay them to rest, or brush them away, and get on with interesting subjects."

The feeling of release didn't last. In July she recorded a "long fantastic Inca-Indian captivity dream in which I was to escape but announced, 'I'll stay here and die with you, Mother.'"

In the past she had often looked for story ideas in what made her angry. Now she was angry about her old unspeakable trouble, the "plight of women in a man's world," but could think of "no alternatives, no 'solutions.'" Her only idea for a story was "the day all women were born as sheep." Even the science fiction apparatus she had once loved no longer yielded ideas or pleasure: "Same old FTL, etc., etc. Aliens, foo."

She wrote one story that winter, long and sad, from an old idea. In "Slow Music" a river of energy has come to Earth; at its banks, people can cast off their bodies and let their souls be carried out into the universe. One young woman has decided she wants to keep her mortal body. She persuades a young man to stay with her, so they can make love, make babies, and die. But in the end they stray too close to the river and are lost.

After this, aside from two minor stories, Alli submitted nothing for publication for the next three years. And though she eventually wrote a number of stories and another novel, nothing was ever as direct, honest, and exciting as her work before she was exposed.

Alli didn't feel she could tell any of this to Bob Harper. Home from the Yucatán in April, she wrote him, "I know, intellectually, that you can help me [. . .] but I don't know it emotionally, if you get what I mean. Some inner gate is shut. I don't know whether the sign on it says Your Tax Dollars At Work Here, or Gone Fishing. Or possibly, Leave me be I can't bear it."

What she needed, she kept thinking, was "to change in some way inside myself." She decided she should try lesbian sex. The day after she wrote Harper, she wrote in her journal, "I want to make love to young women, to make them come, and happy. Maybe then masturbate myself. Sex as activity. It could work. I shall start to mix it with women's groups, looking to actualize this. I really believe I shall. I think I could make my aged self palatable enough. If it was all straight-arrow."

But she didn't do it. Instead she went jogging and signed up for dancing lessons with Ting. She trained as a phone counselor at a local rape crisis center. And Harper and Schehl again suggested she go to a psychiatrist who could prescribe antidepressants.

The first one she went to, in May 1977, was appalled by her drug intake and wanted to get her off it. Alli wrote anxiously in her journal, "If he felt my fatigue after 6 mos withdrawal of amphetamine [in 1974–75] was partly still due to amphetamine withdrawal, how can I ever get 'drug free'—or how measure it?" Later she wrote, "My problem is, I want to be *happy*—like temp. w/morphine; and I fear that all these new things can do is make me endure misery."

She found another psychiatrist who didn't ask her to give up the other drugs. He tried her on various antidepressants, eventually settling on the monoamine oxidase inhibitor Nardil, which helped. In October she wrote Craig Strete, "Doctor is giving me first pink pills, then purple pills, now puce-colored pills, so far nobody will give what I deepest crave, a lead-nose .38 bullet in parietal lobe. I dream about oblivion like other people dream of good sex. Oh jesus for that wonderful instant of knowing: NO MORE. But must not, I know it."

Meanwhile, Ting grew more and more blind in his right eye. Alli asked him if it wasn't "time to go while we were still us." She wanted him to agree to a suicide pact. On July 21 she noted his answer: "Ting agreed to consider suicide in 4–5 years."

Alli never met most of the people Tiptree was close to. She never saw Ursula Le Guin, Joanna Russ, Barry Malzberg; she never shared the promised drink with Ellison, Silverberg, Strete. But in April 1977, Jeff Smith and his wife, Ann, came to McLean to meet Alli and Ting.

Smith had expected to find his idea of a sixty-one-year-old lady writer, and was surprised by the "slim, vital, young-looking" Alli Sheldon who met them at a gas station and guided them back to her house. They arrived tactfully at two in the afternoon and didn't leave until midnight.

> While we were there, she was Tiptree often, the raconteur telling stories with little or no provocation, the speculator running with ideas to logical, illogical and evocative conclusions. Sometimes (particularly when she and her husband clattered around the kitchen fixing dinner) she was Raccoona, the rather dotty retired schoolteacher supposedly in Wisconsin. These were unconscious—whenever she thought about who she was, she was Alice Sheldon, the one who doesn't write science fiction.

Afterward Alli wrote Ursula Le Guin,

> I could see vanishing shreds of Tiptree whirling through the suburban air, evaporating under the impact of a chatty, if erratic McLean matron. [. . .] I don't know if Jeff perceived that Tiptree was hiding somewhere underneath and slightly to the left of the matron, but I could feel it; I've spent so long not being Tiptree, which is to say, me, that it was strange to speak with someone who knows my real self. My "real," daily-life self is a long-elaborated kind of animated puppet show, with its own validity, to be sure—it gets married and holds jobs and does things like that, and tells funny stories (possibly too many)—but those 8 years in sf was the first time I could be *really* real. [. . .] Now all that is gone, and I am back with the merry dumb-show as life, and it doesn't much suit.

In her journal she wrote that the visit had been "profoundly disorienting. It somehow threw me into dreams, into the posture of a past life, without the power." For Smith, who was a kid of twenty-six, she could just manage a meeting in person. For a writer, someone she looked up to, it was impossible. She told Barry Malzberg the Smiths would be the only friends of Tip's to see her in the flesh "for some time, if ever . . . Maybe if I were still a writer it would be different, but I find the idea of coming out of my deep hole to show the grinning corpse around quite unendurable."

Alli was as charming as Tiptree had ever been, but letters had been under her control. To be charming in person cost her too much. In the fall of 1977, editor David Hartwell came to the house in McLean to bring her the Hugo Tiptree had just won for "Houston, Houston, Do You Read?" All afternoon, he recalled, Alli told wonderful stories while Ting watched admiringly. But when Alli invited him to stay for dinner, Ting took him for a walk in the yard and asked him not to accept. "He said she would be exhausted for days afterward."

Tiptree's letter-friendships all changed after the revelation. At first Alli got a lot of supportive mail. Terry Carr wrote to show solidarity and talk about his own experience with a pseudonym. Virginia Kidd said, just before the news broke in *Locus,* that she had heard rumors about Tiptree's identity and didn't care. "What seems important to me is (personally) that you have an absolute right to your privacy and (publicly) that your voice is one of the very few that will turn out to have permanent qualities of excellence, poetry, integrity."

Harry Harrison, as always, suggested meeting for a drink. An occasional pen-friend, the writer Gene Wolfe, saw the news in *Locus* and sent a spontaneous letter of "welcome." Alfred Bester, who didn't even know Tiptree, wrote,

> I was dismayed to hear that you are so annoyed at your cover having been broken that you are threatening never to write science fiction again. Please, on bended knee, I beg, as a dedicated fan and a bedazzled colleague who wishes he had written many of your stories, don't permit your annoyance to let us down. What am I to do if the most brilliant and perceptive of us all casts us into outer darkness?

"Houston" won both the Nebula and the Hugo in 1977, a clear vote of confidence from the writers and fans. The next year, to Alli's joy, "Screwfly" won a Nebula for Raccoona.

There is no sign in the letters of any hostile reaction, and little condescension. But Alli felt raw and exposed; she expected to be denigrated as a woman, and saw it even when it wasn't there. She didn't know how she wanted Tip's friends to react. She didn't like it when they wrote to her; she didn't like it when they didn't. She didn't know how to write back. "Tiptree had a certain epistolary style, which no longer carried any conviction," she later said. " 'Alice B. Sheldon' doesn't have any style except 'Enclosed please find payment.' "

She wanted most of all to be pals again with her first editors, men like Harrison and Pohl, whose approval had pleased her so much. But she hadn't submitted to them in years, they had no more work relationship, and there was no going back to that casual tone. Silverberg had offered her an alternative, coming clean emotionally, but Alli couldn't bear her own or other people's troubles. In October 1977 she wrote Harrison, about a non-SF acquaintance, "Why oh why does everybody I meet feel I am the ideal confidant for their particular lifetime of hell, and treat me to every dangling participle of it? And I say yes, yes, yes, Oh how awful, Oh, my, etc., and they say How you've helped me, you're so strong—and I go home and throw up and throw up."

Alli was angry with Harlan Ellison for a while, believing he had "outed" her. She did not send him a coming-out letter, and he didn't write, though later that year they exchanged notes. He said he hoped he and she could meet, and told her he loved her "for the joyous chaos your Alice-ness has caused among the pig-people." He had no way of knowing she blamed him. He later told her he hadn't written because he had thought she might want to withdraw for a while. He had been afraid her mailbox "would be jammed by the sort of loons who slow down on freeways to gawk at the accidents. I felt you didn't need yet another person to deal with; even if it was only to say, 'I'm still me.' All I'd've said, anyhow, is 'I'm here.' "

But Alli very much wanted to know that Tip's friends were still there. Eventually she heard rumors that Ellison wasn't speaking to her and wrote him to say she considered the friendship over. He got hold of her phone number, but she wouldn't take his call. He sent an admiring, affectionate letter, their friendship was mended, and they went back to exchanging notes. Still, she was always afraid that Tip's friends were disappointed and liked Alli Sheldon less.

Alli did still write to all her young friends: Smith, Dozois, McIntyre,

Yarbro, Strete. Barry Malzberg especially insisted on their friendship, and insisted that Alli keep writing and living. "Damn it if I can go on—and somehow I am, I am after all—then you can. [. . .] You have an obligation to that talent. (When people say this to me about me I laugh hollowly; my only obligation I insist is to be a human being but you already *are*.)" Alli flirted gently with Malzberg, gave advice, and told him that had they been closer in age they might have made trouble for each other. And he admired her, as one depressive admires another, for her courage in continuing to live at all.

Alli could no longer flirt with Ursula Le Guin, and felt awkward writing to her as a woman. One of Le Guin's first responses to the revelation was to ask Alli for writing advice. She said she was "getting an increasing lot of static from the women's movement about how I always write about men," and that the criticism, from Joanna Russ in particular, was

> hitting something unresolved, unsolved, painful inside me [. . .]. The fact remains, that until this MS I just finished this week, I have never really had a woman protagonist; the closest I came is an androgyne, and a couple of times, a marriage. [. . .] Because I couldn't. My Daemon just wouldn't produce a woman-hero. Why not? Why can't I tell the goddam Daemon what to do? Who *is* telling it what to do?

She said she wanted a woman to talk to, a woman who would understand. But Alli was in the Yucatán, and never answered; and Le Guin didn't ask again.

In October 1977, Le Guin wrote, "Do you know, since you write as Alli and tell me facts, in some ways I know less of you than when you wrote as Tiptree and totally disregarded facts!"

Alli read this as a comment on how women friends talk. If Tiptree and Le Guin had met, she replied, Tip would have been all gallantry.

> But when we meet as women, there is the strange come-down of reality, myth lost . . . And I conscious that I come on too strong, a leathered veteran of the wars, yet whiningly vulnerable, my chest visibly open to all the same domestic concerns (bar young, which nature forbade) (or rather, a bloodily inept gynecologist—a detail James would never have permitted to intrude)—plus a wild long biography, complete with

aroma of twice-told tales of exploits found remarkable in the female—but very female—it is all different . . . But it is not, it is the same. Only I hang back, hiding my great paws behind my back, afraid to step too closely into what I know is a field of exquisitely sensitive radar, afraid to damage invisible tentacles. Maybe it's all summed up as, for a woman I come on vigorous (except for the invisible endless times of lying doggo with a cold cloth on my head in a dark room, my sensors overloaded, my heart longing for oblivion. Self-pity—to which Tip would never admit). Whereas as a man I came on gentle.

Another woman . . . woman-to-woman . . . we are all untrained. We have no art at "real" meetings, we start talking about how hard our stoves are to clean . . . It gives me marvellously to think and ponder.

At least with Joanna Russ Alli didn't have to worry about coming on too strong. Even before Tip was outed, after they made up, Alli had been feeling more affectionate toward her argumentative friend. When Russ reported that her consciousness-raising group had accused her of talking too much, Tiptree laughed.

I am as certain that you talk too much as I am that the earth turns. I imagine that when you are consciously *not* "talking too much" you sit there like a smoldering basilisk with ever-larger gouts of smoke coming out of your ears until your "silence" dominates all the talk in the room . . . Or like when the ocean suddenly recedes for miles, leaving the bottom of the bay bare, and people venture forward into the strange, unaware that the odd line on the horizon is a five-mile-high wall of pent-up words rushing down on them with the speed of light. I can just see it.

And Alli didn't have to stop flirting with Russ, although there was the delicate matter of her own sexuality. In July 1977, Alli told Russ about her mother's long-ago attempt to seduce her and in that context confessed, "I guess you could call me a frustrated gay." But she quickly added, "Christ how I hate my aging body, the knobby veined claws that once were hands, the seismic collapse of skin around my mouth."

Russ responded with a love letter.

I like old women with a very special feeling and get all dreamy and erotic about them (an indecent proposal by letter!). Honest. If you only could locate yourself in some youthful Lesbian feminist community (you would soon be bored to death by them, but never mind) they would all crowd round you (in overalls, with shaved heads and multiple earrings) and coo softly, patting you in all sorts of places and saying admiring things about you until you got embarrassed. Truly. [. . .] I wish we could actually meet in the flesh some time some where—we would probably be all prim and stiff and proper unless I had the chutzpah to throw my arms around you and kiss you, which at the moment I would rather like to do!—anyway, perhaps we can, soon, someday?

Consider yourself well and truly propositioned. I was in love with you when you were "James Tiptree Jr." and have been able to transfer the infatuation to Allie Sheldon, who is, after all, the same person. [. . .]

Are you ready to have mad adventures in your waning years?

Russ also urged Alli to explore her sexuality as a source of her depressions. She didn't have to be romantically involved with a woman to be gay, Russ pointed out; "it's rather a matter of one's own internal economy. [. . .] You know, it's *not* disloyalty to Ting; it's not that at all. But to live, knowing that you can never be yourself, that's a very tough thing and enough to make life seem pointless and hopeless."

Alli responded only with a postcard apologizing for having written "such dreary gloop." It was not until three years later that she wrote Russ,

It occurred to me to wonder if I ever told you in so many words that I too am a Lesbian—or at least as close as one can come to being one never having had a successful love with any of the women I've loved, and being now too old and ugly to dare try. Oh, had 65 years been different! I *like* some men a lot, but from the start, before I knew anything, it was always girls and women who lit me up.

After she read this letter Russ asked Alli to come see her in Seattle, where she was teaching. Alli wrote back that she was having heart trouble and was going to spend the winter in New Zealand. They went on exchanging long letters and talking on the phone, but they never met.

If Tiptree's friendships changed, his literary reputation changed utterly after his identity was revealed. Just after the *Locus* announcement, Russ wrote Alli,

> I'm waiting with bated breath to see how many fans "knew all along" and how many "suspected that style wasn't a man's" and how many voices are lifted to tell us that somehow, looking back at what you've written, it isn't, after all, *that* good. . . . I don't think much of the last will happen, actually, but I suspect that fans' writings about you are going to get a shade less chummy.

There wasn't much negative comment, but there was more distance—people didn't know what to think of Tiptree's writing anymore. Quinn Yarbro thought that being read as a woman at all shocked Alli, so that she saw it as more negative than it was.

And Tiptree's reputation did take a dent when *Up the Walls of the World* came out in 1978. Everyone wanted to like the long-awaited Tiptree novel, and most reviewers praised it. In *Analog*, Spider Robinson wrote, "I don't think *tour de force* is too strong; frankly, I'm stunned." Even the contentious Dick Geis reviewed it favorably. But Robinson felt that the "seams showed once or twice"; and no one was as impressed by it as by Tiptree's best shorts. It was nominated for a Hugo in 1979, but Alli withdrew it from the ballot "for personal reasons."

Alli was particularly stung by Algis Budrys's patronizing review in the September 1978 *F&SF*. Budrys wrote that fandom had "awarded all sorts of honors to Tiptree, who remained a distant figure [. . .], while Alice 'Racoona' [*sic*] Sheldon circulated amiably about SF conventions and made clever remarks." He criticized *Up the Walls* for using the present tense and being "overcomplicated," then said that along with "evidence of an intelligent, talented person trying to make something special out of her first novel, and making a series of honest mistakes in the process, we are also given a story of considerable power."

Her stories were still admired, and her new work much in demand. By the 1980s she was even drawing Hollywood interest. New World Pictures, the production company of B-movie king Roger Corman, took an option on "Houston," while the more respectable Carolco Pictures bought the rights to "The Screwfly Solution." (Neither has ever been filmed.) But Alli became very sensitive to slights, especially when she thought anyone preferred Tiptree to Alli Sheldon. A July 1984 *Life* magazine article on women science fiction writers that didn't even mention her upset her. She complained to Bob Mills, "It seems as though all the people whom I'd like to have remember I'm a woman *don't*, and all the misogynists *do*." Mills had recently retired, and Alli had chosen Virginia Kidd as her new agent. She asked them both to write letters to *Life* telling them about Tiptree.

When Kidd explained that Tiptree had probably been left out because he didn't write novels, Alli exploded. Oh, right, she wrote back sarcastically. "I was just sitting where I could see 3 Nebulas and 2 Hugos and something else, and I didn't realise short-story writers are scum." A day later she wrote again, accusing Kidd of wanting Tiptree as her client when "what you have is Sheldon." Alli didn't speak to her old friend for months.

Of course the revelation did change how people read Tiptree. First, it embarrassed a lot of men who had said women couldn't write science fiction. There was then, and to some extent still is, a persistent feeling both in and out of science fiction that women's writing is different from men's and somewhat less equal. Even now, women writers are told off for being "too domestic," or frowned upon when they write fiction that challenges, exhilarates, or disturbs. Women's writing is still seen as less potent than men's. Yet men who didn't think they liked fiction by women had admired Tiptree, and had acclaimed him for the very energy and drive they said women lacked.

Tiptree's performance confronted both men and women with their complicity as readers. Inevitably, the writer's gender influences readers, especially in guessing which side we're supposed to be on. Despite all Alli's worrying at the biological foundations of male and female, her performance reminds us that gender is a social construct, one made by writers and readers both. On "The Women Men Don't See," Le Guin has written,

I remember how, when that story first came out, women read it and were amazed, delighted, jubilant, that a man could write such a story. . . . And then when the author revealed her real name, the revisions of thought, the revelations of prejudice, we all had to go through, to realize that a woman had written such a story.

And Robert Silverberg, of the "ineluctably masculine" comment, told Alli, "You've given my head a great needed wrenching."

For some feminist critics, Tiptree's work is proof that there *is* a women's way of writing. They reread Tiptree as a woman writer who explored women's themes and wrote stories that are "fundamentally about women." The "real" voice in Tiptree's stories belongs to the writer's "true" sex. This has caused some tension around Tiptree's reputation: while feminists have claimed Tiptree as their own, some men have felt that Tiptree has been "stolen from them."

But the revelation of Tiptree's identity works, as in other "passing stories," both to reaffirm and to demolish fiction's "gender line." On one hand, when the person in disguise is unmasked, she is expected to go back to her own people, her own gender. But gender itself has been made suspect: Which is which? Who are "us" and "them"? As Alli once said, "What happens to the value of being Number One in a class of two—if people can't tell the difference?" Or as academic Judith Butler writes, "If gender is constructed, could it be constructed differently?"

Ideally, Tiptree's body of work might be seen as neither male nor female but as (among other things) an exciting, defiant, and comic rejection of gender identity. Tiptree/Raccoona/Alli Sheldon was a person who lived inside her body "as in an alien artifact" and was briefly able to make a free territory in her writing. Surely for both men and women there is something very liberating about Tiptree's performance. Like all cross-dressing it opens up possibilities, taking us past what we thought were the limits of the self. And it symbolizes the imaginative promise of science fiction: that we can think beyond what we already know.

Alli herself never felt she could choose sides. In 1984 she wrote Craig Strete,

I'm half a woman, and the other half a human being—which are not, today, quite the same thing. And whenever I try to vanish into the hermetic, intoxicating world of feminism I find I'm dragging another ABS marked All-Human team, which is so largely male. (Or maybe it's marked, Tiptree.) And when I turn back to the general culture, the world of my own, most private experience tugs at me to turn back and be one with the sisters.

When Tiptree, a woman pretending to be a man, shows men looking at women, this narrative complexity also reflects the way all of us experience our lives. Tiptree's performance reminds us that if writing must be a mirror of the writer's experience, then it is a funhouse mirror of a madhouse experience. It suggests that we all live "5,000 feet underground on a dark day," in stories that remain obscure even to the teller.

But Alli's struggle to write again was long and hard. All the troubles she had had before the revelation got worse: the sense that she could no longer play with her writing or enjoy it, the feeling that she had to write more literally from or about her own experience. Tiptree was gone, she felt. Raccoona, who had been meant to be her "real voice," was silent. For a while she joked about writing under a new pseudonym, Sylvester Mule: Sylvester because she loved the woods, Mule because she was sterile. But sterility is no quality for a writer, and the name yielded no new voice. For the next two years, the door to her unconscious was shut.

She kept seeing death closing in on her, stealing her writing time, stealing Ting. Just after Mary died, in November 1976, she wrote in her journal, "I paid a high price for marrying Daddy, for never breaking the mold. I remain the child, and now terrified of going on. How can I become the support? Not to speak of the survivor . . ."

In December 1977, at Boca Paila, Ting went fishing and got lost all night in a storm. Waiting up for him to come home, Alli went through agonies of worry and grief. After he returned safe she couldn't help wondering, "Is there a story in Ting's adventure?" But later she wrote, "Really my decline dates from the ghastliness of those 24 hrs . . . sitting, waiting, *thinking* . . . I can still see the limp blue-white soaked heavy body being carried in by 2 men, arms dangling."

Ting's daughter Audrey spent Christmas with them that year, and they had a happy time. But in April 1978 Audrey died of a drug overdose in New York. After Markie Sheldon's death in 1974, Ting had tried to get closer to his children, but it was too late, especially for Audrey, whose life Alli called "one each spectacular mess." The death was judged a suicide. Ting took it very hard.

Alli felt she should spend more time with Ting, even if it meant giving up her writing. She wrote Le Guin that Ting was "less and less active, needs more and more of my time, and wishes only to do things *with me*. God help us, we love each other. [. . .] And I myself am 64, slowing. [. . .] I am dying of being wrenched two ways."

In the summer of 1978, with the Lodge sold, the Sheldons spent a month at a fishing camp in northern Maine. There Alli had a vision of a door opening to "writing as me. [. . .] Something cold and hot, clear, different, free. And something to do with hate." In a burst of inspiration she wrote five stories and part of a novel, "some of it old 'Tiptree'-ish, some of it starting to show the new thing. But the 'real' stuff was to follow." Instead, in a fit of resentment and despair (or perhaps, she later thought, fear), Alli threw her story notebooks, stories, and novel into a wood stove. Ting came in, "knocked me aside and tried to save it, but it was thank god too late." And so, she told Le Guin, "I am trying to become nothing."

CHAPTER 39: **WRITING AGAIN (1979–81)**

I think we all contain other people, if we choose to let them speak. The only danger is in coming to believe that they really are "others," not facets of ourselves.

—TERRY CARR TO ALLI SHELDON, 1977

Alli threatened to burn the rest of Tiptree's papers, too, including all his letters. Instead, at the end of 1978, she asked Jeff Smith to come down while she and Ting were at Boca Paila, pack up her office, and store the papers at his house in Baltimore. Alli hoped this would let her start with a clean slate, and was already thinking of making Smith her literary executor.

Her plan to quit writing and take care of Ting was no great success. She showered him with affection, leaving little notes for him around the house saying how much she loved him, reassuring him that tomorrow would be better for them both. But just like Mary years before, she neglected herself. She ate little, subsisting on a steady diet of vanilla custard with frozen raspberries. She started getting ill and having accidents. In the summer of 1978 she fell and broke her wrist. She got a painful case of shingles; her heart was still giving her trouble; the arthritis in her hands got bad again. It was Ting who took care of her: made sure she ate, kept up the household, nursed her through her illnesses. Ting's circle all thought she was a hypochondriac, and that Ting indulged his good-looking wife. Peter Sheldon recalled a "difficult visit" from Alli and Ting. "I don't say it was imagined, but she did say she didn't feel well, and there was an emergency trip to the city to a doctor, racing around—you know, she wanted to be the center of things. I can understand that, but it didn't make things easy."

Apparently Alli was so hard to live with when she wasn't writing that Ting insisted she go back to it. But at the end of 1978 she still couldn't come up with anything new. She kept feeling "something almost there—the tail of something nameless vanishing—when I go after it deliberately, a blank."

In June 1979, Rudolf Arnheim answered a letter from his old friend Alice. "I gather from the name stamp on your envelope that you have given up the anonymity, that James Jr. has changed sex, and the honors due to him are poured upon you in person. Good. You cannot live in permanent identity crisis."

But Alli was in as much if not more of an identity crisis than she had been as Tiptree. For all of 1978 she wrote almost no letters. In April 1979 she wrote Ursula Le Guin in longhand, on colored notepaper: "Tiptree has not given me leave—I think quite rightly—to write you on his old blue typewriter. Indeed, I am wary of writing you at all, until some new true mode develops itself in our proper personae. [. . .] Everything I said was true—all the feelings are still there—yet some mold is broken and a new one yet to form."

Two weeks later, though, Alli wrote, "Do you know, I believe I begin to meet you at last?" Alli was always worrying about how to talk to Le Guin, but of all her correspondences, theirs had the fewest gaps and silences.

As herself, she went on giving people what she thought they wanted. Congratulating Gardner Dozois for something, she began her letter "Hi Luv" and in lieu of champagne sprayed the paper with Norell perfume. She also complained to him about women's writing. "I just finished reading most of the *Analog* "women's issue" and got bored sick I'm sorry to say," she wrote him, a comment she might not have made to a woman.

On the rare occasions when Tiptree's letter-friends came to visit, she went all-out. The Sheldons had the del Reys to dinner once, and Dozois, his wife, Susan Casper, and the Smiths for lunch. Afterward, Alli took a napkin that Dozois had been crumpling, put it in a box, labeled it "Paper napkin shredded by Gardner Dozois [. . .]. My first meeting with a writer," and archived it. A young writer who lived nearby, Somtow Sucharitkul, came to the house to deliver Raccoona's Nebula for "Screwfly" and fell under the spell of this "eccentric old woman" who was both a "favorite grandmother" and a brilliant author.

But just as Tiptree had been a persona, so was the Alli she showed her science fiction friends. Jim Turner, an editor who worked with Alli in the 1980s, observed that everyone who knew her knew a different person. "She was manipulating all of us. I'm not necessarily criticizing her. She was a brilliant woman. She was the most unforgettable person I've ever met. But don't make the mistake of thinking Alli was all sweetness and light."

All this getting along with people cost Alli more than ever, and she preferred to be alone. By the early 1980s, she rarely left the house. Ting did the grocery shopping and went out to lunch with friends; Alli bought clothes from catalogs and kept to herself. Mark Siegel, who interviewed her in 1982, said, "When I was at their house, I got the feeling that it was one of these hobbit holes under the hill that no one ever came to. She never talked about socializing; I never heard the doorbell ring." Peter Sheldon recalled, "She was like a hermit crab. One time when we went down and visited, my wife and I went in the house, and I think it was three or four hours before we discovered where she was, in the middle of the house, in her bed. [. . .] It was like visiting Marlowe in Africa—someone who had gone into the jungle and didn't want to be found."

In good moods, she did talk on the phone. Jeff Smith recalled that he got fewer letters from Alli than he had from Tip, but felt just as close to her because of their long phone calls. Jim Turner knew her as "less an epistolarian than the world's champion long-distance conversationalist." And she did have one regular visitor. Sometime in 1979 Ting decided that Alli needed a secretary, and asked a young woman with an English degree who worked at the Sheldons' travel agency to come over on Saturdays and help Alli organize her correspondence. Donna Risso helped Alli off and on for the next several years. She didn't need the work, but loved being with Alli. When Alli was depressed, she recalled, "we would go weeks or a month or so and I wouldn't see her. And then when I'd come back she'd be fine."

Risso wasn't interested in science fiction, but that only made Alli feel more comfortable. Alli used her as a source, quizzing her about her life and what young people did. "The thing she liked was people who were smart, not boring, willing to go beyond or over the edge, if need be." Sometimes they gossiped about fashion, or Alli told stories about Africa. When she smoked and talked she often got so excited she forgot about her cigarette; Risso would watch her waving her hands with the ash getting longer and longer and wonder when it was finally going to fall. "She was no more an average woman of her day than the man in the moon."

After the very bad year 1978, Alli found more energy and came up with new projects. Ting went down to Boca Paila on his own in the spring of 1979, and Alli bought a tarantula to keep herself company. "His informal name is Lonesome; properly he is Viscount Nostalgie de la Boue. [. . . He] is beautiful, with red knees," she told Le Guin. She also started fighting City Hall. She had received a notice from the Fairfax County Office of Assessments, saying that because she had her own business, writing, she was required to apply for a business license. At her tiny income, the annual fee came to about $10. But the idea of a license to write brought out her combative side. She sent angry letters to local politicians, invoking the Bill of Rights. She unleashed upon Fairfax County the wrath of Harlan Ellison, who contributed a three-page letter of protest. She persuaded a *Washington Post* columnist, Bob Levey, to write a column on her behalf. The fight went on for two years, until Alli went into the hospital for open-heart surgery in 1981 and Ting, who was tired of the whole thing, quietly applied for the license.

Levey became another of Alli's letter-friends, and they occasionally talked on the phone. The Alli he knew was the listener she had been for Bill Davey, the political adviser she had been for Gus Tyler. "She was one of the great readers I've had: so there, so smart, interesting takes on everything I wrote. She really saw the column in a way no one else did. You could tell she was a writer right away. She was excellent at 'walking' an idea, taking it from 1 to 10. She also had a great political instinct: an eye for what political problems could be fixed and how to go about it."

She sometimes talked to Levey about Ting. "She would say how important it was to her to spend the night beside him. She would talk about how every moment with him recaptured what they had together when they were young. I had the impression of a very physical relation between them, great physical passion, even in old age."

But to a science fiction acquaintance, Camilla Decarnin, Alli said that what she felt for Ting was different from "physical love." Instead it was a profound "friendship-love [. . .] for a partner who has shared so much of the struggle of life that you couldn't *be*, separately."

It wasn't until the winter of 1980 that Alli began to write again. That year, for the first time in ten years, the Sheldons didn't go to the cabin at Boca Paila. Their host, Tony Gonzalez, had become mayor of Cozumel, and they liked the place less now that he wasn't there. Besides, Cozumel and Cancún were getting too big, and Boca Paila was too far from medical help. When their lease was up they let the little house go.

Instead, with the money from the sale of 5344 Hyde Park Boulevard and the Lodge, the Sheldons spent the winter of 1980 near Rotorua, New Zealand, at a fishing lodge beside a remote mountain lake. They loved it. They were excited to be in a new place, liked the reserved, practical New Zealanders, enjoyed the relative luxury of the resort, and were dazzled by the landscape. Alli wrote Jeff Smith that it was "the closest approximation of Eden I expect to find."

They thought about emigrating. Ting had been talking for years about New Zealand as a haven from crime, economic collapse, nuclear war, and other near-future disasters. (By now, Ting's idea of financial planning was to stockpile gasoline in the garage, open offshore bank accounts, and hide gold coins in the walls.) They were told emigration would be difficult, and didn't pursue it.

In New Zealand, Alli got back to work. She reconstructed the stories she'd burned in Maine, including three fantasies set in the Yucatán (later published by Jim Turner, at the small press Arkham House, as *Tales of the Quintana Roo*) and two novellas, "Out of the Everywhere" and "With Delicate Mad Hands." They were all published as by James Tiptree, Jr. Alli wrote only one more Raccoona story, a heavy-handed weepie called "Morality Meat."

But they were not "by" Tiptree, in the way the earlier stories had been. Dozois had suggested Alli go on using the byline, even after the truth came out.

> I'm afraid that if you abandon the Tiptree name entirely you may also lose your "tone of voice"—this is a very subtle, almost mystical, matter, but I think it is a real thing [. . .]; that "shadowy presence and voice from under the pancreas" was conjured up to "be" Tiptree, to be a pro-

jection of subconscious functions, and if it can't "be" Tiptree anymore,
it may go away and not come back.

It was too late. The voice had already been slipping before the revelation,
and after the revelation it was gone. None of Alli's later work shows Tiptree's
old authority. The early stories have an assured, almost aggressive insistence
on the rightness of their telling. The later fiction is tentative and distant.
There's less humor, less sex, less voltage. There's too much explaining, too
many long action sequences that don't, like the old ones did, tighten the
story's noose. As Le Guin had said of Raccoona, Alli now had "less control,
thus less wit and power."

She tried recycling old themes (longing for the stars, time travel back to a
lost love, deadly sexual attraction) by giving them to girl protagonists. But the
stories didn't deepen in the process. They don't enter the heart; the pain in
them feels like other people's and not the writer's own. Alli started writing stories that said only "ouch"—like the appalling "Morality Meat," in which abortion has been banned and a "right-to-life adoption center" doubles as a
butcher shop for the wealthy.

Or she wrote superficial fiction like the three *Tales of the Quintana Roo*.
These are light ghost stories about spirits of the sea, told in the first person by
an elderly "gringo" of unnamed sex. The gringo is clearly Alli: a writer and
former experimental psychologist who had been in the Second World War and
had "worked around quite a bit," a passionate conservationist and student of
Maya culture. They are very readable stories, and the book won the World
Fantasy Award. But the fire has gone out of their telling, replaced by wistful
romance and a helpless distress at the pollution of the sea. The narrator
sounds nothing like the colorful "Uncle Tip" of the Yucatán travelogues, as if
Alli as "herself" couldn't acknowledge the part of herself that had made those
stories live.

Alli's two New Zealand novellas are both about girls coming of age. In
"Out of the Everywhere," an alien makes an emergency landing on Earth by
taking refuge in the minds of a newborn girl and her father. The mother dies.
The daughter grows up a strange, neglected prodigy fascinated with mathematics, physics, and the stars. One day the father notices her and buys her a

telescope and a hunting rifle. From then on, brought together by the alien mind they share, they develop a bond. They even start sleeping together, since he is, she says, the only one she has. But in this coming-of-age story, there's no real growing up. Before the daughter has to become an adult with her own sexuality, she returns to her alien form and escapes to the stars.

The other story, "With Delicate Mad Hands," was one of Alli's own favorites. Carol Page begins life as an ugly, abandoned, abused child, "an expert at being unloved." But with energy and skill, she manages to become one of the first women space pilots. She gets there in the only way she can, by enduring the scorn of her male colleagues while serving them as cook, cleaner, nurse, and sexual "waste can." ("We know the men do better with a female along, not only for physiological needs but for a low-status, non-competitive servant and rudimentary mother figure.") Finally, after a superior officer humiliates and rapes her, she kills him and another crewman, steals the ship, and sets off toward the place she has always longed for: empty space. Telepathically guided to a distant planet, she finds the being that has been calling to her all her life from the stars.

"With Delicate Mad Hands" is often heavy-handed. The men are too rotten, the heroine too abused, and the action sequences much too long for the story's delicate payoff. There are too many technical details of retrothrusters, course computers, and oxygen levels. Where Alli had used the apparatus of science fiction to say something new, now she was hiding behind it.

Yet there is a payoff. When Carol and her telepathic friend meet, on a radioactive planet that glows sensuously green and purple from within, the creature holds its hands up to the ship's porthole, and Carol holds her hands up on the other side. Then the creature, who is in some sense female, tells Carol that she has always loved her, "that she—Carol-Page-Snotface-CP-Cold-Pig—had walked all her days and nights embraced by love. [. . .] She had never been alone." Alli thought of this as a lesbian sex scene, and the story as a romance.

But having taken her heroine on such a long journey to find love, Alli could still reach no other closure than her death from radiation poisoning, and her lover's death from empathy. "Delicate" ends where it needs to begin.

―――――――――

By early 1981, Alli was working on another of the manuscripts she'd burned, one she called her "Dead Star" novel. In March 1981, back at the New Zealand resort, she wrote in a journal, "Today, after 2 weeks of struggle, I pronounced that damn 'novel' Dead (for the 2nd time!), tore and burnt up all but pos. useful bits, and buried it away. Trauma." Then she started on it again, with apologies to her hosts for the black spot on their lawn.

In August 1981 she went into the hospital for heart surgery. A failing valve was replaced and she was given a coronary bypass. The operation went well, but the surgeon prescribed medication without asking what other drugs Alli was taking, and Alli ended up back in the emergency room. Between the surgery and the relapse, Alli suffered bouts of memory loss, and it was a very long time before she recovered her old energy.

When she did start working again, she thought she might have found new material at last. She felt that in her earlier writing she had been peeling away layers of herself, like an onion. "I'd peeled myself down to the empty core," she told Charles Platt in 1982. "But then it seemed as though there was a little more of me after all. I found another onion." She also took to heart—probably too much—Algis Budrys's criticism of her "overcomplicated" plots. In writing her second novel, *Brightness Falls from the Air,* Alli concentrated on mastering conventional plotting techniques. She set herself certain limits: as in a detective novel, all the action takes place within a twenty-four-hour period in one setting, a lakeside lodge on the planet Damiem. She constructed a taut showdown between the heroes and the villains. She deployed a whole raft of dramatic devices: the innocent bystander held hostage with a deadman switch ("if I am hurt or killed, she dies"), the erased memory suddenly recovered, the coincidences that are not coincidental, the old-fashioned struggle for the gun. Highly unusual for Tiptree is a big Dickensian finale in which each character gets what he or she deserves.

The lodge is really a ranger station where two guardians, Cory and her husband, Kip, keep watch over Damiem's native creatures. The Dameii are spectacularly beautiful, delicate, humanoid flying insects, like fairy butterflies. They are the source of an exquisite liquor called "Stars Tears," which is distilled from the secretions of their emotion glands. The finest, most sought-after taste in Stars Tears is produced by the emotions pain and fear. Before the planet was guarded, evil humans tortured the Dameii to produce "vintages" for which the Galaxy's wealthy paid fortunes.

This melodramatic denouncement of humanity's crimes (compare the distressing *naturalness* of the killings in "The Screwfly Solution") is intertwined with subtler questions about the nature of beauty and love. A group of tourists has gathered at the camp on Damiem to witness a spectacular aurora caused by the passing of a nova front. It recalls the Lodge in Wisconsin, where Alli had loved to swim naked in the cold lake beneath the northern lights. Yet like Stars Tears the aurora is the result of an evil deed, the destruction of the planet Vlyracocha. The race who lived on Vlyracocha were building a great work of art, which a Federation gunboat captain mistook for a weapon. His crew refused to obey his order to destroy the planet—all except one, his cabin girl, who fired the missiles that blew up the planet and its sun.

In the last light of the murdered star's passing, various events take place. The Dameii are threatened again. One girl searches for her father, another hopes to resurrect her dead sister, and the last Vlyracochan takes his revenge. Alli said one of the book's themes was the danger of caring too much. The cabin girl destroyed Vlyracocha because she loved the mad captain. The Dameii were especially vulnerable because they loved their children. Even the Vlyracochans, it turns out, were dying of a virus of beauty that fed on their souls, leaving them "strangely incapable of hope . . . and yet haunted by unquenchable, unnameable desire."

The ending rejects these passions in favor of ordinary love and life: the surviving characters are able to set aside their unattainable yearnings and pair off into happy couples. As soon as the nova front is past, even the Dameii lose their ethereal beauty and reveal plans to start marketing Stars Tears. When the "unquenchable, unnameable desire" falls away, so does the helplessness, and everything is ordinary and all right. At the end of her life, was this the consolation Alli wanted for herself?

CHAPTER 40: **LOVE IS THE PLAN THE PLAN IS DEATH (1982-87)**

None of the narratives of masculinist, patriarchal apocalypses will do. [. . .]
It's not a "happy ending" we need, but a non-ending.

—DONNA HARAWAY

No one around here goes gently into the night.

—ALLI SHELDON, 1982

In the summer of 1982, the interviewers came. Up to that point Alli had made very little known about herself. Jeff Smith had stitched some of her letters to him into an autobiographical essay titled "Everything but the Signature Is Me," and had published it in *Khatru*. She had been interviewed by phone for an entry in the *Contemporary Authors* reference series, but was still revising the transcript and biography. Now a novelist and critic named Charles Platt asked if he could write a profile, and a junior professor from the University of Wyoming, Mark Siegel, started calling, saying he had a grant to write a book on Tiptree's life and work.

Alli was reluctant at first, though impressed by the grant. To Bob Harper she grouched, "I, A. B. Sheldon, am now regarded as Tiptree's interpreter, or 'contact,' or aunt or something, and a necessary evil. [. . .] Bring on your Platts, your Plotts, your dog-and-pony show—come one, come all. [. . .] Only I'll be under the carpet. They'll have to come on down and 'interview' me there." She asked her agent, Bob Mills, if she could charge them money. But she liked talking about herself too, and, at sixty-six, began thinking she ought to leave a proper record of her life.

Platt hadn't intended to interview Tiptree. A well-spoken young Englishman living in New York, he had done a book called *Dream Makers,* with profiles of SF writers, and was starting a second volume. He recalled, "I didn't like her writing that much. It was too depressing, and it wasn't speculative enough. But I was under pressure from my publisher to 'get more women in the book.' I hate that way of thinking, but that was what I was subjected to. I read a couple of Alice's stories, and even though I didn't especially like them I could see she had a great talent. So, all right, but I wasn't really expecting anything; I knew very little about her. I was just astonished to find that I liked her and Ting so much."

Like everyone who met Alli, Platt was impressed by her background—so much less provincial than most science fiction writers', he thought—and charmed by her warmth. He described her in his profile as "a strikingly beautiful woman" with "compassionate eyes, and a quick smile; her manner is forthright, with a touch of elegance." (Afterward, to Harlan Ellison, Alli rolled her compassionate eyeballs: "Secretly I love it, of course, but there *is* the matter of Truth.") She told her stories, gave her performance, and, when Platt left, collapsed for the rest of the day in a dark room.

She almost insisted on scrapping the profile, on the grounds that she'd been babbling. Instead she did another interview with Platt over the phone, and they ended up becoming friends. Even Ting warmed to Platt, because of his well-bred Englishness, while Platt was impressed with Ting's intelligence, dry humor, and sly nonconformity. Alli asked Platt to interview Ting and help him write a memoir for his children. Platt tried, but said he couldn't overcome Ting's "lifelong habit of downplaying his own achievements—or his reticence about Agency affairs."

Alli flirted with him, Platt recalled. "The only way she knew, really, how to be with men was by flirting. [. . .] She once sent me a picture of herself, and on it she wrote, 'However did I get on B.C.—Before Charles?' I don't think it necessarily meant anything. She just wanted people to like her. At the same time human relationships were a strain. So that made her want to hide from people.

"Yet once she became known by them, she would go all-out. I had more interaction with her, over the profile, than I did with anyone else. She didn't want to do it, but once we started, it had to be done right."

Platt could easily see why Alli had never joined the science fiction community in person. It has been a safe haven for many people, but Platt did not think it would have been one for Alli. "After her death, some people said, 'Oh, if only she'd gone to more conventions, she would have found that the community was willing to provide her the emotional support she lacked, and then she might have found there was more to life.' But the fact is—how can I put this?—her taste and breadth of experience and knowledge of the world was so far beyond the average science fiction convention-goer, it's just laughable that she could have derived very much from these embarrassing events of people dressing up in costumes and firing ray guns at each other. This is a woman who had operated at quite a high level in the CIA and had been all over the world—and also was plagued by demons which could not possibly be erased by a few people gathering around and telling her nice things."

Alli flirted even more with her next interviewer, the young college professor Mark Siegel. She told him he had a great body, like Johnny Weissmuller from the neck down. She was franker with him about some parts of her life, especially her first marriage, though she also told him more exaggerated stories.

Siegel recalled the interview: "She was recovering from open-heart surgery and wore mostly housecoats and robes. A big purplish scar crawled along her breastbone while she smoked Marlboros. The first thing she said was that she could only talk for a little while [. . .]. An hour later she was telling me about how she planned to kill herself. We talked for three days."

Where Platt had been drawn to Alli's knowledge of the world, Siegel admired her philosophy of life and her courage in living through her depressions. He was impressed by her belief in negentropy, and came away feeling that she had written science fiction not in order to express herself (she was not, she had assured him, invested in it in that way) but to express a moral philosophy and deliver a message. He believed her "objective was to write stories that would be fun for people to read but which would also contain at least the germ of a possibility of changing the way they thought and acted. [. . .] She accepted the concessions that seemed necessary, such as writing under a male pseudonym, in order to accomplish that goal." He wrote that the stories' "common point is their concern for justice and for human kindness."

But Siegel was half in love with Alli, and was inclined to see her only as the good daughter. She was concerned about human kindness, but she also warned him, "I qualify as some kind of expert on evil. I'm a loaded gun, an achingly loaded gun wholly unable to get a shot at those who are my enemies." In the end Alli didn't recognize his admiring portrait of her. She wrote Gardner Dozois that Siegel's instincts were "loony," and that she had liked his essay better.

To Siegel she said what she always said, that people could never really connect. Writing about speaking a foreign language, she added, "I have enough trouble communicating in English, even with someone like you. [. . .] Aren't our ideas of what contact with true ETs would be pathetically naive? After the initial pointing and gargling and smiles would come the cold terrible void."

It all made Alli long to be James Tiptree, Jr., again. After Siegel left, Alli wrote Jeff Smith, "I miss the old days so." And that December she wrote again, "Do you know I miss Tip terribly—as a person? I bet you do too. ABS is a poor substitute."

After Alli finished *Brightness Falls* she went back to short fiction, and between December 1984 and December 1986 finished eleven stories. Three linked stories were published by Tor Books as *The Starry Rift*. The rest were published in magazines and in a posthumous collection, *Crown of Stars*. At the same time Alli worked with Jim Turner, her editor at Arkham House, on an illustrated best-of collection titled *Her Smoke Rose Up Forever*.

When the anthologist Lonnie Barbach invited Tiptree to contribute to a collection of erotica, Alli sent her a cheerful story, "Trey of Hearts," about a threesome between a human woman and two aliens in human male shape. The woman, a sales rep waiting at a spaceport for a flight, is approached by a pair of attractive young men with noticeable erections. They explain that they have been given temporary human bodies but have accidentally packed the manual. The bodies seemed to have gone into reproductive mode. Could she help? The story of a threesome was a shock to Alice in her youth, but here she plays it for sweetness and laughter. She also portrays a woman's desire for the male body as vividly as Tiptree ever portrayed men's lust for women—though maybe it helped that the men are really dragons in human form.

John Clute, in his introduction to the first edition of *Her Smoke Rose Up Forever,* wrote that Tiptree had burned out, like a meteor dying in its passage through the planetary atmosphere. Alli herself thought that she had written herself out as Tiptree. But the fact that she could speak only within such elaborate strategies suggests that it was her strategy, not her material, that had failed her. The exposure, the awards, the pressure to write a novel were making it harder for Alli to write even before Tiptree's identity was revealed. After

Alli's death, Gardner Dozois said, "I still believe she might have learned to write as herself. I thought the best work was yet to come." Had she been able to go on writing, she might have experimented until she got her voice back.

But in the end, Alli never found a way in her fiction for a girl to grow up a whole woman. One section of *Brightness Falls from the Air* was conceived as a separate story. In it a strong, fearless girl of fifteen falls from a horse, lapses into a coma, and is declared brain-dead. But her shallow, coquettish twin sister has their brains wired together and devotes her life to sex and sensual pleasures in the hope of getting some feeling through to the lost, free girl. Alli thought for a long time about the ending, but could do no better still than death. The sister reawakens and breaks loose, only to perish, like P. Burke, in the "welter of broken tubes, scars, wires, hoses" connecting her to her beautiful twin.

One of Tiptree's last stories is another bildungsroman for a future girl. Coati Cass is a teenage adventure heroine, a "yellow-head, snub-nose-freckles, green-eyes-that-stare-at-you-level, rich-brat, girl-type fifteen-year-old. And all she's dreamed of, since she was old enough to push a hologram button, is heroes of First Contacts, explorers of far stars [. . .]."

As soon as she gets her first starship, Coati (Raccoona?) runs away from home, finds a mysterious message, and makes contact with a distant race. They turn out to be brain parasites; when a young one named Syllobene takes up residence in her head, Coati has, for the first time, a best friend. But there's a catch. Syllobene hasn't yet learned how to control her race's breeding urge. Untrained, she will go into a frenzy, devour Coati's brain, and release a plague of deadly spores. "The primitive part of myself that contains this dreadful urge is growing, growing, although I am fighting it as well as I can," she cries. "I fear it will soon overwhelm me."

Coati and Syllobene meet Tiptree's usual fate for mothers and lovers: Tiptree's test pilot of female independence saves humanity by crashing her ship and herself into the nearest sun. Among other things, it's another retelling of "The Cold Equations"—only in this version the girl is both pilot and stowaway, and to save the mission must sacrifice herself.

The story is called "The Only Neat Thing to Do."

In the winter of 1986, Ting had a hemorrhage in his one good eye and went almost entirely blind. He could still see a little at the edges, Alli wrote Ursula Le Guin, but the center of his vision was "a great dark smear." He also had a small stroke. He was as lucid as ever, but could no longer read or drive. He played bridge with successively larger decks of cards until he couldn't see them at all. Alli's secretary, Donna Risso, recalled, "He couldn't even take care of Alli at that point. That was a real blow for him."

Alli took care of him as much as she could, and told him constantly how much she loved him. In her last long letter to Jeff Smith, in April 1986, she wrote that with Ting blind,

> there's a shadow on my world too. All the little things suddenly catch you—the beauty of the daffodil blooms, or a new bird at the feeder, or an interesting photo in the news—and you turn to your life-sharer—and—nothing. He can't see, never will see again. [. . .]
>
> And of course there's so much to do—he needs help every 6 minutes, I see his hand futilely seeking something and leap up to help. He tries to make me stop, but I can't. . . . And all the dull things, all the bills to pay and insurance to wrestle with and financial matters—and TAXES—to pick up where he left off, knowing naught about it.

To Camilla Decarnin a few weeks later she wrote, "Time to work—zilch. I cry a lot also."

To Le Guin she wrote, "I haven't been free from self-pity as the days go by and nothing done, but what the hell, writing was my *hobby*, wasn't it?" She tried to prepare to end her days nursing Ting, and told Le Guin she didn't want sympathy. Le Guin told her to go on writing.

In spite of everything, she did. But like Mary, she also tried to escape. In November 1985 she told Le Guin she had been using so much Numorphan that when she ran out she felt bugs crawling over her skin. She had to check into the hospital for three miserable weeks of detox.

She did still like to talk on the phone, and she still went out of her way to befriend younger writers. In the spring of 1986 she wrote a story called "Yanqui Doodle," about a soldier caught up in a hellish Latin American war. While its harrowing scene in a detox ward may draw on Alli's own experience, the story also seems influenced by the Latin American settings of the writer Lucius Shepard. One fall afternoon in 1986, Shepard recalled, Alli called him out of the blue.

"I'd never met her, didn't know anything about her other than her work. She was very generous and gracious to me—she said she liked stories of mine that she'd read. I naturally returned the compliment. We chatted a while about Central America and my travels in the region. She called me a few more times, three more, I think. She always wanted to talk about me or something I'd done. Whenever I tried to turn the conversation to her or her work, she deflected my comments, which makes sense in retrospect, but which I found odd at the time. Once we had quite a long talk about Central American politics. She seemed to know a lot about it—not too many Americans are familiar with names of past presidents of Honduras and Nicaragua. But again, she deflected my questions. The calls would last about twenty minutes. They meant a great deal to me. Less than a month after the final one, she took her own life."

Alli could still, at times, be full of energy and plans. In August 1986 she took a last fishing trip with Ting, this time to Alaska, with the guide helping point Ting in the right direction to cast. Sitting in a cabin deep in the woods on the Talachulitna River, she felt full of life again. To her editor at *Asimov's Science Fiction Magazine*, Sheila Williams, she wrote, "I am bored by the slow pace and ultra-clear style I developed—effect of novel writing. I intend to go back to some of my old short manner, where you hit running and accelerate from there."

But just a few weeks earlier, in a sweltering McLean, she had written Virginia Kidd, "This *is* the silly season, isn't it? God I'll never spend another July in DC above ground."

In the last years of her life, Alli often talked about suicide. She spoke of it to Kidd, to Jim Turner, to David Hartwell. Charles Platt recalled that she occasionally called him sounding not quite coherent—as if she'd had a few drinks—and talked about depression and imagining herself dead. "Very, very morbid stuff." Donna Risso said Alli had written to the Hemlock Society several times, "just to do her research. Alli was big on research—with everything, this included."

She told everyone she would commit suicide when Ting died. In 1984 she wrote Rudolf Arnheim, "Rudi, I am so lucky, so lucky, to have my love still. I look about at the poor left-over ones, I can't imagine how they can live. I shall not. I mean, I shall deliberately never see the sun rise on a world without half of me." Alli mostly did not mention that she was more eager than Ting to go.

David Hartwell recalled, "It was like knowing somebody who drinks a quart of Jack Daniel's before breakfast. You know they're going to die, you just don't know when." Yet he also remembered her "ironic determination to survive in spite of her admitted desire to die."

Barry Malzberg, though, didn't see it coming, partly because he so admired Alli's courage in the face of depression. "She was the darkest writer, but she could still go on. I believed she would show me how, how you could be sixty, seventy, seventy-five, ninety, and still go on. But she finally realized the aliens weren't going to come; she was going to have to do the stinking job herself."

Old friends and colleagues remembered the lively, strong woman they had known and were surprised to hear of Alli's death. Jacqueline Goodnow commented, "Her suicide is still puzzling to me. But that's probably only because I don't know the circumstances. Alice was a very logical thinker once she started from some particular premises."

The premises had been in place for a long time. Alli's suicide note was dated September 13, 1979.

In the fall of 1986, Alli finished "The Color of Neanderthal Eyes," a long story about some of her oldest themes: How can a nonviolent culture defend itself? Why do females mother? In it a mother dies happily in childbirth, knowing that her children will go on. This time Alli seemed almost willing to accept instinct as an explanation.

In February 1987, she sent Virginia Kidd a gentle ghost story called "In Midst of Life." A man who has committed suicide finds himself in an afterlife woven out of the dreams and memories of the dead. He is welcomed there by a polite man in a suit who tells him he too may have anything he dreams or desires, except living people. Then the man gives him a task: to befriend other newcomers, so they won't be frightened or feel alone. In this story, her last, Alli seems to see hope, even in death, in working for others—and promise in her hero's journey to explore the "existential Unknown."

That spring, Platt phoned Alli because he hadn't heard from her in a while. "In characteristic fashion, when I said, 'So, how's things, what's new?' she said, 'Oh, well, things *have* been a little difficult around here, because Ting lost his eyesight, so, hah, you know.' Downplaying domestic crisis to the ultimate degree. She said, 'He just listens to music all the time, really, really loudly because he's deaf, and the noise of Beethoven is driving me up the wall.' And she never normally complained about anything, so if she said that, this was equivalent to saying she felt suicidal.

"So I just talked to her for a long time, and she finally said, 'So, what is it you want?' and I said, 'Nothing, I just called to say hi.' She said, 'Oh, you just called to say hello. Oh, well, that's really nice.' As if it was the first phone call she'd had in weeks where it hadn't been someone wanting something. I could tell she was pretty desperate and I offered to go down there and help. But she refused, and—I never imagined what happened next."

Around the same time, Peter Sheldon came to Washington, and Ting came to see him at his hotel. In the hotel room, Ting broke down and started to cry. He wouldn't say what was wrong. Later Peter thought his father must have been thinking about the pact—or was afraid of what Alli might do. Aside from his eyesight, Ting was not in poor health. He had promised Alli he would die with her when they got too old to live well, but at eighty-four, he was not really ready to go.

Bipolar disorder tends to respond to the seasons. Mania and hypomania are strongest in the summer, depression in the winter, and in the northern hemisphere, May is the peak month for suicide. In May 1987, seventy-one-year-old Alli Sheldon called Sheila Williams, to check whether she had sent Williams a book she had asked for. There wasn't anything strange about her tone, Williams recalled. "I thought at the time it was just somebody being nice. But she must have been cleaning up her papers, making sure she had done something she had promised to do."

On May 18, Alli mailed Le Guin a photocopy of a funny *Smithsonian* article about mistakes students make in history papers. She added a note:

Dearest Starbear,

Can't resist sharing the enclosed with you.

Apologies for the long silence. Life here is on the way down and out. Not to condole, it's been a great one for both.

Love, yrs

Tip/Alli

Late that same evening, Alli phoned a lawyer named James Boylan, a former colleague of Ting's. Boylan had recently done some legal work for the Sheldons, assisting another lawyer, John Morrison, who was the Sheldons' executor. "The night all this happened," Boylan recalled, "I think she forgot I was not really the executor of her estate. She called me around 11:30 and said she was about to kill her husband and herself. She explained to me briefly about their suicide pact. She was very calm, matter-of-fact almost.

"My first reaction was to delay as much as I could. I had seen Mr. Sheldon recently, and he did not appear to me to be depressed; he was not, in my opinion, in the mood to leave the world at that time. I said, 'Does Mr. Sheldon agree with this?' and she said, 'No, he's asleep.' So I reminded her that I was not the executor of the estate, and told her that before she did anything she should call John Morrison. Then I called the police and told them what was happening. John kept her on the phone as long as he could, and then the police got there.

"I got a call then about one in the morning from one of the police officers, who said everything had been worked out and they were going to leave. I said, 'I hope you're right about that. I know these people are very intelligent, and I don't doubt that Mrs. Sheldon will carry out the—thing she started out to do.' But the police seemed to feel they had everything under control.

"And then about three o'clock in the morning Mrs. Sheldon called me back and told me that she had actually killed Mr. Sheldon. I remember she said, 'Jim, I have slain Ting by my own hand and I'm about to take my own life, and for God's sake don't call the police for a few minutes, to give me time to do what I have to do here.' And by this point there was nothing I could do. I did call the police, and they went over and found that both of them were dead."

Alli had waited until Ting slept, and then shot him in the head. Afterward, she made two phone calls. One was to Boylan. The other was to Peter Sheldon. The phone in his bedroom rang in the middle of the night, and Alli was on the line saying she had just shot his father.

She told Peter about the suicide pact, he recalled, "and said she couldn't talk very long because she'd already done this to my father and the police were on the way to the house. I also think she honestly felt that if she didn't go then, they might not be able to meet in the afterlife. I don't think her belief in an afterlife was necessarily religious. I think it was just the idea that something of their relationship, which had been everything to her, would persevere beyond this life. And that there was some magical necessity to leave at the same time, because if they didn't they couldn't find each other.

"I don't think her atheism had anything to do with it. It was a sort of childlike wonder. And I think she had a real interest in the stars, beyond this world: what's it like, what's it going to be like, what's going to happen? She promised to communicate with me after she went, if she could.

"She said I had been extraordinarily helpful. I didn't quite know how, but I guess just giving her strength—maybe even to do this, or to finish it. I wasn't panicking. I realized how fruitless it was even to try to talk her out of doing what she was going to do. It was like talking to a locomotive that was going at 60 miles an hour down a track.

"And she reminded me of a time when I was a kid, up in Wisconsin, when she had let me drive this car they kept up there. It was a huge '36 Buick, and I didn't have a license or anything, but I really wanted to drive the car. So she let me, on the back roads. We came to the end of one of these roads, and I slammed on the brakes, and in the sand on the road this massive car did a complete turnaround and almost turned over. It was a real close one. And she never told anybody that I'd been driving or that it had happened.

"The night she called up, she reminded me of that, that she'd protected me as a teenager. She'd been true to me, and that was important. She didn't betray me." She had kept his secret.

Peter said there was one aspect of Alli's death the police found extraordinary. Ting's death had been bloody and messy, maybe more so than she expected. "So the police told me she wrapped a towel around her head so that wouldn't happen to her. They felt she was learning even up to the very last minute, observing and learning."

The *Washington Post* said the police found Alli and Ting lying beside each other in bed, Alli holding Ting's hand.

The *Post* ran a front-page story on the murder-suicide; the *New York Times* and other papers ran obituaries. Friends called friends to pass on the news. Donna Risso heard about the Sheldons from the evening news and wasn't surprised they had died in the middle of the night. "One in the morning, that was Alli's time."

Le Guin heard from friends before she got Tiptree's last letter. When it came, she recalled, "I felt rather uncanny: here was this light, ordinary thing. You wonder, like Virginia Woolf, did she know very much beforehand what she was going to do? Or was she just, 'OK, this is it, this is enough, the time has come'?" Yet when Le Guin reread Tiptree's work, she felt that it had been changed by the manner of Alli's death. "I think a lot of us didn't realize how bleak her stories are until the end, when we saw that she really meant it."

In an obituary in *Locus,* Gardner Dozois praised not only Alli's brilliance but her ability to love in the face of despair. "She finally gave up on a struggle that there was no way for her to win," he wrote. "[But] what matters is that she herself never relinquished the capacity for caring, no matter what the odds, and that she left for us in her work that same heritage of bravery and compassion, and hope."

A few years later, Le Guin wrote, "Her brilliance and sweetness and quickness and courage burns like fire, it leaves a sense of suffering. She lied to us yet she never betrayed us, never once."

At Alli and Ting's request, there was no funeral, and the bodies were donated to the George Washington University medical school. Later Peter Sheldon received their ashes, which they had asked him to take to the Great Barrier Reef. It was too impractical, so Peter scattered them together in the woods near his house. A few years afterward, he saw the sign his stepmother had promised him. His black cat had been killed by a car, and he had chosen a spot to bury it. "Then something in my mind said no, bury it up near the house. So

I dug a hole, and at the bottom, in the last shovelful, I saw something glitter. It was a little piece of a child's cup, and the design on it was a black cat. It was eerie. I really wondered if Alice wasn't talking to me from beyond the grave."

Alli left Jeff Smith her papers and her library, and made small bequests of money and jewelry to family and friends. She had thought at one point of leaving money to the American Psychological Association, to be used for research on women. But in the end she and Ting left the rest of their estate to the American Friends Service Committee, stipulating that the money should go to women, Native Americans, and the hospice movement. It wasn't the Earth she chose to help in the end, but the human race.

Several of Alli's last stories were published after her death, and her late work was collected in the book *Crown of Stars*. The collection of her best stories that Alli and Turner had assembled, *Her Smoke Rose Up Forever*, was published in 1990. Her work is reprinted in anthologies. The *Khatru* "Women in Science Fiction" symposium became so legendary that it was reissued in 1993, nearly twenty years after its original publication. Tiptree's columns for Jeff Smith circulated in photocopied editions until 2000, when Jeff Smith edited a collection of Alli's nonfiction under the title *Meet Me at Infinity*. A chapbook of Alli's poetry was published in 1996.

The effect of Tiptree's stories can never be the same now as when they were first published in magazines and paperback anthologies. Every time a Tiptree story is reprinted now, it is accompanied by an introduction explaining Tiptree's "true identity." There will never be the same shock that readers had when they first found out and had to go back and reevaluate every word of Tiptree's they had read. But Tiptree's voice sounds as strong as ever: funny, cocky, sometimes angry, always full of wonder.

It is a compassionate voice, too, as Dozois wrote, despite all the deadly endings. Michael Swanwick, who wrote the introduction to a 2004 reissue of *Her Smoke Rose Up Forever*, said, "Even in Tiptree's darkest stuff, you had the feeling that she was on your side. She wasn't doing this to depress you but to protect you. She was giving you bad news you had to know. That was part of what was awful about her suicide. It was exactly what she was trying to protect people from."

Alli didn't flinch, Swanwick said. "She taught us that you can't be afraid to be that bleak. You can't turn away from the implications of a story." Even now, few writers dare confront the human condition as directly as Alli did. The disguise that began as a joke permitted her in the end to write with a haunting honesty about herself, about women and men, about who we are.

Alli often worried that she had been cowardly in publishing under a man's name. A proper feminist, she felt, would have made a point of writing as a woman. Yet Alli's act of claiming science fiction has made other women bolder in taking liberties with the field. Alli enjoyed all science fiction's traditional pleasures, and at the same time she hacked it to make it generate new stories—and to tap into its power.

In 1991, the writers Pat Murphy and Karen Joy Fowler were discussing what they felt was a backlash in science fiction. The genre was moving toward cyberpunk and other kinds of "hard science" fiction, and away from exploring social change. Half as a prank, they decided to start an award for the fiction, by men and women, that they wanted to read: works that explore, expand, and reenvision gender roles. Because most science fiction writers can't live from their work, they decided their award should have a cash prize. Where would the money come from? From bake sales at science fiction conventions, ha-ha. What to call it? They named it after their favorite literary prankster.

From the moment Murphy and Fowler announced it, the James Tiptree Jr. Memorial Award was a huge success. Fans came forward to volunteer at the bake sales, design T-shirts, edit cookbooks. In turn, the award has inspired a new feminist energy within science fiction. Every year, a changing panel of writers and fans chooses the winner and publishes an annotated short and long list. In making their decision, the judges often hold long discussions about what constitutes reenvisioning gender, a debate that in turn raises more questions about what science fiction is and can do.

Alli was never able to imagine a future for women, or for herself. But that doesn't mean her own story is a sad one. In the end, she was able to do what she had always hoped: write, leave behind stories, speak about her longing for that future. The anger and despair, desperation and desire she couldn't express as "herself," she could put into her work. She could speak of her love for "our life and efforts, our strange, tangled, exciting, deplorable, ever-changing condition of profit and loss, trial and dream and struggle." She spoke for women and men. She reminded us to laugh.

Alli believed that great art is only recognized after the artist's death. It is not enough to represent one's own time; an artist must show the limitations of that time, insist we look beyond it, and paint visions of what could be. In her writing and in her life, she accomplished what she hoped. She built a door for us, her future people.

On the near side of that door, a man who doesn't exist sits down at a typewriter. He writes about a woman + machine + alien, journeying to the ends of the universe in search of a way to live. He writes about extraterrestrial eggs, fertilized with the seed of the human mind, waiting to be born into a posthuman world.

He says goodbye as two women, mother and daughter, set out together to explore the infinite cosmos. He watches and waves as they move forward into the free space of the imagination, navigating by the laughter of the stars.

ACKNOWLEDGMENTS

In 1994 I read an article on the Tiptree Award, by Suzy McKee Charnas, in *The Women's Review of Books*. I ended up writing two articles of my own, one for *Ms.* on the award (with thanks to Barbara Findlen) and one for *The Village Voice Literary Supplement* on Tiptree herself (with many thanks to Stacey D'Erasmo). While I was working on that article, I first read some of Tiptree's correspondence. The voice in those letters was funny, self-assured, and utterly arresting. When I came to Tip telling Robert Silverberg that he had shaved and put on lotion to write to his wife, I was hooked.

I met two people who were as excited about a Tiptree biography as I was. One was Gordon Van Gelder, who became my editor at St. Martin's Press. The other was Jeffrey D. Smith, Alli's literary trustee. He gave me access to Alli's papers—meaning he handed them to me and dropped me off at the copy shop. Between them, Gordon and Jeff have contributed years' worth of practical help, long letters, warm friendship, and, in Gordon's case, office supplies. Without these two talented editors, the book could not have been.

Alli's cousin Barbara Francisco, her stepson Peter Sheldon, and his wife, Ann, spoke to me for hours about Alli and helped in many other ways. William and Susan Davey received me in their home, and were also very kind.

Mary Ann Bamberger and Patricia Bakunas, at the University of Illinois at Chicago, helped me find my way in Mary Hastings Bradley's papers. Linda Long and Bernard McTigue, at the University of Oregon; Patricia Owen, Abby Lester, and Laurence Lippsett, Sarah Lawrence College; Andrea Friederici Ross, Brookfield Zoo; Jean-Jacques Eggler, Archives de la Ville de Lausanne; Harriet Memeger, Delaware Art Museum; and Marisa Bourgoin, Corcoran Gallery of Art Archives, were all generous with their time. Michael Valoris of the American Friends Service Committee helped me sort out an estate question. Craig Tenney at Harold Ober Associates discovered Alli's "Ann Terry" submission and was very helpful in tracking Mary's writing career.

Richard D. Walk, Alli's thesis adviser at George Washington University, sent me warm, enthusiastic letters and helped me get in touch with some of Alli's graduate school colleagues, including Jacqueline Goodnow, Lila Ghent Braine, Ann Milne, and Suzanne Hill. The lawyer for the Sheldons' estate, John Morrison, helped me find Ting's colleagues and friends, several of whom spoke to me at length about both Ting and Alli. They included Bob Koke, Walter Pforzheimer (in his famous book-lined home at the Watergate Apartments), Cameron La Clair, James Boylan, and R. Jack Smith.

Charles Platt and Mark Siegel generously let me draw on the transcripts of their interviews with Alli.

Franklin Berkowitz put me in touch with Lucille Lawrentz, Alli's old friend in Wisconsin, and Mary and Milton Martinson, the new owners of Bradley Lodge. The Martinsons helped me arrange interviews with Walter Sternhagen, Sylvia Erwin, Ann Legerski, and others and invited me and my husband, Jan, to stay with them at the Lodge.

Brian Parks, Lotte Hendriks, Nina Ascoly, and Justine Larbalestier read drafts. Linda Gardiner, Robert Legault, and Terence Bailey gave advice. Julia Curry, Ruth Landé, Alyssa Katz, Luigi Mercone, Darrell Moore, and Katherine Pendill all gave me places to stay. Dilys Landé provided emergency babysitting.

At St. Martin's Press, I had expert editing from Jane Rosenman, Michael Homler, Kenneth J. Silver, and Donald J. Davidson, as well as Gordon, who left St. Martin's but came back to work on this book.

A grant from the New York Foundation for the Arts gave me heart.

And I'm deeply grateful to all the many writers, editors, and friends of Alli's who gave interviews, answered questions, let me quote from their letters, sent material for the book, and said they were looking forward to reading it. Thank you to Dr. Claresa Armstrong, Rudolf Arnheim, Jim Baen, Neil Barron, Michael Bishop, Tanya Bresinsky, Steve Brown, Carol Carr, Suzy McKee Charnas, Cy Chauvin, Tayloe Hannaford Churchill, Camilla Decarnin, Gardner Dozois, Albert Dytch, Harlan Ellison, Alan C. Elms, Ed Ferman, Karen Joy Fowler, David Gerrold, William Gibson, Jeanne Gomoll, Cynthia Grabo, Fran Groover, Harry Harrison, David G. Hartwell, Donald G. Keller, Virginia Kidd, Damon Knight, David Lavery, Ursula K. Le Guin, Barry N. Malzberg, Anne McCaffrey, Vonda N. McIntyre, Noel Perrin, Charles Platt, Frederik Pohl, Donna Risso, Mary Rosenblum, Joanna Russ, Darrell

Schweitzer, Lucius Shepard, Robert Silverberg, Helen Farr Sloan, Ann Smith, Inez van der Spek, Craig Kee Strete, Michael Swanwick, Jim Turner, Gus Tyler, Marjorie Kelly Webster, Ted White, Kate Wilhelm, Sheila Williams, Gene Wolfe, and Chelsea Quinn Yarbro.

While I was writing this book I had a son, Eise, and a daughter, Jooske. They helped me miss my deadline, but I still feel lucky they're here. My husband, Jan van Houten, contributed inspired research, an eye for photos, enthusiasm, steady support, and Frisian practicality. Without him I never would have gotten done.

NOTE ON SOURCES

The Mary Hastings Bradley Papers are housed in the Special Collections Department, University Library, University of Illinois at Chicago. They include photos, newspaper clippings, reviews, unpublished manuscripts, date books, and letters, including a few from Alli to her mother.

Another source on Mary's career was the Mary Hastings Bradley file, container 1.4, Society of Woman Geographers records, Manuscript Division, Library of Congress, Washington, D.C. Mary corresponded with other members and returned a questionnaire to the society each year summarizing her activities in the previous year.

Alli Sheldon left her professional papers to Jeffrey D. Smith, her literary trustee. They include journals, unpublished essays and stories, newspaper clippings, and many of Alli's own letters, since she kept copies for reference. These papers are stored in the basement of Smith's house in Baltimore.

Among these papers are several unpublished, and in most cases unfinished, autobiographical manuscripts. The one I have quoted most is "The Relevant Biography" (abbreviated in the notes **RelBio**), a fifteen-page, single-spaced document Alli wrote for her psychologist in 1974 or 1975. Another autobiographical essay, "Everything but the Signature Is Me" (abbreviated in the notes **Signature**), was edited by Jeff Smith from Alli's letters to him and published in 1978.

Alli gave three interviews in her career, and Tiptree gave one. From December 1970 to January 1971, Tiptree gave an interview by mail to Jeffrey D. Smith, who published it in his fanzine *Phantasmicom*; it was later reprinted in *Meet Me at Infinity*. (In the notes it is referred to as **Smith interview**.) In June 1982, Alli gave interviews to Charles Platt and Mark Siegel. I quote from the transcripts of both interviews (abbreviated in the notes **Platt** and **Siegel**). In quoting from Alli's September 1980 interview with Jean W. Ross in *Contemporary Authors*, along with the biographical information Alli submitted, I have used the version that appears in *Meet Me at Infinity*. (It is abbreviated in the notes **CA**.)

Where no other source is given, all citations come from ABSP. Uncited quotations from Alli's journals and unpublished writings and from Alli's, Tiptree's, and Raccoona's correspondence are also taken from Alli's papers.

FURTHER ABBREVIATIONS IN NOTES:

A. Alice Bradley Sheldon
ABSP Alice Bradley Sheldon Papers
HS *Her Smoke Rose Up Forever*
MHB Mary Hastings Bradley
MHBP Mary Hastings Bradley Papers
MMI *Meet Me at Infinity*
R. Raccoona Sheldon
SYMPOSIUM *Khatru 3 & 4, Symposium: Women in Science Fiction*
SWG Mary Bradley file, Society of Woman Geographers records
T. James Tiptree, Jr.
UO University of Oregon Libraries
WWO *Warm Worlds and Otherwise*

WORKS BY ALICE B. SHELDON

Listed here are book-length works or collections in order of publication. All were published as by James Tiptree, Jr. The list that follows gives the short stories in chronological order.

Ten Thousand Light-Years from Home, with an introduction by Harry Harrison. New York: Ace, 1973. (Page references in notes are to 1978 Ace edition). Cited in story list as **TTLYH**.

Warm Worlds and Otherwise, with an introduction by Robert Silverberg. New York: Ballantine, 1975. Cited as **WWO**.

Star Songs of an Old Primate, with an introduction by Ursula K. Le Guin. New York: Del Rey, 1978. Cited as **OP**.

Up the Walls of the World. New York: Berkley Putnam, 1978.

Out of the Everywhere, and Other Extraordinary Visions. New York: Del Rey, 1981. Cited as **OE**.

Brightness Falls from the Air. New York: Tor, 1985.

Byte Beautiful: Eight Science Fiction Stories, with an introduction by Michael Bishop. Garden City, N.Y.: Doubleday, 1985. Cited as **BB**.

Tales of the Quintana Roo. Sauk City, Wisc.: Arkham House, 1986. Cited as **QR**.

The Starry Rift. New York: Tor, 1986. Cited as **SR**.

Crown of Stars. New York: Tor, 1988. Cited as **CS**.

Her Smoke Rose Up Forever, with an introduction by John Clute. Sauk City, Wisc.: Arkham House, 1990. Reissued San Francisco: Tachyon, 2004, with an introduction by Michael Swanwick. (Page references in notes are to 1990 edition.) Cited as **HS**.

The Color of Neanderthal Eyes. New York: Tor, 1990. Tor Double with *And Strange at Ecbatan the Trees* by Michael Bishop.

Neat Sheets: The Poetry of James Tiptree, Jr. San Francisco: Tachyon, 1996.

Meet Me at Infinity, edited by Jeffrey D. Smith. New York: Tor, 2000. Cited as **MMI**.

SHORT WORKS BY ALICE B. SHELDON
IN CHRONOLOGOCAL ORDER BY DATE OF FIRST SUBMISSION

Collections in which the works appear are given in parentheses.

1943

"I Am a WAAC," by Alice Bradley Davey, *Mademoiselle*, June 1943.

1946

"The Lucky Ones," by Alice Bradley. *New Yorker*, November 16, 1946. (*MMI*)

1952

"Phalarope," by Ann Terry. Not published.

1950s

"Please Don't Play with the Time Machine." *Amazing*, Fall 1998. (*MMI*)

1967

"Birth of a Salesman." *Analog*, March 1968. (*TTLYH*)
"Fault." *Fantastic*, August 1968. (*WWO*)
"Faithful to Thee, Terra, in Our Fashion" (original title "Parimutuel Planet"). *Galaxy*, January 1969. (*TTLYH*)
"Your Haploid Heart." *Analog*, September 1969. (*OP*)
"Mama Come Home" (original title "The Mother Ship"). *If*, June 1968. (*TTLYH*)

1968

"Preference for Familiar Versus Novel Stimuli as a Function of the Familiarity of the Environment." By Alice B. Sheldon, *Journal of Comparative and Physiological Psychology*, vol. 67 no. 4, April 1969.
"Help" (original title "Pupa Knows Best"). *If*, October 1968. (*TTLYH*)
"The Last Flight of Dr. Ain." *Galaxy*, March 1969. (*WWO, HS*)
"Meet Me at Infinity." Unsold treatment for *Star Trek* episode. *Eridani Triad* 3 (a *Star Trek* fanzine), 1972.
"Last Night and Every Night." *Worlds of Fantasy* 2, 1970. (*CS*)
"A Day Like Any Other." *Foundation: The Review of Science Fiction* 3, March 1973. (*MMI*)

"Beam Us Home." *Galaxy*, April 1969. (*TTLYH, BB*)

"Happiness Is a Warm Spaceship." *If*, November 1969. (*MMI*)

"I'm Too Big but I Love to Play." *Amazing*, March 1970. (*TTLYH*)

"And I Have Come upon This Place by Lost Ways." *Nova 2*, ed. Harry Harrison, 1972. (*WWO, HS*)

1969

"The Snows Are Melted, the Snows Are Gone." *Venture*, November 1969. (*TTLYH*)

"Through a Lass Darkly." *Generation*, ed. David Gerrold, 1972. (*WWO*)

"The Girl Who Was Plugged In." *New Dimensions 3*, ed. Robert Silverberg, 1973. Hugo Award for best novella. (*WWO, HS*)

"Amberjack." *Generation*, 1972. (*WWO*)

"The Night-blooming Saurian." *If*, May–June 1970. (*WWO*)

"The Milk of Paradise." *Again, Dangerous Visions*, ed. Harlan Ellison, 1972. (*WWO*)

"Painwise." *Magazine of Fantasy and Science Fiction*, February 1972. (*TTLYH*)

"And So On, and So On" (original title "And Shooby Dooby Dooby"). *Phantasmicom 6*, June 1971. (*OP, HS*)

1970

"Mother in the Sky with Diamonds." *Galaxy*, March 1971. (*TTLYH*)

"The Peacefulness of Vivyan." *Amazing*, July 1971. (*TTLYH, BB*)

"The Man Doors Said Hello To." *Worlds of Fantasy 3*, Winter 1970–71. (*TTLYH*)

"I'll Be Waiting for You When the Swimming Pool Is Empty." *Protostars*, ed. David Gerrold and Stephen Goldin, 1971. (*TTLYH, BB*)

1971

"Love Is the Plan the Plan Is Death." *The Alien Condition*, ed. Stephen Goldin, 1973. Nebula Award for best short story. (*WWO, BB, HS*)

"All the Kinds of Yes" (original title "Filomena & Greg & Rikki-Tikki & Barlow & the Alien"). *New Dimensions 2*, ed. Robert Silverberg, 1972. (*WWO*)

"The Man Who Walked Home." *Amazing*, May 1972. (*TTLYH, BB, HS*)

"And I Awoke and Found Me Here on the Cold Hill's Side." *Magazine of Fantasy and Science Fiction*, March 1972. (*TTLYH, HS*)

"On the Last Afternoon." *Amazing*, November 1972. (*WWO, HS*)

"Forever to a Hudson Bay Blanket." *Fantastic*, August 1972. (*TTLYH*)

1972

"The Women Men Don't See." *Magazine of Fantasy and Science Fiction,* December 1973. Withdrawn by Tiptree from Nebula ballot. (*WWO, HS*)

"Angel Fix." By Raccoona Sheldon, *If,* July–August 1974. (*OE*)

"The Trouble Is Not in Your Set." By Raccoona Sheldon. *Meet Me at Infinity,* 2000.

"Press Until the Bleeding Stops." By Raccoona Sheldon. *Khatru 1,* February 1975. (*MMI*)

1973

"Her Smoke Rose Up Forever." *Final Stage,* ed. Edward L. Ferman and Barry N. Malzberg, 1974. (*OP, HS*)

"A Momentary Taste of Being." *The New Atlantis,* ed. Robert Silverberg, 1975. (*OP, HS*)

"The Earth Doth Like a Snake Renew." First submitted as by Raccoona Sheldon, published as by Tiptree, *Asimov's,* May 1988. (*CS*)

1974

"Houston, Houston, Do You Read?" *Aurora: Beyond Equality,* ed. Vonda N. McIntyre and Susan Janice Anderson, 1976. Hugo and Nebula awards for best novella. (*OP, HS*)

"The Psychologist Who Wouldn't Do Awful Things to Rats." *New Dimensions 6,* ed. Robert Silverberg, 1976. (*OP*)

"Beaver Tears." By Raccoona Sheldon, *Galaxy,* May 1976. (*OE*)

"Your Faces, O My Sisters! Your Faces Filled of Light!" By Raccoona Sheldon, *Aurora,* 1976. (*OE, BB, HS*)

"She Waits for All Men Born." *Future Power,* ed. Jack Dann and Gardner Dozois, 1976. (*OP, HS*)

1976

"Time-Sharing Angel." *Magazine of Fantasy and Science Fiction,* October 1977. (*OE*)

"The Screwfly Solution." By Raccoona Sheldon, *Analog,* June 1977. Nebula Award for best novelette. (*OE, HS*)

1977

"Everything but the Signature Is Me." *Khatru* 7, February 1978. (*MMI*)
"Slow Music." *Interfaces,* ed. Ursula K. Le Guin and Virginia Kidd, 1980. (*OE, HS*)
"We Who Stole the Dream." *Stellar 4,* ed. Judy-Lynn del Rey, 1978. (*OE, HS*)

1978

"A Source of Innocent Merriment." *Universe 10,* ed. Terry Carr, 1980. (*OE*)

1980

"What Came Ashore at Lirios." *Asimov's,* September 28, 1981. (*QR*)
"The Boy Who Waterskied to Forever." *Magazine of Fantasy and Science Fiction,* October 1982. (*QR*)
"Beyond the Dead Reef." *Magazine of Fantasy and Science Fiction,* January 1983. (*QR*)
"Excursion Fare." *Stellar 7,* ed. Judy-Lynn del Rey, 1981. (*BB*)
"Out of the Everywhere." *Out of the Everywhere,* 1981.
"With Delicate Mad Hands." *Out of the Everywhere,* 1981. (*BB, HS*)

1984

"Morality Meat." By Raccoona Sheldon. *Despatches from the Frontiers of the Female Mind,* ed. Jen Green and Sarah Lefanu, 1985. (*CS*)
"The Only Neat Thing to Do." *Magazine of Fantasy and Science Fiction.* (*SR*)
"Good Night, Sweethearts." *Magazine of Fantasy and Science Fiction,* March 1986. (*SR*)

1985

"All This and Heaven Too." *Asimov's,* Mid-December 1985. (*CS*)
"Collision." *Asimov's,* May 1986. (*SR*)
"Trey of Hearts." *Meet Me at Infinity,* 2000.
"Our Resident Djinn." *Magazine of Fantasy and Science Fiction,* October 1986. (*CS*)
"Second Going." *Universe 17,* ed. Terry Carr, 1987. (*CS*)

1986

"Come Live with Me." *Crown of Stars,* 1988.

"Yanqui Doodle." *Asimov's,* July 1987. (*CS*)

"Backward, Turn Backward." *Synergy 2,* ed. George Zebrowski, 1988. (*CS*)

"The Color of Neanderthal Eyes." *Magazine of Fantasy and Science Fiction,* May 1988. (*MMI*)

"A Woman Writing Science Fiction." By Alice Sheldon. *Women of Vision,* ed. Denise Du Pont, 1989. (*MMI*)

1987

"In Midst of Life." *Magazine of Fantasy and Science Fiction,* November 1987. (*CS*)

ADAPTATIONS IN OTHER MEDIA

Weird Romance, musical, 1992, based in part on Tiptree's "The Girl Who Was Plugged In." Music by Alan Menken, book by Alan Brennert, lyrics and additional book by David Spencer.

"Houston, Houston, Do You Read?," radio play, aired on National Public Radio in the series *Sci-fi Radio,* February 4 and 11, 1990.

"Yanqui Doodle," radio play, aired on National Public Radio in the series *Sci-fi Radio,* March 18, 1990.

"The Girl Who Was Plugged In," episode of *Welcome to Paradox,* first aired on the Sci-Fi Channel, December 14, 1998.

NOTES

INTRODUCTION: WHO IS TIPTREE, WHAT IS HE?

1 "No one has": Dozois, *The Fiction of James Tiptree, Jr*, unpaginated.

1 "At last I have": Smith interview, MMI, 197.

2 "Paranoia hasn't": "The Women Men Don't See," HS, 122.

2 "shaved and applied lotion": T. to Silverberg, June 8, 1974.

2 "a man of 50": Silverberg, "Who Is Tiptree, What Is He?" WWO, xiv.

3 "It has been suggested": Ibid., xii.

3 "lean, muscular . . . loss": Ibid., xv.

3 "asked me if you were": Russ to T., May 25, 1975.

3 "no woman could": Russ to T., Oct. 28, 1974.

3 "As for me": R. to Jeffrey D. Smith, Feb. 17, 1975.

3 "in a Pentagon sub-basement": T. to Harry Harrison, Oct. 27, 1969; reprinted in Harrison, ed., *Nova 2* (New York : Walker, 1972).

4 "My secret world": A., "A Woman Writing Science Fiction," in Du Pont, ed., *Women of Vision*, 52.

4 "one of the most fascinating": Dozois, *Locus,* July 1987, 63.

4 "Alli was electrifying": Hartwell, ibid.

4 "beautiful alcoholic poet": Signature, MMI, 307.

5 "a kind of explorer-heroine": T. to Albert Dytch, Feb. 1, 1973.

5 "a dazzling and formidable": RelBio.

6 "storm naked": T. to Cy Chauvin, July 25, 1973.

6 "editors wouldn't remember": Signature, MMI, 311.

6 "I cannot make use": Woolf, quoted in Le Guin, "The Fisherwoman's Daughter," 234.

7 Tiptree takes the figure: Haraway, *Primate Visions*, 386.

7 "Certainly let us be": A. to Robert Harper, Jan. 31, 1975.

7 " 'Alice,' it was made clear": A. to Russ, Aug. 26, 1979, UO.

7 "inveterate nicknamer": T. to Russ, Sept. 12, 1975, UO.

8 "PS. I am not": A. to William Paley, July 17, 1973.

CHAPTER 1: THE INNOCENT ADVENTURESS

Much of the information on Carl and Mickie Akeley in this chapter comes from Penelope Bodry-Sanders, *Carl Akeley: Africa's Collector, Africa's Savior.*

9 "And when you see": A. to Mark Siegel, June 22, 1982.

9 "sitting before my dolls' house": "The Story of My Life," notes for lecture, ca. 1953, MHBP.

9 "a well-qualified . . . hour or two": *New York Times Book Review,* Feb. 20, 1921.

10 "the seamy side": "Adventures of a Self Made Author," notes for lecture, ca. 1936, MHBP.

10 "I had the real stuff": Ibid.

10 Victorian ethics: According to the family myth, a longing to fix the world ran in the blood. Mary said she was descended through her mother from a long line of "exhorters" (clergymen and teachers). Alice said she was a closet "educator/missionary/evangelist" whose forebears "were all poor preachers who had terrible theological arguments—the losers would move 200 miles west till they got to Fort Chicago" (A. to Michael Bishop, Jan. 7, 1983).

10 may have been alcoholic: In *Dawn Breaks the Heart,* an autobiographical novel by Alice's first husband, William Davey, a character closely modeled on Alice describes her grandmother as seen through her mother's eyes: "Gina was the holiest woman that ever lived, and the reason for her holiness, it seems, is that she married a drunken doctor who beat her but he died, and she married a sober insurance salesman, who beat her but he lived, so she died" (296).

11 "I also have no such wish": "The Girl from Home," *Good Housekeeping,* Dec. 1911, 765.

12 "Mrs. Herbert Bradley": clipping late 1940, MHBP.

12 "There's always room": A. to Clayton Rawson (editor of mystery book club newsletter who had asked for a biography of Mary), Sept. 11, 1952, MHBP.

12 "silly and self-conscious": MHB, diary (a short-lived attempt), Sept. 1936, MHBP.

13 "you couldn't get close": Francisco, interview with JP, June 1997.

13 "it was understood": RelBio.

13 "where motors": MHB, *On the Gorilla Trail,* 6.

14 "of a vast continent": Ibid., 2.

14 two family friends: Mary's step-uncle, Charles Corwin, had helped Akeley make dioramas for the Field Museum of Natural History in Chicago. Akeley had mounted the animals while Corwin, a painter, did the backgrounds. Among his achievements Carl Akeley was a pioneer of the diorama, displaying animals in natural poses in their own ecosystem.

14 Mickie, too, was a courageous traveler: Later, in 1924, Mickie Akeley went to British East Africa for the Brooklyn Museum, becoming the first woman to lead an African

collecting expedition. She also observed animal behavior and wrote popular magazine articles and books on African wildlife. On the trip with McCutcheon, she adopted a female monkey which she named after McCutcheon, "J.T. Jr." She later wrote a book about J.T. Jr. which Alice, for what it's worth, would almost certainly have read.

15 "seen through the eyes": Carl Akeley to A., Dec. 30, 1920, in MHB, *Alice in Jungleland*.

15 editorials cast doubt: Alice told this to Carl Akeley's biographer, Penelope Bodry-Sanders. It's possible she was exaggerating for dramatic effect. In some ways the controversy was good publicity for the trip—and so was the cute little girl with the bow in her hair. But it is true that in everything she said about Africa, Mary bent over backward to assure her audience that it had been safe to take her daughter.

15 "like a French doll": MHB, *Alice in Jungleland*, 11–12.

16 "a case of *horror vitae*": A., "A Woman Writing Science Fiction," in Dupont, ed. *Women of Vision*, 56.

CHAPTER 2: AFRICA (1921–22)

This chapter is based in large part on Mary Hastings Bradley's books *On the Gorilla Trail* (1922) and *Alice in Jungleland* (1927).

17 "danced along": *Alice in Jungleland*, 43–44.

17 "if I dropped something": Platt.

17 "Some hunters say": *On the Gorilla Trail*, 47. Subsequent quotes come from pp. 3, 34, 34, 39, 49, 45, 51, 57, and 265.

18 Mary had mixed feelings: Other than her comments on progress, Mary wrote surprisingly little about the politics of colonial Africa. She may not have been in a position to speak, since white travelers in the Congo depended on the goodwill of its Belgian administrators.

18 "suffused with sadness": CA, MMI, 337.

21 "It was too big a problem": *Alice in Jungleland*, 33.

22 active volcanoes: The other volcano, Nyiragongo, erupted in January 2002 with a lava flow that buried much of the Congo city of Goma.

22 "a stage setting": *On the Gorilla Trail*, 171. The subsequent quote is from p. 92.

23 "a heartbreaking expression": Akeley, *In Brightest Africa*, quoted in Bodry-Sanders, *Carl Akeley*, 191.

23 wildlife preserve: At Gisenye the Bradleys met a professional hunter and guide, T. Alexander Barns, who was collecting gorillas for the British Museum. Barns wanted to set up a local gorilla-hunting outfit and firmly opposed gorilla preservation. A few years later he was killed by a streetcar in Chicago, confirming Mary's belief that Africa was less dangerous than a city street.

24 "Am I a Batwa?": *Alice in Jungleland*, 106. The subsequent quote is from p. 139.

24 "It was early impressed": RelBio.

25 "shops and hotels": *On the Gorilla Trail,* 233. Subsequent quotes are from pp. 238 and 222.

25 "I think you could say": A. to George Scithers, May 21, 1981.

CHAPTER 3: CHILDHOOD

In writing about Alice's childhood in this chapter I drew on my interviews with Barbara Francisco (June and Sept., 1997) and Walter Sternhagen (July 1998). Quotes not otherwise sourced come from these interviews.

26 "The mother-child interaction": Taped journal, Feb. 1975. In the early 1970s, A. occasionally recorded her thoughts or ideas for stories on tape. Between 1969 and 1975 she made five tapes.

26 "You can understand": "I'm Too Big but I Love to Play," *Ten Thousand Light-Years from Home,* 287–88.

26 "Youngest Explorer": *New York Times,* Mar. 19, 1922, clipping, MHBP.

27 "thrilled to the finger tips": Clipping, no source, Apr. 1, 1922, MHBP.

27 "I was already": RelBio.

27 "My Mummy spent": MHB, *Alice in Jungleland,* 130.

27 "There are some people": Journal, Dec. 8, 1941, Feb. 7, 1976; T. to Joanna Russ, Sept. 22, 1974.

27 "It is true": A. to Dr. K (therapist), Aug. 18, 1955.

28 "For, of course": MHB, *Alice in Jungleland,* 131.

28 "Your father is . . . unloaded on me": RelBio.

28 "You 'taught' me": A. to MHB, Sept. 7, 1961, MHBP.

28 "Very early on": Journal, n.d. [Dec 1975?].

29 "in abeyance": Journal, Apr. 24, 1977.

29 "was marred by dishonesty": A. to Ursula K. Le Guin, Aug. 8, 1979, UO.

29 "an inferior variety": RelBio.

29 "just gave up": Platt.

29 "I was nine": T. to Le Guin, Apr. 29, 1974.

30 "In my family anger": RelBio. A.'s subsequent thoughts on anger come from the same unpublished memoir.

30 "is always for": A. to Clayton Rawson, Sept. 11, 1958, MHBP.

30 "Alice's little uproars . . . intense melancholy": A. to Douglas Buchanan (family doctor), July 17, 1975.

31 "When I was a kid": T. to Jeffrey D. Smith, Sept. 27, 1974, MMI, 271.

31 "I looked in baby-carriages": RelBio.

31 "I didn't tell anybody": A. to Buchanan, July 17, 1975.

31 "I realize": Taped journal, Nov. 30, 1974.

31 "When I feel bad . . . fire": A. to MHB, Sept. 7, 1961, MHBP.

33 "I love it helplessly": T. to Harlan Ellison, Sept. 25, 1973.

CHAPTER 4: CANNIBALS AT HOME (1924–25)

This chapter is based in part on Mary Hastings Bradley's books *Caravans and Cannibals* (1926), *Trailing the Tiger* (1929), and *Alice in Elephantland* (1929).

35 "Mrs. Bradley writes": Chicago Tribune Newspapers Syndicate, brochure for selling syndication rights to *Caravans and Cannibals,* ABSP.

35 "space and beauty": MHB, *Caravans and Cannibals,* 34. Subsequent quotes in this chapter are from pp. 10, 43–44, and 200.

35 "primeval America": A. to Patrick LoBrutto, Dec. 31, 1986.

36 "I haven't taken out": MHB, *Alice in Elephantland,* 6. Subsequent quotes are from pp. 84 and 27.

37 "the official non-intellectual": RelBio.

38 "revealed as a weakling . . . major proportions": Ibid.

38 "There is nothing": Quoted in Nederveen Pieterse, *White on Black: Images of Africa and Blacks in Western Popular Culture,* 65. Nederveen Pieterse notes, "In the [male] literature of exploration Africans are mentioned mainly as part of the landscape, or as obstacles to the exploration." (68)

38 "Finally, I got": Prentiss N. Gray, *African Game-Lands: A Graphic Itinerary,* 29.

38 Western women writers: In *Victorian Women Travel Writers in Africa* Catherine Barnes Stevenson writes that women travelers often "display a special sympathy for and understanding of peoples whose skin color distinguishes them, as women often find themselves distinguished, as the 'other,' the alien." (11)

40 "because of spending": T. to Joanna Russ, n.d. [Oct. 1973].

40 "scared my immature": A. to a women's health organization to which she had sent a contribution, ca. 1985.

40 "I would go to bed": A. to Robert Harper, Oct. 7, 1975.

40 "It wasn't that I": Taped journal, Dec. 1974.

41 "You think of a crucifixion": Platt.

41 "Auschwitz": A. to Russ, Feb. 24, 1980, UO.

41 "I was early impressed": T. to Russ, Mar. 15, 1975.

41 "I got into a good patch": Platt.

42 "As we went for some": Platt.

42 "starving dwarf-children": Comment on "The Last Flight of Dr. Ain," in Harry Harrison, ed., *SF: Author's Choice 4* (New York: Putnam, 1974), MMI, 236.

42 "a man on the steps": T. to Russ, Mar. 15, 1975.

42 matrilineal people: The Minangkabau became another of Alice's "horror-recitals."
    She believed the culture had been wiped out by the Japanese in the Second World
    War, and what to Mary was evidence of women's strength became to Alice proof of
    their vulnerability. In fact, the matrilineal social system of the Minangkabau is re-
    ported to have survived Japanese occupation, the Indonesian war of independence,
    and urban migration with great adaptability.

43 "sidewalks full of gayly dressed people": MHB, *Trailing the Tiger,* 169.

43 "rode a pony": Comment on "Ain," MMI, 235.

CHAPTER 5: CELEBRITY (1925–28)

This chapter is based in part on my interviews with Barbara Francisco; Mary and Milton
Martinson (July 1998) for Alice's riding at the Lodge; and Cynthia Grabo (Aug. 1998).
Quotes not otherwise sourced come from those interviews.

44 "To grow up": "Zero at the Bone," essay on the "death" of Tiptree, written 1977–85,
    MMI, 383.

44 "Jungle Huntress": Clipping, n.d., MHBP.

44 "one of the most gifted . . . peculiarly infectious": Flyer for MHB lectures, ca. 1935,
    MHBP.

45 "Women Brave Jungle Perils": Atlantic City, N.J., *Union*, Feb. 9, 1928, clipping,
    MHBP.

45 "Penetration of Wilds": Providence, R.I., *Bulletin*, Feb. 1, 1928, clipping, MHBP

46 widower: In 1919, Harry and Mary Bigelow had gone on a trip around the world, but
    Mary, who probably knew she had cancer when she left Chicago, fell ill and died in
    Singapore. Typically, Mary Bradley kept her friend Mary Bigelow's diary, with its last
    anxious entries written just before she went in for the surgery from which she did not
    recover.

46 "draped around": Bigelow to A., n.d. [Spring 1930].

46 "Much love": MHB to A., n.d. [Fall 1931?].

47 "I got the feeling": Platt.

47 "awful moment": T. to Eleanora Mills (in office of agent Robert P. Mills), Nov. 8,
    1976.

47 "I couldn't count . . . betrayed their hopes": CA, MMI, 354–55.

47 "A mother so able": Ibid., 354.

48 "Mary foresaw happy years": Ibid., 356.

48 "soon looked like a tool shop": Ibid., 357.

48 The book was used in primary schools: Science fiction writer Chelsea Quinn Yarbro,
    who read *Alice in Jungleland* in grade school in the late forties, experienced it as an ex-
    citing, subversive book, showing that "you could be a kid—a female kid—and have
    high adventure." Yarbro recalled her fourth-grade teacher insisting to the class that it

was fiction, despite Yarbro's protest that the book had photographs (Yarbro interview with JP, Oct. 1996).

48 "the warpage of gifted girls": Moers, *Literary Women*, 197. Alli was thinking of Moers's words when she wrote, "To grow up as a 'girl' is to be nearly fatally spoiled [. . .]." Moers adds, "An excess of early praise for amateur accomplishment may have done more than all the hardships of woman's lot" to doom pretty girls to literary mediocrity.

48 "valued only": RelBio.

49 "his life would have": Woolf, *Diary,* vol. 3, entry for Nov. 28, 1928, 208.

49 "I naively thought": RelBio.

49 "My little hand": Platt.

49 "Alice is a very . . . intervals of intense work": A. school report, Nov. 1, 1927, MHBP.

50 "little Never-Go-to-Bed": MHB to A., n.d. [Oct. 1929].

50 "to try to 'break'": A. to Douglas Buchanan (family doctor), July 17, 1975.

50 "I dreamed horse": A. unfinished essay on riding, 1972.

51 "Just remember": Herbert Bradley to A., Mar. 18, 1930.

51 "All of what": A. to Ursula K. Le Guin, Aug. 28, 1977.

51 "I never permitted": A. to Dr. K, Sept. 25, 1955.

51 "where special sexual": Journal, Nov. 9, 1976.

52 "a large green . . . Our Secret": Signature, MMI, 309.

CHAPTER 6: GIRLS' SCHOOL (1929–30)

Mary and Herbert Bradley saved Alice's letters, and a box of them turned up among Alice's papers. The box also contained Mary's and Herbert's replies and a note from the secretary of Les Fougères to Mary. Uncited quotes come from this correspondence.

54 "There is the vanity training": Russ, *The Female Man*, 151.

54 Les Fougères: Les Fougères was run by the fortyish Mlle Nellie-Rose Chaubert, who had inherited it from her mother. Alice told her parents that Mlle Chaubert had a "best friend," Mlle Courvoisier, who sometimes came with the school on skiing trips.

54 "a little calf . . . queer": A. to parents, Apr. 9, 1930.

55 distance-peeing contest: Robert Koke, interview with JP, May 1996. This story may be apocryphal.

55 "stooges . . . despised": RelBio.

55 "stayed there all day": Platt. Raccoona Sheldon, who claimed to have gone to school with James Tiptree, Jr., mentioned this as one of her childhood memories of him. In Raccoona's version the young Tiptree was "mad at something" (R. to Jeffrey D. Smith, Feb. 17, 1975).

55 "rejoicing to see": A. to Dr. K, n.d. [Sept. 1955].

55 "I woke up": T. to Smith, Apr. 28, 1974.

56 "I was told": A. to MHB, Sept. 7, 1961, MHBP.

59 "seemed always": "The Five-Minute Girl," *Saturday Evening Post,* Jan. 10, 1931; repr., Blanche Colton Williams, ed., *O. Henry Memorial Award Prize Stories of 1931* (Garden City, N.Y.: Doubleday, Doran, 1931), 54. Subsequent quotes are from pp. 55, 60, and 66.

60 "in a steamy . . . didn't know how": A. to Russ, July 16, 1977.

61 "With Mary": Journal, Mar. 23, 1976.

61 "I can't seem": *Ten Thousand Light-Years from Home,* 135. Subsequent quote is from p. 145.

62 "Whatever it was": HS, 80–81.

CHAPTER 7: LIKE A DU MAURIER HEROINE (1931)

63 "The traveling": Symposium, 89.

64 "I am probably": T. to Albert Dytch, n.d. [Dec. 1972].

64 "making those tiny": A. to Max Lerner, June 19, 1956.

64 "hustle out . . . help socially": MHB to Alice Manning Dickey, Apr. 19, 1931, ABSP.

64 "the polite chase": "Possible Beginning for a Memoire," draft, ca. 1977.

65 Then the expedition ran into danger: CA, MMI, 338–39. Alice wrote this fifty years after the event. It's possible she was embellishing for dramatic effect, or that the trip seemed worse in memory. A few months after they got back she wrote her parents, "What a wonderful trip we had. I relive it all often. Oh my dears, we have had a world of happiness all to ourselves" (Nov. 15, 1931).

65 "You keep remembering": A. to Lerner, June 19, 1956. Ewart S. Grogan and Arthur H. Sharp traveled from Beira, Mozambique, to Cairo in one year, 1898. The book they wrote about the trip, *From the Cape to Cairo,* makes no mention of two dead companions.

66 "My own childhood": T. to Craig Strete, Mar. 14, 1976.

66 "Heads, masks. . . . down a fall": Bertha Fenberg, *Chicago Daily News,* July 30, 1931, clipping, MHBP.

67 Brookfield Zoo: Even Herbert did a little writing. The Ober agency recorded one unsold submission: "Article about cost of stocking a zoo together with information about characteristics and love life of the animals." Years later, Alice claimed, she discovered that Herbert had also tried to write for the pulps under a pseudonym.

67 "delighted with her originality": Lillian C. Weaver to MHB, Nov. 3, 1931, MHBP.

67 "so ambitious": Weaver to MHB, Nov. 25, 1931, MHBP.

67 "The task of adjusting": Weaver to MHB, Dec. 10, 1931, MHBP.

67 "Miss Bradley": Clipping, *Chicago Tribune,* Dec. 21, 1934, ABSP.

67 "Alice Bradley, who knows . . . Like a du Maurier Heroine": Clipping, *Chicago Daily News,* July 9, 1932, ABSP.

68 "I do not 'fit'": Journal, Feb. 2, 1977.

68 "I hadn't a clue": A. to Camilla Decarnin, Sept. 16, 1984.

68 "The 2 or 3 great loves": Ibid.

68 "I *like* some men": A. to Joanna Russ, Sept. 25, 1980. Russ responded, "The terrible thing is how all this is *hidden from us*—what *is* a Lesbian, anyhow? It's unthinkable, invisible, ridiculous, Somebody Else" (Sept. 29, 1980).

68 "Tiptree's Dead Birds": Unfinished, unpublished memoir, ca. 1973, describing Tiptree's (and presumably Alice's) first loves. Alice noted in the margin that she had changed the names of the women involved. Otherwise the text is probably, like most of Tiptree's autobiographical writing, more or less factual.

70 "I never": A. to Russ, Feb. 24, 1980, UO.

CHAPTER 8: AMBITION (1931–33)

71 "I like the icy": Quoted in Spalding, *Stevie Smith*, 218–19. Spalding writes, "[Smith's] own isolation was mitigated by her conviction [. . .] that 'there is no part of Nature or the Universe that is not indifferent to Man' " (218).

71 "lunch in Philadelphia": MHB to A., "Thursday eve" [Oct. 1931].

71 "We had great fun": MHB to A., n.d. [Nov. 1931]. Balmer was also a science fiction writer who collaborated with Philip Wylie on the 1933 novel *When Worlds Collide*.

72 "was all 'effortless' ": RelBio.

72 Mary never wrote: As late as 1940 Mary was still planning a book on the third trip, to be called *Black Kings,* and another called *The Fallacy of Colonies* (MHB to SWG, 1940).

73 "Not that you have to earn": MHB to A., n.d. [Feb. 1932].

74 "He *knows*": T. to Craig Strete, June 15, 1976.

75 "the art of pure": A. to Rudolf Arnheim, July 6, 1956.

75 light verse: On a broken clock: "He goes to neither rhyme nor reason; / He rings,—but always out of season. [. . .] I daily promise to replace him, / But somehow I can never face him [. . .]."

75 "would like to be able": Draft of college application, Jan. 26, 1933, MHBP.

75 "the place for": Platt.

75 "reading by flashlight": Lillian C. Weaver to MHB, Feb. 22, 1933, MHBP.

75 "Alice's order . . . housewives": Weaver to MHB, Jan. 20, 1933, MHBP.

75 "I'm stale": A. to parents, n.d.

76 "one dot of life": RelBio.

76 "My life, my death": Platt.

76 "While it makes": RelBio.

CHAPTER 9: "WE HAVE FOUND IT QUITE IMPOSSIBLE TO PERSUADE HER TO LEAD A NORMAL LIFE" (1933–34)

For Alice's Sarah Lawrence career I drew on my interviews with her classmates Tayloe Hannaford Churchill (Aug. 1997), Marjorie Kelly Webster (Aug. 1997), and a woman who wished to remain unnamed (Aug. 1997). In writing about Alice's first marriage in chapters 9 through 12, I quote at length from my interview with the late William Davey (Nov. 1996) and our continuation of that interview in letters (Jan.-Mar. 1997). I quote from Mary Bradley's (briefly kept) diary and her date books for the years 1934–40 (MHBP), in which she jotted down a few words about each day's events. And I quote from Alice's journals and unpublished writings. Unless otherwise noted, all quotes come from these sources.

77 "[She said] she cared": Quoted in Redinger, *George Eliot*, 480. Eliot was holding off Simcox, who was trying to seduce her.

77 "I have terrible times": "Tales of a Paranoid," essay draft, early 1950s.

77 "She painted very, very interesting things": Churchill, who studied art and went on to collect it, was so impressed with Alice's paintings that she bought one. But Alice later took the painting back, saying, "My mother won't allow me to sell this" (Churchill, interview with JP).

78 Alice rewrote her stories: In 1955 she told a therapist, "I have a Munchhausen tendency to embroider, but [. . .] I seldom do distort stories in reaching for effect anymore" (A. to Dr. K, Aug. 18, 1955).

78 "emanating some sort": "The Laboratory of Me," unfinished memoir, 1957.

78 "People came up": Platt.

78 "original, outstanding, pulsating": Sarah Lawrence school report, Dec. 20, 1933 (and, for not working, Mar. 30, 1934), ABSP.

79 "Her habits of eating . . . life": Constance Warren to MHB, Apr. 12, 1934, MHBP.

79 "I fling myself down": T. to Ursula K. Le Guin, May 5, 1974.

79 "and leave it": CA, MMI, 350; Platt.

79 the pressure to have children: A Sarah Lawrence brochure described the college's goals as education, artistic training, community involvement, and "education for women as women. [. . .] When her don asks a Sarah Lawrence student what she expects to be doing five years hence, the answer eight times out of ten is that she hopes to be married with a home and children of her own. There is ample evidence that this generation of young people are doing some serious thinking in regard to the need of more intelligent preparation for marriage. They have made mental note of the tragic mistakes of many of their elders, and want to make a better job of their own lives" (MHBP). The "tragic mistake," apparently, was wanting a career.

80 "so very many who": A. to Joanna Russ, Jan. 15, 1977.

80 "a certain degree of": Havelock Ellis, "Sexual Inversion," *Studies in the Psychology of Sex*, vol. 1, (London: Heinemann Medical Books, 1942), 244. In Alice's generation,

"Sexual Inversion" (first published in 1898 and later revised) was typical early reading for anyone questioning her sexuality. Ellis believed homosexuality was normal but, cultural attitudes being what they were, recommended chastity and self-restraint.

82 "a plump little girl": essay draft, 1981.
83 "something that did not jell": T. to Russ, Oct. 22, 1974.
84 "stops at the point": note on women, 1940.
85 "poise is refreshing": Clipping, no date, ABSP.
85 "a great weakness": RelBio.
85 "Here's to Alice": Clipping, *Chicago Tribune* [Jan. 1935?], ABSP.
86 "She looked at him": *Dawn Breaks the Heart*, 223. Subsequent quotes are from pp. 226, 227, 230, and 231.
88 "When I was made . . . father's heart": Platt.
88 "the Museum of Death": Davey to JP, n.d. [Feb. 1997].

CHAPTER 10: LOVE TROUBLE (1935–36)

In this chapter I draw on the sources for chapter 9, plus interviews with Helen Farr Sloan (Oct. 1996); an old friend of Alice's who did not wish to be named (Aug. 1997); and a woman who knew Bill, and who also preferred to remain unnamed (Sept. 1999). The information on Bill's childhood comes mainly from my interview and correspondence with him. Information on John Sloan comes from John Loughery, *John Sloan, Painter and Rebel* (New York: Holt, 1995).

90 "To love": *The Second Sex*, 517.
90 "You see me": T. to Craig Strete, July 8, 1976.
90 "I did enjoy": A. to Joanna Russ, Aug. 26, 1979, UO.
90 "early opiates": T. to Dick, May 11, 1973.
90 "perhaps three": A. to Dr. K., Sept. 26, 1955.
90 "a brilliant alcoholic": RelBio.
90 "charming": Siegel; "an angel possessed": Siegel and Platt.
91 "very beautiful, as tempestuous": A. to Alfred Bester, Nov. 14, 1983.
91 "a process of rescuing": "The Next Sex," essay draft, ca. 1950.
93 "Out of the beauty . . . delirium": *Dawn Breaks the Heart*, 323. Subsequent quotes are from pages 286–87, 247, 349, and 351.
93 "four feet long": A., "I Told You He Bites," unpublished essay.
93 "Contact with him . . . together": Journal, June 18, 1941.
93 "hereditary nobility . . . belong": Journal, n.d. [late 1930s].
93 "the ability to soup-up . . . powers": Journal, May 27, 1941.
94 the greatest foolishness: "The Human Male," draft, 1973.
95 bloody fistfights: Bill fondly recalled one fight from his time in Berkeley that began in

a bar, over payment for a plate of chop suey, and ended with Bill being pummeled in the parking lot by the bartender, who moonlighted as Max Baer's sparring partner.

95 "of the children's quarreling": MHB diary, Apr. 5, 1935, MHBP. Mary knew of the quarreling already and seemed more concerned about the rumors.

95 "I can't get used to it": Ibid.

95 "Bill dislikes me": MHB diary, Mar. 28, 1935, MHBP.

96 The Bradleys visited: In Santa Fe, Mary pulled off a rare coup: one-upping Bill's father in raconteurship. According to Bill, Randall Davey told them a lovely anecdote about how he'd gone into the yard to sketch some chickens and his favorite chicken had flown up and laid an egg in his lap. Mary took off from the word "lap" and told her own story about the lion that had come to life. "Well, my father's story was just killed, ruined," Bill said, laughing. "Don't you think it's *bad taste* to tell a story about a lion after somebody's told a story about a chicken?"

96 introductory psychology: Alice's professor was Edward Tolman, a prominent specialist in learning theory who, unlike the behaviorists, emphasized animals as actively thinking and perceiving creatures. This notion would be fundamental to Alice's later academic career.

96 "a mechanical farce": Journal, June 15, 1944.

96 "maintaining half": Siegel and Platt.

96 "about which I was . . . damned": "Laboratory of Me," unfinished memoir, 1957.

97 "I long to be touched": Ibid.

97 "a disaster area": T. to Joanna Russ, Sept. 25, 1973.

97 "I am (was)": A. to Russ, Mar. 14, 1980, UO.

97 "the machinery for active sexual pleasure": Journal, Feb. 2, 1976.

97 "To paint an object": Journal, June 24, 1941.

98 "The curious indignity": Journal, Feb. 7, 1976.

98 "going to Venice": Du Maurier said of her feelings for women, "If anyone should call that sort of love by that unattractive word that begins with 'L,' I'd tear their guts out." Forster, *Daphne du Maurier,* 222.

98 "I have yet to meet": "A Short Destructive Inquiry into Modern Aesthetics," unfinished essay.

98 "a touch of lesbianism"; "bohemian chic": Faderman, *Odd Girls and Twilight Lovers,* 82.

98 "the most brave": Ibid., 67.

98 "Since I looked": A. to Joanna Russ, July 16, 1977.

98 talked and talked: Alli once wrote Russ, "If we ever meet/met, we might talk for 72 hours straight and have to be carried apart exhausted, vowing never to go near each other again. . . . You know that almost sick ecstasy of meeting the Sharer. Happens every few years—one has to be very careful of running one's batteries down" (Mar. 14, 1980, UO).

99 "and knowing": Journal, notes for a memoir, Dec. 21, 1982.

100 Alice got pregnant: Alice never discussed her use of contraception. In a letter to JP, Bill Davey declined to comment.

100 "Bill had brought": Siegel, quoted in Mark Siegel, "Love Was the Plan, the Plan Was . . . : A True Story about James Tiptree, Jr.," 7. Siegel brought out Alli's tendency to embellish, and this story is almost certainly exaggerated for dramatic effect.

102 escape the limitations of one sex: Lesbian writers and artists, Teresa de Lauretis writes, "have sought variously to escape gender, to deny it, transcend it, or perform it in excess [. . .]. One way of escaping gender is to so disguise erotic and sexual experience as to suppress any representation of its specificity, [while] another avenue of escape leads the lesbian writer fully to embrace gender, if by replacing femininity with masculinity" ("Sexual Indifference and Lesbian Representation," *Theatre Journal,* May 1988, 159–161). In becoming James Tiptree, Jr., and Raccoona Sheldon, Alice sometimes seems to be escaping, denying, transcending, and performing gender all at once. Her two ways of talking about her attraction to women—translating it into abstract, alien longings and describing it from a man's point of view—correspond to de Lauretis's model.

CHAPTER 11: SEX AND ARGUING (1936–40)

The headnotes to chapters 9 and 10 apply here as well.

104 "Every woman": Joanna Russ to T., Sept. 18, 1973.

104 "the only pleasures": Quoted in Brightman, *Writing Dangerously,* 146.

105 "No sooner had they gone": Clipping, Aug. 7, 1937, MHBP.

106 "I cast aside": A. to MHB, Sept. 7, 1961, MHBP.

106 Alice lied to her parents: A. to parents, n.d., MHBP, Alice's only surviving letter home during this period.

106 lessons from John Sloan: To JP, Bill Davey vehemently denied that Alice had ever studied with his father's friend, although letters from Alice to Sloan, Alice's journal, and Mary Bradley's date book entries confirm it. Bill felt very close to Sloan and may have been possessive of their relationship.

107 "who appear to take": "A Short Destructive Inquiry into Modern Aesthetics," unfinished draft.

108 "chooses to look . . . universal": Journal, 1940. In all Alice's writing until the 1970s she used "he" for "the artist" and "the author." This produced such incongruous constructions as "what the Author (me) is trying to do, and what qualifications he has for the task."

108 "V-shaped . . . blood": Cather, quoted in Moers, *Literary Women,* 258.

108 "I am very strongly": CA, MMI, 393.

109 "As was usual with Vivian": *Dawn Breaks the Heart,* 356.

109 "will acknowledge some": Note on women, 1940.

109 "the personal shit": A. to Joanna Russ, July 31, 1981.

109 "I want to be like": Note, n.d., on stationery from the Seymour, Mary's New York hotel.

110 "exceptional ability": Randall Davey to C. Powell Minnegerode (director of the Corcoran), Jan. 21, 1939, Corcoran Gallery of Art Archives.

110 "Scornful. Eat up": T. to Anne McCaffrey, Sept. 29, 1969. Tiptree was explaining that he wrote fan letters to other writers partly to make up for his former envy.

110 "Fox CE double-barrel": A. to Jeffrey D. Smith, Nov. 24, 1977, and to Alfred Bester, Nov. 14, 1983.

110 "leaping down the rocks": HS, 412. Alli wrote Robert Silverberg that the boy was her young self (Dec. 28, 1976).

111 Ed Ricketts: After *Cannery Row* was made into a musical in 1955, Alice wrote a pseudonymous letter to the *New York Times* saying that she had known Ed Ricketts "back in the 'thirties when I was young and obnoxious," and that in real life he had been an unpleasant character who performed vivisection on cats. "One he insisted on bringing out and putting on the table had been more or less crucified, and it was all quite nasty. [. . .] Steinbeck calls him 'a glorious thinker,' and a lover of women and so forth, the general impression being that he was a pretty saintly type in a lustful way," but "the sad truth is that a more miserable, meaner, tied-up little man you would go far to find." The letter was signed "Ada Lucian Book" (copy in A.'s files, Dec. 1, 1955).

111 "laid off booze": Siegel.

112 " 'excessive detachment' phase": Journal, Dec. 12, 1975.

113 "My contact with negroes": Journal, May 27, 1941.

113 "I never feel . . . illusion": Journal, July 1940.

114 "I am convinced": Unsent, undated letter to friends "John and Mary."

114 "like grey boxcars": Journal, May 29, 1941.

115 "great sacred system": "A Short Destructive Inquiry into Modern Aesthetics."

115 "As an artist I am": A. to Sarah Lawrence Alumnae Association, May 20, 1939, reacting to article in alumnae magazine, Sarah Lawrence College archives.

CHAPTER 12: WAR FEVER (1941–42)

The quotes from Bill Davey come from my interview with him. Some background on the WAAC and the details on the uniform in chapter 13 come from Mattie E. Treadwell's critical, funny, and invaluable book *United States Army in World War II: Special Studies: The Women's Army Corps*. A copy of Alice's enlistment form is in ABSP.

116 "I am not at all": to Thomas Carlyle, May 7, 1822, in *I Too Am Here: Selections from the Letters of Jane Welsh Carlyle* (Cambridge: Cambridge University Press, 1977), 32.

116 "My personal life . . . work": Journal, May 27, 1941.

116 "not a perfect novel": Rose Feld, *New York Herald Tribune,* Mar. 10, 1941.

116 "Author Gives Up": Clipping, n.d., MHBP.

116 published in America: William Davey's novel *The Angry Dust* was published in a Chinese translation in Beijing in 1993, and is scheduled to appear in English, from Wessex Books, in 2006. Another novel, a 3,000-page Second World War epic titled *Splendor from Darkness,* was unfinished at his death in 1999. His published works include *The Trial of Pythagoras and Other Poems* (Paris: Alyscamps Press, 1996) and *Lost Adulteries & Other Stories* (Alyscamps, 1997).

117 "Reaction to the shocks": Journal, May 29, 1941.

117 "Spengler's mania": Journal, June 18, 1941.

117 "I am not adapted": Ibid.

118 "mucking around": Signature, MMI, 308.

118 "He was not *pure*": T. to Anne McCaffrey, Sept. 29, 1969.

118 "One expects painters": From the journal that Alice kept in 1941–42. She later typed it, condensing it and omitting the dates. She called it "Diary of a Whistling Girl," quoting an old saying: "A whistlin' girl and a crowin' hen are sure to come to some bad end. But the girl that whistles and the hen that crows will make her way wherever she goes." In the rest of this chapter, all quotes from Alice's journal are from "Whistling Girl."

118 "on 1 bottle": A. to Joanna Russ, Apr. 16, 1981.

118 "spectacular incidence": A. to Dr. K, Sept. 26, 1955.

118 "whose idea of sex": A. to Robert Silverberg, Dec. 28, 1976.

119 "perceptive enough": CA, MMI, 356.

120 "selfish," a "louse": Poem, n.d., collection of Peter Sheldon.

120 "I came back from": A. to Dr. K, Sept. 25, 1955.

121 "Amazing!": "Whistling Girl."

121 "Do not, please": "Lion and Lamb Lie Side by Side at Institute," *Chicago Sun,* Aug. 9, 1942, ABSP.

121 "works, now on view": Clipping, n.d., courtesy of Peter Sheldon.

121 "eyed it in silence": Smith interview, MMI, 198.

122 "the raucous presses": "Whistling Girl."

122 "That didn't count": Platt.

122 "America deserves expression": *Chicago Sun,* Apr. 25, 1942, MHBP.

122 "not a nurse type": A. to parents, Aug. 13, 1942.

123 "landing the plane": T. to Craig Strete, Sept. 23, 1974.

123 "Think of the humiliation": *Congressional Record,* quoted in Weatherford, *American Women and World War II,* 30.

123 "Are you one of them Wackies?": Treadwell, *Women's Army Corps,* 56.

123 "just another chambermaid": "Whistling Girl."

123 "It was important": Signature, MMI, 308.

123 "[Her] only use for me": T. to Joanna Russ, unsent, filed with draft of "Tiptree's Dead Birds."

124 "slow, heavy quality": A. to parents, Aug. 25, 1942. This is not the same John Michel who was a member of the science fiction group the Futurians.

124 "a hopeless xenophile": T. to Donald G. Keller, May 20, 1972.

125 "the lesbianity": A. to Camilla Decarnin, Sept. 1, 1984. Unattainable, inexpressible, and impermanent love are often seen as recurring themes in lesbian fiction.

125 "I believe it will be": A. to parents, Aug. 12, 1942.

125 "I want work . . . discipline for me": A. to parents, Aug. 13, 1942.

126 "three-inch heels . . . goddamn thing": Signature, MMI, 308–9.

CHAPTER 13: FORT DES MOINES (1942–43)

The quotes from Alice's writing in this chapter come from her journals, especially "Diary of a Whistling Girl" (for the events at Fort Des Moines); a briefly kept date book; her unpublished writings; and her letters to her parents. Most of the letters are in ABSP, but a few (cited in the notes) are in MHBP.

128 "a lady executive": "Whistling Girl." Like the rest of the army, the WAAC was segregated by race: Negro women trained in separate companies at Fort Des Moines.

128 "The girls are *swell*": A. to parents, Sept. 28, 1942, MHBP.

128 "I was South Dishwasher": A. to parents, n.d., ABSP.

131 "Bunny was right": A. to parents, n.d. [Dec. 1942].

131 "Paragraph Ten . . . Format": CA, MMI, 349–50.

131 "has never forgiven": "Tales of a Paranoid," draft. Around this time Alice drew a cartoon titled "A Woman's Version of Genesis." In the sketches Adam shoves Eve aside and snatches the apple for himself, then flings himself flat before an angry God— except for one arm, which he raises to point an accusing finger at his wife. The God who drives them out of Eden wears a military uniform; Adam flees in a business suit, Eve naked except for a cloche hat and a pair of heels.

132 "felt fully alive": RelBio.

132 "Third Officer Alice": Clipping, Mar. 18, 1943, ABSP.

132 "a fact which": Alice Bradley Davey, "I Am a WAAC," *Mademoiselle,* June 1943, MHBP.

133 "The Regular Army": "The Women-Haters," unpublished article, 1946.

133 "My first act": Platt.

133 "It is a question": A. to parents, Mar. 20, 1943, MHBP.

133 "awfully sweet": A. to parents, Aug. 2, 1943, MHBP.

133 "extracted from me": "I Am a WAAC," *Mademoiselle.*

134 "gaining an experience": Ibid.

134 "the lonesomest": T. to Jeffrey D. Smith, n.d. [Oct 1972].

135 Observing the soldiers: That same summer, from an airfield in Illinois, poet Randall Jarrell wrote a friend that "99 of 100 people in the army haven't the faintest idea what the war's about. Their two strongest motives are (a) nationalism . . . and (b) race prejudice—they dislike Japanese in the same way, though not as much as, they dislike Negroes" (quoted in Fussell, 137).

135 "As far as": *Cosmopolitan,* July 1943, 29, MHBP.

CHAPTER 14: IN A PENTAGON BASEMENT (1944)

The background on photointerpretation in Britain comes from Constance Babington-Smith, *Air Spy.* Quotes come from Alice's journals; her unpublished writings, including two completed, unpublished stories and fragments of a novel; and her letters to her parents, all in ABSP.

137 "full of frustrated": Journal, Nov. 22, 1943, summing up the previous year.

138 "one major": T. to Jeffrey D. Smith, n.d. [Oct. 1972].

138 "It looks like . . . first 3 or 4": A. to parents, Nov. 20, 1943.

138 "Once I discovered . . . shark-pack": T. to Smith, n.d. [Oct. 1972].

138 "the jokes": T. to Smith, Nov. 23, 1973.

139 "the mad craving": Journal, Mar. 19, 1944.

139 "Bob is . . . promising": A. to parents, Nov. 14, 1943.

139 "an easy conquest . . . perish": Journal, Dec. 19, 1943.

141 "strange town . . . all the moves": A. to parents, Apr. 22, 1944.

142 "There is this girl": Journal, Feb. 24, 1944.

142 "a sort of mystery": Journal, June 15, 1944.

142 "in Wash. DC": A. to parents, May 1, 1944.

144 "a combination stream": A. to parents, July 25, 1944.

144 "achieve a more democratic": AVC *Bulletin,* ed. Charles G. Bolté, June 1944.

144 Ronald Reagan: Reagan's contribution appeared in the Feb. 15, 1946, issue.

144 "Fundamentally": A. to parents, Apr. 22, 1944.

145 "scar-tissue . . . loneliness": Journal, June 15, 1944.

145 "all of a sudden": T. to Craig Strete, Mar. 1, 1975.

146 " 'Ouch' simply": T. to Strete, June 6, 1974.

146 "I wish you weren't": MHB to A., Apr. 11, 1945, MHBP.

146 "I am so glad . . . one of those": MHB to Bigelow, n.d. [Feb 1945], MHBP.

146 "We have Alice": MHB to Herbert Bradley, Feb. 24, 1945, MHBP.

147 "You know, I'd like": MHB to Bigelow, n.d. [Mar. 3?, 1945], MHBP.

147 "in a tent": MHB to Herbert Bradley, Apr. 4, 1945, MHBP.

147 "my marble . . . lucky you are": MHB to A., Apr. 11, 1945, MHBP.

147 "I am having a horrible": MHB to A., Apr. 16, 1945, MHBP.

147 concentration camps: Mary's credentials as a war correspondent were important to

her, but Alice's later statement that Mary was the "first American woman to inspect and report on some of [the] most hideous of [the] German death camps" (CA, MMI, 336) is misleading. Martha Gellhorn, for *Collier's*, reported from Dachau on V-E Day, and Janet Flanner's article on Ravensbrück ran in the *New Yorker* in April.

CHAPTER 15: TING (1945)

Much of the information on Ting's early life and his army career comes from a memoir draft by Walter Pforzheimer, "*Ave Atque Vale*," and from an unpublished memoir by Ting Sheldon in Walter Pforzheimer's private library. In this chapter I also draw on Alice's journals and unpublished writings; her letters to her parents; and my interviews with Walter Pforzheimer (Nov. 1996), Robert Koke (May 1996), Cameron La Clair (Oct. 1996), Peter Sheldon (several interviews Oct. 1996–July 1998), Charles Platt (June 1997), Barbara Francisco, and Jim Turner (May 1996). Unless otherwise noted, all quotes come from these sources.

149 "The Red Cross . . . expanse": A. to parents, May 28, 1945.

150 "I am getting": A. to parents, June 25, 1945.

151 "care[d] more about": Maier, *Dr. Spock*, 35–36. The words are Maier's, based on his interviews with Spock.

153 Sheldon moved rapidly up the ranks: Charles Platt, who interviewed Ting as well as Alice, had the impression that Ting had "spent most of the war playing bridge, until the end, when he saw his opportunity. And by that time he was so well liked, when he said, 'Do you fellows mind if I lead this little group on this mission to round up some useful Germans?' they said, 'Sure, go ahead.' " Platt admired Ting for his brilliance and unorthodox approach (Platt, interview with JP).

153 "wildly enthusiastic . . . excitement": Babington-Smith, *Air Spy*, 184.

154 "If there is": A. to Robert P. Mills, July 4, 1982.

155 Marriage: Years later, Alli Sheldon told Joanna Russ that she had married "first to Get Away from home—then to Stay Away (after the U.S. Army disbanded). And it has a certain social convenience" (Feb. 24, 1980, UO).

155 "really expected": "Going Gently Down," MMI, 252.

155 "Captain, I have": A. to MHB, May 6, 1968, MHBP.

155 "In a sense": A. to Dr. K, Aug. 18, 1955.

156 "Surely [our marriage] began": A. to Dr. K, Aug. 18, 1955.

157 "plaster eagles . . . parlors": Alice Bradley, "The Lucky Ones," *New Yorker*, Nov. 16, 1946, MMI, 317.

158 Dulles and Helms sharing quarters in Wiesbaden: Powers, *The Man Who Kept the Secrets: Richard Helms and the CIA*, 32.

158 "three volumes . . . hairbrush": A., draft of book on psychology of art. According to Babington-Smith, in *Air Spy*, Alice concluded that the Germans had had much better

cameras but hadn't seen the need to train their interpreters. The Allies had had the better system.

159 "right in the thick": Jim Turner, interview with JP. Alice had seen something of the humanness of war that summer in Berchtesgaden, where she had picked a small book up out of a mud puddle: the private address book of Hermann Goering. Tiptree claimed that it had been full of casual nicknames for German generals, along with the phone numbers of "four masseuses and the Reichstag" (T. to Joanna Russ, Jan. 8, 1974).

159 "The lesson of my time": Symposium, 55.

159 "calm, sensible": T. to Ursula K. Le Guin, Jan. 12, 1973.

159 "To hear the hard": T. to Jeffrey D. Smith, Jan. 29, 1971.

159 "If one of": T. to Smith, Dec. 20, 1970. Smith was interviewing Tiptree by letter for his fanzine *Phantasmicom*. Because this line was illegible in a carbon copy, Tiptree later altered it to read "[. . .] face in his nightmares, for me that face looks much like my own" (MMI, 191).

160 "He gave me": "The Lucky Ones," MMI, 319.

160 "I never did get used to": "The Lucky Ones," MMI, 316. The *New Yorker* edited the piece into its own cooler style. When Alice told the story to Jeff Smith, the habit of saluting colonels became herself nearly blacking Ting's eye every morning when he came out of the bathroom in uniform.

161 "serious, tortured": T. to Smith, Oct. 3, 1971.

CHAPTER 16: GOING UNDERGROUND (1946–47)

Quotes come from Alli's letters, journals, and unpublished writings and my interviews with William Davey, Peter Sheldon, Cameron La Clair, Lucille Lawrentz, and Gus Tyler (July 2000).

162 "Solely in the public interest": Lundberg and Farnham, *Modern Woman*, 370.

162 "Alice received": *Chicago Herald-American,* Jan. 24, 1946, clipping, MHBP.

167 "Suddenly her various": A. to parents, Jan. 18, 1947. The unpublished ghost story is in ABSP.

167 taking photographs: One of Alice's childhood friends in Wisconsin, Lucille Lawrentz, had a sporting goods store in nearby Florence with her husband. Lawrentz remembered that Alice "was always into something, but when she got into photography, then everything had to be pictures, pictures. She came into the store and took pictures of me behind the counter, me at the cash register, me holding up bait. Then Ting had to pretend to be a customer. She'd get up on a ladder and take pictures down, she'd take them from the floor up. Other customers couldn't get in the store. She was so *different*."

167 "The majority said": A. to Rudolf Arnheim, Nov. 10, 1955.

167 "To understand": from one of several drafts of A.'s vision project.

168 "attempting to gain": A. to parents, n.d., ca. 1950.

169 reading up on vision: For fun, Alli also explored some of the odder manifestations of form and color perception. At one point she paid the astronomical price of twelve dollars for a copy of *Thought Forms,* a classic book on auras by the Theosophists Annie Besant and C. W. Leadbeater that included colored pictures of "the aura observed on a mother standing by child's grave, aura of a jealous scullery-maid, aura of a murderer . . . even the aura of a church where Mendelssohn was being played, all very serious and logical" (A. to Rudolf Arnheim, Nov. 13, 1957).

169 started volunteering: She also volunteered for a short-lived organization called Friends of Democracy, which monitored fascist, racist, and communist movements in the United States.

170 "believed that the way": A. to Vonda N. McIntyre, June 10, 1977.

170 "woman is a substitute": Quoted in Doris Kearns Goodwin, *No Ordinary Time* (1994; repr., New York: Touchstone, 1995), 413.

170 "organized movements": Lundberg and Farnham, *Modern Woman,* 25. According to Lundberg and Farnham, women who sought to enter law, industry, or other male fields should be gently discouraged, while the "emphasis of prestige, honor, subsidy and public respect should be shifted emphatically to those women recognized as serving society most fully as women" (370). Not surprisingly, they diagnosed women in the military with a bad case of "penis-envy," and saw the WAC and its sister organizations as "the masculinity complex institutionalized" (215). They also wrote that since it was men's role to provide women with the home life so necessary to their mental health, all bachelors over thirty should undergo psychotherapy. In 1963, in *The Feminine Mystique*, Betty Friedan argued at length with *Modern Woman,* pointing out, among other things, that research showed educated women were more and not less likely to have orgasms.

171 "that of . . . disaster": Ralph S. Banay, M.D., "The Trouble with Women," *Collier's,* Dec. 7, 1946, quoted in A.'s unpublished essay "The Women-Haters."

171 "on a loud": Victor Dallaire, "The American Woman? Not for This GI," *New York Times,* March 10, 1946, quoted in "The Women-Haters."

171 "Incredible how": T. to McIntyre, Jan. 15, 1973.

172 "saying how": A. to parents, Jan. 18, 1947.

172 "kuchen-kids": T. to McIntyre, Sept. 22, 1973. Tip added, "A kimono is something Sex Objects wore in Tiptree's youth."

173 the *New Yorker's:* Getting published there did have the unintended side effect of annoying Bill Davey, who years later still saw it as a personal insult from his nemesis, Mary Bradley. "Mrs. Bradley always wanted to see if she could rub my nose in things, and she got a story of Alice's published in the *New Yorker,* which wouldn't even *read* anything of mine if I got down on bended knee and asked them to. It was a damn poor story, I must say" (interview with JP.)

CHAPTER 17: RUNNING A CHICKEN HATCHERY IN NEW JERSEY (1948–52)

In this chapter I drew on Alli's letters, journals, and unpublished writings and on my interviews with Peter Sheldon. Unless otherwise noted, all quotes come from these sources.

175 "You're afraid": *The Golden Notebook* (1962; repr., New York: Ballantine, 1968), 39. Lessing, born 1919, was Alice's contemporary. Alli read *The Golden Notebook* in 1975 and pronounced it "weepy," featuring "Woman as Kudzu Vine," but impressive in its formal sophistication (T. to Russ, Sept. 12, 1975, UO).

176 "When you candle . . . parding": A. to parents, Jan. 3, 1948.

176 "Poultry Honors to Wife": Clipping, *Newark News,* Feb. 5, 1948, ABSP. To her parents, Alli made a point of explaining away the difference: "The science end was weighted heavier than the business and management end, which is why I nosed him out. He was so sweet—and it's all right, because a man is always given an edge in popular esteem, so my certificates bring me up even."

177 "The fading tapestry": A. to parents, Nov. 7, 1950.

178 "constantly busy fixing": RelBio.

178 joy and fulfillment: Even Alli's progressive friend Max Lerner wrote in the *New York Post* that "a woman is crucially a woman through bearing children and fulfilling herself in them" (May 11, 1953; Lerner, *The Unfinished Country,* 637).

178 "severe convulsions . . . solid": "Laboratory of Me," unfinished memoir, 1957.

179 "*Africa Old and New . . . Stalin*": MHB to SWG, 1952.

179 "Progress more terrifying": MHB to SWG, 1951.

179 bits of a spy novel: A few fragments survive among Alli's papers. Tiptree told Jeff Smith he'd once written "something about a Nazi takeover," but had burned it. "Only good part was where the hero got lost in a cloverleaf" (Sept. 18, 1971).

180 "a rather prosy . . . kingdom of the mind": "The Next Sex," draft.

180 "bored . . . Quisling": "The Trouble with Women," draft.

181 "would go ahead . . . oak": "The Old Little Girls," draft.

181 "Made me feel": A. to Dr. K, Aug. 18, 1955.

181 "are more apart . . . for awhile": "Men and Women," draft.

182 "tenacity of purpose . . . output": *Chess Review* 19, no. 2 (February 1951), 33, ABSP.

183 "the secretion": *Saturday Review,* March 22, 1952, 24.

183 "I salute Mr. Martinez . . . no less": *Saturday Review,* May 3, 1952, 26, ABSP.

184 "forbidden indulgence": "Laboratory of Me," 1957.

185 "She can write": Carl Sandburg to MHB, Dec. 23, 1952, in Mitgang, ed., *The Letters of Carl Sandburg,* 489.

186 "disciplined first-rateness . . . coarse in it": A. to Rudolf Arnheim, May 12, 1958.

188 "in considerable solitude": T. to Joanna Russ, Sept. 25, 1973.

188 "A letter like yours": Italo Calvino to T., Feb. 21, 1970.

188 "The only way": T. to Joanna Russ, unsent, May 24, 1973.

189 "somewhat dubious": A. to "Ed," unidentified colleague in intelligence work, July 1954.

CHAPTER 18: THE AGENCY (1952–55)

Background on the CIA comes from John Ranelagh, *The Agency: The Rise and Decline of the CIA.* I drew in this chapter on Alli's unpublished writings and on my interviews with David G. Hartwell (Nov. 1996), Peter Sheldon, Cameron La Clair, R. Jack Smith (a colleague of Ting's, June 1997), Walter Pforzheimer, Cynthia Grabo, Robert Koke, Gus Tyler, and the transcripts of Alli's interviews with Mark Siegel and Charles Platt. Unless otherwise noted, all quotes come from these sources.

190 "I have a cold mind": A. to unidentified [Max Lerner?], 1952.

190 "illegal, clandestine": Roz Kaveney, "The Science Fictiveness of Women's Science Fiction," 90. In *Trillion Year Spree,* Brian W. Aldiss and David Wingrove write, "In the early fifties [Alice Sheldon] and her husband helped form the CIA. From then on until the mid-sixties she was involved in photo-intelligence work, compiling dossiers on people" (365). "Mid-sixties" adds ten years to Alli's career, and the description conflates the two types of work she did at the Agency. But Alli was also careless about dates. In a letter to SF editor George Scithers in May 1981, she wrote that she had left the CIA in 1962.

190 "You should have seen": David G. Hartwell, interview with JP.

190 "a midwesterner who": T. to Robert Silverberg, Apr. 23, 1971; quoted in Silverberg, ed., *New Dimensions 2* (1972; repr. New York: Avon, 1974), 26.

191 "a rather activist": T. to Ursula K. Le Guin, Apr. 29, 1974.

191 "The CIA parking lot": T. to Harry Harrison, Dec. 5, 1972.

191 director of current intelligence: Ting later moved on to other positions, including director of reconnaissance in the Office of Science and Technology. The National Reconaissance Program was the secret office that oversaw satellite intelligence; the CIA and the Department of Defense were fighting over it, and Ting was brought in because of his diplomatic skills. (Jeffrey T. Richelson. *Civilians, Spies, and Blue Suits: The Bureaucratic War for Control of Overhead Reconaissance, 1961–1965.* A National Security Archive Monograph, January 2003, http://www.gwu.edu/~nsarchiv/monograph/nro/nromono.pdf, accessed July 14, 2005.)

191 insulting caricatures: A. to Joanna Russ, July 31, 1981; Hartwell, interview with JP.

193 "no more moral": CA, MMI, 362.

193 "The Pattern of" etc.: in ABS papers. In a résumé Alli wrote for *Contemporary Authors,* she listed "1954–55, a brief tour of duty on clandestine side working up basic files on Near East" (MMI, 342). This has been misread to mean that Alli spent two

years overseas, although she explicitly told Charles Platt she never left the United States. It does seem to conceal her area of expertise. In her draft biographical sketch for CA, Alli whited out a typed six-letter word and wrote "Near East" over it.

193 "They sent me": In May 1954 Mary apologized to the Society of Woman Geographers for missing a meeting in Washington: "I couldn't combine it with a visit to Alice because my child is off in the wild blue yonder doing God knows what for the government" (SWG). Alli told Mark Siegel that the sinister CIA camp she described in *Up the Walls of the World* was drawn from life.

194 " 'among your peers' ": T. to Russ, Oct. 14, 1976.

194 "deliberate and convinced": A. to Dr. K, Aug. 18, 1955. By that time, the Republicans had extended their witch hunt to "sexual perverts" in government. One of Eisenhower's first acts as president was to sign an executive order mandating the dismissal of homosexuals from government jobs. One of the very few prominent leftists to champion gay rights was Alli's old friend Max Lerner.

194 "to make sure": T. to Ursula K. Le Guin, Jan. 6, 1974. Alli also changed her voter registration to Wisconsin, McCarthy's home state, so she could vote against him.

194 "Boyish clothes . . . shape": "Laboratory of Me," unfinished memoir, 1957.

196 "despite Ting . . . group": Siegel.

196 "overload my circuits": A. to Dr. K, Sept. 25, 1955.

196 "I have no mechanism": A. to Dr. K, n.d. [Sept. 1955].

197 "pop-pop-pop": T. to Craig Strete, Sept. 12, 1974.

197 "fell repeatedly": T. to Philip K. Dick, May 11, 1973.

197 "When I get tolerant": T. to Strete, Sept. 12, 1974.

198 "impersonating": A. to Rudolf Arnheim, May 17, 1955.

198 "second job": A. to Dr. K, Aug. 18, 1955.

198 "a man floating away": A. to Dr. K, Sept. 25, 1955. In some notes Alli made for a novel, she sketched a scene of a clumsy drunk making love to his wife. The woman is lying in bed; the man sits down beside her, landing his full weight on her arm, and begins "covering her mouth with stale saliva—he kissed like a duck quacking," while the pencils in his shirt pocket poke into her breast. "For a moment she forced herself to remain quiet, while he plunged about, and slobbered, uttering baby talk, but then the inevitable happened. The resentment he had hidden boiled over in childish malice, and he sunk his teeth, hard, in her lower lip. She cried out, and he drew back—he was half conscious of the nature of the assault. Shaking with anger, she attempted to cover the situation by an elaborate sneeze, but when he offered to resume his attentions she drew away. He reached for his glass and drank deeply, watching her over the rim. He was now the injured party. Presently he sighed and said, 'Why in hell can't you let yourself go a little for once.' " At the top of the page Alli added, "Probably should change to somebody else—too poisonal."

198 "unsatisfying": A. to Dr. K, n.d. [Sept. 1955].

198 "a little studio": A. to Max Lerner, dated "July 1955" (date added later to carbon).

198 "cater to him . . . setting for his": A. to Dr. K, Aug. 18, 1955.
200 "Damn, you're really": A. to Lerner, "July 1955." The deleted place name was six let-
     ters long. It and Lerner's name were cut out of the carbon.

CHAPTER 19: A DISAPPEARANCE AND A RETURN (1955)

The description of the events at the Lodge comes from Alli's copies of five long letters she
wrote to "Dr. K" in August and September 1955. Quotes are from those letters, from Alli's
journals and unpublished writings, and from her interviews with Platt and Siegel.

203 "I once had": T. to Russ, Nov. 16, 1973. None of Ting's friends—including his
     closest friend, Bob Koke—remembered an episode in which Alli disappeared. Ting
     would have been close-mouthed about something this personal; but this still sug-
     gests a relatively brief disappearance. Besides, Alli would have had to disappear for
     her parents as well, and it's hard to imagine her being out of touch with them for
     long.
203 while Herbert and Mary hovered: One thing Mary did about Alice's home life was
     use it in a story, which she sold to *Ladies' Home Journal*. In "Restive Wife," a daugh-
     ter talks to her mother about her unhappy marriage. The mother identifies with her
     and speaks openly of her own troubles. Together they agree to give their marriages
     one more try.
205 "I was sick to the bone": MHB, *I Passed for White*, 259.
206 "Life moves so": A. to Max Lerner, Mar. 26, 1956.
206 "pure escape": A. to Ting, Mar. 26, 1956.
206 "A symptom . . . into the hole": Journal, Nov. 3, 1955.
206 "I as a person": "Laboratory of Me," 1957.
207 "I am a unique": Journal, June 11, 1956.
207 "You never get [. . .] what is here": A. to Ting, Mar. 26, 1956. Their marriage coun-
     selor apparently didn't discourage their radical desire for an equal marriage. Several
     months of sessions with Dr. K only seem to have made Alli more sure of her right to
     domestic equality.
208 "as we went": Taped journal, July 30, 1973.

CHAPTER 20: LEARNING TO SEE (1956–59)

This chapter draws on my interview with Rudolf Arnheim (May 1996) and especially his
correspondence with Alli, 1956–58. Alli saved Arnheim's letters, and carbons of her
replies, in her professional papers. Most of her other letters from the fifties, including those
to Ting, appear to be lost.

210 "I think the thing": Arnheim to A., June 20, 1956.

211 "natural lucidity . . . tunnel": A. to Arnheim, May 12, 1958.

212 "encyclopedia of curiosities.": Arnheim to A., June 3, 1955.

214 "I suffer . . . agonies": A. to Arnheim, May 12, 1958.

215 "Idiosyncratic energy . . . didn't *see*": Journal, Jan. 20, 1957.

215 "I wonder, has this": Journal, June 30, 1958.

216 "drudgery . . . if you can": A. to Arnheim, Sept. 5, 1957. To St. Augustine, man's greatest happiness lay in the glorification of God. More likely Alli was thinking of St. Thomas Aquinas, who in his *Summa Theologica* wrote, "Aristotle clearly places the ultimate felicity of man in the knowledge of separate substances, obtainable by speculative science." (First part, question 88, article 1.)

217 "What is so 'only' ": Arnheim to A., Sept. 13, 1957.

218 negentropy, and perhaps life itself: Wiener, *The Human Use of Human Beings: Cybernetics and Society.* Alli was familiar with Wiener's work.

219 "To go out": HS, 441. In notes for "On the Last Afternoon," Alli said the man was offered not just immortality but "total escape from the species, which [. . .] can also be the realization of the terrible loneliness among those who are physically of one's kind but not mentally of one's kind" (taped journal, Feb. 1971).

219 "our life and efforts . . . all for": A. to Arnheim, Apr. 21, 1958.

CHAPTER 21: CHEZ WOMEN (1950s)

Unsourced quotes come from Alli's correspondence and from my interview with Barbara Francisco.

220 "All I can say": A. to "Ed," July 1954. A. was defending herself for putting jokes into a professional paper.

220 "Mary Hastings Bradley": *New York Times Book Review,* Mar. 16, 1952.

220 "slim, small woman": Clipping, Sept. 2, 1953, MHBP.

220 *I Passed for White:* The film version starred James Franciscus, who later appeared in *Beneath the Planet of the Apes,* and Sonya Wilde. The poster read, "I look white . . . I married white . . . Now I must live with a secret that can destroy us both!" with the tag line: "Now . . . what will my baby be?"

221 "You just can't write": Friedan, *The Feminine Mystique,* 33.

221 "If we get": Ibid., 46.

221 "her acceptance": *Chicago Daily News,* Apr. 18, 1957, SWG.

221 "Herbert hated": MHB to A., dated "Sunday noon" [May 1961], MHBP.

222 "A Lion's Revenge": Clippings, MHBP.

222 "firmly on the left": T. to Harry Harrison, May 22, 1973.

222 But she had to go back: It was just after Alli left early that she wrote Arnheim her long

letter worrying that she was working selfishly for herself.

222 "I love you so": A. to parents, Sept. 30, 1957, MHBP.

222 "telling the old": A. to Dr. K, n.d. [Sept. 1955].

223 "Sometimes you harangue . . . worlds to penetrate": MHB to A., n.d. [Oct 1957?], MHBP.

224 "primitive biological . . . react against them": Robert Coughlan, "Changing Roles in Modern Marriage," *Life*, Dec. 24, 1956, 109–18.

225 "one side of humanity": unpublished essay on science fiction, late 1960s.

225 "'Ah, stow it'": MMI 69–70. As Tiptree, Alli revised "Time Machine" and sent it to a couple of editors, but it wasn't published until after her death.

226 "Only living room": A. to Joanna Russ, July 31, 1981.

226 "I guess I do": A. to MHB, May 27, 1969, MHBP.

CHAPTER 22: PREDOCTORAL RESEARCH GRANT NO. 10,907 (1960–62)

In writing about Alli's academic career in chapters 22 and 23, I drew on my interviews and correspondence with Richard D. Walk (Nov. 1996–July 1998); my interviews with Ann Milne and Lila Ghent Braine (both June 1997); my correspondence with Suzanne Hill (May 1997); a letter from Jacqueline Goodnow to Dick Walk, answering my questions, which Walk forwarded to me in May 1997; and Alli's correspondence with Rudolf Arnheim (ABSP). Alli's long letter to her mother, dated Sept. 7, 1961 (MHBP), was also an essential resource. Unless otherwise noted, all quotes come from these sources.

229 "My way of finding": A. to MHB, Sept. 7, 1961, MHBP.

229 "visual cliff": In these experiments, Walk and Eleanor Gibson built a glass table, with on one side a shallow platform underneath, and on the other a drop to the floor. They put babies just learning to crawl in the middle, asked their mothers to call to them from the edge, and found that most babies refused to crawl across the "deep" side. This elegantly designed experiment demonstrated that humans are born with depth perception and don't have to learn it, as behaviorists thought, by falling down.

230 "dry-lipped depressions": A. to Barry Malzberg, Nov. 20, 1980.

230 "I resolved to stop": RelBio.

231 "strongly scientific 'hard-nosed'": A., letter of recommendation for a student, Feb. 18, 1964.

231 "I'm afflicted": A. to Alfred Bester, Nov. 4, 1983.

231 "She was very vulnerable": Goodnow to JP, July 10, 2004.

233 "How I love": MHB to A., dated "Sunday noon" [May 1961], MHBP.

233 "nothing seems": MHB to A., dated "Sat morning" [May 1961], MHBP.

233 "There was no 'me'": A. to MHB, Sept. 7, 1961, MHBP.

233 "To admit his death": Journal, Mar 14, 1976.

233 "You know, when": A. to MHB, Sept. 7, 1961, MHBP.
235 "We never seem": MHB to A., Nov. 29, 1963, MHBP.
235 "I keep the 'Jr.'": T. to Cy Chauvin, July 25, 1973.

CHAPTER 23: RAT SCIENCE (1963–67)

See the headnote to chapter 22 for sources.

236 "If you want to": Platt.
237 "Adult humans": Alice Bradley Sheldon, "Preference for Familiar or Novel Stimulation as a Function of the Novelty of the Environment," Ph.D. diss., George Washington University, 1967, ABSP.
238 "It is wrong . . . seen as sin": A. to Robert Harper, Oct. 29, 1975.
238 "wildly affectionate . . . steel table": T. to Jeffrey D. Smith, Nov. 23, 1973.
239 "a major project outline": *Star Songs of an Old Primate,* 234.
239 "bare-faced . . . whole life": Platt.
240 "could barely count": Platt.
240 "Stupid kids": T. to Craig Strete, Sept. 23, 1974. In their evaluations, Alli's students gave her poor marks for organization of lectures but unanimously said she went out of her way to help her students (ABSP).
240 "over-empathy": Journal, Nov. 28, 1976.
240 "She was a wonderfully loving . . . rivalry": Peter Sheldon, interview with JP (Oct. 1996).
241 "like a motor": A. to Robert Harper, Jan. 8, 1975.
241 "adrenal insufficiency": T. to Robert P. Mills, Oct. 14, 1975.
241 "a low-stress-tolerant type": A. to Joanna Russ, Feb. 24, 1980.
242 "Man is not humane . . . frightening him": Platt.
242 "the bloody clowns": Journal (a loose note on Ting), 1980s. Ironically, according to Alli, after Dulles was forced out, "who was it who saw that he was given some information, and not dropped entirely, and whom he finally ended up coming to see? Ting" (A. to MHB, May 6, 1968, MHBP).
242 Vietnam: In Alli's view, one reason Kennedy got the United States into the war was that he hadn't spent enough time around military-intelligence types to discount for occupational psychosis. Whatever else you could say about Eisenhower, he "was the president least susceptible to the Pentagon's insane paranoia. He knew 'em . . ." (T. to Harry Harrison, Dec. 21, 1972).
242 "knee-jerk liberal": T. to Kate Wilhelm, n.d. [Apr. 1974].
243 Wernher von Braun: David Halberstam, *The Fifties,* 613.
243 science fiction: Fantasy flourished too, and Alli discovered Middle Earth. She was never a great fantasy reader, but she was moved by the grandeur and sadness of *The Lord of the Rings.* Her own response to sadness was more along the lines of low com-

edy, but she admired Tolkien's endurance: "His prescription is go on, go on; it stinks, it hurts, but go on" ("Harvesting the Sea," MMI, 265).

CHAPTER 24: THE BIRTH OF A WRITER (1967)

In writing about the start of Tiptree's career in chapters 24 and 25, I drew on my interviews with Harry Harrison (December 1998) and Frederik Pohl (January 1997) as well as Alli's and Tiptree's correspondence. Uncited quotes come from these sources.

246 "The cosmos is": Van der Spek, *Alien Plots,* 112.

246 "Couple of years back": Smith interview, MMI, 195.

247 "Using techniques": Boulter, "Alice James Raccoona Tiptree Sheldon Jr.: Textual Personas in the Short Fiction of Alice Sheldon," 8.

247 "the habit of excessive secrecy": Kaveney, "The Science Fictiveness of Women's Science Fiction," 90.

247 "I'm so spooky": T. to Harry Harrison, May 19, 1972.

248 "Now that she": Arnheim to A., Jan. 3, 1967.

248 "I cannot teach": A. to Arnheim, Nov. 3, 1969.

248 ulcer: Alli later cited poor health as her reason for ending her academic career, but that wasn't a reason she gave at the time.

249 "I was living": Smith interview, MMI, 195.

250 "decided if you were": Pohl to T., July 1, 1968, accepting "The Last Flight of Dr. Ain."

250 "Tiptree kept taking": Signature, MMI, 312.

251 "We really aren't": *Ten Thousand Light-Years from Home,* 56. Subsequent quote from p. 68.

251 Tillie chooses to ally herself: Joanna Russ has pointed out that since there are no other human women in the story, Tillie cannot choose between good and bad women, only between bad women and good men (Russ, "Amor Vincit Foeminam," in *To Write Like a Woman* [Bloomington: Indiana University Press, 1995], 56). Oddly, the Capellans refer to themselves as "Mother"—hence "Mama Come Home." Does Tillie choose men to escape a destructive *maternal* power?

252 "the kind of work": Pohl, unpublished introduction to Tiptree collection *Byte Beautiful,* 1984.

254 two reproductive phases: "Haploid" means having half the normal number of gametes. In haploid reproduction, the organism has a gendered generation, in which a haploid male and female mate. They produce genderless, diploid offspring, which in turn reproduce by budding out more haploid males and females. The haploid generation is in essence living sperm and eggs. On Earth this reproductive system has never gotten further than mosses.

254 "the inherent": John W. Campbell to T., July 27, 1967.

254 "a drive by": T. to Campbell, Mar. 18, 1968.

255 "And then it all sold": Signature, MMI, 311.

CHAPTER 25: DR. JEKYLL AND MR. SPOCK (1968)

On women's pseudonymous writing, see Sandra M. Gilbert and Susan Gubar, *No Man's Land: The Place of the Woman Writer in the Twentieth Century,* vol. 1, *The War of the Words,* and especially Carolyn G. Heilbrun, *Writing a Woman's Life.* Also helpful to me in thinking about women's writing was Marianne Hirsch, *The Mother-Daughter Plot.* For further sources, see the headnote to chapter 24.

257 "In publicly presenting": Sandra M. Gilbert and Susan Gubar, *The Madwoman in the Attic,* 74.

257 "When I was dissatisfied": Quoted in Barbara Reynolds, *Dorothy L. Sayers: Her Life and Soul* (London: Hodder & Stoughton, 1993), 230–31.

257 "while of unpretentious scope": Robert Silverberg, "Who Is Tiptree, What Is He?" WWO, x.

257 "Ain was not": HS, 3.

258 "a fount of hot lava . . . times a day": RelBio.

258 "big hunk . . . heart": Smith interview, MMI, 201.

259 "was elfin": David Gerrold, interview with JP, June 1997.

259 "ideas and phrases": Terry Carr to A., Apr. 5, 1977.

259 "cannot be the business": Southey to Brontë, Mar. 1837, quoted in Barker, *The Brontës: A Life in Letters,* 47.

260 "My Daemon": Ursula K. Le Guin to A., Feb. 7, 1977. Even one of Tip's young feminist friends, Vonda N. McIntyre, who was twenty in 1968, wrote as "V. N. McIntyre" until 1970, when Joanna Russ persuaded her to use her full name (McIntyre to T., Sept. 20, 1973, and to JP, Mar. 26, 2005).

260 "You know, it's": Joanna Russ to T., Aug. 24, 1975.

260 "There is a faint feeling": R. to Amanda Bankier, Dec. 5, 1974.

260 "As Tiptree, I had": "Zero at the Bone," MMI, 381.

261 "Tiptree solved matters": Ibid., 384.

261 "an author only": Quoted in Heilbrun, *Writing a Woman's Life,* 111.

262 never to have told her mother: Later Alli said of Tiptree, "My husband knew. PERIOD. Nobody, but nobody else including mother and my agent knew" (A. to anonymous, Aug. 9, 1981). In CA, Alli wrote, "For eleven years only H. D. Sheldon [. . .] knew who or what Tiptree was" (MMI, 344). This isn't quite true. Alli gave copies of Tiptree's books to one of her few women friends, her old army friend Dilly, and she showed Tip's stories to Rudolf Arnheim. Ting's close friends knew she was writing science fiction. She told Mary she was writing it, too, and may have shown her stories, though she probably didn't tell Mary her pen name.

262 "I'm just not sure": Barry N. Malzberg to T., July 10, 1968.

263 "They just [. . .] look": T. to Harry Harrison, Jan. 7, 1969.

263 "urbane and cosmopolitan": Frederik Pohl, interview with JP.

264 "Confirms my view": A. to Walk, July 15, 1968. Collection of the author.

264 "Like everyone else": T. to Pohl, June 10, 1968.

265 one of Ting's boyhood friends: Nico Llewelyn Davies, the youngest of the five Llewelyn Davies boys, said to be J. M. Barrie's inspiration for Peter Pan and the Lost Boys. Ting had probably been to Amhuinnsuidhe with them before. In 1912, Barrie took the orphaned Llewelyn Davies boys to spend the summer at the castle. They were joined there by Barrie's friend Anthony Hope Hawkins, his wife, Betty, Ting's aunt, and probably Ting as well. See Andrew Birkin, *J. M. Barrie and the Lost Boys*.

265 "I'm grateful": Tape, n.d., found at the Lodge. Courtesy of Franklin Berkowitz.

265 "James Tiptree, Jr., one of our": "Galaxy Stars," *Galaxy,* Jan. 1969, 194.

265 "the touching": T. to Leonard Nimoy, Nov. 12, 1969.

265 "If Spock had a sister—": T. to Harry Harrison, Dec. 11, 1968.

266 "Where in hell": Anne McCaffrey to T., Dec. 17, 1969.

266 "All I had to do": *Ten Thousand Light-Years from Home,* 370. When "Beam Us Home" appeared in the April 1969 *Galaxy,* Tiptree sent a copy to *Star Trek*'s creator, Gene Roddenberry. Roddenberry wrote back, with thanks and a compliment on Tiptree's writing. Before Alli filed his letter with her other correspondence, she wrapped it in plastic to preserve it for the ages.

266 "the perilous . . . Donner Pass": A. to Willard King (Mary's lawyer), Dec. 23, 1968.

CHAPTER 26: FIRST CONTACT (1969)

In this chapter I drew on my interviews with Virginia Kidd (May 1996), Barry N. Malzberg (June 1997), Harlan Ellison (Oct. 1996), and David Gerrold (June 1997), and from Alli's and Tiptree's correspondence in ABSP. Uncited quotes come from these sources.

269 "There does seem": T. to Smith, n.d. [Aug.? 1971].

269 Milford Science Fiction Writers' Conference: The conference was an annual workshop founded in 1956 by Damon Knight, Judith Merril, and James Blish and held in Milford, Pennsylvania, where they all lived at the time. Kate Wilhelm and Virginia Kidd were also associated with the conference, which became an important meeting place for SF writers.

270 "towering, glittering": Smith interview, MMI, 204.

270 "more intelligent": Damon Knight, *The Futurians*, 11.

270 "We were all part": Cy Chauvin to JP, June 1, 1998.

270 "I came to my own": T. to Joanna Russ, Sept. 25, 1973. He made similar remarks to other friends.

270 "the world of": T. to Virginia Kidd, June 16, 1969.

271 "money for jam": Peter Sheldon, interview with JP.

271 "It's probably lèse-majesté": T. to Judy-Lynn del Rey, Oct. 10, 1969.

271 "Yesterday the *Washington Post*": T. to Gerrold, Jan. 3, 1969.

271 "professing [. . .] high regard": Silverberg, introduction to "The Girl Who Was Plugged In," *New Dimensions 3* (Garden City, N.Y.: Doubleday, 1973), 60.

271 "You are like me": A. to Russ, Mar. 14, 1980, UO.

272 "The best way": Malzberg interview. One of the SF writers Tiptree admired and courted in 1969 was Theodore Sturgeon. Later Tip told Craig Strete, "I wrote [Sturgeon] a couple fan letters once that nobody not made out of dead tissue could have ignored, my best charm-the-bird-down prose. He ignored them. [. . .] Of course, maybe I tuned the prose too glittering, sometimes one can make admiration into intimidation." Either that, he wrote, or Sturgeon wasn't reading his mail (Dec. 2, 1975).

272 "Damon, if I'm going": T. to Knight, May 11, 1973.

272 "I start walking": Smith interview, MMI, 204. To Ursula Le Guin, Tip admired Dick's way of "plonking you down in some incredibly complex, totally gaga and insanely believable Ur-world in which the hero proceeds to wander about grumbling over his underwear, while stuff that would make ten short stories for me flashes by, and hero goes on looking for his zipper while cosmic tortures are loaded on him, he tenderly carries Kleenex to berserk devil-women . . ." (Nov. 25, 1972).

275 "You want to lose": T. to Dick, Mar. 10, 1970. Dick approached other writers, too, and Roger Zelazny eventually completed his novel *Deus Irae*.

275 "an offer of . . . seriously": Unsent letter to Ted White, taped journal, Feb. 1971, ABSP. A transcript of the letter was published in the *New York Review of Science Fiction* 63, November 1993.

276 "Absence indefinite": T. to Kidd, Apr. 2, 1969, courtesy of Virginia Kidd.

276 "that fantastic misdirected": T. to Kidd, June 1, 1974.

278 "speculative fiction is hotter": In Harlan Ellison, ed., *Again, Dangerous Visions*, vol. 1, xxi.

279 "She was flowing": WWO, 24. Subsequent quote from p. 36.

280 "I read the first": Brown to JP, Jan. 20 and 22, 1998.

281 "World War II, yeah": T. to Harry Harrison, Oct. 27, 1969. Harrison's biographical note appeared in *Nova 2* (1972; repr. New York: Dell, 1974), 195.

282 "we did the really": Gerrold to T., Nov. 12, 1969.

282 "Did have a bit": Anne McCaffrey to T., Dec. 17, 1969.

283 "You looked fine": A. to Robert P. Mills, Oct. 20, 1974.

CHAPTER 27: THE YUCATÁN (1970)

In writing chapter 27 I relied on Alli's journals (including taped journals) and writing notebooks; my interviews with David G. Hartwell, Peter Sheldon, Ursula K. Le Guin (July

1997), and David Gerrold; and Tiptree's correspondence. Uncited quotes come from these sources.

285 "I don't identify": T. to Barry N. Malzberg, May 10, 1975.

286 home at the end . . . tanned, happy: Joanna Russ thought Alli might have suffered from seasonal affective disorder, so that her mood improved when she got more sunlight.

286 "The ranch owner . . . visit": T. to Vonda N. McIntyre, Feb. 12, 1974.

286 "They watched over": Jeffrey D. Smith, *Science Fiction Chronicle* 8, No. 10, July 1987.

286 " 'platonic marriage' ": A. to Russ, June 12, 1984.

287 "was the single most": David G. Hartwell, *Locus,* July 1987, 63.

287 "would be, (a) . . .": Taped journal, July 30, 1973.

287 "Since the last": A. to Malzberg, Nov. 30, 1980.

287 "The thing about": A. to Alfred Bester, Nov. 14, 1983.

287 "I've lived so deep": A. to Charles Platt, June 19, 1982.

288 "Mother in the Sky": Alli was trying to get in touch with the younger generation, and filled the story with quotes from Rolling Stones songs. Tiptree proudly wrote John Campbell, "I got quite fond of some of it, but my researches damn near got me a summons. Loud is beautiful, if your ears hold out" (June 20, 1970).

288 "write in eight words flat": Brown to JP, Jan. 24, 1998.

288 "It is as cleverly . . . to pieces": Arnheim to A., Jan. 3, 1973.

289 "strikes me as . . . *tell them*": "Do You Like It Twice?" *Phantasmicom* 9, Feb. 1972, MMI, 217.

289 "I felt as though": John Clute, *Washington Post Book World,* Apr. 7, 2002.

290 "I had to take": Smith, interview with JP, May 1995.

290 "I am aware": T. to Joanna Russ, Nov. 7, 1976.

290 "Her arms went up": HS, 40. Subsequent quotes are from pp. 42, 37, and 42.

290 "the vulnerable link": Raccoona Sheldon, "The Screwfly Solution," HS, 13.

291 mating grounds: Alli had originally planned to write about a man watching the monsters mate. The scene is so "fearful" and "awesome" that after he witnesses it "he's totally impotent. [. . .] The human analog is so feeble, so pathetic, and so obviously not a part of one's will that unless the image can be eradicated the human being can't function biologically anymore" (taped journal, Feb. 1971).

291 "The arrival of death": Siegel. The repression of the sexual self in "Your Haploid Heart" seems to echo Alli's own decision to "discontinue sex." Answering a fan letter about "Haploid" in 1969, Tiptree suggested that sex was a stage humans had already half evolved beyond. "We normally regard ourselves as a highly sexualized primate, which of course we are—but in another way we're also a lot of neutral machinery carrying our sexual lives as evolutionary 'prisoners.' "

292 "Like asbestos gloves . . . man": Adrienne Rich, "When We Dead Awaken: Writing as Re-Vision," 40–41.

292 "very xenophilia": Swanwick, Introduction, *Her Smoke Rose Up Forever* (2004), ix.

293 "There's this backward": Smith interview, MMI, 192.

293 "this travesty": T. to Smith, Apr. 22, 1971. He added, "I can't be a pacifist, because if I were an Israeli I would damn well be lurching around with a bayonet; and in World War II there was a genuine Mordor loose in the world. Today the orcs (hawks?) are unfortunately mostly on our side, in our midst . . ."

294 "a writer temporarily": T. to Ted White, Oct. 22, 1970.

CHAPTER 28: A DECADENT INTELLECTUAL FAKED UP IN A WOODMAN'S SHIRT (1971)

295 "I meet somebody": Woolf to Stella Benson, Jan. 12, 1933; quoted in Hermione Lee, *Virginia Woolf* (1996; repr., New York: Knopf, 1997), 5.

295 "whose life forms into narrative": Smith interview, MMI, 196–97.

295 "Writing about your own story": Comment on "The Last Flight of Dr. Ain," in *SF: Author's Choice 4*, ed. Harry Harrison (New York: Putnam, 1974), MMI, 234.

295 "pressing out naked": A., D., n.d. [1945].

296 "storm naked": T. to Cy Chauvin, July 25, 1973.

296 "youthful enthusiasm" . . . story in that: Smith, MMI, 188.

296 "I don't want you": Smith to T., Nov. 19, 1970.

297 "census-type . . . Agnew": T. to Smith, Nov. 29, 1970.

297 "Well, I was born": Smith interview, MMI, 191. Subsequent quotes are from pp. 196, 198, and 197.

297 "Anxious, somewhat": T. to Smith, Dec. 20, 1970, cut from the published interview.

298 "I sympathize": Smith to T., Dec. 3, 1970.

298 "Would really like": T. to Smith, June 3, 1972.

298 "Tip was so warm": Smith, in *Science Fiction Chronicle* 8, no. 10, July 1987.

298 "SEE? . . . anything": T. to Smith, June 22, 1971.

299 " 'I tried this story' . . . other editors": White to JP, May 1, 1997.

299 "Oh, beautiful": HS, 426.

300 "I wish it was": Smith interview, MMI, 202.

300 "refines and darkens": Clute, Introduction, HS, xiii.

300 "I guess it's indecent": T. to Smith, Apr. 16, 1971.

300 "It's not like with you . . . anything l-left": WWO, 20.

301 "to close out": HS, 67.

301 "It's probably no accident": Gibson to JP, Feb. 26, 1998.

301 "I am increasingly": T. to Joanna Russ, May 31, 1975.

302 "produced garrulous": T. to Philip K. Dick, Sept. 10, 1969.

302 "paranoia": Journal, n.d., ca. 1974.

302 "Squatting under a stump": HS, 5.

303 "I have zero feeling": T. to Robert Silverberg, June 8, 1974.

303 "not at all psychoanalytic": T. to Mark Siegel, Mar. 30, 1983.

303 "glamorous adult world": A. to Le Guin, Aug. 28, 1977.

304 "a 'classic' practitioner": Gibson to JP, Feb. 22, 1998.

304 "I resist the demeaning": Ellison, interview with JP.

305 "used to be a fairly seclusive": T. to del Rey, Sept. 9, 1969.

305 "Old, old tourists": "In the Canadian Rockies," *Kyben 1/Phantasmicom* 8, Dec. 1971, MMI, 206–7. Tiptree and Smith titled the column "The 20-Mile Zone," and Tiptree used it mainly to write about his travels. The column, along with other letters and essays by Tiptree (and later Alli), appeared in various forms in various Smith 'zines until he stopped publishing in 1978.

305 "decadent intellectual": "Spitting Teeth, Our Hero—," ibid., MMI, 211–12. Ting had a cameo in the essay, as a "big guy" who was helping take the shutters down—and presumably the driver to the hospital as well.

306 "a major new": in Silverberg, ed., *New Dimensions 2* (1972; repr., New York: Avon, 1974), 26. He also pleased Alli by paying Tip $450, his highest fee so far.

CHAPTER 29: FRIENDSHIPS (1971–73)

For this chapter I drew on Alli's journals and unpublished writings; Tiptree's and Raccoona Sheldon's correspondence; and my interviews with Le Guin, Malzberg, Gerrold, Charles Platt, and Harry Harrison. Uncited quotes come from these sources.

308 "I sympathize": Quoted in Redinger, *George Eliot*, 331.

308 "aggressive admiration . . . answering this": T. to Le Guin, Apr. 17, 1971

311 "Dear Starbear . . . this writing": T. to Le Guin, Jan. 12, 1973. Tip often used his age to excuse his flirtations with women. To Vonda McIntyre, later that year, he wrote, "Oh that Ursula K. Le Guin . . . Thank god I'm an old old primate, I can have my old romances without offense."

312 "Listen—do you": Le Guin to T., Oct. 8, 1973.

312 "radiates something": T. to Russ, Oct. 22, 1974.

312 "But I put": T. to Le Guin, n.d. [Sept. 1973].

313 "He was an extremely charming persona": Le Guin to JP, Jan. 24, 1997.

313 "sort of vast lacuna": Le Guin to A., Nov. 28, 1976.

313 "this man friend": Le Guin, interview with JP.

314 "I mean *stop*": Malzberg to T., May 24, 1974.

314 "capacity for uninhibited": T. to Malzberg, Nov. 22, 1972.

314 "Life is fair": T. to Malzberg, n.d. [Sept. 1969] and (same wording) Apr. 23, 1974.

314 "winning a Nebula": Platt.

314 "I absolutely refuse": T. to Malzberg, Dec. 24, 1972.

314 Pynchon: "His work affects me like having 3 dictionaries dumped in my oatmeal" (A. to Robert Harper, June 4, 1982).

314 "suppressed wild crazy": T. to Harrison, May 11, 1973.

315 "had to brace up": Signature, MMI, 314.

315 "a 12-volt battery": Charles Platt, interview with JP.

315 "I am VERY shy": T. to Le Guin, Apr. 29, 1974.

315 "the question of the personal . . . state the facts": A. to Russ, July 31, 1981.

316 "hopeless sense": "Tiptree's list," a list of stories A. admired, 1970s, unpublished. She was describing Damon Knight's "The Handler."

316 "Probably I should": RelBio.

316 "There is somehow": T. to Le Guin, Mar. 17, 1975.

317 "This is not": "Harvesting the Sea," *Kyben 9,* Sept. 1974, MMI, 260.

317 "running like a deer . . . and the moonlight": "Maya Máloob," *Kyben 3,* Sept. 1972, MMI, 228–30.

318 "I keep trying": A. to MHB, Oct. 16, 1972, MHBP.

CHAPTER 30: THE WOMEN MEN DON'T SEE (1972)

320 "One can speculate": Van der Spek, *Alien Plots,* 171.

321 "Women I think": T. to Smith, May 20, 1972, written just after the anxious letter to Harrison.

322 "I don't have an urge": T. to Vonda N. McIntyre, Oct. 13, 1973.

322 "women over 50": A. to Jo Freeman, June 21, 1973.

322 "for the Lib . . . alive and conscious": T. to Le Guin, Nov. 19, 1973.

322 "how far this wave": A. to Freeman, June 21, 1973.

322 "sadly childish": Journal, May 16, 1972.

323 "I see her first": HS, 121. Subsequent quotes are from pp. 140 and 148.

323 "I hoped somebody would snort": T. to Le Guin, Nov. 19, 1973.

324 "Shit, I knew": A. to Robert Silverberg, Dec. 28, 1976. While she was working on "The Women Men Don't See," Alli showed it to at least one woman friend, possibly her friend Dilly—who has a cameo in it as Ruth's friend, the "director of nursing training at N.I.H." She told Alli she knew plenty of women who fantasized about being taken away in UFOs.

325 "Tip listens": Symposium, 35.

325 "If mankind's": T. to Mills, June 15, 1972. Pohl left Ace shortly after Tiptree signed, partly because the management was unwilling or unable to pay their writers. Tiptree wrote Mills repeatedly, worrying about his $1,500 advance.

327 "bare-faced pain": R. to Edward L. Ferman, Aug. 31, 1972, describing her story "Press Until the Bleeding Stops."

328 "I used to sell": R. to Ferman, Aug. 25, 1972.

329 "technology of chickens . . . corporation": R. to McIntyre, Nov. 27, 1975. Tiptree had also thought of using the hatchery as a setting, but neither persona ever managed to work it in.

329 "a Wisconsinite": R. to Smith, Feb. 17, 1975.

329 "My goodness": R. to Jim Baen, Aug. 22, 1974.

329 "a secret beautiful": *Out of the Everywhere,* 19.

330 "with little hand-written . . . as a woman": White to JP, May 1, 1997.

331 given Raccoona minor stories: Signature, MMI, 312.

331 "klutzy . . . put-down": Le Guin, interview with JP, July 1997.

331 "Raccoona, I think, has": Le Guin to A., Nov. 28, 1976. She added that Raccoona "seems a good deal younger than Tip."

331 *Final Stage*: Searching for ways to be a feminist as a man, Tiptree asked both editors to find more women contributors. Ed Ferman replied that he had heard rumors Tiptree was a woman. Tip countered blandly, "Sorry I can't solve the anthology problem by turning out female."

332 "atrocity without end": HS, 410.

CHAPTER 31: A GLASS GETTING READY TO CRACK (1973)

This chapter is based in part on Alli's journals and unpublished writings, including "The Human Male"; Tiptree's, Raccoona's, and Alli's correspondence; and on my interviews with Chelsea Quinn Yarbro (Oct. 1996), Albert Dytch (July 1998), and Harlan Ellison. Uncited quotes come from these sources.

When Alli gave her papers to Jeff Smith, she stipulated that letters be read only with the permission of the addressee. Because Yarbro did not give me permission to read her letters to Alli, or Alli's to her, her correspondence is absent from this book.

333 "How can we live": T. to Vonda N. McIntyre, Dec. 5, 1973.

333 "[Kate] Wilhelm is": Ellison, ed., *Again, Dangerous Visions,* vol. 2, 432.

333 "I do not": T. to Ed Ferman, Jan. 28, 1973. Ferman later quoted this in his introduction to "The Women Men Don't See," adding, "Well, sf people are a nosy bunch, and we won't give up, but meanwhile there is more than enough to consider in Mr. Tiptree's fiction" (*F&SF,* Dec. 1973).

333 "obviously first-hand": Silverberg, "Who Is Tiptree, What Is He?" WWO, xii.

334 "tall, thin, with an": White to JP, May 5, 1997.

334 "I think of you": Geis to T., July 14, 1973.

335 "I bet you're": Russ to T., Aug. 24, 1975. Tip wrote back, "Are there any physically beautiful writers? You know we're all lumpy. Too earnest in the face." Russ protested, "You? LUMPY? I don't believe it. You are slender and wiry (of course) or your prose is lying."

335 "I type with": T. to Ursula K. Le Guin, June 9, 1974.

335 "I personally have spent": T. to Dytch, Dec. 11, 1972.

335 "I have encountered": T. to Harrison, Dec. 21, 1972.

335 "I have never told": Signature, MMI, 311.

335 "very carefully chosen": A. to Michael Bishop, Jan. 7, 1983.

335 "Ten, fifteen": T. to Smith, Oct. 3, 1971.

336 "I'm getting fairly tired": A. to Harold Ober Associates, Jan. 25, 1973.

337 "the book someone . . . years and energy": Ibid.

337 "Who *are* all these": "The Human Male."

338 "ready to get back": A. to Dorothy Olding, Apr. 19, 1973.

338 "customs, traditions": Russ to T., Nov. 5, 1974.

339 "I tend to think": Symposium, 50.

339 Mothering: Alli planned to argue that females are not passive recipients of male
sperm—the popular view from Darwin on down—but have evolved behaviors that
maximize the viability of their descendants. Alli was ahead of her time here. Thirty
years later, researchers are just starting to look at mothering in evolutionary terms. In
Mother Nature: A History of Mothers, Infants, and Natural Selection, anthropologist
Sarah Blaffer Hrdy emphasizes that female strategies for reproductive success are not
always what we might think of as nurturing or altruistic.

339 "I am beginning to see": T. to McIntyre, July 7, 1974.

339 "lifelong suspicion . . . effects": A., letter to the editor of *Ms.* (copy in ABSP), Oct.
31, 1972.

341 *Roe v. Wade:* Alli told her congressman that she had had an abortion, for medical reasons, and felt no regrets. "The 2- or 3-month embryo is not a human being in any
sense [. . .]. It is really a piece of the mother. [. . .] The embryo (which was shown
me) was a rudimentary blob of flesh slightly bigger than a lima bean. [. . .] I am sure
its soul was still waiting in the pool of souls for assignment; I am *sure* it had none" (A.
to Rep. Joel Broyhill, July 31, 1973).

341 "a road-mending vehicle": T. to McIntyre, Aug. 22, 1975.

342 "extraordinary . . . best work": Draft of review for *Vector,* sent by Brunner to T., early
1974, ABSP.

342 "competitive Lears": A. to Le Guin, "23½ Apr 79," UO.

342 "distinctly unliberated": A. to Curtis Ingham (editor at *Ms.*), July 17, 1974.

342 "We were close": T. to Smith, Nov. 8, 1976, MMI, 302.

342 "I am not 'mother-fixated' ": T. to Smith, Nov. 13, 1976.

343 *Jesus I hate nurses*: T. to Ellison, Sept. 25, 1973. The nurses didn't get along with
Alli very well, either. Ann Legerski, a local woman who cared for Mary, said, "Alice
wasn't like her mother. Alice wanted to get things done quickly, and Mary knew it
didn't work that way" (interview with JP, July 1998).

344 "like a glass": Ellison to T., Nov. 26, 1973. At the same time, Ellison had the same feeling as Harrison: this man's letters were in the wrong register. He remembered David
Gerrold's story and "started to think, god, I just don't think this is a guy" (interview
with JP). It was around this time that he started teasing Tiptree about "he/she."

345 "Grow upward": HS, 298. Subsequent quotes are on pp. 332, 365, 283, and 291.
Robert Silverberg published both Tiptree's and Le Guin's stories in *The New Atlantis
and Other Novellas of Science Fiction* (New York: Hawthorn Books, 1975).

345   Idealistic Lory: In her insightful book *Alien Plots,* Inez van der Spek argues that Lory commits "the sin of innocence," which is "the refusal to acknowledge not only the ambiguity of the world around us but first and foremost the split and composite character of the subject itself. Facing this condition would mean that women start to ponder the meaning of aggression and violence from within" (140). Van der Spek also writes that Lory's "suffering from sexual embodied existence may be so profound that it evokes a fantasy of destructive transcendence of the body" (189).

346   "By the time you": submitted July 8, 1973; published in *Phantasmicom* 11, May 1974, MMI, 255.

CHAPTER 32: "HOUSTON, HOUSTON, DO YOU READ?" (1973–74)

347   "Why don't you write": Le Guin, "The Fisherwoman's Daughter," 234.

349   "Katy drives like": *Again, Dangerous Visions,* vol. 1, 271.

353   "vulnerable and unaware": T. to Le Guin, May 5, 1974.

353   "You seem so *surprised*": A. to Russ, Mar. 29, 1979, UO.

354   "WHY on earth": Russ to T., Mar. 30, 1974. Yet Russ herself, she admitted, was working on a story about a man; and Tiptree responded that he wasn't even talking about p.o.v. "Call off your artillery, all I meant was merely having the female characters do and say realistically."

354   "I was madly": Russ to A., Sept. 29, 1980.

354   "even less manners": T. to Le Guin, May 5, 1974.

355   "I've been corresponding": T. to Smith, Apr. 28, 1974.

358   "in some kind of fancy": Journal, Jan. 1974. Alli thought the ramps came from reading Cordwainer Smith: "unlike 'Alpha Ralpha Boulevard,' back was *up.*" Alli didn't comment on the doctor's name, which recalls both her wartime friend Bob Parsons and Ruth Parsons in "The Women Men Don't See."

359   "his fly open": HS, 172. Subsequent quotes are from pp. 168, 218, and 221.

360   "relaxed, cheery": "Note on 'Houston, Houston, Do You Read?,' " Aug. 25, 1984, MMI, 373. In her reading of primate researchers, Alli saw "the males authority-structuring themselves, the females utilising a fluid, informal, unserious power-structure, or no power structure at all" (T. to Russ, "23–4 Apr 74"). This has since been called into doubt, and certainly wasn't true in Alli's experience of women. Ironically, in the Sheldons' marriage it was Ting, not Alli, who liked to talk.

361   "my own loneliness": T. to Le Guin, July 24, 1974.

361   "each person": "Note on 'Houston,' " MMI, 374.

361   "The clone part": Le Guin to T., May 6, 1976.

361   "cautionary tale": Dozois, www.asimovs.com/discus/messages/2/592.html?#POST 15835, accessed Feb. 5, 2003.

361   "polite, kind isolation": T. to Smith, Aug. 2, 1976. To Le Guin, Tip wrote, "They're

sure to let Lorimer hang around, you know. The hell with the others, I loathe Texans"
(May 14, 1976).

362 "in a world . . . vetting": T. to McIntyre, July 7, 1974.

362 "Left-right": HS, 159.

CHAPTER 33: A TIN ROCKET (1974)

This chapter draws on Alli's journals and unpublished writings; Tiptree's, Raccoona's, and
Alli's correspondence; and my interviews with Barry N. Malzberg and Ursula K. Le Guin.
Uncited quotes come from these sources.

364 "Creative people": Anthony Storr, *Solitude: A Return to the Self* (New York: Free Press,
     1988), 71–72.

364 "PS, this paper": T. to Samuel R. Delany, Feb. 10, 1975, Symposium, 114.

364 "That bruise purple horror": Ellison to T., May 12, 1974.

365 "The sound of soup . . . London": Le Guin to T., Jan. 3, 1975.

365 "HOWEVER": T. to Malzberg, Apr. 18, 1973.

366 "For each man": T. to Le Guin, Apr. 23, 1974.

368 "I can't imagine": T. to Bonnie Leigland (managing editor of *Galaxy/If*), Apr. 12,
     1974. Baen didn't suspect that Tiptree and Raccoona were the same person, but was
     influenced by Tiptree's high regard for this new writer (Baen to JP, July 29, 2005).

369 "I absolutely refuse": T. to Malzberg, Dec. 24, 1972.

371 "Nothing whatsoever amiss": T. to Le Guin, Apr. 29, 1974, UO. The Mailgram that
     Alli sent contained, as standard information, the sender's telephone number. Alli used
     Mailgrams several times for Tiptree's urgent correspondence, giving her real phone
     number, but no one ever tried it. Vonda McIntyre said she wrote it down but never
     dialed it.

373 "All right, Brain": T. to Smith, June 2, 1974.

374 "If I had put . . . flinch": T. to Smith, Sept. 27, 1974, MMI, 271.

375 "Some day I gotta": T. to Silverberg, Apr. 9, 1974.

375 "I can't explain it": T. to Smith, June 2, 1974.

375 "totally meaningless": T. to Kidd, June 1, 1974.

375 "I knew you weren't": McIntyre to T., July 18, 1974. On Sept. 23, Tip wrote McIn-
     tyre he was not anyone famous. "In fact I am not nobody you ever heard of, except J.
     Tiptree Jr." Then he whited out the incriminating "except" and typed in "I am" over
     it.

375 "Rumors circulate": Russ to T., Mar. 29, 1975.

376 "that little twerp": Smith to T., Sept. 6, 1974.

376 "I wish I knew": T. to McIntyre, Sept. 23, 1974.

377 "Tip has been conscious": T. to Mills, Oct. 20, 1974.

CHAPTER 34: A SENSITIVE MAN (1974–75)

379 "Today I sense": RelBio.

379 "there was epidemic": Gibson to JP, Feb. 16, 1998.

380 "family junk": R. to Vonda N. McIntyre, Dec. 5, 1974.

380 "images of corrupt . . . Couldn't": A. to Barry N. Malzberg, Nov. 20, 1980.

382 "the very part": T. to McIntyre, Dec. 5, 1973.

383 "Instead of the lonely": Suzy McKee Charnas, interview with JP, July 1994, in JP, "Feminist Science Fiction," *Ms.*, Nov.–Dec. 1994, 71.

383 "Some women": *Time,* Sept. 23, 1974, reprinted in the fanzine *The Witch and the Chameleon 2,* ed. Amanda Bankier (Hamilton, Ont.: Nov. 1974).

384 "I felt that I knew nothing": Symposium, 7. Images born in science fiction have had other subversive uses: think of the musician Sun Ra, or George Clinton's Mothership and its crew of "Afronauts."

384 "terrifying, empowering": Symposium, 116 (written for the Symposium's second edition, 1993).

384 "If I've called myself": Le Guin to JP, July 7, 2004.

384 "plain social justice": Le Guin to T., July 21, 1974.

385 "I had lost confidence": Le Guin to JP, July 7, 2004.

385 "the dark hard place": Symposium, 115 (1993).

385 "It's easy to avoid": Russ to T., Oct. 28, 1974.

385 "You have obviously": Russ to T., Nov. 5, 1974.

385 "Her style": T. to Russ, Sept. 22, 1974.

386 "may include . . . always indirect": Russ to T., Oct. 28, 1974.

386 "must be authentic": Symposium, 61.

386 "The only thing": Russ to T., Sept. 27, 1975.

387 The symposium: The participants were Smith, Virginia Kidd, Joanna Russ, Ursula K. Le Guin, Kate Wilhelm, Chelsea Quinn Yarbro, Vonda N. McIntyre, Suzy McKee Charnas, Samuel R. Delany, James Tiptree, Jr., fantasy author Raylyn Moore, and African historian Luise White.

387 "just beginning to realize": McIntyre to JP, Nov. 10, 1996.

387 "to be less outspoken": Symposium, 35.

387 "All of us must": Symposium, 105.

387 "The moment you slip": Symposium, 28.

388 "About the either-or roles": T. to Russ, Oct. 22, 1974. Tiptree later assured Russ that "copulation" was "wildly over-rated" and "a fundamentally minor system of human interaction. [. . .] One's personal search for orgasm—even one's search for sexual love—is, in a fundamental view, merely a hobby" (Dec. 11, 1974).

388 "WHY do you say": Russ to T., Oct. 28, 1974.

389 "Of course women . . . mothering?": T. to Russ, Oct. 31, 1974. The theory that orgasm in women has no evolutionary function but is a "side product" (like nipples on men) of male and female parallel development has some currency.

389 "Our view of men": Symposium, 18. Alli took this directly from her draft of "The Human Male." Further quotes from Tiptree's symposium contribution come from pp. 19, 20, and 20–21.

390 Mothering pattern: Despite what he said about men and mothers being patterns that could be present in both sexes, Tiptree was surprised when Delany wrote about sharing the care of his daughter. Do you gaze into your child's eyes? he asked in the symposium. Do you recognize its voice? The men Alli knew best, Herbert and Ting, were not such nurturing fathers.

Tiptree's skepticism about fathers particularly annoyed Ursula Le Guin. Earlier, in *The Left Hand of Darkness*, Le Guin had let her narrator say, "The parental instinct, the wish to protect, to further, is not a sex-linked characteristic" (89). Now, in private, she told Tip sharply that some fathers did change diapers, and that "little bitty shitty people and male parents stare at each other, at extremely short range, with exactly the same total mutual admiration and self-sufficiency as any Madonna and Child in the whole damn Uffizi" (Feb. 25, 1975).

390 "in a sense foreign": T. to Russ, Mar. 15, 1975.

390 Only Le Guin . . . wanted to hear more: Le Guin's insightful 1988 essay "The Fisher-woman's Daughter," about writing and mothering, was written as a response to Tiptree's questions.

391 "Ah, Tip": Symposium, 50. Tip also seemed to be playing into an old SF trope, the woman as bearer of (alien) children. When McIntyre edited *Aurora*, the number of illegal-pregnancy and "exotic means of becoming pregnant" stories she received led her to feel that most SF writers, or even most people, couldn't think of women as anything but "baby machines and nurturers" (Symposium, 36).

Russ's response to such stories was the novel *We Who Are About To* . . . Its narrator is one of a small group of travelers who have crash-landed on an unknown planet. The others hope to found a colony and tell her she must have babies. She says they are far too few to survive and should all just perish gracefully. They attempt force. She kills them all, and dies.

391 "Who are you threatening?": Symposium, 46.

391 "that there are two kinds": Russ to T., Nov. 5, 1974.

391 "I have never held": T. to Salmonson, Nov. 13, 1975.

391 "The sorts of things . . . survive": Taped journal, Jan.-Feb. 1975.

392 "have contributed": Symposium, 87.

392 "Joanna, your piece": Symposium, 93.

392 "Things like being": Signature, MMI, 313.

CHAPTER 35: DEPRESSION (1975–76)

393 "The greatest pain": "Afterthoughts by the Author," *The Best of Philip K. Dick* (New York: Ballantine, 1977), 444.

393 "apathy . . . leaky line": Journal, Dec. 3, 1974.

395 "I would sit out": Platt.

396 "finding myself . . . idiot": A. to Douglas Buchanan, July 17, 1975.

396 "the Second Shoe syndrome": A. to Harper, Oct. 29, 1975.

396 "I have 'deadline-itis' ": Journal, Dec. 30, 1975.

396 "suppressed fury": T. to Le Guin, "4.5 Mar 75."

396 "The intent toward Death . . . waste it)": Journal, June 29, 1975.

397 *Reality* is": A. to Harper, Jan. 23, 1976.

397 "In my head . . . duty to mourn": Journal, Mar. 11, 1976.

397 "a deliberate atrophy": Journal, Apr. 15, 1976.

397 "insert an intellectual 'joint' ": Journal, Mar. 11, 1976.

398 "How can you get angry": T. to Russ, Nov. 7, 1976.

398 "It is my opinion": Russ to T., Nov. 13, 1976.

398 "excessive achievement compulsion": A. to Douglas Buchanan, July 17, 1975.

398 "We and all our works": A. to Harper, Oct. 7, 1975.

399 "[Writing] seems pointless": Journal, July 24, 1976.

399 "my writing work has been": Journal, Mar. 11, 1976.

399 urged his male correspondents: In a letter to fanzine publisher Richard Geis, for in-
    stance, Tiptree gently criticized his "sexist mental freeze," told him why Russ's *Female
    Man* was an important book, and urged him to take another look at feminism. Oddly,
    Geis in his review of *The Female Man* ("Pardon Me, but Your Vagina Just Bit My Penis,"
    Science Fiction Review 14, Aug. 1975) sounds much like Tiptree in the symposium.

401 "There seems to be": R. to Smith, Feb. 17, 1975.

402 "I don't think . . . typewriters": R. to Bankier, July 19, 1975.

402 "You send grim": Malzberg to T., Aug. 6, 1976.

403 "from being a highly": T. to Strete, Feb. 25, 1975.

403 guessed early on: Strete, interview with JP, Nov. 1996.

403 "You are feeling your way": T. to Le Guin, Dec. 11, 1974.

403 "Well, here we are": Le Guin to T., Oct. 31, 1975.

403 "appear quite normal": A. to MHB, July 14, 1975.

403 "It was like squinting": T. to Strete, Nov. 25, 1975.

404 "What is in me": Journal, Nov. 9, 1976.

CHAPTER 36: MARY'S DEATH (1976)

405 "is only good": Journal, Feb. 2, 1977.

405 "The stimulants": A. to Mills, Oct. 14, 1975.

405 "flustered, vague"; "peace" and "normalcy"; "opiate euphoria"; "glorious oblivion":
    Journal, Feb. 9, 1975; May 30, 1977; Feb. 4, 1976; Feb. 25, 1976.

406 "lanky self": "Hilarious Heart Attack," *Khatru 5,* Apr. 1976, MMI, 294. Further
    quotes are from MMI, 297, 300.

406 "makes the": A. to Michael Bishop, Jan. 7, 1983. Bishop was reprinting the essay in an anthology, and had suggested that "gonads" was a male term. Alli took it upon herself to educate him: "For goodness' sake, Mike, *ladies have gonads!!!* What on earth do you think your lady made your child with? Cabbage leaves?"

406 "As to trying": Journal, Mar. 14, 1976. Bob Koke, who was Alli's age and married to an older woman, suggested to Alli that they could end up together. Alli wasn't interested.

407 "the search": Gardner Dozois, *The Fiction of James Tiptree, Jr.*, unpaginated.

407 "a Potemkin world . . . history": T. to Craig Strete, Mar. 14, 1976.

410 "hurts him physically": *Up the Walls of the World*, 91. Further quotes are from pp. 90, 217, and 83.

411 promised not to subdivide: The Lodge's new owners have replaced the tumbledown cabins but kept their promise about the land.

412 "There was, is": quoted in Vendler, "Myths for Mothers."

412 "Her paragraph . . . look at it": A. to Vendler, Oct. 2, 1976.

413 "Rest, rest": Journal, Feb. 2, 1977, quoting an unidentified poet, possibly Loren Eiseley, and substituting (Alli later noted) "cold" for "old."

CHAPTER 37: TIPTREE REVEALED (1976)

This chapter is based in part on Jeffrey D. Smith's account of discovering Tiptree's identity in MMI, 305–6. It also draws on Alli's journals and unpublished writings; Tiptree's and Alli's correspondence; and my interviews with Smith, Harlan Ellison, and Joanna Russ (May 1996). Uncited quotes come from these sources.

414 "letters from Carl Sandburg": T. to Jeffrey D. Smith, Nov. 8, 1976, MMI, 302. This was the letter Tip asked Smith to print.

414 "letters to me . . . memorabilia": T. to Smith (a private letter), Nov. 13, 1976.

414 "man must purify": HS, 17. Subsequent quotes are from pp. 22, 18, and 31.

415 "Here lies": A few years later, Alli wrote Alfred Bester, "I don't romanticise women, as anyone who reads my junk knows—remember the epitaph [in "The Screwfly Solution"]? [. . .] Of course I'm talking about women-in-general, which doubtless, despite long years of attempted objectivity, probably means 'me'" (Nov. 4, 1983).

416 "I didn't expect": Smith, interview with JP. Smith said he couldn't remember who had sent him the postcard.

416 "How great. At last": A. to Smith, Nov. 23, 1976, edited by Smith into the article "Everything but the Signature Is Me," *Khatru 7*, Feb. 1978; repr., MMI, 306.

416 "You used the words": A. to Smith, Nov. 23, 1976 (not in "Signature").

418 "and aside from nearly": McIntyre to A., Dec. 27, 1976.

418 "so they won't": A. to Strete, Dec. 20, 1976.

419 "Christ I worked": A. to Pohl, Dec. 14, 1976. Alli knew about the rejection before she

came out to Pohl, and may have written to him because she wanted to send him the novel.

420 "quite a few": A., "A Woman Writing Science Fiction," *Women of Vision,* 52–53.

CHAPTER 38: "I LIVE IN MY BODY AS IN AN ALIEN ARTIFACT" (1977)

In this chapter I quote at length from Alli's journals, especially from the first half of 1977. I also quote from her correspondence and from my interviews with David G. Hartwell and Chelsea Quinn Yarbro. Uncited quotes come from these sources.

422 " 'I can't adjust' ": WWO, 19.

422 "old lady in Virginia": A., "A Woman Writing Science Fiction," *Women of Vision,* 52.

422 "By definition": A. to Gene Wolfe, Aug. 16, 1984.

422 "And since I have . . . very race": "Zero at the Bone," essay drafted in early 1977, completed in 1985, and published after Alli's death, MMI, 381–82. The title is from Emily Dickinson's poem "A Narrow Fellow in the Grass."

423 "somehow combining . . . imitating Mary": Journal, Feb. 9, 1977.

425 "I know, intellectually": A. to Harper, Apr. 23, 1977.

425 "to change in some way": D., Apr. 23, 1977.

425 "I want to make love": D., Apr. 24, 1977.

426 "slim, vital . . . write science fiction": Smith, "The Short Happy Life of James Tiptree, Jr.," *Khatru 7,* Feb. 1978.

426 "I could see": A. to Le Guin, Apr. 23, 1977. The day after she wrote this letter, Alli made plans in her journal to try lesbian sex—the plans she never carried out.

427 "for some time": A. to Malzberg, Apr. 23, 1977.

427 "What seems important": Kidd to T., Feb. 25, 1977.

427 "I was dismayed": Bester to A., May 2, 1977. Alli answered, "No, it isn't pique about the lost anonymity—although Brendan Gill [in *Here at the New Yorker*] correctly speaks of 'the formidable energy conferred by disguise.' The fact is that I have been for some years fighting an ever-increasing depression, and the well-springs of Tiptree's stories were getting blacker and blacker, and running slower and more slow" (May 11, 1977). The two writers exchanged several more letters in the 1980s.

428 "Tiptree had a certain": CA, MMI, 353.

428 "for the joyous chaos": Ellison to A., Nov. 6, 1977.

428 "would be jammed": Ellison to A., June 3, 1979.

429 "Damn it if I can": Malzberg to A., Aug. 13, 1977.

429 "getting an increasing . . . what to do?": Le Guin to A., Feb. 7, 1977. The book she had just finished was *The Eye of the Heron* (New York: Harper, 1978).

430 "I am as certain": T. to Russ, Oct. 14, 1976.

431 "It occurred to me": A. to Russ, Sept. 25, 1980. Alli's story about her sexuality changed to suit her audience. To Camilla Decarnin, an editor who reprinted "Houston, Houston, Do You Read?" in an anthology of gay and lesbian science fiction, Alli wrote, "I'm gay in a peculiar sense—in my earlier life, when my body had enough energy to explode in physical love, the 2 or 3 great loves of my life were girls. But I hadn't a clue what to *do* about it—remember this is a LONG TIME AGO. Even today I'm susceptible to love-in-the-head . . . But that kind of fascination is a long way from the kind of friendship-love I know best, for a partner who has shared so much of the struggle of life that you couldn't *be*, separately" (Sept. 16, 1984).

   To Charles Platt, who had asked about Don Fenton eyeballing Ruth Parsons's bottom in "The Women Men Don't See," Alli replied, "Well, haven't you ever felt that, standing in a crowded line? I mean, I really don't think I count as much of a bisexual, but I have felt the appeal of rounded flesh" (Platt).

   And to Ursula Le Guin Alli wrote, "And as to flirting, don't be too sure, Madam. Certainly you can't flirt with Alli, who forty years ago may or may not have been a lesbian manqué, but somewhere behind my left shoulder hovers a thin figure in tropical whites with a faded vermillion cummerbund and totally unrealistic dreams of strolling with you, as I said, amidst the Madagascar moonlit where the lemurs weave their ring-tails" (Dec. 4, 1976).

432 "I don't think *tour de force*": Robinson, *Analog,* June 1978, 172–73.

432 "for personal reasons": A. to Hugo committee, July 6, 1979.

432 "awarded all sorts . . . considerable power": Budrys, "Books," *Magazine of Fantasy & Science Fiction,* Sept. 1978, 32–34.

434 "I remember how": Le Guin, in Ursula K. Le Guin and Brian Attebery, eds., *The Norton Book of Science Fiction,* 17.

434 "You've given my head": Silverberg to A., Jan. 10, 1977.

434 "fundamentally about women": Nancy Steffen-Fluhr, quoted in Amanda Boulter, "Alice James Raccoona Tiptree Sheldon Jr.," 15.

434 "What happens to the value": A., autobiographical note, in Patti Perret, *The Faces of Science Fiction,* unpaginated.

434 "If gender is constructed": Judith Butler, *Gender Trouble: Feminism and the Subversion of Identity,* 7. In her book *Bodies That Matter,* Butler argues that a "performance" like Tiptree's is a way to express gender's complexity.

435 "Is there a story": Journal, Dec. 23, 1977.

435 "Really my decline": Ibid., added to entry at unknown later date.

436 "one each spectacular mess": A. to Russ, Apr. 5, 1981.

436 "less and less active": A. to Le Guin, Sept. 21, 1978. In fact A. had just turned sixty-three.

436 "writing as me": Journal, Dec. 22, 1978.

436 "some of it old . . . become nothing": A. to Le Guin, Sept. 21, 1978.

CHAPTER 39: WRITING AGAIN (1979–81)

This chapter draws on Alli's journals, unpublished writings, and correspondence and my interviews with Peter Sheldon, Jim Turner, Mark Siegel (April 1998), Jeffrey D. Smith, Donna Risso (June and Aug. 1998), and Bob Levey (June 1997). Uncited quotes come from these sources.

437 "I think we all contain": Carr to A., Apr. 5, 1977.

437 "something almost there": Journal, Dec. 1978.

438 "I gather": Arnheim to A., June 27, 1979. Alli's own letter is lost: she had stopped keeping carbons, and the original has not turned up among Arnheim's papers. Later Peter Sheldon gave Alli a small photocopier and she began keeping copies again.

438 "eccentric old . . . grandmother": Somtow Sucharitkul, "Alice in Tiptree-land," *Fantasy Review* 10, no. 6, July–Aug. 1987; repr., *Contemporary Literary Criticism,* vol. 50; (Detroit: Gale, 1988), 358.

440 "His informal name": A. to Le Guin, "23½ Apr 79," UO. Alli was working late nights again.

440 Bob Levey: Levey didn't keep Alli's letters. If she kept copies, they were presumably destroyed along with her other personal (non-SF) correspondence.

440 "physical love . . . separately": A. to Decarnin, Sept. 16, 1984.

441 financial planning: According to Peter Sheldon, one of Tiptree's late stories, "The Only Neat Thing to Do," contains coded references to the Sheldons' financial arrangements, including the number of an offshore bank account.

441 "I'm afraid": Dozois to A., Dec. 27, 1976.

443 "an expert": HS, 225. Subsequent quotes are from pp. 228 and 276. The novella's title comes from one of Alli's old Untermeyer favorites, Ernest Dowson's "To One in Bedlam," which begins, "With delicate, mad hands, behind his sordid bars."

444 "I'd peeled myself down": Platt.

445 "strangely incapable": *Brightness Falls from the Air,* 210.

CHAPTER 40: LOVE IS THE PLAN THE PLAN IS DEATH (1982–87)

This chapter draws on Alli's journals, unpublished writings, and correspondence and my interviews with Charles Platt, Mark Siegel, Gardner Dozois (Jan. 1996), Donna Risso, Virginia Kidd, Jim Turner, David G. Hartwell, Barry N. Malzberg, Peter Sheldon, Sheila Williams (Mar. 2005), James Boylan (June 1997), Ursula K. Le Guin, and Michael Swanwick (July 2004). Uncited quotes come from these sources.

446 "None of the narratives": Haraway, "The Promises of Monsters," 110.

446 "No one around here": Siegel.

447 "a strikingly beautiful": Platt, *Dream Makers Volume II,* 257–58. Platt went to

McLean with the editor of *Asimov's Science Fiction Magazine*, Shawna McCarthy, who had arranged the interview.

448 "She was recovering": Siegel to JP, Mar. 8, 1998.

448 "objective was": Siegel to JP, Mar. 21, 1998.

448 "common point": Siegel, *James Tiptree Jr.*, 77.

449 "I have enough": A. to Siegel, Apr. 28, 1983.

450 "welter of broken": *Brightness Falls from the Air*, 278.

450 "yellow-head": *The Starry Rift*, 7. The second quote is from p. 69.

452 "I'd never met her": Shepard to JP, Mar. 24, 2005.

452 "I am bored": A. to Williams, Aug. 5, 1986. Courtesy of Sheila Williams.

453 "It was like knowing": Hartwell, interview with JP, Nov. 1996.

453 "ironic determination to survive": Hartwell, *Locus,* July 1987, 63.

453 "Her suicide is still puzzling": Goodnow to Richard D. Walk, n.d. [May 1997].

455 "Dearest Starbear": A. to Le Guin, May 18, 1987, UO.

457 "She finally gave up . . . hope": Dozois, *Locus,* July 1987, 64.

457 "Her brilliance and sweetness": Symposium, 116 (1993).

459 "our life and efforts": A. to Arnheim, Apr. 21, 1958.

BIBLIOGRAPHY

Aldiss, Brian W., and David Wingrove. *Trillion Year Spree: The History of Science Fiction.* London: Gollancz, 1986.

Babington-Smith, Constance. *Air Spy: The Story of Photo Intelligence in World War II.* New York: Ballantine, 1957.

Barker, Juliet. *The Brontës: A Life in Letters.* London and New York: Viking, 1997.

Beauvoir, Simone de. *The Second Sex* (1953). Repr., New York: Vintage, 1974.

Birkin, Andrew. *J. M. Barrie and the Lost Boys.* New York: Clarkson N. Potter, 1979.

Bodry-Sanders, Penelope. *Carl Akeley: Africa's Collector, Africa's Savior.* New York: Paragon House, 1991.

Boulter, Amanda. "Alice James Raccoona Tiptree Sheldon Jr.: Textual Personas in the Short Fiction of Alice Sheldon." *Foundation: The Review of Science Fiction,* no. 63, Spring 1995.

Bradley, Mary Hastings. *Alice in Elephantland.* New York: Appleton, 1929. With illustrations by Alice Hastings Bradley.

———. *Alice in Jungleland.* New York and London: Appleton, 1927. With illustrations by Alice Hastings Bradley.

———. *Caravans and Cannibals.* New York and London: Appleton, 1926.

———. *The Five-Minute Girl, and Other Stories.* New York: Appleton-Century, 1936. With dust jacket illustrations by Alice Bradley Davey.

———. *On the Gorilla Trail.* New York and London: Appleton, 1922.

———. *Trailing the Tiger.* New York and London: Appleton, 1929.

Brightman, Carol. *Writing Dangerously: Mary McCarthy and Her World.* New York: Clarkson N. Potter, 1992.

Butler, Judith. *Bodies That Matter: On the Discursive Limits of "Sex."* New York: Routledge, 1993.

———. *Gender Trouble: Feminism and the Subversion of Identity.* New York: Routledge, 1990.

Davey, William. *Dawn Breaks the Heart.* New York: Howell, Soskin, 1941.

Dozois, Gardner. *The Fiction of James Tiptree, Jr.* New York: Algol Press, 1977.

Du Pont, Denise, ed. *Women of Vision.* New York: St. Martin's Press, 1989.

Ellison, Harlan, ed. *Again, Dangerous Visions,* vols. 1 & 2 (1972). Repr., New York: Signet, 1973.

Faderman, Lilian. *Odd Girls and Twilight Lovers: A History of Lesbian Life in Twentieth-Century America.* New York: Columbia University Press, 1991.

Forster, Margaret. *Daphne du Maurier.* London: Chatto & Windus, 1993.

Friedan, Betty. *The Feminine Mystique* (1963). Repr., London: Penguin, 1965.

Fussell, Paul. *Wartime: Understanding and Behavior in the Second World War*. New York: Oxford, 1989.

Gilbert, Sandra M., and Susan Gubar. *The Madwoman in the Attic: The Woman Writer and the Nineteenth-Century Literary Imagination*. New Haven, Conn.: Yale University Press, 1979.

————. *No Man's Land: The Place of the Woman Writer in the Twentieth Century*, vol. 1, *The War of the Words*. New Haven, Conn.: Yale University Press, 1988.

Gray, Prentiss N. *African Game-Lands: A Graphic Itinerary*. Boston, supplement to *The Sportsman,* Oct. 1930.

Grogan, Ewart S., and Arthur H. Sharp. *From the Cape to Cairo: The First Traverse of Africa from South to North*. London: Hurst and Blackett, 1900.

Halberstam, David. *The Fifties*. New York: Villard, 1993.

Haraway, Donna. *Primate Visions: Gender, Race and Nature in the World of Modern Science*. New York and London: Routledge, 1989.

————. "The Promises of Monsters: A Regenerative Politics for Inappropriate/d Others." *The Haraway Reader*. New York & London: Routledge, 2004.

Heilbrun, Carolyn G. *Writing a Woman's Life* (1988). Repr., New York: Ballantine, 1989.

Hirsch, Marianne. *The Mother/Daughter Plot: Narrative, Psychoanalysis, Feminism*. Bloomington: Indiana University Press, 1989.

Hrdy, Sara Blaffer. *Mother Nature: A History of Mothers, Infants, and Natural Selection*. New York: Pantheon, 1999.

Kaveney, Roz. "The Science Fictiveness of Women's Science Fiction," in Helen Carr, ed., *From My Guy to Sci-Fi: Genre and Women's Writing in the Postmodern World*. London: Pandora, 1989.

Knight, Damon. *The Futurians*. New York: John Day, 1977.

Le Guin, Ursula K. "The Fisherwoman's Daughter," in *Dancing at the Edge of the World* (1989). Repr., New York: Harper & Row, 1990.

————. *The Left Hand of Darkness* (1969). Repr., London: Futura, 1981.

————, and Brian Attebery. *The Norton Book of Science Fiction*. New York and London: Norton, 1993.

Lerner, Max. *The Unfinished Country*. New York: Simon & Schuster, 1959.

Lundberg, Ferdinand, and Marynia F. Farnham, M.D. *Modern Women: The Lost Sex*. New York and London: Harper, 1947.

Maier, Thomas. *Dr. Spock: An American Life*. New York: Harcourt, Brace, 1998.

Moers, Ellen. *Literary Women* (1976). Repr., London: Women's Press, 1978.

Nederveen Pieterse, Jan. *White on Black: Images of Africa and Blacks in Western Popular Culture*. New Haven: Yale, 1992.

Perret, Patti. *The Faces of Science Fiction*. New York: Bluejay Books, 1984.

Phillips, Julie. "Feminist Science Fiction." *Ms.,* Nov.–Dec. 1994.

————. "Mars Needs Women: The True Fiction of James Tiptree Jr." *Voice Literary Supplement,* Sept. 1996.

Platt, Charles. "James Tiptree, Jr." In *Dream Makers Volume II: The Uncommon Men and Women Who Write Science Fiction*. New York: Berkley, 1983.

Powers, Thomas. *The Man Who Kept the Secrets: Richard Helms and the CIA*. New York: Knopf, 1979.

Ranelagh, John. *The Agency: The Rise and Decline of the CIA*. New York: Simon and Schuster, 1986.

Redinger, Ruby V. *George Eliot: The Emergent Self*. New York: Knopf, 1975.

Rich, Adrienne. *Of Woman Born: Motherhood as Experience and Institution*. New York: Norton, 1995.

————. "When We Dead Awaken: Writing as Re-Vision." In *On Lies, Secrets, and Silence*. New York: Norton, 1979.

Ross, Jean W. Interview with Alice Sheldon, *Contemporary Authors*, vol. 108. Detroit: Gale Research, 1983. Reprinted in *Meet Me at Infinity*, 2000.

Russ, Joanna. *The Female Man* (1975). Repr., Boston: Beacon Press, 1986.

Sandburg, Carl. *The Letters of Carl Sandburg*, ed. Herbert Mitgang. New York: Harcourt, Brace, 1968.

Siegel, Mark. *James Tiptree Jr*. Mercer Island, Wash.: Starmont House, 1985.

————. "Love Was the Plan, the Plan Was . . . A True Story About James Tiptree, Jr." *Foundation: The Review of Science Fiction*, no. 44, Winter 1988/89.

Smith, Jeffrey D., ed. "If You Can't Laugh at It, What Good Is It?," interview with James Tiptree Jr. *Phantasmicom* 6, June 1971. Reprinted in *Meet Me at Infinity*, 2000.

————., ed. *Khatru 3 & 4, Symposium: Women in Science Fiction*. Baltimore: Nov. 1975. Reprinted, with additional material edited by Jeanne Gomoll, Madison, Wisc.: SF3, 1993.

Spalding, Frances. *Stevie Smith*. New York and London: Norton, 1988.

Stevenson, Catherine Barnes. *Victorian Women Travel Writers in Africa*. Boston: Twayne, 1982.

Treadwell, Mattie E. *United States Army in World War II: Special Studies: The Women's Army Corps*. Washington, D.C.: Office of the Chief of Military History, Department of the Army, 1954.

Van der Spek, Inez. *Alien Plots: Female Subjectivity and the Divine in the Light of James Tiptree's A Momentary Taste of Being*. Liverpool: University of Liverpool Press, 2000.

Vendler, Helen. "Myths for Mothers." *New York Review of Books*, Sept. 30, 1976.

Weatherford, Doris. *American Women and World War II*. New York: Facts on File, 1990.

Wiener, Norbert. *The Human Use of Human Beings: Cybernetics and Society*, rev. ed. Garden City, N.Y.: Doubleday, 1954.

Woolf, Virginia. *Diary*, vol. 3. London: Hogarth Press, 1980.

INDEX